"I AM YOU"

"I AM YOU"

*The Hermeneutics of Empathy
in Western Literature,
Theology, and Art*

Karl F. Morrison

PRINCETON UNIVERSITY
PRESS

All Rights Reserved
Library of Congress Cataloging in Publication Data will be
found on the last printed page of this book

ISBN 0-691-05510-6

Publication of this book has been aided by the
Whitney Darrow Fund of Princeton University Press

This book has been composed in Linotron Aldus

Clothbound editions of Princeton University Press books
are printed on acid-free paper, and binding materials are
chosen for strength and durability. Paperbacks, although
satisfactory for personal collections, are not usually
suitable for library rebinding

Printed in the United States of America by
Princeton University Press,
Princeton, New Jersey

To the Memory of
W. F. *and* Minnie Mitchell
who sheltered my father
when he was orphaned

and

to John *and* Emmet
who from the beginning
entered into this work
with me

CONTENTS

LIST OF ILLUSTRATIONS

On a lily tremble
Two droplets, clear and round
They melt together and plunge
Into the flower's deep cup.

Friedrich Hebbel,
"Ich and Du," in
*Oxford Book of
German Verse*,
ed. H. G. Fiedler
(Oxford, 1911),
p. 392.

PREFACE

MUCH CAN BE TOLD from a single word. Long ago, the German philosopher Fichte (1762–1814) wrote a celebrated treatise on the human condition. However, Fichte's actual title, *Die Bestimmung des Menschen*, was vastly unclear. He intended to proclaim his confidence that, from its origins, the human race had slowly and unconsciously, but steadily, advanced from tribalism toward global unity; the word *Bestimmung*, denoted something fixed, a "goal" or "destiny." But there were other connotations. The English translator reduced the possible meanings of *Bestimmung* to one. He rendered Fichte's title as *The Vocation of Man*. Indeed, one note of uncertainty implied by "vocation"—the chance that the call might not be heard or might be misheard—was also present in Fichte's treatise.

Many of the circumstances that caused him doubt are still with us. As he looked about him, Fichte saw universal strife. Evidence for the cruelty of the human race to its own abounded in the carnage of battle for which armies went to the trouble of crossing continents and seas, in fratricidal civil wars, in governments conducted by force and fraud to enrich the few from the agonies of the many, and even in the cross-purposes, mistrust, and self-love that stirred up the conflict of good against good for the sake of good. Fichte refused to accept such evidence as proof that the entire existence of humanity was an empty game without beginning or end, perhaps a game devised by a malign god to be played out, as in a theater, simply to amuse himself.

Throughout the bitter divisions of the world, he saw a different kind of play in which even hatred sprang from a secret thirst for love, a kind of play in which thought, love, and hate existed in and through one another. The destiny of the human race was its harmonious unity. The vocation to humanity was a call to each conscience to live up to its duty, in freedom, to enlarge the union of sympathy that actually existed among human beings, a mysterious union transcending time and space. Fichte described that union as an ever-repeated play in which individuals perceived, understood, and loved themselves only in others. While the play worked through its unaging, ceaseless round, it nevertheless advanced because, hour by hour, the circle of humanity enlarged with new life and love. The *Bestimmung* of humanity even in and through strife was a call to conscience and to joy.

YET, AN ARRESTING THING about some doctrines of sweetness and light is the sharpness of the talons that they can display when balked. Intolerance was also part of the tradition for which Fichte argued. Ironically, Fichte himself conceived his broad and generous idea of human unity in such a way as to gain a conspicuous place for himself in the annals of anti-Semitism and, indeed, a reputation as the only one among German Romantic philosophers who set forth "with bitter sharpness" doctrines of hatred toward the Jews.[1] The chief evidence for this conclusion is a passage of four pages in a vast oeuvre; but the message of those few lines is plain.

The passage occurs in a treatise written early in Fichte's career, full of praise for the French Revolution. There, he contended that resistance to assimilation made the Jews "a state within a state" in every country where there was a Jewish population. Because of its separatism, he asserted, this international state was hostile to the political orders within which it existed. Continually at war with them, and contemptuous of rights existing under sanctions other than their own, particularly of those deriving from Christian precepts, Jews, he continued, would take advantage of civil rights to trample roughshod over the rights of others. He concluded that, despite their alleged contempt for human rights, Jews must enjoy them because they were human beings; but that, because of their subversive hostility to legitimate political orders, they should be denied civil rights. He saw only one way in which the tensions between dominant orders and the Jewish "state within a state" could end and the Jewish obstacle to human unity be overcome—namely, the conquest of a homeland for the Jews and the deportation of them all to it.

Since Fichte's day, some commentators have seen fit to heighten the severity that is in this passage recontextualizing it with partial quotations and with juxtaposed statements by other writers who were racial anti-Semites. Yet, the bulk of Fichte's writings, and his entire subsequent career, including his term as rector of the University of Berlin, have also been thought to display both a progressive mitigation of his ideas about Jewish separatism and forthright official action on his part against anti-Semites.[2] Once uttered, words can have lives independent of their authors'. Controversy over Fichte's position in 1793 and later is important evidence of the mingling of repugnance and engagement in the tradition that he espoused; for it will be part of our story, together with the fact that throughout the career of that tradition, hatred often proved to be as powerful and necessary

[1] Frank Schirrmacher, "Prozess mit tödlichem Ausgang: Ein wichtiges Symposion über Judentum, Antisemitismus und deutsche Literatur," *Frankfurter Allgemeine Zeitung*, 17 March 1987, p. 27.

[2] An example of the editorial techniques employed to locate Fichte among the rabid anti-Semites occurs in Eleonore Sterling, *Judenhass. Die Anfänge des politischen Antisemitismus in Deutschland (1815–1850)* (Frankfurt a. M.: Europäische Verlagsanstalt, 1969), p. 128. For a discussion of the matter that is generous to Fichte, see Alfred D. Low, *Jews in the Eyes of the Germans: From the Enlightenment to Imperial Germany* (Philadelphia: Institute for the Study of Human Issues, 1979), pp. 143–54. I am obliged to Professors Gavin Langmuir, Steven M. Lowenstein, and Ms. Phyllis Jestice for helping me understand Fichte's position concerning the Jews in 1793 and the controversy about the positions that he assumed later in his career.

a bond in human society as love. Indeed, we are only now beginning to speak of the hatred at the heart of the erotic metaphor of male dominance and female submission with which, through the centuries, the bonding of "I" and "you" was explained.

"What am I myself," Fichte asked, "and what is my *Bestimmung?*" To us, it may seem more appropriate to define humanity with the uncertainty of the call that may be misheard or not heard than with the confidence of a destiny, slowly but inexorably achieved through the ages, notably when what was thought to be the call of destiny has led to genocide. In the generations since Fichte's death, conflicts yet more terrible than those he knew, and yet more destructive to any idea of the inherent dignity of human being, have come to pass, conflicts that his own words were used to support. The part of the Western tradition that enabled him to speak of a destiny for humanity—indeed, of human perfectibility—has been largely effaced. Designated keepers of the human conscience have striven for what divides, rather than magnifying what is common. Yet the part of the tradition that enabled him to speak of a vocation to humanity remains and finds hearers, not least among those who greatly suffer.

In this book, I have tried to sketch out the historical contours of that tradition which, now ever more urgently, calls us to humanity but now promises no destiny, a tradition whose call often most tantalizingly is what is unspoken in the things that are said.

THIS ESSAY CONTINUES lines of inquiry begun in my study, *The Mimetic Tradition of Reform in the West.* Obligations incurred in writing *"I Am You"* therefore duplicate those that I gratefully acknowledged when the earlier work was published. I am mindful of the many extraordinary acts of speculative and practical empathy with which John B. Wolf and Emmet Larkin, not sparing themselves, helped me to find ways and words to speak of ideas that had once been taken as profound and evident truths, but that had long since fallen from common discourse. Martin Marty and William H. McNeill also proved courageous and resourceful companions in my long journey. It would be wrong not to mention once again the understanding and encouragement that, over the space of nearly twenty years, I received from Miriam Brokaw, as one book led, by no means inevitably, to another.

Of course, entirely new obligations have been incurred in writing this essay. It was begun at the University of Chicago and completed at the University of Kansas. I am under heavy obligations to both universities for the opportunities that they opened to me to pursue my studies and to sift them out in discussions with students and colleagues. The University of Kansas has most generously assisted me with grants from funds attached to the Ahmanson-Murphy professorship in medieval and Renaissance history, and (for research set forth in the chapter, "Schleiermacher's Anthropology") with a grant from the New Faculty Research Fund (#3549-20-5038). While I was still a newcomer to Kansas, these grants fortunately made it possible for John Lomax to help me as a research assistant. The task of final revisions was appreciably lightened by the award of a fellowship from the John Simon Guggenheim Memorial Foundation. I am deeply grateful for this institutional support and for Dr. Lomax's discerning and kindly assistance.

A number of the chapters in this study began life as lectures. Without recounting each occasion individually, I should like to think that those who gave me the opportunity to pursue these inquiries will find their confidence repaid; the depth and range of the following work was enriched by comments and suggestions that they gave me.

Early in the work, I had the good fortune to discuss ideas of common interest with Arthur Mann, Mary Rall, and Linda Seidel. Later, Jaroslav Pelikan, as a reader for the Princeton University Press, gave me the benefit of a thorough review. In the last stages of revision, I profited from the incisive suggestions of an authentic hermeneuticist, Alan Sica. I thank them for their compassionate toughness of mind at decisive moments in composition.

The present version of the work owes much to the careful and perceptive editorial eye of Brian R. MacDonald.

It is also a pleasure to acknowledge the gracious permission that I have received to reproduce the following materials: from Richard Kay, for permission to reproduce his poem "On Watching a Bird and Fruit Painted in Colors on Silk by Wu Ping," from *Saltatim*, a collection of his poems; from Theofanis Stavrou, on behalf of Nostos Books, for permission to use "Guernica," from Kóstas Kindínis' *Poems: Reinvestigations and Descent from the Cross*, translated by Kimon Friar; from New Directions Press, for permission to quote some lines from Babette Deutsch's translation of the poem, "Was wirst du tun, Gott, wenn ich sterbe?" in her translation of Rilke's *Das Stundenbuch*; from the Direktion der Bayerischen Staatsgemäldesammlungen for permission to include illustrations of van der Werff's *Children Playing before a Sculptural Group with Hercules*, and Maass's *View of the Rubens Gallery in the Alte Pinakothek, Munich (1895)*; from Prälat Dr. Sigmund Benker, on behalf of the Diözesanarchiv des Erzbistums München-Freising, for allowing the inclusion of the engraving by J. Mörl, after Cosmas Damian Asam, of the interior of Freising Cathedral after the renovations by the Asam brothers, Cosmas Damian and Egid Quirin; from the Metropolitan Museum of Art, for permission to reproduce Rembrandt's *Aristotle with a Bust of Homer*; from Stanley Moss for permission to include a reproduction of Luca Giordano's *Carneades with a Bust of Paniscus*; from the Norton Simon Museum of Art at Pasadena, for permission to reproduce Jusepe de Ribera's *The Sense of Touch*; and from the Portland Art Museum, for permission to reproduce the *Portrait of the Sculptor*

Antoine Coysevox, by an anonymous painter in the circle of Pierre Mignard (1612–95).

Finally, among these righteous deeds, I record with thanks that other authors will understand the assistance of Marnie Veghte and Elizabeth Bitoy, at the University of Chicago, who prepared early stages of some sections of the manuscript, and Sandee Kennedy and Beth Ridenour, at the University of Kansas, who prepared the final rescension. It was not easy for them.

THE VENTURE OF this essay has demonstrated many ways in which the isolation of personality can be bridged, through friendship, for example, or common dedication. It has also demonstrated that one's independent vision may be impervious even to wise and tender counsel. For the rest, I return, as any author might, to a vision that Fichte also shared, a vision of understanding transforming itself into empathy by play, that is, so to speak, of understanding understanding. Laying aside the vengeful, divisive edge that his love could assume, Fichte wrote: "The 'I' who speaks in this book is by no means the writer. My wish is that the reader may become the 'I' who speaks—that readers may understand what is said here, not merely in a historical sense, but really and actively talk with themselves while reading, pause to consider here and there, draw reckonings, and form decisions, as does the readers' *alter ego* in the book. For, thus, by their own work and reflection, purely out of themselves, readers may develop the actual ways of thinking for which a mere blueprint is set forth in this book, and build them in their hearts."[3]

[3] Johann Gottlieb Fichte, *Die Bestimmung des Menschen*, preface, in *Johann Gottlieb Fichte's sämmtliche Werke*, 1. Abt., 2. Bd (Berlin: Veit, 1845), p. 168.

ABBREVIATIONS

Corp. Christ., *ser lat.*	*Corpus Christianorum, series latina*
CSEL	*Corpus Scriptorum Ecclesiasticorum Latinorum*
Mansi	Giovanni Dominico Mansi, *Sanctorum Conciliorum Nova et Amplissima Collectio*
Migne	J. P. Migne, *Patrologiae Cursus Completus*
PG	*series graeca*
PL	*series latina*
MGH	*Monumenta Germaniae Historica*
in usum schol.	*Scriptores rerum Germanicarum in usum Scholarum*
Conc.	*Concilia Aevi Karolini*
Conc. Suppl.	*Concilia, Supplementum*
Ldl	*Libelli de Lite*
SS	*Scriptores*

INTRODUCTION

THE HISTORY OF compassion is yet to be written. With the studied art-lessness of his age, Bernard de Fontenelle (1657–1757) lightly touched the starting point—a common humanity. "All human faces in general," he wrote, "are of the same model, and yet the Europeans and the Africans have two particular models: nay, commonly every family has a different aspect. What secret then has nature to show so much variety in a single face? Our world, in respect of the universe, is but a little family, where all the faces bear some resemblance to each other. . . ."[1] In this essay, I attempt a rough sketch of features that a portrait may eventually display.

With a certain irony, Fontenelle advocated the rational empiricism that suppressed feeling in science, including the study of humanity and its artificial world of culture. For, according to him and other empiricists, intrusion of feeling into observation, reflection, and verification was exactly what had brought science under bondage to theology. They set out to expel what we know as the pathetic and affective fallacies from the world of knowledge, leaving it to reason molded by experience. By contrast, a medieval writer admired the spiritual discipline by which one person could bear the sufferings of another, "if not in body, then by compassion of mind."[2] Empiricists argued that the imaginative use of sentiments, including compassion, told more about the observer than about the phenomena observed, tainted reflection, and predetermined results of verifying experiments. By feelings, one turned the vision inward on the fabrications of one's own mind, instead of outward, upon the world as it was. Truth, for them, was empirical and physical. Consequently, truth was grounded in physical separateness, and not in affective union.

One of Fontenelle's analogies highlights just this difference between compassion and empiricism. He imagined nature as a great opera house. The audience luxuriated in the illusions of the stage, ignorant of the machinery backstage that produced them. It did not see the stage as it was. And yet, the engineer offstage thought of nothing but the "wheels and

---

[1] Bernard de Fontenelle, *A Week's Conversation on the Plurality of Worlds*, 6th ed., trans. Aphra Behn, J. Glanvil, John Hughes, and William Gardner (London: Bettesworth et al., 1737), third evening, pp. 90–91. The ideas in this essay are a further development of inquiries set forth in my earlier study, *The Mimetic Tradition of Reform in the West* (Princeton: Princeton University Press, 1982). Historical reasons for assuming continual cross-references among the arts (including literature, theology, and the visual arts) are elaborated more fully there than they could be in the present work.

[2] Cosmas of Prague, *Chronica Boemorum*, 2. 4 (*MGH in usum schol.*, p. 89).

movements [that] are hid to make the representation the more agreeable."
The engineer was like the empirical philosopher, searching into the wheels
and springs that nature had so completely kept out of sight "that we have
been a'guessing at the movement of the universe." Because Descartes had
revealed that there was no movement, even an intellectual one, without
material causation, "to see Nature as she really is, you must stand behind
the scenes at the opera."[3]

This contrast between the affective response of the ignorant audience and
the empirical knowledge of the skilled engineer, between empathetic participation and detachment, enriched the natural sciences. But its very
triumphs there, establishing working norms of correct and incorrect
methods, have biased discourse in those lines of humanistic inquiry that, at
some stage in their histories, have aspired to be scientific. The success of
natural science's war against pathetic and affective fallacies, transferred into
historical inquiry, has blinded us to truths of empathetic (or compassionate)
bonding and to long traditions of inquiry that sought to understand them.
It is not the first, or the last, instance in which one art has seduced another.

Martin Buber's celebrated book, *I and Thou*, exhibits the results of this
transference of detachment from the sciences to the humanities. In that
book, Buber (1878–1965) contended that every person discovered the self in
relationships with others. One became conscious of oneself as a person, an
"I," Buber wrote, by dealing with another person, a "you." Could one
break through the separateness of individual personality, he asked, moving
beyond the relationship between separate "I"s and "you"s to an identity in
which "I am you"? Mystics thought that this occurred in the union of
human souls with God. But Buber specifically asserted that the identity
taught by one of them, Meister Eckhart (ca. 1260–1327), could never exist,
except perhaps in some peripheral sense.[4]

By dismissing Eckhart, Buber set himself not only against one writer, but
even more against the tradition in which Eckhart stood. Further, he took no
account of the elaborate critical system that conveyers and defenders of the
tradition had developed to verify their conclusions by experimentation, and
to protect themselves against the private delusions of heretics or eccentrics.
He may have done this because, although steeped in a profound spirituality,

---

[3] *A Week's Conversation*, first evening, pp. 7–8.

[4] Martin Buber, *I and Thou*, trans. Walter Kaufmann (New York: Scribner's, 1970), pp.
134–35. Buber himself referred to "the familiar mystic verse, 'I am you and you are I' " (*I and
Thou*, p. 133). On Buber's view that empathy impaired individual judgment and that it could
lead to a "temporary loss of ego" (i.e., of personal wholeness), see Robert L. Katz, *Empathy:
Its Nature and Uses* (Glencoe: Free Press, 1963), pp. 39, 89, referring to Buber's *Between Man
and Man*. Principles encased in the sentence "I am you" are denied from another point of view
in a poem protesting against the efforts of colonial rulers to impose their own patterns of
speech, behavior, and thought on alien subjects. The poem defiantly asserts, "I am not you."
Adam Small (?), "Africa's Plea," quoted in Cosmas Desmond, *Persecution, East and West:
Human Rights, Political Prisoners and Amnesty* (Harmondsworth: Penguin, 1983), p. 21.

he did, in considering human dialogue, stress rational faculties and pragmatic experience almost to the exclusion of the passions. He may also have
argued as he did because the kinds of personal union summed up in the
sentence, "I am you," seemed to challenge doctrines of personal freedom
and integrity that were vital to Buber's inmost religious and philosophical
commitments.

Of course, Buber's position was not the only offspring of the Enlightenment. Some could actually use the words, "I am you," while scorning any
form of compassion. The alliance of empiricism and materialism, signaled
by Fontenelle's statement that philosophy had become "very mechanical,"[5]
engendered mechanistic conceptions of human society, governed by laws of
physics. Buber relentlessly opposed the sort of collectivism that Aldous
Huxley later described in his novel, *Brave New World*.

Huxley in fact used the sentence, "I am you and you are I," to epitomize
the annihilation of personal uniqueness in the regimented and standardized
society of the imagined future. By satire, Huxley took his stand with Buber.
At a crucial moment, he quoted verses from Shakespeare's poem, *"The
Phoenix and the Turtle."* Shakespeare described the union of two lovers in
one essence, a union that confounded reason by assimilating the distinctive
features of separate personalities. Huxley's protagonist, Bernard Marx,
judged the poem to be "just a Solidarity Service hymn," such as the one
containing the verse "I am you and you are I." A misfit in the collectivism
of the Brave New World, Bernard Marx defiantly asserted "I am I," and, to
his grief, he lived continually subject to the loneliness and the vexations of
self-consciousness. His anguish was the price of regarding each personality,
including one's own, as unique. Huxley insisted that the moral greatness
and true progress of Western civilization demanded that price. He satirized
the ethical poverty and sterile repetitiveness that came from denying the
integrity, the dignity, and the pathos of each person, whether personality
were annihilated by absorption into a social whole or by assimilation into
the private union of two lovers. But Huxley misread *"The Phoenix and the
Turtle."* The union of lovers that it described was not the self-annihilation
celebrated by Solidarity hymns in the Brave New World. In fact, *"The
Phoenix and the Turtle"* stood in the very philosophical tradition that Buber
had discounted.[6]

The sentence "I am you" and the tradition that gave it meaning did
indeed provide alternatives to the individualism defended by Buber and
Huxley. It set forth alternative modes of identity that were worked out over

---

[5] *A Week's Conversation*, first evening, p. 10.

[6] Aldous Huxley, *Brave New World* (London: Longmans, 1977), chap. 4, pt. 2, and chap. 5,
pt. 2, pp. 60, 73–75. The sterility of the liturgy employing the sentence "I am you and you
are I" is echoed in the destructive orgy with which the book concludes, chap. 18, pp. 205–206.
I am grateful to Mr. Andrew Morrison for directing me to these passages.

many centuries, both in discussions of humanity and of God, and in continual reflection on marriage, friendship, rivalry, and the arts.

The three words in the sentence, "I am you," conceal a miniature universe, part of which is opened to view in the following pages. The sentence was not a paradox coined through spontaneous invention by a few clever writers in various epochs; rather it was the signature of a continuing theme in western culture. Part of the universe hidden in the sentence is intellectual or spiritual; part of it is historical. There are, perhaps surprisingly, structural parallels with the empiricist method that, to use Fontenelle's figure of speech, replaced the audience with the engineer. Some of those parallels, including efforts to avoid self-delusion by experimentation, should become apparent in the following chapters.

EMPIRICISM, represented by Fontenelle, and the tradition summed up in our sentence, "I am you," were mental exercises that followed parallel lines from observation, to reflection, to experimentation. Likewise, they led, not to the solution of problems, but to awareness that all understanding falsifies, and to wonder before the unknowable whole, of which the knower, apprehending without comprehending, was part. The movement of knowledge was crowned not by intellectual closure but by a kind of rapture. Nature, Fontenelle realized, with its amazing powers of self-concealment, cast a shadow of uncertainty over all scientific theories; all were provisional, pending future discoveries. There were limits of science beyond which human wit could not pass. Even when one realized that the universe was like backstage machinery, or a watch, "and depend[ed] only upon the just disposing of the several parts of the movement," knowing was crowned with feeling: with an admiration at the sublimity of the thing. But that sublimity concealed many secrets, including how it was that humanity had a single face.[7]

I cannot here speculate whether these parallels arose because empiricism and the affective doctrines that it opposed actually sprang from the same rationalist stock, or whether, in their conflict, the fighters took on, as often happens, the ways of their enemies. For the moment, it is perhaps enough to indicate that the concept of empathetic participation is of general, if unacknowledged, currency.

Remembering that "civilization arises and falls as play,"[8] I suggest that, while the concept of participation and what it has to say about life has largely been ignored in recent times by positivist sciences, so doubtful of human solidarity, it has remained vigorous in other areas of inquiry and expression. The phrasing, "I am you," may indeed be unusually condensed,

[7] *A Week's Conversation*, first evening, pp. 10–11; third evening, p. 92; sixth evening, p. 179.

[8] Johan Huizinga, *Homo Ludens: A Study of the Play Element in Culture* (Boston: Beacon Press, 1950), foreword, n. p.

or elliptical, but, through the concept of empathy, its meaning is evident in branches of biology, sociology, social psychology, psychiatric theory, education, and esthetics. It is also entirely familiar in mystical theology. The empathetic discipline of "feeling oneself into the other" is cultivated in some professions as a stimulus to the creative imagination, a tool of therapy, and a goad to social action.[9]

The ideas encased in our sentence have something of value, not only for historians of religion and community, and for others concerned with ideas of personal wholeness, but also for those who study esthetic bonding through the visual, literary, and performing arts, and, above all, for those intrigued by hermeneutics, the art of understanding. For surely, in the interplay of author, performer, and audience, empathetic participation is the common ground from which all arts—including the art of understanding—spring, and, in fact, from which comes the art that is a negative value in every art. As noted, Aldous Huxley employed the sentence, "I am you and you are me," to epitomize the suppression of personality in modern technological culture. But he was consciously appropriating the signature of a religious tradition that taught the perfection of each personality by participation in the being of others. That tradition has pervaded many literary currents. Some expressions are popular and occult, as are the novels by Carlos Castañeda. Others, like the writings of Martin Heidegger, are recondite and philosophical. What has been called "the literature of the second self" is abundant.[10]

The present essay is a contribution toward bridging the gap between areas of inquiry in which the tradition is current and those in which it has lapsed. Admittedly, the tradition in literature is now largely limited to writers who hold to some kind of immanentism, and chiefly to writers of fiction. Novels (for example, those of Thomas Mann and Hermann Hesse) are replete with recastings of the concept of unity through empathetic participation, or with parodies of it.[11] But fiction teaches lessons that historians ignore at the cost of diminishing the truth. Oddly, a medieval lawyer, Baldus de Ubaldis, writing about corporations, suggested the lesson that I am drawing. Corporations, he wrote, were personalities only as legal fictions. But legal fictions are real facts. "Fiction," Baldus wrote, "imitates nature. Therefore fiction has a place only where truth can have a place."[12] Hermann Hesse brought the lesson home: "We shall not forget that history, however much

---

[9] See the convenient survey in Katz, *Empathy: Its Nature and Uses*, pp. 1–2, 17, 28, 30–31, 77, 82, 119.

[10] I employ the title of a book by Carl F. Keppler: *The Literature of the Second Self* (Tuscon: University of Arizona, 1972).

[11] For example, see Thomas Mann's *The Transposed Heads: A Legend of India*, trans. H. T. Lowe-Porter (New York: Vintage Books, 1969), pp. 6, 30, 82, 110, 112. The book is a parody on the Indic doctrine that "distinctions between the I and the you" are illusory.

[12] Ernst H. Kantorowicz, *The King's Two Bodies*, 2d ed. (Princeton: Princeton University Press, 1969), p. 306.

sobriety, goodwill, and objectivity we bring to bear in the writing of it, still remains invention, and that fiction is its third dimension."[13] This character also belongs to another kind of historical reflection: the kind that in every age, and not only by the noblest passions, has impelled the human heart toward unity through love and conflict.

MY FIRST CONCERN is to demonstrate that the subject is a real one by establishing the various meanings that the sentence had, meanings that its history gave it. Most of the following discussion, however, concerns mimetic explanations of how it was possible to think that "I" could become "you." These explanations were drawn from essential facts of reproduction in human nature itself, from reproduction of the human species through individual events of sexual procreation, and from reproduction of general ideas through production of individual tools, or works of art, according to design.

The point of departure for us is the primordial distinction between body and spirit, and between the two corresponding ways of giving form—procreation and composition. These are the origins of what I have called the biological and esthetic paradigms of assimilation. Reflections on assimilation through, or by analogy with, biological relationships posed the conceptual models of the individual organism in which many members became one, and of the genetic, or sexual, bonding in which two became one flesh. Reflection on esthetic assimilation likewise led to two variations: the first, the formal assimilation of parts in the wholeness of a single composition, and the second, the bonding through feelings of a viewer with something in the work of art.

Both paradigms therefore explained what gave existing things their coherence, and how other beings were drawn into and participated in that inward unity. As reflections on human nature, from two different points of view, they also proved to be two variations on the theme of love, the affect that, in countless perplexing forms, was the key to physical, intellectual, and spiritual union. In its portrayal of male dominance and female submission, the biological paradigm also illustrates the hatred, perhaps suppressed, that could be part of love. These paradigms did not rest in the earliest geological stratum of ideas. The venerable distinction between flesh and spirit came before them; and before even that was the playing out of unformed but formable experience, a playing out that was unseeable and unsayable, and that eventually gave rise to the distinction and to the organizing paradigms. Here, it is enough to say that the biological and esthetic paradigms had roles to play in the continuing tension between the works of the flesh

[13] Hermann Hesse, *Magister Ludi (The Glass Bead Game)*, trans. Mervyn Savill (New York: Ungar, 1967), chap. 1, p. 44.

and those of the spirit, not only in theology, but also in the running debate in so many areas about the relation between nature (or life), a synonym of flesh, and art, a synonym of spirit.

The paradigms drawn from biology and art converged; both indicated how the many could become one. Ominously, they were models of form-giving strife: the first, through male dominance; the second, through the imposition of form by the artist on recalcitrant matter. In both fields of study, progress was made by inquiring into the contrast between the repet-itiveness of reproductive processes and systems and the singularity of the individual beings that, by assertion of dominance, were brought into the world. In the course of discussion, I suggest that biological and esthetic facts of individual existence were woven into broad theories about the cognitive evolution of society through struggle, and, indeed, into the movement of that evolution itself.

The discrepancy between timeless repetitiveness and time-bound individ-uality intruded both antihistorical and historical aspects into this reflection. As historical documents, esthetic or mystical texts are artifacts of times past. But, to the kindred heart, even centuries distant, the experiences that they portray are not of time. Martin Heidegger (1889–1976), the existen-tialist philosopher, provided an elaborate analysis of this ambivalence in his discussion of history as the recurrence of the possible, of time as part of the act of handing down and repeating the possible through existential choice, and of existential choice as a moment of insight in which one is freed both to appropriate the possibility that can be repeated and to disavow the dead remnant of the "past" working itself out in "today." The task of thinking, he wrote, was not an adventure so much as a homecoming. Heidegger's theories elucidate some reasons why theories of how the "I" could become the "you" could be regarded both as historical and as hostile to history.

Indeed, the anachronism in the sentence "I am you" and the experience of the sentence across the ages provide an opportunity to test Heidegger's assertion that the task of the historian is to make "manifest the 'universal' in the once-for-all." Consequently, I have attempted to take account both of the historical and of the antihistorical nature of the sentence by organ-izing the discussion topically, and, on individual topics, providing one spec-imen of patristic (or medieval) thought and a parallel specimen of nine-teenth- or twentieth-century thought.

My strategy is to move from the sentence, "I am you," as a historical artifact (Chapters 1, 2), to patterns of understanding that enabled inter-preters to make the sense of the sentence (Chapters 3–5), and finally to ways of understanding the enterprise of understanding that lay at the bedrock of the tradition under review, considering first verbal (Chapters 6–8) and then visual (Chapters 9–12) ways of understanding understanding.

NOT ALL WAYS of thinking solve problems. Some, to the contrary, deepen the riddle of life. The simple declarative sentence, "I am you," summed up a tradition in which the logic of questioning led searchers beyond the closure that answers could provide. At some moments, closure appeared to be within sight; but time and again the questioners found that "every definition is a negation" (*omnis determinatio est negatio*) and, in their need, began afresh. The questions were larger than the sum of all possible answers.

If taken literally, the sentence points toward an inward communion beyond the external bonds of association in society, and beyond dialogue between "I" and "you" as separate persons. It points toward an identity beyond relationship, a common human identity that enhances the separate identities of individual persons. The ethics of transcendent communion do coexist with those of personal identity in Western culture and, not infrequently, in the same minds. In the present essay, I indicate the meanings, the history, and the implications concerning personal identity that are built into the sentence. But I have been primarily concerned with ways of understanding both the event and the experience of understanding itself. In important ways, reflection on the event and experience of play yielded the raw materials out of which empathetic understanding was formed. Consequently, at some points in the following account, understanding is virtually synonymous with play.

Some play disgusts; some understanding repels. The records of history are strewn with incidents in which even recognition that all human beings display varieties of a single face, that the whole universe is "but a little family," and, above all, that any understanding falsifies has not called forth humble or generous ways. Convinced that God created the human race in his own image, St. Ephrem the Syrian (ca. 303–73) still sang of a freedom to choose compassion or inhumanity, a freedom that may indeed be a tragic flaw, but yet in its great power soars beyond the reach of thought or faith.

> See his goodness! Though he could have made us beautiful
> by force, without labor, he labored in every way
> that we might become beautiful by our own will,
> painting our own beauty,
> with colors gathered by our own free will.
> If he himself had made us fair, we would have been only an image
> blocked out, and beautified by another artist,
> as he saw fit, with the colors of his palette.[14]

---

[14] *Hymns of the Faith*, 31. 1; adapted from J. B. Morris, trans., *Select Works of S. Ephrem the Syrian* (Oxford: J. H. Parker, 1847), p. 206.

PART I
THE CONTENT OF
THE SAYING

For, by usage all that is loved draws its lover into its own nature, whence the Philosopher said, "Usage becomes a second nature." Thus it is when a shoot of pear is grafted to an apple stock. After it becomes established, the apple bears according to the nature of the pear in such a way that afterwards the two together are rightly called a pear, and they produce the fruit of the pear.

John Fortescue, *De Laudibus Legum Anglie*,
chap. 5, ed. S. B. Chrimes
(Cambridge, 1942), p. 16.

ONE

The Positive Content

THIS CHAPTER and the next constitute a dossier for the incredulous. Readers familiar with the language and tradition of empathy may well begin with later chapters. However, for many, the world of empathy, ways of thinking about it, and the vocabulary it requires are unknown. To provide some guidance, I have cast these chapters on positive and negative contents in a fairly schematic way. Attempting to keep the schema from beginning in categories and ending in catechesis, I have supplied numerous illustrations at most points. In this way, I hope to provide a systematic introduction to a subject that flies in the face of widespread convictions about personal separateness and, by the weight of illustrations, to assure the skeptical that the propositions at issue in this essay actually belong to a common heritage of Western culture. I hope, by schema and illustrations, to prepare a secure point of departure. At any rate, these chapters should suggest that the sentence, "I am you," was not an occasional accident of phrasing invented by whimsical writers, but rather the signature of a long and many-formed hermeneutic tradition. It had a history. At the beginning, I must emphasize that the sentence did not make its sense. Interpreters made sense of it, and they were able to do that because of their common heritage.

THE SENTENCE "I am you" is reminiscent of Vedic theology. It reflects the propositions that God (*Atman*) inhabits all things and, particularly, that the human soul is identical with Atman. Parallels have been drawn between Vedic theology and doctrines of Western scholars who taught that human personality was subsumed in a higher, perhaps divine, unity.[1]

---

[1] Richard Reitzenstein, *Poimandres: Studien zur griechisch-ägyptischen und frühchristlichen Literatur* (Leipzig: Teubner, 1904), p. 17 (first prayer to Hermes, 11, 20–21; second prayer to Hermes, 7; third prayer to Hermes, 11). See also the *Gospel of Eve*, quoted in Epiphanius of Cyprus, *Panarion* 26.3 (in *Die Griechischen christlichen Schriftsteller der ersten drei Jahrhunderte*, vol. 25: p. 278). *Gospel of Thomas*, 108 (James L. Robinson, ed., *The Nag Hammadi Library* [Leiden: Brill, 1977], p. 129). Late in the second century, Irenaeus of Lyon recorded that a Gnostic adept named Marcus employed the sentence both in its spiritual and in its erotic senses. According to Irenaeus, Marcus preyed on women of station, saying to each, "Adorn yourself as a bride expecting her bridegroom, so that you may be I and I, you," with the aid of magic and philters. Seduction followed. *Against Heresies*, I. 7. 2 (I. 13. 3.) (William Wigan Harvey, ed., *Sancti Irenaei Episcopi Lugdunensis Libri Quinque adversus Haereses . . .*, vol. 1 [Cambridge: Cambridge University Press, 1857], p. 118). I am obliged to Mrs. Jayarani Fedson for referring me to a later use of the sentence "I am you" in a collection of hymns to Viṣṇu. See A. K. Ramaṇujan, *Hymns for the Drowning: Poems for Viṣṇu by Nammaḷvar* (Princeton: Princeton University Press, 1981), p. 89. As noted previously (Introduction, n. 11), Thomas Mann parodied this tradition in *The Transposed Heads: A Legend of India*.

Indeed, the sentence "I am you" appears to have entered European literature at a moment, and in a place, notably susceptible to Indic theology. To my knowledge, the sentence was first used in religious texts composed in the eastern Mediterranean basin, during the second century after the birth of Christ.[2] Some of these texts were composed by non-Christians; others, by Christians. All belong to cults that combined features of many religions and philosophies into secret doctrines and rituals. The sentence "I am you [and you are I]" appears as an occult formula or incantation expressing unity of the initiates with their gods.

The eclectic Greek culture that gave rise to these texts was open to Indic ideas, and such was particularly the case in Egypt, where some, and perhaps all, of these texts were written. In his account of early Church history, Eusebius of Caesarea (ca. 260–ca. 340) asserted that, during the second century, there were many Christian preachers—"evangelists of the Word"— in East Africa and India. One of them, Pantaenus (died ca. 200), returned to Alexandria and became head of the catechetical school, a position that enabled him to form the thinking of men who subsequently laid the foundations of Christian theology. Pantaenus had converted to Christianity from Stoicism, which taught a divine immanence resembling on some counts that taught by Vedic theology. What he taught as a Christian may have been informed by resonances in his mind between Stoic and Vedic doctrines.[3]

However, the sentence summed up ideas that had long been present in Western thought and belief, and that persisted long after the second century of the Christian era. If this had not been so, the sentence would have been yet another exotic ritual formula, imported and discarded because it had no

See also a statement attributed to the Islamic mystic, Bayazid Bastami: "I went from God to God until they cried out from me in me, 'O thou I.' " G. van der Leeuw, *Religion in Essence and Manifestation: A Study in Phenomenology*, vol. I (New York: Harper and Row, 1963), p. 503.

[2] On the story that Indian cosmology passed to the Egyptians and from them to Pythagoras, see Philostratus, *Life of Apollonius of Tyana* 8. 7 (Loeb ed., vol. 2, pp. 302–303, 205). On Greeks journeying to learn from Indian sages, see ibid., 1. 2; 1. 18; 3. 19 (Loeb ed., vol. 1, pp. 6, 49, 269). On Indian and Scythian prisoners of war, see Lucian of Samosata, *On the Parasite*, 52 (Loeb ed., vol. 3, p. 304). On the story of Dionysus's Indian expedition in late antique Egyptian literature, see Albin Lesky, *A History of Greek Literature*, trans. James Willis and Cornelis de Heer (New York: Crowell, 1966), pp. 816–19. One should also bear in mind the perennial question of whether and (if so) how much Plotinus, the founder of Neoplatonism, owed to oriental philosophy.

[3] Eusebius, *Ecclesiastical History*, 5. 10–11; 6. 13. Rufinus of Aquileia (ca. 345–410/11) described a later philosopher, Meropius of Tyre, who took his two sons with him to India in quest of wisdom. He carefully educated his sons. On the return voyage, their ship was captured off the coast of Abyssinia, and all aboard were killed except the sons. One of them eventually went to Alexandria and was sent back to Abyssinia as a missionary by Bishop Athanasius the Great. The other made his way home to Tyre, where he served as priest. Rufinus heard the account of their adventures from the latter. *Historia Ecclesiastica*, 1. 9 (Migne *PL* 21: 478–80).

roots in the Western tradition. There is no need to look afar to Vedism, Buddhism, or Sufic mysticism for broad structures of thought that gave meaning and long life to the sentence.[4] Centuries of thought and experience had prepared such structures in the West, encompassing other kinds of unity in addition to that between humanity and God.

Once adopted in the West, the sentence "I am you" became a motif of those already existing structures. As such, it has persisted until the present time. To illustrate the various structures of thought summed up in the sentence, their antiquity, and their persistence, I shall consider the different strands of thought woven together in John Donne's (1573–1631) *Meditation 17*. After identifying those strands, I shall sketch their pedigrees in Western thought.

In *Meditation 17*, Donne asserted the identity of the living with the dead. "Never send to know for whom the bell tolls," he wrote. "It tolls for thee."[5] Actually, the bell was tolled for the specific person whose funeral was in progress. But Donne believed that the bell was "passing a piece of [himself] out of this world." He adduced several reasons.

The first was sacramental. "The Church is catholic, universal, so are all her actions." By baptism, a child is "connected to that head which is my head too, and engraffed into that body whereof I am a member."

To this, Donne added metaphysical reasons. He invoked the philosophical argument that the world had, in God, its first cause and final goal. "All mankind," he wrote, "is of one Author, and is one volume," each life being an individual chapter. Death was not the destruction of a chapter, but rather a translation under God's hand, the very hand that "shall bind up all our scattered leaves again for that library where every book shall be open to one another." Donne's other metaphysical reason was drawn from the ancient philosophical category of substance. There was, he assumed, one substance of humanity in which all human beings participated. "No man is an island, entire of itself; every man is a piece of the continent, a part of the main. If a clod be washed away by the sea, Europe is the less. . . . Any man's death diminishes me because I am involved in mankind."

Finally, Donne combined a theory of knowledge (epistemology) with ethics. "The bell doth toll for him that thinks it doth."[6] However, people who hear the bell may not recognize that it tolls for them. They may not know that the tolling of the bell is a sign applying to them at all. They may

---

[4] E.g., Nikos Kazantzakis, *Report to Greco* (New York: Bantam, 1966), p. 370 (chap. 25); see also p. 98 (chap. 12).

[5] Charles M. Coffin, ed., *The Complete Poetry and Selected Prose of John Donne* (New York: Modern Library, 1952), pp. 440–41.

[6] Donne appears to have modified this view in *Meditation 23*, where he argued that "even in pleasures and in pains there is a propriety, a *Meum* and *Tuum*" excluding empathetic participation, though not fellow-feeling. Coffin, *The Complete Poetry and Selected Prose of John Donne*, pp. 456–58.

misread a particular occurrence of the sign. The identity of the dead with the living was not self-evident; it had to be grasped by processes of thought. Further, recognition was not enough. The lessons signified had to be desired and assimilated. Donne wrote, to be sure, that a man was united to God from the moment when he recognized that the bell tolled for him, but he went on to describe the ethical consequences. Recognition entailed willingly assuming the affliction of the dying to one's own profit, "if, by consideration of another's danger, I take mine own into contemplation and so secure myself by mankind my recourse to my God, who is our only security."

Thus, Donne wove together a number of strands to justify his idea of common identity. These strands enabled him to think of several kinds of personal union. Because of sacramental theology, he was able to think of believers in personal union with Christ, their common head, and of believers in union with one another through their unity in Christ's body. His metaphysical reasoning enabled him to think of personal union of man with God through the participation of effects in their causes (God being the first cause—the single Author—of the world), and of each human being with all others through participation in the substance of humanity. On epistemological (and ethical) grounds, he was also able to conceive of personal union of man with God through recognition of a common humanity and willing application of its moral consequences.

Moreover, it is evident that Donne distinguished between potential and actual identity. His theology taught him that identity inhered in the sacramental bond uniting believers in, with, and through Christ. His metaphysics taught him that identity inhered in nature, specifically in its causal order and in substances. However, these truths did not exist for those who did not know and desire them, any more than the bell tolled for those who ignored or misread its signal. Even those who perceived the grounds of union had to move in a complex process from potential to actual identity— by sacramental action repeated until death; by enduring the movement of egress, dispersion, and reunion through which the hand of God bound up "all our scattered leaves again"; by desiring the affliction that matures and ripens such people, making them fit for God; and finally by embracing misery as a treasure that brings them "nearer and nearer our home."

In fact, the web of ideas that guided Donne postulated an identity of the "I" with the "you" that coexisted with and enhanced personal separateness. This ambiguity is implicit in two paradigms of unity on which Donne's ideas centered: the biological unity of members in one body (as in the Church as the body of Christ), and the esthetic unity of parts in a whole composition (as in chapters of a book).

As we shall see, both the biological and the esthetic paradigms actually consisted of two components, the one static and the other dynamic. The static component of the biological paradigm characterized the organic assimilation of many members in one body. Its dynamic component had to do with the genetic process of procreation, by which individual bodies, in their organic integrity, joined into one to produce others, male dominance and female subordination being always asserted. The static component of the esthetic paradigm derived from analogy with the combination of disparate elements in a single artistic composition. The dynamic component concerned the processes of knowing and feeling by which a spectator, or hearer, absorbed and was absorbed into a work of art. In the event, both paradigms were perspectives on the same subject: human nature in its multiplicity and unity. From this common subject they gained their common preoccupation with the emotions (or affects) as the means of bonding and, in particular, with love, the most complex and powerful of all affects whether in nature or in art, the created second nature of human existence.

Either in the biological or in the esthetic paradigm, the identity achieved was selective. It extended to particular aspects of existence having to do with heart and mind, rather than an all-encompassing unity of the material world, such as is the case, for example, in pantheism. (These paradigms of unity also figured in theories about society, as we shall in Chapter 5.)

This partial common identity was achieved by mediation. The "I" and the "you" were separate until a mediating act was performed uniting them in the crucial aspects. This act might be a sacrament (reenacting the historical mediation of Christ). It might be the causal act of procreation by which humanity was conveyed, or the providential act of "translation" by which estrangement from God in this world was changed into union with God in the next. It might be the mediating act of recognition and acceptance by which one person desired to participate empathetically in the affliction of another, making it his own. In all cases, it was an act of understanding, that is, of interpretation. Finally, mediation was itself possible because the "I" was intrinsically like the "you" in the aspects that permitted identity. The processes through which the "I" and the "you" moved by degrees from remote to close likeness and finally to identity were mimetic as well as hermeneutic.

Donne's intellectual tradition illustrated the ambiguous coexistence of selective identity with personal separateness with a variety of metaphors. In *Meditation 17*, Donne himself employed the metaphor of grafting. There were many others: the drop of water in a cup of wine, the heat in a bar of iron, the grains kneaded together into one loaf of bread, the manifestation of an archetype in a copy, the kindling of many candles from one and the same fire, the harmony of voices in song, and the act of eating and digestion by which the flesh of one body was transformed into that of another.[7] The

[7] Paulinus of Nola (353–431) provides an unusual metaphor when he describes the faithful as being "sewn on" to God. *Ep.* 29: 3 (*CSEL* 29, p. 249). Cf. his musical metaphors in *Carm.* 21: lines 269–344, and *Carm.* 27: lines 69–92 (*CSEL* 30, pp. 167–69, 265–66).

list is a long one, but its very length may serve to emphasize the ambiguous teaching of the tradition of which Donne stood, an ambiguity that operated even when Donne admonished each of the faithful to move from likeness to identity with Christ, to be Christ's image "or not His, but He."[8]

I have identified a number of strands of thought that enabled Donne to compose *Meditation 17*. It remains, however, to indicate the ancestry and the career of his reasons, the kinds of identity that those reasons made conceivable to him, and the crucial role of mediation through stages of likeness toward identity; a mimetic strategy was embedded in each of the four reasons.

DONNE'S THINKING followed generally the division between works of the flesh and works of the spirit. The first category had two fields of inquiry—sacramental and metaphysical; the second category had only one but that field of inquiry was the most complex—epistemology.

Ideas about sacramental union were of primary importance to the biological paradigm. Several kinds of sacramental unity were recognized in classical and postclassical antiquity. The first was inspiration, or divine possession. Plato regarded inspiration as a sacred madness of which the highest form—philosophic madness—was like a continual initiation into perfect mysteries,[9] a movement by which the soul was absorbed into the divine beauty, rhythm, and harmony that it saw, loved and imitated. The second and third kinds of sacramental unity were indeed enacted in mystery cults. Such unity might come about through eating consecrated elements, as devotees of Dionysus ate the raw flesh of a bull consecrated to the god and given his name. In this case, rituals of dedication and naming were thought to identify the god with the bull through sympathetic magic, enabling the flesh of the bull, transformed into that of the god, to be transformed yet again into the flesh of the initiate. Sacramental unity might also be achieved through rituals of personification. Evidently, when Apuleius (fl. 150) was initiated into the mystery cult of Isis, he was costumed as the god Horus, "adorned like the sun, and set up in the place of a statue, [and] the curtains being suddenly opened, I was exposed to the sight of the people."[10] Likewise, the Jewish theologian, Philo of Alexandria (fl. 40), described the High Priest's liturgical vestments as an elaborate symbolic representation of the universe. From the moment when he was clad in that image of the world, the High Priest was obliged "to bear about the pattern of it in his mind, so that he shall be in a manner changed from the nature of a man into the nature of the world and . . . become a little world himself."[11]

---

[8] *The Crosse*, lines 35–36 (Coffin, *The Complete Poetry and Selected Prose of John Donne*, p. 234).

[9] *Phaedrus*, 249, 265.

[10] *Metamorphoses*, 11. 24 (Rudolf Helm, ed. [Leipzig: Teubner, 1968], p. 286).

[11] *Life of Moses*, 2. 26. 135 (Loeb ed., vol. 6, p. 515).

Whether by inspiration, or by mimetic rituals of dedication or personification, the nature of the believer was absorbed, or transformed, into that of the divinity. The epistles of St. Paul demonstrate that these methods of personal union through sacraments entered the theology of the early Church. By the indwelling Spirit, Paul wrote, "I am crucified with Christ. Nevertheless, I live; yet not I, but Christ liveth in me" (Gal. 2:20). The Eucharistic elements, Paul taught, became the body and blood of Christ, consumed by the faithful to salvation and to damnation by those who discerned not the Lord's body (1 Cor. 11:23–29). Baptism was considered a mimetic ritual by which, being baptized into Christ and Christ's death, the initiate would also be in the likeness of his resurrection (Rom. 6:3–5). The believer personified—"put on"—Christ (Rom. 13:14; Gal. 3:27).

Thus, well before the sentence "I am you" entered European literature, complex sacramental grounds by which interpreters could make sense of it were prepared. The ritual incantations in non-Christian hermetic texts affirmed that the believer was transformed into the divinity by likeness— by knowledge, by the god's name hidden as a charm in the believer's heart, or by the fact that the believer was the image of the god. All these grounds, anticipated in pre-Christian thought, were embedded in Christianity. However, Christianity had added a dimension of sacramental unity that was not directly anticipated: not only a primary unity between devotee and god, but also a secondary unity among believers.

Repeating Scriptural doctrine, Donne offered to this secondary unity when he wrote of the Church as the body of Christ. "For as we have many members in one body," St. Paul had written, "and all members have not the same office; so of another," through bonds of love (Rom. 12:4–21; 1 Cor. 12:12–27; 13:1–13). It was possible to write of this union as a "convisceration" of believers with one another and with Christ.[12] St. Augustine (354–430) imagined Christ contemplating the ever-growing body of the faithful and saying, "In me, they are also I," and the believers bending grammar to affirm, for their part, "He is we."[13]

Normally, the sacramental union of believers in the body of Christ was associated with their eating his body and drinking his blood in the Eucharist, a parallel with Dionysiac practice. However, through the centuries, Christians occasionally, but persistently, reversed this sacred cannibalism, teaching that believers were consumed by Christ and digested into his body,

[12] Paschasius Radbertus (ca. 790–ca. 859), De corpore et sanguine Domini, 19 (Corp. Christ., continuatio mediaevalis, 16, p. 101). De charitate, 2 (Migne PL 120: 1464).

[13] Tr. in Joan., 21, 7–8 (Corp. Christ., ser. lat., pp. 216–17). Tr. in Joan., 118, 5 (Corp. Christ., ser. lat., p. 618): "quoniam in me, etiam ipsi sunt ego." Tr. in Joan., 111, 6 (Corp. Christ., ser. lat., pp. 632–33): "Aliter enim est in nobis tamquam in templo suo, aliter autem quia et nos ipse sumus, cum secumdum id quod ut caput nostrum esset, homo factus est corpus eius sumus." Serm. 134: 8 (Migne PL 38: 742): "Iam vero si nos ipsos adtendamus, si corpus eius cogitemus, quia et nos ipse est.   Ergo et nos ipse, quia ipse caput nostrum, quia totus Christus caput et corpus."

became bone of his bone and flesh of his flesh. Christ consumed the faithful at his altar, wrote one twelfth-century commentator, just as a falcon devours a dove, "for one bird cannot be incorporated into another bird so long as it keeps its former life."[14] The Vedic origins of the sentence "I am you" contained an inner logic that disclosed itself again in this portrayal of a devouring god; for Viṣnu also, allowing himself to be eaten by the believer, devoured the soul of the believer by his grace.[15] That distant yet indomitable logic appeared again in T. S. Eliot's portrayal of Christ as a ravening tiger, coming "in depraved May" to devour us.[16]

There is no need to pursue the ground of sacramental unity in Christian theology through the centuries, to the assertion of Gerard Manley Hopkins (1844–89) that, reborn in the faithful, Christ

[14] Gerhoch of Reichersberg, Tr. in Ps. 22: 5 (Migne, PL 193: 1051). Cf. Marcelle Thiébaux, The Stag of Love: The Chase in Medieval Literature (Ithaca: Cornell University Press, 1974), pp. 46, 60–66. For similar passages by two of Gerhoch's contemporaries, see Anselm of Havelberg, Dialogi, 3. 20 (Migne PL 188: 1244): ". . . quia in illo prius per aquam baptizati, postea eum esuriendo et sitiendo spiritualiter potamus"; and Bernard of Clairvaux, Serm. in Cant., 71. 3. 5–7 (J. Leclercq, C. H. Talbot, and H. M. Rochais, eds., Sermones Super Cantica Canticorum, 36–86 [Rome: Editiones Cistercienses, 1958. S. Bernardi Opera, vol. 2], pp. 217–18): "Nam si manduco et non manducor, videbitur in me ille esse, sed nondum in illo ego." Bernard describes how believers eat Christ, and how they, in turn, are prepared, chewed, swallowed, digested, and assimilated as they are conformed to Christ. Julian of Norwich, A Revelation of Love, ed. Marion Glasscoe (Exeter: University of Exeter, 1976), no. 75, pp. 90–91: ". . . for the thriest of God is to have the general man into him, in which thirst he hath [drawyn] his holy that now be in bliss, and gettand his lively members, ever he drawith and drinkith, and yet he thirstith and longith." See also below Chapter 4 at n. 15. For modifications of this theme, see Augustine, Conf., 7. 10. 16 (Corp. Christ., ser. lat. 27, pp. 103–104): "Cibus sum grandium: cresce et manducabis me, nec tu me in te mutabis sicut cibum carnis tuae, sed tu mutaberis in me." Conf., 7. 18. 24 (Corp. Christ., ser. lat. 27, p. 108): "Ego sum via veritatis et vita et cibum, cui capiendo invalidus eram, miscentem carni." See below Chapter 7, n. 234. Cf., with the texts of Paul, the following "secret sayings of the living Jesus," in the Gnostic Gospel of Thomas: "Logion 7. Jesus said, 'Blessed is the lion which becomes man when consumed by man; and cursed is the man whom the lion consumes and the lion becomes man. — — Logion 11. The dead are not alive and the living will not die. In the days when you consumed what is dead, you made it what is alive." The Nag Hammadi Library in English, pp. 118–19. See also John Donne's metaphor of a consuming fire:

> . . . alas the fire
> Of lust and envie have burnt it heretofore,
> And made it fouler; let their flames
>   retire,
> And burne me o Lord, with a fiery zeale
> Of thee and thy house, which doth in eating heal.

Divine Poems, 5 ("I am a little world made cunningly"), in Coffin, The Complete Poetry and Selected Prose of John Donne, p. 249. Compare Peter Damian's statement, Sermo 6: De sancto Eleucadio (Migne PL 144: 537), that, through the dust of the Golden Calf, which they drank, the Hebrews absorbed Satan, though he had tried to absorb them into his members: "Sic, sic, ille vitulus per ignem zeli, ac aciem verbi, aquamque baptismatis ab eis potius absorptus est quos conatus est absorbere: in eos ipse transfusus est, quos in sua, hoc est diabolica, tentaverat membra transferre."

[15] Ramaṇujan, Hymns for the Drowning, pp. 67–69, 76–77.

[16] T. S. Eliot, "Gerontion," in The Waste Land and other Poems (New York: Harcourt, Brace, and Jovanovich, 1934), pp. 19, 21.

> . . . comes to be
> New self and nobler me
> In each one and each one
> More makes, when all is done
> Both God's and Mary's Son.[17]

The motif of sacramental unity can be traced in many diverse strands. The motif appears, for example, in novels by Carlos Castañeda, in which disciples of the Nagual, or mystic master, become one and the same because they are one being with the Nagual, and part of him.[18] The motif also appears in the literature of social work. When Dorothy Day (1897–1980) explained her motivation for devoting her life to alleviating the plight of the poor, she turned to the literature of Christian spirituality and, above all, to sacramental theology. Drawing on these sources, she wrote, "I suffered not only my own sorrow but the sorrows of those around me. I was no longer myself. I was man.   I was that mother whose child had been raped and slain. I was the mother who had borne the monster who had done it. I was even the monster, feeling in my own heart every abomination."[19] Enough has been said to establish that a sacramental ground for thinking that one could move beyond likeness and beyond relationship to personal union was present in European culture from classical antiquity onward, and that it found a secure and permanent shelter in Christian theology.

METAPHYSICS was the second field that contributed to the biological paradigm of assimilation. To be sure, the metaphysical ground for thinking that "I" could become "you" claims the same antiquity and persistence as the sacramental. It originated in philosophical discourse about the One and the Many, longrunning discourse that already could seem otiose and hackneyed, if not childish, even in fourth-century Athens.[20] Yet, there was no way to evade the issue if one began, as Plato and Aristotle did, from the assumption that the world was a cosmos, a whole composed of many parts and governed by a primordial harmony—in other words, that all individual things were essentially one. In that case, one had to grapple with the ironic marvel that "the one is many and infinite, and the many are only one";[21] the whole was identical with its parts.[22] But, on different metaphysical grounds, Plato and Aristotle argued that it was also possible for parts to be considered identical among themselves. Because ideas about the very being

---

[17] "The Blessed Virgin Compared to the Air We Breathe," lines 68–72, in W. H. Gardner, ed., *Gerard Manley Hopkins: A Selection of His Poems and Prose* (Harmondsworth: Penguin, 1954), p. 56.

[18] See *The Second Ring of Power* (Harmondsworth: Penguin, 1979), pp. 16, 19–20, 62–63, 58, 72, 74, 210; *The Eagle's Gift* (New York: Pocket Books, 1981), p. 218.

[19] Dorothy Day, *From Union Square to Rome* (New York: Arno Press, 1978), p. 6.

[20] Plato, *Philebus*, 14–15.

[21] Plato, *Philebus*, 14.

[22] *Theatetus*, 203. Aristotle, *Rhetoric* 2.24. 1401a.

of things was fundamental to assumptions built into the sentence, "I am you," a detailed survey of guiding propositions is in order.

Both philosophers argued that causation gave the key to the ironic identity between the One and the Many and that, in this regard, generation was a particularly important mode of causality. Plato's explanation was unusually complex. According to the myth of creation that he set down in the *Timaeus*, God made the world as an artist produces a work, standing outside the composition. Creation was not the production of material elements (which already existed in chaos without divine action), but the imposition of order and proportion. This God achieved using three "natures": an intellectual pattern, or archetype; the space in which the world was formed; and the world itself, the created copy. Plato described the archetype as a father ("the thing of which the thing generated is a resemblance"), space as a mother ("that in which generation takes place"), and the world as their child ("that which is in the process of generation").[23]

The continual process of generation defines the world,[24] although the world is the image of God, who was neither generated nor generating.[25] The causal process of generation sustains the world's likeness to God, who stood outside the world and yet who, as "the best of causes," determined the process[26] and, as cause to effect, imparted his divine attributes (including immortality) to the world, to the lesser gods whom he created, and to human souls.

Plato's doctrines allowed for the identity of parts and whole on several counts. The first derived from his esthetic theory that an image participated in its archetype, a theory that he built into his doctrine of cosmic order. The actual world participated in its divine pattern. God created only one world, realizing that to create more than one would be to diminish the resemblance of the copy (the world) to the pattern (himself). However, the pattern itself was composed of subordinate Ideas, or Forms, which had many earthly copies. For example, the Idea of humanity was reflected in individual human beings. They were human precisely because they were informed by the archetypal humanity. The many were one by participation in their universal form.

But how did this participation occur across the gulf that divided the intellectual archetype from the material world? The gulf was mediated, according to Plato, by love (in this case, Eros), a natural attraction of the imperfect towards its perfect self. A lover is seeking the other half of himself, which can only be the good. His quest leads to transformation, or as Plato wrote, "birth in beauty." Conception and generation are an immortal

---

[23] *Timaeus*, 50.
[24] *Timaeus*, 29.
[25] *Timaeus*, 29–30, 92.
[26] *Timaeus*, 29.

principle in the mortal creature . . . because to the mortal creature, generation is a sort of eternity and immortality," always leaving a new existence
in place of the old.[27] All the quests and conflicts of this life are stirred up by
love for immortality—an identity that people seek in the procreation of
children and in giving birth to intellectual conceptions of art and justice.
But only a few could enter into the greater and more hidden mysteries of
love that led true philosophers to find their other half in archetypal beauty,
and that enabled them to procreate not images but realities of beauty, and
to achieve such immortality as a mortal could. Plato's metaphysical ground
for identity therefore coincided with his sacramental one.

Aristotle argued that Plato's doctrine of forms completely voided the
question of where formative motion came from, and that it consequently
annihilated the study of nature.[28] Aristotle rejected Plato's esthetic dualism
of archetype and copy and, with it, the dualism of mind and matter. He
replaced Plato's three tier schema—God, archetypal world, and material
world—with a unified concept of world order, but one in which the process
of generation remained crucial to the identity of the parts with the whole.

As a geometer, Plato was primarily concerned with abstract form; as a
biologist, Aristotle was primarily concerned with the concrete specimen.
Whereas Plato had argued that individuals found their true being in universal archetypes, Aristotle insisted that universals existed only as they
were realized in actual individuals. Thus, for Aristotle, the principle of identity had to lie in the transmission of life, rather than in the duplication of
form.

His unified conception of the world enabled him to conclude that God was
the beginning and the end of that transmission, and that he was immanent
in it, rather than transcendent above it, as Plato taught. As the unmoved
mover, God's continual action sustained the chain of causality in nature, the
circular progress of generation and decay by which living creatures came to
be and passed away, only to be replaced by others of the same genera and
species. As the final end of the cosmos, God was the goal toward which the
ceaseless procession of creatures moved.

The emotional and mystical element of love was banished from Aristotle's genetic theories, which, correspondingly, made room for identity at
points rather different from those allowed by Plato's esthetic doctrines.
Instead of Plato's archetypes, Aristotle postulated substances as the generic
and specific forms that shaped the matter of which individual beings were
composed. His doctrine of substances enabled him to think that all members
of a species were one in kind, though many in number. Thus, Callias and
Socrates could be considered one man through the substance of humanity.[29]

[27] *Symposium*, 205–207.
[28] *Metaphysics*, 1. 9. 992b.
[29] Cf. *Metaphysics*, 7. 10–11. 1034b–1037a.

Such was "the One beside the Many, which is a single identity within them all."[30]

In the line of procreation by which life was conveyed, a more limited identity could be affirmed between parents and their children, and among brothers. "Parents love their children as themselves," Aristotle wrote, "for these are, deriving from them, like separated other selves.   Brothers love each other as being born of the same parents. For their identity with them makes them identical to each other. That is why people talk of the same blood, the same stock, and so on. They are, therefore, in a sense, the same thing, though in separate individuals."[31]

Aristotle's broadest metaphysical ground for identity, however, was the immanence of God in the world as the ordering principle of its parts, as the source of its life, and as its ruler.[32] An extremely unclear distinction between passive and active intellects proved to be important in this regard. Aristotle emphasized the difference between the passive and mortal intellect in the human soul, and the active and immortal intellect that made all things, that came "from outside," and that awakened the passive intellect to realize its potentiality in action.[33] Aristotle's meaning was fiercely debated over the centuries, but some commentators concluded that the active intellect was indeed the Unmoved Mover, and that the thoughts of men were in some sense the self-realization of God.

Of course, the metaphysical grounds of identity explored by Plato and Aristotle had long lives, and experienced many transformations in Western theology and philosophy. Plato's concept of an archetypal humanity by participation of which all men were one played an important role in doctrines of Christ. Donne took up this theme in his analogue between the multiplicity of lives and the unity of mankind, on the one hand, and the multiplicity of chapters and the unity of the book that they composed, on the other. But Donne also drew on a commonplace of Christian doctrine. For centuries, interpreters had asserted that, although the books of Scripture were many, they had been written by one Spirit. Thus, they were rightly counted as one book being informed by the same Spirit, even as many churches were one Church, or, as Milton put it,

> as in an organ, from one blast of wind,
> To many a row of pipes
> the sound-board breathes.[34]

As long as these metaphors explained how things came to be, they belonged to the biological (or engendering) paradigm. When they explained

---

[30] *Posterior Analytics*, 2. 19. 100a.
[31] *Nicomachean Ethics*, 8. 12. 1161b.
[32] *Metaphysics*, 12. 6. 2–12. 7. 12. 1071b–1072b.
[33] *On the Soul*, 3. 5. 430a. *On the Generation of Animals*, 2. 736b.
[34] E.g., Gerhoch of Reichersberg, *Tr. in Ps. 26:* 2 (Migne *PL* 193: 1182). *Tr. in Ps. 150:* 6 (Migne *PL* 194: 996). Milton, *Paradise Lost*, I. 708–709.

how things stirred the affects of the spectator or hearer and produced unity between the audience and something in the work of art (including the artist), they belonged to the esthetic paradigm. This followed from the ability to consider things from a carnal or from a spiritual perspective. It was by some participation such as these metaphors ambiguously conveyed, some theologians argued, that human beings were one with Christ, though only the redeemed could go further and participate in his divinity.[35] Aristotle's teachings on identity in substance were preserved in scholastic philosophy and literature.[36] It pervades all doctrines, even widely disparate ones of theology and sociology, that posit "the original unity of mankind," and that can, therefore, imagine a "primordial empathy" imparted to each human being.[37] Drawing on this tradition as expounded by the German philosopher, Schopenhauer, Jorge Luis Borges asserted that "what one man does is something done, in some measure, by all men." Every man is all men. "When a man recites Shakespeare, he is Shakespeare," and when he discourses on Goethean doctrines, he is Goethe.[38] But perhaps the longest career of all belonged to Aristotle's doctrines of immanence. Eventually fused with other teachings derived from Stoicism and Neoplatonism, they gained prominence in western European mystical thought with the rise of Aristotelianism, from the late twelfth century on. The active intellect became the divine spark that illuminated the mind, and that realized a potential identity with God. On this reasoning, for example, Meister Eckhart asserted, "God is the same one that I am," and again, "God made all things through me."[39] These conceptions gained new vigor among German philosophers of the pre-Romantic and Romantic eras. Subsumed in the

---

[35] For examples of the idea that all human beings comprised one man, see Augustine, *City of God*, 10. 14 (*CSEL* 40, pt. 1, p. 470). Leo I, *Serm. 12*: 1. 2; 63. 6. 7 (*Sources chrétiennes, serm. 82*, vol. 200, pp. 150–56; *serm. 50*, vol. 74, pp. 82–84.) Of course, this idea, like that of original sin, found theological support in the doctrine that the entire human race descended from Adam.

[36] Otto of Freising, *Gesta Friderici I. Imperatoris*, 1. 5 (*MGH SS in usum schol.*, pp. 16–18). For parallels in Boethius, and in the commentaries of Otto's contemporary, Gilbert de la Porrée, on Boethius, see my article, "Otto of Freising's Quest for the Hermeneutic Circle," *Speculum*, 55 (1980) p. 228 n. 31. See Thomas Aquinas, *Comm. in Nic. Eth.*, 8. 12 (*Opera*, vol. 21 [Parma ed.], p. 288). Aristotle's teaching on identity between parents and children is also reflected in Dante's comment on Bertran de Born, who alienated King Henry II of England from his son. In Hell, Bertran's condign punishment was to carry his own head like a lantern (*Inferno, canto* 28, lines 125–26):

> And they were two in one and one in two.
> How this can be, He knows who is [in Hell] obeyed.

On Wolfram von Eschenbach's assumptions that brothers are one flesh, and that a father and his two sons are all one, manifest in three parts, see Robert Levine, "Wolfram von Eschenbach: Dialectical 'Homo Ludens,' " *Viator*, 13 (1982), pp. 199–200.

[37] Katz, *Empathy*, p. 63.

[38] *Ficciones*, ed. Anthony Kerrigan (New York: Grove, 1962), pp. 10, 19, 120–21.

[39] Rudolf Otto, *Mysticism East and West*, trans. Bertha L. Bracey and Richenda C. Payne (New York: Macmillan, 1970), pp. 28, 119.

World Soul, Herder (1744–1803), felt an intense union with the entire cosmos:

> To the lowest creature
> My sense feels and tastes and stretches.
> All beings are in harmony
> With me, yes, I am they.[40]

Likewise, Fichte (1762–1814) taught that all beings in the world were united through a common participation in the all-generating life of the Absolute, although, in their mutual relations, they were separate individuals. Each was connected with the One who alone existed; all life was the life of the Absolute. Thus, "In all the forms outside me, I behold myself again beaming back to me from them, divided and separated into the greatest diversity, as the morning sun, broken and rebroken into a thousand dewdrops, glitters back toward itself."[41] Fichte imagined himself exclaiming to the Absolute: "Sublime, living Will, named by no name, encompassed by no concept! Well may I raise my spirit to thee, for you and I are not divided. Your voice sounds within me; mine resounds again in you."[42]

Now we turn from the genetic paradigm, which dealt predominately with works of the flesh, to the esthetic paradigm, which dealt, by and large, with those of the spirit. For our purposes, the contributions of epistemology to the esthetic paradigm were far more intricate than those of sacramental and metaphysical thought to the biological one. Apart from sacramental and metaphysical grounds of identity, Donne advanced an epistemological (and ethical) reason for identifying an "I" with a "you." Identity was established by an act of recognition and desire by which one person empathetically participated in the condition of another. In this regard, too, Donne affirmed a tradition that antedated the introduction of the sentence "I am you" into European literature and that persisted long after his own day, a tradition more complex than the ones previously discussed but dependent on the ontological.

Again, the origins of the tradition were present in Plato and Aristotle. Plato taught that, like the eye, the soul became what it saw.[43] It participated in the divine archetypes because, before it entered the body, it had wandered in the celestial regions, being imprinted with images of what it saw, as seals are set in wax. In this world, sensation was caused by streams of particles

---

[40] "Die Schöpfung." Cf. "Das Ich," 1. 82ff. Bernard Suphan, ed., *Herders sämmtliche Werke*, Bd 29 (Berlin: Weidmann, 1889), pp. 444, 137. See previous discussion in the Preface.
[41] *Die Bestimmung des Menschen*, 3 (Fritz Medicus, ed., 3rd ed., [Leipzig: Meiner, 1921], p. 151).
[42] *Die Bestimmung des Menschen*, 3 (Medicus, ed., pp. 139–40).
[43] *Republic*, 6. 508–509.

moving from objects into the body. There, they formed impressions—of sight, hearing, and so forth—that the mind integrated, operating according to its own powers (including recollection of the archetypes). Through those impressions, it contemplated the universals.[44]

Opposing Plato's doctrine of innate ideas, Aristotle insisted that the mind was a blank slate when it entered the world, and that it was written upon by experience. Yet he too argued that a basic likeness between knower and known was a condition for knowledge. The thinking part of the soul, he wrote, had to be potentially identical in character with the object of knowledge, without being the object. The acts of knowing and thinking made this potentiality actual. As it reflects on the images presented to it, "the mind which is actively thinking is the objects which it thinks," or, in other words, "thought shares the nature of the object of thoughts."[45] Thus, the known object becomes part of the knower.

From their beginnings, theories of empathetic participation through knowledge were applied, not merely to the exalted identity that could be achieved between human beings and God, but also to various kinds that could exist among human beings. Identity through empathetic participation remained a theme in the literature of love and friendship. Thus, Aristotle wrote that a friend was "another I," and that friends were "one soul abiding in two bodies."[46] Long after, Ben Johnson (ca. 1573–1637) took up what had become a continuous theme in Western literature, writing of two friends "that either grew a portion of the other."[47] I reserve a fuller discussion of this theme to the chapter on amorous sympathy.

It was easy for Christian writers to assimilate these theories of knowledge, and for mystics to apply to one's knowledge of God the principles that "the intellect becomes what it can grasp," and that, when one person knows another, "I am made in you."[48] Love is "the transforming of the desire into the loved thing itself," wrote Richard Rolle (ca. 1300–ca. 1349). "Every lover," he added, "is assimilated to the beloved.   [The soul], completely absorbed in its longing to love Christ, and Christ alone, transforms itself into its Beloved."[49] Meister Eckhart wrote, "the eye in which I see God is the same eye in which God sees me. My eye and the eye of God is one eye,

[44] *Timaeus*, 64–68. *Theatetus* 184–85.

[45] *On the Soul*, 3. 4, 7. 429–30, 431a–b. *Metaphysics* 12. 7. 1072b.

[46] *Nicomachean Ethics* 9. 4. 1166a. Diogenes Laertius, *Lives of Eminent Philosophers*, "Aristotle," 20 (Loeb ed., vol. 1, p. 463).

[47] "Ode on Sir Lucius Cary and Sir Henry Morison," in *The Complete Poetry of Ben Johnson*, ed. William B. Hunter, Jr. (Garden City, N.Y.: Doubleday, 1963), p. 227. See also Eve's words to Adam in Milton's *Paradise Lost*, IV, 487–88: "Part of my soul I seek thee, and thee claim / My other half. . . ."

[48] John Scotus Eriugena, *Periphyseon*, 1. 9 (quoting Maximus the Confessor); and 4, 9 (Migne *PL* 122: 449–50; 780).

[49] Richard Rolle, *The Fire of Love*, chap. 17, 32, trans. Clifton Wolters (Harmondsworth: Penguin, 1981), pp. 99–100, 144.

and one vision or seeing, and one knowing, and one loving,"[50] a metaphor that Ralph Waldo Emerson (1803–82) employed centuries later when he wrote that he felt himself a transparent blind and all-seeing eyeball "part and parcel of God."[51] Implanted in the Neoplatonic doctrine that man, as lover, was transformed into God, the beloved—the soul "is itself what it loves"—[52] this exalted theory of divinization through knowledge received new vigor through the scholarly revivals of the fourteenth and fifteenth centuries. Pico della Mirandola (1463–94) declared that, at the climax of the soul's ardent ascent, "roused by ineffable love as by a sting, like burning Seraphim rapt from ourselves, full of the divinity, we shall no longer be ourselves, but He Himself who made us," a vision paralleled in the final sections of Castiglione's *Courtier*.[53] Unlike Pico and Castiglione, St. John of the Cross (1542–91) gave this common idea specifically Christian meaning. Addressing Christ, he wrote, "Let us so act that, by means of this exercise of love, we may come to see ourselves in Thy beauty: that is, that we may be alike in beauty, and that Thy beauty may be such that, when one of us looks at the other, each may be like to Thee in Thy beauty, and may see himself, in Thy beauty, which will be the transforming of me in Thy Beauty; and thus I shall see Thee in Thy beauty and Thou wilt see me in Thy beauty, and Thou wilt see Thyself in me in Thy beauty, and I shall see myself in Thee in Thy beauty; so that thus I may be like Thee in Thy beauty and Thou mayest be like me in Thy beauty, and my beauty may be Thy beauty, and Thy beauty my beauty, and I shall be Thou in Thy beauty and Thou wilt be I in Thy beauty. . . ."[54]

A second area in which epistemology contributed to the esthetic paradigm is the literature of impersonation. I have already alluded to the place that impersonation had in sacramental rituals. The bonding of personifier and personified was an enduring theme, not only in the *theatrum sacrum*, but also in the secular theatre. In the twentieth century, it still seemed essential to the director Stanislavski (1863–1938). In his writings on the theatre, he described how, by careful training, the actor absorbed the character that he

---

[50] *Serm. 12*, on *Eccl.* 24:30, in J. Quint, ed., *Meister Eckharts Predigten*, vol. I (Stuttgart: Kohlhammer, 1958), p. 201; and *Rechtfertigungsschrift*, 9. 19, in Augustinus Daniels, *Eine lateinische Rechtfertigungsschrift des Meister Eckhart* (Münster-i-W.: Aschendorff, 1923. *Beiträge zur Geschichte der Philosophie des Mittelalters*, Bd 23, Hft 5), p. 42.

[51] "Nature," in *Emerson's Complete Works*, vol. 1 (Boston: Houghton-Mifflin, 1884), p. 16. I am obliged to Professor Arthur Mann for this reference.

[52] Plotinus, *Enneads*, 6. 8. 18.

[53] Pico della Mirandola, "Oration on the Dignity of Man," 16, adapted from Ernst Cassirer et al., *The Renaissance Philosophy of Man*, (Chicago: University of Chicago Press, 1948), p. 234. Castiglione, *The Courtier*, 4. 70.

[54] *Spiritual Canticle* 35. 3 (*The Complete Works of St. John of the Cross*, vol. 2, trans. E. Allison Peers [Westminster, Md.: Image Books, 1957], p. 157). John of the Cross's words recall, in part, a widely read Cistercian composition of the twelfth century, *De Spiritu et Anima*. Making up his text out of a mélange of patristic quotations, the author anticipated life in the Heavenly Jerusalem, "cum videbimus te in te et nos in te et te in nobis visione et felicitate perpetua" (chap. 60 [Migne *PL* 40: 825]).

was to play and made it his own. Careful observation and knowledge was required, a movement "by creative emotions" from "the realm of the external, the intellectual into that of the inner, spiritual life." By that movement, the actor made the desires and feelings of others "part of his very self." The greatest actors, Stanislavski wrote, absorbed not only their parts, but also the soul of the play, and they synthesized "themselves with the playwright."[55]

The point to be made is that this "transfiguration or metamorphosis" by which the actor personified others resulted from a method of analysis grounded in imitation of models observed in real life. The method was both a cognitive and an affective process; it was mimetic. Because it required inward assimilation of character, this kind of impersonation differed from the external kind attached to those who represent others. For example, if a master is honored in his servant, it does not necessarily follow that the servant has absorbed his master's character.[56]

In its epistemological outlines, Stanislavski's method had a venerable antecedent, outside the theater, at the very center of European religious and political thought, namely, in the doctrine that legitimate popes personified the Apostle Peter—that each in his time was "living Peter." Of course, in liturgical drama and in political action, the Petrine doctrine had theological and sacramental aspects for which Stanislavski's method provided no counterpart. Yet the two doctrines of impersonation overlapped in their insistence that the personifier enacted a role, that his enactment required conformity of thought and emotions with models taken from life, and, finally, that this mimetic discipline merged the actor with the character that he enacted, and with the soul, and the author, of the play. Actors could play many parts. Thus, on epistemological grounds, Bernard of Clairvaux (1090–1153) wrote of the pope's numerous roles: in primacy, he was Abel; in governing, Noah; in patriarchate, Abraham; in orders, Melchisedech; in dignity, Aaron; in authority, Moses; in judgment, Samuel; in power, Peter; and, by anointing, he was Christ.[57]

---

[55] Constantin Stanislavski, *Creating a Role*, trans. E. R. Hapgood (New York: Theatre Arts, 1961), pp. 25, 50, 78, 226, 231–32. On epistemological grounds, authors may also assume the identities of their subjects. For a particularly clear statement of this identification, see Cynthia Ozick, as quoted in the *New York Times* magazine, 10 April 1983: "Leaving graduate school at the age of 22, disdaining the Ph.D. as an acquisition surely beneath the concerns of literary seriousness, I was already Henry James. When I say I 'became' Henry James, you must understand this: though I was a near-sighted 22-year-old woman infected with the commonplace intention of writing a novel, I was *also* the elderly, bald-headed Henry James." A parallel instance occurs in Hermann Hesse's novel, *The Glass Bead Game*, trans. Mervyn Savill (under the title *Magister Ludi*) (New York: Ungar, 1967), p. 235, in which the Music Master became so "impregnated with music . . . [in] all the parts and organs of his body, into the pulse and breathing, into spell and dream, until he was now only a symbol, an apparition, a personification of music."

[56] Cf. Augustine, *Tr. in Ev. Johan.*, 54. 3 (*Corp. Christ., ser. lat.*, 36, p. 460).

[57] Bernard of Clairvaux, *De Consideratione*, 2. 8. 15; see also 4. 4. 12 (J. Leclercq and H.

The literatures of friendship and impersonation set forth variations on the epistemological theme of empathetic participation. Despite the improbability that the themes of empathetic identity would intersect with materialism, an instance of that intersection did occur in the thought of Ludwig Feuerbach (1804–72), whose materialist philosophy inspired Karl Marx and Friedrich Engels. Feuerbach imbibed mystical theology from the writings of Jakob Boehme (1575–1624) and Herder,[58] and, despite his revolt against religious pietism and the supernaturalism of Hegelian philosophy, he invested some elements of theology in his materialist doctrines of society. For example, he was able to write that, considered separately, in and for himself, an individual man was only man, but "man with man—the unity of I and you—is God."[59] Feuerbach affirmed that the separateness among individuals was real. He insisted that each person achieved consciousness of the self only by experiencing that distance. Still, what distinguished human beings from brute animals was not self-consciousness but consciousness of the species,[60] and the ethics consequently specific to human nature required the sacrifice of one's self-being, the surrender of self to another. The individual personified the species, and had corresponding obligations. This was learned through love. "In loving, . . . I bind my being to the being of another; I exist only in the other, with the other, and for the other. Not loving, I exist only for myself. But when I am loving, I posit myself for another. . . . The being of the other is my being." In this way, one gained through love the consciousness of humanity as a species—the unity of man with man—that was the basis of all philosophy, moral law, and truth. "The other is *per se* the mediator between me and the holy idea of the species."[61]

In a related sense, the philosopher, Wilhelm Dilthey (1833–1911) employed the sentence "I am you" as a clue to the tacit assumptions that sustain cultural unity.[62] In fact, there was a long precedent for the secularism of Feuerbach and Dilthey.

Their use of the esthetic paradigm lightly moved into an area that theologians explored when they posed questions about God's feelings, and about

---

M. Rochais, eds., *Tractatus et Opuscula* [Rome: Editiones Cistercienses, 1963, *S. Bernardi Opera*, vol. 3], pp. 423, 457–58).

[58] See *Gedanken über Tod und Unsterblichkeit*, ed. Werner Schuffenhauer (Berlin: Akademie, 1981. *Ludwig Feuerbach: Gesammelte Werke*, Bd 1), p. 229, referring to Boehme as "*grosser Prophet*." Feuerbach also adverted extensively to Boehme in *Das Wesen des Christentums*, ed. Werner Schuffenhauer (Berlin: Akademie, 1973. *Ludwig Feuerbach: Gesammelte Werke*, Bd 5), p. 180 and passim.

[59] *Grundsätze der Philosophie der Zukunft*, no. 62 (*Ludwig Feuerbach: Kleinere Schriften*, Bd 2 [1839–46], ed. Werner Schuffenhauer [Berlin: Akademie, 1970. *Ludwig Feuerbach: Gesammelte Werke* Bd 9], p. 339).

[60] *Das Wesen des Christentums*, p. 28.

[61] *Gedanken über Tod und Unsterblichkeit*, p. 338; *Das Wesen des Christentums*, p. 278.

[62] *Entwürfe zur Kritik der historischen Vernunft*, in *Wilhelm Dilthey: Gesammelte Schriften*, Bd 7 (Berlin: Teubner, 1927), pp. 191, 208.

the dependence of the Creator upon his creation. Their teachings embodied a quandary that had grown familiar to theologians, one, in fact, that leads back to the point at which we began: the unities of God and the world. Suppose the statement "I am you" describes an identity between God and actual men and women, in the changing historical circumstances of their lives and in their variable knowledge. Then, theologians had asked, is it possible that God is, in some sense, dependent upon his creatures, or altered by identity with them? Was it possible to apply to God an observation that Aristotle made concerning human craftsmen? "Every man," Aristotle wrote, "loves his own handiwork better than he would be loved by it if it came alive, and this happens perhaps most of all with poets. . . . The cause of this is that existence is to all men a thing to be chosen and loved, and that we exist by virtue of activity [i.e., by living and acting] and that the handiwork is in a sense the producer in activity . . . ; for what he is in potentiality, his handiwork manifests in activity."[63]

I consider, in some detail, the subject of empathetic participation in art in Part IV. For the moment, it may be helpful to identify several doctrines about epistemology as applied to works of art that contributed to an identification between God and creation. Two can be briefly mentioned. The first, that stated by Aristotle, identified the artist with his work. The artist was considered to be in the work, or, as Aristotle wrote, the artist's ideas and skill were thought to receive material existence in it. Another doctrine taught that the subject, not the artist, informed the work. The portrait did not merely represent the subject but partook of the nature and dignity of the person represented. The cornerstone of all sympathetic magic, this primordial belief justified veneration of imperial images in the late Roman Empire. As St. Athanasius of Alexandria (ca. 295–373) wrote, "In the image is the shape and form of the Emperor, and in the Emperor is that shape which is in the image. For the likeness of the Emperor is exact; so that a person who looks at the image sees in it the Emperor; and he again who sees the Emperor recognizes that it is he who is in the image. And from the likeness not differing to one who after the image wished to view the Emperor, the image might say, 'I and the Emperor are one; for I am in him

---

[63] *Nicomachean Ethics*, 9. 7. 1167b–1168a. See Callistratus, *Descriptions* 2 (Loeb ed., Philosotratus, *Imagines*, p. 385). Callistratus describes the statue of a baccante that "by its outward shape keeps its own creator alive." See the comment attributed to the naturalist and painter Andrei Avinoff (in 1945–46). Referring to a watercolor that he had just finished, he is reported to have said: "The odor of the rose seemed to flow from the end of my brush as I painted. I became the rose." Alex Schoumatoff, "Personal History (The Schoumatoff Family—Part II)," *The New Yorker*, 3 May 1982, p. 103. In the twelfth century, the Abbot Suger of St. Denis spoke of this unity accomplished through the mediacy of the artisan. Writing of God as the author and Solomon's Temple (as a type of the abbey church of St. Denis, which he had just rebuilt), Suger wrote: "Identitas auctoris et operis sufficientiam facit operantis." *De Consecratione*, chap. 2, in Erwin Panofsky, *Abbot Suger on the Abbey Church of St. Denis*, 2d ed., ed. Gerda Panofsky-Soergel (Princeton: Princeton University Press, 1979), p. 90.

and he in me; and what you see in me, that you see in him, and what you have seen in him, that you see in me.' Accordingly, he who venerates the image, in it venerates the Emperor also; for the image is his form and appearance."[64] Desecration of imperial statues was equated with assault upon the person represented and could be ruthlessly punished.[65] The same doctrine of sympathy between the subject and the work of art sanctioned the veneration of sacred icons.[66]

The other epistemological doctrines require somewhat fuller notice—for example, the identification made between artist and subject. The identification of the artist with the work of art concerned the making of the work. The identification of the artist with the subject concerned what the work manifested, and it taught that the work manifested the artist, disguised as the subject: in other words, it was a concealed self-portrait. This doctrine was more profound than Buffon's assertion "style is the man himself", for it both included and penetrated beneath the level of style. The theory that the mind became what it knew or contemplated was one component. Another was the theory that art and education existed to correct the deficiencies of nature, and to form habits of thought and action as a second nature. Aristotle applied these components to his discussion of the credentials of poets.

However, it was crucial for Aristotle that the effects of a poetic work—its power to achieve a bonding between audience and portrayal—depended on the artistry of the individual poet.[67] The poet was an imitator; he represented actions and agents.[68] But the manifestation in the work was the genius, or inspired madness, of the poet himself. In their common task of imitation, many made mistakes; poets varied in skill and judgment. Few had, and none could learn, the crucial use of metaphor, "an intuitive perception of the similarity in dissimilars."[69] To be sure, the poet did not perform his task of imitation when he addressed the audience directly, but only when he spoke under the guise of his characters.[70] But it was his skill in metaphor that enlivened the drama, his enactment of the story that the characters portrayed, his emotions that the drama imparted to the audience.[71] There were, Aristotle wrote, three ways of disguising the artist's

---

[64] *Against the Arians*, III. 5 (trans. from *Nicene and Post-Nicene Fathers*, ser. 2, vol. 4 [New York: Christian Literature Company, 1892], p. 396 [adapted]).

[65] E.g., the threat of mass execution and deportation issued against the Antiochenes as described in John Chrysostom's twenty-one homilies *On the Statues*.

[66] See Catharine P. Roth, trans., *St. Theodore the Studite on the Holy Icons* (Crestwood: St. Vladimir's, 1981).

[67] *Poetics*, 1454b.

[68] *Poetics*, 1448a.

[69] *Poetics*, 1459a.

[70] *Poetics*, 1460a.

[71] *Poetics*, 1455a, 1460a.

voice[72]; but, in all, the poet himself was the manifestation in the work of art, the unseen spirit that spoke in different voices through the characters and imposed on them the work of dramatic action. Centuries later, Leonardo da Vinci (1452–1519) captured a similar identification of artist and subject when he wrote that painting "compels the mind of the painter to transform itself into the very mind of nature."[73]

The last epistemological doctrine about art that contributed to the esthetic paradigm by identifying God and creation grew out of a stance that I have already considered. The viewer became what he beheld. The knower was transformed into the object of knowledge. Aristotle applied this self-identification to drama. For the audience at a tragedy experienced the emotional catharsis of pity and fear because it vicariously entered into the drama being enacted before it. St. Augustine's writings are replete with allusions to the entrance of the viewer into the work of art, notably with reference to the theater. Perhaps the most elaborate is his reference to a scene in Terence's play *The Eunuch*. There, a young man asserts that a painting of Jupiter in the act of adultery induced him to reenact the scene with his own fornication. Of the many levels of emotional bonding present in this text, Augustine most dreaded that the audience would enter into the action of the boy in the play even as he entered into that of the picture.[74]

Each of these doctrines—identification of the artist with the work, identification of the subject with the work, identification of the artist with the subject, and identification of the beholder with the work—has survived into modern times. In each, the principles encased in the sentence, "I am you," apply.[75]

---

[72] *Poetics*, 1448a: to "speak at one moment and at another in an assumed character" as Homer did; to remain the same from beginning to end without change; and to "represent the whole story dramatically, as though they were actually doing the things described."

[73] Kenneth D. Keele, *Leonardo da Vinci's Elements of the Science of Man*, (New York: Academic Press, 1983), p. 131.

[74] *Ep*. 91: 4 (*CSEL* 34, pt. 2, pp. 429–30). *Conf.*, 1. 16 (*CSEL* 33: 23). *City of God*, 2. 7; 8. 26 (*CSEL* 40, pt. 1, pp. 68–69, 402–404). See below, Chapter 5 at nn. 19, 49.

[75] For identification of the artist with the work, see Charles Dickens, *A Tale of Two Cities*, preface. Katz, *Empathy*, p. 29, on Shakespeare and Balzac. James Joyce, *A Portrait of the Artist as a Young Man*, chap. 5 (London: Granada, 1983), p. 194: "The personality of the artist passes into the narration itself, flowing round and round the persons and the action like a vital sea." See also John Ruskin's comment, "Adore a falcon as did the Egyptians and paint it as never would he who sees it in a feathered biped, because the ecstasy which you have experienced will pass through your hands into the picture, and will give it the power to communicate to others the same transport." Cited in Lionello Venturi, *History of Art Criticism*, trans. Charles Marriott (New York: E. P. Dutton, 1964), p. 180. For identification of the subject with the work, see Hermann Hesse, *Narzissus and Goldmund*, chap. 11, trans. Ursule Molinaro (New York: Bantam, 1971), 164. Carving a statue of St. John, which is really a portrait of his friend, Narzissus, Goldmund became convinced that Narzissus was actually working through his (Goldmund's) hands to represent an image of his own (Narzissus's) being. For identification of the artist with the subject, see Hesse's identification of the Music Master in *The Glass Bead Game*, above n. 55. Kenneth Clark, *What is a Masterpiece?* (New York: Thames and Hudson, 1981), p. 16: "[Titian] has become Aretino." Modern expressions of this doctrine are legion.

We are now able to return to the subject of theological tradition. From Christian antiquity onward, these four modes of esthetic identification enabled writers to identify God with creation for the following reasons: first, as artist, he was actualized in his work; second, as subject (that is, the invisible model of perfection of which the visible world was an image), he informed his work; third, the continual creation by which God sustained the world was the act by which he contemplated himself in the mirror of the world; and finally, rational creatures (including mankind), contemplating their maker and model, became the object of their contemplation, the source from which they came and the end to which they returned.

Over the centuries, a series of Christian theologians and philosophers did progress from asserting the identity between God and human beings to teaching the dependence of God on his creatures. Indeed, these were writers who followed Aristotle, in emphasizing the immanence of God in the created world, rather than following Plato in stressing God's transcendent detachment above and outside it. In the ninth century, John Scotus Eriugena (ca. 815–ca. 877), by far the greatest theologian in the West between Augustine of Hippo and Amselm of Canterbury, taught that God was ignorant of his own nature until, and inasmuch as, he saw it manifested by "theophanies" in the world. Meister Eckhart likewise insisted that God became God in his creatures. The culminating voice in this theological tradition was Hegel's (1770–1831), proclaiming that stages of history occurred as the Absolute Spirit repeatedly came to new stages of self-consciousness, mirroring itself to itself in events of this world.[76]

Two further examples from painting will suffice. Referring to every painting as a summation of the artist's experience, Wassily Kandinsky wrote, "In each picture is a whole lifetime imprisoned, a whole lifetime of fears, doubts, hopes and joys"; See *Concerning the Spiritual in Art*, trans. M.T.H. Sadler (New York: Dover, 1977), p. 3. The contemporary British painter, Adrian Stokes once wrote, "Art must always show, to some degree, an integration of ourselves that cannot be separated from the integration imputed to our objects," and Lawrence Gowing has given unusual immediacy to the identification of artist and subject in a number of self-portraits in which "the image on the picture surface was formed over the negative imprint which remained after paint had been sprayed over Gowing by assistants as he was strapped to that surface." See Richard Morphet, *The Hard-Won Image: Traditional Method and Subject in Recent British Art* (London: The Tate Gallery, 1984), pp. 40, 44. For identification of the beholder with the work, see the eighteenth-century doctrine that viewers, abstracted from their own circumstances, entered into paintings and other objects of contemplation, in Michael Fried, *Absorption and Theatricality: Painting and Beholder in the Age of Diderot* (Berkeley: University of California, 1980), pp. 119–22, 130, 141. In its essentially Platonic conception, that the mind becomes the object of its contemplation, this doctrine also figures in the literature of theosophy, for example, in the writings of George William Russell (AE): Robert Bernard Davis, *George William Russell ("AE")* (Boston: Twayne, 1977), pp. 86 and passim. Heinz Höpfl, *A.E. (George William Russell): Dichtung und Mystik. Versuch eine Deutung von A.E.'s mystischer Weltanschauug* (Bonn: Peter Hanstein, 1935. *Bonner Studien zur englischen Philologie*, Heft. 23), esp. pp. 56–73. It also characterizes twentieth-century doctrines of esthetic empathy. See Katz, *Empathy*, pp. 3–5, 9, on "the annihilation of the subject in the object." See below, Chapter 12, n. 9.

[76] On John Scotus Eriugena, Meister Eckhart, and Hegel, see my study, *The Mimetic Tra-*

In quite different ages, poets captured the possibility that God's vital dependence on his handiwork went beyond empathetic identification. In the seventeenth century, Angelus Silesius wrote,

> I know that without me
> God can no moment live;
> Were I to die then He
> No longer could survive.[77]

In the twentieth century, Rainer Maria Rilke (1875–1926) repeated the theme:

> What will you do, God, when I die?
> When I, your pitcher, broken lie?
> When I, your drink, go stale or dry?
> I am your garb, the trade you ply.
> You lose meaning, losing me.

> What will you do, God? I am afraid.[78]

Drawing from this tradition, Feuerbach and Dilthey advanced to secularism, arguing that God and humanity were identical,[79] that "God" was in fact a projection of the needs, powers, and experiences at the heart of common human life. In this mood (acknowledging an eclectic reliance on venerable precedents), I. B. Singer (1904–) wrote that he had built "a private God" for himself, a God conforming exactly with Singer's own intellect, emotions, experience and imagination. As an artist and scientist, this God kept on experimenting, improving Himself in the experiences of men and women. Singer's God was not cruel, and this reduced "all problems concerning God . . . to a single one: 'Why the suffering?' The answer is: Without suffering there is no art. Suffering and joy represent the ele-

---

dition of Reform in the West (Princeton: Princeton University Press, 1982), pp. 168–70, 205–206, 318, 321. For the metaphor of history as a picture gallery displaying representations of the spirit, see below Chapter 8 n. 117; Chapter 11 n. 10.

[77] Angelus Silesius (Johannes Scheffler, 1624–77), Cherubinischer Wandersmann, 1. 8 (Hans Ludwig Held, ed., Angelus Silesius: Sämtliche poetische Werke, vol. 3 [Munich: Hanser, 1949], p. 8). Thomas Aquinas rejected the possibility of dialectical exchange between God and man. He agreed with Dionysius the Areopagite that mutual likeness could exist among things of the same order, but not between things of higher and lower orders. Moreover, when likeness was derived from one order of existence to another (as from a man to a statue), it inhered in the copy, not in the model. "We say that a statue is like a man, but not conversely; so also a creature can be spoken of as in some way like God, but we can not say that God is like a creature." Summa Theologiae, I. Q. 4, A. 3.

[78] "Was wirst du tun, Gott, wenn ich sterbe?" in Babette Deutsch, trans., Poems from the Book of Hours "Das Stundenbuch" by Rainer Maria Rilke (Norfolk, Conn.: New Directions, 1941), p. 31.

[79] Feuerbach, Gedanken über Tod und Unsterblichkeit, pp. 207–208.

ments upon which is based the divine drama. God, the Creator, is Himself the universal sufferer. Our suffering is His suffering. We are He."[80]

I HAVE NOW considered three ways in which sense could be made of the statement, "I am you": sacramental, metaphysical, and epistemological. These fields of inquiry contributed to two broad paradigms for organizing ideas about assimilation. Based on the fundamental distinction between flesh and spirit, and inspired by the two essential means of human reproduction, propagation and composition, the biological and the esthetic paradigms were pervasive and enduring. They provided ways to think about the static existing form and the dynamic forming action. Thus, the biological paradigm consisted of two components: the organic, concerned with individual things as they are in their composite integrity, and the genetic, portraying living things as they reproduce themselves. Human sexuality was an important element in the genetic part of the paradigm. The corresponding components in the esthetic paradigm were the formal, concerned with the wholeness and coherence of a work of art and the compositional, purporting to explain how viewers or hearers (including the artist) could become one with something in the work that might not be present in its formal structure. Even this rapid survey leads to a few conclusions.

First, Martin Buber contradicted substantial elements in the Western intellectual tradition when he criticized Meister Eckhart for teaching an identity between God and man that never really existed (see the previous discussion in the introduction).

Second, the sentence "I am you" has led us to four areas in which relationships were thought to shade into real identity. All of those areas were expressed or implied in Donne's *Meditation 17*. Cosmology was expressed in the doctrine that God inhabits all things, and therefore that God and the world are, in some sense, identical. Sacramental theology was expressed in the teaching that bonding occurred between the divinity and the believer and, through the divinity, among believers. Metaphysics was expressed in the proposition that all humanity comprised one human being, an idea of primordial unity that was applied most directly to parents and children. Epistemology was expressed in the identity between knower and known (or subject and object), a proposition that ramified through doctrines affirming the identity of lover and beloved, actor and character (impersonation), and—a cluster of ideas that dealt with art—artist and work, subject and work, artist and subject, and beholder and work.

Third, the sentence, "I am you," was accepted in Western literature because it epitomized answers that philosophers and religions had long

[80] "What is God to Do—Discuss His Book with every Reader?" *New York Times*, 18 May 1979, p. A-29. On one precedent, see D. F. Dudow, " 'My Suffering is God.' Meister Eckhart's *Book of Divine Consolation*," *Theological Studies*, 44 (1983), pp. 570–86.

given to extremely varied, but common, human needs. It was a formula, or slogan, that concisely expressed well-known and elaborate patterns of thought and belief.

Fourth, the sentence persisted in Western literature, partly because it encapsulated many common experiences in which two, or many, became one, partly because it was canonized in authoritative texts of the tradition, partly because it affirmed longed-for unity beyond the divisions of individual existence, and even beyond the collective association in which "I" + "you" = "We."[81]

WE CAN NOW go further in sketching out, in a preliminary way, a conceptual diagram for the following discussions. Beyond these conclusions, the examples given above suggest some broad characteristics of the tradition—or rather the strands of the Western tradition—in which the sentence "I am you" took root. Within Western culture, the sentence and the patterns of thought that it epitomized originated in ancient Greece. Neither sentence nor patterns of thought owed essential meaning or content to the other two fonts of the Western intellectual tradition, Old Testament Judaism and Roman thought. To be sure, both contributed elements to the conception structure as it took shape. The account in *Genesis* of God's creation of man in his image and likeness, and of his breathing his own spirit into Adam's nostrils proved to be especially important to allegorical aspects of the structure. But the origins of the sentence and its meaning were Greek. True to that beginning, the sentence and its meanings retained their cogency among people who moved easily in the intellectual heritage of Greece, and who worked in inquiries of high abstraction, rather than the forensic and social inquiries in which both Old Testament Jews and Romans of the classical and postclassical periods most notably distinguished themselves.

Another characteristic relates to the career of the sentence and its message of personal union. As the references above indicate, sentence and message remained current among writers who fell under the sway of certain strains of Platonism and Aristotelianism. Taken up into the sacramental theology of the Church, they also found an intellectual and institutional shelter through the doctrines and social affiliations of mystics, including religious orders. Thus, they passed, with permutations, into the writings of modern philosophers, particularly those of the German Idealist school. Both

[81] Lucien Goldmann, *The Human Sciences and Philosophy*, trans. Hayden V. White and Robert Anchor (London: Cape, 1969. Cape Editions 30), p. 28. Even the reflections of Gabriel Marcel culminate in the equation "I" + "you" = "We." Despite his emphasis on participation of the "I" and the "you" in one another, they do not pass beyond relationship, or dialogue, to merge into unity. In fact, they achieve freedom to be "other." Even the most intimate relationship of prayer "is the ultimate affirmation of the reality, 'we are.' " Seymour Cain, *Gabriel Marcel* (South Bend: Regnery and Gateway, 1979), pp. 35–39, 43, 46–47, 55, 95.

the sentence and the concept of personal union were ridiculous to writers of other philosophical commitments. Marx castigated the Young Hegelians for confusing the "I" with the "you."[82]

A further characteristic relates to the cogency of the sentence. The grounds of argument that I have discussed—sacramental, metaphysical, and epistemological—were hardly evidence and (much less) proof. What made the arguments convincing? It is clear that, through the ambiguities of metaphor, they are all—even those derived from the biological paradigm—esthetic arguments in that they deal with transformation, and that, in most instances (if not in all, implicitly), they taught a personal union achieved through the affects. Union progresses through stages of knowing, desiring, and enjoying or emulating the other. The arguments found their vindication in the esthetic closure of joy.

Not only the arguments, as structures of thought, but the accumulated writings and the traditions that conveyed them, were ratified in the same way, that is, by feeling in the moment of esthetic closure. There is an obvious analogue with drama. There, too, Plato argued, conviction was a matter of inspiration, not of art. He portrayed all the participants in a dramatic performance as iron rings, suspended in a chain from a magnet. The God, or Muse, is the magnet. A poet, the interpreter of the God (perhaps one, like Homer, long dead) would be the first ring, and from him the force of attraction would run through intermediate links—interpreters of the first interpreter, rhapsodes, actors, dancers and chorus masters—to the spectators. What moved them all was not knowledge or technical skill, but inspired, ecstatic love, an emotion of the mind that transcended the senses and the passions.[83] Similarly, Aristotle's doctrine on the cathartic self-identification of spectators with the action in tragic drama required, first of all, a poet of special gifts, or a touch of madness, and, secondly, an esthetic participation by spectators in the play as though it were reality.[84] The play became a transparent medium through which spectators relived a poet's vision and, in so doing, regained his original inspiration.

The experience of esthetic closure became a continual assurance of truth in the tradition with which we are dealing. It characterized classical rhetoric, when aspiring scholars were admonished to imitate and rival great poets and writers of earlier centuries, for "from the great natures of the men of old there are borne in upon the souls of those who emulate them . . . what we may describe as effluences, so that even those who seem little likely to be possessed are thereby inspired," and led to the sublime.[85] The same assur-

---

[82] Karl Marx, *Die heilige Familie* 6. 3. f., in *Gesamtausgabe*, Abt. I. Bd 3, (Frankfurt-a.-M.: Marx-Engels Archiv. 1932), pp. 318–19, especially against Bruno Bauer.

[83] *Ion*, 533–36.

[84] *Poetics*, 1455, 1461.

[85] "Longinus," *On the Sublime*, 13. 2 (W. Rhys Roberts, ed. and trans. [Cambridge: Cam-

ance by esthetic closure characterized Christian doctrine, when, by imitation, disciples were thought to absorb the faith of their masters, as though it were their master's blood transfused into their veins.[86] It characterized theories of art in the eighteenth century, when Winckelmann insisted that "imitation of the ancients is the only way for us to become great and inimitable," recapturing the inspired virtues of the Greeks.[87] It characterized spiritual experiences in every age, including one recounted by Simone Weil (1909–43). Captivated as she read the metaphysical poetry of George Herbert, she wrote, "I used to think that I was merely saying beautiful verses; but though I did not know it, the recitation [of Herbert's poem, *Love*] had the effect of a prayer. And it happened that as I was saying this poem [in 1938] . . . Christ himself came down and He took me."[88]

I have referred to some authors who excluded supernatural action and

---

bridge University, 1935], p. 81). Cf. Erasmus, *Praise of Folly*, chap. 25 (trans. Hoyt Hopewell Hudson [Princeton: Princeton University Press, 1970], p. 71): "As for these stilted, insiped verses they display on all occasions (and there are those to admire them), obviously the writer believes that the soul of Virgil has transmigrated into his own breast." On the theological doctrine that the spirit of Christ, or the Holy Spirit, was infused into the souls of believers, notably into those of exegetes, see Brian Stock, *The Implications of Literacy: Written Language and Modes of Interpretation in the Eleventh and Twelfth Centuries* (Princeton: Princeton University Press, 1983), pp. 442–43 (particularly concerning Bernard of Clairvaux). Because the Holy Spirit was regarded as the "spirit of the prophets," much the same conception informed statements such as Gregory the Great's that the spirit of Elisha was in Benedict of Nursia's breast. *Dialogues*, 2. 13, 4 (Adalbert de Vogüé, ed., *Sources chrétiennes*, vol. 260 [Paris: Cerf, 1979], p. 178).

[86] Cf. Hilary of Arles, *Sermo de vita Honorati* 36 (Samuel Cavallin, ed., *Vitae Sanctorum Honorati et Hilarii Episcoporum Arelatensium* [Lund: Gleerup, 1952. Publications of the New Society of Letters at Lund, 40], p. 75). Honorius has just commented that God begat him through Honoratus for the people of Arles. Cf. the sense of unity represented by Hermann Hesse in *The Glass Bead Game*, trans. Mervyn Savill (under the title *Magister Ludi*), p. 199, at the point where Joseph Knecht, now the head of his order, reflects upon the relationship that, as a youth, he had with his Music Master. He identified himself alternately both with the young student and with the old Master until "in the course of this fluctuating interchange of personalities, there came a moment when he was both of them together, simultaneously master and small pupil, or rather, he stood above both of them, the originator, conceiver, leader and spectator of the circle. . . ." See also Quintilian's advice to orators that a father seeking redress from a court for some dire loss should "transfuse a portion of his own sorrowful feeling into the breasts of his audience" (*Institutes*, 11. 1. 53). But in many relationships, including that of master and disciple, transfusion of feelings could occur even when one of the principles was absent. Cf. Ambrose of Milan, *Ep. 18*: 33 (Migne *PL* 16: 1022): "Let no one flatter himself because he is absent. He who joins himself to others in mind is more present than he whose assent is given by bodily presence. For it is more to be united in mind than to be joined in body."

[87] *Gedanken über die Nachahmung der griechischen Werke in der Malerei und Bildhauerkunst* (H. Uhde-Bernays, ed., *Kleine Schriften zur Geschichte der Kunst des Altertums*, vol. 1 [Leipzig: Insel, 1925], p. 60).

[88] Letter to Joë Bousquet, *Pensées sans ordre concernant l'amour de Dieu* (Paris: Gallimard, 1962), p. 81. Cf. Hermann Hesse, *The Glass Bead Game*, trans. Mervyn Savill (under the title *Magister Ludi*), p. 461: "I sensed at each waking moment the Redeemer at my side and felt his strength flowing into me; and when I had fully recovered I was sad because I could no longer feel his presence."

who read "holy books" without being convinced of their authenticity. They too have framed their versions of personal union by making the works of earlier writers their own, and by participating in the "effluences" of their genius. For them too the works of art became transparent mediums through which clues appeared, revealing a profound unity and coherence at the heart of life. For them too conviction that there could be a personal union (of whatever kind) sprang from esthetic closure in the perception, desire, and joy of love.

The discussion thus far has elaborated some conclusions that I tentatively set forth in discussing Donne's *Meditation 17*. Two points will recur throughout the following discussion. First, whether in sacraments, or by metaphysical processes, or through empathetic participation, the unity of "I" and "you" required an action that mediated the distance between the two. Secondly, in every case, this act of mediation was imitative, that is, mimetic. Esthetic closure of the distance came by moving through stages of increasing likeness to the point of identity. Finally, these mimetic processes were tautological. The goal that a person chose was a projection of his character, that is, of his inmost needs and capacities. Mimetic transformation had its origin and its end in the mind of the beholder. Mimetic transformation was proportionate to commitments that transcended thought and words, that is, to faith that moves in love toward its object. Donne's bell did not toll for everyone, but only "for him that thinks it doth."

This tautology underscores a distinction between one-sided (or esthetic) empathy and two-sided (or interpersonal) empathy. However, even in the exchange of dialogue, a tautology exists; for, like any other object of knowledge, the perceiver's capacity limits his power to assimilate the "other" as that "other" really is. Although the "I" may recognize the freedom of the "you" to escape, the "you" that merges with the "I" is still a fraction incorporated into the "I's" circle of knowledge.[89]

Aldous Huxley also witnessed to this hermeneutic circle. As we said, Huxley satirized the propositions "I am you and you are I" as teaching a collectivism in the Brave New World that annihilated individuality. He therefore misrepresented the content that long centuries had given to the sentences. Yet, steeped as he was in religious knowledge, Huxley accurately invested the propositions with sacramental, metaphysical, and epistemological meanings. He set them in a hymn sung at a liturgical ceremony parodying the Christian Eucharist, and indeed recalling charges of sexual promiscuity that pagans had hurled at the Christian agape, or love-feast, in late antiquity. Like Donne, Huxley recognized that the union of "I" and "you" depended, not on the externals of an elaborate sacramental order, but on an

---

[89] For the distinction between esthetic and interpersonal empathy, see Katz, *Empathy*, pp. 92–93.

inward act of faith. His protagonist, Bernard Marx, went into the ceremony knowing that he would fail to achieve the promised union again, just as he had done before. He joined the others in ecstatically proclaiming the advent of the Greater Being and in enacting an orgiastic union. But disbelief prevailed; he neither heard the advent that he proclaimed nor experienced the inner consummation that the orgy promised.[90]

Culminating in tautology, the mimetic processes return again and again, as they must, to the mind of the viewer—to one side of a relationship. They turn, not to the spectacle, but to the spectator. Love, too, can be one-sided. The Platonic love of an image for its archetype, the love of a craftsman for his handiwork, and the love of living persons for others in long-dead generations and cultures are examples. Unrequited love is also common among human beings who live in the same time and place. Even when love is two-sided, as between parents and children or among friends, it may take different forms; it is proportionate to the temperament and capacity of the lover, not to the character or merits of the beloved. Thus, the three terms—the lover, the beloved, and love, "a certain life that couples two things or that seeks their coupling"[91]—can be thought about separately.

The evidence of the following chapters will indicate repeatedly that, in some relationships, it was thought possible for a loving "I" to become "you" without a mutual exchange of affection, and that, in others, for "I" to become "you" through exchanges of quite disparate kinds. The focus of this essay is on the mediating third term (namely, understanding as love, or another affect acting with love's bonding strength). The biological paradigm of male dominance and female submission is a reminder, however, that hatred, overt or suppressed, could be subsumed in bonding by love.

Eventually, I shall take account of the partnership of love and hatred, and of the acknowledgment that human bonding could be sealed in the violence of ecstasy by hatred masquerading as love. However, I must turn first to the strategy of proof, in order to round out this discussion of the content of the sentence. Whether according to the biological or the esthetic paradigm, whether actually or metaphorically referring to the works of the flesh or those of the spirit, the cogency of the sentence, "I am you," depended largely on negative elements, which characterize its mimetic nature. To prepare for the next stage of discussion, let me now summarize the negative elements that have been implied in the discussion thus far.

Mimetic processes that consummated the union of "I" and "you" passed from visible things to invisible—for example, from the visible instruments of a sacrament to invisible identity between the worshipper and his god. It followed that visible things must be regarded as, in some sense, trans-

[90] Huxley, *Brave New World*, chap. 5, p. 2, pp. 73–75.
[91] Augustine, *De Trinitate*, 8. 10. 14 (*Corp. Christ., ser. lat.*, 50 A, pp. 290–91).

parent, in much the same way as physical gestures can be screens of feeling. Art had to be used to conceal art—in fact, to negate itself—so that the mind of the viewer, or hearer, could move freely beyond the physical object to the truth that it represented, beyond physical to psychological mimesis. The viewer matched this act of self-negation with one of his own, willing suspension of disbelief.

Whether by physical or by mental representations, the effect of the mimetic processes that we have considered was to make intellectually (or spiritually) present what are physically absent. (In art, a portrait represents its absent sitter. Mimetic sacraments render absent divinities present. Similarly, in metaphysics, causal chains present distant parts of sequences, and, in epistemology, ideas bring absent objects of thought to mind.)

The goal of mimetic processes was self-extinction—to reduce the symmetry of "I" and "you" through stages of diminishing likeness and increasing identity. (Of course, the mimetic asymmetry could also be reduced by movement in the opposite direction, through stages of increasing unlikeness.) Such are some negative aspects of the strategy of proof that have already appeared and that, in fact, expressed its predicamental nature.

TWO

The Negative Content

> Through non-formal contemplation, I am inclined to
> believe that it is the existence of intangible elements, the
> negative, in architectonic forms which makes them come
> alive, become human, naturally harmonize with one
> another, and enable us to experience them with human
> sensibility.
>
> Amos Ih Tiao Chang, *The Tao of Architecture*
> (Princeton: Princeton University Press, 1956), p. 9.

THE SENTENCE, "I am you," had a positive content, made up of what was
understood: propositions drawn from sacramental theology, metaphysics,
and epistemology. These propositions converged into two broad paradigms,
corresponding with flesh and spirit, that provided ways to explain how
many became one, but they were by no means self-evident. The grounds of
their validity went beyond logical, and even empirical, proof. They
extended to yet more general doctrines that defied the law of contradictions
and, indeed, that prescribed negation and the coincidence of opposites.

The positive content of the sentence (the formal propositions) was what
was understood; the negative content consisted not only of propositions
but, even more, of methods of understanding that made it possible to reach
those propositions. We have already seen that esthetic assimilation could
come about between a viewer or hearer and something that was not present
in a formal composition of a work of art, and the unseeable and unsayable
aspects of organic union and genetic reproduction are countless. There is an
element, perhaps the most important of all, that is reminiscent of Zen in
both paradigms. For the negative content completed the paradigm, whether
biological or esthetic, whether in the realm of flesh or in that of spirit. Perhaps because both paradigms were shot through with eroticism, filling in
the gaps and silences with what the heart needed or dreamed, the negative
content was common to both. But it was especially prominent in the esthetic
paradigm and, most precisely of all, in the part of the esthetic paradigm that
dealt with understanding: that is, hermeneutics or epistemology.

In the chapters that follow, I shall provide detailed examples of how positive and negative contents combined in the thinking of some individual

writers. At this point, I propose to define in general terms the negative content of the sentence, "I am you."

THE TERM *hermeneutic gap* sums up the negative content of an inquiry into understanding. The hermeneutic gap is the question encased in any answer, even when the actual answer does not correspond with the question that provoked it. As a literary device, it operates under many guises—for example, in the hidden associations at the heart of a riddle or a metaphor, in the vanished clues that have to be recovered to solve a murder mystery, or in the enigmas of allegory. A hermeneutic gap in this sense—a lack of information—arouses curiosity; it stimulates the imagination. Deprived of information needed to complete the pattern emerging before him, a reader or interpreter becomes a co-creator of the text in the process of reading. He enters into the text, and into the author's mind, trying repeatedly to fill in the gap. Masters of rhetoric play on this response, deliberately creating verbal or logical predicaments to ensnare their audiences, to hold them on the edges of their seats.

The words *sign, symbol,* and *sacrament* indicate a yet more fundamental predicament at the heart of all communication: the need to read between the lines, to fathom what is unsaid in the words, in order to grasp the message in the text. Where there is the chance of understanding, there is also the chance of misunderstanding, accidental or calculated; and misunderstanding shades into the spectrum of incomprehensibility. The effort to explore the silence in the words was, fundamentally, an attempt to bridge the distance between speaker and hearer that made both understanding and misunderstanding possible.

The hermeneutic gap is not an exclusively literary phenomenon. As a challenge to enter into an object of understanding, and into the creative process by which that object was produced, it is universally experienced. Using visual methods, the celebrated Rorschach test demonstrates how the mind creates a hermeneutic gap even when none was intentionally built into an object; and the impulse to define and plunge into gaps of understanding is part of the dynamic in all arts. In Part Four, I shall indicate that the limitations of the medium itself constituted a fundamental part of the hermeneutic gap in painting.

The hermeneutic gap, then, can be counted as part of any inquiry, including the complex interrogation that culminated in the sentence, "I am you." However, the hermeneutic gap itself was defined by concepts of the human condition and by methods of association. I now turn to these other, subsidiary negative contents.

THE POINT OF DEPARTURE must be the estrangement between individuals that is the precondition of all communication. Without distance, identity would prevail, and there would be neither the need nor the possibility of communication, of bridging the gap between partners in the human dialogue. Need is implicit in this estrangement, need that can be satisfied by participating in the lives of others. Ludwig Feuerbach captured the universal negativity at the heart of participation when he wrote: "Every single human being who exists outside of me is a hole, an emptiness, a gap in me. I am an entirely perforated essence. My whole being is a pore. Every essence like mine that exists independently [of me] punctures me, wounds me. In every human being, I simply observe what I lack. Other human beings are nothing other than the objective, independent pores of my own self as observed outside of me. And so all things are porous, full of void, open spaces."[1]

Portrayals of bonding through love took this negative porosity for granted. Were not friends "one soul in two bodies"? The biological paradigm made the erotic bonding of friendship applicable to other contexts. Was not a lover, seeking the good of the beloved as though it were his own, "set outside himself and made to pass into the object of his love"?[2] Gottfried von Strassburg (fl. 1210) portrayed Tristan and Isolde as sharing "a single heart and one desire," "one mind, one heart and a single will between them." "We are one life and flesh," Isolde says. "Let me see my life in yours . . . may you see yours in me, your other self, Isolde."[3] Describing the "unity of heart and soul" is his Cistercian monastery, Aelred of Rievaulx (ca. 1110–ca. 1167) described a moment when he perceived a mutual filling conditioned by emptiness: "The day before yesterday," he wrote, "as I was walking the round of the cloister . . ., I found in that multitude of brethren no one whom I did not love and no one by whom, I felt sure, I was not loved. I was filled with such joy that it surpassed all the delights of this world. I felt indeed my spirit transfused into all and the affection of all to have passed into me. . . ."[4]

Finally, erotic bonding also provided a way of visualizing the inmost life of each person. Conflicting emotions; the divergence of reason, feeling, and will; and the rival authorities of intellect and senses—all added up to a jangled disharmony of spirit. Consciousness (and conscience) require an internal division between the judging self and the judged self, another instance in which "I" and "you" confront each other, each in its own needfulness, this time inside a single mind. Erotic bonding served to explain how the different faculties of mind—the subject and the object in the command,

[1] *Gedanken über Tod und Unsterblichkeit*, ed. Werner Schuffenhauer (Berlin: Akademie 1981. *Ludwig Feuerbach: Gesammelte Werke*, Bd 1), p. 257.

[2] Thomas Aquinas, *Summa Theologiae* Ia. Q. 20. A. 2, on Aristotle.

[3] Gottfried von Strassburg, *Tristan*, trans. A. T. Hatto (Baltimore: Penguin, 1967), chap. 15, 16, 28; pp. 195, 200, 282.

[4] Aelred of Rievaulx, *Spiritual Friendship*, trans. Mary Eugenia Laker (Kalamazoo: Cistercian Publications, 1977), chap. 3: 82, p. 112.

"Know thyself"—could achieve unity. Writers concluded that that unity was a coincidence of opposites, such as when a form-giver (a male) unites with a form-receiver (a female) to engender progeny. When these figures of thought and speech were employed to explain how a person came to be at one with himself (as it was, for example, by Augustine and, much later, by Ludwig Feuerbach), they witnessed to an idea of spiritual androgyny.[5]

Conveniently yielding to the ardor of his age for making lists, Bernard of Clairvaux identified five ways in which participation through love made it possible for the self to be communicated: five ways, in other words, in which interpreters could make sense of the sentence, "I am you." The predominance of the biological paradigm is notable. They were conjugal, when husband and wife become one flesh; moral, when a virtuous man is at one with himself; by accord, when, in charity, a multitude is of one heart and soul; by desire, when the soul, clinging to God in desire becomes one spirit with him; and by condescension, when the Word of God was incarnated by union with the clay of human flesh, and two natures united in one person.[6]

Aelred referred to the process of filling as the transfusion of himself into others and the pouring of others' affections into him. But these complementary movements, of self-emptying and being filled, were also recognized in other contexts. Bernard's reference to the Incarnation posited the double movement of self-emptying and being filled. Yet other examples indicate that these movements could also occur (as in the case of parted lovers) when one party was absent. Dialogue was unnecessary in such cases, because discipline and habits of mind rendered the absent one present.

To speak of Christ, the primitive Christians, friends, and lovers, is also to speak of suffering, that is, to take up the esthetic paradigm. "Without grief, it is not possible to live in love" (sine dolore, non potest in amore vivere). In some forms, therefore, the concept of participation reversed the positive and negative poles of pleasure and pain. Self-emptying is painful, but the literature of asceticism (including the ascetic discipline of love) emphasizes the joy of pain that led to union and, indeed, the glorious passion of union in which rapture and agony were identical. In the ascetic's quest for happiness, pain is a positive value. The bliss that martyrs would enjoy in paradise, Augustine wrote, would be adorned by the dazzling white scars on their risen and glorified bodies.[7] Negation itself becomes a positive value.

A distinctive method of associating ideas underlies the concept of partic-

[5] See below, Chapter 5 at nn. 59, 80, 108, 109, 111, 131.

[6] Bernard of Clairvaux, De Consideratione, 5. 8. 18. (J. Leclercq and H. M. Rochais, eds., Tractatus et Opuscula [Rome: Editiones Cistercienses, 1963. S. Bernardi Opera, vol. 3], pp. 482–83).

[7] H. I. Marrou, The Resurrection and St. Augustine's Theology of Human Values (Villanova: Villanova University Press, 1966. The Saint Augustine Lecture, 1965), p. 28.

ipation. Between the fourth and the twelfth centuries, the classical terms of association—*likeness, contiguity,* and *contrast*—were in full vigor, and their interplay was one contribution of epistemology to the esthetic paradigm.

Even by way of introduction, a special comment on this subject is needed. Of the three categories, contrast is the hardest to understand as earlier generations understood it. David Hume (1711–76) kept likeness and contiguity as categories of association, but he substituted cause-and-effect relations for contrast, which (as contrariety) he regarded as a mode of likeness.[8] When he wrote about the beautiful and the ugly in art, Croce (1866–1952) reduced the beautiful and the ugly to mutually exclusive terms, to categories of absolute difference, rather than to categories of association by contrast. He dismissed the entire idea of association by contrast and an extensive body of philosophical literature on the subject. "For Aesthetic does not recognize the sympathetic [the beautiful] or the antipathetic [the ugly] or their varieties, but only the spiritual activity of representation."[9] Perhaps the clearest measure of how thoroughly the earlier force of association by contrast has been lost occurs in James George Frazer's (1854–1941) celebrated division of "sympathetic magic" into two varieties: "homeopathic or imitative" and "contagious." The first works by likeness, the other, by physical contiguity. Frazer defined no variety of sympathetic magic that corresponded with contrast.[10]

Croce's reduction of the beautiful and the ugly to mutually exclusive terms of difference brushed aside many strands in art criticism that employed them as terms of association. One example is the ancient theory of the sublime, revived in the classicism of the seventeenth and eighteenth centuries. That theory recognized that the antitheses of beauty and ugliness, calm and tumult, pleasure and torment, coincided in experiencing the sublime. For then, what was ugly could become intensely beautiful; the attraction and repulsion of the holy were at one. Christianity provided another strand in which contrast was a medium of esthetic association, rather than one of dissociation. Augustine of Hippo praised the repellant awkwardness and rusticity of literary style in the Scriptures as expressing a supreme eloquence beyond the powers of worldly rhetoricians. He reveled in the ugliness of Christ's mangled and tormented body on the cross as manifesting supreme beauty.[11]

Likewise, Frazer's restriction of sympathetic magic to "imitative" and

---

[8] *A Treatise of Human Nature,* I. 5.

[9] Benedetto Croce, *Aesthetic as Science of Expression and General Linguistic,* 2d ed., trans. Douglas Ainslie (London: Macmillan, 1922), p. 88.

[10] *The Golden Bough: A Study in Magic and Religion* (New York: Macmillan, 1923), chap. 3, pp. 11–47.

[11] *Serm. 43*: 5–7 (Migne *PL* 38: 256–58).

"contagious" varieties, with no category of contrast, left much out of account. Frazer himself described rituals of exaltation that ended in humiliation and death (e.g., the slaying of the King of the Saturnalia) and rituals of humiliation that ended in exaltation and life (e.g., the enactments of death and resurrection in initiation rites). There are also other rituals—"rituals of rebellion"—in which societies enact their own inner conflicts precisely to avert the social disruptions that would occur if the defiance of authority that they represented actually took place outside the controlled environment of sacred liturgy. Yet others manifest the demonic side of the sacred. The use of euphemism in blessings and curses is a further instance in which magic employs association by contrast. Indeed, contrast pervades all sympathetic magic, associating strictly regulated ceremonies with "the actual messiness of human life."[12]

David Hume's substitution of causal relations for contrast indicates a broad change of thinking that permitted writers in such different fields as Croce and Frazer to discount or ignore association by contrast. To speak of causes and effects is to speak of action, of a relationship that an outside observer can detect between an agent and something acted upon. Causality is an outward phenomenon, an empirical category of association, just as likeness and contiguity may be.

Contrast is also an outward phenomenon, and an empirical category, when it is used to distinguish and to divide; but when it is used to associate and to combine (as in the examples just given), it transcends experience. In theories of the sublime, or of the manifestation of beauty in ugliness, and in rituals of exaltation reversed into death or of abasement reversed into life, contrast is not an act but a state, not a phenomenon but a process, not a calculated antithesis but an innate sympathy.

Hume's substitution of causality for contrast indicates a general shift toward empirical, or positivist, ways of thinking, a change in cultural norms that later expressed itself in the rejection by Croce and Frazer of contrast as a term of association. Contrast was excluded because it did not serve positivist norms of association. In fact, the whole original constellation of likeness, contiguity, and contrast was held together by assumptions that came from the very world of thought and belief against which the empiricists rebelled, denouncing it as rank superstition. Thus, even as they omitted contrast as a term of association, empiricists also omitted nonpositivist connotations of likeness and contiguity: for example, connotations of spiritual likeness and unlikeness, and of proximity and distance that were not defined by time or space (including emotional proximity and distance). In retaining

[12] Cf. John Skorupski, *Symbol and Theory: A Philosophical Study of Theories of Religion in Social Anthropology* (Cambridge: Cambridge University Press, 1983), p. 91.

likeness and contiguity as terms of association, they actually kept only the positivist fraction of the total meaning that those terms had originally held.

A visual metaphor may be helpful. Empiricists visualized the world as a chain of causes and effects that were phenomena, even accidents. Their world was two-dimensional. They rejected a far more complex, three-dimensional way of visualizing the world—namely, the belief that the world was not a chain of events, but rather a sphere of life, continually unfolding from itself and enfolding upon itself, a sphere in which contrasting poles were identical because, in its ceaseless unfolding and enfolding, its center was everywhere and its circumference, nowhere.

A modern positivist understanding of contrast as irreconcilable difference would keep us from recognizing how it was possible, following the esthetic paradigm, to associate opposites as poles in a single entity, or as in some sense identical. Esthetics, a logic of feeling, could override reason, a logic of analysis. Differences could be proportional, not absolute. How can there be evil in a good world? "God uses our ills for his own good purposes," John of Salisbury (ca. 1115–80) wrote. "Just as in a painting, a black or smutty color, or some other such feature, looked at by itself, is ugly, and yet considered as part of the whole painting it is pleasing, so things which separately examined seem foul and evil, yet when related to the whole appear good and fair, since He adapts all things to Himself whose works are all exceedingly good."[13] The coincidence of opposites—positive and negative values—is as complete in John's use of contrast as it was when Luther (ca. 1483–1546) wrote: "God must become a devil before he can be God, and we must make the trip to hell before we come to heaven. We can not become God's children without first becoming the children of the Devil. For the Devil must already have said and done everything before God says and does it."[14] Contrasts that are identical in this way are hard to visualize in the two-dimensional straight line of a chain of events. But they are easy to conceive in a concentric order visualized as "an infinite sphere the center of which is everywhere, the circumference, nowhere." According to this order, polar opposites are united by a kind of natural sympathy, an amorous sympathy or possibly (in Spinoza's term) a "malevolent sympathy." By sympathy, opposites of good and evil, subject and object, and even hunter and victim become one.

In the unfolding and enfolding concentric order, contrast remains, but as an aspect, even as proof, of participation through sympathy. Identity was

---

[13] *Polycraticus*, 8.18.

[14] *Der 117. Psalm ausgelegt, 1530* (E. Thiele, ed., in *D. Martin Luthers Werke. Kritische Gesammtausgabe*, vol. 31, pt. 1 [Weimar: Böhlaus Nachfolger, 1913], p. 249): "Und Summa, Got kan nicht Got sein, Er mus zuvor ein Teufel werden, und wir konnen nicht gen himel komen, wir musen vorhin ynn die helle faren, konnen nicht Gottes kinder werden, wir werden denn zuvor des Teufels kinder. Denn alles was Gott redet und thut, das mus der Teufel geredet und gethan haben."

posited in the same sense as when writers affirmed that a virtuous person became god, or that every true Christian was Christ. Identity in this union did not mean equivalence, interchangeability, or indistinguishability. Likewise, identity in the sphere whose center was everywhere and whose circumference was nowhere was a matter of modulation. It was proportional. I have already said that contrast was a state, rather than an act, a process rather than a phenomenon, a sympathy rather than an antithesis. Now, I can add that by recognizing proportional identity, arguments from contrast excluded "either/or" categories and enabled people to think of individuals *both* as themselves *and* as proportional modes of another's being. Augustine captured one example of this interplay when he described the union of teachers and students in their investigations of Scripture. By coupling of hearts, he wrote, students "are affected while we are speaking and we are affected while they are learning. We dwell in one another; and, thus, it is as though they speak in us what they hear, and in them we learn after some fashion what we teach."[15]

The interplay of positive and negative values—whether in the biological or esthetic paradigm, in works of the flesh or the spirit—underscores the essential character of participation as play bridging the gap of need between individuals. To be sure, it could be in deadly earnest. But it was still a game in which, as Huizinga put it, "the player . . . felt himself transformed into another ego which he did not so much represent as incarnate and actualize."[16] Clearly in this game, as Huizinga wrote, "holiness and play always tend to overlap. So do poetic imagination and faith."[17]

Thus, the hermeneutic gap, arising in the separateness of human existence, was to be filled. The means of filling was a hermeneutic circle, through which, by methods of association—including, particularly, association by contrast—a dynamic play came about, allowing the knower to assimilate the known. The focal point of this esthetic was the spectator, not the spectacle. To provide some idea of the range of enterprises shaped by this concept of understanding, I now turn to associative interplay of positive and negative values in games of love and rivalry, in the interpretation of texts through the silence of words, and in the assimilation of pictures through the emptiness of paintings. To be sure, we speak of empty words and silent paintings and reverse the adjectives as though they were synonyms. But I hope to demonstrate that this usage rests on false analogies.

    [15] *De cat. rud.*, 12.17 (*Corp. Christ., ser. lat.*, 46, p. 141). *Tr. in Ev. Johan.*, 21.7.8 (*Corp. Christ., ser. lat.*, 36, pp. 216–17).
    [16] Johan Huizinga, *Homo Ludens: A Study of the Play Element in Culture* (Boston: Beacon, 1950), p. 145.
    [17] *Homo Ludens*, p. 140.

PART II
PATTERNS OF
UNDERSTANDING

THREE

Amorous Sympathy: John Donne

THUS FAR, I have indicated some features of the strategy of proof that interpreters use to make the sense of the sentence "I am you." I have used Donne's *Meditation 17* as the point of departure, and indicated that principles of human solidarity expressed there derived from a tradition that began in classical antiquity and that extended, with many changes, into modern times.

To demonstrate that those principles, and the supporting strategy of proof, actually served to organize a whole picture of the world, I shall have to go further, from the sentence to the patterns of understanding that made the sentence possible. I have already indicated the direction of the argument by discussing two comprehensive paradigms of assimilation: the biological and the esthetic, reflecting the primordial division in Western thought between flesh and spirit. The tradition of amorous sympathy—and the roles played in it by those paradigms—is so evident in the literature of friendship and romance that, at the outset, I shall only provide one example of its impact. I shall continue and enlarge the discussion of Donne's thought, a bridge indeed between the medieval and modern writings. Focusing more sharply than before on Donne's erotic and spiritual poetry, I shall indicate the scope of application that the principles of human solidarity had for him and, by implication, for other, later writers who partook of the same tradition as he.

In Chapter 5, I shall indicate how pervasive and long-lasting the theme of amorous sympathy was: I shall consider how one writer at each end of our chronological range, Augustine of Hippo at the beginning and Ludwig Feuerbach at the end, made amorous sympathy, with special emphasis on the component of sexual bonding in the biological paradigm, the keystone of thought about social unity. However, the road we have to travel is far from straight. Before we reach the goal of social theories, we shall need to examine how doctrines of bonding through conflict, or malevolent sympathy, complemented and enlarged those of bonding through love. Indeed, anticipations of these darker tones will appear in the following discussion; they may even be implied, though unintended, in Donne's use of the biological paradigm, with its assumption of male dominance and female subordination.

Except for a few references, I am not going to speak about Donne's sermons; for to speak about them in detail would carry us into the dense thickets of sixteenth- and seventeenth-century homiletic conventions. The focus of my remarks is a poem by Donne that appears to be an academic exercise, lacking any emotional depth at all: "To Mr. Tilman after He had taken Orders." After exploring the strategy of proof implied in that one poem, I shall indicate the fuller contours of that strategy and the principles that it sustained in other works by Donne.

FIRST, I MUST SAY, parenthetically, a word about different ways of thinking about personality; for characteristics that one attributes to personality naturally define ways in which one thinks about human bonding, through friendship, for example.

Despite important qualifications, the "discovery" of the individual—the *uomo singolare* or *unico*—persists in the myths of historiography as a characteristic achievement of humanism, no matter that the continuing revolt of the medievalists has moved the event back from the fourteenth century, where Burckhardt put it, to the eleventh or twelfth century, no matter that the correspondence between the term and historical reality has been challenged. The "discovery" of personality allegedly resulted from modifying a received paradigm—in this case, made up from ancient and patristic ideas—to suit contemporary circumstances. However, individualism was only one notion of personality in the repertoire offered by the classical tradition. Certainly, there was present the concept of the individual will, operating in the tragic grandeur of its isolation, and the loneliness of this concept reinforced the atomistic incommunicability of bodies taught by materialist philosophers. So too was present an array of collectivist notions, according to which the individual reason was subsumed into the universal. Apart from will and reason, the ancient world recognized the appetites as faculties of the soul. Correspondingly, there was a third possibility that combined features both of individualism and of collectivism. This third possibility neither left personality isolated and incommunicable in the will, nor transcended it with general reason. Instead, it permitted individual persons, while remaining themselves, to be fused with others in heart, in spirit, or in soul. Through the centuries, the signature of this appetitive or sympathetic union was the simple declarative sentence, "I am you." The emphasis in this third concept was not on what personality was but on how it changed—how one personality was grafted onto another. The means of assimilation was likeness, and the process of bonding was the imitative movement from likeness toward identity. The idea of mimesis therefore opens a window on this third way of thinking about personality, as exemplified in John Donne's poetry.

For the moment, I recall—merely to illuminate by contrast—Burckhardt's widely discounted theory that the Renaissance discovered and perfected the idea of the *uomo singolare* by dissolving the "faith, illusion and childish prepossession" that, he said, constrained medieval writers to be conscious of themselves "only through some general category."[1] I contrast with this theory the pain that Donne felt at a moment when the strands of his life seemed to have come unraveled: ". . . to be no part of any body," he wrote, "is to be nothing. At most, the greatest persons, are but great wens, and excrescences; men of wit and delightfull conversation, but as moalles for ornament, except they be so incorporated into the body of the world, that they contribute something to the sustentation of the whole. . . . Such as I am, [I am] rather a sicknesse and disease of the world than any part of it."[2]

DONNE, IN FACT, used the sentence, "I am you," and variants of it, to describe the bonding of friends and lovers. However, the predicamental ideas that made it possible to think about the mimetic union of persons can be found elsewhere, in verses at the end of the poem "To Mr. Tilman after He had taken Orders." After considering this text, I shall place it in the wider setting of Donne's general esthetic ideas, and, by means of those ideas, indicate how the assumptions and underlying strategy of proof in the poem to Tilman related to the passions expressed in the "I am you" verses. The interplay of biological and esthetic paradigms should become evident in our discussion of Donne's easy oscillation between flesh and spirit.

Edward Tilman, a man of genteel poverty, was ordained in 1618 as deacon and, the next year, as priest. Whether Donne ever met the man is not known; he did read a poem that Tilman had written expressing, on the ground of personal unworthiness, his reluctance to be ordained. Donne's response has nothing to do with the content of Tilman's poem. Clearly, Tilman's verses served Donne as an excuse to reconsider the doubts that beset him before his own ordination three years earlier than Tilman's (1615). Having gained assurance in the meantime, Donne concluded his poem:

> Maries prerogative was to beare Christ, so
> 'Tis preachers to convey him, for they doe
> As Angels out of clouds, from pulpits speake;
>
> These are thy titles and preheminences,
> In whom must meet Gods graces, mens offences,
> And so the heavens, which beget all things here,
> And the earth our mother, which these things doth beare,

---

[1] *The Civilization of the Renaissance in Italy*, vol. I, pt. 2, chap. 1, trans. S.G.C. Middlemore (New York, 1958), p. 143.

[2] *Letters* 18, 20 (Charles Edmund Merrill, Jr., ed., *Letters to Several Persons of Honor* [New York, 1910], pp. 44, 51). R. C. Bald, *John Donne: A Life* (Oxford, 1970), p. 230. It has long been recognized that Donne stood, and acknowledged himself as standing, in a classical tradition that looked to Augustine of Hippo, Bernard of Clairvaux, and Thomas Aquinas as preeminent spokesmen. See Mary Paton Ramsay, *Les doctrines médiévales chez Donne, le poète métaphysicien de l'Angleterre (1573–1631)* (London: Oxford, 1917), p. 283.

Both these in thee, are in thy calling knit,
And make thee now a blest Hermaphrodite.[3]

For reasons that will become apparent, these verses refer to a situation rather more complex than the "I am you" verses; for Tilman was being described both as the subject and as the means of personal bonding.

Donne normally aimed for poetic closure, saving his best, summary epigram for the last lines. The curious term, "blest hermaphrodite," can therefore be assumed to summarize the entire poem. What does it mean? To be sure, a hermaphrodite is, after a fashion, the union of an "I" and a "you." Is Donne's term more than a piquant, but banal, turn of phrase to indicate a union of opposites, like the "strange hermaphrodites" of work and play with which Donne adorned a wedding poem?[4]

At first glance, the poem to Tilman has little mimetic content, and none at all in these concluding lines. On first reading, the biological paradigm (in its sexual, erotic, and mythological elements) would appear to comprise Donne's sense of the fusion of "I" and "you" in a hermaphrodite. Certainly, the sexual content of the lines relates them not to the "strange hermaphrodites" of the marriage poem, but, far more closely, to Donne's pious wish to dedicate a poem to the memory of Elizabeth Drury on each anniversary of her death:

Immortal Maid, who though thou should'st refuse
The name of Mother, be unto my Muse
A Father, since her chast ambition is,
Yearly to bring forth such a child as this,

extending her progeny through generation after generation of her praises "until man vanishes."[5]

The specifically erotic content in the lines to Tilman recall Donne's reference to conjugal union in "The Canonization":

The Phoenix ridle hath more wit
    By us, we two being one, are it.
So to one neutrall thing, both sexes fit,
    We dye and rise the same and prove
    Mysteries by this love.[6]

The two become one phoenix: "each is both and all."[7]

The mythological content in the verses to Tilman appears to allude to the

---

[3] Lines 41–43, 49–54.

[4] "Epithalamium made at Lincoln's Inne," line 30.

[5] "Of the Progresse of the Soule—The Second Anniversary," lines 33–36.

[6] "The Canonization," lines 23–24. On Wolfram von Eschenbach's assertion that a lady and her champion were one person, "both maid and man," see Robert Levine, "Wolfram von Eschenbach: Dialectical 'Homo Ludens,' " *Viator*, 13 (1982), pp. 197–98.

[7] "Epithalamion, or Marriage Song on the Lady Elizabeth and the Count Palatine being Married on St. Valentine's Day," lines 85–89.

legend of Hermaphroditus, the son of Hermes and Aphrodite, whose body fused with that of the nymph, Salmacis. Indeed, Donne cross-referenced this legend with that of the phoenix, when he applied Ovid's line on the Hermaphroditus-Salmacis union, describing the phoenix union of male and female, as "one neutral thing." Ovid had written: "The body and the nymph were not two, but a double form, that could be called neither woman nor boy, since merged, they seemed both and neither."[8] By reference to the maternal earth and the engendering heavens, Donne also appears to allude to the myth of Gaea, the primeval earth-goddess, and Uranus, her son and husband.

Yet, on closer inspection, all these allusions turn out to be inappropriate or false. The sexuality in the poem to Tilman is plainly figurative; hermaphroditism represents something spiritual, a point at which the biological and esthetic paradigms moved from being mutually reflective to being equivocal. Eroticism, physical or spiritual, is quite absent. The apparent mythological allusions are least satisfactory of all. Donne celebrates the fecundity of preachers, replicating, through the blessings in their words, "Maries prerogative to bear Christ," and the cosmic fecundity of earth impregnated by heaven. Nothing could be further from the myth of Hermaphroditus, who invoked a curse on the lake where he was infused with Salmacis, depriving of their virility all men who swam in its waters. Likewise, the legend of Uranus and Gaea is not really appropriate to Donne's message. The birth of the Titans, Cyclopes, and other monsters; Uranus's cruel imprisonment of his children; the castration of Uranus by his son Cronus at Gaea's urging; and, finally, the birth of the furies from black blood dripping from Uranus's severed member evoke scenes of terror far from the unspeakable joys that Donne ascribed to the priesthood. The consubstantiality of the persons of the Trinity did not permit an easy transference from the Father, as begetter, and the Son, as begotten, to Cronus as begotten and begetter. Clearly, the "blest hermaphrodite" belonged to a frame of reference that is not immediately suggested by the words "classical tradition."

What made Tilman's blessed hermaphroditism—the union of "I" and "you"—thinkable and convincing? Let us reassemble our scraps of evidence: the Blessed Virgin, the engendering heavens and parturient earth, the cross-reference between the phoenix and the hermaphrodite, and the hermaphrodite itself. These scraps do indeed form a pattern. They are drawn from alchemy, an occult art in which Donne was deeply read. The Blessed Virgin, the phoenix, and the hermaphrodite were all synonyms for the philosopher's stone,[9] and the "blessed and sacred" art of alchemy was

---

[8] *Metamorphoses*, 4, lines 378–79.

[9] Cf J. van Lennep, *Art et alchimie: Étude de l'iconographie hermétique et de ses influences* (Brussels: editions Meddens, 1966), p. 22.

considered a way of spiritual perfection by many, including notably Para-
celsus, whose works Donne owned and absorbed.

Donne's reference to heavens and earth is drawn from the recipe for the
production of the philosopher's stone. The principal ingredients were two.
The male, or active, ingredient—fire—was represented by the sun, the King
and Father. The female, or passive ingredient—purest mercury containing
an equal proportion of sulfur—was earth. The protracted stage of heating
required was referred to as the bath of Mary, the Jew. Sitting together in
the bath, the King and the Queen were fused into the child that was them
both. Alchemists believed that metals contained seeds that the all-engen-
dering heat of the sun caused to germinate and be born in the womb of the
earth through a process of vaporization, recombination, and condensation.
They proposed to repeat and to accelerate this process in the laboratory.
Thus, in producing the philosopher's stone, they believed that they dealt
with living materials: with the earth (a body) containing fertile seeds; with
the *aqua viva* (the soul) that, under heat, tortured and disintegrated the
body; and finally with repurged quicksilver (the spirit) that was used in the
process of vaporization and coagulation to produce transmutations, to purge
and spiritualize the body until body and soul became one with spirit. In
general, therefore, alchemy demonstrated that materially different bodies
were not incommunicable; to the contrary, they could be "concorporated"
into spirit by processes of decomposition, coagulation, and fixing. Empirical
science as Donne knew it proved that "I" could become "you" and gave
formulas for the transformation.

The production of the philosopher's stone was thought to do more than
reproduce natural processes at an accelerated pace. In its combination of
body, soul, and spirit, and in its drama of physical torture, disintegration,
and spiritual reconstitution, it was thought to reproduce three passions and
three resurrections: those of matter, of humanity, and of Christ.[10]

The great property of the philosopher's stone was its fecundity, or its
"seminal essence," expressed in the power to reproduce its own purity in
metals, converting all metallic bodies into gold; to heal all dead and living
bodies without other medicine; and to impart perfection to all things. It
could not prevent the death of the body, but, rendered into the solution of
the *elixir vitae*, it cleansed the body of impurities and decay, renewed
youthful powers, and prolonged life. Thus, by analogy, Donne portrayed
Tilman both as the subject of fecund healing and as the medium of fecund
healing to others, between heaven and earth.

Naturally, alchemists who regarded their art as a religious enterprise,
sacred in its essence and effects, considered these doctrines secret, to be

[10] Lennep, *Art et alchimie*, p. 21 (Andreas Libavius, *Commentarius Alchymiae*, pars 2, lib.
4 [Frankfurt: Peter Kopf, 1606], p. 58). On Donne and alchemy, see Ramsay, *Les doctrines
médiévales chez Donne*, pp. 272–80.

revealed only to the virtuous, only to those whose feelings and purposes were harmonious with the sacred purposes of their art. Only the fewest of the few could penetrate the hiddenness of truth. In unworthiness and ignorance, most human beings could even hold the philosopher's stone in their own hands without discerning its powers.

Placing Donne's verses to Tilman in an alchemical frame of reference emphasizes their relevance to the priesthood that Donne and Tilman shared. Of course, it establishes parallels with other works using the biological paradigm, in which, for example, Donne wrote of the sun, by whose "male force is all we have begot,"[11] and in which he compared the "cherishing heart" of his mistress's "best loved part" with

> The Chymick's masculine equall fire,
> Which in the Lymbecks warme womb doth inspire
> Into th' earths worthless durt a soule of gold.[12]

The main advantage is that the alchemical frame of reference helps define the place of mimesis in a poem to Tilman that at first glance has little mimetic content. Indeed, it alerts us to disguised mimetic allusions that, together with explicit ones, establish a conceptual unity running throughout the poem and sustaining the hermaphroditic fusion of "I" and "you."

Mimesis was the scientific method of transforming "I" into "you." The mimetic content in the verses to Tilman consists chiefly in the nature of alchemy and its place in the poem, in the metaphors of the poem, and in ways of thinking about different levels of perception that Donne employed to define Tilman's position.

I have already hinted at the mimetic character of alchemy. As indicated, alchemical processes were thought to replicate passions and resurrections, not only those of matter, but also those that humanity and Christ experienced to correct the deformities that sin intruded upon human nature.

More generally, in the gap between nature and art, alchemy was thought closer to nature than to art because it used natural relations and processes. According to one account, the preliminary operations in the production of the philosopher's stone refined forms of natural products. Nature departed and art began with the combination of two of those products, the "second oil," or "sperm of the metals," annointing the solidified "menstruum," or "milk of the virgin," and joining with it in one body.[13] Alchemy derived its

---

[11] "Of the Progresse of the Soule—The Second Anniversary," line 12.

[12] *Elegy 8*: "The Comparison," lines 35–38. See also "Of the Progresse of the Soule—The Second Anniversary," lines 493–95.

[13] Cornelius Alvetanus, *De Conficiendo divino Elixire sive Lapide Philosophico*, in *Theatrum Chemicum*, vol. 5 (Strassburg: Zetzner, 1660. Reprint, Turin: Bottega d'Erasmo, 1981), pp. 815–21. I am greatly obliged to Professor Allen Debus for this reference and for other alchemical information.

essential power from nature, and yet what was perfect for the objectives of
nature was imperfect for those of art. Thus, four kinds of relationship
between alchemy and nature were possible. First, by taking its materials
from her, alchemy entered into partnership with nature in enterprises, such
as farming, to which nature gave the first impulse. Moreover, it imitated
nature in enterprises to which art gave the first impulse, such as the production of the philosopher's stone. Further, it supplemented the deficiencies
of nature by perfecting those natural products that nature left imperfect,
and by inventing new things to satisfy the needs of life. Finally, it surpassed
nature by using decay and putrefaction, which were the end in nature, as a
transition to another, and more perfect, state.[14] Thus, like all mimetic arts
(including rhetoric, poetry, and painting), alchemy imitated nature to correct and surpass her.

Recognizing the mimetic allusion to the transformation of an "I" into
another with which Donne concluded the poem also indicates that he established a thematic unity through his metaphors: the plowman, imitating and
cultivating nature; steel, responding to the pull of a lodestone; coins
stamped with an old image, counterstamped with a new one and thus given
new valuation; paintings of angels; and, finally, the hermaphrodite. The
metaphors converge at one point: the organic assimilation explained by the
biological paradigm, and its genetic effects. These and other nonmimetic
metaphors in the poem (the new vintage, the merchant ship setting sail with
lowly staples and returning laden with luxuries of the Orient) are all
employed to express transformation from one mode of existence to quite a
different, higher one: the gains surmounting expression, the joys passing
speech that Tilman achieved by entering holy orders. Throughout, the
emphasis is on the fecundity of the new state. This is true even of the steel-
magnet metaphor; for, as an anonymous writer said:

> If iron to the load-stone be not put certeinly,
> It will decrease wonderfully;
> The species of all things both more and less each one,
> Are maintained by reason of multiplication;
> Then if they be not multiplied they decay.

The iron must multiply through the application of the magnet, or decay.[15]

The importance of the mimetic metaphors is twofold.[16] They indicate that
Tilman had assumed a new and fecund character, or *persona*, an ambiguous

---

[14] Libavius, *Commentarius Alchymiae*, pars I, lib. 3, chap. 1, 3, pp. 244, 247.

[15] Elias Ashmole, *Theatrum Chemicum Britiannicum*, ed. Allen G. Debus, *The Sources of
Science*, no. 39 (reprint, New York: Johnson Reprints, 1967), chap. 5, p. 412. On coin stamps
as imparting value, see Donne's "The Second Anniversary," lines 369–70, and *Elegy 10*: "The
Dreame," lines 4–5.

[16] Bald, *John Donne*, p. 302.

one, for he remained the same man as before. The hand that he placed on the holy plow was the same as he had turned to secular occupations. He was the same steel, though now moved in unfamiliar ways by the magnet; the same coin with a new valuation; the same speaker, "new feathered" as angels are "with celestial love"; "the same materials" spiritualized and transmuted into the hermaphrodite.

Furthermore, the mimetic metaphors indicate how, by mediation, this ambiguous *persona* was achieved. They all point to the complex mediative event that transformed, or "repersonalized," Tilman, namely, his priestly ordination. In a sense, the poem really has two subjects mentioned and distinguished in its last lines: the priestly calling and the priest himself, the "blest hermaphrodite." Priesthood subsumed diaconate. Unlike Tilman, Donne was ordained deacon and priest on the same day, and his poem contains allusions to the actual consecration rituals for both orders and to Scriptural passages associated with those orders.[17]

Donne's emphasis on "the titles and preeminences" of the calling repeat the ordaining bishop's reference to the "high dignity" and "great excellency" of the vocation "whereunto it hath pleased God to call you";[18] and his grandiose parallel with royal service—the priest as "embassadour to God and destinie" (line 38)—plays on *ambassador* as a translation of *apostolos*, an allusion to the apostolic duties prescribed in New Testament lessons appointed for the liturgies and repeated in instructions to, and prayers for, ordinands. Donne's description of the priest's duty to "blesse the poore beneath [the pulpit], the lame, the weake" (line 44) alludes to the liturgy

---

[17] The Scriptural allusions are as instructive as the parallels with the actual ordination liturgies. The two metaphors with which the poem begins—the plowman and the vintage—allude, respectively, to the material and the spiritual status of the priest. The plow refers to the irrevocable decision that Tilman had made. "And Jesus said unto [a disciple]: No man having put his hand to the plow and looking back is fit for the kingdom of God" (Luke 9:62). In a more practical vein, it also refers to the right of a priest to receive sustenance from his congregation, a right to "livings" that was tenaciously exercised by English clergy in Donne's time and that enabled Donne as Dean of St. Paul's to engage in soothing pluralism after his long lean years. The relevant Scriptural text was 1 Cor. 9:9–10. The metaphor of vintage—change through fermentation—referred to the change in Tilman's mind and evoked both the Scriptural analogue of new wine in old bottles (Mark 2:22), and the spiritual intoxication of the apostles after the descent of the Holy Spirit at Pentecost (Acts 2:13). The contempt of the "foolish world" for holy orders, as it whiled its time away "in dressing, mistressing and complement" evoked the reading from Acts 20, appointed for the consecration of priests; and, of course, St. Paul's query "hath not God made foolish the wisdom of this world," (1 Cor. 1:20), and his awful sentence that faithless men did not glorify God, "but became vain in their imaginations, and their foolish heart was darkened. Professing themselves to be wise, they became fools," and idolaters, given up by God to "vile affections," the unnatural affections and "lusts of their own hearts" (Rom. 1:21–24). The ordination liturgy prescribed that ordinands be instructed to set aside, so far as they could "all worldly cures and studies" in order to save God's children living "in the midst of this naughty world." *Second Edwardian Prayerbook*, in Ernest Rhys, ed., *The First and Second Prayerbooks of King Edward The Sixth* (London: Everyman's Library, 1932. Theology and Philosophy no. 448), p. 454.

[18] *Second Edwardian Prayerbook*, ed. Rhys, pp. 454, 455.

for the ordering of deacons: "it is his office where provision is made to search for the sick, poore, and impotent people of the parish and to intimate their estates, names and places where they dwell to the curate, that by his exhortation they may be relieved by the parish or other convenient alms."[19] Donne's words—"celestial love," "gainings [that] do surmount expression," "joyes [that] pass speech"—incorporate allusions to the "Veni Creator Spiritus," the hymn invoking the descent on priestly ordinands of the Holy Spirit "the love so clear," "heavenly gift of God most high which no tongue can express," "the fountain and the lively spring of joy celestial."[20]

Appropriately, there are strong parallels between the texts of ordination rituals and Donne's references to the production of the philosopher's stone, the "blest Hermaphrodite." The testing and purification of elements in the alembic according to formula correspond with the rubric that no man execute the office of deacon, priest, or bishop "except he be first called, tried, and admitted according to the form here following."[21] The hermaphrodite's fecundity had a parallel in the doctrine that consecration was to enable the ordinand to serve God "in holiness and pureness of living," and "in innocency of life," and, through the "wholesome and godly examples and patterns" of his life, to enlarge "God's blessed kingdom."[22]

One especially notable parallel with alchemical process was that this purity was conveyed by a spiritual annointing, just as the "body" and "soul" in the alembic were transmuted by "anointing" with rarefied quicksilver; for mercury is an "unctuous vapor," a "living, active, spiritual principle."

However, the key to Tilman's new *persona* fusing "I" and "you" lies elsewhere. I have already emphasized the importance of sacramental theology in Donne's thought about bonding (Chapter 1). A remnant of pre-Reformation theology was Donne's view that ordination conferred a sacramental seal in the soul, through which the believer participated in the priesthood of Christ. This is evidently the meaning of his lines (15–18):

> And as new crowned kings alter the face,
> But not the monies substance; So hath grace
> Changed only Gods old image by creation,
> To Christ's new stamp, at this thy coronation.

The doctrine of the sacramental seal was certainly conveyed by Donne's early Catholic education; the personal impact of his Jesuit uncles; his readings in divinity at Hart Hall, Oxford, a hospitable place for Catholics; or his

[19] Ibid., p. 447.
[20] Ibid., p. 452.
[21] Ibid., preface, p. 438.
[22] Ibid., pp. 444, 455, 457.

later study of scholastic theologians, including Thomas Aquinas. Tilman's new *persona* was mediated to him by the image of Christ in his heart.

As our discussion of *Meditation 17* (Chapter 1) prepared us to expect, we have found that sacramental reasoning was crucial to Donne's use of the biological paradigm of assimilation. But we have noted points at which the esthetic and biological paradigms became not only mutually reflective but also equivocal. We must now recognize that sacramental reasoning also had implications for the esthetic paradigm—that is, for the realm of the spirit as well as for that of the flesh. Like all sacramental actions, ordination was mimetic: the outward, physical acts of the consecrator were to replicate the inward, spiritual acts of the Holy Spirit, the implanting of Christ's image in the soul. The correspondence between Donne's poem and the liturgy of ordination (including related Scriptural passages) illuminated the process of "repersonalization" that Donne expressed in his ambiguous, mimetic metaphors. They also replicate the three stages of union with God that, Donne believed, could be known in part on earth, but perfected only in heaven: "inexpressible association" (still very distant in this life), assimilation (like association, "not near enough" here below), and identification.[23] In fact, Donne assumed that these stages of transformation occurred in the bonding of the mind (or soul) with human beings as well as with God.

How did they apply to his ideas about sacramental bonding in ordination? At this point, sacramental reasoning linked with the epistemological content of the esthetic paradigm. The process took place in Tilman's heart and mind. His "diviner soul" caused him to put his hand to the holy plow; the fermenting of the new vintage, the "new thoughts and stirrings" were within his mind; the seal was set in his soul. The new thoughts and character did not come about through a dialogue, or exchange, between Tilman's "I" and another's "you," in which both were altered by mutual recognition and self-recognition. The change was one-sided, in Tilman alone.

In the second place, the inward change expressed itself in action that was scorned by the world. The altered soul perceived that what the world confided in was mere dust, and that what it derided was the source of inexpressible joy and nobility. This inversion of values defied natural reason; it transcended the autonomous will. It was a response to feeling, to the pull of new motions, a response that followed on the ecstatic elevation of celestial love. It was esthetic, rather than rational or voluntary.

Consequently, the process by which Tilman gained his new *persona* was inaccessible to the many. The theological knowledge that elucidated it was specialized, as was the astronomer's lore mentioned by Donne. The passionate commitment that put it into action inverted common values and

[23] *Sermon 2*, in Evelyn M. Simpson and George R. Potter, eds., *The Sermons of John Donne*, vol. 9 (Berkeley: University of California Press, 1958), p. 89.

subjected the person so acting to scorn and disrespect. The joys that repayed it were one-sided, incommunicable.

Finally, the sacramental seal, the image in the soul, that communicated the new *persona* was administered only to those recommended by their learning and virtue, who had been "tried, examined, and admitted according to the form" prescribed, and to each of them individually. This image in the soul, too, ordinands were unable to communicate unless, subsequently, they were as bishops empowered with all seven gifts of the Holy Spirit.

Plainly, the transformative process posited degrees of likeness mediated between the human soul and the divine archetype, and the mediation of likeness was calibrated according to degrees of esthetic perception. Here, the epistemological grounds for bonding in spirit, according to the esthetic paradigm, that we earlier found in Donne predominate over the metaphysical (Chapter 1). To carry the discussion one step further, the stages of the "repersonalization" process correspond with modes of perception. *Perception* in this case, is equivalent with *participation*. The lowest level is that of signification. Words signify to all, but to those unprepared to give them spiritual content, they have no higher meaning. The second mode of perception is the symbolic. The symbolic mode is accessible to those who recognize the figural content of images, verbal and otherwise, and whose emotions may draw them from the figure to the reality. An affective, esthetic mediation is possible. The third mode of perception is the sacramental. The sign, or figural, representation is also the reality. Inward vision discerns the reality beneath the veil and participates in it. Participation by perception is both mediated—through signs and figures—and immediate. Intellectual communication shades into affective communion; esthetic closure occurs; a new *persona* is grafted to the old.

Such are the levels of participation opened to others by Tilman's mimetic office as mediator, or "embassadour to God and destinie." Donne played on a wide range of possibilities given him by the biological and esthetic paradigms. The scornful and disrespectful world neglects as mere signs his words and the "wholesome and godly examples and patterns" of his life. For it, esthetic participation goes no further than hearing the sounds of the words and understanding their literal meanings. Words and examples could not mediate or convey Christ to the "foolish world." The poor, the lame and the weak beneath the pulpit participated in the blessing of which Tilman's words were figures. But his fecundity as a "blest Hermaphrodite" was effective only in sacramental union.

WE HAVE FOUND that the sacramental, metaphysical, and epistemological grounds of bonding that informed Donne's *Meditation 17* (Chapter 1) were also at work in the poem to Tilman, with considerable emphasis given to the esthetic components of epistemology. However, the relatively few verses of that poem did not give the scope for a complete display of Donne's strategy of proof. Before I go on beyond the poem "To Mr. Tilman," a word about the fuller contours of Donne's general esthetic orientation will help to explain in particular why he found the esthetic paradigm cogent and will also suggest how he was able to consider the biological and esthetic paradigms in some sense equivocal, moving between flesh and spirit as though in the same idiom. An elaborate concept of human faculties, physical and spiritual, lay behind the three-tier hierarchy of perception and the corresponding degrees of participation or "repersonalization." There is no need to explore this subject in detail. I should, however, recall Donne's insistence that mediation was a universal law of nature. God had "denied even to angels the ability of arriving from one extreme to another without passing the mean way between."[24] In the human physical constitution, bodies were engendered by carnal intercourse; souls were created and infused by God into them. As "the thin and active part of the blood," spirits were "of a kind of middle nature between soul and body," uniting the organs of the body to the faculties of the soul.[25] Through their mediation, sensory perceptions were translated into spiritual; for example, "the picture in the eye" was translated into "the picture in the heart."[26]

It followed, as Donne wrote, that

> souls must descend to affections
> and to faculties which sense may reach and apprehend.[27]

Donne was able to reconcile the soul's descent to mediating faculties with the dominance of the affects by holding that love was the composite of all virtues.[28] But his language was sometimes extreme. In his religious writings, the dominance that Donne assigned to the affects expressed itself not only in the subordination of reason to the appetites, converging in faith,[29] but also in the ultimate futility of the scientific (or pseudoscientific) knowledge in which he took deep and abiding interest.[30] Will and reason hesitated to embrace salvation; the passions demanded that God ravish them.[31]

In summary, Donne held, with Thomas Aquinas, that the cognitive

---

[24] Prayer from Evelyn M. Simpson, ed., *Essays in Divinity*, Book I (Oxford: Clarendon, 1952), p. 37.

[25] *Sermon 12*, in George R. Potter and Evelyn M. Simpson, eds., *The Sermons of John Donne*, vol. 2 (Berkeley: University of California Press, 1955), pp. 261–62.

[26] Below, at nn. 69, 70, 79, 82.

[27] "The Extasie," lines 59–68.

[28] To the Countess of Huntingdon: "That unripe side of earth," lines 129–30.

[29] To the Countess of Bedford: "Reason is our soules left hand," line 1. John Carey, *John Donne: Life, Mind and Art* (New York: Oxford University Press, 1981), p. 231.

[30] Carey, *John Donne*, pp. 247, 253.

[31] *Holy Sonnet 14*: "Batter my heart."

power moved only through the appetitive powers, especially the intellectual appetite (or will), but that the will itself moved through sensory appetites.[32]

It is also important to note that, among the senses, sight was, for Donne, the noblest.[33] But, just as Donne subordinated the deliberative power of reason and the deciding power of will to the assimilative powers of the affects, or appetites, he subordinated direct sensory data gained by the eye of the body to the assimilative vision of the inward eye:

> . . . our sense
> Strong objects dull; the more,
>   the lesse wee see.[34]

Again:

> Churches are best for prayer
>   that have least light.
> To see God only, I go
>   out of sight.[35]

Donne realized that the "negative values" of a painting were crucial— the blanks that the eye of the viewer fills in, the dark or neutral patches that accentuate and enliven vivid sections, the contexts that the painting evokes in the viewer. The "negative values" are exactly what give a picture its meaning and mediating function, and what permit a viewer to see more in it than is demonstrably there. Idolatry occurred, Donne recognized, through failure to see through the mediating picture to its "negative qualities," thus worshipping "the image without relation to the prototype and first pattern. . . ."[36]

The general importance of negative values to the strategy of proof that Donne used as a writer and theologian is evident, and, quite naturally, negative values form the nucleus of his three tiers of inward participation: association (by signs), assimilation (by symbols), and identification (by sacraments or, more generally, sacramental participation). Donne's love of self-torturing paradox, his equivalent of chiaroscuro in Baroque and mannerist architecture; his "excess / In seeking secrets, or Poëtiqueness,"[37] whether in the unseen design within the world, or in the soul hidden within the

---

[32] *Summa Theologiae*, Ia. Q. 20. A. 1.

[33] "An Anatomie of the World—The First Anniversarie," line 354.

[34] "The Dreame," lines 8–9.

[35] "A Hymn to Christ at the Author's last Going into Germany," lines 29–32. A very strong statement of the priority that Donne (in contrast with Ben Jonson) gave sight, and of Donne's interest in painting, occurs in Norman K. Farmer, Jr., *Poets and the Visual Arts in Renaissance England* (Austin: University of Texas, 1984), pp. 19–26.

[36] "Ignatius His Conclave," in Charles M. Coffin, ed., *The Complete Poetry and Selected Prose of John Donne* (New York: Modern Library, 1952), p. 336.

[37] "The Litanie," 8, lines, 70–72.

body, or in God's image in the soul; his assumption that, of the three components of the soul, the (vegetal and) sensual created with the flesh, being material, were negative, while the spiritual, or intellective, infused by God, was positive[38]—all indicate how fundamental "negative values" were to Donne's general awareness of the interplay of opposites, and to his quest for "the picture in the heart" or "the face in the mask."[39]

Donne was fascinated by the unseen power of magnetism. To him, magnetic attraction and repulsion did not seem to work in opposite directions. Instead, he imagined positive and negative poles as constituting a cosmic force "to draw and fasten sundered parts in one."[40] Likewise, when he described his emotions, Donne portrayed a unified interlacing of sympathies and antipathies. He characterized the most joyful emotion, love, as warfare, anguish, and martyrdom, often pursued in grief or jealousy when the beloved stood hopelessly apart through absence, indifference, or death. He raised the unconscious hatred of such balked ardor to conscious discourse when he wrote:

> Yet, love and hate me, too,
> So, these extreames shall neithers office doe;
> Love me, that I may die the gentler way;
> Hate mee, because thy love is too great for mee;
> Or let these two, themselves, not me decay;
> So shall I, live, thy Stage, not triumph bee;
> Lest thou thy love and hate and mee undoe,
> *To let mee live, O love and hate mee too.*[41]

When he spoke of his ardor for God, Donne also portrayed the coincidence of opposite emotions:

> Those are my best dayes,
> When I shake with fear.[42]

Doubt and "the sin of fear" were complements of Donne's faith.[43] And he transferred to the soul's union with God characterizations of violence used earlier in his life to describe erotic death in the ravishment and ecstasy of carnal union.

It was a theological commonplace that, by virtue of his perfect simplicity, God was the coincidence of all opposites. This idea reinforced the conviction that the divine nature was unsearchable and ineffable, and that the positive

---

[38] Ramsay, *Les doctrines médiévales chez Donne*, p. 222.

[39] "The face in the mask," a reference to God's presence in the world, occurs in "A Hymn to Christ on the Author's Last Going into Germany," line 6, p. 257.

[40] "An Anatomie of the World: The First Anniversary," lines 221–22.

[41] "The Prohibition," lines 17–24.

[42] *Divine Poems*, 19: "Oh, to vex me, contraries meet in one," line 14.

[43] Cf. "A Hymn to God the Father," line 13.

affirmations of theologians about God always implied their own denials, as inadequate propositions. The "negative" (or apophatic) way necessarily complemented the "positive" (or cataphatic) way of theological discourse.

Declaring the perfection of his own, complex love, Donne took up the language of the negative way:

> If that be simply perfectest
> Which can by no way be exprest
> > But *Negatives*, my love is so.
> > To All, which all love, I say no.
> If any who deciphers best,
> > What we know not, our selves, can know,
> Let him teach mee that nothing. . . .[44]

Pervaded as it was by imagery of disguise and of the coincidence of opposites, Donne's "excess in seeking secrets" ferreted out negative values on each of the three levels of participation. On each level, the mind (or soul) worked as sculptors, do,

> As perchance, carvers do not faces make,
> But that away, which hid them there,
> > Do take,[45]

freeing the image that nature had hidden in the stone.

In his poem, "The Crosse," Donne played on all three levels. On the level of association (or signs), he pointed to the family of cruciform designs in the visible world. On the level of assimilation (or symbol), he spoke of Christ's cross as the archetype to which all other cruciform patterns witnessed. On the level of identification, he admonished the soul to free the image of Christ that had been hidden within it, "And be his image, or not his, but hee."[46] The degree of identification implied in these words—the degree to which "I am you"—must be stressed. Donne turned graphically to the level of identification in "The Litanie," addressing Christ:

> O be thou nail'd unto my heart,
> > And crucified againe,
> Part not from it, though it from thee would part,
> But let it be, by applying so thy paine,
> Drown'd in thy blood, and in thy passion slaine.[47]

[44] "Negative Love," lines 10–16.
[45] "The Crosse," lines 33–34. For other, similar metaphors drawn from sculpture and painting, see Rugoff, *Imagery*, pp. 108–109.
[46] "The Crosse," lines 35–36.
[47] "The Litanie," 2 ["The Sonne"], lines 14–18.

"The blood of my Savior," Donne wrote, "flows in my veins."[48]

It would be possible to go further in discussing the broad contour of Donne's strategy of proof and to indicate the roles of the world (or sin), the flesh (or death), and Satan as negative values in Donne's thought. However, enough has been said to establish some of the negative values in his ideas about the human soul, and how they figured in his works.

The point to be made is that, whether in the biological or the esthetic paradigm, Donne's sensitivity to the unifying force of negative values reflected the priority that he gave to vision, among the senses, and, correspondingly, to his fascination with the art of painting.

At this point, I part company with those who hold that Donne "never visualize[d] or suggest[ed] that he ha[d] any pleasure in looking at things."[49] This view may be justified if one refers only to Donne's citations of visual beauties in nature. But it is far from understandable if one recalls the importance that painting had in his life. At moments throughout his career, he had his portrait painted, from the one (possibly by Hilliard) as an eighteen-year-old dandy with sword and large, bejeweled, cruciform earring, to the one of Donne in his shroud that Donne commissioned so that he could contemplate it from his deathbed envisioning what he was soon to be, a painting that Donne also meant to serve as a model for his tomb effigy. Portraits of himself aside, Donne began assembling, no later than 1605, a collection of paintings that numbered more than eighteen by the time of his death.[50] Metaphors from painting are frequent in his works, and, toward the end of his life, he defended the use of religious pictures in churches against Puritan iconoclasts.[51] He recognized the transformative power of painting, whether hesitantly, as he did in referring to alchemy:

> . . . so many angled figures
> in the book
> Of some great conjurer that
> would enforce
> Nature . . . from her course[52]

or playfully, as he did in alluding to "witchcraft by a picture," or seriously, as when he spoke of redemption:

> Then doth the Crosse of Christ work
> fruitfully

---

[48] *Sermon 9*, in George R. Potter and Evelyn M. Simpson, eds., *The Sermons of John Donne*, vol. 2 (Berkeley: University of California Press, 1955), p. 210.

[49] Carey, *John Donne*, p. 131, quoting Rupert Brooke.

[50] Bald, *John Donne*, pp. 150–51, and pp. 563–67, Donne's will.

[51] Bald, *John Donne*, p. 498. See also Rugoff, *Imagery*, pp. 108–109.

[52] "The Bracelet," lines 33–36. Cf. Lennep, *Art et alchimie*, p. 32, on the importance of alchemy to Western art.

> Within our hearts, when we love
>   harmlessly
> That crosse's pictures much, and
>   with more care
> That Crosse's children, which our
>   crosses are.[53]

If Donne were not responsive to the sensory beauty of painting—and this has not been demonstrated—then he profoundly experienced through the mimetic art an esthetic response of another kind. He acutely knew that all art is sensual. The sensual impact was subordinate to associative feelings that it stirred through its "negative values." This stirring, of course, permitted visual—or verbal—images to be filled with symbolic and sacramental content.

THUS FAR, I have examined the mimetic content of one poem that addresses the special circumstances of priestly ordination, and I have sketched general contours of Donne's esthetic, and highly predicamental, strategy of proof that the poem to Tilman took for granted. The keystone of the poem is a reference to a mimetic art, alchemy, which Donne employed as an analogue of ordination. A considerable use of metaphors described the ambiguity of mimetic action, all illuminating by analogy the grafting of one *persona* onto another by ordination. Finally, broad outlines have appeared of the mimetic process of bonding by participation that Donne evidently believed at work in ordination. The participation was one-sided, not dialogic. "Christ's new stamp" passed to Donne; no reciprocal stamp passed from Donne to Christ. The participation was inward but neither rational nor voluntary. It was mediated by third terms between the "I" and the "you," between Christ and the soul, and even between the body and the soul. It was esthetic, advanced by feelings stimulated by visually keyed associative devices. Furthermore, stages in the process of bonding by participation could be distinguished according to the degree of esthetic, or affective, closure they achieved: none at the significatory stage, partial at the symbolic stage, full at the sacramental stage, where likeness merged into identity. The shaping of Donne's thought according to biological and esthetic paradigms of assimilation has been evident throughout.

As I now turn to the verses in which Donne specifically used the sentence, "I am you," or some variant, three questions remain concerning the application of his predicamental strategy of proof. Was this concept of personal bonding by participation part of Donne's general thinking about human relations, or was it limited to the special case of ordination? Did he accept kinds of personal bonding other than mimetic participation? Given the

---

[53] "The Crosse," lines 61–64.

interplay of personal and traditional values, what did Donne's concepts of personal bonding by participation owe to classical antiquity?

The second question is the simplest to answer. In the broad range of his works, Donne considered many kinds of personal bonding: with God, with Christ, with others through God, with moral exemplars, with a sibling, with a lover (or a friend), with all humanity, and, sportively, with men, animals, insects, and fruit inhabited across the centuries by the same soul, through metempsychosis.

The grounds of bonding vary. Not all are mediated, mimetic, affective, or participatory. The most obvious distinction is between those that occur through a change in the soul (esthetic) and those that are specifically physiological or generally part of the order of natural existence in which the soul may be part (biological). Among the latter are the relations of brother and sister, one "by their bloods," or even the flea that sucked blood both from Donne and from his beloved, and

> swells with one blood made of two.
>
> Oh stay, three lives in one flea
>   spare,
> Where we almost, yea more than married are.
> This flea is you and I, and
>   this
> Our marriage bed, and
>   marriage temple is.[54]

Likewise, no change was required by the theory that individuals were one in their species, a doctrine, as we saw, set forth in *Meditation 17*: "No man is an island, entire of itself; every man is a piece of the continent, a part of the main. . . . Any man's death diminishes me, because I am involved in mankind. And therefore never send to know for whom the bell tolls. It tolls for thee."[55] Even when bonding did occur in the soul, it need be neither affective nor mimetic nor participatory. Metempsychosis, as part of natural order, required no change in the soul, as it passed from the apple that Eve ate through emperor, packhorse, spider, and melon to Donne. "She [the soul] is he [Donne]," but no transmutation of the soul had occurred.[56]

Donne's exalted vision of the heavenly Jerusalem also evokes a spiritual order in which—the old nature having already been perfected—bonding without further change is in the nature of things: Donne envisioned the "joy of our society and conversation in heaven. . . . where all soules shall

---

[54] "Upon the Translation of the Psalmes by Sir Philip Sydney, and the Countess of Pembroke, his Sister," line 15; the siblings are also one by the Holy Spirit. "The Flea," lines 3–13.
[55] *Meditation 17.*
[56] *Metempsychosis: The Progresse of the Soule*, epistle.

be so intirely knit together, as if all were but one soule, and God so intirely knit to every soule, as if there were as many Gods as souls."[57]

Even when one turns to the instances in which Donne applied the sentence "I am you," or its variants to an acquired bonding of souls (as in friendship), there would appear to be a marked exception to the one-sidedness of participatory transformation that I noted in the poem to Tilman, and thus to other characteristics that I identified. Donne's use of words with the prefix *inter-* suggests dialogue. He wrote of the intergrafting of outward senses, of hands and eyes, that prepared for the interanimation of love by which soul flows into soul,[58] and the interassurance of the mind by which two loving souls are one, even when lovers part.[59] He imagined his three souls (vital, animal, and intellective or immortal) "emparadised in you, in whom alone I understand and grow and see."[60] A consummate dialogue appears to be described in Donne's lament for his dead beloved:

> And wee were mutuall elements
> > to us
> And made of one another
> My body then doth hers involve
> And those things whereof I consist
> > hereby
> In one abundant grow and burdenous
> > And nourish not, but smother.
> My fire of passion, sighes of ayre,
> Water of teares and earthly sad despaire,
> > Which my materialls bee.[61]

Yet that reciprocity was not inevitably part of love. Love might not be returned. "I must love her, that loves not me," Donne once lamented.[62] Lovers could be parted by distance or by death. It might be comforting to think "that absent lovers one in th'other be,"[63] or that the dead survived in the living, that

> They who one another keep
> Alive, ne'r parted bee.[64]

---

[57] *Sermon 4*, in Evelyn M. Simpson and George R. Potter, eds., *The Sermons of John Donne*, vol. 7 (Berkeley: University of California Press, 1954), p. 139.

[58] "The Extasie," lines 4, 9, 41, 59.

[59] "A Valediction: Forbidding Mourning," line 19. Carey, *John Donne*, p. 270.

[60] "Valediction: Of my Name, in the Window," lines 25–27.

[61] "The Dissolution," lines 1–11.

[62] "Loves Deitie," line 7.

[63] *Elegy 16*: "On his Mistress," line 26.

[64] *Song*: "Sweetest love, I do not goe," lines 39–40.

But mutual exchanges had ceased. Although reciprocity might stimulate love, what one loved, in reciprocal or in nonreciprocal relationships, was an image assimilated to one's heart.

Separation could leave that image to melt away in the body's elemental fire.[65] The affections of the beloved could wander, and then the visual reminders of the former lover, "love's magic," would cease to speak to her, assuring her, in his voice, "Here you see me, and I am you."[66] Even the image of the Crucified had been deformed in the sinner's heart, and must be restored before by grace Christ could recognize him and the man turn his face again to his Redeemer.[67]

There was no reciprocity between a portrait and its subject. A young man, departing on a long and hazardous venture, might give his portrait to his beloved. When he returned, weatherbeaten, scarred, wasted, would his beloved receive him, or yearn for the man in her picture and memory?[68] It was possible to love the "faire impression in my faithful heart" more than the beloved herself.[69]

How was that inward picture formed? The image of God was a special case, impressed on the soul by the same Creator who infused it into the body. Other inward images were formed by using the array of visual mnemonic data the world presented and that were inventoried in Donne's verses: the physical closeness of friends and lovers, a golden chain, a bracelet of hair, a name carved into a windowpane that the beloved saw overlayed by her own reflection, a portrait. All formed "pictures in our eyes."[70]

There were also words that triggered mental associations—the images and interlacings of images—in Donne's poetry. Poetry, like painting, was a mimetic art, and, in a well-known statement, Sidney employed this analogue to describe the impact that poets meant to have, combining the abstractness of philosophers with the concreteness of historians. "Whatsoever the philosopher saieth should be done, [the poet] gives a perfect picture of it by some one, by who he presupposeth it was done, so as he coupleth the general notion with the particular example. A perfect picture, I say, for he yieldeth to the powers of the mind an image of that whereof the philos-

---

[65] "Heroicall Epistle: Sapho to Philaenis," lines 10–11.

[66] "Valediction: On my Name, in the Window," lines 11–12, 61–66.

[67] "Goodfriday, 1613. Riding Westward," lines 41–42. Cf. *Sonnet 13*: "What if this present were the world's last night?" lines 2–3:

> Mark in my heart, O Soule, where
> Thou dost dwell,
> The picture of Christ crucified. . . .

[68] *Elegy 5*: "His Picture."

[69] *Elegy 10*: "The Dreame," lines 1–2.

[70] "The Extasie," line 11. Cf. "Witchcraft by a Picture," line 2.

opher bestoweth but a wordish description, which doth neither strike, pierce, nor possess the sight of the soul so much as that other doth."[71] The poet translated his feelings into words. The reader followed a mirror-image of the process, transforming the poet's words into his own feelings. Thus, poetry was a means for transforming pictures in the eye into pictures in the heart. Donne himself alluded to the ways in which his verses could "strike, pierce [and] possess the sight of the soul" when he presented them as "a picture or bare sacrament."[72]

In this statement, I have come again to the modes of assimilative participation that I found in the poem to Tilman: significatory (words), symbolic (verbal or visual images), and sacramental. Donne's phrase "bare sacrament" requires comment. The "mere" or "bare" sacrament of the Eucharist was made up of the material elements and the words of consecration. However, they were neither the reality (the *res*), the supernatural presence filling the elements and words, nor the effect of the sacrament. Donne's hope that the "merit of love" would be bestowed upon him through the "bare sacrament" of his words (lines 14–15) presupposed that reality and effect could be added. Thus, Augustine and, citing him, Thomas Aquinas, had taught that words became the form of a sacrament, not because they were said, but because they were believed[73]—that is, not because of the minister, but because of the participant. How then was this transubstantiation through faith to be achieved?

First, notably in the biological paradigm (which pertained actually or metaphorically to works of the flesh), it required acceptance of "negative values"—in this case, hidden correspondences, an underlying unity that made the variety of things into a vast code of mutually illuminating signs and symbols.

> If all things be in all,
> As I think, since all, which
> were, are, and shall
> Bee, be made of the same elements,
> Each thing, each thing implies
> Or represents.[74]

Moreover, especially in the esthetic paradigm (which pertained actually or metaphorically to works of the spirit), it required concentrated, ardent desire to be assimilated to the subject that the sign or symbol represented, even at the cost of change in one's own identity:

---

[71] Philip Sidney, *The Defense of Poesie* (London: Ponsonby, 1595) p. Div.
[72] To Mr. T. W. [Thomas Woodward], "At once, from hence," line 12.
[73] *Summa Theologiae*, IIIa. Q. 60. A. 7.
[74] *Satyre 5*: lines 9–12. See also "The Storme," lines 69–72.

Likeness glues love; and if
that thou so do
To make us like and love,
must I change to?[75]

In his later life, Donne complained that the ardent concentration that could lead from verbal to unitive prayer was broken for him by trifles. The likeness that glued love could not occur if the heart lacked intensity, if it were distracted, as Donne described himself at prayer, suddenly finding his attention scattered by "a memory of yesterday's pleasures in an anything, a nothing. . . ."[76]

Finally, ardent self-surrender—the passage from likeness to identity with the object of love—demanded assimilative action. This conformity could be described as sexual propagation:

. . . by that remorse
Which my word's masculine persuasive
force
Begot in thee. . . .[77]

It could be described as a reverberation in the mind like that in "bels of the purest metal,"[78] or as the continual joy moving artists as they mediated between the images in their minds and those on their canvasses, of

. . . Painters that do take
Delight, not in made work, but
whiles they make.[79]

At the most exalted level—that between the soul and Christ—Donne compared faith active in love with music:

A sinner is more music when
he prayes
Than spheares or angels praises be

Heare thyself now [O Christ], for thou
In us doth pray.[80]

[75] "Change," lines 23–24. The answer here is a cynical demurral, which, however, is contradicted by Donne's "I am you" poems.

[76] Sermon 10, in Evelyn M. Simpson and George G. Potter, eds., The Sermons of John Donne, vol. 7 (Berkeley: University of California Press, 1954), pp. 264–65.

[77] Elegy 16: "On his Mistress," lines 3–5.

[78] Problems 7.

[79] Elegy 15: "The Expostulation," lines 57–58.

[80] "The Litanie," lines 200–201.

Evidently, faithful action, assimilating the lover to his beloved, *is* the "image in the heart," the power that transformed signs and symbols into sacraments. In human relations, the sacrament was not indelible; the image could fade. In relations with God, the sacramental seal, like the primordial image in the soul on which it was counterstamped, could be marred, but not effaced. God's lodestone continued to stir new motions in Donne's steel.

I, FOR ONE, cannot escape the conclusion that the poem to Tilman incorporated a predicamental strategy of proof that extended to other works of Donne, to his erotic verse as well as to his sermons. That pattern of thought was constructed around the biological and esthetic paradigms, which it was able to use either reflexively or equivocally. The poem to Tilman assumed a process of bonding in the soul by participation that added a *persona* to Tilman's original one, without suppressing it. The transformation was not dialogic, but one-sided. It was esthetic, instead of rational or voluntary. It was produced by mimetic action of the affects, compared with, and convincing because of, the mimetic art of alchemy, and described (though not exclusively) by mimetic metaphors. Finally, the process advanced as the soul moved by mediation toward identity with the other through stages of likeness. Those stages corresponded with participation through significatory, symbolic, and sacramental perception.

In reviewing other compositions by Donne, in which the bonding of "I" and "you" figured, we found a number of bondings that were neither participatory nor esthetic-affective, nor mimetic. Only bondings in the soul involved the affects and mimetic action. We also found that the dialogue of "love's exchanges" was not in fact what bonded souls. Guided by the principle that likeness passed from subject to image—that the image participated by likeness in the subject—and not vice versa, Donne considered that the union of "I" and "you" was a one-sided assimilation that could occur and survive without the physical presence of the "you." But participation indeed required presence. The key agent in transformation was the image of the beloved that the lover had formed in, and presented to, his own soul.

Donne understood that image as a pattern of action with which the receiving soul conformed, or to which it resonated. It was mediated to the soul by significatory, symbolic, and sacramental perception, and it was impressed there by faith active in love. These assumptions were expressed, as they were in the poem to Tilman, by analogies with mimetic arts (notably, painting and poetry) and by the use of mimetic metaphors to recreate the transformation that "love's alchemy" had produced.

There are differences between the verses to Tilman and other compositions. These can be attributed to the premise that Tilman was both subject and medium of participatory bonding. As medium (a blest hermaphrodite), he corresponded with word, or picture, or "bare sacrament," those other mediating thirds through which two became one. Other texts, including *Meditation 17*, likewise addressed particular circumstances and, in those texts, Donne combined mimetic and nonmimetic bondings to suit the theme at hand.

I have dealt, therefore, with predicamental ideas by which Donne generally organized his thoughts about human personality. But it is essential to recall, however briefly, that Donne spoke from amidst a long tradition. It is easy to identify the remote sources of Donne's various kinds of bonding. Metempsychosis descended to him from the Pythagoreans; bonding by blood or by membership in the human species, from Aristotle; bonding through God, in all and all in all, from the Stoics; the fusion of two souls into one through friendship, from Aristotle and many later writers, including Cicero. This list could be extended, but, if it did not widen beyond philosophy and belles lettres, it would omit the body of materials in which the sentence "I am you" and its associated doctrines of mimetic bonding first appeared. I refer to Gnostic and hermetic literatures, to the literary currents in which they combined, and to theurgic practices associated with them and with other mystic cults in antiquity.

Gnostic and hermetic practices employed statues of the gods as, in some sense, images of the Image of God through which a believer could assimilate divine likeness and, drawn to God as iron is to magnets, become a medium between earth and heaven.[81] The believer's inward likeness to the divine "you" was the God's presence—*persona*, or name—in his heart.[82]

Something of the sort was recalled by Apuleius, "a person," as he said of himself, "initiated into many sacred mysteries of the gods," who claimed also to subscribe to Platonism with its doctrine of innate ideas, images of eternal verities set like seals in the mind. Carefully guarding the greater secrets, Apuleius described a mnemonic device, an image of Mercuriolus, called Basileus, that he carried with him among his books. He addressed prayers to it on festal days, and presented offerings of incense and wine, and, occasionally, victims, entering through it into communion with the one whom Plato first called Basileus, ". . . the cause of the whole nature of things, the ordering principle (*ratio*) and the primal source" comprehended by no place, by no time, by no function, and therefore thinkable by few, expressible by none."[83]

Early modern Europe had assimilated and transformed such ideas into its own systems of belief. There were many channels by which hybrid Gnostic-hermetic ideas, infused with Neoplatonism, reached Donne. Christian her-

---

[81] *The Cup or Monad*, s. 11; *On the Adoration of Images*, in G.R.S. Mead, *Thrice Greatest Hermes*, vol. 2 (London: John M. Watkins, 1949), pp. 91, 287.

[82] *An Invocation to Hermes as the Good Mind*, s. 11; *An Invocation to Lord Hermes*, s. 11, in Mead, *Thrice Greatest Hermes*, vol. 1 (London: John M. Watkins, 1949), pp. 85, 89.

[83] *Apologia*, chap. 63–65.

meticism was widespread, and Giordano Bruno had developed a non-Christian hermeticism through which the adept attracted cosmic powers into his personality by imaginative concentration on their images, reflecting "within his mind the whole universe in the ecstasy in which he bec[a]me one with the Powers."[84] Bruno taught his doctrines in England, and his books overlapped with alchemical literature with which Donne was familiar. His living presence was still recalled in the circles in which Donne moved.

But there were older channels. Early in the career of the Church, the mysteries of Platonic love and those of Gnostic and hermetic piety were blended with what Donne may have heard described at his ordination: "And without doubt, great is that mystery of godliness. God was showed in the flesh, was justified in the Spirit, was seen among the angels, was preached unto the Gentiles, was believed on in the world, and was received up into Glory" (1 Tim. 3:16). Donne was as aware of the carnal rites of "love's deitie" as, through alchemy and hermeticism, he was of the Gnostic components in his thinking. He tactfully, if hermaphroditically, omitted both when he wrote of his pre-Christian heritage:

> Temples were not demolish'd,
>   though profane.
> Here Peter Jove's, there Paul
>   hath Dian's fane.
> So whether my hymne you admit or chuse,
> In me you've hallowed
>   a pagan Muse.[85]

In his anatomy of the mimetic participation by which that hallowing occurred in individuals, Donne also provided a model of how Renaissance society transmuted itself, not according to the actual pattern of antiquity, but according to the image of antiquity that it had taken to its heart. He also tapped the primordial source of esthetic and moral evolution itself.

For reasons previously stated, I shall at the moment allow Donne to stand alone as representative of patterns of understanding that taught bonding through amorous sympathy. But Donne's own references to conflict and contrariety point to another piece in the puzzle. Before describing how this broad understanding of love was capable throughout the long period under review of being woven into theories of social unity (Chapter 5), I must turn to a less-recognized aspect of the tradition of participatory bonding, one that, employing the biological and esthetic paradigms, sounded the full range of erotic passion, tender and savage, implied by the word "evolution."

[84] Frances A. Yates, *Giordano Bruno and the Hermetic Tradition* (New York: Vintage Books, 1969), p. 326.
[85] *To the Countess of Bedford*: "T'have written then," lines 13–16.

FOUR

Malevolent Sympathy

A   AUGUSTINE: PLAY AND ENMITY

In the *Lyra Apostolica*, I have said that, before learning to love, we must "learn to hate," though I had explained my words by adding "hatred of sin."

John Henry Newman, *Apologia pro Vita Sua*
(New York: Modern Library, 1950), p. 73[1]

IN THE FIRST two chapters, I established a dossier on the sentence, "I am you," the signature of a tradition. With the discussion of amorous sympathy, the inquiry went a level deeper. From the sentence, we moved to patterns of interpretation, including a strategy of proof, that made the sentence possible. Those patterns circled around two common paradigms, the biological and esthetic, both dealing with the formal coherence of separate things, and with the dynamic by which it becomes possible for many individuals to participate in the same coherence and thus to become one. Evidently, in the tradition represented by John Donne, those two paradigms, procreational and compositional, could be rendered both mutually reflexive and equivocal. Both could imply conflict: the biological through male dominance and female subordination, and the esthetic, through the struggle of the artist to impose form on matter. Later (in Chapters 6–12) this excavation into ideas will go still deeper, moving to the enterprise of understanding itself, in verbal and in visual expression. Then, we shall consider how understanding was understood in such a way as to answer the needs (amorous and malevolent) for human bonding. We are moving from the product to the means and, finally, to the enterprise of interpretation. At the moment, however, we still have to consider another fundamental way in which bonding was understood—namely, bonding by malevolent sym-

[1] Cf. Leszek Kolakowski, *Religion* (New York: Fontana, 1982) p. 198: ". . . we really know what is good by knowing what is evil and we know evil by doing it. In experience, evil has to come first as against the sequence represented in theological speculation. And the first evil I can know is the evil in me, whereas evil in others (again: as distinct from natural facts) is derivative."

pathy. Here too the biological and esthetic paradigms served to organize thought, even when love appeared under the guise of hatred.

The legacy of the ancient world recognized that strife could be a condition and a means of union, and that human bonding could take place through emotions antithetic to love. Under the weight of that legacy, even David Hume, applying the universal solvent of skepticism to bonds among things, affirmed that contrariety was a mode of resemblance.[2]

From the beginning of philosophy, it had been taught that the world was a harmony composed of natural sympathies and antipathies, and that, indeed, harmonious unity was sustained by strife, by the very forces that held things apart. Some ancient philosophers argued that, like the peoples of whom T. S. Eliot wrote, the very elements were "united in the strife which divided them."[3] Realizing that to embrace the good was also to forsake the evil—that cleaving to the good and spurning the evil were two aspects of the same action—moral writers, too, understood that antipathies shaped personal behavior and identity as much as sympathies. Ancient tragedians manipulated the empathetic participation of audiences by engaging them with pity (or compassion) and repelling them with terror. Likewise, the union of the worshipper with the holy combined the *fascinans* with the *tremendum*.

Even in rhetoric, "the perception of incompatibility is essential to the interpretation of the message in the case of metaphor"—or, as Aristotle said, the perception of similarity in dissimilars.[4]

Thus fortified in so many areas, the ancient tradition demonstrated that conflict, rivalry, and hatred were means of assimilation as well as of estrangement. Bonding through "malevolent sympathy" could occur by stages, through conversion from love to hatred, or *vice versa*, or, in such changes of heart as that portrayed by Shakespeare, when Juliet's love for Romeo—her "only love"—sprang from her hatred for the Montagues—her "only hate":

> Prodigious birth of love it is to me
> That I must love a loathed enemy.[5]

The classical tradition also recognized that estrangement and bonding might be simultaneous. Conflict, even hatred, can be mixed with love, not least in the violence of ecstatic union. Torn with love and hatred, Catullus anticipated Romeo's agony of "brawling love [and] loving hate . . . misshapened

---

[2] *Treatise of Human Nature*, I, 1.5. 6–7.

[3] "Little Gidding," III. 1. 174. *Four Quartets* (New York: Harper and Row, 1971), p. 56.

[4] Paul Ricoeur, *The Rule of Metaphor*, trans. Robert Czerny et al. (Toronto: University of Toronto Press, 1975), p. 186. Aristotle, *Poetics*, 1459a.

[5] *Romeo and Juliet*, I. 4.

chaos of well-seeming forms."[6] Even where love is absent, emulation can lodge the object of antipathy in the enemy's heart. Writing on jealousy, St. Cyprian drew from his own pre-Christian experience when he observed that, whereas an enemy could evade his jealous persecutor, the persecutor could not escape his prey. Envy kept his adversary always within him tied and bound to his heart with the inescapable chains of his own fervent zeal.[7] Appropriating a Platonic doctrine, a modern writer echoed the same idea: ". . . it is the nature of hatred, as it is the nature of love, to change us into the likeness of that which we contemplate."[8] What is sometimes called the "imitation of the agressor" could be either the assimilation of the predator to his prey, or *vice versa*. The literature of rivalry from antiquity to the present day is replete with instances in which the identification of enemies' lives was so intimate that the destruction of the one was the destruction of the other.[9]

These scattered vestiges of the ancient world—in cosmology, ethics, and psychology—entered the Christian tradition. However, much more than these elements was in play when, as the philosopher Karl Jaspers observed, "Time and again after the combat, indeed during it, Nietzsche seems to stop fighting, to turn toward the enemy, to transform himself, so to speak, into the enemy—not wanting to annihilate him, but wishing him to endure, wanting even Christianity to endure, against which, after all, he had repeated Voltaire's 'Ecrasez l'infame'."[10]

Nietzsche's familiarity with classical literature prepared his mind for the play of attraction and repellence, and of love mixed with pity, fear, and hatred with which he both assimilated and scorned Christianity. But, in the long course of time, those ancient perceptions that bonding did occur through conflict had merged with Christian doctrines that conflict was the precondition of bonding. Nietzsche's transformation of himself into "the enemy" displays many of those Christian teachings: hatred of the world as a preliminary to encompassing the world, the ascetic inversion of pain and pleasure by which God's strength was perfected in the weakness of his ath-

---

[6] Catullus, *Carm. 85. Romeo and Juliet*, I. 1.

[7] Cyprian, *De zelo et livore*, chap. 9 (*Corp. Christ., ser. lat.*, 3A, pp. 79–80).

[8] George William Russell (AE.), quoted in Robert Bernard Davis, *George William Russell ("AE")* (Boston: Twayne, 1977. Twayne's English Authors Series, no. 208, 1977), p. 102. See also the reference to AE in Michael Farrell, *Thy Tears Might Cease* (New York: Knopf, 1969), p. 520: "We become like what we hate." I am grateful to Professor Emmet Larkin for drawing my attention to Farrell's novel.

[9] Carl F. Keppler, *The Literature of the Second Self* (Tucson: University of Arizona Press, 1972), pp. 21–22, 28–29. See also the statement of G. K. Chesterton's fictional detective, Fr. Brown, that he was able to solve crimes because he was able to imagine himself inside the murderer. The act of imagination, he said, was "a religious exercise"; through it, he became the murderer. G. K. Chesterton, "The Secret of Father Brown," and "The Secret of Flambeau," in *The Penguin Complete Father Brown* (Harmondsworth: Penguin, 1981), pp. 464–66, 584.

[10] Karl Jaspers, *Nietzsche and Christianity*, trans. E. B. Ashton (Chicago: Regnery, 1961), p. 91.

lete, the ascetic or martyr; unity through the counterpoint of opposites (for example, good and evil); and victory through defeat, specifically the redemptive sacrifice of the savior, which reversed the roles of victor and vanquished. Of course, a common relationship bound these teachings together. For they were all part of the peculiarly Christian doctrine about nature and art. They explained how, as an artist, God reformed the corrupted nature of the elect into a new and perfect creation, by, through, and in his suffering Word, or art.

At some stages during "the Christian centuries," European art itself expressed this complex center of faith. Bernard of Clairvaux bore witness to this center when he denounced Cluniac sculpture for its elaborate contortions, its *"mira quaedam deformis formositas ac formosa deformositas"* (amazingly deformed beauty and beautiful deformity). As Meyer Schapiro commented, "the fact that medieval art is full of such incongruities, accidental and designed, and can tolerate the unfinished and the partial, points to a conception of the beautiful in art fundamentally different from the ancient."[11] Inasmuch as art is intended to engage the empathetic participation of viewers, the "amazingly deformed beauty and beautiful deformity" of some Romanesque art also points to a concept of association through contrast quite different from pre-Christian doctrines, a conception that also made possible Nietzsche's bonding with Christianity through hatred.

I submit that the elaborate and conscious method of association, analyzed in earlier chapters, lay behind that concept. By reference to interpretations that Augustine of Hippo placed on Scriptural accounts of Jacob's rivalry with his brother, Esau, and of his wrestling match with the angel, I propose to illustrate how the method was applied to hostile relationships.

However, before approaching those particular examples, a wider context needs to be defined for Augustine's understanding of malevolent sympathy in the light of the mutually reflexive, and occasionally equivocal, eroticisms taught by the biological and esthetic paradigms.

AUGUSTINE'S GAMING BOARD

Augustine described in meticulous detail the dark crisis that ended in his conversion. It began with the arrival of Ponticianus, who recounted to Augustine and his friend, Alypius, the conversion of St. Antony. He told them how the saint's example had recently been followed by two soldiers, and the women betrothed to them, in Trier. The narrative sequence there-

---

[11] Meyer Schapiro, "On the Aesthetic Attitude in Romanesque Art," *Romanesque Art* (New York: G. Braziller, 1977), pp. 8, 23–24. I am grateful to Professor Linda Seidel for directing me to this essay. Schapiro quoted Bernard of Clairvaux's famous statement in his *Apologia*, 12. 28 (J. Leclercq and H. M. Rochais, eds., *Tractatus et Opuscula* [Rome: Editiones Cistercienses, 1963. *S. Bernardi Opera*, vol. 3], p. 104).

fore intensified through a series of conversions, culminating in the moment
when Augustine snatched up a copy of the Apostle Paul's letters, opened it
randomly to Romans 13:13, and, in rending distress of heart, applied it to
himself.

The detail in this account to which I draw particular attention is that,
when Ponticianus arrived, Augustine and Alypius were sitting at a gaming
board, on which the text of the Apostle's letters had been placed. In fact, to
underscore the dramatic connection of play with spiritual understanding,
Augustine loaded the portrayal of his conversion with details of play: an
unknown children's game involving the singsong chant, "Take and read";
imitation of a model (St. Antony), bibliomancy, and the decisive codex
taken from a gaming table. (Although Augustine did not identify the kind
of play for which his gaming board was designed, it is worth recalling that
another early Christian writer lamented the dice table as one of the
Tempter's snares, together with idolatry, prostitution, drunkenness, and
murder.)[12]

The description of Augustine's conversion was plainly one of the great
moments in his spiritual history. With all the skill of a rhetorician and an
admirer of the theater manqué, he composed a dramatic account calculated
to move the reader; no detail, including that of the gaming board, was inad-
vertent. But the significance of this apparently casual bit of scenery requires
a wider context, which is also the context into which Augustine and the
Church Fathers placed bonding through love and rivalry.

Christians recognized that the union between a believer and the object of
belief rested on probabilities. It belonged to a language of interrogation. No
doubt, they considered the probabilities of faith as true as some now regard
the probabilities of mathematics. They found the same bonding process at
work in the mysteries of nature and in those of Scripture, a process of love,
enacted through conflict, through likeness, and through contiguity achieved
through the skill and affective intimations of the interpreter. However,
their unifying actions were understood as stochastic, as they would have to
be, dealing with surprises, and they described those actions in analogues of
games of skill, of imitation, and, above all, of risk. The fact must be emphasized that they drew those analogues from forms of play that they condemned.

Speculative play in Scriptural understanding was, in the first instance, a
game of love—in fact, a game of love's hide-and-seek. Unlike Philo of Alex-

---

[12] Conf., 8, 6, 14 (Corp., Christ., ser. lat., 27, p. 121): "supra mensam lusoriam." Cf. De
aleatoribus (once falsely ascribed to St. Cyprian), chap. 5 (CSEL 3, pt. 3, p. 97). On the connection between play and dramatic exposition in a much later text, see Giuseppe Mazzotta, The
World at Play in Boccaccio's Decameron (Princeton: Princeton University Press, 1986). For
further discussions of Augustine's game metaphors, see below, n. 19; Chapter 5 at n. 49;
Chapter 6 at nn. 83, 100.

andria, who wrote of his mating with the liberal arts, Christian authors portrayed themselves as brides in quest of Christ, their spouse. But the spouse, not his coy mistress, flirted. The truths of Scripture were mysteries hidden by God in order to stir up desire, to "fuel the fire of love," to enhance delight by the difficulty and surprise of discovery, and finally to raise the heart through the agitated fires of love to the quiet of contemplation.[13] Above all, the greedily amorous carnality in the Song of Songs was taken as a secret model of spiritual eroticism.

The Fathers found much other support for this conviction in Scripture itself, not only in assertions by St. Paul, such as that things kept secret from the beginning of the world had been revealed to Christians (Rom. 16:25), but also in Christ's deliberate use of parables to conceal his doctrines (Matt. 13:13, 34; Luke 8:10) and in his commands to keep miracles secret (e.g., Matt. 8:4; 16:20; 17:9) and to fast and do alms in secret "unto thy Father which is in secret" (Matt. 6:16–18).

Augustine's account in the *Confessions* of his spiritual formation recalls how, repelled and baffled by the hiddenness of Scripture, Augustine gradually became inflamed with love for Christ the bridegroom—how, again and again, God concealed himself from Augustine or repelled him in order to humble him, even as smitten with love and fear, and groaning in the torments of his desire, Augustine stretched toward consummation in the divine embrace.[14]

Love's stochastic play of hide-and-seek, of denial and concession, had other aspects that included hostile emotions, including hatred, and they were described in analogues of amphitheater, theater, and circus. For Christians, hardly any place of worldly amusement was more abhorrent than the amphitheater, the scene of martyrdom. And yet, Tertullian (ca. 160–ca. 240), the earliest of the Latin Fathers, was able to glory in the mutilation and slaughter of his co-religionists in the arena. Fists staggered; heels kicked; boxing gloves mangled; whips gashed; swords killed. In the arena, fighters did not lament their pain, but sought it, knowing that the crown of victory would close their wounds, and the palm, hide their blood; confident, too, that remembrance would confer a kind of eternity upon them. So it was with martyrs, Tertullian wrote. God had chosen them to triumph by courage over the devil, whom they had spurned by faith. No one complained against the superintendent of the games in the arena. Why should any one complain against God for his barbarity? "Does God lust for man's blood?" Yes, Tertullian answered, if man lusts for a sure salvation, a second birth. Tertullian rejoiced that divine wisdom not only murdered her chil-

---

[13] Augustine, *Ep. 55*: 11. 21; 137. 5. 18 (Migne *PL* 33: 214, 524). *Contra Mendacium*, 10. 24 (Migne *PL* 40: 533–35). *Serm. 51*: 3. 4—4.5 (Migne *PL* 38: 335–36).

[14] E.g., *Conf.*, 2. 6, 13–14; 4. 12. 18–19; 4. 15. 24–25; 6. 5. 8; 7. 10. 16 (*Corp. Christ., ser. lat.* 27, pp. 23–24, 49–50, 52–53, 78–79, 103–105).

dren, but tortured them by fires and punishment, and butchered herself in Christ. Pagan gods were appeased by human sacrifices. "If our God too, in order to have something called sacrifices of his own, had required martyrdoms for Himself, who would have reproached Him for the funereal religion, and the mournful rites, and the altar pyre, and the undertaker priest? Who would not rather have counted happy the man whom God devoured?" By martyrdom, one proved the "love [that] covers a multitude of sins" (1 Pet. 4:8).[15]

When persecution ended, martyrs continued to be idealized through their cults, and, indeed, asceticism was cultivated as a substitute for the martyrdom that Tertullian had praised as the "baptism of blood." Asceticism made it possible for believers to prove their love through martyrdom not once, but daily in the mortification of flesh and contrition of heart. Early Christian rigorists had abhorred the disciplined cultivation of slaughter, "as an exercise and an art," by professional gladiators, their feeding of their bodies with strong food, their magnificent development of brawn and muscle so that they might die a harder death for the gratification of spectators.[16] They loathed the struggles in which naked men entwined their bodies, wounding one another in "abominable embraces."[17]

Yet such were models that the Fathers applied to themselves in their speculative play, strenuously training for the contest, and boldly stripping to grapple with their enemies.[18] Augustine thought of the rhetorician's subdued style, of which he was a master, as a naked fighter, "crushing the sinews and muscles of his foe and with his most powerful limbs overcoming and destroying falsehood," and Jerome portrayed himself in his theological conflicts as a warrior fighting to the death.[19]

After he had undergone dreadful struggles with temptation, Antony was left by the tormenting demons, and Christ appeared to him. "Where were you?" Antony asked, "Why did you not come sooner to soften my pains?"

---

[15] *Scorpiace*, chap. 6–7 (*Corp. Christ., ser. lat.* 2, pp. 1081–82). See above Chapter 1 at nn. 14–16.

[16] Cyprian, *Ep. 1*: 7, 8 (to Donatus) (Migne *PL* 2: 210–16).

[17] Pseudo-Cyprian, *De spectaculis*, chap. 8 (*CSEL* 3, pt. 3, p. 10).

[18] Gregory of Nyssa, *Life of Moses*, 2. 36. 44 (Jean Daniélou, ed., *Grégoire de Nysse: La vie de Moïse* [Paris: Cerf, 1955]. *Sources chrétiennes*, vol. 1*bis*, pp. 41, 43).

[19] Augustine, *De doctrina Christiana*, 4. 26. 56. See also the metaphor of a powerful and richly armored warrior, applied to the grand style: ibid., 4. 20. 42 (Migne *PL* 34: 109, 117). Jerome, *Ep. 49*: 12–13; 50. 5 (*CSEL* 54, pp. 367–70, 393). The theme of union with Christ through struggle was capable of many variations. See Benedicta Ward, trans., *The Sayings of the Desert Fathers* (London: Mowbray, 1975), p. 75, no. 13. John the Dwarf was troubled that he found himself "in peace, without an enemy." He consulted an old man, who "said to him, 'Go, beseech God to stir up warfare so that you may regain the affliction and humility that you used to have, for it is by warfare that the soul makes progress.' So he besought God and when warfare came, he no longer prayed that it might be taken away, but said, 'Lord give me strength for the fight.' "

Christ answered: "Antony, I was here, but I wanted to watch you fight."[20] Christ himself, always the superintendent of the games, was also the consummate athlete, the conqueror of death, crowned with the victor's wreath, and bearing the trophy of the cross.

The Fathers denounced the play of the theater too, whether comedy, tragedy, or mime. Attended by sensuous, enervating music, ancient crimes were relived; adultery was learned while it was seen; men were emasculated by the debauched effeminacy, surpassing the obscenity of prostitutes, performed before their eyes. All was deceit and pretense on the stage; but the spectators enacted what they saw. "Men imitate the gods whom they adore, and to such miserable beings, their crimes become their religion."[21]

Still, just as they appropriated the agonistic play of the amphitheater to their lives, so too the Fathers embraced the imitative play of the theater to describe their spiritual love.

To be sure, imitation figured also in the gladiatorial games, reenacting to the death, with every refinement of theatrical ingenuity, various modes of bloodletting recounted by history and myth. More directly relevant to Christian liturgy was the fact that imitation was also an essential part of rituals performed by mystery cults, such as the initiation rite described by Apuleius, in which he portrayed the god Horus.[22] Other Church Fathers may, like Augustine, have witnessed and been engrossed by public enactments of pagan cults, even as they were by theatrical performances.[23] At any rate, in Christianity as in other mystery religions, the drama of liturgy was infused with concepts of theatrical imitation. The priest enacted the role of Christ; the people enacted the roles set forth in the Scriptural readings for the day. They also participated in a cosmic liturgy: "Is it not true that those very songs which God's choirs of angels sing in heaven are the songs which we on earth utter in harmony with them?"[24] The entire patristic doctrine of consecration, of moral conversion through emulation, and of hierarchic discipline and order is infused with analogues to the theater's enticement of spectators to pleasure through imitation, to reformation according to the models enacted before them.[25]

[20] Athanasius, *Life of Antony*, chap. 10 (Migne *PG* 26: 860). For an echo of this passage in Bede's *Life of Cuthbert* (chap. 37), see Gerald Bonner, " 'The Holy Spirit Within': S.Cuthbert as a Western Orthodox Saint," *Sobornost*, 1 (1979), p. 18. For Augustine's characterization of Christ as the superintendent of athletic bouts, see below Chapter 6 at n. 84.

[21] Lactantius, *Divine Institutes*, 6. 20 (Migne *PL* 6: 706–13). Cyprian, *Ep. 1*: 8 (to Donatus) (Migne *PL* 2: 211–16). Pseudo-Cyprian, *De spectaculis*, chap. 6 (*CSEL* 3, pt. 3, pp. 8–9). Augustine, *City of God*, 6.5 (*Corp. Christ., ser. lat.* 47, p. 172): "Ubi sunt ludi scaenici nisi in rebus divinis, de quibus hi libri tanta sollertia conscribuntur."

[22] Chapter 1 at n. 10.

[23] Chapter 5 at n. 19.

[24] John Chrysostom, *In Heb. Hom.*, 14. 1. 2 (Migne *PG* 63: 111).

[25] Lactantius, *Divine Institutes*, 6. 20 (Migne *PL* 6: 706–707, 710–13). Cf. col. 707: "spectator et particeps fiat." On the impossibility of historical imitation and the necessity of moral,

Finally, the Fathers also applied to their game of love the metaphor of the hated circus. "What else does the practice of the circensian games contain but levity, vanity, and madness? For the souls [of spectators] are hurried away to mad excitement with as violent an impetuosity as that with which the chariot races are carried on there, so that they who come for the sake of seeing the spectacle now themselves exhibit more of a spectacle when they begin to shout, to be thrown into paroxysms of excitement, to jump from their seats." Their faces, the image of God, were disfigured with lust as those of the contestants were by wounds. Often, the tumult between circus factions ignited street warfare and revolt, for no place was "more merciless than the circus, where people do not spare even their rulers and fellow citizens."[26]

And yet the Apostle Paul had applied the racing metaphor to himself: "I have fought a good fight, I have finished my course, I have kept the faith. Henceforth, there is laid up for me a crown of righteousness which the Lord, the righteous judge, shall give me at that day; and not to me only, but unto all them also that love his appearing" (2 Tim. 4:7–8). With this precedent, the Fathers portrayed themselves as runners in the race of virtue against vice. But they were also tumultuous spectators and vicariously participated in the contests of others. Gregory of Nyssa (ca. 331–ca. 396) introduced his *Life of Moses* with a scene evocative of mob cruelty and civic warfare: "At horse races, the spectators intent on victory shout to their favorites in the contest, even though the horses are eager to run. From the stands, they participate in the race with their eyes, thinking to incite the charioteer to keener effort, at the same time urging the horses on while leaning forward and flailing the air with their outstretched hands instead of with a whip. They do this not because their actions themselves contribute anything to the victory, but, in this way, by their good will, they eagerly show in voice and act their concern for the contestants."[27]

Even to mention the amphitheater, theater, and circus is to invoke a stochastic form of play that ran throughout all social strata: gambling. These three institutions of the ancient world existed for the spectator: "This is not glory, but folly," a Christian wrote of one game. "Take away the spectator, and you have shown its emptiness."[28] By contrast, gambling engaged the participants, not vicariously, but directly. Gambling was a dominant form of social mingling that cut across all class lines, both in the Greek and Latin cultures of late antiquity and, as Tacitus reported, also among the Germanic

---

see Gregory of Nyssa, *Life of Moses*, pref. 14; 2. 49 (Daniélou, ed., pp. 5, 45). See John Humphrey, *Roman Circuses: Arenas for Chariot Racing* (Berkeley: University of California Press, 1985).

[26] Lactantius, *Divine Institutes*, 6. 20 (Migne *PL* 6: 706–708). Cf. Tertullian, *De spectaculis*, chap. 16, 18 (*Corp. Christ.*, ser. lat. 1, pp. 241–42, 243).

[27] Gregory of Nyssa, *Life of Moses*, pref. 1 (Daniélou, ed., p. 1).

[28] Pseudo-Cyprian, *De spectaculis*, chap. 8 (*CSEL* 3, pt. 3, p. 11).

tribes where, in their passion, men who cherished liberty above all else, gambled their wives and children and themselves into slavery with a cast of the die.[29] Caesar used a phrase understood everywhere and in every generation when he said that the die was cast when he took his irretrievable step across the Rubicon. Before the conversion of the Empire to Christianity, a most zealous caster, the scholar-emperor Claudius, wrote a book on the art of playing with dice.[30]

An early Christian writer lamented that the devil presided over the dice table, using it to incite anger, perjury, devious talk, rabid friendship, and discordant brotherhood and drive gamblers into poverty, disgrace, and crime. They practiced the very art with which the devil had thrust his image forward for idolatrous worship; for, before it stretched out across the board, the caster's hand sacrificed to the devil, rejecting the art of the Lord, which gains instead of losing. Bishops, he wrote, were slack in rebuking dice players, and, indeed, they associated themselves with them directly. The hand that, purified from human wrongs, imposed on foreheads the protecting sign of Christ and consummated the divine sacraments, was snared once more in the coils of the devil from which it had been freed. The sound of the rattling dice covered the silence of the player's incestuous defilement. After the Christianization of Rome, despite repeated legislation, the emperor Justinian grieved that he had found deacons and priests and even bishops "beloved of God" who had no shame about playing with dice or most ardently mingling with spectators at such games, polluting their hands, ears, and eyes with the damned and forbidden play. Significantly, Justinian continued to condemn clerics for avidly following the horse races, and mingling in the audiences at theatrical shows and animal fights, the very spectacles that, at baptism, they themselves commanded new Christians to forsake with all demonic pomp and worship.[31]

Being "an image of war," the practice of gambling in amphitheater, theater, and circus reflects on the metaphors that the Fathers drew from those areas to describe their quest for God. Moreover, gambling was, like events in the amphitheater, theater, and circus, a religious activity, not in the abstract and solemn way of public cult, but in the earthy, passionate bargaining of the player with the powers that controlled the play—bargaining through fasting, prayers, luck-enticing vows, good-luck amulets, and curses.

Infused with religion, the psychology of gambling pervaded all the metaphors that I have mentioned. All the games of conflict, imitation, and skill were games of hazard. The psychology of gambling is a mentality in which

---

[29] *Germania*, chap. 24 (Loeb ed., p. 166).

[30] Suetonius, *Claudius*, chap. 33 (Loeb ed., p. 64).

[31] *De aleatoribus*, chap. 1–11 (*CSEL* 3, pt. 3, pp. 93–103). *Corpus Iuris Civilis, Codex Iustinianus*, I. 4. 34. *De episcopali audientia*, ed. Paul Krüger (Berlin: Weidmann, 1900), p. 48.

the player may stake all on winning but actually seek to atone for an unspoken guilt by losing; in which the player derives from risk an ecstasy of pleasure mingled with pain, an erotic joy in a sense of the uncanny (which is to say of fear); in which the thrill of joy and fear comes from the possibility of surprise through a sudden and antirational "change of fortune"; and, often, in which players disguise their own motives from themselves and may even mask the disguises.

The other forms of play that I have mentioned were ingrained in the thoughts and feelings of the Fathers through their youthful enthusiasms and through the continuing ardor of their fellow believers. Augustine never lost, but merely sublimated, the "love of play" that, reflecting on his boyhood, he associated with the competitiveness of ballgames, with "wrestling" in the "arena" of his school, and with the foolish delights of the stage.[32] As bishop, he inventoried the pack of renegades, fornicators, and gamblers in the Church, the same crowds who, filling the churches on feast days, thronged to pagan theaters.[33] Another writer grieved that, with the Eucharistic Body of Christ still in them, Christians rushed from the altar to the exhibitions of idolatry at the public games, by way of the brothel.[34] "Where," they say, "are these [spectacles] prohibited [in the Scriptures]? On the contrary, both Elijah as the charioteer of Israel, and David himself danced before the ark. We read [in Scripture] of psalteries, horns, trumpets, drums, pipes, harps, and choruses. Moreover, the Apostle, in his struggle, puts before us the contest of the Caestus, and of our wrestling against the spiritual things of wickedness. Again when he takes his illustrations from the racecourse, he also proposes the reward of the crown. Why, then, may not a faithful Christian man look upon that which holy writ portrays?"[35]

Unlike the other games of hazard that I have mentioned, the play of chance was brought into the Church, and in a way that emphasized the questioning nature of the other games. Both Old and New Testaments sanctioned it as the casting, drawing, or reading of lots. Indeed, according to Scripture, lots were cast during Christ's crucifixion, and at the election of Matthias, precisely so that Old Testament prophecies might be fulfilled.[36] Although he recalled with shame the confidence that, as a young man, he had had in reading lots,[37] as bishop Augustine recognized that God spoke through lots, as well as in other ways.[38] He thought it was better for Christians to read lots from the pages of the Gospels than to consult demons, although he disliked the practice in matters concerning the vain things of

---

[32] *Conf.*, 1. 9. 15; 1. 19. 30; 3. 2. 2–4 (*Corp. Christ., ser. lat.* 27, pp. 8–9, 16–17, 27–29).

[33] *De cat. rud.*, 25. 48 (*Corp. Christ., ser. lat.* 46, pp. 171–72).

[34] Pseudo-Cyprian, *De spectaculis*, chap. 5 (*CSEL* 3, pt. 3, p. 8).

[35] Pseudo-Cyprian, *De spectaćulis*, chap. 2 (*CSEL* 3, pt. 3, p. 4).

[36] Ambrose, *Exposit. Ev. Sec. Luc.* 1. 21–23 (*Corp. Christ., ser. lat.* 14, pp. 17–18).

[37] *Conf.*, 4. 3. 5 (*Corp. Christ., ser. lat.* 27, p. 42).

[38] *Serm.* 12: 4 (*Corp. Christ., ser. lat.* 41, pp. 167–68).

this life.[39] But, he judged, when warfare threatened a church, it was best to decide by lot whether, or which, clerics should stay, and which, if any, should flee to safety. Perhaps, he wrote, those who are better will choose to lay down their lives for their brethren, and those whose lives are less useful will decide to save themselves by flight. These decisions would be challenged. "Therefore, as it is written, 'The lot suppresseth contentions, and determineth even between the mighty' (Prov. 18:18)." It was wise for God to decide in such doubtful cases whether the better should be called to the fruit of passion and those of weaker spirit, and less profit to the Church, be spared. But, in such cases, Augustine insisted, none could exclude himself from participating in the reading of lots.[40]

Gambling worked its way into Christian symbolism; for, like the phoenix and the thornbush, dice were symbols of Christ's passion. According to Isidore of Seville (ca. 560–636), some considered the casting of dice itself an allegorical art, because they played on a figured board across divisions called "past, present, and future."[41]

The interrogation of God by casting or reading lots from Scripture was also allegorical, at least in the moral sense; for, opening themselves to the ever-fresh astonishments of God's inscrutability, Christians judged events in Scripture prefigurative, and prescriptive, of events in the lives of present men, women, and communities.

I have now indicated ways in which Christian writers described the speculative play by which, through Scriptural understanding, they associated themselves with the promises of blessing that they believed they found concealed in nature and in sacred history. Hatred was balanced by love; despair, by hope; and guilt, by pardon. But symmetry was imperfect. For, in the surprises of love's hide-and-seek, fear could not be matched with security but only with promise. Thus, love was a game of probabilities, a game of burning, insatiable hunger, played in the blindness of faith, at risk. For "faith is the substance of things hoped for, the evidence of things not seen" (Hebr. 11:1).

It is not surprising that rivalry, and hatred, became defining characteristics of love, and that writers imagined themselves bonded in need to their rivals, indeed, to those who hated and persecuted them. Their doctrine of love hinged on interrogation without answers, on the sadness of experience that contradicted expectations, reintegrating the sense of life by shattering it. However, the openness of interrogation without answers was decisively important; for it delivered Christians from the vicious circle of projecting into Scripture their own expectations, their own answers to their own ques-

[39] *Ep. 55*: 20. 37 (Migne *PL* 33: 222).
[40] *Ep. 128*: 12 (Migne *PL* 33: 1018).
[41] *Etymolog.*, 18. 60. 1.; 18. 65. 1 (W. M. Lindsay, ed., *Isidori Hispalensis Episcopi Etymologiarum sive Originum Libri XX*, vol. 2 [Oxford: Clarendon, 1911], n. p.).

tions. Their stochastic doctrine of interrogation emphasized the negative values, the hermeneutic gaps, of the art of interpretation. In the terms of Christian exegetes, they demanded the self-emptying of the interpreter. This kenosis delivered the interpreter from the presumption of acting as a ventriloquist to Scripture and made real, all too real, "the creative negativity of true questioning, which is essentially the negativity in experience, that reaches and transforms, in the heart of the hermeneutical experience."[42]

Something of the sort was implied by Augustine when he portrayed the dramatic moment of his conversion, the fateful text of Paul resting on a gaming board.

Bearing in mind this context of malevolent sympathy in the game of love, I now turn to the specific interpretation placed by Augustine on the rivalry between Jacob and Esau.

AUGUSTINE AND MALEVOLENT SYMPATHY

Augustine's pattern of understanding reflected the circumstances of his life. In a revealing aside, Augustine remarked how easily he was distracted by the fascination of the hunt. Although he no longer went to the circus to watch predatory chases, he would stop his horse, he wrote, and pause in rapt attention to see a hound chasing a hare through an open field. Often, at home, he would watch lizards catch flies, or spiders entangle them in webs. There was a parallel with his own life. As a controversialist, Augustine himself was a hunted hunter. His enemies among the Donatist bishops raged against him, arguing "that he was a wolf to be killed in defense of their flock, and that there could be no doubt at all that God would forgive the sin of any man who killed him." Although, in the frenetic violence of the Donatist controversy, ambushes were laid for him, Augustine escaped. Yet the bonding of hunter and victim, which he personally and long experienced, entered into his deepest thinking about human relations.[43]

I shall speak first about the visible structure of Augustine's interpretations—that is, his montage of narratives—and then about his unifying, but unseen, framing devices of association. At first we shall be concerned chiefly with a particular use to which Augustine put the esthetic paradigm, namely, his effort to disclose the inner coherence of Scripture as a supreme work of art. But it must also be said that his doctrine that all the saved, whether they lived before or after Christ, were united by love in one city, which was also the body of Christ, and were joined to Christ in fecund spiritual mar-

[42] Richard E. Palmer, *Hermeneutics: Interpretation Theory in Schleiermacher, Dilthey, Heidegger, and Gadamer* (Evanston: Northwestern University Press, 1969), p. 233.

[43] Augustine, *Conf.*, 10. 35. 57 (*Corp. Christ., ser. lat.* 27, pp. 185–86). Possidius, *Vita Augustini*, chap. 9, 12 (Migne *PL* 32: 41, 43).

riage, brought into play the erotic content both of the esthetic and the biological paradigms, which is also to say, the conflict implied in male dominance and female subordination, and in the artist's imposition of form on
matter. There are many passages in which the eroticism of Augustine's
organic and genetic vocabulary is obviously prerequisite to that of his
exalted esthetic idiom. For Augustine, as for Donne long centuries afterwards, the two paradigms were both mutually reflexive and equivocal.

But this was not so for the three modern writers with whose understanding of malevolent sympathy I wish to compare Augustine's. For them,
the tension between nature and art could not be resolved by a graceful elision of metaphors or patterns of association. In their works, the biological
paradigm existed as a foil for the esthetic one, and a synonym of evil. The
three works to be considered are all essays in sexual frustration. In their
preoccupation with creative conflict, the three modern writers rejected the
mutuality, which came so easily to Augustine, between sexual consummation and artistic composition, and which he both used and mistrusted.

In this chapter, therefore, I shall concentrate on Augustine's use of the
esthetic paradigm and reserve to a later chapter (Chapter 5) a discussion of
his use of the biological one. Thus, for the time being, the oscillation in
Augustine's mind—characteristic also of Donne, but not of the three twentieth-century authors—between works of the flesh and works of the spirit
must be implied, rather than stated.

As we shall see at the end, the pattern of understanding that enabled him
to think of bonding by malevolent sympathy was dominated by negative
values. These values enabled him to employ, with decisive effect, association by contrast in his doctrines of bonding. Augustine gave primary importance to the transfer of identity from one person to another. Jacob disguised
himself as Esau, thereby deceiving their father, Isaac, into giving him the
blessing due the firstborn. At the time, the transfer was fraudulent by
intent. In the long run, because it testified to the mystery of Christ's
bearing the sins of others, it was prophetically true, and it was confirmed as
such by Isaac. The angel carried the *persona* of God[44]; and, when he
bestowed his blessing on Jacob and gave Jacob, "he who supplants" a new
name, Israel, "he who sees God,"[45] the transfer was authentic. The premise
that Jacob and the angel assumed the identities of others, whereas Esau did
not, enabled Augustine, following the esthetic paradigm, to detect in the
Scriptural accounts many narratives that turned on impersonation. By a
series of equations, he moved from the narrative of rivalry between
brothers, first, to the contrast between body ("the carnal man") and soul
("the spiritual man"); second, to the contrast between Jews (still mired in

---

[44] *Serm. 5: 6 (Corp. Christ., ser. lat.,* 41, p. 57).
[45] *Serm. 122 (72):* 3 (Migne *PL* 38: 681–82).

carnal understanding of the Scriptures) and Christians (to whom God had imparted spiritual understanding of Scripture); third, to the contrast between the first man, Adam, "of the earth, earthy," and Christ, "who is from heaven, spiritual"; and, finally, to the contrast between the elect and the reprobate. The rivalry of Esau and Jacob thus encapsulated the rivalry of the two sides of human nature, carnal and spiritual, whether within any individual heart or in the broad sweep of sacred history.[46]

Jacob's struggle with the angel permitted further reflections. As they wrestled "until the breaking of the day," the angel touched the hollow of Jacob's thigh and disjointed it. At length overcoming the angel, Jacob refused to let him go until the angel blessed him, leaving his thigh withered. By assuming Esau's identity, Jacob had supplanted him in his primacy and inheritance, but he had also incurred the deadly rage of his brother, which he appeased only after he had passed some years in a distant land, and at great cost. When the angel transferred his identity (as God's impersonator) to Jacob, Jacob became a "type" of Christ. Being lamed, he also assumed the typology of the flesh that Esau had carried. By a reversal of roles, he was both blessed and lamed, both victor and vanquished. This ambiguity enabled Augustine to place Jacob on both sides of the conflict between body and soul. Accordingly, in the wrestling, the angel carried the *persona* of God. His struggle with Jacob signified Christ's passion, Augustine wrote, because the Jews (carnality) had overcome Christ (spirituality) as Jacob overcame the angel.[47] In his withered member, Jacob personified (as did Esau) Jews and bad Christians, people of carnal vision, whereas in his blessedness, he personified true believers, a duality that would end only after death when, in the heavenly city, Jacob, the supplanter, would be entirely transformed into Israel, "he who sees God."[48]

Augustine's method of association therefore produced a montage of narratives. If the coherence of the esthetic paradigm is presupposed, those narratives generally corresponded with the four levels of interpretation with which Augustine tried to unfold the hidden sense of Scripture. At the *historical* (or literal) level, Jacob supplanted Esau and wrestled with an angel. At the *etiological* level, the events in the life of Jacob witnessed to the universal causality of sin and redemption, namely, to the redemptive process, set in motion by Adam's disobedience and accomplished by Christ's self-sacrifice, that constituted sacred history. Further (and still on the etiological level), they illustrated how the Jews caused the Christians to supplant them, for if the Jews had not been inwardly blinded, Christ would not have been

---

[46] *En. in Ps.* 136: 18 (*Corp. Christ., ser. lat.*, 40, pp. 1975–76).

[47] *City of God*, 16. 39 (*Corp. Christ., ser. lat.*, 48, p. 545).

[48] *Serm.* 5: 4, 8 (*Corp. Christ., ser. lat.*, 41, pp. 55, 59). *Serm. 122 (72)*: chap. 3–4 (Migne *PL* 38: 681–83). *City of God*, 16. 35, 39 (*Corp. Christ., ser. lat.*, 48, pp. 540, 549).

crucified.[49] On the *analogical* level, the typological equivalence between Old Testamental and New Testamental figures was disclosed (Esau equals Jews; the lamed part of Jacob equals Jews crucifying Christ; and the blessed part of Jacob equals Christ). The prophecy applied to the descendents of Esau and Jacob that "the elder shall serve the younger" (Gen. 25:23) corresponded with Christ's eschatological prophecy, "the last shall be first and the first last" (Luke 13:28–30). The *allegorical* (or mystical) narrative revealed the equivalence of the duality of carnal and spiritual natures, represented by Esau and Jacob, and by the lame and blessed parts of Jacob with the duality of every faithful soul in this world, and with the Church. The line of carnality extended to unconverted Jews and wicked Christians. The eventual transformation of the double Jacob-Israel into the single Israel in paradise bespoke, allegorically, the purgation of the Church of all impurities at the Last Judgment.[50]

It is striking that Augustine repeated, at each narrative level, the scenario characteristic of tragedy: pathos, discovery, periptery, and epiphany. On the historical levels at least, his portrayal lacks tragic effect—that is, it fails to arouse pity and fear—according to Aristotle's prescription because, first, Jacob's conflict with Esau arose from an evil deliberately perpetrated by Jacob himself, not from a great error in judgment; second, consequently their story could be read as the passage of a bad man from misery to happiness; and third, it was a trait of comedy according to Aristotle for "the bitterest enemies in the piece (e.g., Orestes and Aegisthus) to walk off good friends at the end, with no slaying of anyone by anyone."[51] On the allegorical, or mystical level, even the dreadful fate of the damned should not have conveyed the "tragic pleasure" of pity and fear. Being an act of justice, the fall of the bad from the relative happiness of this world into the misery that they deserved should inspire rejoicing, instead of fear or compassion, except for the fact of suffering itself.[52]

However, it is also evident that Augustine did intend the sufferings of the damned to arouse the tragic effect of compassion and terror, because awareness of one's own sinfulness and of the small number of the predestined rendered the agonies of the damned a potential mirror for each Christian, the object of empathetic participation, not merely monstrous but also productive of cartharsis through compassion and fear.[53] The multiplicity of Augustine's narratives also makes evident that for his interpretation (as for

[49] *Serm. 122 (72)*: chap. 4 (Migne *PL* 38: 683).

[50] The historical, etiological, analogical, and allegorical levels are those specified by Augustine himself (instead of the literal, anagogical, mystical, and moral applied by other exegetes). See Karl F. Morrison, " 'From Form into Form': Mimesis and Personality in Augustine's Historical Thought," *Proceedings of the American Philosophical Society*, 124 (1980), pp. 286–87.

[51] *Poetics*, 1452a–1453a.

[52] Cf. *Poetics*, 1452b, 1453b.

[53] *Poetics*, 1453b.

tragedy, according to Aristotle), the characters were included for the sake of the action. At the highest levels of narrative abstraction, where lessons were drawn that applied to every Christian life, characters, indeed, were unnecessary, just as "a tragedy is impossible without action [i.e., a plot], but there may be one without character. The tragedies of most of the moderns," Aristotle added, "are characterless."[54] It was on this level of moral conduct that Augustine wished the cathartic effects of pity and fear to be strongest. Thus, elements of tragedy do penetrate through the various narratives that Augustine extracted from the stories of Jacob's conflict.

In the account of Jacob's conflict with Esau, the sequences of pathos to discovery to periptery to epiphany are laminated and visible, each through the others. The struggle of Esau and Jacob in the womb crowned by Jacob's deception of Isaac (pathos), the disclosures of Jacob's plot and his flight (discovery-periptery), and the reconciliation between the brothers (epiphany) is seen through the etiological sequence of Adam's disobedience (pathos), the Fall and expulsion from Eden (discovery-periptery), and the advent and second coming of Christ, the new Adam (epiphany). Further, the historical and etiological narratives are visible through the anagogical one of persecution of the Church by the Jews and the Roman Empire (pathos), the pacification of the Church (discovery-periptery), and the long-deferred supplanting of the Jews by the Christians, notably in the Diaspora (epiphany). All other narratives are read through the allegorical, which follows the sequence of daily conflict between flesh and spirit both in each Christian and in the Church (pathos), illumination by faith and progress through conversion until death (discovery-periptery), and direct vision in Paradise (epiphany). Each movement from pathos to epiphany ends in happiness for the elect and misery for the reprobate—in the supplanting of Esau, cast down because of his fleshly concupiscence for a bowl of lentils; in the disinheritance and dispersal of the Jews because of their faithlessness; and in the eternal misery of the damned because in Adam they committed the crime of crimes, which Christ did not remit for them.

Of course, the account of Jacob's struggle with the angel also displays this lamination of narratives, each following the tragic scenario and conveying the "tragic pleasure" of empathy: catharsis through pity and fear.

Thus far, I have only considered the elaborate structure of narratives on the surface of Augustine's texts. True to the formal coherence required by the esthetic paradigm, underpinning all the levels of personal identification and harmonizing them was Augustine's powerful concept of a bonding between nature and art, a bonding through which God, the sculptor, melted down humanity's old, flawed nature and recast it into a new, supremely

---

[54] *Poetics*, 1450a.

beautiful form.[55] As ever, art used nature to perfect and surpass nature. Now, I must turn to the framing devices that enabled Augustine to think that these highly diverse narratives were united, a problematic infrastructure that permitted him to visualize how the redemptive fusion of nature and art worked.

The different narratives in this montage were held together by a network of impersonations in which roles were transferred and even reversed. the play of association that allowed Augustine to construct that network was by no means self-evident, nor, consequently, were the conclusions that he drew from the Scriptural account of Jacob. When, in order to deceive Isaac, Jacob slipped kid skins over his hands, masquerading as his hairy brother, he perpetrated not a lie but a true mystery, because his act signified Christ's assumption of sins (that is, the hairy skins) that were not his own.

Not everyone could see that Jacob's supplanting of Esau corresponded with the Church's supplanting of the Jews. The associations that elucidated these mysteries were not evident to the principals in the events; Jacob (and Rebecca) intended to deceive Isaac.[56] Nor did the fortunes of Esau and Jacob themselves reflect the transfer of primacy. For, after he received Isaac's blessing, Jacob fled into a distant land and tended the flocks of others, to escape his brother's rage, while Esau remained at home, became rich, and ruled in abundance. Jacob, the hunter, became the hunted. Moreover, at their reconciliation, the elder did not serve the younger. It was Jacob who reverenced his brother from afar off and delivered up lavish peace offerings. Indeed, far from being evident to the principals, Jacob's supplanting of Esau became apparent only after the lapse of many centuries, when Jacob (in the form of Christians) filled the earth and ruled nations and kingdoms, when the Christian Roman Empire expelled Esau (in the form of Jews) from his homeland and forbade Jews to enter Jerusalem.[57] Even then, the composite montage that Augustine detected behind a network of impersonation was hidden from "heretics, schismatics, scatterers of the Church, [and] mockers of Christ."[58] It was not evident to the Jews, the elder who served the younger, the Christians, by uncomprehendingly bearing the sacred books from which the Church lived, and who unwittingly blessed Christ, whom they denied.[59] It was not evident to the world that hated Christ and his elect.[60]

---

[55] *Enchir.*, 23 (89) (*Corp. Christ., ser. lat.* 46, p. 97). *City of God*, 22. 19 (*Corp. Christ., ser. lat.*, 48, p. 838). Cf. *En. in Ps.* 6: 5 (*Corp. Christ., ser. lat.*, 38, p. 30): "Dum autem nos convertimus, id est mutatione veteris vitae resculpsimus spiritum nostrum. . . ." Here, too, the emphasis is on God as the ultimate sculptor. For Augustine concludes: "Sana me ergo, inquit [psalmista], non propter meritum meum, sed propter misericordiam tuam."

[56] *Contra Mendacium*, chap. 24 (*CSEL*, 41, p. 500).

[57] *Serm.* 5: 5 (*Corp. Christ., ser. lat.*, 41, pp. 55–56).

[58] *Tr. in Ev. Johan.*, 11. 13 (*Corp. Christ., ser. lat.*, 36, p. 118).

[59] *En. in Ps.* 136: 18 (*Corp. Christ., ser. lat.*, 40, p. 1975). *City of God*, 16. 37 (*Corp. Christ., ser. lat.*, 48, pp. 541–42).

[60] *Tr. in Ev. Johan.*, 87. 2 (*Corp. Christ., ser. lat.*, 36, p. 544).

In these regards, Augustine turned from the formal to the dynamic aspects of the esthetic paradigm, from the inner coherence of Scripture as a work of art to the bonding that could occur between readers of Scripture and the unspoken content of the text. The plausibility of Augustine's "montage technique" therefore rested on "negative values," on expectations and assumptions not present in the literal text. Augustine recognized that fiction and reality necessarily mixed as long as human beings "saw through a glass darkly" (1 Cor. 13:12), being limited to perceive through the senses and to think and speak indirectly through the medium of words, rather than seeing them face to face, and communing without the reflective mediation of words. These "negative values" illuminated the faith in this world that anticipated sight in the next.

An esthetic of very wide application was in play. For Augustine saw the whole scope of history as a formal composition, a poem or song. God, its author, achieved its exquisite beauty, "by the opposition of contraries, arranged, so to speak by an eloquence, not of words, but of things." Those admirable antitheses were created by a common act—mimesis. For, just as the saved imitated God in righteousness, so the reprobate imitated him perversely. The dread sentence of reward and punishment informed the antitheses of the composition with justice, "the supreme and true beauty." And that justice expressed the eternal and unsearchable wisdom of God, which deployed even the agonies of the damned, yet more incredible than the joys of the saved, for the beauty of the work.[61]

As he linked the components of his montage, Augustine employed the three modes of association set forth by Aristotle and canonized in the rhetorical tradition: likeness, contiguity, and contrast. These modes of association gave the infrastructure its cohesion. A few examples of each will suffice. Etymology was a tool for establishing likeness. That Esau was also referred to as Edom, which, Augustine thought, meant "blood," enabled the bishop to make his vital association of Esau with carnality.[62] Likeness of conduct also served as a means of association, as when Augustine identified the angel with Christ because, like him, he lay down and took up his power at will and abstained from anger under attack.[63] Augustine argued from likeness of use that, when he put hairy skins on his hands, Jacob prefigured Christ, who put on the sins of others.[64] Association by contiguity likewise

[61] See Conf., 2. 6. 14 (Corp. Christ., ser. lat. 27, p. 24). De Musica, 6. 11. 29; 6. 13. 40 (Bibliothèque augustinienne, lre série, vol. 4, pp. 424, 444). En. in Ps. 44: 3 (Corp. Christ., ser. lat. 38, p. 496). City of God, 11. 18; 15. 21 (Corp. Christ., ser. lat. 48, pp. 337, 487). Ep. 138: 5 (Migne PL 33: 527). Contra Adimantium Manichaei Discipulum, 41. 47 (Migne PL 42: 204–206). In general, see Jaroslav Pelikan, The Mystery of Continuity: Time and History, Memory and Eternity in the Thought of St. Augustine (Charlottesville: University Press of Virginia, 1986). I am obliged to Mr. Stanley Rosenberg for referring me to Pelikan's book.

[62] En. in Ps. 136: 18 (Corp. Christ., ser. lat., 40, p. 1976).

[63] Serm. 122 (72): 3 (Migne PL 38: 682).

[64] Contra Mendacium, chap. 24 (CSEL, 41, p. 51).

took many forms, often crowned by surprise at what could be believed although it was impossible. By contiguity—the presence of the "entire mass" of humankind in Adam—the human race as a whole perished because of Adam's disobedience; also by contiguity—God in Christ and believers in Christ—redemption occurred.[65] Metaphors of organic unity (vine and branches, head and members) expressed this kind of association by contiguity.[66] Plainly, however, contiguity need not be a matter of spatial or temporal juxtaposition. Indeed, Augustine's arguments from contiguity emphasize the greater weight that he assigned to the astonishments unlocked through association by contrast.

Augustine acknowledged that, in its historical context, Jacob's deception of Isaac was a lie. He recognized that Esau and Jacob were twins, conceived by one act of generation, offspring of one seed, two sons in one womb.[67] But the contiguity that provided correct spiritual association shockingly transcended and reversed these historical contiguities. In the order of truth, Jacob's deception and the conflict between Esau and Jacob—the bifurcation of carnal and spiritual peoples—were contiguous to Christ's redemptive sacrifice, rather than to their historical contexts. Thus, surprisingly, what was false in the historical order could be true in the prophetic order.

Association by contrast pervaded Augustine's montage of impersonations, not merely in the literal sense that Esau's fall was Jacob's rise.[68] Jacob's historical lie that was prophetic truth invited Augustine to demonstrate that the tools of rhetoric commonly served the object of association by contrast. Intellectual association by contrast and personal bonding by conflict witnessed to a common principle of likeness in contrariety. Technical devices such as antiphrasis dazzled the imagination by indicating the direct opposite of what one said, and parables, tropes, and metaphors likewise enhanced the joy of discovery by using contrariety to obscure meaning.[69] Rhetoric demonstrated not only that the mind could know through calculated surprises of contrasts but also that opposites could be identical in signification.

The erotic aspects of the esthetic paradigm were very pronounced. When Augustine discussed Jacob's wrestling match with the angel, he explored a similarly paradoxical identity of reference in the emotional sphere. The wrestling match, he wrote, elucidated Christ's command, "Love your enemies" (Matt. 5:44; Luke 6:27). Grappled to Christ, personified by the angel, Jacob exemplified how the faithful Christian, if he cleaved fast to Christ, would, when wrestling with enemies, love them. A complex emo-

---

[65] *Tr. in Ev. Johan.*, 87: 2–3 (*Corp. Christ., ser. lat.*, 36, pp. 544–45).

[66] *Tr. in Ev. Johan.*, 87. 1–2 (*Corp. Christ., ser. lat.*, 36, pp. 543–44).

[67] *City of God*, 16. 36 (*Corp. Christ., ser. lat.*, 48, p. 540). *En. in Ps.* 136: 18 (*Corp. Christ., ser lat.*, 40, p. 1975). *Tr. in Ev. Johan.* 11. 10–11 (*Corp. Christ., ser. lat.*, 36, pp. 116–17).

[68] *En. in Ps. 136*: 18 (*Corp. Christ., ser. lat.*, 40, pp. 1975–76).

[69] *Contra Mendacium*, chap. 24 (*CSEL* 41, pp. 499–500).

tional chiaroscuro was in play. In another connection, Augustine insisted that Christians were obliged to a perfect hatred of evil men, namely, to hate the vice and love the man. Christians were to love their enemies for what was good in them, and to hate them for what was evil.[70] Commenting on Jacob's struggle with his angelic adversary, Augustine admonished his people to be perfect even as God was perfect, loving their enemies. But the chiaroscuro was also in play in this model. For God loved his creatures, even when he hated them for the defects that he did not create.[71] So, too, in love, he chastised them with famine, sicknesses, pestilence, and death.[72]

In his *Tractates on the Gospel of John*, Augustine applied the same principle of bonding through love and hatred, exemplified in Jacob's conflict with the angel, more broadly when he turned to the relationship between Christians and the world. In mind-bending paradox, he asserted that the whole world was the Church, and that the whole world hated the Church. That is, the world hates the world; the enemy hates the reconciled; the damned, the saved; the impure, the justified. How, he asked, does the world of perdition love itself and hate the world of redemption? It loves itself, he answered, with a false love, not with a true one. Therefore, it falsely loves itself and truly (but unconsciously) hates itself.

> "For whoever loves iniquity hates his own soul." But the world is said to love itself because it loves the iniquity by which it is iniquitous; and, again, it is said to have hated itself because it loves what is harmful to itself. Therefore, it hates the nature in itself, and loves vice. It hates what has been done through the goodness of God; it loves what has been done in it through free will.
>
> Wherefore we are both forbidden—if we rightly understand—and commanded to love [the world]. That is, we are forbidden, where it is said to us, "Do not love the world"; but we are commanded where it is said to us, "Love your enemies." They are the world who hate us. Therefore, we are also forbidden to love in it what it loves in itself, and we are commanded to love in it what it hates in itself, namely God's handiwork, and the diverse consolations of his goodness. Indeed, we are forbidden to love the vice in it, and we are commanded to love the nature, although it loves the vice and hates the nature, so that we may love and hate it rightly, although it loves and hates itself perversely.[73]

The role that malevolent sympathy played in the redemptive fusion of nature and art is evident in these doctrines. Also evident is how malevolent sympathy entered into Augustine's literal, etiological, anagogical, and alle-

---

[70] *City of God*, 14. 6 (*Corp. Christ., ser. lat.*, 48, p. 421). *Contra Faustum*, 19. 24 (*CSEL* 25, pp. 522–25).

[71] *Tr. in Ev. Johan.* 35. 34 (*Corp. Christ., ser. lat.*, 36, p. 319).

[72] *Serm. 5:* 2 (*Corp. Christ., ser. lat.* 41, pp. 51–52).

[73] *Tr. in Ev. Johan.* 87. 2–4 (*Corp. Christ., ser. lat.*, 36, pp. 544–45).

gorical narratives: at each level, the act of bonding was sealed by a single emotion manifested both as love and as hatred, just as the fusion of nature and art advanced through a contrapuntal rhythm of hatred and love until God, as love, was all and all in all. Plato observed that tragedy and comedy were cognate arts, both of them combining pleasure and pain, fear and love, and that they were governed by the same genius (*Philebus* 50; *Symposium* 223). Augustine's teaching on bonding similarly identified love and hatred in the redemptive fusion of nature and art, just as he also identified the four Stoic "perturbations of soul"—desire, joy, fear, and sorrow—as different names for love.[74] In his frame of reference, tragic bonding through catharsis of pity (or compassion) and fear could be regarded as an effect of love.

The discussion about the structure of narratives and the unifying infrastructure of association thus far has shown that Augustine's montage of narratives—all versions of the redemptive fusion of art and nature—was composed by a method of association. That method consisted of three modes of association: by likeness, by contiguity, and, especially, by contrast. Its coherence and veracity depended on "negative values" accessible to the eye of faith, but hidden from heretics, schismatics, and unbelievers; and those "negative values" were detected most notably in surprises revealed through association by contrast.

Augustine portrayed all history as the warfare of two cities, each united by the emotion of love, although they cherished different objects of love. Correspondingly, his method of exegetical association resolved itself into discourse on the method of emotional association that unified those cities, particularly, the city of God. Love was the keystone for both methods, but such was his awareness that contraries could be identical, that Augustine conceived of hatred, fear and, sorrow—as well as joy and desire—as manifestations of love. In fact, Augustine depersonalized his doctrine of love. In a way reminiscent of the "characterlessness" of some of his narrative levels, human beings went away and perished; they abided only in God. Moreover, one loved eternal verities (God or virtue) and hated vices in a person, rather than making the person himself the object of emotion. Thus, Augustine's doctrine of emotional bonding was abstract. Friends were loved in God and God in them; and enemies were loved for the sake of God (*propter te*). Therefore, one could, unknowingly, love a person whom one cast off, or perhaps hate a person with whom one broke bread and lived in common.[75]

These abstract, depersonalized ideas circle around a doctrine of participation that is implied in all that I have said concerning Augustine's method of association. Augustine's teachings about the use of contrast in rhetoric pre-

---

[74] On Plato, see Chapter 4 (B) n. 82. Cf. *Symposium*, 223. *City of God*, 14. 7 (*Corp. Christ., ser. lat.*, 48, pp. 421–23).

[75] *Conf.*, 4. 9. 14; 4. 12. 18 (*Corp. Christ., ser. lat.*, 27, pp. 47, 49). *Tr. in Ev. Johan.* 90. 2–3 (*Corp. Christ., ser. lat.*, 36, pp. 551–53). See below, Chapter 7, n. 228.

disposed him to expect actual association by contrast in the nature of things. Likewise, his mastery of tropes predisposed him to think that, in actual things, the part epitomized the nature of the whole, much as a relic, part of the body of a martyr, encased the sanctity of the whole. Of course, his doctrine of participation was cosmic in scope. The idea of participation in moral nature enabled Augustine to distinguish between the merely external ties of community and the inward merging of communion. According to Augustine, persons are loved or hated in proportion to their participation in virtue, that is, in God. Augustine's cherished metaphor of light (learned, like the doctrine of participation itself, from Neoplatonism) elucidated his doctrine that all creatures derived their being from God, the Light of lights, many lamps taking their fire from one flame, and that their degree of being depended on their proximity to the source of light.

Augustine's esthetic linking of narratives required this concept of participation. The transference of identity from one actor to his impersonators was plausible only if one assumed that the actor and his impersonator participated (or communed) in the same virtue or vice, that they were, in some degree, one in spirit. Moreover, participation was proportionate, and it could come about through stages, as indicated by the process by which Jacob was converted into Israel, and by the slow movement through which Christians supplanted the Jews, fulfilling the prophecy that "the elder shall serve the younger." The ambiguity of proportionate participation is indicated by the point at which Augustine declared that Jacob, both lamed and blessed, epitomized in his own person the conflict between carnality and spirituality, represented also by the rivalry of Jacob (signifying spirit) against Esau (signifying flesh).

Further, participation could be one-sided. Jacob was bonded to Isaac by his blessing, to Esau by conflict, and to the angel by blessing and conflict. But the identities of Isaac, Esau, and the angel were conveyed to Jacob, not his to them. Likewise, converted Jews assumed the character of Christians without conveying their own identity to Christ.

Throughout, participation occurred through the mimetic act of mediation. Indeed, Augustine's account is an essay in how illusory mimesis—Jacob's masquerade as Esau and the angel's pretense of being a man—mediated the way to authentic, transformative mimesis, namely, to mimesis through which two quite disparate historical events participated in the same truth, or a person was transformed by conversion into the likeness of what he had hated. The "tragic pleasure" of catharsis through pity and fear required mimetic participation in the hearts of the audience.

Guided by the doctrine of participation, Augustine was able to discount historical context as a tool of association, although, with varying rhetorical purposes, he employed it on occasion. Association in terms of moral nature became an exercise in timelessness and placelessness, just as, in reference to

truth, Jacob was closer to Christ, whom he prefigured, than to Isaac, whom
he deceived. For this reason, Augustine was able to detect astonishing role
reversals in sacred history, when the part that a person played in the context
of history was quite inverted in that of prophecy: that is to say, when, from
its storehouse of "negative values," association by contrast presented yet
another paradox to the dazzled eye of faith. So it was that Jacob was found
to be as the Apostle Paul said of himself, "a deceiver, yet true" (2 Cor.
6:8), but not in his own time. In the prophetic order, above all, participation
revealed contariety as a model of likeness.

Augustine's interpretations of Jacob's struggles indicate four ways in
which, he thought, "art" could produce participatory bonding of one person
to another by way of moral nature. The first was dialectical. Augustine
plainly recognized that each party to conflict was both active and passive.[76]
It was particularly in the dialectical union of the action that role reversals
occurred—for example, in the historical narrative, when Jacob was both
victor and vanquished in his conflict with the angel, and in the allegorical,
when Christ was both vanquished and victor in his crucifixion. The second
way of participatory bonding was by feud. Each party was both transgressor
and avenger. Gain for the one was loss for the other. An alternating pattern
of debt and retribution was established that became the entire narrative
unless ended by an action, outside the rules of the feud, that destroyed the
feuding relationship. Bonding by feud characterized the relationship of Esau
and Jacob between the time of Isaac's deception and that of their extravagant
reconciliation. It also characterized the pattern of debt and retribution that
constituted Augustine's portrayal of history as a drama of redemption. The
third way of participatory bonding disclosed in these texts is by substitution. By this means, in the historical narrative, Jacob supplanted Esau, and
the angel carried the persona of God. In the analogical, or allegorical, narrative, Christians were substituted for the Jews. The last way of participatory bonding indicated by Augustine is by transference. In the historical
narrative, Isaac and the angel transferred their blessings to Jacob and thus
conveyed to him their identities—Isaac, that of patriarch, and the angel,
that of Christ's impersonator. On the anagogical and allegorical levels,
transference by blessing divinized the humanity of Christ, and the
humanity of believers who participated in Christ.[77]

This survey of how Augustine used the esthetic paradigm to organize his
"montage technique" provides some indications of how Christian ideas
about bonding through conflict went beyond those embedded in pre-Chris-

---

[76] Cf. the statement of Meister Eckhart: "Acting and being acted upon are two equally primary principles, but are one motion." "Response to the list of forty-nine Articles," in *Meister
Eckhart: The Essential Sermons, Commentaries, Treatises, and Defense*, trans. Edmund Col-
ledge and Bernard McGinn (New York: Paulist Press, 1981), p. 73.

[77] E.g., above, Chapter 1 at n. 13.

tian traditions. Augustine took the stories of Jacob as elucidating, among other things, Christ's command, "Love your enemies." His discussion led not to the suppression of conflict but to uncompromising strife, in which Christians struggled to the death against the carnality in others that they hated in themselves. The injunction to love one's enemies was one aspect of the injunction to hate the world, and of the insistence that the world hated the Church, even when world and Church were identical.

Further, Jacob's conflict with Esau illustrates the centrality of the feud to Christian doctrine. Even in the incomplete comments that he made on the subject in the texts just considered, it is apparent that, for Augustine, the interminable cycle of debt and retribution was at the heart of historical process. Without it, human society generally, and Christian society specifically as conceived by him, would end. As has been asserted in another connection: "Feud bears the same relationship to social order as blasphemy to the Christian religion: they are both the negation of a specific structural arrangement which would cease to exist were the possibility of negation removed."[78]

Beyond love of enemies and the feud, the account of Jacob illustrated for Augustine the event of conversion, as bonding through strife. In the texts just reviewed, Augustine adverted to the conversion of Jacob, the supplanter, still bearing in his lameness the infirmities of carnal men and unbelievers, into Israel, "he who sees God." Strife, represented by Jacob's struggle with the angel was an essential part of his bonding through conversion. In one text, Augustine emphasized the point by paralleling the transformation of Jacob into Israel with that of Saul, the persecutor, into Paul the Apostle.[79] The Church itself was being converted from its condition as world hating world into the heavenly Jerusalem where there was no longer desire and aversion, but charity was all in all.

Because they center on the interplay of nature and art—that is, on creation—Augustine's discussions of Jacob are ultimately all variations on the theme of suffering, particularly on that of suffering caused by the loss of paradise. The accursed world had been plunged into bondage; the redeemed world yearned for its promised freedom, its new creation. Augustine's concept of bonding through strife culminated in the creative act that was also the epitome of suffering to redeem the loss and destroy the bondage—that is, in sacrifice. Love of enemies, feud, and conversion all converged in the liberating passion of Christ, and also in the duty of faithful Christians to imitate his sufferings, even as they applied the lash of correction to the wicked, even as, like Christ, they humbly became obedient unto death in conflict against the multitude of the wicked that encompassed them. The

[78] Jacob Black-Michaud, *Feuding Societies* (Oxford: Blackwell, 1975), pp. 68, 88, 120.
[79] *Serm. 122 (72):* chap. 6 (Migne *PL* 38: 684).

doctrine of deliverance through sacrificial bonding was crystallized in the liturgies of Eucharist and baptism, by which believers entered into Christ's death and resurrection. In other writings, Augustine set forth the ascetic inversion of pleasure and pain as one aspect of liberating sacrifice, even as he proclaimed the Church's duty to persecute heretics and unbelievers in the atoning work of love. Participatory bonding through strife ran through the Christian paradoxes of death and life, poverty and riches, obedience and freedom, humility and glory, defeat and victory, all disclosed in the savior, a mediator, though rejected and alone, who triumphed by being slain. Not surprisingly, Augustine's ideas about nature and art bonded through conflict add up to an essay on power.

These traits certainly appear when, in Jasper's words, Nietzsche "seems . . . to transform himself into the enemy," that is, into Christianity. If the chiaroscuro, the accidental and designed incongruities of twelfth-century art, expresses a complex doctrine of bonding, so too does the art of other periods that practiced the interplay of multiple narratives; that esteemed the virtues of grace, complexity, variety and difficulty; and, above all, that delighted in the surprise of identity in contradiction.[80] As an identifiable way of thought and expression, these attitudes gave primacy to the affects and feelings: they were esthetic. The interplay of antipathies and sympathies that they conveyed hinged on the tension between flesh and spirit, tormenting enslavement from which one could escape only through further suffering. Freedom lay in the lonely sacrificial agony of the mediating creator. He was slain by his own creation, by the very work that he had made in his own image and likeness, that he embraced in love for its nature and rejected in hatred for its defects, and that, by dying, he gained power to make again new and free.

All lines of Augustine's doctrines about bonding through conflict converged at this point. Here and now, the work is in the Creator and he is in it, but their union is flawed, and in two dimensions. There is always something unspoken in the creative word, something rebellious in its uttered image. There is always the Creator's hatred for flaws introduced into his work by others, always hatred by the work for standards of perfection that condemn it. The agony of poetic distance remains. And so the Creator submits to be destroyed by his creature—he in it and it in him—so that an identity surpassing union can be achieved, the violence of poetic closure mediating between them.

I HAVE SURVEYED the pattern of understanding, organized around the esthetic paradigm, that made possible Augustine's concept of how human beings, on the one hand, and nature and art, on the other, were bonded

---

[80] Cf. John K. G. Shearman, *Mannerism* (Baltimore: Penguin, 1967), pp. 25, 41, 84.

through malevolent sympathy. That concept had several dominant characteristics, conforming with the strategy of proof outlined in earlier chapters.

It depended upon association by likeness, contiguity, and (especially) contrast.

These modes of association enabled Augustine to create a montage of multiple narratives. However, he recognized that the associative links connecting those narratives depended on "negative values"—that is, on assumptions and beliefs not present in his texts. Those "negative values" were not accessible to the many—to the condemned world—but only to the elect. And even for the elect, believing but not yet seeing, perception and knowledge remained a mixture of fiction and reality.

The associations that he drew connecting the narratives in his montage were affective and esthetic. They hinged on emotions and feelings.

The bonding of identities that he taught occurred when one person participated in (partook of) the feelings of another and so the two become one in spirit.

Throughout these teachings was a concept of suffering through loss, suffering epitomized and conveyed through the warfare of flesh against spirit.

Gaining power to become children of God, the elect were destined to be freed from the bondage of that conflict, freed as they entered into the suffering of the mediator and creator, destroyed by his handiwork.

This summary would be incomplete if I did not add that participatory bonding through conflict, as Augustine portrayed it in the texts reviewed above, was a bonding of men. Women had supporting roles—Rebecca, the mother both of Esau, the bad, and of Jacob, the good, who inspired Jacob to supplant her other son by deceiving Isaac, his father and her husband; Leah and Rachel, Jacob's wives, and their respective handmaidens whom they gave to Jacob for progeny.[81] But Jacob's bonding is with his father (by transference), with his brother (by feud and substitution), and with the angel personifying Christ (by dialectic). The power and powerlessness of women and the contrariety of their likeness belonged to another order of existence from those of men.

Matched rivalry might well pit men against men: the classic rivals in Western culture—Hercules and Antaeus, Cain and Abel, Esau and Jacob, Judas and Jesus, and Romulus and Remus—were men. Lacan's three psychologically formative moments are also of interest: the "weaning complex," which imprints the character with "primordial ambivalence" toward the mother; the "intrusion complex," in which the self constructs itself by jealousy towards siblings; and the "Oedipus complex," in which rivalry

[81] *En. in Ps. 136*: 18 (*Corp. Christ., ser. lat.*, 40, pp. 1975–76). *Contra Mendacium*, chap. 24 (*CSEL*, 41, p. 499). *City of God*, 16. 38 (*Corp. Christ., ser. lat.*, 48, pp. 543–44). *Serm. 5*: 4 (*Corp. Christ., ser. lat.*, 41, pp. 53–54). *Tr. in Ev. Johan.*, 11. 11 (*Corp. Christ., ser. lat.* 36, pp. 116–17).

with the father is both repressed and sublimated into an "ego-ideal." Augustine's treatments of his parents, his brother, and his son in the *Confessions* afford other lines of speculation.

In his use of the biological paradigm, Augustine applied the hatred and fear that entered into the relationship of male dominance and female subordination as he knew it in the environment of childhood, an environment, he recalled, in which wives were frequently bludgeoned until their eyes were swollen shut and alcoholism was endemic among them. We should recall his account of how God prepared his soul for its spiritual marriage with torments and beatings.

However, the points to be made are first that, in the literature of rivalry (as represented by Augustine's texts), participatory bonding by conflict was male bonding, and, second, that male bonding has also been the dominant, if not the exclusive theme in the literature of friendship from antiquity until the present day. Power figured as large in the self-assertion of malevolent sympathy as it did in the self-surrender of friendship.

I propose that Augustine's mannerist "obsession with *difficultà*,"[82] which was also an obsession with creative freedom, and the concept of bonding through conflict, as incompletely framed in antiquity and expanded by Christian writers, has figured very prominently in nineteenth- and twentieth-century literature, especially that dealing with the tension between nature and art, and, moreover, I suggest that the montage technique employed by Augustine, together notably with the method of association by contrast, has also persisted in the literature of empathetic participation. The linkage, by way of eroticism, between the biological and the esthetic paradigms of creativity and conflict, which I have thus far only suggested, also remained a powerful device for the organization of ideas about human relations.

I propose to illustrate this continuity with reference to three works: James Joyce's *A Portrait of the Artist as a Young Man*; Luigi Pirandello's *Henry IV*; and Thomas Mann's *Doctor Faustus*. In each of these, medieval sources were employed to portray bonding through malevolent sympathy, and from those sources, fragments of the biological and esthetic paradigms were derived, but only to magnify esthetic union, open to the few, and to discount biological union, in which all participated. Despite their extreme differences, the one from the others, and despite their profound originality, each also displays the drama of esthetic loss and redemption, and the tantalizing mixture of fiction and reality, exemplified by Augustine. Here, I shall mention only the apex of Augustine's doctrines, the destruction of the mediating creator in and by his creation.

An incisive critic of James Joyce has summarized what needs to be said.

---

[82] Shearman, *Mannerism*, p. 41.

"Individuals," he wrote, "must be sacrificed, if there is ever to be another cosmos. 'Except a grain of wheat fall into the earth and die, it abideth by itself alone,' says the gospel of Saint John, 'but if it die, it beareth much fruit.' A hard saying, but not a hopeless one. It is not only the burden of the manifold texts of *Finnegans Wake*; it is, explicitly or implicitly, the text which the most serious and percipient of modern writers have expounded with an ever-increasing urgency. . . ."[83] Taking Nietzsche as the unspoken model of *Doctor Faustus*, and recognizing that Nietzsche's conflict against Christian morality was "an event within Christianity,"[84] Thomas Mann applied a sentence from the Gospel to his version of the Faust story. "It is a great saying," he wrote, "that he who lays down his life will gain it . . . a saying that has no less native right in the spheres of art and literature (*Dichtung*) than in that of religion."[85] With this conviction, Mann took, as a symbol of the composer redeeming society by his music, Jacob, wounded and blest, in conflict with the angel.[86]

B   THREE TWENTIETH-CENTURY TEXTS:
JOYCE, PIRANDELLO, AND THOMAS MANN

THE PATTERN OF understanding malevolent sympathy, represented by Augustine of Hippo, can be traced down to the present day, together with the strategy of proof that sustained it. Like any living heritage, it was capable of many forms. In the following sections, I shall describe how the concept of empathetic participation, as conveyed by it, characterized three quite different writings of the twentieth century: James Joyce's (1882–1941) autobiographical *A Portrait of the Artist as a Young Man* (1916), Luigi Pirandello's (1867–1936) play, *Henry IV* (1922), and Thomas Mann's (1875–1955) novel *Doctor Faustus: The Life of the German Composer Adrian Leverkühn as Told by a Friend* (1947).

Some points of correspondence with Augustine's doctrines on bonding through conflict are readily apparent. The esthetic paradigm of bonding is certainly given prominence, although Augustine employed the esthetic and the biological paradigms as complementary and even equivocal ways of organizing his ideas, whereas the three modern writers used the biological paradigm in order to dismantle it and, with great care, to reuse some of its elements to enlarge the esthetic one. In this regard their understandings of the relation between nature and art differed from Augustine's and, of

[83] Harry Levin, *James Joyce: A Critical Introduction*, 2d ed. (New York: New Directions, 1960), p. 204.

[84] "Die Entstehung des *Doktor Faustus*: Roman eines Romans," *Gesammelte Werke*, Bd 11 (Oldenburg: Fischer, 1960. *Reden und Aufsätze*, 3.), p. 272.

[85] Ibid., p. 147.

[86] *Doctor Faustus: The Life of the German Composer Adrian Leverkühn as told by a Friend*, trans. H. T. Lowe-Porter (New York: Vintage, 1971), pp. 57 (Beethoven), 507 (Bruckner).

course, from Donne's. For them, the paradigms were by no means mutually reflexive or, consequently, capable of being equivocal.

The correspondence with Augustine's ways of organizing his ideas is evident in the preoccupation of the three modern works between art and suffering, and to be precise, between the ascetic inversion of pleasure and pain as the condition of creative life. They weave the history of "the Christian centuries" into their narratives. They build their characterizations of creative suffering as essays on freedom, played out in the tension between nature and art. Moreover, they portray that tension in language and symbols drawn from the Christian theology of sin. As a result, the drama of freedom, as described by them, reveals its kinship to the struggle between flesh and spirit, not as in the natural antipathy of substances envisioned by some Greek philosophers, but as the story of corruption and depravity within the mind characteristic of Augustinian doctrine.

Apart from these points of narrative orientation, others, in the very structure of discourse, are apparent. I have selected these works in part because of their self-conscious dependence on texts and ideas drawn from the theological system that Augustine did much to create. Thus, the fragmentary esthetic paradigm that they exhibit should stand out all the more clearly by comparison with the broad and comprehensive structure that Augustine employed.

One striking feature that the works have in common, and that comparison with Augustine (and Donne) reveals, is the exquisite care that the authors took to discredit the biological paradigm of creativity and conflict in order to magnify the importance of the esthetic one. It is by no means a case of dismissing out of hand, or even arbitrarily demolishing, an unacceptable way of thinking. It is rather a calculated reworking of materials in which the act of demolition was actually part of the act of construction, with elements of the demolished system being appropriated, recut, and built into the chosen one.

The motives that informed this understanding are evident if one compares the themes of redemption set forth by the three modern writers with that taught by Augustine. For, whereas Augustine believed that the sickness of the world was genetic and its redemption achieved by a Savior who participated by nature in the weakness of all, the three modern writers held that the sickness of the world was cultural, and that redemption was open to the fewest of the few who cut themselves free from the culture, the artificial second nature, of the masses.

The syntax and vocabulary for speaking about human bonding through conflict remained, together with stylized affective responses inculcated by the Western tradition (part of the moral examples taught through literary education). They found one use in fiction, but in fiction as a branch—perhaps, as Hermann Hesse wrote, the third dimension—of history. Augustine set forth his glosses on the conflicts of Jacob with Esau and the angel as explorations of hidden truths in sacred history. The authors to whom we now turn continued to deploy, as he had done, the perceived human need for unity with others by means of rivalry and strife; the theatrical appeal of the tragic scenario to a reader to reexperience emotions in the text; and the imaginative power through the narrative structure, language, and stylized responses of discourse to go beyond historical events, penetrating them to discover a wider poetic truth within them. For those writers, as for Augustine, negative values were paramount in the portrayal and in the creative reexperience of bonding through the play of repellant attraction.

Indeed, the three works particularly recommend themselves to this discussion precisely because they are studies in play. Joyce's *Portrait* represents the play of the artistic imagination in the act of discovery; Pirandello's *Henry IV*, the enactment of bafflement as the norm of intellectual life, an inescapable prison in which every person is sentenced to solitary confinement; and Mann's *Doctor Faustus*, the redemption of the artist through the play of artistic composition and performance that destroy him. All represent play both as a means to understand what can be understood and as the fleeting instant and experience of understanding itself. As they draw with repugnance on the biological paradigm and with favor on the esthetic one, they give an anatomy of play itself, the playing of the play, so to speak, not only the outward gestures, but also the inward motivations. It is hard to overemphasize the importance of association by contrast to the integrative work of understanding, even when the outcome of understanding is ironically located in failure. Not the least in their repertoire of contrasts is that between the paradigms themselves or, as the authors plainly understood, between flesh and spirit.

Even when they disavowed the Christian tradition, Joyce, Pirandello, and Mann employed its patterns of understanding in these three works, whether their theme was freedom and power, as it was for Joyce and Pirandello, or freedom and beauty, as for Mann. The contention here is that their debt to the tradition is evident, not only in obligations that they acknowledged but, even more, in the method of association by contrast that allowed them to portray empathetic participation through hatred, anger, and fear.

JAMES JOYCE, *A Portrait of the Artist as a Young Man*

More completely than the works by Pirandello and Mann, Joyce's *Portrait* explores the play of understanding that moves unspoken within the lines of a text. Combining the erotic components of biologic and esthetic paradigms, his book has a deceptively simple core: it is an essay on "suffocated anger."[1] Let us begin with his narrative orientation. In the nature of things, discussing the tragic scenario in which Joyce cast the narrative entails discussing also the language (the words and syntax) of repellant attraction. Joyce describes his own life up to the age of twenty, portraying himself under the name, Stephen Dedalus. One fascination of the book is that it illustrates a process of bonding through antipathy, as Joyce wished to recall living through it. For the book charts how Joyce revolted against the Church in pain, wrath, and pride and yet found his mind "supersaturated with the religion in which [he said he] disbelieved[d]" (p. 216). His decisive break with the Church came when he rejected a vocation to the priesthood, yet afterward he conceived of himself as a "priest of the eternal imagination" performing a Eucharistic transubstantiation of "the daily bread of experience into the radiant body of everliving life" (p. 200). Throughout his account, two modes of bonding occur: by feud, in his various conflicts, and by transference, notably in his concept of artistic inspiration. The emotions that served as the instruments of bonding were chiefly terror and pity, which could be aroused even by the experience of beauty (pp. 186–87).

By his choice of the name "Stephen Dedalus," Joyce indicated the centrality of pain in his story. As the story unfolds, the emphasis falls on Dedalus, the mythological figure who, driven by love of his distant homeland, escaped his prison by inventing wings and flying triumphantly across the sea, an image of freedom that Joyce combined with resurrection from the dead (p. 154). Yet, this triumph was crowned with suffering. As the epigram of his *Portrait*, Joyce used a verse by the Roman poet Ovid, who wrote that Dedalus "turned his mind to unknown arts" in order to achieve flight. Beyond the line quoted by Joyce, Ovid added: "he studied nature." Still, those arts proved to be "disastrous" (*damnosas*). Dedalus taught them to his son, Icarus, who, pressing them beyond their limits, was killed. According to Ovid's account, Dedalus "repudiated his arts" (*devovitque suas artes*), as he recovered Icarus' corpse from the sea and entombed it.[2]

Together with this mythological allusion, Joyce's assumed name contains a reference to the protomartyr, St. Stephen, Dedalus' namesake and patron, whose name was also carried by a vast expanse of Dublin (St. Stephen's Green), a city that is also the mysterious presence permeating this and all of Joyce's writings (pp. 145, 224). In hagiography and cult, the martyrdom of Stephen was crowned with triumph, in contrast with the triumph of Dedalus, which was crowned with death. Naturally, the same contrast of suffering and victory dominates the portrayal of Christ, the suffering victim and triumphant judge, that Joyce included in a sermon that profoundly

---

[1] James Joyce, *A Portrait of the Artist as a Young Man* (London: Granada, 1977), p. 146.
[2] *Metamorphoses*, 8. 188–215. See, apart from the epigram, Joyce's tribute to Dedalus, pp. 162–63.

stirred the young Dedalus (pp. 105, 109–10). Here, as in the example of St. Stephen, powerlessness is transcended with great power, but, as in that of Dedalus, the creator is undone by his creature. So, too, were the Irish patriots, recalled by Joyce, who, including Parnell, were betrayed, reviled, or abandoned by their own (pp. 35–37, 184).

True to the Augustinian heritage, Joyce imagined martyrdom as a glittering triumph over, or apotheosis of, the animality of humanity's carnal nature (pp. 103, 106, 128, 186).

Like Pirandello and Mann, Joyce used the esthetic paradigm to cast his story in the tragic scenario that was used long before by Augustine in his glosses: pathos, discovery, peripetry, and epiphany. Like them, he restricted his narrative to the historical level, excluding etiology, analogy, and allegory (or mysticism), not as aspects of the narration, but as definable levels of narrative.

Thus, by comparison with Augustine's works, Joyce's *Portrait* exhibits an attenuated version of the esthetic paradigm. However, Joyce's orientation of historical narrative, in the tragic scenario, is unusually elaborate, in that the full tragic scenario does not run throughout the *Portrait* but instead repeats itself three times. The book consists of five chapters, which, in turn, comprise three parts, each of which reaches a climax in a revelatory crisis from which there is no return. The first part (chapters 1 and 2) portray Dedalus's life from each childhood until the age of sixteen. The stage of pathos describes his physical and psychological suffering at school, his acute sense of bodily weakness and inferiority, the pain that he endured through abuse of power, and the angry divisions in his family over the dual question of Irish nationalism and Church authority. At the stage of discovery, Dedalus, who had once felt that he was being prepared to carry on the conflicts that his father had waged, found himself coldly detached from the elder Dedalus and his companions, for the young man had never been touched by the joy of companionship "nor the vigor of rude male health nor filial piety." He recognized his dominant emotion as "a cold and cruel and loveless lust" illuminating his dead childhood (p. 88). Further, when, despite generosity with a small sum of money he had gained, Dedalus was unable to enhance the lives of his family, he perceived with great clarity "his own futile isolation" (p. 90). At the peripetery, he sought release for the "angry lust" stirred up by his sense of powerlessness and isolation. At the epiphany, he found his partner in sin, a prostitute, but only after his being had been penetrated by "a presence subtle and murmurous and a flood filling him wholly with itself," an agonizing penetration that freed from him a "wail of despair . . . a cry for an iniquitous abandonment" (pp. 91–92).[3]

In the second part of the book (chapters 3 and 4), Joyce portrays his

---

[3] On the brevity of this experience, p. 136.

detachment from the Church. At the stage of pathos, Dedalus endured great spiritual agony as a result of his carnal sin, which he regarded a crime worse than murder (p. 130). Powerful sermons delivered at his school on the endless agonies of the damned stirred contrition in his heart and led him not only to seek priestly absolution but also to impose upon himself a self-lacerating penance of physical and spiritual mortification. He dreamed of entering the priesthood and of being purified by holy orders (p. 144). At the stage of discovery, he realized with shame and sorrow that he would never escape his "restless feeling of guilt." The periptery followed, when, urged by the Jesuit director of studies in his school to consider a priestly vocation, he quickly and without regret declined the very thing for which, in penance, he had longed. In the complex epiphany, Dedalus experiences detachment from a band of religious; he is afflicted by pain and pity at the sight of his classmate's naked bodies at the seaside, feelings that stimulated the "dread [in which] he stood of the mystery of his own body" (p. 153). The central act of the epiphany was the "ecstasy of fear" that raised his soul in flight above the earth, purified it, made it luminous, and commingled it with spirit. Constructing this episode in exact symmetry with the epiphany that closed the first part, Joyce paralleled the earlier "wail of despair" with Dedalus's ecstatic desire to utter "the cry of a hawk or eagle on high, to cry piercingly of his deliverance to the wind"—a silent cry, for "the cry of triumph which his lips withheld cleft his brain." Rising "from the grave of boyhood," his soul had cast off "her graveclothes" (p. 154). Continuing the symmetry with the first epiphany, Joyce then introduced, corresponding with the episode of the prostitute, Dedalus's profane joy at the sight of a girl on the beach, a girl of mortal beauty yet bearing the colors of the Blessed Virgin, and away from whom he walked in his ardor for "recreat[ing] life out of life," without breaking "the holy silence of his ecstasy" (p. 156).

The third part of the book (chapter 5) resumes the tragic scenario, beginning with the pathos of Dedalus's disaffection from his family, his sense of the triviality of his studies at University College, Dublin, and barriers to his communication both with other male students there and with the Jesuit dean of studies. The stage of discovery occurs in the long discourse on esthetics and on the esthetic emotions of terror and pity that forms the centerpiece of this section. Here, Joyce transposed the stages of periptery and epiphany, treating the periptery as a denouement of the entire book. Immediately following the esthetic discourse, the third epiphany, like the other two, includes the elements of spirituality and carnality, in that order. Awaking from sleep, Dedalus felt irradiated by the flame of inspiration. He himself, the artist, was the counterpart of the Blessed Virgin. "In the virgin womb of the imagination, the Word was made flesh" (p. 196).[4]

---

[4] See also Dedalus's recollection of experiences in prayer, p. 136.

Suffused with Eucharistic imagery, his thoughts formed verses, some of which his lips murmured, and "then stopped. The heart's cry was broken" (p. 197). After writing down the verses, he turned his thoughts to his beloved, against whom he gradually aroused a "rude brutal anger [that] routed the last lingering instinct of ecstasy from his soul," shattering his image to bits and flinging them to the winds. But, in his contempt and mockery of her image, he realized that "his anger was also a form of homage" (p. 199). As his thoughts of her passed from mood to mood, he felt sexual desire awaken; and the epiphany ends with an erotic fantasy (p. 201). The transposed periptery, serving as a denouement, follows. Resuming the theme of isolation, it culminates when Dedalus finds that he is conscious of a radical detachment from all others, even from himself as he used to be (pp. 216–17). He decides to embrace a life of loneliness, without "even one friend," and to leave his family, University College, and Dublin, so as, through solitary writing, "to forge in the smithy of [his] soul the uncreated conscience of [his] race" (p. 228).

Cast into high relief by Joyce's assault on the part of the biological paradigm that dealt with sexual procreation, the dynamic of esthetic reproduction took on particularly sharp contours. The frustration of the dynamic provided by the biological paradigm and the power of the alternative provided by the esthetic one (in the composition of a work of art) is a dominant feature of the *Portrait*. Joyce constructed many of the individual sequences in his story as montages, frequently held together by little else than the verbal devices of which he was a master.[5] Indeed, the three parts of the book, each following the tragic scenario, constitute a montage of the whole. For, although they follow one another in chronological order, the narrative is set forth in them as a series of mutually reflective episodes, rather than as a single, unfolding plot.

On the surface, they might appear to be episodes in the progressive isolation of the artist. But, although the sublimation of Dedalus's hostile emotions precluded overt bonding by love, it established a disguised bonding that expressed itself in sexual ambivalence and in the portrayal of Dedalus's emotional formation as a counterpart of religious conversions and, indeed, of priestly vocation.

Many passages play on the theme of incommunicability. In acute class-consciousness, sharpened by the financial distress of his father's household, Dedalus perceived barriers of comprehension between Protestants and Catholics (pp. 33–34), between himself and English culture (even in the mind of an English convert to Catholicism) (pp. 171–72, 227), between himself and "the hidden ways of Irish life" accessible to the peasants whose

[5] See Harry Levin, *James Joyce: A Critical Introduction*, 2d ed. (New York: New Directions, 1960), pp. 186–87.

"dull piety" and bodily smells repelled him from the altar (pp. 16, 96–97).[6] The constant emphasis on Dedalus's pride adds to the theme of incommunicability. For, through the sin of pride, Satan denied God service, and in his overpowerful pride, "the rebellious pride of the intellect," Dedalus repeated that denial of service and estrangement (pp. 108, 122, 215). Over and over, Joyce depicted incommunicability and pride leading to the isolation of the artist. Even as a child, Dedalus felt "different from others. He did not want to play" (p. 60). In his spiritual pride, he always "conceived himself as being apart in every order" (p. 146). He felt content only when he was alone with the fictions of his own mind, ignored, alone, and happy in his ecstasy, near "the wild heart of life" (p. 155). Even the learned materials, part of the common legacy of Western culture, out of which he hoped to create a philosophy of beauty, were esteemed by his age no higher than "heraldry and falconry" (p. 163).

THUS FAR, we have considered two entwined elements: the narrative orientation (cast in the tragic scenario) and the language (syntax and words) that Joyce used to portray malevolent sympathy. We now turn to the third element, drawn from the tradition that Augustine did much to form—namely, stylized affective responses, portrayed in the text in which readers were expected to participate. Isolation was part of Dedalus's emotional coldness. In the first lines and pages of his book, Joyce introduced the motif of physical coldness, exemplified first of all by the change from warmth to cold in bedwetting (p. 7). In these pages, heat is a sign of impending or actual pain, sickness, or conflict. Burning heat was associated with punishment, shame, agony, and fear, as later it was with the fires of hell, and with the fiery flakes of self-accusation that pricked Dedalus to remorse (pp. 110–15, 118, 130). Quivering with dreadful awareness of his guilt and impending agonies among the damned, Dedalus could see that God burned with love for humanity. Yet, even that burning love was a sign of hellfire's terrible anguish as well as of grace; for God "would not be God if He did not punish the transgressor" (p. 122).

Coldness, cruelty, and lovelessness characterized the lust that impelled Dedalus (p. 88). His youthful ardor subsided into "a cold, lucid indifference . . . a cold indifferent knowledge of himself" (p. 96). At the end, Dedalus was left alone in "cold sadness" (p. 223). Coldness, in this book, is associated with powerlessness and fear (e.g., pp. 17, 42, 88).

The root of Dedalus's overmighty pride and of his cold isolation was self-contempt. This appeared in a conviction of his own inward filth, as a result of his carnal sin with the prostitute (e.g., pp. 111, 117, 125–26, 131–32)

---

[6] See also Joyce's comments on the sexual practices of peasant women (pp. 165–66) and his contempt for the "priested peasant" to whom his beloved made her confession (p. 200).

and, later, in a sense that, in the broad sweep of his imagination "his mind bred vermin" (p. 211). It appeared also in a sense of masculine inadequacy when measured against his father (pp. 87–88) and of smallness and weakness amidst the hard, muscular bodies of his adolescent classmates, who terrorized him. This intimidating sense of vulnerability repelled him when he saw them naked (pp. 8, 153, 221) and made him willing, in his anger against his beloved, to release her to some imaginary athelete who "had black hair on his chest" (p. 211).

Intimidated by the animal strength of other males, Dedalus dreamed of overpowering a woman, violating her innocence with his "brutelike lust" (p. 107; cf. p. 64). Yet, the violence of this desire also expressed complex feelings. The *Portrait* begins with the very young Dedalus being set at odds by his mother, who promises that he will apologize for an unspecified action, and by an older woman who taunts and curses him with blinding by an eagle, who would tear out his eyes unless he apologized to her (pp. 7–8). He was mocked by other boys because he kissed his mother at bedtime, and he could not decide whether it was right or wrong to kiss her, or why "people [did] that with their two faces" (pp. 13–14). In one of the many symmetries of the book, Dedalus balanced this early vignette on kissing with an episode in the last chapter, where Dedalus defends the pain that he will add to his mother's sufferings by not receiving communion at Easter, pointing out that Pascal and St. Aloysius Gonzaga refused the kisses of their mothers, and that Jesus himself publicly treated his mother with disdain (p. 218).

Despite the eroticism of many passages in the *Portrait*, despite the episode with the prostitute and the hint of a continuing romantic liaison, Dedalus's pattern of behavior was withdrawal from women. The deliberate contrast between frustration of biological reproduction and the fecundity of esthetic is everywhere present, and Joyce elaborated it with exquisite nuances. At most, he only endured "an embrace [that] he longed to give" (p. 144). He was aware of a "dark shame of womanhood," even in his beloved; he imagined the sexual liberties of Irish peasant women and the infidelities of young wives (pp. 165–66, 203, 210). As a youth, he did not flirt; in his penitential exercise, he "shunned every contact with the eyes of women," (pp. 70, 137), while devoting himself to the veneration of the Blessed Virgin (pp. 96–97, 107, 132, 135, 143, 148). Even after he abandoned the Church, he yearned to embrace "the loveliness that has not yet come into the world," (p. 226), on the one hand, evading even his beloved, "temptress" as she was (pp. 195, 198–99, 201), and, on the other, believing that he had never been wooed by any woman's eyes (p. 215).

Dedalus's sense of loneliness and pollution, of intimidation and rejection by males and females produced a bonding with both and led to sexual ambiguity. Conscious of his masculinity, Dedalus took note, generally with disapproval, of feminine traits in other men.[7] Yet, Dedalus was also attracted by Cranly's "dark, womanish eyes," his handsome face and strong, hard body. Dedalus thought of Cranly's sensitivity to "the weakness of [women's] bodies and souls," and of Cranly's willingness to condescend to women and protect them with his "strong and resolute arm." He himself "thrilled" to Cranly's touch (pp. 221, 223).

Dedalus's identification with women through physical and spiritual vulnerability is explicit in the three epiphanies. Employing in each the femininity of the soul, Joyce described how, before coition with the prostitute, "he suffered the agony" of "penetration" by "some dark presence moving irresistibly upon him from the darkness," "a flood filling him wholly with itself" (pp. 91–92). At the spiritual ecstasy following his decision not to become a priest, "a wild spirit passed over his limbs," and his soul cast off "her grave clothes" (p. 154). At the time of his penance, the mystic invitation caressing the soul and calling her forth to espousal had given Dedalus the sense of "newly born life" within him. Similarly, in the third epiphany, just as Gabriel came to the Virgin's chamber, his own soul was filled and "in the virgin womb of the imagination, the Word was made flesh" (pp. 136, 138, 196).

When he wrote that Dedalus's anger against his beloved was "a form of homage" (p. 199), Joyce expressed both the ambivalence in one particular relationship, but also the sexual ambivalence in his feelings about himself, which combined traits of brute lust, perceived as masculine, with weakness and self-surrender, perceived as feminine.

Again and again, Joyce identified anger as the crucible of this ambiguity. He spoke of anger against his family, leading to "wounded pride and fallen hope and baffled desires" (p. 85; for anger against his mother, see p. 137). When his father's property was sold to satisfy creditors, he sensed anger with himself and with the change of fortune that was infusing squalor and insecurity into his world. With his father in Cork on the day of the sale, he was humiliated both by comparisons drawn by others between his father and himself and by his father's own jibes. "Wearied and dejected by his father's voice," he heard nothing around him except as there reverberated in it "an echo of the infuriated cries within him" (pp. 85–86).[8]

---

[7] E.g., p. 39 (on "Lady Boyle"), pp. 140–41 (on the femininity of the Capuchin habit), p. 181 (on the "womanish care" with which the dean gathered his cassock). Cf. the boyishness of a woman, p. 220.

[8] Other references to the elder Dedalus enlarge this same theme. The father ridiculed his son in Cork by referring to him as "an ugly likeness" of his grandfather (p. 86). After the young Dedalus had been painfully and unjustly beaten in school, his father had a hearty laugh about the incident with the priest who had applied the blows (pp. 66–67). As a schoolboy, the young Dedalus felt sorry for his father "a shrewd, suspicious man" (p. 83) because he was not a magistrate, as the other boys' fathers were (p. 24), and, as a student at University College, he was condescendingly amused when his father called him a "lazy bitch" (p. 159). Joyce's adoption of the Dedalus myth, which leaves a father grieving over the death of a son, killed

At school, occasional abuse that he received at the hands of classmates filled him with "suddenwoven anger." The shame, agony, and fear of corporal punishment, which Dedalus regarded as unfair and cruel; the inculcation of a sense of failure and squalor that formed part of the method of instruction; and the awareness of being enveloped by "malignant joy" when physical or mental castigation fell upon him filled him "always with unrest and bitter thoughts" (pp. 72–73). Characteristically, Joyce wrote of the ease with which he divested himself of this anger, of a power which made "anger and resentment fall from him" (pp. 77, 80), so that, although he was often beset by anger, it quickly slipped away from him and never became an "abiding passion." Love, or what he recognized as lust, had also penetrated his being, but it too fell away, "leaving his mind lucid and indifferent" (p. 136; see pp. 91–92).

Joyce acknowledged that this divestiture of anger was an act of suppression, a deliberate concealing of anger or pride with silence, an "immense" exercise of will to stifle its expression (pp. 137, 144). Imagining his face as it might be if he became a priest, he saw it tinged with "suffocated anger" (p. 146). Indeed, he found in his Jesuit teachers the practical discipline for crushing the "pride and anger in [his] heart," and models of a chill, ordered, and passionless life without joy or hatred, cold, detached, and indifferent, like a stick in its master's hand (pp. 114, 145–46, 169–70).

Evidently, Dedalus's suppression of anger derived from this sense of loneliness and powerlessness. It belonged to the same complex pattern of behavior as discipline of bodily mortification and spiritual contrition that he undertook after the episode with the prostitute. That discipline required voluntary loss and promised, in compensation, atonement for guilt. Leading to cold, emotional indifference without either love or hatred, the suppression of anger also required voluntary loss and provided, in compensation, immunity to the emotional ravages of a person convinced of his weakness, ugliness, and impurity. In one sermon on repentance, a preacher warned Dedalus and his classmates that the greatest torment possible for the created soul was "the pain of loss" (p. 118).

Whereas the preacher spoke of the damned, Dedalus's strategy of suppression counterbalanced emotional loss in this world. First, it denied loss by erecting a defense of apathy. Second, it circumvented loss by permitting the soul to bond with the objects of its dread and anger. For those emotions were suppressed, not killed; and they allowed Dedalus to assimilate to himself the masculine brutality that he feared and desired and the feminine weakness that he despised and exemplified. Dedalus's strategy also permitted him to abandon his vocation to the priesthood, yet to portray his

through his rash and disobedient abuse of the father's invention, is germane to these passages, as is the invocation of Dedalus as "old Father" in the concluding entry of A Portrait.

vocation as a writer, "a priest of eternal imagination" (p. 200), in Eucharistic symbols; to leave the Jesuits, yet to take as his own their emotional detachment and their tool of cunning (cf. p. 169; on the "legendary craft" of the Jesuits, see p. 222).

The persistent and elaborately articulated repudiation of eroticism set forth in the biological paradigm in favor of that set forth in the esthetic one permitted Joyce to exorcise biological metaphors and symbols and to reappropriate them, cleansed and adapted to his purposes. Certainly, each of the three epiphanies in the *Portrait* left Dedalus "lonelier than the last."[9] However, each epiphany is also a step forward in Dedalus's esthetic conversion, an advance in his vocation to the "priesthood" of art. Thus, Joyce passed from the infusion of "some dark presence" in the first epiphany, penetrating him from the darkness (p. 91), to the commingling with spirit in the second, which lifted him in ecstatic flight and made radiant his eyes and limbs (p. 154), and finally to the impregnation of "the virgin womb of the imagination," when, in the afterglow of "the white flame . . . deepening to a rose and ardent light, . . . the word was made flesh" (pp. 196–97).

Evidently, in the course of the *Portrait*, Dedalus passed from belief to disbelief, but just as his anger toward his beloved was an act of homage, so too was his departure from the Church. Joining the Protestants, he argued, would destroy his self-respect (p. 220; cf. pp. 39–40), and he acknowledged a residual loyalty in the scholastic doctrines that he formulated about art, in poetry that he quoted and songs that he sang, and in his sense that he was "born to be a monk," or perhaps a heretical friar, doubting yet faithful, like the thirteenth-century Franciscan, Gherardino da Borgo San Donnino (fl. 1260) (pp. 198–99).

Joyce knew very well that the concept and experience of the affects that he portrayed was molded—and therefore stylized—by ecclesiastical tradition. Dedalus's conversion to heresy, his calling to the "priesthood of the eternal imagination," left his mind "supersaturated with the religion in which [he said he] disbelieve[d]." In its combination of suppressed emotion with detached intellectualism, it formed a mirror image of another conversion that powerfully shaped Joyce's thinking: namely, the conversion of John Henry Newman to the Roman communion. Newman was the founder of University College, Dublin, where the last stage of Dedalus's conversion occurred, and there are similarities between Newman and the Jesuit dean of studies who inspired Dedalus with "desolating pity," and the cause of whose conversion Dedalus speculatively dissected, casting himself as the elder brother of the prodigal son (pp. 171–73).

Unflattering as the analogies may be between Newman and Joyce's dean of studies, the fact remains that, in the *Portrait*, Joyce quoted Newman

---

[9] Levin, *James Joyce, A Critical Introduction*, p. 53.

three times and referred to him twice more, once as the "greatest writer" in prose (pp. 73–74, 149–50, 160, 171).

Reading "the cloistral silver-veined prose of Newman," (p. 160), one can easily see many points of correspondence between Newman's conversion to Rome and Dedalus's to art. As a child, Newman thought of himself as an angel, a parallel with the winged figures of Dedalus (and Lucifer) in Joyce.[10] At school, he refused to play games, and he may well have anticipated the trouble with his eyes that became acute in 1817. At the age of fifteen, Newman, like Dedalus at the age of sixteen, experienced a crisis consisting of four simultaneous events: his father's bankruptcy and the removal of the family to another house, a severe illness, a religious crisis, and leaving school. In his illness, Newman "was terrified at the heavy hand of God which came down upon [him]," and he endured much that was "awful and known only to God."[11] His Calvinism plunged him into dread of eternal punishment, but it also conveyed to him a sense of his own election, and detachment from his immediate surroundings.[12]

Dedalus's crisis sent him to a prostitute but left him with the combination of lust and celibacy noted previously. Newman's crisis left him with a commitment to celibacy, which, during the next thirteen years, he was intermittently tempted to break.[13] Newman's preference of intellectual over moral excellence at Oxford, and his commitment to the intellectual exercises of dogma as fundamental to religion; his assertion that he did not seek, but was sought, by friends; his sense of being driven back into loneliness (before 1826 and after 1841); the separation from his family and friends who regarded him as a traitor for his contributions to the Tractarian Movement; his indifference to those committed to his charge; his obstinate choice of estrangement in order to remain true to his vocation, cherishing only the relationship of the soul to God, solitary with solitary (*solus cum solo*)—all have exact parallels in Joyce's account.[14] Finally, like Newman's *Apologia*, Joyce's *Portrait* ends as the protagonist leaves his college forever, entering upon a life in which he could defend himself only with "silence, exile, and cunning."[15] Of course, there was a further parallel that could not have been lost on Joyce between the long period when ecclesiastical authorities stifled Newman's writings and enterprises by their suspicion, hatred, or indifference (1845–64), and Joyce's early years as a writer when legal verdicts of obscenity, blasphemy, and treason greatly hampered the publication of his works. Similarities so complex are hardly accidental.

[10] John Henry Newman, *Apologia pro Vita Sua* (New York: Modern Library, 1950), p. 33.

[11] *Autobiographical Writings*, ed. Henry Tristan (London: Sheed and Ward, 1957), pp. 150, 268.

[12] *Apologia*, p. 37.

[13] *Apologia*, p. 38.

[14] *Apologia*, pp. 42, 45–46, 75, 100–12, 149, 203.

[15] *Portrait*, p. 222.

Joyce's assimilation of Newman's esthetic model as stylist and as convert expressed his entire strategy of empathetic participation in narrative orientation and language, as well as in stylized affective responses portrayed in the text for the participation of his readers. We may now describe how Joyce transposed these three elements into a moral level of reader response, which we first encountered in Augustine.

The theme continuing through all the stages of Dedalus's conversion is pride, together with its dark side, powerlessness. In the early stages, Dedalus sought to counterbalance the terrors of his weakness with the pride of the Church's power. The Jesuits were wealthy; they could promote their own (pp. 65–67). They could inflict agonizing corporal punishment on children unjustly and cruelly, without remorse, indeed laughing heartily about it with the parents of charges they had punished (p. 67). As to the great of this world, the clergy had "cursed [Parnell] to death" (p. 37). They had the "awful power," greater than any king or emperor, "to make the great God of heaven come down upon the altar . . ." (p. 143). This pride, above others, echoed the pride in Dedalus's own heart.

As he became convinced that his guilt of sin was unforgivable and his pollution beyond cleansing, his powerlessness turned to other prides. He always had the power to deny and destroy, the power in the "rebellious pride of the intellect" to refuse to serve as Lucifer and Adam had done (pp. 98, 108, 122, 138, 215). He had the power to spurn the one thing that was needful—the salvation of the soul (p. 102). But Dedalus's task was to turn this self-destructive act into art. He discovered that "his soul lusted after its own destruction" (p. 96). "He would create proudly out of the freedom and power of his soul. . . ." (p. 154). He would resume Newman's "proud cadence" (p. 150) but in the vernacular of the profane.

The motif of the suffering creator, destroyed yet triumphant, was evident in his choice of the name Stephen Dedalus, and at every crisis of his narration, Joyce portrayed Dedalus's suffering as variations on one theme: "the pain of loss . . . the greatest torment which the created soul is capable of bearing" (p. 118). In childhood, losses sustained through powerlessness aroused anger. The characteristic demand of the feud for compensation was futile. God, burning with love for humanity, could and must visit the punishment of his anger on transgressors (pp. 112, 122–123). The feud's interminable cycle of debt and retribution established the framework of bonding, and, as we have seen, Dedalus was bonded to the very objects of his anger. His inability to gain compensation by matching force against force, led him to disguise that cycle by suppressing both love and hatred—the emotions of desire for the good and loathing for the bad. By stages clearly marked with "epiphanies," he developed a strategy of moral detachment; however, this strategy left the way open to esthetic bonding through the "tragic emotion" that combined pity and terror (p. 186).

It is striking that this *Portrait* of gradual isolation is crowned by a discourse on empathy. Step by step, drawing on and expanding materials from Aristotle and Thomas Aquinas, Joyce set forth three stages in the instant of esthetic apprehension, three stages of analysis leading up to that instant, and, finally, three stages in the production of a work of art, beginning with the esthetic apprehension by the artist when he conceives the work and ending with the esthetic apprehension by the artist when he conceives the work and ending with the esthetic apprehension by the audience when the work is done. All esthetic apprehension, he asserted, was static. Moreover, it escaped the dichotomy of carnal and spiritual; for, arising, to be sure, in perception of sensory things, it transcended carnal attraction and repulsion. It was evoked by two aspects of the same action—pity (the apprehending mind's union with a human sufferer) and terror (its union "with the secret cause of suffering"). This poetic or mystical union with pain was inward.[16] From the soul's prison gates, art could draw forth an image of the beauty that it conveyed (p. 187).

Joyce understood the dyad of nature and art specifically as life and art. This dyad runs throughout Joyce's comments on bonding. He considered life and art, in turn, as aspects of the yet more comprehensive duality of flesh and spirit. Each part of a dyad required the other. Thus, carnal life without spirituality amounted to the "dull gross voice of the world of duties and despair," represented by the lives of other members of his family, whom he tried and failed to approach (pp. 90, 149, 151). Spiritual life without carnality was represented by the priesthood as in the "inhuman voice that had called him to the pale service of the altar" (p. 154). This "life" that Joyce intended when he wrote about life and art was not any particular mode of existence, but rather the force that drew him in rapture close to its own "wild heart," that called him "to love, to err, to fall, to triumph, to create life out of life" (pp. 155–56), a call that was realized when the word was made flesh "in the virgin womb of his imagination" (p. 196).

The first kind of empathetic participation that Joyce identified, under the category of life and art, was that between life and the artist, exemplified in his epiphanies, notably in the second and third. Less abruptly than in ecstatic epiphanies, it also occurred in the process by which the artist, contemplating an object, passed from the synthetic moment when his attention was arrested by the object—"the esthetic image"—as an individual thing (*integritas*), to the analytic moment when, fascinated by the harmony of the object (or "esthetic image"), he categorized its parts and the rhythm of their interrelation (*consonantia*). It moved, finally, to the esthetic moment when the singular wholeness of the "esthetic image," the "supreme quality

---

[16] Cf. p. 184: "You can be a poet or a mystic after."

of beauty," was conceived in his imagination. This was the first, or lyric, form of art (pp. 192–93).

The second kind of empathetic participation occurred between the artist and the work that issued from his immediate apprehension of beauty. Speaking of literature, Joyce described how the personality of the artist flowed into the narrative that he was creating, and how it encompassed the characters and action, at length filling each character "with such vital force that he or she assumes a proper and intangible esthetic life." The work takes on a life of its own, while the artist, estranged from his now independent narrative, "remains within or behind or beyond or above his handiwork, invisible, refined out of existence, indifferent. . . ." This is the second, or "epical," form of art (pp. 194–95).

The final kind of empathetic participation occurs between the audience and the "esthetic life" that the artist infused into the characters in his narrative. Through this third, or "dramatic," form of art, "the esthetic image" in the narrative was "purified and reprojected" from the audience's imagination. In the cycle between the work and the audience, the image becomes life, thus completing the "mystery of esthetic" that began with the artist's first perception. Like the "mystery of creation," the "mystery of esthetic" ends in the creation of life out of life through a process that Joyce described as conception, gestation, and reproduction (pp. 190, 193–94).

Each of these "forms" of art, or empathetic bonding, took place through participation: the artist, conceiving the life in the "image"; the characters in narrative, gestating the artist's personality; the esthetic image in the work, reproduced in the imagination of the audience. The mystical terms with which Joyce described Dedalus's epiphanies convey the intensity of the artist's immediate participation in life at the moment of conception. It is also clear that participation in the "esthetic image" at every stage was mimetic.

As Joyce set forth the esthetic image in the *Portrait*, the dramatic experience of beauty followed the tragic scenario, and the primary stimuli of mimetic participation were pity and terror. Thus, Joyce portrayed Dedalus's conversion as a movement from burning shame and fear to the coldness of "suffocated anger."

In his epiphanies, Dedalus experienced esthetic unions: at the first, his involuntary cry was "a wail of despair"; at the second, in his ecstasy of fear, it was a silent cry of triumph that cleft his brain; and the third, it was the heart's broken cry. Joyce refers to several kinds of empathetic participation familiar in Christian tradition, including sacramental union through the Eucharist and ordination and imaginative union, through devotional exercises, with Christ, his crucifiers, and the damned (pp. 123–26, 133, 145). These he laid aside when, believing in the love of God, he yet realized his own incapacity for love and hatred, his own failure to love God, even though he was, and remained, able to unite his will with the will of God (pp. 136, 217). From the literature of mysticism and scholastic philosophy, he retained bonding by transference, exemplified in the three epiphanies, when he was penetrated, commingled, or filled with spirit. While these unions exalted and irradiated Dedalus's mind, they also confirmed his inability to "merge his life in the common tide of other lives" (p. 138). They led to a sundering of his relationships, to a destruction of the "person he used to be," and even to the refinement "out of existence" that artists experienced in their works (cf. pp. 150, 216–17, 221). Dedalus's sexual ambiguity and vocation to the priesthood "of eternal imagination" were monuments of bonding that occurred through the mimetic conflict of powerlessness and pride. His doctrine of esthetic bonding expressed the subtler, but no less ferocious, mimetic conflict of the soul lusting for a union, in the pity and terror conveyed through art, that would consummate its own destruction.

Nor were these the only empathetic bondings through conflict that characterized a writer in English, for whom English always had the strangeness of an acquired language,[17] a theorist attempting to compose as his masterwork an esthetic philosophy out of medieval texts—"monkish learning"—that were veiled to "so poor a Latinist as he" (p. 163).

In retrospect, Joyce's acknowledgement of his debt to the Christian heritage of malevolent sympathy should be emphasized in language (both syntax and words), in the moral stylization of affective responses, and, fundamentally, in narrative orientation. Indeed, much of the suffering in Joyce's narrative depends upon the explicit use made of the antitheses of sin and purity, guilt and innocence, flesh and spirit, at the heart of bonding by feud, and of the paradigm of bonding by transference, in mystical union, reproduced in Dedalus's epiphanies. The English conquest of Ireland is the backdrop of much of Dedalus's sense of foreignness with his language, religion, and compatriots (pp. 163–64, 171–72, 183–84, 224–25, 227). The *Portrait* is illuminated with references to, or quotations of, medieval writers.[18] Steeped in the discipline and doctrine of the Church, from which he slowly and incompletely withdraws, Dedalus portrays himself as a "doubting monk" (pp. 160, 190, 198–99). The esthetic doctrines that Dedalus expounds are "applied Aquinas" (p. 190).

Above all, Joyce derived from Christian doctrine the paradigm of the creator powerless, abandoned, tormented and destroyed, yet coming again triumphantly in power and in great wrath. For Joyce, the paradigm was not

---

[17] Dedalus declined to master the Irish language as part of the nationalism that he rejected (pp. 164, 172, 184).

[18] Venantius Fortunatus (p. 190), *Agincourt Hymn* (p. 198), Cornelius Agrippa (p. 203), Gherardino da Borgo San Donnino (p. 199), Geraldus Cambrensis (p. 207), Augustine of Hippo (p. 213), Dante (p. 227). See also pp. 20, 153–54.

biological but esthetic; for him, the two paradigms could not be equivocal, as they occasionally were in Augustine's thinking. For Joyce, the promise of art was not freedom and beauty, as it was for Mann, but rather freedom and power. It was his model of the afflicted and triumphant creator, already at work in Joyce's mind, that led him in *Ulysses*, to portray himself both as Stephen Dedalus, the counterpart of Lucifer, and as Leopold Bloom, the counterpart of Christ.[19] Dedalus's perception that his soul lusted after its own destruction was a stage in his progression toward this moment when the work of composition, the creator's deliberate self-refinement out of existence by increasing participation, or absorption (pp. 193–94), could be depicted both in the crime, the moral suicide of the fallen angel, and in its atonement, the redeemer's self-sacrifice.

PIRANDELLO'S *Henry IV*

Whereas Joyce's anatomy of play led to artistic creation as a form of individual redemption of the artist, Pirandello's led to irony of art that destroys as it creates. Of the categories discussed thus far—narrative orientation, language, and portrayed and anticipated affective responses—Joyce employed the first two to serve the last. For Pirandello, however, narrative predominated. Pirandello's "dark comedy," *Henry IV*, is an essay in rivalry.[20] At first glance, its narrative orientation exemplifies the impossibility of participatory bonding. But, to the contrary, as the drama runs its course, it demonstrates how personalities are shaped and bonded precisely by mutual repugnance—that is, by malevolent sympathy. The particular mode of empathetic participation that it sets forth is union by substitution.

The field of action in the play flashes with hostility. The drama depicts an Italian nobleman of the twentieth century. Impersonating the eleventh-century German emperor, Henry IV, in a masquerade pageant, he was thrown from his horse and struck his head on a stone. Thereafter, for many years, he created an illusory court around him, forcing anyone who entered his ambit to play the role of a person who had actually been in the medieval emperor's circle. Thus, Pirandello made the action in his play allude to an unusually strife-filled reign in imperial history—one, moreover, that called forth two Italians as the staunchest foes of the German ruler—namely, Pope Gregory VII and the Countess Mathilda of Tuscany. At the very beginning of the play, Pirandello reminded the audience of the many bitter conflicts that beset the emperor. He brought them directly on stage by making the focus of action a pair of portraits, the one, of Henry IV, and the other, of

[19] Levin, *James Joyce: A Critical Introduction*, p. 116.

[20] John Louis Styan, *The Dark Comedy: The Development of Modern Comic Tragedy*, 2d ed. (Cambridge: Cambridge University Press, 1968), pp. 137–56, 259–60, 298.

"his most ferocious enemy," Countess Mathilda of Tuscany.[21] Much of the tension in the play hinges on the ardor that, before his "madness," the modern counterpart of Henry IV had felt for the modern counterpart of Mathilda, and that she repulsed with mockery and fear—a passion for a dream that blazed forth again in catastrophic frustration at the end of the play.

Pirandello, like Joyce, did not ignore the biological paradigm. Instead, his elaborately articulated refutation of it formed a context in which the integrative functions of the esthetic paradigm stood out all the more sharply. Indeed, the trivialization of sexuality is part of the unrelieved isolation in which Pirandello's characters appear to live. The modern "Mathilda's" general contempt for men, the modern "Henry IV's" (alleged) sexual promiscuity, and the confused transference of his passion for Mathilda to her daughter exclude romantic union. However, the denial of romantic bonding is only one aspect of Pirandello's categorical denial that communication, much less communion, is at all possible. The mother and the daughter strongly resemble each other in appearance, but they are divided by the mother's dominance and by gossip stirred up by the mother against them both.[22] Throughout, characters perceive situations and each other in idiosyncratic ways. Each person is unknown to the other and lives in "his own different and impenetrable world."[23] As Pirandello stated in another play, *Six Characters in Search of an Author* (written at the same time as *Henry IV*), each person might think that he understood another, but he was deceived.[24] What was tragedy for one was a joke for another.[25] Indeed, using a device that Brecht called the *Verfremdungstechnik*, Pirandello characteristically disrupted communication between the stage and the audience, challenging, reversing, and baffling the logic of action that he had induced the audience to read into the enactment. It was even impossible for actors to absorb into themselves the characters that they portrayed.[26]

Still, for Pirandello, all facets of incommunicability in his play—in narrative and in language—added up to a classical, indeed, an esthetic unity achieved through the use of a paradigm derived from ancient writers and their modern continuators. That unity did not occur through "logical development," but through what Pirandello called "the whole life of the work," a life preserved in the play's form.[27] The "whole life of the work" tran-

[21] Eric Bentley, ed., *Naked Masks: Five Plays by Luigi Pirandello* (New York: Dutton, 1952), p. 146.

[22] Ibid., pp. 175, 179, 182, 199–201, 207.

[23] Ibid., p. 193.

[24] Ibid., p. 224.

[25] Ibid., pp. 190, 193, 201.

[26] *Six Characters in Search of an Author*, in Bentley, ed., *Naked Masks*, pp. 245, 254–57.

[27] "Preface" to *Six Characters in Search of an Author*, in Bentley, ed., *Naked Masks*, pp. 371–74.

scends the isolation of characters; it appears in the interconnectedness of narrative levels, which, in turn, manifests a bonding of characters by substitution. The stylized affective response of bonding in rivalry portrayed in the text and anticipated in spectators appeared in this rather attenuated form, and without the moral sense that it had in Augustine or in Joyce.

There are three narrative levels, all of them historical. The first depicts Henry IV, the eleventh-century emperor. The second, Henry IV, the twentieth-century impersonator; and the third, the retinue and companions of the impersonator. The first and the third exist for the sake of the second. Pirandello employed his play as a critique of society, contending that the madness of "Henry IV" was saner than the sanity of the contemporary world. Further, he deliberately evoked the strife-filled reign of the emperor as an analogue to the circumstances of his impersonator. However, his objectives did not require him to expand these aspects of his work into independent moral or analogical narratives.[28] Further, of the three historical narratives, the story of the eleventh-century emperor has neither logic nor movement. Its function was to provide a reference point of warfare, hatred, mockery, and pity. Likewise, the narrative from the vantage points of the modern "Henry IV's" entourage was "built up all round him."[29]

In a deeper sense, the two auxiliary narratives serve the esthetic unity of the play in a strictly classical way—that is, by accentuating the unities of time and action. Working as a playwright, between nature and art, Pirandello keenly sensed the "conflict between life-in-movement and [artistic] form." In nature, the conflict ends destructively. Life pervading the form of the human body slowly "kills that form." However, in art, the form of a composition preserves the life within it and delivers it up fresh and vigorous as often as the book is read or the play, performed. "The work of art . . . lives forever in so far as it *is* form."[30] This tension between the fluidity of life and the fixity of artistic form afflicts "Henry IV." One result of his madness is that, for him, time stopped at the moment of his injury. Pirandello used many devices to express the torment of sensing the diminution of life, year by year, indeed, of hearing life and time flee together in the throbbing pulse of one's own arteries. "Henry IV's" demented retreat into the eleventh century gave him the illusion of freedom from this terror, the sense of being transposed "out of the world, out of time, and out of life," into history, which was changeless, "fixed forever."[31] His companions, two of whom were present at the ill-fated pageant, conspire to cure him by a

---

[28] See Pirandello's specific rejection of symbolic, allegorizing art, in "Preface" to *Six Characters in Search of an Author*, in Bentley, ed., *Naked Masks*, p. 365.

[29] Bentley, ed., *Naked Masks*, p. 174.

[30] Preface to *Six Characters in Search of an Author*, in Bentley, ed., *Naked Masks*, pp. 371–72.

[31] Bentley, ed., *Naked Masks*, pp. 189, 195.

shock, intended to "shake" his mental watch and "get it going again."[32]
Unknown to them, "Henry" had (he thought) actually recovered from his
madness some years earlier. He chose to continue his fictional life, thereafter centered upon a fictional madness, because it delivered him from anx-
iety of time, and, equally, because it enabled him to play the puppeteer with
other people, forcing them to enact the roles that he assigned.[33]

Such are the materials out of which Pirandello constructed the tragic scenario of pathos-discovery-peripetery-epiphany. However, the stage of
pathos—the twelve years of "Henry's" madness—ended eight years or so
before the play began. In fact, it extended to the time before the pageant
when "Henry," scorned by others and raging against himself, was repulsed
with mocking fear by Mathilda. The stage of discovery occurs when
"Henry" discloses to his retainers that he has not been mad for years and
declares that, because they now know that he is sane, he cannot continue
the fiction.

The peripetery that follows is very complex. To restore Henry IV's sense
of time, his would-be benefactors proposed to recreate the moment when
his "watch" stopped. The portraits of "Henry" and "Mathilda" were souvenirs of the pageant. The plan was to shock "Henry IV" back into time by
substituting for the portraits the living people whom they represented—or,
more accurately, young people who resembled them as they were when the
portraits were painted. The surrogates, indeed, were generational "replace-
ments" of the original subjects: the son of "Henry's" sister and "Mathilda's" daughter. Ironically, the surrogate "Henry" has achieved a relationship with the surrogate "Mathilda" that "Henry" sought and failed to
establish with "Mathilda": they are engaged to be married. These surrogates were carefully placed within the picture frames instead of the portraits. The trap was sprung. Abruptly, "Henry" and "Mathilda" "as [they]
were then" confront "Henry" and "Mathilda" "as [they] are now."[34]

The shock perpetrated by those who wish to cure him, however, leads to
a peripetery in which Pirandello made it impossible to tell whether "Henry"
had relapsed into insanity, whether he had ever really left it, or whether he
had moved further into the time-ebbing world of the sane, that "continuous
everlasting masquerade, of which we are the involuntary puppets," living
out our "madness so agitatedly, without knowing it or seeing it."[35] His
jarred mental "watch" does indeed resume at the moment when it stopped,
but in an unforeseen manner. The two companions who had been at the
catastrophic pageant, many years earlier, were "Mathilda" and Belcredi.
Then, "Henry" had courted and been spurned by "Mathilda." Goaded by

[32] Ibid., p. 178.
[33] Ibid., p. 189.
[34] Ibid., p. 207.
[35] Ibid., pp. 205–206.

his companions in the pageant, his horse had reared and thrown him. Soon after the fall, he had reentered the revels, his face a mask of insane fury, drawn his sword, and threatened one or two of the others, who reacted, hitting "him with their whips and fans and sticks."[36] Now, in the epiphany, the aged "Henry" resumes that action, seizing in ardent passion "Mathilda's" daughter as embodying the dream that he had years before seen in "Mathilda," and, drawing his sword, he kills Belcredi, his chief tormenter, long his rival for Mathilda's favors, and, lastly, the denier of his madness. Henry completes the sword-thrust that he began fifteen—or was it eighteen?—years earlier.[37]

Pirandello's treatment of time contributed to the organic union of the three narratives by establishing unity of action.[38] He served the same object by his use of medieval materials and negative values. His quotation from the early twelfth-century biography of Henry IV[39] establishes a parallel between the characterization of the emperor in that biography as an innocent victim, glorified, martyr-like, by sufferings, and that of "Henry IV" as a perennial butt of scorn, whose affliction was his best defense. The assignment of roles in the eleventh-century masquerade around Henry also established points of correspondence between the narratives. "Henry IV" corresponds with the unfortunate, yet heroic emperor. "Henry's" recently deceased sister, who prompted the attempt to cure him, corresponds with the emperor's mother, also named Agnes, who, until her death, supported him. "Mathilda" plays two roles: those of the Countess Mathilda of Tuscany, the emperor's great enemy, and of the Duchess Adelaide, the mother-in-law of the emperor. (Adelaide is known to German historians as the Margravin, or Countess, Adelheid of Savoy, a kinswoman of Mathilda. Merciless in her intrigue and warfare, Adelheid was one of the dominant figures in Italian politics until her death in 1091, and marriage to her daughter, Bertha, provided Henry IV a major foothold in Italy. As early as 1073–74, she was found among Gregory VII's adherents, although she interceded with the Pope for her son-in-law at Canossa.) Frida, her daughter, impersonates both "Mathilda" and "Mathilda's" impersonation of the eleventh-century countess. Finally, in the pageant, Belcredi, Henry's rival and victim, took the role of Charles of Anjou, a figure entirely detached from

---

[36] Ibid., p. 159.

[37] Ibid., pp. 153, 203, 207–208.

[38] But this element in *Henry IV* was part of Pirandello's ironic manipulation of the "Aristotelian" unities, which included an attack upon Aristotle's doctrines that there could be a drama without characters, but not characters without action; that characters should be credible, good, appropriate, and consistent; and that a tragedy imitates an action that is complete in itself.

[39] Bentley, ed., *Naked Masks*, p. 196, quoting the anonymous *Vita Henrici IV. imperatoris*, chap. 8 in *MGH, SS in usum scholarum*, p. 28. The date of Henry IV's audience with Gregory VII at Canossa is given as 25 January 1071 (Bentley, ed., *Naked Masks*, p. 142), possibly a typographical error for the correct year, 1077.

the life of the Emperor Henry IV, and yet a suitably antithetic figure, because, in alliance with the papacy, which Henry had opposed, Charles had destroyed the Empire, which Henry had preserved. In the medieval masquerade, the play within Pirandello's play, Belcredi is cast as Peter Damian, a correspondent of the Margravin Adelheid of Savoy, who prevented Henry from dissolving his marriage to Adelheid's daughter (1069) and attempted to enlist Adelheid in enforcing obedience to the ideals of the Gregorian reform. An ascetic cardinal, he was also a friend of the man who, after Damian's death, became the archenemy of Henry IV, Pope Gregory VII. Since Gregory is not portrayed, Belcredi-Damian stands as his surrogate.

The unspoken historical sympathies and antipathies represented by these impersonations constitute a large part of the negative values in the play. Together with them, one must repeat, is Henry's chief antagonist, Gregory VII. Of course, other negative values modified the esthetic paradigm that informed Pirandello's anatomy of the play. The persecution mania of "Henry IV" reflects the mental illness of Pirandello's wife, which lasted from 1904 until her death in 1918, and of which Pirandello himself was the chief victim. In 1922, when *Henry IV* was written, the violent rivalry of Empire and Papacy and the savagery of a mad ruler in Italy were calculated to recall Mussolini's anticlericalism and the profligate violence culminating in his March on Rome and assumption of office (23 October 1922). Aristotle's definition of tragedy and the Sorellian doctrine of violence as a unifying element in art and society are among the other negative values that figure in the play without figuring in the text. However, for the theme of bonding the historical sympathies and antipathies evoked by impersonations were primary, and these provided a very attenuated testimony to the tradition of stylized affective responses represented by Augustine and Joyce, a testimony void of moral content.

Evidently, in a work where impersonation is everything—and in which there are instances of impersonations of impersonations—bonding by substitution is part of the dramatic action. The action demands that the affinities in a relationship persist, even when one or more parties to it are replaced—when, for example, Frida is substituted for her mother. In general, the emotions by which characters are related on all Pirandello's narrative levels are hostile: pity (which Pirandello elsewhere described as a "specially ferocious form of cruelty"),[40] anger, grief, and, above all, terror.

Apart from the passion that inspired "Henry IV's" unhappy courtship of "Mathilda," love appears but briefly in the devotion of a servant,[41] perhaps also in the relationship between "Henry" and his sister,[42] and of Frida and

---

[40] *Six Characters in Search of an Author*, in Bentley, ed., *Naked Masks*, p. 224.
[41] Bentley, ed., *Naked Masks*, p. 196.
[42] Ibid., pp. 153, 199.

her fiancé, di Nolli.[43] Not love, but harsher affects, shape the dramatic action. Yet, like the Verfremdungstechnik, Pirandello used them to achieve empathy, even if it was his distinctively bitter compassion.

Bonding by substitution is evident in the enactment of roles at the ill-fated pageant, and in the masquerade of "Henry IV's" court. It is also evident in Pirandello's striking use of the paintings mentioned earlier, iconic substitutes for "Henry" and "Mathilda," which, in the "shock episode," are themselves replaced by living surrogates.

Substitution links characters on the three narrative levels; bridging generations and centuries, it creates the intricate network of ambiguities underpinning the entire play. In addition, contemporary rivals are also bonded by substitution. Pirandello's central metaphor of the portraits indicates as much. For "Henry IV," the portraits are mirrors, rather than paintings, and they project living images into a world that, receiving them, also comes to life.[44] In another connection, Pirandello wrote that performance brought before the eyes of the audience his "own fantasy in the act of creating."[45]

"Henry IV" likewise projects his fantasies into the living world. Freed by insanity from the terrifying masquerade of life,[46] he made others captive to his fiction, working as a puppeteer, pulling the wires on his entourage as though they were marionettes, or as the master of the revels, forcing the others to mask or unmask themselves and appear before him as he wished.[47] The world that he created around him was a mimetic substitution for his fantasy.

Association by likeness and by contiguity were crucial to Pirandello's dramatic irony as the metaphors of pageant and painting amply demonstrate. However, it was association by contrast that produced the esthetic unity of the drama itself.[48] The living images that "Henry IV" projected into the world, and the world that came to life around them had no existence other than conflict. In the unity of their action, active and passive were one. Their interplay was the life within the form of the play, just as, taken together, the characters were the drama and the drama was in them—that is, in the contrasting passions that drove them to perform, to be torturer and tortured.[49]

In Pirandello's play, the three elements of portrayal that we have been considering—narrative orientation, language, and stylized affective re-

[43] Ibid., p. 198.

[44] Ibid., p. 145.

[45] "Preface" to Six Characters in Search of an Author, in Bentley, ed., Naked Masks, pp. 373–74.

[46] Bentley, ed., Naked Masks, p. 208.

[47] E.g., ibid., pp. 146, 189, 207.

[48] See Pirandello's explicit mockery of argument from likeness, ibid., pp. 150–52.

[49] Cf. "Preface" to Six Characters in Search of an Author, and Six Characters in Search of an Author, in Bentley, ed., Naked Masks, pp. 219, 366, 370, 372.

sponses—did not witness to irony that led to salvation through suffering as they did in Augustine, or to irony that led to the creation of art, as in Joyce. For Pirandello, they taught the bonding of malevolent sympathy, to be sure, but with a bleak and sterile irony.

The special irony in the esthetic paradigm as realized in *Henry IV* is at least threefold. In substituting his fantasies for the everyday world, "Henry" himself had to play a role. By a confusion of parts, he became the puppet of himself,[50] thereby producing the effort by others to cure him and the catastrophe that ensued. The second irony was that, while "Henry" imagined himself as the puppeteer and master of the revels, he remained an "involuntary puppet" of time. Although, in his madness, he freed himself from the anguish of life ebbing away through the years, still, in his body, he carried the marks of age, artlessly camouflaged with paints and dyes. Thus, Pirandello depicts several intricate role reversals, in which "Henry" was both victim and avenger, free and captive, victor and vanquished, tormenter and tortured. He suffers through his own creation, which in fact was a mimetic substitute for Pirandello's own "torment of spirit."[51]

The final irony is that the conflict between life and form leads, in this portrayal of nature, to death. Life kills form as it must in nature, whereas the drama, "the work of art, lives forever in so far as it *is* form."[52]

THOMAS MANN, *Doctor Faustus*

Like Joyce and Pirandello, Thomas Mann provided, in *Doctor Faustus*, an anatomy of play both as a means to understand and as the swiftly past event and experience of understanding itself. Like them, he too emphasized the erotic aspects of the biological paradigm only, by way of dismissing it in a portrayal of sexual frustration, to magnify the eroticism in the esthetic paradigm of bonding, and indeed to expand it with analogues and metaphors transferred from the repertoire of the discounted model. Of the three authors, Thomas Mann used the method of association by contrast in the most varied and programmatic fashion in narrative orientation, language, and the stylized affective responses Mann portrayed and into which he expected his readers to enter. The text of *Doctor Faustus* itself, and an extensive account of the circumstances under which Mann wrote that novel,[53] provide detailed information about the source and character of that method.

The very choice of Faust as a subject required the use of theological mate-

---

[50] *Six Characters in Search of an Author*, in Bentley, ed., *Naked Masks*, pp. 213–14.

[51] Cf. "Preface" to *Six Characters in Search of an Author*, in Bentley, ed., *Naked Masks*, p. 369.

[52] Ibid., p. 372.

[53] "Die Entstehung des *Doktor Faustus*: Roman eines Romans," in Thomas Mann, *Gesammelte Werke*, Bd 11 (Oldenburg: Fisher, 1960. *Reden und Aufsätze*, 3.), pp. 145–301.

rials. Although, in one passage, German humanism is dismissed as "pure Middle Ages," geocentric and anthropocentric, and thus hostile to modern science, Mann drew heavily on medieval texts and ideas in characterizing his hero, the composer, Adrian Leverkühn, and, of course, "the Devil, as the background hero of the book."[54] Inasmuch as *Doctor Faustus* is a call for the liberation of art (specifically, music) from the fetters of bourgeois individualism, Thomas Mann looked back to the prebourgeois era, when, he believed, people were freer than ever again to yield themselves to their inward visions and feelings, exactly because they received from the Church an absolute, external frame of intellectual reference.[55] Thus, many elements in the story derive from the pre-Renaissance era: texts that Leverkühn employed in his musical compositions,[56] the locations in which Mann set the greater part of his account, and the characterizations of Leverkühn himself.[57] For the subject of association by contrast, however, other borrowings were of greater moment. These include interpretation of art, the profane, and the sacred; the concept of the world (which, for Mann, was culture) as contaminated and in need of purification, sick and in need of healing; and, finally, the concept of redemption through a creator who, in his agonies "bears the suffering of the age."[58] Mann's borrowings from the Middle Ages included the means by which he characteristically associated contrasting, or opposing, terms, namely, dialectic. For, in medieval texts (including writings by Augustine of Hippo and Thomas Aquinas), he found evidence for arguing that the wicked and the holy were one, united dialectically (pp. 100–103).[59] As will become apparent, he used dialectic as the key for reconciling the historical, as well as the moral, antinomies of life.

Some points of coincidence between Mann's association by contrast and that represented by Augustine of Hippo can be regarded as fortuitous, including the "mingling of fiction and reality" to produce a montage of different narratives.[60] There are in *Doctor Faustus* matters of great concern to Mann to which terms such as *allegory* and *symbol* may rightly be

---

[54] "Die Entstehung des *Doktor Faustus*," p. 191.

[55] *Doctor Faustus: The Life of the German Composer Adrian Leverkühn, as told by a Friend*, trans. H. T. Lowe-Porter (New York: Vintage, 1971), p. 369.

[56] Provençal and Catalan lyrics of the twelfth and thirteenth centuries (pp. 161–63), Dante's *Divine Comedy* (epigram and p. 163), the *Malleus maleficarum* (p. 233), *Gesta Romanorum* (pp. 305 ff.), unspecified works by Mechthild of Magdeburg, Hildegard of Bingen, and the Venerable Bede (pp. 336–37), an Old French metrical version of the vision of St. Paul (p. 394), Freidank (pp. 471–72).

[57] For example, Leverkühn wrote in a small monkish hand (p. 221), and he masqueraded as the twelfth-century composer, Perotinus the Great (p. 372).

[58] "Die Entstehung des *Doktor Faustus*," p. 203.

[59] Mann considered dialectical structure one of the salient characteristics of *Doctor Faustus*. See "Die Entstehung des *Doktor Faustus*," pp. 194, 213. Wilhelm Kantzenbach, "Theologische Denkstrukturen bei Thomas Mann," *Neue Zeitschrift für systematische Theologie und Religionsphilosophie*, 9 (1967), pp. 201–17.

[60] "Die Entstehung des *Doktor Faustus*," pp. 165, 167.

applied, but, by contrast with Augustine's array of interpretive levels, Mann's allegory, or symbolism, operated only on the level of history. Among the concerns that he represented figuratively is the risk that, ever pressing beyond the limits of the possible, art (particularly music or the novel) might achieve its own sterility (p. 259).[61] A second concern that Mann represented figuratively in *Doctor Faustus* was the isolation of the artists and the arts from the community, ominously measured against the urgent need of art, if it were to live, to enter and draw upon the common consciousness of the community. However allegorically or symbolically Mann portrayed these and other impelling concerns in *Doctor Faustus*, he did not construct narratives around them, in the fashion of a speculative theologian. Rather, he built them into two narrative levels, both of which were (or purported to be) historical: the fictional life of Adrian Leverkühn, including a portrayal of German culture between 1880 and 1940; and the actual history of Germany from the decades before the first World War until the last days of the second. *Doctor Faustus*, Mann wrote, "is a book about Germanness" (*Deutschtum*).[62] On both narrative levels, he worked out the twofold historical theme of the nearness of sterility to creativity, and of people's inborn power to doubt, which predisposed them to ally with the devil.[63]

As an esthetic structure, therefore, the narrative montage in *Doctor Faustus* lacks elements corresponding with Augustine's etiological and allegorical (or mystical) narratives. Although Mann certainly implied an analogical connection between the two narratives, he did not work out the analogical correspondences fully enough for a complete analogical narrative to emerge. Reduced to two historical narratives, the montage correspondingly demanded a relatively homogeneous apparatus of negative values to unify it. In the putative biography of Leverkühn, the sequence of pathos-discovery-periptery-epiphany was easy to follow. The stage of pathos began with Leverkühn's youthful pilgrimage from theology to philosophy and, finally, to music. It was stamped with his asceticism. It ended when he sought and achieved the syphilitic infection that released his genius (1905–06).[64] The stage of discovery followed in his conversation and pact with the devil, "the angel of death" (1912).[65] Thereafter, in the periptery, Leverkühn withdrew to the isolation of Pfeiffering, where he lived and composed for nineteen years (1912).[66] At the epiphany, Leverkühn unveiled his great work, an oratorio entitled *The Lamentation of Doctor Faustus*, to a select

[61] Ibid., p. 205.
[62] Ibid., p. 291.
[63] Ibid., p. 187.
[64] *Doctor Faustus: The Life of the German Composer Adrian Leverkühn*, chap. 15–16, 19.
[65] Ibid., chap. 25.
[66] Ibid., chap. 26.

company of guests and, in the process, suffered a syphilitic stroke from which he never recovered (1930).[67] In the denouement, Leverkühn spent the ten years remaining to him in a moribund, or comatose, existence, until he died on 25 August 1940.

Mann portrayed the narrative of German political history in a sketchy fashion. Frequently switching between Germany at the time of particular events in Leverkühn's life and Germany at the time that Mann (or the narrator, Zeitblom) was actually writing (1943–45/7), Mann deliberately created a lag between the dramatic stages of Leverkühn's biography and those of recent German history. The pathos in German history began in 1914, with the outbreak of World War I or, more distinctly, in 1919, with the collapse of the German Empire. Attended by political and economic distress and pervasive uncertainty, the era of bourgeois humanism, which had begun at the end of the Middle Ages, came to an end.[68] After an interval of recovery, during the 1920s[69] the pathos deepened in 1939–40. Then, intoxicated with early victories, Germany reeled forth to keep the pact sealed with her own blood, a pact that conferred upon her freedom and power and exacted her destruction. The novel ends with Leverkühn's death and burial, coinciding with this tragic venture. Mann had no need to describe in detail his country's experience of World War II. In allusions to the period 1944–45, it is evident that the stages of discovery and periptery have occurred, and that an epiphany, corresponding with Leverkühn's destruction as an artist, was at hand.

The linkages between the historical narratives exist in the text. They are positive and do not need to be read into the text, as negative values do. They consist, as Mann wrote, of a counterpoint between "the fate of the hero and other inhabitants of the book" and "Germany's catastrophe."[70] Leverkühn's devotion to theory rather than practice parallels Germany's willingness to live only on theory, and thus to study evil.[71] His demonism and compact with the devil parallels the bent of "the German soul," and his insistence that art must be purified by rebarbarization paralleled the Fascist call for the rebarbarization of culture.[72] Finally, the fatal blow that he sustained beneath the statue of Nike (or Victory) as he presented his greatest work echoes the hopeless and utter destruction that Germany brought upon herself "at the height of her dissolute triumphs" (p. 510).

Certainly, there are negative values in the esthetic structure organizing *Doctor Faustus*, not least the actual sound of serial music. Mann's account

---

[67] Ibid., chap. 47.
[68] Ibid., chap. 34.
[69] Ibid., chap. 36.
[70] "Die Entstehung des *Doktor Faustus*," p. 232.
[71] *Doctor Faustus: The Life of the German Composer Adrian Leverkühn*, pp. 44, 68, 143, 403, 453 on Adrian; p. 482 on Germany.
[72] Below, after n. 81.

of the novel's composition inventories a host of books, conversations, and experiences, including his wartime broadcasts against the Nazis, that entered into its fabric. A preliminary sketch, composed as early as 1901, and forty pages excised from the penultimate draft would also count as negative values.[73] The life of Nietzsche, never mentioned by a name in the novel, was nevertheless, the model for Leverkühn's biography, and a continuing preoccupation of Mann throughout the time when he was writing the novel.[74] The works that Marlowe and Goethe wove out of the Faust story and the complex heritage of Christian theology on creation, fall, atoning sacrifice, and redemption also formed part of the general culture that, without specific allusions in the novel, made *Doctor Faustus* conceivable to Mann and comprehensible to his audience.

However, the point is that Mann did not use negative values to link narratives in the book, as Augustine did, and that one must look elsewhere for survivals of the Christian method of association by contrast represented by Augustine.

Repeatedly, Mann portrays the inaccessibility of great art and the isolation of the artist. Leverkühn's use of parody and irony, as well as his calculated dissonance, made his music cold "even repellent and revolting" to the majority (pp. 56, 151). As he struggled, always on the frontier of the imaginable, each achievement further beyond the pale than earlier ones, he himself despaired "of executing the impossible" (p. 259). Although some defenders stepped forward, audiences walked out of performances of Leverkühn's works. His songs remained unsung. Of his two greatest works, the *Apocalypsis cum figuris* was performed only once and then denounced as "a mockery of art," and *The Lamentation of Doctor Faustus* was never performed, "a buried, forbidden treasure" (pp. 263, 377, 485). Leverkühn himself was aloof and detached from those around him by "his armor of purity, chastity, intellectual pride, and cool irony" (p. 147). Others offered him their devotion; but, knowing love only as an emotion "from which the animal warmth has been removed" (pp. 69, 218), Leverkühn generally evaded the reciprocal bonds of affection, driven more and more by temperament and illness into the seclusion of his darkened room. He reached out from his isolation only twice: first, to a friend who betrayed him and, second, to a child who died in unspeakable pain.

However, Mann did portray various kinds of esthetic bonding. In his music, Leverkühn drew together calculation and expressivism, strict obedience to convention and freedom of play. The bourgeois triumph of the Renaissance had broken these doublets apart. Reproached both for esotericism and for "cultural Bolshevism," he also fused the advanced art of the elite

---

[73] "Die Entstehung des *Doktor Faustus*," pp. 155, 156.
[74] Ibid., pp. 165–66, 198, 300.

and the enjoyable art of the lower social orders, which Romanticism had sundered (pp. 320–22, 339, 389).

His pact with the devil promised a yet more improbable combination of opposites. Latent in his neglected works, the recombinations of what history had divided would in time be discovered. The healthy would assimilate the products of Leverkühn's disease, syphilitic madness, and have no need to become mad. In them, he would "become healthy" (p. 243). Bonding between individuals and their communities was vital to Mann's theme. His severest criticism was against bourgeois individualism. Even the masterpiece, the triumphant utterance, was rejected by "emancipated art" (p. 239). The symbol of Leverkühn's ideal was the oratorio *Doctor Faustus*, which was entirely a choral work, without solos; for collectivism was the antithesis of bourgeois culture (pp. 373, 487). Mann therefore portrayed various kinds of personal bonding; but many of them hinged on contradictions as basic as that the health and vigor of life depended on the morbidity of the artist, a sickness that made him "brother of the criminal and the madman" (p. 236).

One kind of personal bonding provided by the esthetic paradigm—that between the author and his work—is among the primary negative values in *Doctor Faustus*. The two major characters in the novel, Leverkühn, the composer, and Zeitblom, the narrator, in fact represent two aspects of Mann himself, the artist ever probing the extreme spiritual limits of his art,[75] and the conservative, bourgeois critic.[76] In fact, the pairing of Leverkühn and Zeitblom reproduces the pairing of contrasts that Mann drew between himself and his brother, Heinrich Mann, as well as the use of the "doublet" by other writers. Hermann Hesse, too, portrayed the dialogue of two voices within himself when he divided the action between two characters, as in *Narziss und Goldmund* and in the *Glassbead Game*, which latter Mann read during the composition of *Doctor Faustus*. There, as in Mann's own work, *The Transposed Heads*, the paired actors portray the tension of carnal and spiritual in the individual artist.[77] In *Doctor Faustus*, they similarly represent the tension between law and miracle (cf. p. 18), criticism and invention: that is, between the dead art of humanist conventions and the "genius-giving disease" of living art that renewed culture but that, for the artist, was full of suffering and "infused with the angel of death" (cf. pp. 239–42, 497). The give-and-take of this dialectic ruled even the morbidity

[75] See Mann's own comments on Leverkühn and Zeitblom, ibid., pp. 169, 203, 247, 285, 299.

[76] See Inge Diersen, *Untersuchungen zu Thomas Mann: Die Bedeutung der Künstlerdarstellung für die Entwicklung des Realismus in seinem erzählerischen Werk* (Berlin: Aufbau-Verlag, 1960), pp. 304–305.

[77] The device is very ancient. See Bruno Bettelheim, *The Uses of Enchantment: The Meaning and Importance of Fairy Tales* (New York: Vintage, 1977), pp. 90–96, on "tales of two brothers" exemplifying "the contradictory aspects of the personality."

of genius; for, in its boldest and most eerie convolutions, Leverkühn's was the music of one who never escaped conventions of his native place and age (p. 83).

The importance of association by contrast, through dialectic, to Mann's narratives is indicated by the superficial nature of association by likeness and association by contiguity in his story. In a long section on protective imitation in insects, the resemblance of natural markings on shells to human writing, and chemically produced imitations of natural forms (pp. 14–20), Mann reiterates the point that likeness does not form a bond. It may, indeed, indicate "weird, half-hidden associations" (p. 13). But outward resemblance could ambiguously conceal poison with beauty, a concealment that some employed for black magic and others, for the Eucharist. The mimicry of nature by chemistry produced lifeless crystals, "pathetic imitations of life," that, though capable of movement, were dead. Again, when Mann wrote of the use of mimetic devices (including echo) in music (p. 60), and of music as "almost the *imitatio Dei*" (p. 78), he was writing of a purely formal—that is, superficial—association, rather than one that produced an inward bonding.[78]

Mann used association by contiguity to a similar effect, and here his departure from the biological paradigm was sharp. Women in *Doctor Faustus* co-exist with men, but their role is to serve. In her affair with Rudolf Schwerdtfeger, Inez Institoris reversed the proper roles of men and women by demanding exclusive possession of him, but, in so doing, she betrayed the morbid passions that eventually impelled her to murder her lover (p. 349). Under the characterization of women as temptresses and practitioners of black arts (pp. 105–11), the other women move through *Doctor Faustus* as subordinate actors. Throughout their long years of comradeship, Leverkühn never spoke with Zeitblom "of love, of sex, of the flesh" (p. 146). As "the hunted hunter," he sought out his "Esmeralda" first in a house of prostitution and, that failing, in a hospital precisely to be contaminated by possessing her flesh (pp. 154–56).[79] Serenus Zeitblom himself engaged in a minor affair, not out of passion so much as curiosity, pride, and a desire to imitate the openness of classical culture in sexual matters (pp. 146–47). Even the incestuous Queen in a story taken from the *Gesta Romanorum*, who laments her dead brother-husband as her "second I," is portrayed chiefly as an instrument of procreation, as much as "object of use" as "Esmeralda," the diseased prostitute (pp. 155, 317–19). The asso-

---

[78] Mann, of course, intended a thematic connection between the piercingly sorrowful effect of echo in baroque music (adapted by Leverkühn in *The Lamentation of Doctor Faustus*) and Leverkühn's ill-fated nephew, nicknamed Echo (pp. 479, 486). See also Mann's statement that the friendship between Leverkühn and Rüdiger Schildknapp hinged on "the likeness in the color of their eyes," i.e., "upon an indifference as profound as it as light-hearted" (p. 171). Cf. the likeness between the eyes of Leverkühn and his mother (p. 22).

[79] On Augustine as the hunted hunter, see above Chapter 4 at n. 43.

ciation of men with women by contiguity was therefore formal, or superficial.

So far as Leverkühn was concerned, the same could be said of his association with other men. He was deceived in his "homoerotic" relations with Schwerdtfeger, his "alter ego," the person toward whom, for the first time, Leverkühn felt human warmth; for Schwerdtfeger, having wooed him with a lover's coquetry, betrayed him (pp. 415, 436).[80] His young nephew's agonizing death thwarted Leverkühn's only other ardor, and, in his delirium, Leverkühn fancied that he had murdered the child who trusted him (p. 501). Seen from Leverkühn's point of view, both these apparent bondings resolved into actual contiguity.

Still, Mann did envision a mysterious bonding of persons reminiscent of the ancient biological doctrine that all human beings were one by virtue of their common substance, a surprising "and always somewhat unnatural" transformation that negated "the singleness of the individual soul" in the polarity of "the I and the not I" (p. 415). This was not based on carnality, as when, in marriage, "the twain [became] one flesh," a phenomenon that required, not the fusion, but "the strangeness of I and you," lust for the flesh of another that would be nonsensical if the "I" and the "you" were, in fact, "one flesh" (pp. 187–88). Rather, it was the kind of spiritual bonding through polarity that enabled a teacher to be "the personified conscience of the pupil" (p. 180), and that enabled Zeitblom to identify himself with Leverkühn so thoroughly as to feel that, after Leverkühn's death, he, Zeitblom, could imagine living for him and in his stead (p. 253).

This spiritual bonding of a quasi-biological nature was also, indeed, a bonding of opposites. Throughout, Zeitblom stressed his dislike for Leverkühn's materials and judgment, and yet he wrote *libretti* for the composer, thus becoming part of the music that he loved and hated (cf. pp. 161, 164, 184). As the narrator, Zeitblom also, in a sense, became the characters that he portrayed, including Leverkühn.[81]

On a level transcending personality, spiritual bonding also occurred in nationalism. The "national character" or "the soul of the nation," as fatefully exemplified by the Nazi era in Germany, and in the collective feelings that pervaded any culture, disguised and manifested themselves through individual artists as though through masks (pp. 117, 135, 481–82).

Each of these kinds of bonding became known through conflicting emotions, both creative and destructive. Zeitblom cherished Leverkühn in his heart with "love full of fear and dread" (pp. 452, 505; for fearful love and grief, cf. p. 67), and the joy that he felt in love was tempered also by jealousy of others who sought Leverkühn's friendship (pp. 316, 323, 351, 421).

---

[80] See "Die Entstehung des *Doktor Faustus*," p. 208.

[81] I owe the observation concerning Zeitblom's union, though his *libretti*, with Leverkühn's music to Professor Philip Paludan.

Thus, love, fear, and hatred mingled in Zeitblom's attachment to Leverkühn himself as well as in the emotions stirred in him by one of Leverkühn's compositions (p. 378). Constructive and destructive emotions likewise mingled in Zeitblom's comments on bonding through "the German soul," a bonding that subsumed even the originality of the artist into "a common consciousness" (pp. 117–18). Love was counterbalanced by fear, pride by shame. Impelled by a "feeling for religion," by a yearning for religious intoxication combining the holy and demonic, the Germans displayed their "tragic soul" in the catastrophes of World War II. Their "love belong[ed] to fate—to any fate, if only it be one, even destruction kindling heaven with the crimson flames of the death of the gods" (pp. 118, 174–75, 452, 480–82).

The word *polarity* is a key to Mann's complex doctrine of association by contrast, whether according to the esthetic paradigm or to some vestige of the biological one. Human nature, as he understood it, was full of contradictions. The antinomies of life rendered life essentially equivocal, and located "true passion only in the ambiguous and the ironic" (pp. 9, 123, 193, 242). "Relationship," he wrote, "is everything. And if you want to give it a more precise name, it is ambiguity" (p. 47).[82] Leverkühn's greatness consisted in revealing the profound antinomies of life, "a making unlike the like" (p. 378). His last and greatest work, *The Lamentation of Doctor Faustus*, an ode to sorrow, was the negation of Beethoven's *Hymn to Joy* (pp. 478, 487, 490).

Throughout *Doctor Faustus*, Mann repeatedly turned to irony as the means by which art advanced. It was by irony that Leverkühn strove to unite the contraries of elite and popular music, irony so extreme in his hands that critics denounced its mocker as "antipathetic to the artist mind," blasphemous, and nihilistic (pp. 275, 321).

The creative power of irony was valid because, in Mann's world, opposites coincided and became identical. What were antipathies from one point of view were sympathies from another. Evidently, this was true of disease and health, and of life and death, just as Leverkühn's procreative act with the prostitute both purified and contaminated him with the disease that released his art and that slowly killed him. It was necessary, as Kleist said,

---

[82] Cf. p. 304, attributing to Plato the statement that comedy and tragedy "grow on the same tree, and a change of lighting suffices to make one into the other." See above, Chapter 4 (A) n. 74. The statement attributed by Mann to Plato does not occur literally in Plato's texts. My colleague, Professor Sesto Prete, has suggested that the origin of Mann's statement may be a translation of Plato. He refers, as an example, to an English translation by J. L. Davies and D. J. Vaughan (London, 1852, p. 88), where the following words occur: "for even two branches of tradition, which are thought to be closely allied, are more, I believe, than can be successfully perused together by the same person, as, for instance, the writing of comedy and tragedy. . . ." I am very much obliged to Professor Prete for this suggestion, pointing to an intermediate stage of translation between Plato and Mann.

for Adam again to eat the forbidden fruit of the tree of knowledge, so that he might fall from guilt into his original state of innocence (p. 308).

By far the chief ambiguity in Mann's story was that between good and evil. Mann provided a statement of the philosophical argument that the devil was in fact a necessary emanation and concomitant of God, just as the freedom to sin was inseparable from the creative act. Everything exists and occurs in God, including apostasy from him (pp. 100, 131). Theology delivered up this proposition; but logic also required the "dialectic association of evil with goodness and holiness" (p. 103). God had to create the world "saturated with evil"; for without evil the universe would be incomplete. Lacking the mutual contrast of good and evil, the one or the other might exist, but it would have no meaning, and the lack of their reciprocal action would despoil the world of God's power to create good out of evil, thus also diminishing God's glory (pp. 103-104). Natural science provided yet another ground for identifying the opposites of good and evil. The scientist disclosed the cosmos as amoral, empty of God. Morality existed not in the material world but only in the psychic world of humanity. Still, human morality, like humanity itself, originated and developed precisely in biological evolution; growing in the abominable void of physical creation, the good was the flower of evil, blossoming chiefly in wrong (pp. 273–74). Mann considered good and evil, the godly and the satanic, as two aspects of the same creative and life-giving event.

His treatment of cultural polarities of "good" and "bad" is similarly dialectical. He regarded old and new, the regressive and the progressive, as one in human experience, fused and interpenetrated with one another, notably in the creation of works of art, for which, given the weight of collective norms, personal inspiration could never be "altogether new" (pp. 143, 252, 263, 372, 376, 438). This was particularly true when the artist created anew by returning to the primitive basis of all art (pp. 62–63, 381).

Zeitblom and Leverkühn parted ways on this point. For Zeitblom, the representation of conservative bourgeois humanism, culture and barbarism were antitheses. His "bloodless humanism"[83] equated barbarism with humanity's natural bestiality, suppressed and negated by the arts of culture. Zeitblom found it "painful and mortifying" that the rebellious force of animal instinct dragged the human mind down into bestiality, although human carnality could be beautified and purified by spiritual exaltation. Zeitblom therefore equated barbarism with the "soulless instinct" of the flesh and culture with the artificial refinement of spirit through sentiment. Yet, opposites coincided in his antithesis of soulless instinct and intellect. For, he asserted, intellectual pride was largely devoid of soul, incapable of

[83] "Die Entstehung des *Doktor Faustus*," p. 249.

beauty and spiritual exaltation (pp. 147–48). Leverkühn's cold and mocking intellectuality, he judged, was at one with naked animal instinct.

Leverkühn responded that the polarity of culture and barbarism was a stereotype perpetrated by bourgeois civilization. "Mind and spirit," he said, were not moved by the abstract, or spiritual alone; they were stirred most profoundly of all "by the animal sadness of sensual beauty" (p. 414). However, he judged, civilization had lost its instinctive, primitive basis, and it would have to be rebarbarized to regain its capacity for culture (pp. 59–60). For this reason, the objective of art was to cut through the pretentions of self-glorifying fictions of play that intruded themselves between the viewer and nature. "Only the non-fictional is still permissible [in music], the unplayed, the undisguised, and untransfigured expression of suffering in its actual moment" (p. 240). The barbaric was "in life and nature" at the heart of humanity and feeling (p. 217). In its secularization, since the Renaissance, European culture had denied the mystic passion—the passion concerning the absolutely questionable—from which genuine inspiration derived (pp. 237, 242–43). Turning from the religious cult that nurtured this creative feeling and in which reason and magic became one wisdom (p. 194), culture made a cult of itself (p. 243). Seeing only culture in religion, it transformed even the Church into an organ of bourgeois liberalism, concealing "the daemonic character of human existence." However that character still lurked in older, conservative theological traditions (pp. 88–90, 243).

Thus, Leverkühn asserted that bourgeois civilization found its true antithesis in collectivism, not in barbarism (that is, in animal instinct) (p. 373). Zeitblom's antithesis of culture and barbarism made him dread the revolution and dominance of the masses as "the destruction of culture" (p. 339). Zeitblom said that Bolshevism, which never destroyed art, was infinitely preferable to Fascism, with its zeal, uncharacteristic of the masses, for eradicating censored works of art. Leverkühn's linkage of collectivism and barbarism permitted him to envision a time when, by returning to its priestly and primitive origins (p. 374), art would not languish as the dying monopoly of an isolated elite, but would pervade and serve the whole community (p. 322).

To his horror, Zeitblom, the spokesman for "bloodless humanism," found the polarity of culture and barbarism resolved in the same way by esthetics and political spokesmen who advocated "bloody barbarism," contending that great beauty could only spring from brutal instincts[84] and that the dictatorship of the part or the interests of the community justified the ruthless destruction of individuals (pp. 287–89, 365–67, 370, 372). True to the elitism and individualism of the bourgeois, Zeitblom found in the

[84] Cf. ibid., p. 249.

instinctual savagery and primitivism of Leverkühn's music both an "inaccessibly unearthly and alien beauty" and a musical counterpart of the "dialectical process" that culminated in Hitler's "world rejuvenating barbarism, revelling in atrocity." Yet he recognized that the triumph of Fascism would have destroyed Leverkühn's work and deprived him of his artistic immortality (pp. 173, 322–40, 366, 373–74).

When Mann turned to the antitheses of art itself, particularly in music, he reconciled them dialectically, just as he did the antitheses of good and evil, whether moral or cultural. Form and content, he wrote, were "absolutely one and the same" in music, as in no other art (p. 61). Yet he insisted that his novel had to become that of which it dealt, namely, constructive music.[85]

In all the arts, he wrote, "the subjective and the objective intertwine to the point of being indistinguishable" (p. 190). This is especially so when the inherited conventions of art manifest themselves under the mask of an artist's individuality (p. 135), or when the reverse occurs, and the greatness of an individual (e.g., Beethoven), surmounting tradition, outgrows the merely personal and subjective and enters into the myth and objectivity of collective life (p. 53). The structure of music itself exemplified the dialectical resolution of opposites as, for example, when the successive intervals of notes were transformed into the simultaneity of the chord, and the discordance of notes "contrasting and conflicting" with each other yielded the polyphonic harmony of the chord (pp. 73–74). Leverkühn's compositions carried this dialectical resolution to unusual heights. In them, the heat of expressionism and cold calculation "play[ed] into each other," expressivism encompassing counterpoint and the objective structure of the work alive with feeling (p. 178).[86] The most complex and ingenious devices were employed to "purify" the complicated into the simple, to apprehend the simplicity at the foundation of all being (pp. 152, 321–22)—the simplicity that was the conflict in an artist's nature between chastity and passion from which his work grew (p. 152).

Thus, Mann ended with an ambiguous assessment of the esthetic paradigm, one that might have led him to discount it, as he had discounted the biological paradigm. However, the consequence of abandoning esthetic bonding, and thus works of the spirit as well as those of the flesh, were such that Mann accepted suffering as the cost of dialectical tension. In art, the creator bore this cost as he mediated the union of opposites. Exultation and

---

[85] Ibid., p. 187.

[86] See Mann's comment on the *Apocalypsis cum figuris* (*Doctor Faustus: The Life of the German Composer Adrian Leverkühn*, p. 375): "The whole work is dominated by the paradox (if it is a paradox) that in it dissonance stands for the expression of everything lofty, solemn, pious, everything of the spirit; while consonance and firm tonality are reserved for the world of hell, in this context a world of banality and commonplace."

misery, self-veneration and self-horror, joy and despair were the artist's lot as mediator. Yet, overarching this alternation of moods was the pain of isolation from the warmth of ordinary human life, the anguish of disease, the sufferings of composition, always in despair of exceeding earlier norms and in disgust for all but the impossible (cf. pp. 259, 458). Mann recalled Beethoven, "the afflicted artist" (p. 57) whose *Hymn to Joy* Leverkühn revoked with *The Lamentation of Doctor Faustus*, and Schubert, whose genius, touched with death, unfolded in "grandly self-tormenting" songs (p. 77). Leverkühn's deliberate self-infection with "creative, genius-giving disease," the agonies of body and mind that ensued, and his self-mockery were landmarks of his "wrestling with music and its sacred difficulties," as Jacob wrestled with the angel, a conflict in which, like Jacob, he was both victor and vanquished, both blest and afflicted. In the same way, seeking "Esmeralda" so that he could be infected by her, he had been both hunter and hunted (p. 154).[87]

Scripture afforded a higher analogue. In reversing Christ's cry in Gethsemane, "Could you not watch one hour with me?", Leverkühn "transform[ed] that cry of human and divine agony" into an assertion of prideful human confidence (pp. 490–92; on Beethoven, cf. p. 58). But, in dialectic above all, contrariety is a mode of likeness. Leverkühn sought freedom by rebelling in strict obedience to rules (e.g., pp. 193, 239, 241, 379, 488). Even reversing Christ's cry, Leverkühn's suffering had a "Christlike character" (p. 483). Obedient to the rules of music, he suffered unto death to purify music in order that it might perform its work of redemption, purifying culture, and bringing into existence an innocent art, an "art without anguish" (p. 322). Thus, pleading to God in his music for atonement of sin (p. 266), Leverkühn stepped forward to "atone with his blood for the weaknesses and sins of the time, including his own. . . . a sacrifice by which the old Adam is put away and from which in unity a new and higher life will be wrested. . . ." Adam had sinned and fallen into guilt through pride. By Leverkühn's arrogant pride, might not Adam, or another Adam, "eat a second time from the tree of knowledge in order to fall back into the state of innocence" (pp. 300, 308)? Leverkühn's story portrays this redemptive "self-destruction," this "sacrifice of love."[88]

CONCLUSION

The texts by Joyce, Pirandello, and Mann, which I have examined, indicated both the continuity, and the dispersal, of the heritage of empathetic participation, in the distinctive category of malevolent sympathy. Taken by itself,

[87] Mann applied the analogy of Jacob and the angel explicitly to Beethoven and Bruckner (pp. 57, 407) and implicitly to Leverkühn (p. 360).

[88] "Die Entstehung des *Doktor Faustus*," pp. 147, 244, 250.

any of the three twentieth-century texts displays but a fraction of the elaborate pattern of understanding that Augustine unfolded in his comments on Jacob's struggles.

They provide three anatomies of play as the event and experience of understanding. Unlike Augustine (and Donne), they went to great lengths, elaborating narratives of sexual frustration, to reject the biological paradigm of bonding and set forth the esthetic paradigm as the key to the coherence of play—the rules of the game, as it were. The two paradigms could not be mutually reflective, much less equivocal, as they had been for Augustine. The turning aside from dominance through biological eroticism in favor of dominance through esthetic is especially notable.

To be sure, there are striking similarities to Augustine's expositions. Above all, the texts acknowledge the facts that empathetic participation can occur through feelings of hatred, anger, and fear and that the bonding occurs in proportion to the capacity of the assimilator. They also agree that participatory bonding occurs through imitation, in heart or mind, of the object of hostile or painful feelings. This act of mimetic participation can occur through one or more modes, which I have roughly identified as dialectic, feud, substitution, and transferral. Yet another similarity, and a particularly notable one, given the extreme diversity of these texts, is the lonely, or esoteric, character of the assimilation. It occurs in the loneliness of the heart, and it results in the estrangement and isolation of the assimilator. Further, the texts that have been examined portray this paradoxical bonding that isolates as an aspect of art's mission to reform and perfect nature, a mission that leads to freedom and triumph through the destruction of the creator by his work. Finally, the texts have in common with Augustine the effort to engage their readers through a narrative composed of montages, through which the tragic scenario of pathos, discovery, periptery, and epiphany plays itself out. They have in common stylized affective responses set forth in the texts into which readers were expected to enter, the syntax and vocabulary of discourse about bonding, and methods of narrative orientation. These similarities, together with the deliberate use of medieval data, place the modern texts in the tradition represented by Augustine.

However, the dissimilarities underlying the disjunctures in paradigm between Augustine's doctrines and those exemplified in the twentieth-century texts are also conspicuous. The most obvious of these derive from explanations of suffering. Augustine believed that man was made for happiness and that misery was visited upon him as punishment. Divine justice intruded misery, including death, into human nature, which sin had deformed from its original goodness. By reforming them according to its own image and likeness, divine mercy would redeem only a few from this just condemnation and restore to them the happiness for which they were made. Augustine therefore cast suffering and redemption from it in a moral context. Human misery and the predicament of good and evil were, for him, aspects of the same subject. As universals, they cut across all distinctions of time, place, class, and nation. To say that art—in this case, the art of the Creator-Savior—corrected and reformed nature was to say, first, that sin had deformed human nature by prideful transgression, guilt, pollution, disease, bondage, powerlessness, and shame, all of which blocked the soul's participation in virtue; and, second, that, in the elect, grace and faith reformed nature so that the soul could participate in virtue, as it was made to do, by humble obedience, innocence, purity, health, freedom, power, and glory.

Augustine's elaborate, many-tiered, montage of narratives was designed to engage his readers; to lead them through the universal moral drama played out in individual sufferings; and, if possible, to reproduce it in them, as they followed Augustine in linking the tiers of narrative and, thereby, in the experience of moral transformation. Given Augustine's rhetorical doctrines, the obscurity and difficulty of negative values linking the narrative levels were important didactic tools for arresting his readers, exciting them in love to search for Scriptural treasures hidden from the many, and promising them the joy of consummating, through inward struggle, union with the good that was concealed in the text. Spiritual catharsis was part of conversion to the good and an object of Augustine's narrative structure.

The esthetic structure of the three twentieth-century works present rather a different picture. Of course, the theology of sin and redemption is essential to the narratives in Joyce's *Portrait* and Mann's *Doctor Faustus*. However, Joyce portrayed it as the source of intense hatred, anger, and fear and as part of Dedalus's early life that he suppressed, even as he sublimated his hostile emotions. Mann employed it to illustrate the guilt, or sinfulness, that must be embraced as the inescapable cost of human creativity. For Pirandello, as well as for Joyce and Mann, human suffering was neither change intruded into a primordially happy nature nor a symptom of moral turpitude. "Life is pain," Mann wrote, "and we live only as long as we suffer."[89]

Such moral issues as Joyce, Pirandello, and Mann present in these three works concern the esthetic experience and mission of the artist. They are not universal. Indeed, the three authors characterize them primarily as matters of individual concern to the artists, estranged and isolated even from social and personal relationships, and secondarily as products of class structure.

Suffering, not happiness, is the natural condition of the human race, and doctrines concerning the pain of existence, though esoteric, were set in lim-

[89] Ibid., p. 241.

ited esthetic contexts, rather than in a universal moral one. This difference
in orientation led to differences in narrative strategy between Augustine
and the three twentieth-century authors. Levels of allegorical and mystical
narrative had no place. Even when, as in *Doctor Faustus*, more than one
narrative are in play, they are parallel, or intersecting, lines of historical
exposition, rather than excursions into nonhistorical kinds of meaning.
Consequently, the task of linking different levels of narrative values did not
occur. Because the narrative or narratives remained on the historical level,
it was not necessary to engage the reader in moving from literal to allegorical meanings. The chain of events in the narrative itself established such
linkages as were needed.

There was a further consequence. Augustine had deployed his repertoire
of modes of bonding—by dialectic, feud, substitution, and transference—in
part to establish points of correspondence through all the stages of his
ornate narrative structure. Thus, the structures of the narrative montages
in the three twentieth-century works lack some essential features of Augustine's portrayal of empathetic participation through conflict: the full range
of meanings, and the sense of coordination through negative values, among
various modes of bonding. Finally, it must be added that the three twentieth-century writers did not address their readers didactically, as Augustine
had done. They anticipated that their tasks would be accomplished when the
reader experienced through empathetic participation a "tragic pleasure" to
which neither catharsis nor moral transformation nor happiness was essential. This, too, was a consequence of narrowing personal union to the historical dimension.

We are now in a position to return to the theme of amorous sympathy,
exemplified for us at the outset by John Donne. Enlarged by ideas of
bonding through malevolence, ideas of bonding through love provided basic
theories of social, as well as of personal, union. But it is important to
remember that the paradigms of bonding through love, whether biological
or esthetic, implied strife for dominance: the first, the dominance of male
over female, the second, that of artist over matter. And where strife is
implied, there also is hatred. I shall consider this amplified aspect of our
theme, again taking Augustine as a representative of thought at the beginning of our chronological span. I have chosen Ludwig Feuerbach to represent thought toward the end of that span.

FIVE

Implications for Social Unity:
Augustine and Feuerbach,
with a Digression on Darwin

IN PREVIOUS CHAPTERS, it has become evident that, whether by amorous or malevolent sympathy, the empathetic identity of "I" and "you" did not exist from the start, except potentially. The dominant patterns of understanding required what was potential to be made actual by a process of transformation that narrowed the distance of relationship until it closed. Closure came through affective bonding in which love, conflict, and hatred could combine. In the present chapter, I explore the implications of the patterns of understanding empathy by which interpreters made the sentence make sense for social unity. To illustrate the continuity of ideas about the hermeneutic enterprise in this regard over a long time I discuss two authors, Augustine of Hippo and Ludwig Feuerbach, because both of them deliberately employed the signature, "I am you," to elucidate their theories of society and held up their theories as antidotes to what each considered the prevailing moral decadence of his age. The connecting link between them may well have been another fiery excoriator who rejoiced in battle against what he judged prevailing decadence: Martin Luther. For, despite his rejection of established religious norms, Feuerbach considered himself Luther's heir. The example of Fichte (discussed in the preface) does not let us escape from the question of how doctrines of harmony justified conflict and even persecution.

Augustine defined a people as "a gathering of a rational multitude brought into association by communion, of one accord, in the objects of their love."[1] At the beginning of our inquiry, we noticed that the reasons for thinking that "I" could become "you," although they were many, comprised two paradigms: the biological grounded in the coherence of individual organisms and in the dynamic of procreation, and the esthetic, grounded in the formal unity of individual works of art and the dynamics of affective absorption. These paradigms corresponded with the ancient distinction between flesh and spirit, and with the two characteristic human means of form giving through dominance: procreation and composition.

---

[1] *City of God*, 19. 24 (*Corp. Christ., ser. lat.*, 48, p. 695): "populus est coetus multitudinis rationalis rerum quas diligit concordi communione societas."

Both explained strife for dominance, and thus the combination of amorous with malevolent feelings. The two dynamic principles united the individual with the species. We have already considered in some detail the esthetic paradigm as employed by Augustine and its later history, and have made evident the esthetic informing the love that united many into one people. We will now discuss the biological paradigm, its points of equivalence with the esthetic paradigm (notably through the play of eroticism in its many forms), and its duration in the history of ideas. We shall also consider the oscillation that it made possible between works of the flesh and those of the spirit.

I suggest later that the concept of esthetic and biological bonding introduced by Augustine entered into this intellectual heritage out of which Charles Darwin (1809–82) shaped his paradigm of genetic evolution. Darwin's contemporary, Ludwig Feuerbach, exhibited his debt to Christian doctrine more directly than Darwin. He, like Augustine, regarded love as the unifying bond of culture and the characteristic feature of the human species. Discarding the propositions of Christian dogma, Feuerbach limited himself to the sphere of nature, rather than oscillating, as Augustine had done, between natural and supernatural. Yet even this simplified way of thinking distinguished, as Augustine's had done, the positive values set forth in philosophical propositions and the negative values of poetic experience that they purported to define. Feuerbach's approach, like Augustine's, required an assimilative structure of analogy and metaphor to reconstruct an ineffable, and in that sense negative, poetic act in the positive language of reason. Love and conflict made up the bonding process. We shall find that the reasons why Friedrich Engels (1820–95) judged Feuerbach's " 'most beautiful passages' in praise of this new religion of love [to be] almost unreadable today" were rooted in a long tradition, encompassing Augustine, from which Engels had consciously, but not completely, detached himself in his own enterprise of social renewal.[2]

AUGUSTINE

Augustine's whole concept of bonding encompassed three kinds, or degrees, of love through which "I" could become "you": carnal love directed toward the sensory world, mental (or intellectual) love directed toward the world of thought, and spiritual love directed toward God. He imagined the soul passing through these levels by an imitative process that was biological as well as esthetic.

The dynamic of procreation was fundamental to Augustine in every major area of theology. At the heart of this doctrine were the convictions

[2] *Ludwig Feuerbach und der Ausgang der klassischen deutschen Philosophie,* chap. 3. Karl Marx-Friedrich Engels, *Werke,* Bd 21 (Berlin: Akademie—Marx-Engels Archiv, 1962), p. 285.

that all life sprang from the same external source and that it was reproduced through all levels of creation by love. God filled the material bodies of this world, but they did not fully contain him. Augustine was repelled by philosophers who taught that God was a World-Soul, "a kind of womb of nature containing all things in Himself so that the lives and souls of living things are taken . . . out of His soul . . . and therefore [that] nothing at all remains which is not part of God." And yet, Augustine himself insisted that God was the Life within all souls, "the Life of lives."[3] Through the love that he was, God created the world and conveyed life to it, and, through the same love, he regenerated the souls of the elect, quickening them from animal to spiritual life.[4] Augustine also thought that the human race had a single origin and that the impulse of love reproduced the species in its individual members. God made Adam the source of all human life to confirm the unity of the human race.

To be sure, there was an archetype of human nature,[5] according to which the human species was not subject to death.[6] But Adam's sin put a great distance between that archetype and all humankind. In Adam, all die. "For we all were in that one man when we all were that one man who fell into sin by the woman who was made from him before the sin. For not yet was the particular form created and distributed individually to us in which we as individuals were to live, but already the seminal nature was there from which we were to be propagated; and this nature being vitiated by sin and bound by the chain of death and justly condemned, man could not be born of man in any other condition."[7] All human beings were present in Adam; through the ages, all women in travail gave birth to Adam.[8]

Love deriving from this common origin informed the mutual affection of spouses and their longing for children and preserved "the bonds of marriages, kindreds, and relations."[9] Augustine's teaching on the genetic reproduction of the human race from a single ancestor opened various possibilities of personal union. It enabled him to argue that humankind was one collective person, and that the history of the world could be considered the education of one individual, personified in the people of God.[10]

However, lessons imparted through Augustine's struggle to cast off the

[3] Conf., 1. 3; 3. 6; 10. 6 (CSEL, 33, pp. 3, 52, 234). City of God, 4. 12 (Corp. Christ., ser. lat., 47, p. 110).
[4] Tr. in Ev. Johan., 9. 8; 23. 5–6; 27. 8 (Corp. Christ., ser. lat., 36, pp. 95, 234ff., 408). De Trinitate, 5. 16. 17 (Corp. Christ., ser. lat., 50, pp. 226–27).
[5] Cf. De Trinitate, 9. 6. 9 (Corp. Christ., ser. lat., 50, p. 301).
[6] City of God, 13. 15 (Corp. Christ., ser. lat., 48, p. 306).
[7] City of God, 13. 14 (Corp. Christ., ser. lat., 48, pp. 305–306). Cf. En. in Ps. 84: 7 (Corp. Christ., ser. lat., 39, p. 1165): "We were not yet we, but we were in Adam."
[8] De sancta virginitate, 6. 6 (CSEL, 41, p. 240).
[9] De fide rerum invisibilium, 2. 4 (Corp. Christ., ser. lat., 46, pp. 4–5).
[10] City of God, 10. 14; 12. 21–23, 27; 13. 14 (Corp. Christ., ser. lat., 47, p. 288; 48, pp. 376–81, 383–84, 395–96).

materialism of Manichee doctrine diverted him from completely working out the biological paradigm. His writings display many instances in which he modified, or turned aside from, the carnality of the biological paradigm, although, as we shall see, he was eventually able to spiritualize both paradigms. Thus, shrinking from a relapse into the materialism of his youthful beliefs, which would have mired him once more in works of the flesh, he turned from biological to esthetic reasoning, refusing to identify parents and children, as Aristotle had done (see Chapter 1 at n. 31). However, Augustine refused to identify man or human nature with the physical body. Men were called, he wrote, to be gods, not men.[11] The defining characteristics of man were spiritual, not carnal. Therefore, identity among human beings hinged on spiritual affinities to each other and, ultimately, to God. Augustine's detachment from his father, and his assertion that there was nothing of himself but sin in his own son,[12] sharply contrast with his statement that his life had been made one with that of his mother, Monica.[13] However, Augustine explained his identification with Monica as deriving not only from physical descent but far more from the spiritual conversion that occupied the first thirty-one years of life. He imbibed the name of Jesus with his mother's milk,[14] and she was an unswerving promoter of his long, digressive spiritual odyssey, giving birth, Augustine wrote, to his salvation.[15]

Augustine's esthetic (rather than biological) identification with Monica therefore resembled the bond with a friend to whom Augustine became "another he." Truly, Augustine wrote, a friend was "half of one's soul. For I felt that my soul and his soul were one soul in two bodies. . . ."[16] Friendship was built up gradually by outward signs proceeding from the hearts of those loving and of those loving in return until one was made of many. Hence, the loss of a friend's life was also the death of the living.[17]

Thus, identity of "I" and "you" among human beings posited a uniform human nature conveyed through carnal descent, but it could not be realized without a mediating act of mental (intellectual) love, any more than their spiritual union with the Life of their lives could be realized without the mediation of God's love in the person of Christ and in the sacraments. Augustine taught that these three modes of identity—carnal, intellectual, and spiritual—coincided when spiritual progeny were begotten by baptism

[11] *Tr. in Ev. Johan.*, 1. 1. 3–4 (*Corp. Christ., ser. lat.*, 36, p. 2).

[12] *Conf.*, 9.6 (*CSEL*, 33, p. 207).

[13] *Conf.*, 9. 12 (*CSEL*, 33, p. 221). See also *De Beata vita*, 1.6 (*Corp. Christ., ser. lat.*, 29, p. 68).

[14] *Conf.*, 3. 4 (*CSEL*, 33, pp. 49–50).

[15] *Conf.*, 1. 11 (*CSEL*, 33, pp. 15–16).

[16] *Conf.*, 4. 6 (*CSEL*, 33, pp. 72–73). For Aristotle's use of this definition, see above, Chapter 1, at n. 46.

[17] *Conf.*, 4. 8–9 (*CSEL*, 33, pp. 74–75).

in the Church; but he knew very well that from the outset, at the most basic level of physical perception, the quest for identity might be biased against both the intellectual love that united friends and the spiritual love that permitted union with God.

In fact, the carnality of the biological paradigm was as inescapable as it was treacherous for Augustine. For knowledge of one's world began with the bodily senses, and with "carnal images" imprinted on the mind by sensory perceptions. Augustine took pains to document how easy it was to be drawn by them into empathetic participation in gladiatorial contests, as was Augustine's friend, Alypius: "for, at the instant when he saw the blood [of a fallen gladiator], he drank in the savagery . . .; he was delighted with the wickedness of conflict and intoxicated with bloody joy."[18] Augustine's own spiritual venture gave alarming reasons to mistrust carnal images. As a young man, Augustine himself felt the same powerful engagement as Alypius in theatrical performances and in the "images of vice"—public liturgies and obscene games—celebrated in honor of the gods and goddesses.[19] He later realized that participation in these events nurtured in him "various and shadowy loves"[20] and an ardent delight in loving and being loved and, most of all, in enjoying the body of his lover.[21] Yielding, he played into the hands of demons who used liturgical and theatrical spectacles to induce men and women to join them in their crimes by imitating the licentious conduct and events portrayed.[22]

The difficulty for Augustine was that even spiritual knowledge began in carnal images. The *Confessions* is itself a grand structure of carnal images composed by Augustine to serve his ministry of preaching.[23] But the transition from carnal to mental and, further, to spiritual identification depended on the will and capacity of the reader. The *Confessions* could be read in idle curiosity; read with a "brotherly mind," loving what was to be loved in Augustine, lamenting what was to be lamented, and applying his experience to amend their own lives;[24] or read on a higher level, disclosing behind "signs corporally pronounced and things intellectually considered" something more—"the simple love of God and neighbor proclaimed in such manifold sacraments and innumerable languages." Behind the carnal images of spoken words and the intellectual vision that elucidated them, some readers could detect and participate in the ultimate negative value in his text—namely, the love in which God gave men all their works and

[18] *Conf.*, 6. 8 (*CSEL*, 33, pp. 127–28).
[19] *City of God*, 2. 4, 26 (*Corp. Christ., ser. lat.*, 47, pp. 37–38, 61–62). For a scene in Terence's *The Eunuch* that stuck in Augustine's mind, see below n. 49.
[20] *Conf.*, 2. 1 (*CSEL*, 33, p. 29).
[21] *Conf.*, 3. 1 (*CSEL*, 33, p. 44).
[22] *City of God*, 2. 7, 24–25, 27 (*Corp. Christ., ser. lat.*, 47, pp. 40, 58–63).
[23] *Conf.*, 1. 1 (*CSEL*, 33, p. 2).
[24] *Conf.*, 10. 3–4 (*CSEL*, 33, pp. 227–30).

formed one living soul of the faithful, using his preachers and ministers as he renewed their mind according to his own image and likeness.[25]

As he considered the passage from carnal images to spiritual knowledge, Augustine himself moved toward a reconciliation of the biological and esthetic paradigms. Augustine recognized that the number of persons who could pass from positive evidence of carnal interpretation to the negative level of spiritual understanding was very small; they were the elect whom God regenerated by his grace.[26] However, Augustine also had a clear concept of the process by which the transition took place in the individual mind, and how individual transitions constituted a whole—the human species or the people of God. He portrayed the individual and collective movements in the two closely meshed ways that we first encountered in discussing John Donne's *Meditation 17*.

Both paradigms began with the fundamental distinction of lover, beloved, and love, "a certain life that couples the lover and what is loved, or seeks that they be coupled."[27] Love was a turning of the will that had many faces. When it yearned to have what was loved, love was desire. When it had and enjoyed its object, love was joy. Fleeing from obstacles, it was fear; and, feeling weighed down by impediments, love was sadness. Turned to evil objects, love was evil; turned toward good, it was good. In all its characters—desirous, joyful, anxious, or sad—it was sanctified when turned toward God.[28] Augustine was intensely conscious of the contending loves that might co-exist in the same heart.[29] He knew the complex emotions of a man who loved what should not be loved and, in blatant self-contradiction, hated his ill-directed love.[30] However, the fact remained that love was in the mind of the lover, not in the object of love.

Esthetic ways of reasoning predominated over biological when Augustine posited the inwardness and subjectivity of love. His emphasis normally fell on the spectator, rather than the spectacle. Augustine recognized many kinds of relationships in which one-sidedness prevailed. He knew that it was possible to love friends of friends, contemporaries whom one had never met but on whose characters and careers one wished to pattern one's own.[31] His doctrine that there were archetypal virtues gave him another reason for loving people whom he did not know. For example, Augustine wrote, he

[25] *Conf.*, 13. 31, 34, 36 (*CSEL*, 33, pp. 382–83, 385–87).

[26] *De bono viduitatis*, 23. 28 (*CSEL*, 41, p. 341).

[27] *De Trinitate*, 8. 10. 14 (*Corp. Christ., ser. lat.*, 50, pp. 290–91). See also Augustine's definition of knowledge as "a kind of life in the reason of the knower." *De Trinitate*, 9. 4. 4 (*Corp. Christ., ser. lat.*, 50, p. 297).

[28] *City of God*, 14. 7. 9 (*Corp. Christ., ser. lat.*, 48, pp. 422–23, 427–30).

[29] *Conf.*, 4. 14; 8. 5; 8. 9–10; cf. *Conf.*, 2. 1 (*CSEL*, 33, pp. 29, 81, 178, 187–91).

[30] *City of God*, 11. 28 (*Corp. Christ., ser. lat.*, 48, p. 348).

[31] An example is Augustine's admiration for the orator, Hierius, to whom he dedicated his first treatise (now lost), *On the Beautiful and the Appropriate*. *Conf.*, 4. 14 (*CSEL*, 33, pp. 81–82).

loved the Apostle Paul, not as a man, but because of his righteous mind—
that is, because his love conformed with a steadfast and unchangeable pattern.[32] Thus, it was possible to love not only great figures like Paul but also
any virtuous person whom one never knew, and indeed to love persons with
whom, through misjudgment, one refused to break bread.[33] At the highest
level, believers could only love Jesus and God without knowing them face
to face.[34]

Even among brethren, one knew the love with which he loved more than
the brother whom he loved.[35] The soul, loving itself, remained a great
depth, hidden even to itself.[36] Thus, love did not consist in the positive
values of knowledge; for clearly it was possible to know someone (or something) without loving him (or it).[37] Love did not consist in the positive
values of belief; for the devil believed in God without loving Him.[38] Love
did not consist in the positive experience of a mutual exchange between the
lover and the beloved; for the beloved might be, at most, an imaginary
portrait in the mind of the lover.[39] Love did arise from a susceptibility in
the mind of the lover to beauty, a negative value in the positive composition
of a person or object. In terms reminiscent of Feuerbach's description of a
porous soul, participating in others through its needfulness (see Chapter 2
at n. 1), Augustine wrote that beauty was the cause of love, drawing the
soul to objects of its love, and quickening in it a desire to be one with them.[40]

Love therefore arose in a sense of esthetic need and distance; it was also
consummated in a sense of esthetic filling and closure. Augustine described
the soul cleaving to temporal things "with the adhesive of love"; or idola-
trously adhering to its own fictions, "deceived by an immature and perverse
love of reason."[41] But, eventually, it would find corporal and intellectual
closure insufficient. Beyond them, most exalted above itself and most
inward in God, the Life of its life, it might end its restless search in the
vision of God, the Beauty that it had loved in beautiful things, and be rapt,
absorbed, and enfolded into the intimate joys of eternal life, full of the love
that was God, all in all.[42]

[32] *De Trinitate*, 8. 6. 9; 8. 9. 13 (*Corp. Christ., ser. lat.*, 50, pp. 279–84, 289–90).

[33] *Tr. in Ev. Johan.*, 90. 2–3 (*Corp. Christ., ser. lat.*, 36, pp. 551ff.).

[34] *De Trinitate*, 8. 4. 6; 8. 5. 7 (*Corp. Christ., ser. lat.*, 50, pp. 274–75, 277).

[35] *De Trinitate*, 8. 8. 12 (*Corp. Christ., ser. lat.*, 50, p. 286).

[36] *En. in Ps. 41*: 13 (*Corp. Christ., ser. lat.*, 38, pp. 470–71). *Conf.*, 4. 13 (*CSEL*, 33, pp. 81–82).

[37] *De Trinitate*, 8. 4. 6 (*Corp. Christ., ser. lat.*, 50, p. 275).

[38] *Tr. in Ev. Johan.*, 83. 3 (*Corp. Christ., ser. lat.*, 36, p. 536).

[39] On Paul and Jesus, see *De Trinitate*, 8. 4. 7; 8. 5. 7 (*Corp. Christ., ser. lat.*, 50, pp. 275–77).

[40] *Conf.*, 4. 10; 4. 13 (*CSEL*, 33, pp. 76, 80).

[41] *Tr. in Ev. Johan.*, 40. 4; 74. 1 (*Corp. Christ., ser. lat.*, 36, pp. 351, 513). *De Trinitate*, 1. 1. 1 (*Corp. Christ., ser. lat.*, 50, p. 27).

[42] *Conf.*, 1. 1; 9. 10 (*CSEL*, 33, pp. 1–2, 217). *City of God*, 22. 30 (*Corp. Christ., ser. lat.*, 48, p. 865).

For the few who received it, this ultimate closure lay in the future. While in the world, the soul was in transition, ambiguously loved by God as it would become and hated by God as it was.[43] In ironic conflict between its present and future states, it moved in a process of transmutation "from form into form."[44] Quite naturally, Augustine imagined this process as an analogue to the making (and remaking) of a work of art. For the soul was an effigy, modeled in the image of God, and God, the "great artist" who had originally made the world and humankind, was again at work as a sculptor correcting the ravages of sin.[45]

The biological and esthetic paradigms were two perspectives on the same love, which was a love of dominance, the first the perspective of the flesh, and the second, that of the spirit. It was the love that impelled the individual soul "from form into form" toward esthetic closure with God. But that love was part of a far grander modeling process, also characterized by the struggle of coming into being, both procreative and compositional. Augustine imagined, not merely the physical world, but also the historical world as an artistic composition, a poem, or a painting that was gradually being completed, or a song whose parts were the lives of individual men.[46] Wicked men failed to detect the broad pattern taking shape within events. Turning aside from God, they were blind to his handiwork. They loved their own private interests, mistaking parts for the whole[47] that was visible dimly and partially to the saved, but clearly and fully perfected in the eyes of God. Augustine's biological and esthetic reasoning consequently enabled him to combine the most intimate impulses of the heart with the grandest movements of history.

Whether in the soul or in great historical action, the struggle of transition, impelled by love, was mimetic. The pattern of understanding dominated by the strategy of mimesis explained how "I" could become "you." Augustine rebuked those who censured Christian celibates on the basis of

---

[43] De Trinitate, 1. 10. 21 (Corp. Christ., ser. lat., 50, p. 59). Similarly, Augustine taught: "Whoever loves men ought to love them either because they are righteous or so that they may be righteous. For so also he ought to love himself. . . ." De Trinitate, 8. 6. 9 (Corp. Christ., ser. lat., 50, p. 283). Cf. also Augustine's teaching that "he who lives according to God owes toward evil men a perfect hatred, in such fashion that he shall neither hate the man because of his vice, nor love the vice because of the man, but hate the vice and love the man." City of God, 14.6 (Corp. Christ., ser. lat., 48, p. 421). One should hate the wicked because they are wicked but love them because they are men: En. in Ps. 138: 28 (Corp. Christ., ser. lat., 40, p. 2010). See also De doctrina Christiana, 1. 59 (CSEL, 80, p. 23), where Augustine taught that man was to be loved because of God, while God was to be loved for His own sake.

[44] De Trinitate, 15. 8 (Corp. Christ., ser. lat., 50A, p. 480).

[45] City of God, 22. 19, 30 (Corp. Christ., ser. lat., 48, pp. 838, 862). Cf. Conf., 1. 11 (CSEL, 33, p. 17).

[46] For the analogue with a poem, City of God, 11. 18; for that with a painting, City of God, 11. 23; for that with a song, Conf., 11. 28 (Corp. Christ., ser. lat., 48, pp. 337, 342. CSEL, 33, p. 308).

[47] Conf., 3. 8 (CSEL, 33, p. 58).

misinformation; they imitated what they thought, he wrote, instead of what they saw.[48] Yet this imitation of subjective rather than objective reality was at the heart of his own doctrines, which focused on the spectator, rather than on the spectacle. The pattern of imitation might be very complex, even in the love of carnal images. To illustrate his contention that the examples of the gods provoked immoral behavior, Augustine recalled a scene from Terence's comedy, *The Eunuch*. Terence portrayed a young man who sanctioned his own adultery by referring to a fresco that depicted Jupiter's descent into the lap of Danaë. The young man boasted that in his licentiousness he "imitated God."[49] Augustine detected at least five stages of imitation in this example. At the beginning, he found not Jupiter, a god, but men to whom divine honors were paid after death.[50] In their lying ways, poets later ascribed the misdeeds of "most wicked men" to gods, so that crimes might no longer be considered crimes.[51] This was the first stage of imitation. The second occurred in the mind of the artist who made the painting; the third, in the mind of the author who wrote the play; and the fourth in the mind and action of the young man portrayed in the play. Augustine's censures were aimed at the fifth stage, in the minds and actions of those (including himself) who saw the play or other theatrical and religious spectacles that purported to give divine sanction to fornication with carnal things against God.[52]

Augustine also regarded imitation as the act of bonding among friends. His experience taught him, however, that imitation could unite friends in carnal associations that "made one out of many" by inflaming the souls with evil desires.[53] Consequently, when he spoke of imitation among friends as a means by which the ravages of sin were corrected, he posited the "true friendship" established by love that the Holy Spirit diffused in the hearts of the elect.[54] Man mediated to man. (It is worth recalling that, of the large cast of characters portrayed in the *Confessions*, only six were women, and only one, Augustine's mother, was mentioned by name and counted among the companions in his process of conversion.) "For between the folly of man and the most pure truth of God, the wisdom of man is set, as something in the middle."[55] Through a common linkage of charity, the wise man imitated God; and the foolish imitated the wise.[56]

[48] *De bono viduitatis*, 22. 27 (*CSEL*, 41, p. 339).
[49] *City of God*, 2. 7 (*Corp. Christ.*, ser. lat., 47, p. 40). *Conf.*, 1. 16 (*CSEL*, 33, p. 23). For further discussions of Augustine's use of game metaphors, see chapter 1 at n. 74; Chapter 4 at nn. 12, 19; Chapter 6 at nn. 83, 100.
[50] *City of God*, 8. 26 (*Corp. Christ.*, ser. lat., 47, pp. 246–49).
[51] *Conf.*, 1. 16 (*CSEL*, 33, p. 22).
[52] Cf. *Conf.*, 1. 13 (*CSEL*, 33, pp. 18–19).
[53] See *Conf.*, 13. 21, "aemulatio viri ab amico est," and *Conf.*, 2. 9, on the theft of pears through "nimis inimica amicitia"; see also *Conf.*, 4. 8 (*CSEL*, 33, pp. 42–43, 74–75, 369).
[54] *Conf.*, 4. 4 (*CSEL*, 33, pp. 68–69).
[55] Cf. *Conf.*, 13. 21 (*CSEL*, 33, p. 369).
[56] *De utilitate credendi*, 33 (*CSEL*, 25: 41).

At every level, union of the lover and the beloved occurred through imitation of subjective reality. At every level, this movement was dynamic, but only in its full range did its struggles end in the restoration of man from deformity to wholeness that was both personal and collective. Augustine's esthetic doctrines permitted him to assert that the individual person was the basic element of collective unity and, in the general scheme of salvation, to maintain the principle that the whole was identical with its parts. However, even though these doctrines addressed compositional aspects of salvation, they did not elucidate the practical method by which, according to the New Testament, salvation was gained—that is, by regeneration. The effect of incorporation, as esthetic union, was illumination.

The doctrine of regeneration, effacing the taint of original sin conveyed through carnal procreation, a normative doctrine of Christian orthodoxy, compelled Augustine to return repeatedly to the biological paradigm, although he subordinated it to the esthetic one, as he subordinated flesh to spirit. Together with the esthetic, compositional paradigm, he employed an organic, procreative one, delighting in ways to render them complementary, and even equivocal. From this second perspective, unity existed, not among parts and whole, but between members and body; and the mimetic act of bonding "I" and "you" was not artistic modeling but genetic procreation. The principle of unity in the biological paradigm was function; that in the esthetic one was harmony. The effect of incorporation, as biological union, was fecundity in good works.

Clearly, the biological and esthetic ways of visualizing the bonding process were not sharply distinguished in Augustine's mind. The two ways of thinking coincided at many points. Basically, Augustine failed to distinguish between form and function. When he considered the structure of the body, for example, he was so struck by the symmetry and proportion of its parts, that he could not decide "whether, in creating the body, greater regard was paid to utility or to beauty," although, in the end, he thought that the balance tipped in favor of beauty. He was convinced that every member, even internal organs hidden within the comeliness of the skin (as impiously disclosed by anatomists' knives) contributed to the beauty of the whole, and some parts (for example, a man's beard) that had no useful purpose were ingeniously designed as ornaments.[57]

Augustine's esthetic and biological paradigms also coincided in positing the descent of humankind from a single prototype—namely, the image of God, embodied in Adam. Whether viewed as a process of reformation or as

---

[57] *City of God*, 22. 24 (*Corp. Christ., ser. lat.*, 48, pp. 849–51). Cf. *Conf.*, 13. 28 (*CSEL*, 33, pp. 380–81), emphasizing not the utility, but the beauty of individual members and their yet greater beauty in combination.

one of regeneration, correcting the ravages of sin was a restoration of that image.

A third point of coincidence was the immanence of God. Augustine's esthetic paradigm portrayed God as the Beauty informing all beautiful things. His biological paradigm portrayed him as the formative energy in the act of procreation. At the Creation, God gave humankind sexual organs and fertility, the congenital power to propagate the species, but he imposed no necessity of procreation. After Adam's fall, he imposed reproduction after the fashion of animals as a curse, but reproduction required more than sexual intercourse. Neither male nor female generated progeny; neither conveyed genetic form. God himself gave the increase "by that energy wherewith 'He worketh hitherto' " (John 5:17). He caused "the seeds to develop and to evolve from certain hidden and invisible folds into the visible forms of this beauty that we see [whether in human beings or in insects]. Coupling and connecting in some wonderful fashion the incorporeal and corporeal natures, the one dominant, the other submissive, He makes a living creature."[58] Thus, according to the esthetic paradigm, God was the informing principle of beauty; according to the biological paradigm, he was the principle of genetic conformity.

Above all, Augustine's esthetic and biological paradigms coincided in portraying love as an impulse to union through dominance. His elision between form and function, his theory of descent from a common prototype, and his doctrine of immanent form (or formative energy) found their dynamic center in his concept of love as "a kind of life" coupling, or seeking to couple, the lover with the object of his love.

Again, in the biological paradigm as in the esthetic one, the individual mind was the basic component of Augustine's theories about collective union. Throughout, he was guided by the principle that there existed inside each human mind a "wedlock" of contemplation and action.[59] The distinction between the sexes, in which "the two became one flesh," through the dominance of the male and the submission of the female, typified this erotic bonding. Augustine identified these two elements as the male principle, the rational part of the soul, appointed to rule, and the female principle, the appetitive part, appointed to be subject.[60] Each consisted of diverse faculties,

[58] *City of God*, 22. 24 (*Corp. Christ., ser. lat.*, 48, p. 847–48). See also *Conf.*, 1. 6 (*CSEL*, 33, p. 8), "aut ulla vena trahitur aliunde, qua esse et vivere currat in nos, praeter quam quod tu facis nos, domine. . . ." Cf. *En. in Ps.* 138: 7 (*Corp. Christ., ser. lat.*, 40, p. 1994): "For no one is born unless God form him in his mother's womb, not does any creature have a maker [*plasmator*] other than He." See below Chapter 6, n. 48.

[59] *De Trinitate*, 12. 12. 17–19 (*Corp. Christ., ser. lat.*, 50, pp. 371–73).

[60] *De opere monachorum*, 32. 40 (*CSEL*, 41, p. 594). See *Conf.*, 13. 32 (*CSEL*, 33, pp. 384–85). *De Trinitate*, 12. 3. 3 (*Corp. Christ., ser. lat.*, 50, pp. 357–58). In *De Trinitate*, 12. 12. 17–19 and 12. 13. 20–21 (*Corp. Christ., ser. lat.*, 50, pp. 371–72, 373–74), Augustine explicitly refused to follow other writers in identifying the female principle with the bodily senses.

but it was through the interplay of intelligence (including memory) and desire that the mind conceived and gave birth to knowledge. There were, Augustine wrote, three moments in which the will (as love) coupled them, each time engendering a "species" of knowledge. At the first, love coupled a material body with the senses of the perceiver, begetting sensory perception (or images) in his body. Next, it joined sensory images with memory, begetting recollection. Finally, it united recollection with mental intuition, begetting thought (or knowledge). Love united both the faculties of the mind, the generative principles of mind, and the modes of knowledge engendered, the parent with the offspring.[61]

Just as male and female were one flesh, so intellect and desire were one mind.[62] Instead of two parents, therefore Augustine actually posited a single parent—mind, consisting of intellect and desire. He went further and taught that desire and love were the same impulse; for "the same appetite that made one long to know of a thing becomes the love of the thing once one knows it while this appetite-turned-into-love holds and embraces its well-pleasing off-spring (that is, knowledge [*notitia*]) and unites it to its begetter."[63]

Augustine's esthetic argument from archetypes permitted him to argue that one person knew other minds by knowing his own and, indeed, that one could understand something about the archetype of human minds by examining it as an image of the Trinity.[64] His reasoning about the procreation of knowledge in the individual mind gave him a genetic paradigm by which he could elucidate the unity of the three divine persons, and reject the analogy that some had drawn between the Father's eternal begetting of the Son and carnal procreation by male and female.[65]

However, a person's innate love was inadequate to reveal that the dynamic trinity in the soul was the image of the divine Trinity;[66] for, just as the soul could deform, but not reform, itself,[67] so human love was generative but not regenerative. Through the Holy Spirit, God diffused a greater than human love in the hearts of the elect. From that moment, God began to be their Father, although he had predestined and loved them from

[61] *De Trinitate*, 11. 9. 16; 14. 6. 8; see also *De Trinitate*, 11. 2. 2–3 (*Corp. Christ., ser. lat.*, 50, pp. 353, 334–37; 50A, pp. 430–32).

[62] *De Trinitate*, 12. 3. 3 (*Corp. Christ., ser. lat.*, 50, p. 358).

[63] *De Trinitate*, 9. 12. 18 (*Corp. Christ., ser. lat.*, 50, p. 310).

[64] *De Trinitate*, 8. 6. 9; 14. 8–19 (*Corp. Christ., ser. lat.*, 50, pp. 283–84, 435–59).

[65] *De Trinitate*, 12. 5–6. 5–8 (*Corp. Christ., ser. lat.*, 50, pp. 359–63). Cf. *De Trinitate*, 15. 6. 10 (*Corp. Christ., ser. lat.*, 50A, p. 472), where Augustine equates the Father with the lover, the Son with the beloved, and the Holy Spirit with the love proceeding from and common to both. For Feuerbach's analogy between the doctrine of the Trinity and conjugal relations, see below n. 109.

[66] *De Trinitate*, 15. 24. 44 (*Corp. Christ., ser. lat.*, 50A, p. 522).

[67] See *De Trinitate*, 14. 16. 22 (*Corp. Christ., ser. lat.*, 50A, p. 451).

before the creation of the world.[68] As they turned to him, their very substance was changed for the better, and they gained power to become children of God, indeed, to be transformed into him.[69]

According to his esthetic paradigm Augustine argued that the formation (or reformation) of the soul followed a mimetic process. So, too, according to his biological paradigm the process of spiritual reproduction was mimetic. This was true of the reprobate as well as of the redeemed. Through the erotic bonding in their minds, the reprobate imitated Satan in self-love and became his children.[70] Through the erotic union in their minds, the elect imitated Abraham in love of God and became the spiritual seed of Abraham, sons of God.[71] Abraham prefigured Christ. As Augustine considered the genetic power of imitation, he found that the real contrast was not between the disobedience of Satan and the faithfulness of Abraham but between Satan, the mediator of death, and Christ, the mediator of life. Satan's mimetic tactics were shams and delusions. He masqueraded as an angel of light. He invented rituals and magical incantations, "sacrilegious imitations," and deployed his legions of devils to perform stupendous miracles, promising the purification of the soul, but actually reproducing his own spiritual death in each person's physical and spiritual death. Christ's mediation consisted in leading his followers through death to life. He assisted not only by the sacramental cure for sin that he brought, but also by the example of humility and obedience unto death that he set, reproducing the life that he was in those whom he engendered in the Church.[72]

Always the same, and always singular, the phenomenon of birth suggested a further aspect of imitation to Augustine. Each natural birth recapitulated Adam.[73] Each spiritual rebirth sacramentalized in baptism recapitulated the experience of the "human race as a whole," first born of Adam, "evil and carnal," and then grafted into Christ, by regeneration, "good and spiritual."[74] Augustine also thought of this "grafting" into Christ as the birth of Christ in the womb of every redeemed soul.[75]

As Augustine reflected upon the history of the elect in the world, he observed that this double recapitulation—of carnal birth and spiritual rebirth—in individual events was the process that constituted the body of Christ. The patriarchs and prophets of the Old Testament made up part of

[68] *De Trinitate*, 5. 16. 17 (*Corp. Christ., ser. lat.*, 50, pp. 226–27).

[69] *De Trinitate*, 5. 16. 17 (*Corp. Christ., ser. lat.*, 50, pp. 226–27) *Conf.*, 7. 10 (*CSEL*, 33, pp. 157–58).

[70] *Tr. in Ev. Johan.*, 42. 10, 15 (*Corp. Christ., ser. lat.*, 36, pp. 369–70, 372–73).

[71] *Tr. in Ev. Johan.*, 2. 13–16; 108. 5 (*Corp. Christ., ser. lat.*, 36, pp. 17–19, 617–18). *City of God*, 16. 25–27 (*Corp. Christ., ser. lat.*, 48, pp. 529–32).

[72] *De Trinitate*, 4. 10–13. 13–18 (*Corp. Christ., ser. lat.*, 50, pp. 178–86). *Tr. in Ev. Johan.*, 48. 6; 54. 7; 80. 1 (*Corp. Christ., ser. lat.*, 36, pp. 415–16, 462, 502).

[73] Above, n. 8.

[74] *City of God*, 15. 1 (*Corp. Christ., ser. lat.*, 48, p. 453).

[75] *De sancta virginitate*, 2. 2, 5. 5 (*CSEL*, 41, pp. 236, 239).

that body, although they lived before the birth of Christ in the flesh; they were like an infant's hand, emerging first from the womb, but still attached to the whole body.[76] Through faith and baptism, new additions were made daily to the body of Christ, while "bonded and knit together by every constituent joint, the whole frame grows through the due activity of each part, and builds itself up in love."[77]

Augustine's biological recapitulation theory therefore led him to conclude that the individual member existed for the welfare of the whole body, and that modifications introduced by the recapitulative process in individual persons occurred for the benefit of the human race, or at least for the representative part of it elected to salvation. By means of such modifications to individual persons—for example, to Abraham, David, and Christ himself—the people of God moved from each stage in the history of the world to the next, accumulating in itself the beneficial variations of earlier generations and preparing for those yet to come.[78]

Generation, as Augustine wrote, establishes relationship.[79] His doctrine of procreation identified some ways in which one could move beyond relationship to identity. Those ways coincided with others encased in his esthetic paradigm of bonding such as the elision between form and organic function; descent from a single archetype; the immanence of informing Beauty or energy; and the mutual dependence of part and whole, an esthetic assumption that had its genetic counterpart in the interdependence of member and body or of individual and species.

So far as the typology with which Augustine described spiritual procreation was concerned, the point of identity between male and female was reached in his emphasis on maternity—the maternity of each redeemed soul giving birth to Christ;[80] the maternity of the Apostle Paul generating sons through the Gospel and nourishing them with milk; the maternity of Christ, and of God, giving their milk to suck.[81]

However, Augustine's view that people imitated what they saw with the eye of the mind introduced an element into his doctrines of genetic bonding for which there was no obvious counterpart in his esthetic paradigm—namely, perfectibility through conflict. The esthetic paradigm permitted Augustine to imagine a composition (a poem, or painting, or statue, for

---

[76] De catechizandis rudibus, 19. 33 (Corp. Christ., ser. lat., 46, p. 158).

[77] City of God, 22. 18, quoting Ephesians 4:16 (Corp. Christ., ser. lat., 48, p. 837).

[78] De utilitate credendi, 9 (CSEL, 25, pp. 12–13).

[79] De Trinitate, 5. 6. 7; 5. 16. 17 (Corp. Christ., ser. lat., 50, pp. 211–12, 224–25).

[80] Above, n. 75.

[81] On Paul, see Conf., 13. 22; on Christ, Conf., 7. 18; on God, Conf., 4. 1 (CSEL, 33, pp. 64, 163, 370). Cf. Augustine's inversion of the roles of Adam and Eve and of Christ and Mary in saying "by woman came death, by woman life." See Joseph Vogt, "Ecce ancilla Domini. Eine Untersuchung zum sozialen Motiv des antiken Marienbildes," Vigiliae Christianae, 23 (1969), p. 256.

example) that would be gradually refined, perhaps by severe reconstructive methods, struggling against its own defects until it was perfected at the end of time, a movement by which the "I" of the sinner was assimilated to the "you" of Christ. The struggle of the artist to dominate matter was at the heart of this paradigm.

His biological paradigm, constructed on the analogy of male dominance and female subordination, portrayed a different kind of conflict: that of a collective body moving toward perfection both by growth and by conflict with internal as well as external enemies. The two peoples engendered by their imitation of opposite objects of love—the children of the devil and those of God—confronted each other in bitter hostility. Some of the Church's enemies appeared to be clearly identifiable; such were pagans and Jews, who persecuted the martyrs. But hidden among them there had been and were still hidden "those destined to be fellow-citizens" of the City of God, men who like the Apostle Paul became confessors of the faith that they had persecuted. There was also a lack of clarity inside the Church; for "the city of God has in her communion, and bound to her by the sacraments, some who shall not eternally dwell in the lot of the saints." Some had not yet shown their true colors; others, evidently Christians in name only, thronged the churches one day with the faithful and crowded into the theater the next day with the godless. Still others, like the Donatists, had fallen into open schism. Yet even they might eventually be reclaimed.[82]

The Church endured conflict with persecutors and with wolves masquerading as sheep of Christ's fold. Persecution proclaimed the Gospel of Christ through the signs and wonders with which God attended the torments and deaths of the martyrs, and by which he later converted the peoples who had slain them with demonic fury and the kings who had laid the Church desolate.[83] Likewise, conflicts arising from schism profited the Church in the perfection of virtue, discipline, and doctrine.[84]

Augustine returned repeatedly to a special area of conflict, that between the Church and heretics. Under the name of Christ, he wrote, heretics obstinately defended their depraved and pestilential teachings against the Church's sound doctrine. When they gained coercive powers, they were able to visit temporal persecution upon true believers. They were also able to aggrieve pious hearts because they blasphemed the Christian name, the sacraments, and the Scriptures while they professed to venerate them. But this most bitter conflict embued the saints with great fecundity; for it perfected the Church in wisdom by leading her to define wholesome doctrine,

---

[82] *City of God*, 1. 35; 18. 49 (*Corp. Christ., ser. lat.*, 47, pp. 33–34; 48, pp. 647–48). *De catechizandis rudibus*, 14. 21; 19. 31 (*Corp. Christ., ser. lat.*, 46, pp. 145–46, 155–56). *Ep. 185*: 1. 2, 7. 31, 10. 43 (CSEL, 57, pp. 2, 28–29, 37–38, and passim).

[83] *City of God*, 18. 50 (*Corp. Christ., ser. lat.*, 48, p. 648).

[84] See citations of *Ep. 185* in n. 82.

in patience by subjecting her to suffering, and in benevolence by exercising her "persuasive doctrine or terrible discipline," which latter might extend to inciting secular rulers of persecution.[85] (See discussion in Chapter 6 after n. 95.)

The genetic bonding that, according to Augustine, composed the history of the world took place in an environment of intense competition, rivalry that was particularly severe among those who claimed the name of Christ. Augustine believed that the perfection of the human species in the Church advanced through the accumulated beneficial variations that this bitter interspecific rivalry produced, first in individual men and women and, gradually, in the entire community—variations by which the "I" of the persecutors was changed into the "you" of the persecuted.

Enough has been said to indicate that Augustine's two paradigms of bonding centered on a theory of mimetic change. Love was a mimetic action in the mind of the lover, a dynamic mediation by which the lover sought assimilation with the beloved. Through the assimilative structure set forth in his esthetic and biological paradigms of bonding, Augustine applied the enigmatic assumptions that we found to be characteristic of the negative values in the bonding process (see Chapter 1, after n. 91).

First, he contended that one could be assimilated to invisible things by means of visible signs, symbols, and sacraments.

Second, he argued that signs, symbols, and sacraments represented (or made present) realities that were absent.

Third, he insisted that art must be used to conceal itself, if one were to participate in the realities that were both manifested and concealed by signs, symbols, and sacraments. This negation by which works of art became transparent could occur only if a viewer had already performed an act of self-denial by suspending his disbelief. Likewise, it was only by self-surrender that one offered visible proofs of invisible loving, or that, in a knitting together of hearts, the "I" could be perfected in the love of the "you."[86] But this insight had a pathos of its own; for friends were limited, and they separated in anger, in indifference, or in death. The only love in which one could be continually perfected, without grief of separation, was the love of God.

Fourth, he taught that disclosing and participating in the hidden content of representations depended on the capacity of the individual. Thus, as in unraveling the mute poetry of a picture, the kind and degree of mimetic action that occurred depended on the expectations that the "I" (the lover or beholder) read into the "you" (the beloved or the sign, symbol, or sacra-

---

[85] *City of God*, 18. 51 (*Corp. Christ., ser. lat.*, 48, p. 649). *Conf.*, 7. 19 (*CSEL*, 33, p. 165). *Ep. 185*: 2. 7, 2. 11, 6. 21 (*CSEL*, 57, pp. 6–7, 9–10, 19, and passim).

[86] Cf. *Conf.*, 4. 9 (*CSEL*, 33, p. 75). *De fide rerum invisibilium*, 2.4—3.5 (*Corp. Christ., ser. lat.*, 46, pp. 4–8).

ment). Love arose from a sense of beauty that, in its highest form, contradicted the senses. Such love extolled the beauty of Christ's mangled body and embraced the beauty of justice exemplified by the martyrs. The eye shrank in horror from the bodies of martyrs, their limbs torn apart, their bowels chewed open by wild beasts. There was little whole, little to love, in them except "the whole beauty of justice."[87] Some could not behold the invisible things of God manifested by visible creation.[88] Heretics misread the signs, blasphemed the symbolic language of Scripture, and received condemnation through the sacraments.[89]

Fifth, mimetic action in the mind of the lover produced diminishing likeness to the beloved as he approached identity in esthetic closure. If God were the object of love, this movement led to union with the Life of man's life, to the divinization to which man was called. If the physical world or vain human imaginings were the object of love, it led to ever greater estrangement from God, that is, to "immortal death."[90]

Largely by allegorical exegesis, Augustine unlocked these enigmas, reconstructing in logical sequence and verbal narrative the poetic act of faith working in love. By the assimilative structure of figural exegesis, he was able to mediate between the positive objective structure of theological propositions and collective norms and the negative pole of a most inward and ineffable experience. His esthetic and biological paradigms belonged to that assimilative structure or pattern of understanding. Using them, Augustine was able to explain how the "society" of the saints was built up by countless most inward acts of love through which the City of God begot its citizens.[91] Mimesis was a strategy of continual advance through conflict. Thus, the personal and social implications of the sentence, "I am you" were interdependent. The ornate conception of psychosocial renewal that Augustine delivered against what he considered the morally sick society of Rome passed through many transformations after his day.

THE PATTERN of understanding that enabled Ludwig Feuerbach to think the sentence, "I am you," was far less elaborate than the one that lay behind Augustine's doctrines. Feuerbach excluded the divine intervention in human affairs from some heavenly sphere beyond this world; for him, relationships were material and secular. Still, he needed some explanation for human bonding that performed in his theories the unifying functions that the doctrine of God performed in Augustine's. He found that explanation

[87] *Serm. 44*: 1–3 (Migne *PL*, 38: 258–60). *En. in Ps. 64*: 8 (*Corp. Christ., ser. lat.*, 39, p. 831).
[88] *De Trinitate*, 15. 6. 10 (*Corp. Christ., ser. lat.*, 50A, p. 472).
[89] Cf. *De symbolo ad catechumenos*, 8. 16 (Migne *PL*, 40: 636).
[90] *City of God*, 6. 12 (*Corp. Christ., ser. lat.*, 47, p. 184).
[91] *City of God*, 15. 1, 2; 19. 5 (*Corp. Christ., ser. lat.*, 48, pp. 453–55, 669–70).

in his conception of the human species and its reproductive processes. His functional substitution of the species for God was by no means unprecedented or unparalleled. It made contact with Augustine's theories in the rationale that they offered for genetic bonding; and indeed, one of his contemporaries, Charles Darwin, also pursued secular lines of inquiry that, in its teachings on morphology of the species, duplicated some important features of Augustine's pattern of understanding. To smooth the transition from Augustine's theology to Feuerbach's materialism, I shall digress briefly to indicate some resemblances between Augustine's and Darwin's conceptual paradigms.

Augustine wrote as a theologian about the human mind and heart. Darwin wrote as a naturalist about the physical existence of plants and animals, including the human species. It would be vain to seek analogies in the materials about which they wrote, or in the objects that they wrote to achieve. However, there are paradigmatic relationships between the two theories of transformation, possibly because both Augustine and Darwin believed that they were describing systems of biological reproduction in which the procreation of individuals altered and perfected the species by a process of selection.

For Darwin, the history of the species was a continual modeling process. Each species began with a single prototype. In response to the physical environment and, especially, to competition ("most severe between those forms that are most nearly related in habits, constitution, and structure")[92] genetic modifications were introduced. Variations appeared in individuals; changes best adapted to dominance within the conditions of existence remained, conveyed to subsequent generations through alterations of habit or physical structure. The fittest survived. Modifications that were unsuited, or inadequately suited, to the environment perished, as did transitional forms that had been superseded. Natural selection worked by accumulating slight, successive, favorable variations. Each individual was imprinted by the collective formation of the species, and each recapitulated it in the process of maturation. Embryos commonly revealed "the prototype of each great class," but a second phase of formation followed gestation in the womb. Darwin taught that "the adult differs from its embryo, owing to variations having supervened at a not early age [in past individuals a long time ago] and having been inherited at a corresponding age [in living individuals of each generation]. This process, while it leaves the embryo almost unaltered, continually adds, in the course of successive generations, more and more difference to the adult. Thus, the embryo comes to be left as a sort of picture, preserved by nature, of the former and less modified condition of the species."[93]

[92] *The Origin of the Species*, chap. 4 (New York, 1872?, from the 6th ed.), p. 112.
[93] Ibid., chap. 7, 11, pp. 240, 366.

Thus, the language of the esthetic paradigm was used in Darwin's account of biological evolution. Each individual recapitulated the prototype and the experience of the species, and each contributed to the changing formation of the species through the modifications that he himself sustained and passed on to his descendents. Individual modifications occurred for the benefit of the whole community. Consequently, "nature is prodigal in variety, though niggard in innovation."[94]

Darwin believed that the process of transformation had not ended. Through the work of natural selection, progress toward perfection continually advanced, always evolving as it had evolved in the past "endless forms most beautiful and most wonderful."[95]

Darwin applied the term "mimesis" to one, quite limited phenomenon, defensive adaptations in the appearance of some species. However, the esthetic strategy of mimesis, as I have defined it, is evident in his broad theories on the transmission and modification of form. His theory of unity of type corresponds with Augustine's doctrine of archetypes, specifically of Adam and Christ as prototypes of his two species, the reprobate and the elect. Darwin's theory that morphologic features advanced as individuals adapted to conditions of existence (including especially competition) corresponds with Augustine's idea of the beneficial effects of conflict on the City of God, and particularly of fecundity in the saints produced by the interspecific enmity of heretics. Darwin's theory of the survival of the fittest parallels Augustine's teaching that each person knew and loved according to his own capacity, that only a few were able to receive the world of God and that, among them, there were gradations of enlightenment. Darwin's theory that the individual was imprinted with the experience of the species, manifesting it in two stages (in the womb and in later maturation) coincided with Augustine's belief that the saved recapitulated Adam in their carnal births and Christ in the spiritual rebirths. Both writers insisted that the individual was modified for the good of the species, and that the advance toward perfection was cumulative and continual. However, the biological progress that Darwin envisioned in physical evolution, and which he organized and described in esthetic terms, had no imaginable end, while the spiritual progress anticipated by Augustine would end at the Last Judgment.

A final and crucial analogy exists in the role assigned by the two writers to selection. The fixed judgments of divine election performed in Augustine's doctrine of salvation a function corresponding with the trial and error of natural selection in Darwin's theory of the survival of the fittest and, through them, of the species. However, there is also a point of dissimilarity, namely, that regarding the individual's power to choose. By what means did he receive the modifications visited upon him? Darwin portrayed change

[94] Ibid., chap. 15, p. 487.
[95] Ibid., conclusion, p. 505.

as an involuntary and perhaps unwitting adaptation to conditions. Discussing modifications in the human mind, however, Augustine portrayed man as seeking his own transformation, as he moved falteringly and with the clouded eye of faith toward identity with the divine object of his love.

To illustrate the longevity of some ideas of regeneration that Augustine set forth, I now turn to another exponent of reform, Ludwig Feuerbach. Feuerbach repudiated Augustine's theology, although he claimed to be the legitimate heir of Luther, one of the greatest Augustinians. Yet, like Augustine, he was able to employ the signature, "I am you," to summarize his conviction that the basis of social unity was the esthetic and biological closure of love, a closure, after stages of conflict that issued in incorporation, with its fruits, illumination and fecundity.

FEUERBACH

Feuerbach regarded Christianity as part of the social degeneracy against which he rebelled. Yet he rejected theology, not religion. He maintained that religion expressed processes of thought and feeling by which human society was composed. With Christianity as his prime example, he argued that, by studying the processes manifested in religion, men could turn them to the advantage of politics. He anticipated that, consequently, politics as the "religion" of the state would achieve the perfection (or divinization) of the human race.[96]

Feuerbach considered love the great bond that formed religion and gave it its bonding power. Wishing not to destroy religious tradition so much as to secularize it, he embodied in his own theories of social unity elements of the very theology that he censured. However, his revisions entailed radical simplifications of what theologians, including Augustine, had taught about love.

He discarded the propositional structure of dogma, and the collective norms, of the Church. There was no need, Feuerbach argued, to posit either a supernatural dimension or, consequently, divine revelation giving access to it. He accepted as authentic only "materials which can be appropriated through the activity of the senses." He rejected the argument that human life was bound to some primordial idea or archetype that cryptically and imperfectly informed events. Events produced images (or ideals); they did not reflect them.[97] Thus, Feuerbach argued, the elaborate scheme of communication through symbols and sacraments, taught by theologians, did not correspond with the actual conditions of knowledge. The kind of veiled

[96] Sidney Hook, *From Hegel to Marx: Studies in the Intellectual Development of Karl Marx* (New York: Humanities Press, 1958), pp. 221, 243, 255.

[97] E.g., on Christ as a signifier, *Das Wesen des Christentums*, ed. Werner Schuffenhauer (Berlin: Akademie, 1973. *Ludwig Feuerbach: Gesammelte Werke*, Bd 5), pp. 441–42.

mediation between the sensory world and an invisible order that symbols and sacraments purported to achieve was, in fact, a circular reflection of the human mind upon itself. Indeed, Feuerbach did not clearly distinguish symbols from sacraments;[98] both, he argued, were created by our imaginative powers. Doctrines proclaiming their efficacy fulfilled wishes or dreams corresponding with human states of mind, but (closing the circle) those states of mind were themselves dependent on the significance that was assigned to the material elements out of which the symbol or sacrament was physically made.[99] Even the most exalted symbols and sacraments purported to consecrate everyday relations and events—such as marriage and friendship, cleansing and nourishing—things that should be sacred in and of themselves. Ritual and cult, in particular, sacrificed the real mysteries of human existence to imaginary, illusory ones.[100]

Thus, Feuerbach eliminated two of the three levels at which, Augustine argued, "I" could become "you." He excluded supernatural identification of "I" and "you." Only the level of identification within physical nature remained. It occurred through significance, through what Augustine had called "carnal images." Augustine had justified the levels of symbols and sacraments by arguing that the eye of the mind and the eye of faith could detect truths prior to, and within, the world accessible to the eye of the body. The eye of faith received the enlightenment that disclosed the truth that physical and intellectual truths reflected. Feuerbach argued that theologians had been correct in teaching that the unitive force of love worked through sensory images. They erred, he said, by intruding the element of faith, which cast up the two tiers of illusion beyond the level of material signs. They hypothesized "supernatural significance," but they were actually dealing with creatures of their own imagination.[101]

Moreover, Feuerbach argued, "faith active in love," the subjective core of theology, was malign. Faith limited, defining an exclusive community. Love universalized, embracing all. Faith defined and isolated its objects, including God. Internally consistent, it was "imprisoned within itself"; and, through the restrictions and assurances of its dogma, it gratified the need of the believer for dominance over others, for the sense of control.[102] Thereby, it contradicted love, which was free and all-embracing. Christianity, Feuerbach judged, had sacrificed love to faith. The "malignant principle" of faith had abolished "the natural ties of humanity." As Augustine had demon-

---

[98] *Das Wesen des Christentums*, p. 450, calling Baptism and the Eucharist both symbols and sacraments. See also ibid., chap. 25, pp. 406–407.

[99] Ibid. pp. 401, 404.

[100] Ibid., pp. 445, 450–51, 453–54.

[101] Ibid., pp. 401–402.

[102] Ibid., pp. 409, 416.

strated in justifying the persecution of schismatics, it sophistically vindicated deeds of hatred, calling them deeds of love.[103]

By confounding love with faith, he argued, Christian theologians had
constructed a massive edifice of doctrine. The doctrine itself was illusory,
but it contained important lessons, concerning the negative values in
human bonding. "God is the revealed interior, the expressed self of man;
religion is the solemn unveiling of man's hidden treasures, the disclosure of
his most inward thoughts, the open confession of his love-secrets."[104] At
the heart of human nature, there was a disconsolate feeling of loneliness
and a call for unity. With its dogmatic formulas about God, theology
addressed this need for "a union of beings most inwardly loving one other."
It reflected both the need and the comforting redress that human nature
itself possessed. In theology, feeling was "exalted to that level on which it
can see itself mirrored and reflected in God, its own mirror. God is the
mirror of man."[105]

Bridling love by faith, Christianity intruded religious cult and doctrine
between individuals. It had given the name of love to cruel acts of fanati-
cism; it had corrupted morality by its sophistic reasoning. But it provided a
massive and long-lived example of needful human nature at work, projecting a theoretical image of a person's sense of disunion within himself
and with other people, of his ardent need for unity, and of the mimetic
strategy of love by which personal separateness could be mediated and unity
achieved by modeling practice on theory.

Feuerbach insisted that sexual relations were the ground from which
feeling and discourse about "I" and "you" arose. "Where there is no 'you,'
there is no 'I,' but the difference between 'I' and 'you,' the primary condition of all personality, of all consciousness, is only real, living, ardent, as
the difference between man and woman."[106] "Man and woman together
first constitute the actual man; man and woman together is [sic] the existence of the race, for their union is the source of multiplicity, the source of
other men. Hence, the man who does not deny his manhood . . . knows
and feels that he is a fragmentary being, which needs [to be added to]
another partial being for the making up of a whole: of true humanity."[107]
This insight into human needfulness, Feuerbach argued, gave a key to
Christian doctrines of the Trinity. Christianity denied and repressed the
sexual instinct, with the result, however, that it created an image of God
idealizing the proceative union of male and female.[108]

[103] Ibid., pp. 435–38.
[104] Ibid., p. 46.
[105] Ibid., pp. 127, 149.
[106] Ibid., pp. 177–78. See Engels's comment that love between the sexes was one of the
highest forms, if not the highest form, of practice in Feuerbach's new religion. *Ludwig Feuerbach*, chap. 3, in Marx-Engels *Werke*, Bd 21, p. 283.
[107] *Das Wesen des Christentums*, pp. 290–91.
[108] Cf. *ibid.*, pp. 65–66, and below, n. 109.

Although dogmatic formulas about the Trinity defined three persons, Feuerbach wrote, they expressed only two principles: the "I" (the begetting Father) and the "you" (the begotten Son). Theologians had defined the personality of the Holy Spirit unclearly, as a vague personification of the love between Father and Son, reusing ideas about identity that they had already employed in defining the personalities of the Father and the Son. "Love in and by itself belongs to the feminine sex and being," and it was represented by the femininity of the Son, a "passive, suffering receptive being," "half man, half woman," by contrast with the Father, "the active principle of masculine spontaneity." The Son was "the feminine feeling of dependence in God." However, to make the feminine component more explicit, theologians introduced the Virgin Mary, "a real being," who personified the "womanly tender heart," "the mother's heart," that already beat in the Son. Christian theologians objectified and idealized the sexual relations and genetic fecundity that they repressed. "Religion," Feuerbach asserted, "is man's consciousness of himself in his empirical totality, in which the identity of self-consciousness exists only as the multiply-related, complete unity of 'I' and 'you'."[109]

Augustine's intuition of God's maternity was cast in direct opposition to writers who described the Trinity in analogues of human sexuality.[110] Still, his description of the divine persons as lover (the Father), beloved (the Son), and coupling love (the Holy Spirit) did anticipate Feuerbach's analysis. When Augustine discussed the operations of the mind as an image of the Trinity, he plainly described them as male and female principles united by love and generating various species of knowledge. He regarded the procreating trinity in the soul as replicating the eternal generation of the Son.

Feuerbach preserved this figural relationship between archetype and image, but he inverted it, arguing that the dogma of eternal generation was a projected image, not only of human sexuality, but also the creative interplay within the mind, which was both subject and object, both "I" and "you" to itself.[111]

Elucidating the movement of love by which "I" and "you" become identical, Augustine employed two paradigms. His sexual metaphors belonged to the biological paradigm but they coincided in many respects with assumptions set forth in his esthetic paradigm. On balance, Augustine subsumed his arguments in a general strategy for closing esthetic distance.

The same kinds of paradigms and the same emphasis on esthetic closure recurred in Feuerbach's teaching. The traces of biological paradigm of male dominance and female subordination are already evident. I now turn to the

---

[109] Ibid., pp. 130–49.

[110] Above, n. 65.

[111] *Das Wesen des Christentums*, pp. 29, 166–67. *Gedanken über Tod und Unsterblichkeit*, ed. Werner Schuffenhauer (Berlin: Akademie, 1981. *Ludwig Feuerbach: Gesammelte Werke*, Bd 1), pp. 302–11.

esthetic one and to the point at which the two paradigms intersected. Analyzing the conception of God was analogous with analyzing the relationship between a portrait and its subject. The conception of God (the portrait) reflected human personhood (the subject) back for its own contemplation.[112] It revealed the "holiness and goodness of human nature," qualities that one could perceive in the concept of God or in other people through "esthetic feeling, esthetic understanding."[113]

Love arose in the negative value of distance, or need; it sought closure. To satisfy the need, one had to follow the way of negation, just as one did in scrutinizing a picture for meaning. "If you possess the meaning of the picture, you no longer need the picture."[114] At the moment of negation, the work of art becomes transparent, disclosing itself as a shape and illuminated by Spirit. The figural veil is penetrated; the reality is observed and absorbed by the viewer; being becomes beauty in this manifestation, or reflection in the sensory world and in the mind that perceives its epiphany.[115] In an individual's life, the external realization of this spiritual negation is death,[116] the moment at which the significance of one's life is manifested and wholly surrendered to others.[117]

As in any quest for esthetic wholeness, pain was the feeling of distance (or estrangement), joy, that of closure (or union).[118] The ultimate feeling of union with "a being that is distinct from and yet also at one with the self" represented in doctrines of God was "nothing except the essence of feeling enraptured and enchanted with itself, intoxicated with joy, blissful in itself."[119]

Like Augustine, Feuerbach rejected the self-absorbed delights of narcissism. He repudiated the concept of the world as without a center, fragmented into as many worlds as there were individuals, a concept that he regarded as characteristic of his own day.[120] The dual character of death both as negation and as manifestation (or affirmation) proved that there was a universal reality prior to human individuality, a reality of which even personhood was a figural manifestation, in which one became through love "deeper and more than a person," and to which one must inevitably surrender his personhood.[121] That prior reality was the human species.

---

[112] *Gedanken über Tod und Unsterblichkeit*, pp. 209–10.
[113] *Das Wesen des Christentums*, p. 68.
[114] *Gedanken über Tod und Unsterblichkeit*, p. 228. Cf. ibid., p. 188, arguing that history finally grasped the meaning of the "picture" of the doctrine of the resurrection of the body, and, in so doing, dissipated the picture.
[115] Ibid., pp. 392–93.
[116] Ibid., p. 240.
[117] Ibid., pp. 312–17, 332–34.
[118] Ibid., p. 229.
[119] Ibid., p. 214. *Das Wesen des Christentums*, pp. 40–41, 43.
[120] *Gedanken über Tod und Unsterblichkeit*, pp. 263–64.
[121] Ibid., p. 215.

In the species, Feuerbach found the all-unifying principle of life, the life of lives, that Augustine had found in God. "The species infuses love into me."[122] This infused love was the comprehensive love-in-general that manifested itself in the self-surrender of particular loves, to be sure, but that could also lead one to live for the common good, becoming assimilated with objects above the finite self, and rendering one's life a continual sacrifice.[123] Consciousness of unity with and in the species revealed that "all in one [and] one is all. This is the secret of life, of the unity of the soul and the body. The one as many is the body; the many as one is the soul."[124]

Feuerbach's paradigm of sexual reproduction and his use of it as a pattern for identity between "I" and "you" was keyed to his concept of the species, with the esthetics that it entailed. The Church Fathers had reasoned that, in the body of Christ, there was a community of abilities; what belonged to one member belonged to all others.[125] Feuerbach too reasoned by analogy with the body. Its components were not parts but members, acting reciprocally to generate one product—life.[126] Similarly, in the species, what one individual lacked was supplied by another. Individual existences were single phenomena of one vast, organic system.[127] Love was the emotion by which this system mediated between separate existences to establish their cohesion. It was the movement by which, through feeling, each "I" bound himself to the existence of another, so that the being of the other became his own.[128]

Just as love was "the middle term" between the universal and the individual,[129] so "the other human being is the bond between me and the world."[130] It was in love—which (as previously noted) Feuerbach regarded as "essentially feminine"—that one became conscious of qualities in oneself that Feuerbach judged to be feminine: passive dependence, suffering, and compassion (or empathetic participation in the sufferings of others).[131] But it was also in the self-giving of love that one manifested and recognized the male principles of spontaneous and generative action.

Much of Feuerbach's attention centered on mutual exchanges of love between man and woman and among friends. But his idealization of the biological species gave him a wider esthetic framework in which "I" and "you" could move beyond relationship to identity through the interplay of

[122] *Das Wesen des Christentums*, p. 442.
[123] *Gedanken über Tod und Unsterblichkeit*, pp. 337–40.
[124] Ibid., pp. 214, 253–54.
[125] E.g., Pope Gregory I's *Cura Pastoralis*, 3. 10 (Migne *PL* 77: 63–64).
[126] *Gedanken über Tod und Unsterblichkeit*, p. 295.
[127] Ibid., pp. 303–308 and passim. Cf. *Das Wesen des Christentums*, pp. 274–75.
[128] *Gedanken über Tod und Unsterblichkeit*, pp. 228–30. See also *Das Wesen des Christentums*, p. 441.
[129] *Das Wesen des Christentums*, p. 99.
[130] Ibid., p. 165.
[131] See ibid., pp. 109, 117–21, 164–65. Above, n. 109, on the feminine nature of Christ.

positive and negative values, the framework of history. Augustine described the body of Christ as an organism continually growing toward perfection, composed of individual persons and developed by the reproductive act of mimesis repeated in every redeemed soul. Likewise, Feuerbach considered the species as an organism steadily perfecting itself through the ages, an existence composed of all individual existences and advanced by the regenerative act of mimesis through which each mind assimilated what it saw in objective manifestations (its rational knowledge) to its subjective life (its feelings).

From one viewpoint, the formation of the individual was the cause, and the formation of the collective body, the effect. From another viewpoint, these roles were reversed. The two processes permeated one another. The irreducible unit in either formation—personal or collective—was dialogue in the mind. There, the species was realized, procreated, and perfected.

The doubling of the self into objective and subjective into an inward "I" and an inward "you" could occur only at an advanced stage of culture.[132] Thinking and feeling, like every present event, were conditioned by the past.[133] They were not products of the past, and so detachable from it, as a work of art is detachable from the craftsman who produces it; for any present event, including the dialogue within the mind, subsumed its history, the ground of its being and of its transformations.[134]

Just as the inward assimilative dialogue itself could occur only at an advanced stage of culture, so too history conditioned the ways in which the dialogue was conducted. In the general advance of humankind, each stage mediated possibilities from the one before to the one after it, breaking down what had been considered cultural limits of the species and reconstituting new limits of the conceivable and the possible. In their turn, these too were overcome and superseded.[135]

Change, Feuerbach wrote, was not a shift of superficial appearances, but an engendering of essential concrete mutations. This engendering impulse was humanity, or Spirit, or love, "a real love that has flesh and blood, that reverberates as a universal force through all that lives."[136] Within the organic totality of culture, this force modulated itself in individuals, recollecting and mediating at every moment the accumulated alterations of consciousness, the expanded possibilities of existence. Such was the force that enabled Feuerbach to entrust the study of human nature, which Christianity had pursued through mythic images, to the sciences of psychology,

[132] *Das Wesen des Christentums*, pp. 28–29, 166–67.
[133] See *Gedanken über Tod und Unsterblichkeit*, p. 262.
[134] Ibid., pp. 286–88, 303–308.
[135] *Das Wesen des Christentums*, pp. 269–70.
[136] Ibid., p. 100.

physiology, and anthropology. "History is life," he concluded, "and life is history; a life without history is a life without life."[137]

Feuerbach therefore considered history as a dynamic and continuing act of mimesis (specifically, recollection), by which culture recalled, assimilated, and transformed its character.[138] Like "works of genuine art," culture contained within itself (that is, in its historical nature) grounds of its existence.[139] Yet, history was not a completed work of art, but rather a creative process that was its own end, its own creation.

Reasoning in these terms, Feuerbach kept some guiding assumptions about assimilative structure that had characterized Christian theology, even though he excluded the means of identifying the supernatural through symbols and sacraments.

Among these assumptions was the role of conflict encased in the two primary paradigms used to explain bonding—the biological and the esthetic. Indeed, Feuerbach's own writings illustrate assimilation through conflict. The structure of his most celebrated book *The Essence of Christianity*, comprises a systematic inventory of basic articles of the Christian faith. The entire doctrine of love, which I have just described, exemplifies his assimilation to the enemy. Internally, his teachings posited conflict as a condition of union. This was notable in two regards. The first marks his portrayal of the movement toward union as a struggle against the finitude of the person. All finitude, he contended, was negation. Thus, all the circumstances that defined individual life as such—experience, space and time, reason, and goals of every sort including, ultimately, death—also negated the individual. Love was the struggle to transcend the finitude of individual life, its "total negativity." The second regard in which Feuerbach's doctrines posited conflict was in their dialectical character. The realization that the individual was "nothing without and outside the object of [his] love"[140] produced a dialectical tension between lover and beloved that ended only in death or, rather, in that moment of utter self-surrender when the individual yielded himself up to the ultimate union of "I" and "you" in God, understood both as the life and as the death of the human species.

Limiting the identity of "I" and "you" to the level of natural, sensory existence, he still brought esthetic and biological paradigms into convergence, giving predominance to the esthetic. He still shaped his thinking according to the five enigmatic assumptions concerning negative values that informed Augustine's thought and that, indeed, characterized the tradition of empathetic participation as a whole.

---

[137] *Gedanken über Tod und Unsterblichkeit*, p. 287.

[138] See ibid., p. 334, where Feuerbach refers to recollection as a digestive process by which the Spirit transforms finite beings into itself.

[139] Ibid., p. 291.

[140] Ibid., pp. 342, 344.

First, he considered that the bonding of "I" and "you" took place by passing from visible to invisible things. Although he gave first importance to sensory data, his object was not the visible body but the "invisible sensible reality" that it encased, namely, life itself.[141] Particular sensory loves derived from and led toward the universal love conveyed by the species, the engendering process that was humanity and that was more real than any individual person.

Second, Feuerbach also argued that the mimetic process of bonding rendered present things that were absent. He condemned some results, such as the images and myths of theology, which expressed things that were absent because they were nonexistent. He praised other results, such as the recollection and digestion by which culture relived and assimilated its past and extended the limits of human possibility.

Third, self-negation was essential to bonding "I" and "you." Art had to conceal itself to be convincing; the viewer must suspend his disbelief. Feuerbach's whole doctrine of bonding required self-negation in the form of self-giving love, leading to a climax in death, when one surrendered oneself entirely to the recollection of others. His biological rationale also called for a unity of members dominated by "absolute interpenetrability [and] transparency in which one [component] does not darken the other . . . but rather in which one purpose penetrates everything."[142]

Fourth, Feuerbach was guided by the assumption that participatory bonding brought with it diminishing likeness, as "I" and "you" moved toward identity, toward the moment when there would remain only "the manifestation of love."[143]

Fifth, Feuerbach agreed that the process of participatory bonding was not self-evident. The mute poetry concealed in a painting was not obvious to all. Likewise, even while he professed to be the philosopher of the common man, Feuerbach taught that the process of bonding was accessible neither to the uneducated nor to many of the learned whom misconceptions and delusive philosophical commitments blinded to the actual order of things. The bonding of "I" and "you" was potential in all human relations, but not realized for all.

Evidently, as an exponent of reform, Feuerbach was the product and the interpreter of change that Augustine had also expressed. Theirs were patterns of understanding that informed doctrines about art and society with the same promise of wholeness through conflict for dominance and the same creative irony. In the first chapters of this book, I have explored the contents of a simple, declarative sentence, "I am you." I have now considered patterns of understanding through amorous and malevolent sympathy that

---

[141] Ibid., pp. 294–95.
[142] Ibid., p. 297.
[143] *Das Wesen des Christentums*, p. 115.

made that sentence thinkable, and extended its call to harmony through conflict, not only to the individual heart, but also to society as a whole. In the last two parts of this study, I shall go deeper, to the ideas about the enterprise of understanding itself that gave substance to the mediating patterns that we have now described.

PART III
UNDERSTANDING UNDERSTANDING:
THE SILENCE OF WORDS

Understanding is a re-discovery of the "I" in the "you."
This identity of spirit in the "I," in the "you," in every
subject of a community, in every system of culture, [and]
finally in the totality of spirit and of universal history
makes the co-ordination of the diverse efforts in humane
disciplines (*Geisteswissenshaften*) possible. The knowing
subject is here one with its object, and the object is the
same on every level on which it can be perceived and ana-
lysed.

Wilhelm Dilthey, "Die Aufgabe einer Kritik der
historischen Vernunft," in *Wilhelm Diltheys
Gesammelte Schriften*, Bd 7
(Leipzig: Teubner, 1927), p. 191.

INTRODUCTION

A SMALL clue can sometimes unfold into a great mystery. We began with a short declarative sentence, a concrete, but microscopic, artifact of Western culture. After unpacking the rather dense contents of its three monosyllables, we considered the patterns of understanding that made the sentence possible. Now, we have seen that those patterns are not the end of the trail. We have been dealing with a nest of puzzles, and only now are we able to approach its center. The patterns of understanding, including strategies of proof, are mediators of the sentence, not its source. We must go further to the understanding that lay within those patterns and strategies, indeed, to the understanding of understanding. Thus, we are moving from a small, concrete artifact through methods of artifice to the original materials out of which the artifact was made.

The paradigms of creative conflict that enabled interpreters to make sense of the sentence "I am you" were deeply rooted in philosophical and theological tradition. But it is one thing to understand a statement and quite another to accept it. In the career of our sentence, acceptance came from feeling; indeed, feeling preceded understanding. Minimizing the chance that the sentence "I am you" was not an empty play on words or self-delusion therefore required a strategy prior to methods of expression, a strategy made up both of logical propositions (drawn from coherent structures of philosophy, theology or both) and of esthetic, or poetic, intimation.

We have repeatedly encountered the application of that strategy as proof. Rhetoric could satisfy the demands of proof. But, as verification, the strategy dealt not only with what was demonstrable but also with what was authentic, and it was continually required to test its own adequacy as a means serving the end of authentication. The irresoluble tension between the demonstrative and the self-critical functions of the strategy is a dominant theme of the following two sections on understanding understanding. The first is on the medium of words; the next, on that of painting. For, as Hegel pointed out, only the two senses of hearing and sight have undergirded authenticating theories of perception. The other senses—smell, taste, and touch—give access to what is pleasant. But hearing and sight alone give access to the beautiful in art, and thus to the esthetic enjoyment capable of being described and authenticated in theories of understanding.[1]

In the section on words, by considering three writers, very distant from each other in time and point of view, I hope to demonstrate the convincing

[1] *Dialogi*, 2. 16 (Migne *PL* 188: 1187).

power that the strategy retained for some discerning critics through the
centuries. In their works, the three writers—Augustine of Hippo, Gerhoch
of Reichersberg, and Friedrich Schleiermacher—also displayed both the
adaptability of the strategy of understanding understanding to the demands
of different writers and of diverse cultural contexts, and the resources that
sustained interpreters as the logic of their questions continually moved
them beyond the finitude of answers.

The title of this section deserves some explanation. In the *Phaedrus* (274–
76), Plato spun a myth out of the invention of writing. He evoked a curse
over the cradle of the new skill. It would, he said, produce forgetfulness,
and, because they delivered not truth but a semblance of truth, written
words "neither [spoke] for themselves nor [taught] the truth adequately to
others." Written speeches, he continued, were like paintings. They preserved a "solemn silence," and they were contorted at will by readers who
might or might not understand them. From his own perspective, Bishop
Anselm of Havelberg (ca. 1099–1158), like Plato, placed the event of
meaning in the mind of the interpreter as, from its initial ignorance, the
understanding moved over things that could be seen to the formation of
words, and then to the formation of visible letters on the visible parchment.
There, he said, they spoke as they kept silent, and kept silent as they spoke,
arousing a reverse sequence, from visible to invisible, in the mind of the
reader, according to his capacity.[2] Like Plato, Anselm perceived that words
were silent until the reader made them speak as far as he was able to fathom
their hidden contents and that, even then, they could keep their own
secrets.

That is also to say that all interpretations in some degree falsify their
objects, for a simple reason: by selectively identifying, appraising, and
reconstituting the details of the object, each interpreter must bring to bear
the shifting patterns of the interpreter's own knowledge and an ordering
vision foreign to the object itself. Inevitably, interpreters see both more and
less than is there; more, because they may indeed understand the object
better than the maker, and less, because they can not recover the unspoken
and unspeakable elements that prompted makers, given the options of
acting or not, to call things into the world, to inform those particular beings,
rather than any others, with their inward visions, and to enable others to
participate in the vision in the work, one in heart and mind with them.
Thus, the task of authentication was always more difficult to accomplish
than that of description.

The content of the sentence, "I am you," expressed play. The paradigms—biological and esthetic—by which the sense of the sentence was

---

[2] *Vorlesungen über die Aesthetik*, Bd 1, 5th ed. of Jubiläumsausgabe (Stuttgart: Fromann,
1971), pp. 67–68.

made followed rules of the game. But something was prior even to these paradigms or rules, for they only distinguished, as rules of play do, between meaningless and meaningful actions, and established degrees of meaning. Before the paradigms was the venerable distinction between flesh and spirit, another rule, and even before that the unformed but formable play out of which the game and its rules of artifice gradually emerged. The same play in the playing continually tended to shift the game and change the rules by refining technique, multiplying exceptions, increasing handicaps. Just as some questions exceed the sum of all possible answers, so the possibilities of some play is greater than the sum of all confining forms. Game and rules, the works of artifice, could change; but play continued, the playing of the play that allowed the rules to be, to be performed, and continually to be put to the test and that could bend, stretch, and change the rules. Self-critical understanding of verbal and visual understanding was the playing of the play that gave rise to the rules, or paradigms, with which we have thus far been concerned, and to the modifications that they experienced through the centuries. Even the rule that distinguished between flesh and spirit was not impervious to change as play went on. We must now turn from the rules to the playing.

SIX

Rhetoric Swallowed up in Hermeneutic:
The Case of Augustine

ANYONE WHO REFLECTS on the assimilation of alien symbols into early Christian thought can see that what the Fathers read in the pagan texts before them was quite different from the meanings that they read into those texts. Their approach to scriptural exegesis was often similar. The Fathers' primary concern was not what Scripture said but what they thought it meant, and sometimes, more precisely, not what Scripture meant but what understanding Scripture meant. The subject of the present chapter is what understanding Scripture means; my title is taken from Todorov's observation that Augustine changed the Western tradition of symbols by subsuming rhetoric in hermeneutics.[1] The issue is the degree to which rhetoric's power to prove was subject to a higher, critical power to authenticate.

Perplexities encountered by commentators on Moses' vision of the burning bush give a point of departure. That incident exerted a continuing fascination on commentators because it purported to disclose one of the deepest mysteries, the very being of God.

Several texts, from the beginning and the end of the period in which I have an interest brought me to ask, "What does understanding Scripture mean?" Indeed, the Jewish commentator, Philo of Alexandria, anticipated a Christian perplexity when he wrote that the angelic form in the midst of the flaming bush spoke to Moses "in a silence more distinct than any voice."[2] Gregory of Nyssa imagined the sensory equivalent in sightless vision, when he taught that Moses beheld the revelations opened to him "with a seeing that consists in not seeing," his mind penetrating into the "luminous darkness" of God, beyond knowledge and comprehension.[3] At the end of the period, Teresa of Ávila (1515–82) recognized the difficulties for verbal communication presented by Moses' experience. At moments of spiritual exaltation, she wrote, when "the faculties are so completely absorbed that we might describe them as dead, and the senses as well, how can the soul be said to understand this secret?" Beyond understanding, it

---

[1] Tzvetan Todorov, *Theories of the Symbol*, trans. Catherine Porter (Ithaca, N.Y.: Cornell University Press, 1982), p. 57.

[2] Philo, *Life of Moses*, 1. 12. 66 (Loeb ed., vol. 6, p. 310).

[3] Gregory of Nyssa, *Life of Moses*, 2. 163 (Jean Daniélou, ed., *Grégoire de Nysse: La vie de Moïse* [Paris: Cerf, 1955]. *Sources chrétiennes*, vol. 1 *bis*, p. 80).

was inappropriate, Teresa added, for those who received such sublime visions "to understand them in such a way that they can describe them." To illustrate these points, she recalled Moses, who, she said, "could not describe all that he saw in the bush, but only as much as God wished him to; yet, if God had not revealed secret things to his soul in such a way as to make him sure of their truth . . . , he would not have taken upon himself so many and such arduous labors."[4] We can visualize all this as a nest of separate boxes, centering on the flash of revelation. All three authors point to one disequilibrium between God's revelation and Moses' perception, and to a second between the ineffable manifestation and the words of Scripture. There is, of course, a third, between the words of Scripture and the perception of the reader; and a fourth between the words of one interpreter and the understanding of another. If the meaning of Scripture was thus obscured at the source, what did understanding the Scripture mean?

To clarify this question, I turn once more to texts by Augustine of Hippo. The arresting aspect of his commentaries on the incident at the burning bush is not lucidity but the array of perplexities that he found by collating the account in Exodus with New Testament allusions.[5] Deft allegory could elucidate *significatio secreti* in the miraculous fact of a bush that burned without being consumed. Moral theology could clarify why, when Moses asked his name, God gave two, quite different, replies. But ingenuity was not enough to explain why, according to one account, the Lord appeared to Moses, and, according to others, an angel appeared to him. Were all true? If an angel appeared to Moses, how did Moses speak to the Lord, as he was reported to have done? Trinitarian theology posed another considerable difficulty. Were all persons of the Trinity present in the burning bush when God revealed his name as "the God of Abraham, Isaac, and Jacob"? Perhaps God had appeared in an angel, just as he appeared in fire, smoke, and sound, and, indeed, just as the mind (*anima*) appears in something other than itself, the voice. Both the conflicting accounts and the Trinitarian question could be resolved at one stroke if it were assumed that the Lord who appeared in the bush was the Son, the second person of the Trinity, in his ministry as angel.[6]

As his resort to alternative interpretations suggests, Augustine recognized that he had not conclusively dispelled the perplexities. He had, he wrote, neither the capacity nor the time to try to unfold the volumes (Augustine here deliberately used the word for "scrolls") of God's mysteries. Multiple meanings were possible, including some unintended by

---

[4] *Interior Castle*, 6.4 (E. Allison Peers, trans. [New York: Doubleday, 1961], pp. 150–51).

[5] Exodus 3:2–4, 17. Acts 7:30–34. Matthew 22:32. Mark 12:26. Luke 20:37. Hebrews 11:16.

[6] *Serm.* 6: 1–5. *Serm.* 7. 1, 4–6 (*Corp. Christ., ser. lat.*, 41, pp. 62–64, 70, 73–75). *De Trinitate* 2. 13. 23 (*Corp. Christ., ser. lat.*, 50, pp. 110–12).

Moses, the author, if only they accorded with the rules of faith, truth, and piety. There might be meanings hidden to Augustine, *sacramenta* in the Old Testament that he did not understand. As to these, he could only ask, seek, and knock that they be opened to him.[7] Even Moses, interrogating God and hearing words from the bush, was inflamed to go beyond words to sight, and "said to the God with whom he spoke, 'Show my thyself.' "[8]

Strangely, but characteristically, Augustine found no difficulty in the thought that, as he interrogated God, Moses' mind had been raised up in ecstasy and had seen truth not conveyed in what was said in the text of Scripture.[9] This discrepancy, also commented on by Gregory of Nyssa and Teresa of Ávila, might appear to have been a major barrier to understanding the account of Moses at the burning bush, even greater than the perplexities that Augustine explained away. Certainly, it excluded any recovery of the intent guiding a (supposed) author of Scripture. The reasons why Augustine did not include it among his perplexities are woven into his general concepts about mind, speech, and Scripture. I shall return to this curious aspect of Augustine's commentary at the end of the chapter.

Inability to fathom the depths of Scripture is a persistent motif in Augustine's writings. At least in part, it arose from the Father's conviction that language, including the words of Scripture itself, was caused by "the abyss of the world and the blindness of the flesh."[10] Here, "we mortals do not know the hearts of mortals," not even the hidden depths of our own hearts. But, in paradise, "when the shadows of this mortality and corruption shall have passed away," the Lord will illuminate what darkness had hidden, and manifest the thoughts of the heart, and "our thoughts also shall be visible to all."[11]

Even in this world, the words of Scripture were not needed by those who lived according to faith, hope, and charity, except to teach others; for "the charity of Christ surpasseth all knowledge." Many, Augustine wrote, lived in solitude, without books, yet their great holiness and virtue was partial by comparison with that in paradise, where "there will be no more reading of the Gospel to us; but after all pages of reading and the voice of reader and preacher have been taken away, He who at this time has given us the Gospel will Himself appear to all who are His. . . ."[12]

Thus, the object of study was not the words of Scripture but the truth in

---

[7] *Serm.* 6: 8. *Serm* 7: 3 (*Corp. Christ., ser. lat.*, 41, pp. 67, 71–72). *Conf.*, 12. 24 (*Corp. Christ., ser. lat.*, 27, pp. 233–34), on Genesis 1:1, another text attributed to Moses.

[8] *Serm.* 7: 7 (*Corp. Christ., ser. lat.*, 41, p. 76).

[9] Ibid.

[10] *Conf.*, 13: 23 (*Corp. Christ., ser. lat.*, 27, p. 262).

[11] *De Trinitate*, 1. 8. 17 (*Corp. Christ., ser. lat.*, 50, p. 50). *Enchiridion*, 32. 121 (*Corp. Christ., ser. lat.*, 46, p. 114). *City of God*, 22. 29 (*Corp. Christ., ser. lat.*, 48, pp. 861–62).

[12] *De Doctrina Christiana*, 1. 39. 43; 2. 41. 62 (*Corp. Christ., ser. lat.*, 32, pp. 31, 75–76). *Tr. in Ev. Johan.*, 22. 2; 35. 9 (*Corp. Christ., ser. lat.*, 36, pp. 223, 332–33).

the words. Understanding Scripture required exceeding the letter of Scripture, as controversialists did when they used non-Scriptural words to define
the persons of the Trinity.[13] It also required accepting the fact that the
opacity of the flesh intervened between the authors of Scripture and their
readers. The intent of an author might well be so thoroughly hidden that
no interpreter could be sure of recovering it. The result was a multiplication
of interpretations. "This obscurity," Augustine wrote, "is beneficial,
whether the sense of the author is at last reached after the discussion of
many other interpretations, or whether, though that sense remain concealed, other truths are brought out by the discussion of that obscurity."[14]
The truth in Moses' words was true whether Moses understood it or not.[15]
How could one fathom the intent of a person who is absent or dead, when
even someone present and alive might carefully hide many things?[16] If
Moses appeared and said to the host of interpreters, "I thought this," they
still could not see, but only believe, the truth in his words.[17]

Indeed, God tempered holy Scripture to convey truth in a diversity of
meanings—"a great abundance of most true meanings"[18]—all given to
build up charity. Augustine wrote that, if he had been Moses, he would
have wished God to give him such eloquence and skill in weaving texts
together that those unconvinced of the truth in his narrative would not
reject the words out of hand, and the convinced could understand, each
according to his own capacity, drawing new meanings out of the same
words.[19] Yet, despite their useful abundance, the thoughts of men were
vain, nor should one be tempted, by delight, to tarry among them. Rather,
one must stretch forward to the moment when the multitude of interpretations would cease, when God, as one, would remain "all in all," and the
whole company of the redeemed would say one thing without end, praising
him in one, having been made in him.[20]

Augustine's satisfaction with the multiplicity of interpretations and his
insistence on charity as an informing principle of exegesis did not lead him
to conclude that all interpretations were equivalent. The Jews knew the Old
Testament Scriptures, but their disbelief in Christ cast a veil over the eyes
of their hearts. Thus, Philo, "a Jew of great learning, whom the Greeks

---

[13] *De Trinitate*, 15. 26. 47 (*Corp. Christ., ser. lat.*, 50A, p. 528).

[14] *City of God*, 11. 19 (*Corp. Christ., ser. lat.*, 48, pp. 337–38). *De Doctrina Christiana*, 3.
27. 38 (*Corp. Christ., ser. lat.*, 32, pp. 99–100). *Conf.*, 12. 24, 30 (*Corp. Christ., ser. lat.*, 27,
pp. 233–34, 240).

[15] *De Doctrina Christiana*, 4. 11. 26 (*Corp. Christ., ser. lat.*, 32, p. 134). *Conf.*, 12. 24 (*Corp.
Christ., ser. lat.*, 27, p. 234).

[16] *De Utilitate Credendi*, 5. 11 (Migne *PL* 42: 73).

[17] *Conf.*, 12. 25 (*Corp. Christ., ser. lat.*, 27, p. 235).

[18] *Conf.*, 12. 25, 31 (*Corp. Christ., ser. lat.*, 27, pp. 236, 240). *De Doctrina Christiana*, 1.
36. 41 (*Corp. Christ., ser. lat.*, 32, p. 30).

[19] *Conf.*, 12. 26, 31 (*Corp. Christ., ser. lat.*, 27, pp. 236, 240).

[20] *De Trinitate*, 15. 28. 51 (*Corp. Christ., ser. lat.*, 50A, p. 535).

speak of as rivaling Plato in eloquence," could not understand the symbols pointing to Christ, and he committed to writing interpretations of gross carnality. The Jews did not understand what they knew. The veil of ignorance was also over the hearts of the Manichees, who knew both Testaments.[21] Even among Christians, learning did not equate understanding. God revealed his truth to babes and the simple, and hid it from the wise.[22] There were few who could strain forth into the secrets of Scripture, and to whom could be entrusted hidden meanings that the multitude could not grasp and, indeed, that should not be exposed to the many.[23]

These, the fewest of the few, had wisdom from beyond themselves; "for whatever kind of excellent genius they have, unless God be present, they creep upon the ground."[24] They searched for truth as unlearned men, emptying themselves by prayer so that God might fill them.[25] Adverting to the parable of the sower, Augustine wrote that he was scarcely even the basket into which Christ placed, and from which Christ scattered, his grain. "Pay attention, not to the usefulness of the basket," he wrote, "but to the charity of the seed and the power of the sower."[26]

These ideas create immense difficulties for theories of meaning. Meaning presupposes a "sender" and a "receiver." Yet, Augustine taught, the heart of any person was a hidden abyss even to himself. Who could penetrate the thought of another, or know what he was doing inside his mind, or look within his heart? By outward signs, to be sure, people conversed; but they did so as one abyss calling to another. The preachers of God's words called to the abyss, even as also the abyss of the human heart called to the hidden and dreadful abyss of God's judgments.[27]

In ordinary human discourse, many elements came into play as the meaning in the words was formed in the heart of the speaker, embodied in the words of his mouth, uttered in his voice, heard by the ears of the listener, and received in the listener's heart. In the teaching of sacred doctrine, the yet more complex—indeed, miraculous—illumination occurred by which listeners heard the word of God through the speaker.[28] But there was no force inevitably uniting these elements as links in a dependable chain of

---

[21] *Contra Faustum*, 12. 4; 12. 39 (Migne *PL* 42: 255–56, 274–75). *Tr. in Ev. Johan.*, 24. 5 (*Corp. Christ., ser. lat.*, 36, p. 246).

[22] *Conf.*, 7. 9, 21; 8.2, and freq. (*Corp. Christ., ser. lat.*, 27, pp. 102, 111, 114).

[23] *De Utilitate Credendi*, 7. 16 (Migne *PL* 42: 76). *Tr. in Ev. Johan.*, 24. 6 (*Corp. Christ., ser. lat.*, 36, p. 247). *De Doctrina Christiana*, 4. 9. 23 (*Corp. Christ., ser. lat.*, 32, p. 132).

[24] *De Utilitate Credendi*, 10. 24 (Migne *PL* 42: 82).

[25] *De Utilitate Credendi*, 7. 16 (Migne *PL* 42: 76). *En. in Ps. 41*: 8 (*Corp. Christ., ser. lat.*, 38, p. 465). *De Doctrina Christiana*, 4. 15. 32 (*Corp. Christ., ser. lat.*, 32, pp. 138–39).

[26] *De Disciplina Christiana*, 1. 1 (*Corp. Christ., ser. lat.*, 46, p. 208).

[27] *En. in Ps. 41*: 13–15 (*Corp. Christ., ser. lat.*, 38, pp. 470–71. See also *Conf.*, 13. 13 (*Corp. Christ., ser. lat.*, 27, p. 249).

[28] Augustine, *Serm.* 120 (Migne *PL* 38:677–78).

transmission. The unilluminated misunderstood the speaker's meaning; the illuminated received it in diverse ways.

This approach is indeed a strange hermeneutics. It displays the familiar characteristics of hermeneutics. It enters into words. It seeks to understand, explain, interpret, and criticize. Yet it denies the "common hermeneutical assumption that an interpretation is authentic when it corresponds to what was originally the author's own interpretation and restores it without transformation."[29] Indeed, Augustine's remarks appear to anticipate Heisenberg's uncertainty principle. By observation, the viewer changes the phenomenon. In fact, Augustine's hermeneutics, banishing certainty of recovery and illumination, glories in a stochastic doctrine of multiplicity. Further, it is not unusual that Augustine's hermeneutics dealt with what was unsaid in the words. Other hermeneutics, too, have recognized the unsayable and the unthought in what was said. When he reflected on these things, Heidegger asked, "What are poets for?"[30] Perhaps, it is significant that Augustine did not ask, "What are interpreters of Scripture for?" What is remarkable is that, for him, authentic hermeneutical discourse was wordless, and even lacked such extension in time as speech requires.

Let us draw a few strands together: The perplexities that Augustine identified in understanding Scripture arose on two counts. The first was "the blindness of the flesh," notably as expressed in the discrepancy between words and thought. This was a general barrier, both to knowledge and to communication. Augustine's insistence on the inaccessibility of one mind to another through words is striking in a rhetorician and, moreover, in a man who celebrated "the marvellous nimbleness which has been given to the tongue and the hands, fitting them to speak and write" as testimonies to the providence of the Creator.[31]

The second count on which perplexity arose was particular, namely, the hiddenness of Scripture itself. These negative values define Augustine's hermeneutics as much as his positive assertions; for although they were impediments, they also had to be numbered among the circumstances that made communication both necessary and possible.

Consequently, I suggest, understanding Scripture meant two contradictory things: first, the estrangement of each human being from God and neighbor, and, second, the renewal through charity of unity with God and with other redeemed souls in God. Augustine defined charity as the move-

---

[29] Robert Denoon Cumming, "The Odd Couple: Heidegger and Derida," *Review of Metaphysics*, 34 (1981), pp. 493–94. Professor Gary Shapiro kindly called my attention to this article.

[30] "What are Poets for?" in Martin Heidegger, *Poetry, Language, Thought*, trans. Albert Hofstadter (New York: Harper and Row, 1971), pp. 89–142.

[31] *City of God*, 22. 24 (*Corp. Christ., ser. lat.*, 48, p. 850).

ment of the soul toward the object of love.[32] Negative values were still to be reckoned with so long as that movement fell short of perfect unity.

To say that understanding Scripture meant both estrangement through sin and union through charity does not fully answer the question, "What does understanding Scripture mean?" For understanding Scripture also meant itself. This second level of understanding will help us grasp the interplay of positive and negative values in Augustine's hermeneutics. Let me explain.

Augustine consistently defined signs as sensual things.[33] Accordingly, the movement of the mind, in understanding, could not be called a sign. Yet, as is evident from what has been said thus far "the action of the mind" of a person who made sensual signs (such as words) was itself an *actio significativa*.[34] It had meaning in part because it was "the truth [or lack of truth] within the words"[35] that one chose and used to convey to another's mind, insofar as he was able, the movement of his spirit.[36] In a deeper sense, understanding also had meaning because reflecting upon the act of understanding—understanding understanding, as it were—turned the attention of the mind and the feelings to objects of thought that understanding denoted by likeness, contiguity, or contrast. One of those objects of thought denoted by understanding understanding was the Trinity, in whose image the mind was made. In the act of seeing itself through itself, the understanding actualized that image and contemplated its divine archetype as it remembered, understood, and loved itself.[37] When it actualizes the image of the Trinity in this fashion, the mind becomes the meaning that it begets, rather as, in Augustine's theology, God the Father uttering himself begot the Word that was his equal in all things.[38]

The soul's act of self-reflection therefore signified, as image signifies archetype, and, by actualizing itself as image, the image participated in the archetype. By its movement of self-reflection, the soul was both "sender" and "receiver." In this sphere of meaning, as in Scriptural interpretation, it was possible for everything to signify, but for the signs to go unrecognized,

[32] *De Doctrina Christiana*, 3. 10. 16 (*Corp. Christ., ser. lat.*, 32, p. 87).

[33] *De Magistro*, 8. 24 (*Corp. Christ., ser. lat.*, 29, pp. 183–84). *De Doctrina Christiana*, 2. 1. 1 (*Corp. Christ., ser. lat.*, 32, p. 32). See Jaroslav Pelikan, *The Mystery of Continuity: Time and History, Memory and Eternity in the Thought of Saint Augustine* (Charlottesville: University Press of Virginia, 1986), pp. 18–26 (on memory and forgetting), 123–39 (on sign, event, and sacrament).

[34] Cf. *De Trinitate*, 2. 6. 11 (*Corp. Christ., ser. lat.*, 50, p. 96). *De Doctrina Christiana*, 2. 2. 3 (*Corp. Christ., ser. lat.*, 32, p. 33).

[35] *De Doctrina Christiana*, 4. 11. 26 (*Corp. Christ., ser. lat.*, 32, p. 134).

[36] *De Doctrina Christiana*, 2. 2. 3 (*Corp. Christ., ser. lat.*, 32, p. 33). See also the mind (*anima*) in the voice, *Serm.* 7: 4 (*Corp. Christ., ser. lat.*, 41, p. 73).

[37] *De Trinitate*, 14. 7. 10 (*Corp. Christ., ser. lat.*, 50A, p. 434). *En. in Ps. 41*: 7 (*Corp. Christ., ser. lat.*, 38, p. 465).

[38] *De Trinitate*, 15. 14. 23 (*Corp. Christ., ser. lat.*, 50A, p. 496). Cf. *De Trinitate*, 15. 11. 20 (*Corp. Christ., ser. lat.*, 50A, p. 489).

except by those who knew immediately the objects that they signified.[39] Understanding signs that were made to signify (as in Scripture), however, differed from the act by which observers (or spectators) foisted meaning upon things that had no meaning (as in superstitious practices such as augury).[40] Like Scripture, the process of understanding was full of secrets.

Augustine portrayed understanding as a study in discontinuities issuing from the dichotomy of body and soul. The bases of thought were random sensory impressions absorbed in memory "as though in a belly" for later rumination.[41] Thought occurred in a throwing movement, as something formable but not yet formed was tossed back and forth among the impressions of what was already known. It was formed as a concept—what Augustine called "the true word," "the inner word," or "the word of the mind"[42]—when, by the spinning motion with which it was hurled, it took on likeness to the known. It was "reified," known and thought in the same manner, and spoken in the heart without a vocal word, even without the thought of a vocal word in any language.[43] In this preverbal utterance, knowledge is spoken as it really is.[44]

Thus, the mind began with the sensory perceptions that it had in common with beasts, and ascended to "the rational cognition of temporal things."[45] In this progression, the mind displayed its triune resemblance to the Trinity; for it engaged memory, understanding, and will. Also portrayed as desire or love, will was the bond between memory and understanding; for, whether in physical or in intellectual perception, will directed the sight of the eye to an object, thus producing vision.[46] Consequently, Augustine defined understanding as "that by which we understand while we are thinking: that is, when, after things that had been present to the memory but were not being thought have been recovered, our thought is formed; and [it] further [includes] that will (*voluntas*) or love (*amor*) or desire (*dilectio*) which unites this offspring (knowledge) and parent (*ratio*) and is in a certain fashion common to both."[47]

When he discussed sexual reproduction, Augustine distinguished (as we

---

[39] Cf. *Tr. in Ev. Johan.*, 24. 6 (*Corp. Christ., ser. lat.*, 36, p. 247). *De Utilitate Credendi*, 13. 28 (Migne *PL* 42: 85).

[40] *De Doctrina Christiana*, 2. 24. 37 (*Corp. Christ., ser. lat.*, 32, p. 60).

[41] *De Trinitate*, 12. 14. 23 (*Corp. Christ., ser. lat.*, 50, p. 377).

[42] *De Trinitate*, 14. 14. 20–15. 25 (*Corp. Christ., ser. lat.*, 50A, pp. 448–52).

[43] *De Trinitate*, 15. 15. 25 (*Corp. Christ., ser. lat.*, 50A, p. 499). Cf. Augustine's reference to the rhythm of heard music resting "without tempo in some secret and deep silence" in the mind. *De Trinitate*, 12. 14. 23 (*Corp. Christ., ser. lat.*, 50, p. 377). Cf. *De Trinitate*, 15. 11. 20 (*Corp. Christ., ser. lat.*, 50A, p. 487).

[44] *De Trinitate*, 15. 11. 20 (*Corp. Christ., ser. lat.*, 50A, p. 488).

[45] *De Trinitate*, 12. 15. 25 (*Corp. Christ., ser. lat.*, 50, p. 379).

[46] *De Trinitate*, 12. 15. 25; 13. 20. 26; 14. 8. 11 (*Corp. Christ., ser. lat.*, 50, p. 379; 50A, pp. 418–19, 436–38).

[47] *De Trinitate*, 14. 7. 10 (*Corp. Christ., ser. lat.*, 50A, p. 435).

saw) two formative acts. The first, performed by a man and a woman, was propagative. The second, performed by God, was conformative. God gave the essential form to the offspring in the womb and coupled the spiritual and corporal natures.[48] When Augustine considered the begetting of the "true word" in the mind—"the word before any sound, before any thought of sound,"[49] he detected conformation by God only when, having progressed from sensory perception to knowledge, the mind moved further from knowledge to wisdom—that is, from rational cognition of temporal things to intellectual cognition of eternal things, which latter required participation in God.[50]

In rational cognition, the mysterious instant when the mind's eye was formed, or conformed, with the object of contemplation could be described as a rapid flash of light flooding through the mind (*animus*) and quickly withdrawing into its secrets, leaving vestiges in the memory from which vocal words were formed.[51] I repeat that conformation of image with archetype included participation of the image in the archetype. As image, the mind's eye became that with which it was conformed. This transformation into likeness was true of understanding in general. Understanding Scripture required, in addition, a yet higher mystery.

Augustine insisted that those who sought the will of God must study and memorize the text of Scripture, even if they did not understand it.[52] Even though God himself signified by the words in Scripture, he was able to divide the gift of desire for study from that of understanding.[53] Insofar as expositors understood and spoke the truth, they did so by divine inspiration, by God's working in them.[54] To be sure, what they saw through God's spirit, he saw, and what they spoke through his spirit, he spoke, though, dwelling in eternity, he did not see or speak, as they did, in time.[55]

Augustine described the joy of this inward enlightenment and participation of God in many ways. He recalled how, as he walked in the streets, he would sometimes hear bands of musicians playing in front of houses where lavish celebrations were underway. Walking by desire in this world, a person sometimes heard the joyfulness of an inner and intelligible sound, such that all external sounds were cast aside, and was snatched up into the most inward places, while still bearing the fragility of the flesh. Following

[48] *City of God*, 22. 24 (*Corp. Christ., ser. lat.*, 48, pp. 847–48). See above. Chapter 5, n. 58.
[49] *De Trinitate*, 15. 12. 22 (*Corp. Christ., ser. lat.*, 50A, pp. 493–94).
[50] *De Trinitate*, 12. 15. 25; 14. 8. 11; 14. 19. 26 (*Corp. Christ., ser. lat.*, 50, p. 379; 50A, pp. 436–38, 457–59).
[51] *De cat. rud.*, 2. 3 (*Corp. Christ., ser. lat.*, 46, pp. 122–23).
[52] *De Doctrina Christiana*, 2. 9. 14; 4. 5. 8 (*Corp. Christ., ser. lat.*, 32, pp. 41, 121).
[53] *Conf.*, 13. 24 (*Corp. Christ., ser. lat.*, 27, p. 363). *De Doctrina Christiana*, 3. 37. 56 (*Corp. Christ., ser. lat.*, 32, pp. 115–16).
[54] *Conf.*, 12. 25; 13. 37 (*Corp. Christ., ser. lat.*, 27, pp. 235, 272).
[55] *Conf.*, 13. 29 (*Corp. Christ., ser. lat.*, 27, p. 268).

the sweet and hidden delight of that sound, he tracked the instrument that sounded and, withdrawing from every noise of flesh and blood, came to the house of God.[56] The erotic metaphor of begetting also entered into the formation of this "inner word" in understanding Scripture. Our darkness, Augustine lamented, had been stripped of the garment of God's light. "Give yourself to me, my God, and give yourself to me. Behold. I love, and, if it is too little, may I love more powerfully, beyond measure, so that I may know by how much love I fall short of that which is enough, so that my life may run into your embraces, nor be turned aside until it is hidden in the hiding place of your countenance."[57]

Adverting, as he often did, to 2 Corinthians 5:6–7—"whilst we are at home in the body, we are absent from the Lord; for we walk by faith, not by sight"—Augustine habitually distinguished between sight and faith—that is, between the perception of God by direct vision that the redeemed would enjoy in paradise, and perception of him through indirect signs and sacraments of faith in this world. He applied a similar distinction to preverbal and verbal modes of understanding. As concerns the body, he wrote, seeing and hearing were two separate senses: in the mind (*animus*) they were the same, and inward discourse was vision.[58] Because the sight of thinking so closely resembled the sight of knowing, the "word of the mind" had such truth as was humanly accessible; for that which was in knowledge was also in the word, and that which was not in knowledge was not in the word.[59] Just so, after the resurrection, the redeemed would see each other's thoughts.[60]

This identity through participation was not possible when the preverbal word of thought was rendered into verbal signs. In the mind, knowledge could be spoken according to its true being. But this was not so in sounds and other signs that could be heard or seen by the body.[61] The slow, intricate unfolding of speech belonged to an order entirely different from that of the rapid flash of understanding, and different even from that of the vestiges that that flash left, by its swift flight, in the memory. Augustine was oppressed by awareness that, through words, he could not enable his hearers to understand all that he understood; the sounding words of his tongue could not convey the inward delights of his heart.[62] When his subject was the ineffability of God, his words fell so far short of what he wished

[56] En. in Ps. 41: 9 (Corp. Christ., ser. lat., p. 467).
[57] Conf., 13: 8 (Corp. Christ., ser. lat., 27, p. 246).
[58] De Trinitate, 15. 10. 18 (Corp. Christ., ser. lat., 50A, p. 485).
[59] De Trinitate, 15. 11. 20 (Corp. Christ., ser. lat., 50A, p. 488).
[60] Above n. 11.
[61] De Trinitate, 15. 11. 20 (Corp. Christ., ser. lat., 50A, pp. 486–488). Cf. De Trinitate 15. 15. 24 (Corp. Christ., ser. lat., 50A, p. 498).
[62] De cat. rud., 2. 3 (Corp. Christ., ser. lat., 46, pp. 122–23). De Doctrina Christiana, 1. 13. 12; 2. 13. 19 (Corp. Christ., ser. lat., 32, pp. 13, 44–45).

to say that, when he had spoken, he felt he had done nothing more than wish to speak.[63]

Nor could understanding Scripture be conveyed by spoken words to those who were blind to the signs of Scripture. Thus, when challenged by the question "Where is thy God?" the pagan could display his idol to Augustine's fleshly eyes; but the pagan did not have the inward eyes to which Augustine could show his God. The sower cast his seed among those who despised, censured, or derided him.[64] Not desiring truth, the unbelieving Jews were far from Truth itself, even while they stood beside Christ and heard his voice.[65]

The ceaseless movement of thought by which things lived and died as they entered and slipped out of memory, the throwing of "formless yet formable" perceptions here and there among existing impressions and concepts, characterized the imperfection of this life. For, in paradise, just as the thoughts of the redeemed would be open to the sight of all, so too their thoughts would no longer go and come from some things to others, but they would see their knowledge entire, at a single glance.[66] The sounds of words were incommensurable with the sight of knowledge. They were, like the flames in the burning bush, a corporal apparition that existed to signify something and then to pass away.[67] But they signified only to the converted, only to those who could participate in the realities that they represented.

Augustine repeatedly asked what purpose could be served by translating into words the visions disclosed to the eye of the heart. The individual preacher could only be grieved when his soul slipped away from the contemplative sweetness of God's house, thwarted by the inadequacy of his speech to convey to others his inward joy,[68] and burdened by the rapid volleys in the mind and the ebb and flow of memory. But, for Augustine, love—holy or perverse—encompassed the individual in a wider society. "Charity," he wrote, "which holds men together in a bond of unity, would not have a means of infusing souls and virtually mixing them together if men could teach nothing to men."[69] Interpreting Scriptural understanding in words was, in fact, an extension of the charity that drew the interpreter to read Scripture and that illuminated his inward vision. Had not Christ descended to the weak to gain the weak? Likewise, the charity of the

---

[63] *De Doctrina Christiana*, 1. 6. 6 (*Corp. Christ., ser. lat.*, 32, p. 9).

[64] *En. in Ps. 41*: 6 (*Corp. Christ., ser. lat.*, 38, pp. 463–64). *De Disciplina Christiana*, 13. 14 (*Corp. Christ., ser. lat.*, 46, p. 223).

[65] *Tr. in Ev. Johan.*, 48, 3 (*Corp. Christ., ser. lat.*, 36, pp. 413–14).

[66] *De Trinitate*, 15. 15. 24; 15. 16. 26 (*Corp. Christ., ser. lat.*, 50A, pp. 498, 501).

[67] Cf. *De Trinitate*, 2. 6. 11 (*Corp. Christ., ser. lat.*, 50, p. 96).

[68] *De cat. rud.*, 2. 3 (*Corp. Christ., ser. lat.*, 46, pp. 122–23). *En. in Ps. 41*: 10 (*Corp. Christ., ser. lat.*, 38, p. 467).

[69] *De Doctrina Christiana*, pref., 6 (*Corp. Christ., ser. lat.*, 32, p. 4).

preacher, after descending to discourse in words, returned strengthened into its inmost places.[70] Clashing in charity, the host of interpretations set forth by different writers sifted ever more finely the obscure texts of Scripture and progressively disclosed the Truth to which they all witnessed.[71] Charity was supremely an act of participation.

In the movement of participation that charity was, neither speaking nor learning was the task of isolated individuals. "When the good faithful speak to others who are good and faithful, both speak what is their own, for God is theirs, and those things that they speak are His." For "every man is a liar; insofar as men are not liars they are not men, since they are gods and sons of the Most High."[72] Even more, as men speaking to men, preachers exemplified the call of abyss to abyss; yet, like the Apostle Paul, they called, not in their own voices but, to use the Psalmist's metaphor, in the roaring voice of God's cataracts.[73] As for those who heard in charity, Augustine portrayed Christ saying, "When one of the least of mine learns, I learn."[74]

I have come again to charity, but with a difference. We now perceive that understanding Scripture—and, even more, expounding Scripture—remained exercises in interrogation. Why interrogation? Human discourse was necessary and possible because of the hiddenness of one soul from another. Discourse was also defined by other negative values—for example, the discontinuities in the cycle of receiving and uttering. There were discontinuities between things and perceptions of things, between perceptions and understanding, and between understanding and words. These remained formidable negative values. The cycle itself was being bracketed at each end by the gulf between soul and body. Beyond these defining negatives, the yet more impenetrable negative value of God's inscrutability defined the enterprises of understanding and expounding Scripture. Thus, Augustine distinguished between the human mind, questioning in this world and contemplating in paradise. He yearned for the light of heaven, in which there would be no question. Then, the mysteries of God "need no more be given tongue by us in words of faith and sounding syllables, and we may imbibe them in that silence with most pure and burning contemplation." No longer would words be needed and no longer would they fall short of understanding; no longer would understanding be something attempted rather than achieved.[75]

[70] De cat. rud., 10. 15 (Corp. Christ., ser. lat., 46, pp. 137–38).
[71] City of God, 11. 19 (Corp. Christ., ser. lat., 48, pp. 337–38). De Doctrina Christiana, pref., 8–9 (Corp. Christ., ser. lat., 32, pp. 5–6).
[72] De Doctrina Christiana, 4. 29. 62 (Corp. Christ., ser. lat., 32, pp. 166–67). En. in Ps. 115: 3 (Corp. Christ., ser. lat., 40, p. 1654).
[73] Conf., 13. 13 (Corp. Christ., ser. lat., 27, p. 249).
[74] Tr. in Ev. Johan., 21. 7–8 (Corp. Christ., ser. lat., 36, pp. 216–17).
[75] De Trinitate, 15. 25. 45 (Corp. Christ., ser. lat., 50A, pp. 523–24). De cat. rud., 25. 47 (Corp. Christ., ser. lat., 46, p. 171).

Augustine frequently underscored his distinction between faith in this world and sight in the next by referring to Matthew 7:7: "Ask and it shall be given you; seek and ye shall find; knock and it shall be opened unto you" (also Luke 11:9). He concluded two of his major works, *On the Trinity* and the *Confessions*, with this interrogative command,[76] and he contrasted his quest with the efforts of those who not only did not knock, but even barred the door to Christ.[77]

To question was not to doubt. Storm-tossed, Peter in his dread saw Christ walking upon the waves. The Lord said, "It is I. Fear not." "If it be you," Peter said, "command me to come to you across the water; thus I prove whether it is you, if you can do in your word what you yourself can do." Christ said: "Come." And "the word of Him who commanded was made the power of him who heard." Yet, as he walked upon the waves, Peter, becoming fearful, began to sink, crying out, "Lord, I perish." Christ reached forth his hand, and raised him, saying, "O thou of little faith, wherefore did you doubt?" So, too, Christians, feeling in tribulation that they were "cast out from before [God's] eyes," should cry out to him, not with their lips, but inwardly with the heart, where God heard the voice of prayer. They should cry in fear and trembling, but not in doubt.[78]

Here too understanding Scripture converged with the participatory movement of charity. For, in one text, Augustine wrote: "Now, this is the true faith of Christ, which the Apostle speaks of, 'which worketh by love'; and, if there is anything that it does not yet embrace in its love, it asks that it may receive, seeks that it may find, and knocks that it may be opened to it."[79] In another text, he wrote "To the love of God we are invited by the Gospel, where it is said, 'Ask, seek, knock,' [Matt. 7:7], by Paul, when he says, 'that ye, being rooted and grounded in love may be able to comprehend' (Eph. 3:7), and by the prophet, when he says that wisdom can easily be known by those who love it, seek for it, desire it, watch for it, think about it, nurture it [cf. Sap. 6:12–16]."[80]

Thus, as participation, understanding Scripture was its own meaning, first, through the affects, in charity, and, second, through cognition, in questioning.

Augustine's discussion of the affective and cognitive sides of understanding are rich in connotations that point to meanings within meanings. The description of thought as a throwing movement, a volley back and forth, came naturally to his mind. As a boy, he played ball in a highly

[76] *De Trinitate*, 15. 28. 51 (*Corp. Christ., ser. lat.*, 50A, p. 534). *Conf.*, 13. 38 (*Corp. Christ., ser. lat.*, 27, p. 273).
[77] *Tr. in Ev. Johan.*, 2. 9 (*Corp. Christ., ser. lat.*, 36, p. 16).
[78] *En. in Ps. 30*: 10 (*Corp. Christ., ser. lat.*, 38, pp. 219–20).
[79] *Enchiridion*, 31. 117 (*Corp. Christ., ser. lat.*, 46, p. 112).
[80] *De Moribus Ecclesiae*, 18. 24 (Migne PL 32: 1325–26).

competitive spirit, flogged by a schoolmaster for playing, tormented with rage and envy toward the winner.[81] Discussion of letters always recalled to his mind schoolroom floggings as manifestations of love, both of his parents and of schoolmasters. To become expert in a subject, one learned it by great pains, he wrote, "and he who loved you gave you over to those pains; in loving he had you flogged" to learn letters. The association with flogging and love pervaded Augustine's account of God's dealing with him in the years of his conversion and in his overarching doctrine that fear was necessary in learning to live well.[82] Training in letters also brought to mind associations with the wrestling school (*palaestra*) and theater.[83] Constant reflection on, and exposition of, Scripture brought to mind analogues of wrestling and racing; doctrinal controversy was an analogue of battle. Christ was the "master of the bouts."[84]

To use Augustine's terms, these impressions, largely of games in amphitheater, theater, and circus, had been stored up for rumination in the memory. He had thrown his "unformed but formable" perceptions of knowledge among them until, by an interplay of memory, understanding, and desire, his hermeneutics (the concept of understanding Scripture) was begotten, having the form or image of the knowledge from which it was born[85] and, like all images, participating in the nature of its archetype.

It is no accident that the form, or image, was so clearly one of play— especially competitive play—to one who confessed an intense "love of playing" in childhood[86] and who singled out as two indices among many of the height that culture had reached in his own day the amazing spectacles exhibited in theaters, incredible except to those who saw them, and the contrivances for capturing, killing, or taming wild beasts.[87] For Augustine's whole portrayal of understanding Scripture defines a game in which some are masters and others are at different stages of proficiency, a game of competition accented by deception, misread signals, and surprises, set off by its rules in a ritual time and space that were in but not of the world. The game was one in which paradoxes were resolved in enigmas, and contraries became identical. It gave each participant a role to learn and play, a position to master on the field—a role or position that, for the duration of the game,

---

[81] *Conf.*, 1. 9 (*Corp. Christ., ser. lat.*, 27, p. 9).

[82] *De Disciplina Christiana*, 11. 12; 12. 13 (*Corp. Christ., ser. lat.*, 46, pp. 219, 220–21).

[83] *Conf.*, 1. 19 (*Corp. Christ., ser. lat.*, 27, p. 16). For further discussion of Augustine's metaphors of play see Chapter 4 at nn. 12, 19; Chapter 5 at n. 49; and below n. 100.

[84] *De Doctrina Christiana*, 4. 26. 56 (*Corp. Christ., ser. lat.*, 32, p. 162). Tr. in *Ev. Johan.*, 35. 9 (*Corp. Christ., ser. lat.*, 36, p. 322). Cf. *Conf.*, 6. 9 (*Corp. Christ., ser. lat.*, 27, p. 81), on the use of an unspecified metaphor from the circensian games to correct Alypius. On Christ as "agonotheta magnus," *De Symbolo*, 3. 9 (*Corp. Christ., ser. lat.*, 46, p. 192). On battle metaphors, see, for example, *C. litt. Petil.*, 3. 11. 12–3. 13. 14 (Migne *PL* 43: 354–55).

[85] Cf. *De Trinitate*, 15. 12. 22 (Corp. Christ., ser. lat., 50A, p. 493).

[86] *Conf.*, 1. 19 (*Corp. Christ., ser. lat.*, 27, pp. 16–17).

[87] *City of God*, 22. 29 (*Corp. Christ., ser. lat.*, 48, p. 849).

transcended his natural character. It was a game of ultimate risk, a game that acquired its own order, its own meaning, in play. "The concept of play," Huizinga wrote, "merges quite naturally with that of holiness."[88]

Augustine cognitively described this play as the oscillation between image and archetype. "Whoever therefore can understand the word that precedes, not only sound, but even the images of sounds that are turned over by thought . . . can already see through this mirror and in this enigma some likeness of that word of which it was said, 'In the beginning was the Word, and the Word was with God, and the Word was God.' "[89]

But the affect of charity kept the cognitive questioning that led from image to archetype clear of doubt. Augustine described the search in this play of hide-and-seek as panting, or as hungering and thirsting. An example occurs in his description of the spiritual ecstasy that he experienced together with his mother. With words, he tells how, panting for the fountain of life, they thought about the coming eternal life of the saints, which "neither the eye hath seen, nor the ear heard, nor hath it arisen in the heart of man." Swept up by burning affection, Augustine and Monica silently passed through inward thought over created things, transcending their own minds. Straining forward beyond the things in which they loved God to God himself, they attained by a sudden stroke of the heart to eternal wisdom that speaks not through the tongue of the flesh, or the voice of an angel, or enigmas of similitude, but through itself. For an "instant of understanding," they perceived in their ecstasy of love how it might hereafter ravish and absorb its beholder and hide him forever in its inmost joys. They heard wisdom speaking and they sighed; leaving there the first fruits of their spirits, they returned to the sounds of their mouths, where words begin and end.[90]

The play of image and archetype was a visual analogue of that between word and meaning. I can now return to the curious facts that, when Augustine commented on the episode of Moses at the burning bush, he neither concerned himself with the intent of the author of the Scriptural text nor weighed the discrepancy between what Moses saw at the bush, when his mind was raised in ecstasy, and what he was thought to have said in Scripture.

From the preceding discussion, it is possible to grasp why understanding this text of Scripture was conterminous with the cognitive and affective meaning derived from the text. For Moses was not the sender of the meaning, but rather, like the readers of Scripture, a recipient. His interrogation of God at the burning bush exemplified the faithful questing of true Christians for the archetypical Word of which the "word of the mind" was

[88] *Homo Ludens. A Study of the Play Element in Culture.* (Boston: Beacon, 1955), p. 25.

[89] *De Trinitate*, 15. 10. 19 (*Corp. Christ., ser. lat.*, 50A, p. 485).

[90] *Conf.*, 9. 10 (*Corp. Christ., ser. lat.*, 27, pp. 147–48).

an image, and verbal words, remote and carnal signs, and for the direct vision that superseded types and shadows.

Interrogating God, Moses learned his name: "I am who am." Then, "inflamed with desire to see what is, he said to the God with whom he spoke, 'Show me thyself.' " This was a cry in which fear entwined with revelation, not with doubt.

Like Peter, sinking into the waves, Moses cried in his ecstasy of fear, "I am cast away from before your eyes."[91] He was driven to despair by the name, "I am who am," perceiving at a flash how entirely different God was from human beings, and how powerless he himself was in the presence of perfect Being. But, as Christ raised Peter from the waves, so God raised Moses up from despair by revealing his second name: "I am the God of Abraham, the God of Isaac, and the God of Jacob": that is to say, immutable in the perfection of being, God yet did not wish to be apart from changeful mortals. "If we can after a fashion seek God and inquire into Him who is—and, indeed, 'He is not afar off from any of us: For in Him we live and move and have our being' [Acts 17:27–28]—let us therefore wordlessly (ineffabiliter) praise His being and love His mercy."[92] The participatory act of understanding is its own meaning, understanding that is interrogation through love that began in fear.

His enemies found Augustine's approach to authenticating the sense of Scripture repellent. Given the Father's emphasis on interrogative play, and on the stochastic nature of the entire enterprise of understanding, it is easy to grasp how one of them, the Donatist bishop, Petilian of Cirta, denounced him as a "mere dialectician," by implication a forger of lies,[93] and one, moreover, given to the skepticism of the Academics, neither affirming nor denying his objections, raising up uncertainty in the place of certainty, preventing readers from believing what was true, and, indeed, making them consider such things most doubtful.[94]

With the ear of an expert controversialist, Petilian took up one of Augustine's favorite illustrations for play, the relation between image and archetype, to illustrate his point. "Falsehood often imitates truth," Petilian wrote, "by walking in its steps." Augustine's lying and devious representations were like the simulation of a true man by his portrait,

> expressing with its colors the false appearances of truth. And, in the same way, the bright clarity of a mirror catches the face, so as to represent the eyes of him who looks into it. Thus, it presents his own face to every person who goes by so that the very features of the person

[91] Augustine applied Ps. 30: 22 to Peter in En. in Ps. 30: 10 (Corp. Christ., ser. lat., 38, pp. 219–20), and to Moses, Serm. 7: 7 (Corp. Christ., ser. lat., 41, p. 76).

[92] Serm. 7: 7 (Corp. Christ., ser. lat., 41, p. 76).

[93] C. litt. Petil., 3. 16. 19 (Migne PL 43: 356).

[94] C. litt. Petil., 3. 21. 24 (Migne PL 43:359).

meet themselves in return. The pure falsehood of a clear mirror is able to bring it about that the very eyes that see themselves think of themselves as though they were in another person. Even when a shadow stands before it, it doubles the images, dividing its unity in great part by lying. For is this not true because the representation (*figura*) lies?[95]

Petilian's charges that Augustine's hermeneutics proved, but did not authenticate, recall the familiar accusation that identified heresy with idolatry. Heretics, it was said, took the silver and gold of word and meaning that they had by nature and turned them into idols made up from their own hearts. They bowed down and worshipped the meanings that they had made in the image and likeness of themselves, rather than the authentic sense of Scripture that they had received. Augustine's hermeneutics had absorbed the play of conflict. Using the visual metaphor of the mirror to illuminate his insistence that Augustine's hermeneutic consisted of rhetoric and skepticism, Petilian threw down the rebuke of idolatry. The rebuke fell, not on the enterprise of verbal expression, but exactly on the preverbal stage of vision—the "sight of knowing" and the "sight of thinking"—where, Augustine judged, understanding occurred. The flash of understanding, in which the mind saw itself through itself, in which the mind became the meaning that it begot, took on dangerous colors. Petilian argued that the dangers were not only spiritual. For, in his view, Augustine's "idolatry" reprojected conflictual play from hermeneutics back again onto society. (See previous discussion in Chapter 5 after n. 84.)

Petilian considered Augustine still a Manichee and entered other serious objections against his character, his associates, and his career. However, Petilian's most bitter accusations arose from the discrepancy that he perceived between the call for peace to which the gentle skepticism of Augustine's detachment of words from thought contributed, and the call for persecution that the Father's concept of ecclesiastical discipline eventually sustained. The play of meaning was war. Augustine reconciled the discrepancy by arguing that persecution was a work of love, part of the warfare that spirit waged against flesh, a strife that the righteous waged against themselves and against their carnal neighbors, not in hatred, but in love.[96] "The correcting punishment, therefore," Augustine wrote, "is not evil, though the wrongdoing be evil. For indeed, it is a cutting iron, but that of a doctor's incision, and not that of an enemy's wound."[97] But Petilian saw that the hand of the slaughterer glistened with blood at the instigation of Augustine's words, and that Augustine himself was a "persecutor and butcher," a true son of the devil, transforming himself into the likeness of

---

[95] *C. litt. Petil.*, 2. 26. 60 (Migne *PL* 43: 279–80).
[96] *C. litt. Petil.*, 2. 68. 154 (Migne *PL* 43: 307–308).
[97] *C. litt. Petil.*, 3. 4. 5 (Migne *PL* 43: 320).

an angel of light, uttering the names of peace and unity while he waged war with kisses.[98]

When Augustine looked into Scripture with the eyes of his heart, did he mistake the reflection of his rhetoric for the authentic Word of God? Such is one possible conclusion, if understanding Scripture means itself.

At the burning bush, God revealed to Moses with one name ("I am who is") what he was in himself, and with the other ("I am the God of Abraham, the God of Isaac, and the God of Jacob") what he is toward humans. The first bespoke fear; the second, hope.[99] So too, Augustine's act of understanding Scripture, in charity and in interrogation, had double aspects; the first turned toward God and those at one with him, and the other toward these who, like Petilian, were not of the Lord's house or body. A harsh love, a coercive questioning lies behind Augustine's gentle words.

> When therefore our Lord Jesus Christ shall come, and, as the Apostle Paul also says, will bring to light the hidden things of darkness, and will make manifest the thoughts of the heart . . . no prophet shall be read to us, no book of an apostle shall be opened, we shall not require the witness of John, we shall not need the Gospel itself.   What shall we see when these aids have been removed?   I beseech you, love with me; by believing, run with me . . .; let us pant for our home above. . . . What shall we see then? Let the Gospel now tell us: "In the beginning was the Word, and the Word was with God, and the Word was God." (John 1:1)   "Behold, now are we the sons of God, and it doth not yet appear what we shall be; but we know that, when he shall appear, we shall be like him; for we shall see him as he is" (1. John 3:2).   I am about to lay aside this book, and you too are going to depart, every man to his own house. It has been good for us to have been in the common light, good to have been glad therein, good to have rejoiced therein, but when we part from one another, let us not depart from Him.[100]

These words of benign play—searching, finding, running, and the rebound of image and archetype—also contained the play of battle. Augustine welcomed the flames of hatred from his enemies that proved his conscience pure in the sight of God. He rejoiced and was exceedingly glad in the abuse and persecution that his enemies heaped upon him. By understanding Scripture, did he not participate in—that is, become—the authentic truth of Scripture? Understanding replicated the humiliation of Christ; it brought him to put on the armor of God and, if need be, fight to the death alone and against odds to defeat the devil by loving God's ene-

---

[98] C. litt. Petil., 2. 8. 17; 2. 17. 38; 2. 93. 202 (Migne PL 43: 263, 270, 324).

[99] Serm. 7: 7 (Corp. Christ., ser. lat., 41, p. 76).

[100] Tr. in Ev. Johan., 35. 9 (Corp. Christ., ser. lat., 36, pp. 322–23).

mies, thereby proving the love that united him in the body of Christ, and participating in the life that God was. Hatred answering love was needed to complete and authenticate his spiritual understanding of Scripture. Nothing more was needed from men. "Cursed be the man that trusteth in man," (Jer. 17:5), he wrote, quoting Jeremiah for Petilian's edification. If the hearts of his enemies were not converted to peace, yet would his peace rebound upon himself.[101]

[101] *C. litt. Petil.*, 3. 2. 3; 3. 6. 7–3. 7. 8; 3. 11. 12—3. 13. 14; 3. 49—3. 59. 71 (Migne *PL* 43: 348, 351–52, 354–55, 378–83.

SEVEN

Diagramming the Hermeneutic Circle: The Example of Gerhoch of Reichersberg

THE "STRANGE HERMENEUTICS" practiced by Augustine was a massive apparatus. Its power to convince derived, in part, from its comprehensiveness—that is, from its ability to encompass, digest and absorb the most disparate elements. All agreed that the cycle of understanding consisted of a vicious circle when understanding did not go beyond rhetorical demonstration. For then it became little more than a ventriloquist's trick, the same person interrogating the text and responding for it. But, when the cycle produced authentic understanding, it was never self-reflective, because it depended on powers, insights, or visions that did not originate in the interrogator, but that came to him by empathetic participation in another. Authentic understanding was never independent. The dispute between Petilian and Augustine illustrates how easily what appeared to one author a hermeneutic circle might appear to his critics a vicious one. Distinguishing hermeneutic from vicious circles was all the more difficult because understanding was regarded as affective, not linguistic, and also because a distinction was drawn between understanding as an instantaneous (and incommunicable) flash of insight, and interpretation as the constructive work of inquiry, reflection and discourse that followed, as memory follows event.

Yet, the hermeneutics of empathy (and even eroticism) that Augustine employed to read between the lines, and within the silences of the words of Scripture, was not the fragile invention of one person. It belonged to the general heritage of Western culture, and, in many forms, it long continued to shape concepts of understanding, one of the most characteristic human acts. The distinction between authentic understanding (nonlinguistic) and rhetorical demonstration (linguistic) persisted, and so too did ideas about relations between constitutive events of understanding and recollective enterprises (and modes) of interpretation that arose from them. Quite naturally, this tradition continually and restlessly debated the conditions that made authentic understanding possible, and, thus, the relationship of the understander to the object of understanding, through empathetic participation. Conflict was built into the hermeneutic method as a ratifying component.

To illustrate the persistence of the "strange hermeneutics" after the age of the Church Fathers, I propose in this chapter to diagram the hermeneutic circle conceived by Gerhoch of Reichersberg (1092/93–1169). His writings were conspicuous for their extensive use of the biological and esthetic paradigms of conflict for dominance. He employed them repeatedly to sustain his effort to pierce through formal knowledge and its organizing structures, as through a shell of rhetoric, and to participate in the authentic and authenticating experiences of which forms of knowledge were thought to preserve but memories.

Almost exactly midway between Augustine and Schleiermacher in the long chronology of theological hermeneutics, Gerhoch is best known as a vociferous advocate of Church reform, but many diverse enterprises were woven into his life. From the beginning of his literary career (1126) onward, he was a tireless proselytizer for the communal discipline practiced by Augustinian canons. An intricate trail of undertakings as teacher, reformer, and diplomat preceded Gerhoch's conversion to the canonial discipline and his debut in the arena of literary controversy. He was a man of extremely varied cultural accomplishments, an enthusiastic and skilled producer of theatrical spectacles (at least before he converted to an austere way of life), an imaginative and accomplished artist, and a master of psalmody, as well as a theologian, liturgist, and administrator. He passed the greater part of his life in southern Germany, at first in the dioceses of Augsburg and Regensburg. Under Pope Innocent II's patronage, he was eventually installed as provost of the Augustinian house at Reichersberg, in the diocese of Salzburg (1132), where he presided until his death, except for a time when the troops of Frederick Barbarossa expelled him for defying the emperor's antipope.

He served his contemporary popes in numerous capacities during his first half-century; he frequently visited Rome. In 1152, Pope Eugenius III gave him his most splendid task, a mission of reform to Hungary and Russia. The mission never became more than a fair dream. At Eugenius's death (1152), Gerhoch's service as a laborer in the papal vineyard went into sudden and permanent eclipse. In 1162, he attended Bishop Eberhard of Salzburg when he waited upon Barbarossa at Pavia, explaining their continued defiance of the Antipope, but the period of his wide travels and exalted diplomatic connections had already ended when Eugenius died. Even earlier, he had grieved to find a canker gnawing at the very heart of the Church, the see of Peter.

Gerhoch's political ventures and his extensive writings witness to his movement in the same circles as Bernard of Clairvaux, Otto of Freising, and Rupert of Deutz. But his eager desire to establish close rapports with great spiritual teachers of his day was always disappointed. He was quick to imagine heretical tendencies in others. Some found the scent of heresy faintly rising from his own immense learning, tireless energy, and prophetic zeal. He remained a strangely isolated figure in the literary and doc-trinal history of his time.

Although he was one of the principal exemplars of learning in the twelfth-century Renaissance in Germany, Gerhoch did not alter the course of intellectual history, as Augustine had done and as Schleiermacher later did. He was, rather, a "symptom, a critic, and a mirror of his age."[1] Indeed, so far as can be determined, his writing found no audience outside his own day and monastery. He expressed a common intellectual tradition; and, with exceptional completeness, he illuminated the connecting tissues of that tradition. The distinguishing characteristics of Gerhoch's work were fortui-tous, in the temperament of the man and the character that his oeuvre assumed randomly as it grew. He was able to set forth an unusually keen and detailed sense of esthetic unities in knowledge, thanks, first of all, to his continuing struggle to tame and cleanse (and not to suppress) his own sen-suality, and, second, to his discerning experience of the visual arts, music, drama and liturgical drama, and rhetoric. Further, the wide scope and variety of his writings also provide a rich sampling of approaches to the experience of esthetic bonding through interpretation. Other writers—Meister Eckhart, for example—employed the theology of participation in strikingly original and idiosyncratic ways and thereby shifted the direction of thought. Gerhoch can be regarded as a representative writer because he represented a common viewpoint with great clarity and completeness. It is at least possible that the completeness of the structure of thought, which sets Gerhoch apart from others, resulted from his devotion throughout most of his career to a single enterprise, a set of commentaries on the Psalms.

Composed long after the patristic era, when Augustine's guiding ideas about understanding had been disseminated into the common heritage, composed also in comparative isolation after his own period of wide travels and residence at the papal court, Gerhoch's voluminous commentaries on the Psalms yield a fully articulated specimen of the self-critical methods of authentication that tradition gave him. They also disclose the instability that the gap between authentication and rhetorical demonstration intro-duced into political action as well as into theological discourse.

Turning now to the hermeneutic circle according to Gerhoch, I shall organize my diagram according to what was considered the greatest safe-guard against falling into a vicious circle; namely, dependence. For Ger-

[1] Peter Classen, "Der Häresie-Begriff bei Gerhoch von Reichersberg und in seinem Umkreis," in Willem Lourdaux and D. Verhelst, ed., *The Concept of Heresy in the Middle Ages (11th–13th C.)* (Louvain: University Press, 1976; Medievalia Lovaniensia, ser. 1, Studia 4), p. 39. On Gerhoch's place in the general context of the diffusion of scholastic doctrines and methods, see Peter Classen, "Zur Geschichte der Frühscholastik in Österreich und Bayern," *Mitteilungen des Instituts für österreichische Geschichtsforschung*, 67 (1959), pp. 249–77. Mr. Bruce Brasington kindly drew my attention to this article.

hoch, dependence explained why those who authentically understood Scripture were few, though interpreters were many. It explained the esthetic (and nonlinguistic) character of understanding. And it lay at the heart of the conditions that made authentic understanding possible, for dependence of the understander on the object of understanding, often portrayed in terms of erotic play, was the essence of the whole hermeneutic enterprise.

THE FEWNESS OF UNDERSTANDERS

The tension between demonstrative knowledge and authenticating understanding was of a piece with Gerhoch's concept of the Church as a charismatic communion. At every stage in the evolution of his thought, Gerhoch was guided by a vision of the Church modeled on the account of the apostolic community given in the book of Acts: "Now the multitude of those who believed were of one heart and soul, and no one said that any of the things that he possessed was his own, but they had everything in common" (Acts 4:32). Gerhoch normally altered this verse to read that the multitude of believers were of one heart and soul in God.

Gerhoch was a polemicist for the *vita apostolica*, rediscovered and restored in his own day, he thought, by canons regular who lived according to the Augustinian *Rule*. As such, he quite naturally turned again and again to the Scriptural portrayal of the apostolic Church, including, particularly, the utter dependence of the post-Pentecostal Church, as described in Acts, on the gifts of the Holy Spirit. Yet, keenly aware of betrayals and divisions in the apostolic Church itself,[2] Gerhoch accepted strife over Scripture in his time as part, and indeed as vindication, of his hermeneutic experience. Gerhoch realized that his doctrines were inaccessible to the majority of professed Christians. He reached those doctrines by what he called "leaps of understanding" that brought spiritual masters to heights of contemplation inaccessible to the simple, and certainly to the enemies of the faith such as Jews, pagans, heretics, and false Christians.[3] Gerhoch considered himself in a small minority, the blessed few who, by grace, excelled in leaps of spiritual understanding. Only one in thousands, he wrote, had the combination of prudence and faithfulness required by a Scriptural expositor, and, certainly

---

[2] *Tr. in Ps. 64*, chap. 40, 71, 124. Migne *PL* 194: 33. *MGH, Ldl* 3, pp. 470, 472. On Gerhoch's life and work, see Peter Classen, *Gerhoch von Reichersberg: eine Biographie* (Wiesbaden: Steiner, 1960). For a fuller discussion of Gerhoch's reform ideology, and his deliberate use of paradox as a rhetorical device, see my article, "The Church as Play: Gerhoch of Reichersberg's Call for Reform," in Stanley Chodorow, Richard Fraher, and James Ross Sweeney, eds., *Festschrift Brian Tierney* (Ithaca, N.Y.: Cornell University Press, forthcoming).

[3] *Tr. in Ps. 21*: 1 (Migne *PL* 193: 991), comparing orthodox teachers with harts. It was their duty, Gerhoch wrote, to administer vigorously to those beneath them what they learned leaping on the contemplative heights. On the enemies of the faith, see e.g. *Tr. in Ps. 71*: 5 (Migne *PL* 194: 320).

philosophers and others steeped in worldly and sacred doctrine lacked it.[4]
Not everyone had faith; not everyone believed the Gospel.[5] Truth was not
revealed by God, not by majority vote. Had not the majority chosen Ba-
rabbas and rejected Christ?[6] Few walked with God, as Enoch did. Few burned
with zeal for the house of God, as Elijah did, when he first brought the
sacrifices of false priests to nothing and then cut the priests' throats. Associating himself with the prophets and with the Apostle Peter, Gerhoch
gladly endured isolation, persecution, and even the charge of heresy for the
doctrines that he taught.[7]

Convinced that Christ inhabited the faithful, and regarded by his
brethren at Reichersberg as in union with God,[8] he felt that he wrote under
compulsion, forced onward by an outpouring of the waters of eternal life,
an outpouring that manifested its purity in a river, as though of liquid gold,
falling over the sanctuary of St. Michael, where he wrote and where he
customarily sat to meditate on the Psalms.[9] Gerhoch also had the comfort
of celestial vindication. An enemy learned from a terrifying vision that his
stubborn opposition to Gerhoch had involved him in sin against the Holy
Spirit, and, dying unreconciled, he begged Gerhoch in a vision to absolve
him beyond the grave.[10]

As an expositor, Gerhoch invoked the Holy Spirit to enable him, in his
exegesis, to preserve the authentic understanding with which it had
informed the text of the Psalms, and indeed that the same Spirit that
inspired the Psalms would inflame his tongue with the flames of spiritual
fire. He trusted that God would govern his spirit and his pen.[11] But the
assimilation of others to God through the means of his work required that
they already be inhabited by the Holy Spirit, drawn together "in unity and

---

[4] *Ep. 3* (Migne *PL* 193: 490).

[5] *II. Thess.* 1:8, 3:2, quoted in prologue to the *vitae* of Berengar and Wirto (Migne *PL* 194: 1428).

[6] *De aedificio Dei*, chap. 145 (*MGH, Ldl* 3, p. 186). Classen, *Gerhoch von Reichersberg*, p. 195.

[7] E.g., *Dial. de cler. sec. et reg.* (*MGH, Ldl* 3, pp. 203–204, 232, 236, 239) (144,000 to be saved). *Tr. in Ps. 64*, chap. 79, 106, 120, 167 (Migne *PL* 194: 57, 71, 79. *MGH, Ldl* 3, p. 492). E. Sakur seriously mutilated the texts of several major treatises by Gerhoch when he omitted theological sections from the *MGH* edition. Consequently, references in these notes to Ger-hoch's commentary on Ps. 64, *de aedificio Dei*, and *de investigatione Antichristi* will cite the *MGH* edition when possible and other editions when necessary.

[8] *Annales Reicherspergenses, Chronicon Magni Presbyteri* (a. 1169) (*MGH, SS* 17, p. 492).

[9] *Tr. in Ps. 54*: 24 (Migne *PL* 193: 1672).

[10] *Tr. in Ps. 34*: 8 (Damian Van den Eynde and Odulph Van den Eynde, eds., *Opera Inedita*, 2, pt. 1 [Rome: Pontificium Athenaeum Antonianum, 1955–56. *Spicilegium Pontificii Athe-naei Antoniani*, 9], pp. 358–60). This edition will hereafter be cited as *OI*. Volume I (*Spici-legium Pontificii Anthenaei Antoniani*, 8) and volume II, pt. 2 (*Spicilegium Pontificii Athenaei Antoniani*, 10) were published in Rome in 1955 and 1956, respectively.

[11] *Tr. in Ps. 31*, prologue; *Tr. in Ps. 34*: 27–28 (*OI*, 2, pt. 1, pp. 8, 402). *Princeps mundi* (*Liber de simoniacis*), no chapter number (*MGH, Ldl* 3, p. 241). *Expositio super canonem*, prologue (*OI*, 1, p. 3).

peace, which is the bond of perfection."[12] There were, he acknowledged, many who could not penetrate to the spiritual word inside the husk of his carnal words. Those carping critics against whose siren songs he had to stop his ears could not enter into his apocalyptic moment with him;[13] nor could kings entranced by sorcerers, poets, and philosophers and blinded by them to the wisdom preached by the Lord's servants; nor could the world as a whole, captivated by lies.[14] Few, he knew, believed. Only they, dependent on divine illumination, could see the direction of events as he portrayed them, and those few were all by overwhelmed by the vast majority in the Church, the wicked, as the Jews had been in their Babylonian captivity.[15]

The Character of Understanding

The esthetic (and nonlinguistic) character of understanding according to Gerhoch cast his argument from dependence into high relief. For, at this crucial point, the danger of falling from understanding into ventriloquism was acute; the pit of the vicious circle yawned at the interpreter's feet.

Characteristically, Gerhoch found the hermeneutic event essentially the same, whether the object being interpreted were a painting or a text. The same "habit of mind" and "discipline of morals" came into play; for the true goal of inquiry into any work was not its "positive values"—that is, the material composition—but its "negative values"—that is, contents of a picture that were unseen and unseeable, or contents of a text that were unsaid and unsayable.[16]

Sensuality was the basis of Gerhoch's esthetics; morality (justice, or righteousness) was its goal.[17] But obedience and self-denial were required to reach the goal of goodness from the beginning of sensual perception. In

---

[12] *Princeps mundi* (*Liber de simoniacis*), chap. 23 (*MGH, Ldl* 3, p. 260). *Tr. in Ps. 34:* 8 (*OI,* 2, pt. 1, p. 360).

[13] *Tr. in Ps. 51*, prologue to *Pars VI* (Migne *PL* 193: 1609).

[14] *Tr. in Ps. 64*, chap. 139, 144 (*MGH, Ldl* 3, pp. 480, 482).

[15] *Tr. in Ps. 64*, chap. 64, 79 (*MGH, Ldl* 3, p. 468. Migne *PL* 194: 57).

[16] *Tr. in Ps. 8:* 1 (Migne, *PL* 193: 740): "Ecclesia dicitur torcular, quia in ea verbum divinum sono et intellectu, figuris et earum significatis, quasi vinaceo et vino quasi amurca et oleo compositum est; quod cum eodem sono fertur ad aures aut etiam per litterarum, seu picturarum vel etiam totius mundanae fabricae figuras ingeritur visui, et ita ipsum verbum visu vel auditu comprehensum, quasi in torculari discernitur: dum soni auditi et figurae conspectae foris manent, intellectus vero ad interiora manans, et in lacu memoriae diligenter exceptus inde transit ad habitum mentis et morum disciplinam quasi in cellam vinariam, de qua dicit sponsa: 'Introduxit me rex in cellam vinariam, ordinavit in me charitatem' " (*Cant.* 2: 4).

[17] As indicated below (at nn. 25–55), Gerhoch's senses of sight (visual display and beauty) and hearing (rhetoric and music) appear to have been acute. His olfactory sense may also have been alert, at least to bad odors, to judge from the frequency with which he employed metaphors of fetor for wrong belief or personal unworthiness. E.g., *Tr. in Ps. 26:* 8 (Migne *PL* 193: 1199). *Tr. in Ps. 147:* 9 (Migne *PL* 194: 977). *De aedificio Dei*, chap. 164 (fetor and contamination of a corpse), chap. 181 (*MGH, Ldl* 3, pp. 194, 201). *Princeps mundi* (*Liber de simoniacis*), chap. 33 (fetor and contamination of a corpse) (*MGH, Ldl* 3, p. 271).

search of wisdom, authentic teachers spurned carnal prudence, which was hostile to God; and they lovingly submitted to be ruled, not by their own understanding, but by that of others. Rejecting the world and their own senses, they followed the understanding that was according to God, even in matters that seemed absurd to human understanding.[18] By obedience, or dependence, they transcended sensory perception and the finitude of individual judgment, and penetrated to the negative, and true, value encased in the work of art.

Thus, when he thought about esthetic experience, Gerhoch was not concerned with the work of art as an object of sensual perception so much as with its intelligible contents. The essential part was its integrating force, a part that corresponded with the invisible point at the center of a circle, the imperceptible adhesive coordinating of separate members into a single body, and the soul in the body.

By using analogy rightly, one could pass beyond physical objects or events (the lowest stage in the hierarchy of feeling), apprehend the negative values integrating them, and through the affects ("the assent of the mind")[19] become assimilated to those values. Gerhoch's description of contemplating a painted crucifix will illustrate the method of assimilation that he took for granted—namely, assimilation through analogic transference.

The lowest level of analogy was the sensory one, recognizing the painting as an image (*imago depicta*). The second level was intellectual, recognizing the image as that of a poor and needy man (*quem certa figurat imago*). The third level was spiritual, recognizing the man in the picture as Lord and God (*in depicta imagine Christi crucifixi Deum intelligis*). At this third level, the believer passed beyond what was accessible to the sense of vision (*supra id quod vides*), and beyond the equivalences that the intellect could make the image. The Lord was seen by the heart when "with sound faith you know him to be God whom you see as man." The last stage was affective. It was reached when the soul, in obedient love, identified itself with the God in the man in the picture. At this level, analogies of sensory art fell away. Seeing God face to face, the viewer became like him, inflamed by the Holy Spirit as metal, losing its own form, assimilates the form of the fire that melts it.[20]

---

[18] *Tr. in Ps. 29:* 10 (Migne *PL* 193: 1273–74).

[19] On the "assent of the mind," *Tr. in Ps. 136:* 8 (Migne *PL* 194: 908–909).

[20] *Tr. in Ps. 40:* 14 (Migne *PL* 193: 1486). *Tr. in Ps. 72:* 19, 20 (Migne *PL* 194: 350). He commented that pictures representing Jesus on his mother's lap helped visualize the principle that the kingdom of God is within us, and that pictures showing Christ on the cross between the Blessed Virgin and John illustrated how Christ combined the affective (female) speculative mode with the intellective (male) speculative mode. *De investig. Antichristi*, 2. 73 (Friedrich Scheibelberger, ed., *Gerhohi Reichersbergensis Praepositi Opera Hactenus Inedita* [Linz: Quirein, 1875], p. 333). See below nn. 20, 88, 150, 171. Cf. Gerhoch's insistence that a *pictura hominis* has to be a *vera pictura; De investig. Antichristi*, 2. 1 (Scheibelberger, ed., p. 188). Gerhoch occasionally referred to painting as a metaphor for elements of a structure that were

Gerhoch described the fullness of this assimilative participation in the physically sightless sleep of contemplation. He recalled a priest who, after the rigors of the night office, fell asleep "in a sweet sleep," sitting at the foot of a crucifix. But, while he slept, his heart kept watch. With the sound of rushing wind, a radiant presence, like a gold coin, crashed through the glass window at his head. It left the glass unbroken; but the presence itself scattered into golden particles that filled the entire house. They enveloped him like a shimmering cloud and entered the receptacle of his body and soul through every pore, filling him with their great sweetness and leaving him permanently endowed with spiritual fortitude.[21]

In his comments on seeing a crucifix, Gerhoch actually described a tautology. Because the soul, as a vessel, had already been filled with grace and enlightened by faith,[22] it could fill the picture with meaning. As it did, it participated again with the God-in-man in the picture; and it was again filled with the meaning that it had read into the picture.

Just as the soul was a receptacle to be filled, so too the painted crucifix was a receptacle to be filled by the negative values that the viewer could project into it.[23] Having been unable to discern the God in Jesus, the poor and needy man, the stubbornly disobedient Jews presumably were unable to pass beyond the second level of analogy hidden in the crucifix.[24] In antiquity and the Renaissance, writers argued over the "deficiencies" of painting. By comparison with sculpture, they argued, its two-dimen-

---

ornamental and instructive, but not structural as were columns. E.g., *Tr. in Ps. 27*: 2 (Migne *PL* 193: 1225). *De aedificio Dei*, chap. 43, 45 (*MGH, Ldl* 3, pp. 162–63). *Princeps mundi* (*Liber de simoniacis*), chap. 18 (*MGH, Ldl* 3, p. 256). He used a metaphor from painting to illustrate the forgiveness of sins: "Similitudo trahitur a cera, cui impressa est deformis imago, qua deleta reformatur cera ad exprimendam pulchram imaginem." *Tr. in Ps. 50*: 3 (Migne *PL* 193: 1684). He compared contemplation of his sins with looking at a horrific picture: " 'Et peccatum meum contra me est semper,' hoc est, quasi imago horribilis stat contra me, quam 'semper' apertis et clausis oculis aspicio, et orando et plorando annihilare cupio." See also his reproach to the Romans for commissioning a picture that showed an emperor performing groom's service to a pope. The picture, he wrote, witnessed to Rome's character as a new Babylon, where the proper duties of pope and emperor were confused, and St. Peter's command, "Fear God; honor the king," was ignored. *De investig. Antichristi*, 1. 72; *De Quarta Vigilia Noctis*, chap. 12 (*MGH, Ldl* 3, pp. 393, 511–12). Cf. the celebrated painting in the Lateran depicting Lothar III receiving the imperial crown in return for rendering homage to Pope Innocent II. Otto of Freising, *Ottonis et Rahewini Gesta Friderici Imperatoris*, 3. 10 (*MGH, SS in usum scholarum*, p. 177). While describing events of 1157, Otto (or his continuator, Rahewin) referred to umbrage that Frederick took at the painting on an earlier visit to Rome (1154–55), and Pope Hadrian IV's promise at that time to remove it. The fact that Gerhoch's comments on the picture occur in treatises written not long after 1157 may indicate that some account of it reached him perhaps indirectly from a member of the imperial expedition in that year. He may, of course, have seen it himself. See also n. 88.

[21] *De investig. Antichristi*, 1. preface (*MGH, Ldl* 3, p. 306).

[22] Below, nn. 78, 113.

[23] Cf. Paulinus of Nola, *Carm. 27*: lines 511–15 (*CSEL* 30, p. 285). "Whoever sees these [pictures] recognizing what is true in the empty figures feeds his faithful mind with an image that for him is by no means empty." See Gerhoch's description of his own commentary on Psalm 64 as a chamberpot. *Tr. in Ps. 64*, chap. 75 (Migne *PL* 194: 55).

[24] *Tr. in Ps. 40*: 14 (Migne *PL* 193: 1486).

sionality was deficient, further removed than three-dimensionality from the world it pretended to represent. By comparison with poetry, it was deficient in its muteness, and in portraying only one act, and one perspective. By contrast, poetic narrative spoke and moved, portraying a whole in its full diversity. Two-dimensionality, muteness, and single-image portrayal left much to the imagination. But these "deficiencies" provided exactly the vessels that, in the twelfth-century, Gerhoch found packed with negative values, to which loving obedience gave access, and that served him as tools of assimilation through analogical transference.

In fact, Gerhoch the rhetorician was not drawn to the visual arts, with their vernacular of line, color, and mass, so much as he was to the aural arts of speech and psalmody. To these arts he devoted his life. As a rhetorician, he was able, in his reflections in speech and psalmody, to distinguish between the rhetorical and the authentic. Evidently Gerhoch delighted in aural rhythms and harmonies. In addition to his expert training in rhetoric, he had a wide and precise knowledge of different modes of psalmody.[25] The great work of his life, extending over the space of more than twenty years (1144–1167/68), was his commentary on the Psalms; he also wrote exegeses of songs found in other books of the Old Testament. He envisioned the saved as a great, harmonious chorus.[26] He also imagined them—mixing two favorite metaphors—as "a new song made of living stones (that is, the elect)," a new song of praise to God that could only be sung "in the Church of the saints."[27] The discipline of psalmody[28] was used as a metonym of religious discipline as a whole, the life of obedience. String and wind instruments represented the four cardinal virtues (prudence, fortitude, justice, and temperance). The timbrel, with its dry, taut hide, represented the drying, mortifying, and crucifying of the flesh.[29] Gerhoch identified singing with other aspects of religious discipline—with writing[30] and other acts of spiritual endeavor (learning, teaching, reading, and in every way sowing and protecting the seed of the psaltery),[31] with the interplay of active and contemplative lives,[32] with spiritual warfare and parturition,[33] and, of

---

[25] E.g., *Expositio super canonem*, "Evangelium" (*OI*, 1, pp. 6–7).

[26] *Tr. in Ps. 66*: 3 (Migne *PL* 194: 157).

[27] *Tr. in Ps. 95*: 1; *Tr. in Ps. 149*: 1 (Migne *PL* 194: 579, 989).

[28] *Tr. in Ps. 70*: 24 (Migne *PL* 194: 310–12), "disciplinata psalmodia," "disciplinate psallentes," "forinseca psallendi disciplina."

[29] *Tr. in Ps. 91*: 4; *Tr. in Ps. 97*: 5, 6; *Tr. in Ps. 149*: 3 (Migne *PL* 194: 564, 591, 990).

[30] *Tr. in Ps. 51*, prologue to *Pars VI* (Migne *PL* 193: 1609). The identification of psalmody with writing is exemplified by the occasional appearance of neumes over Scriptural and liturgical texts in Gerhoch's commentary on the Psalms. Classen, *Gerhoch von Reichersberg*, pp. 115–16.

[31] *Tr. in Ps. 147*: 7 (Migne *PL* 194: 976).

[32] Gerhoch frequently used this metaphor. E.g., *Tr. in Ps. 9*: 12; *Tr. in Ps. 32*: 3; *Tr. in Ps. 46*: 7–8; *Tr. in Ps. 67*: 33; *Tr. in Ps. 103*: 33; *Tr. in Ps. 104*: 2; *Tr. in Ps. 137*: 1; *Tr. in Ps. 143*: 9 (Migne *PL* 193: 961, 1323, 1580. Migne *PL* 194: 220, 581, 621, 634, 911, 959).

[33] *Ep. ad quasdam sanctimoniales* (*OI*, 1, p. 370). *Tr. in Ps. 54*: 20: (Migne *PL* 193: 1656).

course, with the splendor of the liturgies, in which religious spent so much of their daily lives.[34]

Many associations enabled the aural arts to prevail over visual ones in Gerhoch's thinking. Still, he believed that the same assimilative method of analogic reasoning through obedience was at work both in painting and in psalmody. In psalmody, the sensual level of perception consisted of music and words. But, for Gerhoch, the music, despite the opulent pleasure it gave the ears, was secondary to the words. It was possible to be led into sin, as Augustine had observed, by delighting more in the song than in what was sung. The words remained primary, even though the sweetness of song, mixed with melodious instruments, could be added to temper their austerity, as David, the psalmist, and men in Gerhoch's own time had done.[35] But Gerhoch did not mean the words on the page.

Gerhoch's primary distinction between exterior (or carnal) senses and interior (or spiritual) ones had profound implications.[36] "Word," he wrote, was a similitude for the Son of God. It could be understood to apply to mental operations in three ways: the word of the mouth (e.g., "man"), the literal sound; the word of the heart, the mental image (e.g., of a man), corresponding with the sound of the spoken word; and the word of the mind, which was the abstract, intellectually defined category of the particular instance designated by the spoken word (e.g., "man" as an *intellecta substantia*). Before we do anything, we first speak it by the word of the mind, because we put things in order by making thought. And we visualize with imaginary images (of the heart), whatever we think of (in the abstract). In these two ways, we illustrate how the word begets its like. "And so the Son and Word is called the image and likeness of God."[37]

Gerhoch recognized that moral discrepancies occurred between the words spoken externally by the tongue, and the word uttered inwardly by the heart. It was possible to bless with the mouth and curse with the heart. When such duplicity, or multiplicity, occurred, the mouth spoke, but did not confess.[38] A "good Psalm," Gerhoch wrote, was made up by coordinating strings, sound, and the movement of fingers. Strings represented the drying up (or mortification) of the flesh; sound, the virtues of the heart;

---

[34] *Princeps mundi* (*Liber de simoniacis*), chap. 17 (*MGH, Ldl* 3, pp. 255–56). *Tr. in Ps. 40:* 2 (Migne *PL* 193: 1473). *Dial. de cler. sec. et reg.* (*MGH, Ldl* 3, p. 228).

[35] *Tr. in Ps. 41:* 5 (Migne *PL* 193: 1504–1505). *Tr. in Ps. 5:* 13 (Migne *PL* 193: 706). *Tr. in Ps. 68:* 13; *Tr. in Ps. 118:* 54. *Zain* (Migne *PL* 194: 240, 768–69).

[36] E.g., *Tr. in Ps. 32:* 2; *Tr. in Ps. 41:* 5 (Migne *PL* 193: 1322–23, 1505).

[37] *Tr. in Ps. 44:* 1 (Migne *PL* 193: 1565).

[38] *Tr. in Ps. 65:* 17 (Migne *PL* 194: 144–45). See also *Tr. in Ps. 77:* 16 (Migne *PL* 194: 450–51). On the use of words as disguise, *Tr. in Ps. 24:* 2 (Migne *PL* 193: 1098): "Sed iam ego disciplinis eruditus non in me ipso, non in foliorum id est verborum vanis tegumentis, ut Adam 'confido,' sed 'in te, Deus meus, confido'. . ."

the movement of the fingers, expression of those virtues in external actions, good works.[39]

If even faith, which can move mountains, is dead without authenticating charity, how much more is psalmody?[40] In the discipline of psalmody as in that of prayer, it was essential that the words uttered by the mouth conform with those of mind and spirit, that the heard prayer or song be infused by the affects, for Christ "loves the warmth of heart, rather than the beauty of words, in psalmody."[41]

Like pictures, psalms and the words that composed them were vessels to be filled.[42] They might be costly and beautiful, but empty;[43] or they might be abused with unworthy contents. Every Mass celebrated by heretics was like the incantations of the wizards who performed their magical tricks before Pharaoh; heretical Masses had the spoken words and visible signs of a sacrament, but not its content of orthodox faith.[44] Those who prayed or sang Masses with the concept of worldly lucre in their minds and the hunger for it in their hearts, and whose main goal was to acquire precious raiment, delicate food, or gold and silver, were idolaters, worshipping the idol of lucre in their minds.[45] Such men—priests and pontiffs—were animal men, lacking the Spirit and God's plenty, even though they sacrificed and communicated at his table.[46] Orthodox believers who sang in body, mind, and spirit might find the Psalms partly full, or empty, if they sang without the concentrated fervor of devotion.[47] When their obedience was imperfect, orthodox and pious singers could be distracted by carnal imaginings or vain,

---

[39] *Tr. in Ps. 146:* 1 (Migne *PL* 194: 973).

[40] *Tr. in Ps. 1*: Gloria (Migne *PL* 193: 657). A hymn contains three things. In (1) praise, there is (2) confession, and (3) the warmth in the joy of the loving singer. For unless the song is sung in joy, it is not a hymn; he does not sing who does not love. *Tr. in Ps. 72:* 1 (Migne *PL* 194: 337).

[41] *Tr. in Ps.*, prologue to *Pars III* (*OI*, 2, pt. 1, pp. 3–4). *Tr. in Ps. 34:* 3b (*OI*, 2, pt. 1, pp. 347–48). *Tr. in Ps. 70:* 8 (Migne *PL* 194: 286). *Expositio in Cant. Moysis,* 1 (Migne *PL* 194: 1019).

[42] *Tr. in Ps. 70:* 22 (Migne *PL* 194: 367). Gerhoch knew that the same Psalm might have quite different meanings when sung on two separate occasions. Context gave meaning. *Tr. in Ps. 37:* 2–5 (*OI*, 2, pt. 2, p. 588). For the unusual depiction of Scriptures as a "vessel of death," see John of Salisbury, *Historia Pontificalis,* chap. 13. Marjorie Chibnall, ed., *John of Salisbury's Memoirs of the Papal Court* (London: Nelson, 1956), pp. 28–29: "Sic et singuli scripturas sacras inveniunt vasa mortis; non tamen quod ille venena habeant, sed illi corruptos et toxicatos afferunt sensus." See also John of Salisbury's assertion that Christ was hidden in the letter of Scripture. *Policraticus,* 7. 12 (C.C.J. Webb, ed., vol. 2 [Oxford: Clarendon, 1909], pp. 137–38, 147).

[43] *Tr. in Ps. 70:* 24 (Migne *PL* 194: 310).

[44] *Expositio super canonem,* "Collatio missae" (*OI*, 1, p. 16). Gerhoch had no more regard for Masses sung by heretics (i.e., Nicolaites) than if they had been sung by pagans. *Dial. de cler. sec. et reg.* (*MGH, Ldl* 3, pp. 215–16).

[45] *Tr. in Ps. 43:* 22 (Migne *PL* 193: 1555). See also *Dial. de cler. sec. et reg.* (*MGH, Ldl* 3, p. 233).

[46] *Tr. in Ps. 64,* chap. 172 (Migne *PL* 194: 114).

[47] *Tr. in Ps. 70:* 24 (Migne *PL* 194: 311–12).

wandering thoughts.[48] Gerhoch found also that when he was sleepy in body or mind, he did not sing with mind and body, his attentiveness could be distracted, and he could be grievously saddened by fear that his prayer would be rejected, unheard by God.[49]

Thus, Gerhoch considered words and psalms as vessels to be filled according to the capacity of the speaker (or hearer), just as he regarded the painted crucifix as a receptacle to be filled with analogies according to the capacity of the beholder. God had abundantly filled the Psalms and their words with the wine of truth and the oil of charity.[50] The leap of understanding from the sensory words to the spiritual contents was not possible for all, or equally possible for those who found them. For not all, or all in equal measure, could in obedience use the method of analogy authentically to detect and assimilate the negative values in the psalms and their words.

One negative value in them was silence. The monastic discipline of contemplative silence naturally associated the Psalms with silence in Gerhoch's experience. The association was also natural in dealing with God, a subject that could be apprehended but not comprehended, and with a joy that could neither be expressed nor passed over entirely in silence.[51] It was natural that silence, a central feature of monastic discipline, appeared to Gerhoch not as a sterile void but as a fecund capacity. Gerhoch recalled a rhetorical figure, the elipsis, which enabled a speaker to say more by leaving a necessary word unspoken than by inserting it.[52] The soul cried to God with the inner voice, not in the clamor of words, but in the vehemence of desires; it sang to him when the bodily lips were closed.[53] Words and acts of charity merely followed and manifested the silence of this cry and jubilation. In silence, angels and archangels joined the human choirs in praising God.[54]

Greater negative values were the art, and the artist, in the Psalm. The art of music was in the ingenious mind, in the wise heart; and, without leaving the mind and heart, it went forth in admirable work. It went forth onto parchment, when the rules to be obeyed by small and large instruments in measure, number, and weight were written down. It went forth in a gross, corporal fashion through musical instruments, so that the unskilled could sweetly feel the subtle, invisible art by sight, touch and hearing. But the invisible exemplar remained in the ingenious mind. Gerhoch employed this analogue to elucidate how the Word of God could be both in the mind of

[48] On carnal imaginings, n. 84. On vain thoughts, *Tr. in Ps. 1*: Gloria (Migne *PL* 193: 655).
[49] *Tr. in Ps. 54*: 20 (Migne *PL* 193: 1657).
[50] *Tr. in Ps. 70*: 22 (Migne *PL* 194: 367).
[51] *Tr. in Ps. 26*: 6 (Migne *PL* 193: 1195). *Tr. in Ps. 146*: 5 (Migne *PL* 194: 975).
[52] *Tr. in Ps. 54*: 20 (Migne *PL* 193: 1663).
[53] *Tr. in Ps. 26*: 7 (Migne *PL* 193: 1197). *Tr. in Ps. 137*: 1 (Migne *PL* 194: 911).
[54] *Tr. in Ps. 9*: 15 (Migne *PL* 193: 763). *Tr. in Ps. 148*: 1 (Migne *PL* 194: 984–85). *Expositio super canonem*, "Sanctus," "collatio missae" (*OI*, 1, pp. 10, 15).

God and in the world, modulating it according to number, weight, and measure.

Christ was the Word full of all art. He was the art and music of God, hidden at first from the many, but latterly rendered visible and audible though the incarnation, just as wisdom, or music, exists first in the mind and later in the instrument, while remaining also in the mind.[55]

From grammar, Gerhoch drew another illustration of how the Word, or art, of God, functioned as a negative value in works of art. In grammar, he wrote, there were many elements that did not sound unless they were joined to, and sounded with vocables: these mute or semivocal letters were therefore called consonants. Likewise, human prayers were mute and inaudible letters in heaven unless the Word made flesh, the entirely and more than entirely vocal Word, were mixed with human consonants.[56]

Gerhoch affirmed that the artist unified the work and seized the attention of others by infusing it with his own nature (*ingenium*). People praised and loved the artist in his work, rather than the work itself. So much the more, Gerhoch wrote, should they love and praise God, the artist, in his works; for, beginning with nothing, he created not only the world but even the materials from which he made it.[57] Likewise, when the regenerate soul was inflamed with the Holy Spirit, the created work was informed with the nature of its Creator, just as, when metal is liquified in fire, it loses the forms of its own nature and takes on the form of the fire itself.[58] This reasoning enabled Gerhoch to argue that, although their bodies were buried in peace, Apostles still lived through their examples of life, their symbol of faith, and their written doctrines, as well as through their abiding benefactions.[59] Likewise, David and the other psalmists were present in the affects that informed their writings.[60] The telling fact for Gerhoch was that the Psalms manifested not only the art in the psalmists' ingenious minds but also the divinity inhabiting them, Christ, the "true David," or the Holy Spirit "who preached by the mouth of the holy prophets."[61] The examples, writings, and benefactions of the Apostles manifested both the arts in their own minds and divine Truth.[62]

[55] *Tr. in Ps. 19*: 3; *Tr. in Ps. 56*: 10 (Migne *PL* 193: 959, 1705–1706).

[56] *Tr. in Ps. 19*: 2 (Migne *PL* 193: 914). See also Bernard of Clairvaux, *De Diligendo Deo, 7. 22* (Jean Leclercq and H. M. Rochais, eds., *Tractatus et Opera*. [Rome: Editiones Cistercienses, 1963. *S. Bernardi Opera*, vol. 3], pp. 137–38): "Sed enim in hoc est mirum, quod nemo quaerere te valet, nisi qui prius invenerit. Vis igitur inveniri ut quaeraris, quaeri ut inveniaris. Potes quidem quaeri et invenire, non tamen praeveniri. Nam etsi dicimus: 'Mane oratio mea praeveniet te,' non dubium tamen quod tepida sit omnis oratio, quam non praevenerit inspiratio. Dicendum iam unde inchoet amor noster, quoniam ubi consummetur dictum est."

[57] *Tr. in Ps. 27*: 2 (Migne *PL* 193: 1224). *Tr. in Ps. 144*: 4 (Migne *PL* 194: 964).

[58] *Tr. in Ps. 72*: 19–20 (Migne *PL* 194: 349–50).

[59] *Tr. in Ps. 5*: 7 (Migne *PL* 193: 694).

[60] *Tr. in Ps.*, prologue (Migne *PL* 193: 633–36).

[61] *Tr. in Ps.*, prologue to *Pars I* (Migne *PL* 193: 626).

[62] *Tr. in Ps. 5*: 7 (Migne *PL* 193: 694) Cf. *Tr. in Ps. 43*: 2 (Migne *PL* 193: 1534): Orthodox

Gerhoch's assumption of negative values thus led him to the same circularity of obedient subordination in regard to psalmody as it did in regard to the painted crucifix. The work of art was a receptacle filled by its authenticating negative values. In the crucifix, these were the man depicted and the God in the man. In Psalms, and the words of Psalms, the negative values were, primarily, the art of the psalmist, the psalmist, and the God in the psalmist. The receptacle held these contents, but not for all, or for all equally. By pursuing analogic equivalences with the obedient eye of faith, the viewer, or the singer, had to recover them or, in effect, to fill the vessels, not according to their capacity, but according to his own.

The soul of the viewer or singer was itself a receptacle, and what it contained determined the contents that it could discern by analogy in the work of art. Parallel chains of analogues existed in the soul and in the work of art. In turn, the soul assimilated its own internal images to those in the work by analogic inference. Finding in the work analogues of what it had in itself, the "receptacle of the heart"[63] was replenished by partaking of what it found. "Showing my heart to you as an instrument of psalmody, I shall sing to be filled, and I shall be filled to sing, to you, O Lord. I shall sing, I say, and singing to my capacity, I shall be filled. Filled, I shall be made a vessel among 'the vessels of the Psalms,' " filled with the spirit of wisdom and understanding, with the spirit of counsel and fortitude, with the spirit of knowledge and piety; and the spirit of the fear of the Lord "will fill me from 'the vessels of the Psalms,' " which vessels, Gerhoch added, had been turned and rounded by the fingers and hand of God.[64]

Gerhoch therefore set up the leap of spiritual understanding as a cycle of affective assimilation in which love was cognate with obedience; and he supported that cycle by a method, also circular, of analogic inference. Through affective bonding, it was possible to put the same Psalm into the mouth of David, the prophet; of Christ, the true David; or of the Church (or any person in the Church), the body of Christ. For, in the one Church, all became one person, dedicated to the praise of God.[65] A speaker assumed the *persona* of the one by whose authority he spoke, or by whose inspiration he was filled. This event of personification, Gerhoch wrote, occurred daily in church. Standing in the midst of the people, a lector could proclaim, "I

---

believers, hearing the Church Fathers with their external sense, heard the Lord with their internal.

[63] Cf. *Tr. in Ps. 68*: 31 (Migne *PL* 194: 266), "in vasis cordium."

[64] *Tr. in Ps. 70*: 23 (Migne *PL* 194: 308–309).

[65] On Christ, the true David, e.g. *Tr. in Ps. 26*: 6 (Migne *PL* 193: 1196). On Gerhoch's frequent statement that "ego vel ego ecclesiastica persona" uttered a verse in a Psalm, e.g., *Tr. in Ps. 50*: 20, *56*: 4, *60*: 3, *70*: 18–19, *118*: 21. *Guimel*, 105. *Nun* (Migne *PL* 193: 1665, 1697, 1769. Migne *PL* 194: 301, 745, 794). Cf. *Tr. in Ps. 31*: 4b (*OI*, 2, pt. 1, pp. 34–35): "ego David vel ego paenitens ut David." Also *Tr. in Ps. 65*: 8 (Migne *PL* 194: 130). On the unity of the Church as one person in God's praise, *Expositio super canonem*, "communicantes" (*OI*, 1, p. 40).

am the God of Abraham and the God of Isaac and the God of Jacob. . . ."
But the lector neither proclaimed himself truly God, nor did he tell a lie.
For by voice he assumed the lordship of him whom he served by reading.
The hermeneutic circle was closed; the vicious circle, evaded. Likewise,
because they were filled with the Holy Spirit, the writers of Scripture were
drawn above themselves, as though they were quite outside themselves, and
so they could write about themselves as though they were not themselves.[66]

The Conditions of Understanding

The dependence that safeguarded the hermeneutic enterprise from the error
of self-reflection was written into the most basic conditions of understanding. For human beings were ultimately dependent upon their Creator
for their very existence, for their place in cosmic order, and for the distinctively human faculties that made understanding possible. Gerhoch took
these grounds of dependence for granted. But he was preoccupied with the
related conditions that enabled the few to go beyond knowledge (or interpretation) to authentic understanding, and, thus, transcending their animal
(or creaturely) faculties to become one with their own Creator.

The authentic hermeneutic experience (by contrast with the rhetorical
exercise) was in fact a reexperience by the understander of an author's state
of mind, and even of the Holy Spirit informing that state of mind. Evidently, the expression of interpretation was yet more complex than the
event of understanding. Reexperiencing emotions in the text was possible
because of the fundamental order of created existence, encompassing not
only the author and the interrogator of the text, but also all things that
were; because of the uniform composition of human nature particularly of
the soul, that made empathy and compassion possible; and also because of
the dynamic of play through which effective participation was achieved.
Finally, it was possible because of a call to participation that the interpreter
heard from within the text. I now turn to these broader aspects of the hermeneutic experience.

Ontology

The leap of spiritual understanding between the artist-in-the-work and the
interpreter required that both have a common nature. When God was the
artist-in-the-work, the interpreter's nature had to be transformed.

The entire world was permeated by the God from whom every order of
existence, "from the highest archangel to the lowest earthworm," derived
its being, and whose power and justice governed every particle of creation
from end to end, from the depths of the abyss to the heights of heaven,

---

[66] *Tr. in Ps.* 77: 1 (Migne *PL* 194: 436–37).

from the beginning of time to the consummation of ages.[67] God had made, and still made, the world so admirably that nothing was superfluous or inappropriate, down to the least worm.[68] Only a "sightless mind," he wrote, that had no regard for the whole would find fault with any part of the world, made, as it was, so that nothing was superfluous or unsuitable. To consider the parts separately would be like thinking about the nose, or any eye, alone; they could only be repellent taken in isolation, though they partook of, and contributed to, the beauty and utility of the whole.[69] The Son of God was manifest in this ordering of creation, "the mirror of creation," from the one end to the other, and the Holy Spirit manifested his judgment in the "mirror of creatures" by cooperating with the holy and elect in their good works.[70]

God was the life of the soul, just as the soul was the life of the body.[71] The great ontological question for Gerhoch was how the nature of human beings could be transformed into the nature of God. Evidently, the sacraments, notably the Eucharist, were means of this ontological change. The bread and wine were sanctified and changed into something else, and those who participated worthily in them were saved, being changed into Christ's body.[72] But the words and outward forms of consecration did not perform this double transformation. Rather, the Eucharistic bread became the Lord's body, into which the Word of God was "transfused," by faith in Christ's passion, resurrection, and ascension. Through unity of faith, catholic ministrants of the sacrament were at one with the Master of Truth, as branches on the vine, abiding in Christ and living from his spirit. Even if their morals were reprehensible, Christ spoke in them. Whatever they did was done by Christ and confirmed by his Spirit. Christ lived in the salvation of those communicating with them, so long as by faith they adhered as branches to Christ as their one vine. Likewise, unity of faith awakened the active effect of the sacrament among communicants, an effect that was merely passive, or latent, in sacraments of heretics, even when celebrated according to the prescribed form.[73] Participants were changed into gods by believing in God.[74] They were not "natural gods," as Christ was; but, chosen by God, they were "adopted gods," participating by faith in his divinity,[75] adhering in their truthfulness to the true God, and conforming their wills with his.[76]

---

[67] *Tr. in Ps. 70*: 18–19; *Tr. in Ps. 76*: 4; *Tr. in Ps. 118*: 129, *Fe*; *Tr. in Ps. 144*: 11 (Migne *PL* 194: 302–303, 425, 808, 966).

[68] *De aedificio Dei*, chap. 1 (Migne *PL* 194: 1193).

[69] *Liber de aedificio Dei*, chap. 1 (Migne *PL* 194: 1193).

[70] *Tr. in Ps. 39*: 5 (Migne *PL* 193: 1457).

[71] *Tr. in Ps. 70*: 17 (Migne *PL* 194: 300).

[72] *Princeps mundi* (*Liber de simoniacis*), chap. 25 (*MGH, Ldl* 3, p. 262).

[73] *Princeps mundi* (*Liber de simoniacis*), chap. 24–25 (*MGH, Ldl* 3, pp. 261–62).

[74] *Tr. in Ps. 32*: 4 (*OI*, 2, pt. 1, p. 112).

[75] *Tr. in Ps. 9*: 20; *Tr. in Ps. 49*: 1 (Migne *PL* 193: 766, 1595).

[76] *Tr. in Ps. 9*: 21 (Migne *PL* 193: 768). *Tr. in Ps. 33*: 2–5 (*OI*, 2, pt. 1, pp. 176, 221).

With an image familiar in writings of monastic spirituality, Gerhoch commented that, as those given to immoderate drinking of strong wine lose their wits, so too, inebriated with the fullness of God's house, the human minds of God's elect change into the divine.[77]

The Composition of the Soul

Given a common nature, bonding between the understander and the artist-in-the-work required a common impulse and directive. The body was a receptacle for the soul, which moved, ruled, and sensitized it.[78] Likewise, God had formed the rational soul as a vessel to contain understanding of his commands, understanding that was itself to be filed with faith. Indeed, so distinct was this concept of the soul as a receptacle that metaphors of filling provided the symbolic framework of the contrasting parallels between true and false Christians that Gerhoch drew in his masterpiece, the commentary on Psalm 64 that he presented to Pope Eugenius III.[79] Gerhoch emphasized

[77] *Tr. in Ps. 35*: 9 (quoting Gilbert de la Porrée). *Tr. in Ps. 37*: 2–5, (*OI*, 2, pt. 2, p. 597).

[78] *Tr. in Ps. 145*: 1 (Migne *PL* 194: 969). Cf. *Tr. in Ps. 68*: 31 (Migne *PL* 194: 266), "in vasis cordium." *De investig. Antichristi*, 1. preface (*MGH, Ldl* 3, p. 306), "totum receptaculum corporis et animae illuis."

[79] *Tr. in Ps. 118*: 73. *Jod* (Migne *PL* 194: 779). On the stages in the composition of Gerhoch's commentary on Psalm 64, see Damian Van den Eynde, *L'Oeuvre littéraire de Géroch de Reichersberg* (Rome: Pontificium Athenaeum Antonianum, 1957. *Spicilegium Pontificii Athenaei Antoniani*, 11), pp. 93–107. A provisional inventory of the contrasting parallels of metaphors of filling used in Gerhoch's commentary on Psalm 64 follows. On the key doctrine that Christ emptied himself and assumed human nature into God, *Tr. in Ps. 64*, chap. 88, 89 (Migne *PL* 194: 61–62).

For the eating metaphor, see *Tr. in Ps. 64*, chap. 110 (Migne *PL* 194: 73). (Gerhoch argues that the redeemed pass into the body of Peter by instant obedience just as did the unclean animals, killed and eaten by him.) *Tr. in Ps. 64*, chap. 172 (Migne *PL* 194: 114). (Christ is the fatted calf on which the blessed feast, and the Holy Spirit is its fat.)

On spiritual inebriation, *Tr. in Ps. 64*, chap. 105 (the blessed), 139 (the reprobate) (Migne *PL* 194: 76, *MGH, Ldl* 3, p. 480). There are many references of this sort.

On the metaphor of pure raiment in which the righteous, having been cleansed, were reclothed. *Tr. in Ps. 64*, chap. 99, 172, 173 (Migne *PL* 194: 67, 115).

On the temple in which the righteous were living stones, *Tr. in Ps. 64*, chap. 81–85 (Migne *PL* 194: 58–60).

On the good as valleys, or river channels, filled with abundance, or with God's pure waters, *Tr. in Ps. 64*, chap. 104–20 (Migne *PL* 194: 69–80). One and the same river of God flows in all spiritual men. *Tr. in Ps. 64*, chap. 64, 79 (*MGH, Ldl* 3, p. 468. Migne *PL* 194: 57).

On sexual metaphors of filling, see *Tr. in Ps. 64*, chap. 104, 120 for analogies between the earth as female and plowing as the act of the male in coition. *Tr. in Ps. 64*, chap. 123, 152, 171 (Migne *PL* 194: 81; *MGH, Ldl* 3, pp. 485–86; Migne *PL* 194: 114).

On the good as abundant fields, *Tr. in Ps. 64*, chap. 123, 152, 171 (Migne *PL* 194: 81, *MGH, Ldl* 3, pp. 485–86. Migne *PL* 194: 114).

On the saved as the contents of Lord's granary, *Tr. in Ps. 64*, chap. 121, 171 (Migne *PL* 194: 80, 114). See also chap. 23 (*MGH, Ldl* 3, p. 450), where Gerhoch equates two receptacles, (1) the valley of humility with (2) the reed baskets in which the Apostles gathered the fragments of the five loaves.

On the year of plenteousness, *Tr. in Ps. 64*, chap. 122 (Migne *PL* 194: 80).

On the evil as arid fields filled with thorns and thistles, *Tr. in Ps. 64*, chap. 120–23 (Migne

the soul as capacity for transformation—as a receptacle to be filled with
altered or new life—when he referred to the mind as a stomach or a womb.[80]

Capacity and deficiency were two sides of the same coin. But how was the
receptacle of the mind to be filled? It could be filled with illusions introduced
by the senses. Gerhoch distinguished the *animus*—reason, male, the interior man created after the image of God—from the *anima*—sensuality,
female, captivated by visible and carnal things. The animus sought invisible
things, such as truth, goodness, justice, and wisdom; but the anima troubled
it, as Eve, yielding to the serpent, troubled Adam. From the womb of
memory, the anima drew images left by the carnal senses, poisonous illusions that intruded spiritual fornication upon the inner man, even when he
was singing the Psalms or at prayer.[81]

To fill the intellect in this way was to realize only man's animal capacity.
Following St. Paul's distinction between the "animal man" who "receiveth
not the things of the Spirit of God," and the "spiritual man" who, having
the mind of Christ, "judgeth all things," (1 Cor. 2:14–16), Gerhoch repeatedly contrasted "animal men," who had no knowledge of the eternal and
supreme good, with those whose understanding had been filled with the
Holy Spirit and whose interior selves had been renewed according to the
image and likeness of God.[82] If the shepherds at Christ's nativity had not
believed the angel who brought them glad tidings, they would not have
been made gods; rather, not even remaining men, they could have ceased
to be rational men and become brute animals, as Herod, the slayer of the
innocents, was in the cruel bestiality of his unbelief.[83]

PL: 79–82).
On the evil as befouled channels of adulerated waters, *Tr. in Ps. 64*, chap. 127–29, 133, 135,
136, 139 (*MGH, Ldl* 3, pp. 473–75, 478–79, Migne *PL* 194: 92. *MGH, Ldl* 3, pp. 479–80.
On the wicked as fish, playing in the turgid and drying waters of Babylon's river or
devouring other fish, *Tr. in Ps. 64*, chap. 94, 138 (Migne *PL* 194: 65. *MGH, Ldl* 3, p. 479). See
also Gerhoch's statement that the continent were like fish because they did not procreate by
coition, an analogy without reference to the waters in which the fish live. *De investig. Antichristi*, 2. 20 (Scheibelberger, ed., p. 231).
On the evil as men blinded by the smoke of a seething cauldron (Jeremiah 1:13), *Tr. in Ps.
64*, chap. 64, 65 (*MGH, Ldl* 3, pp. 466–67).
On the Church as a splendid temple, like the temple of the Jews, glittering with gold on the
outside, but filled with corruption, *Tr. in Ps. 64*, chap. 169 (Migne *PL* 194: 113). Cf. the temple
of Christ's body, *Tr. in Ps. 64*, chap. 88, 89 (Migne *PL* 194: 61–62).
[80] For the metaphor of the stomach, see *Tr. in Ps. 77*: 16; *Tr. in Ps. 121*: 7–8 (Migne *PL*
194: 451, 813). For the metaphor of the womb, see *Tr. in Ps. 7*: 15 (Migne *PL* 193: 737). *Tr.
in Ps. 136*: 8 (Migne *PL* 194: 909), "in vulva mentis conceptae." *Exposit. super canonem*,
"praefatio" (*OI*, 1, p. 7). *Tr. in Ps. 33*: 15b. (*OI*, 2, pt. 1, p. 289). *Tr. in Ps. 35*: 25. (*OI*, 2, pt.,
2, pp. 421–22).
[81] *Tr. in Ps. 1*: Gloria; *Tr. in Ps. 41*: 6 (Migne *PL* 193: 656–57, 1505–1506). *Tr. in Ps. 136*:
8 (Migne *PL* 194: 908). *Tr. in Ps. 37*: 7 (*OI*, 2, pt. 2, pp. 628–29).
[82] *Tr. in Ps. 34*: 3b (*OI*, 2, pt. 1, p. 338). Those who are not inwardly renewed according to
the image and likeness of God remain in their old state, and they are rightly called "homines
vel iumenta." *Tr. in Ps. 35*: 7c–8a (*OI*, 2, pt. 2, p. 432).
[83] *Tr. in Ps. 32*: 4 (*OI*, 2, pt. 1, p. 111). On Herod as "homo ille, immo bestia," see *De*

Gerhoch occasionally distinguished between domesticated animals, such as oxen, sheep, and cattle, and wild beasts, such as wolves, lions, and bears. Gentle and obedient, the blessed could be considered animal men filled with blessing, while men of bestial heart were animal men filled with God's curse.[84] But, in general, man's animal sensuality and the carnal images stored in the memory were, for Gerhoch, most closely associated with sexual concupiscence "common to us with cattle and pigs, beasts and birds."[85] In act and in memory, the five senses served the "wicked," "most foul," and polluting lust that dominated the whole body and that found its throne in the loins.[86]

Thus, Gerhoch regarded animal men as damned by their blindness to things of the Spirit, even when they were expert in secular letters, trained in that wisdom that, being earthly and animal, is fettered to things of this world.[87] He took pains to represent the animal deformities of the human soul in pictures,[88] illustrating visually how the soul could conform with ravening beasts in ferocity, with soaring birds in self-exaltation, and with other brute animals in the degrading loss of human reason and piety. On earth, there were many beasts such as he represented masking their savage ferocity and serpentine coils with a human appearance, and playing even in the Church the role of the beast that in Paradise had been more cunning than all other animals.[89]

If the spiritual capacities of the soul were filled, what was human became god. If the animal capacities of the soul were filled, no ontological transformation occurred; there could be no union of heart and soul in God. In either case, filling the receptacle of the mind was the task of faculties other than those of the receptacle itself (i.e., intellect, counsel, and will). Behind the baneful effects of carnal images there was an original delight felt through the five senses,[90] recorded with images in the memory. The association of delight with the remembered images gave birth to offspring when the mind embraced the subjective image of the objective reality that it desired. Concupiscence motivated the erotic bonding of mind with image, and that

---

investig. Antichristi, 1. 44 (*MGH, Ldl* 3, p. 351). Occasionally, Gerhoch employed animals as analogues illustrating patterns of human behavior, or as apocalyptic types expressed in actual human beings. E.g., *Dial. de cler. sec. et reg.* (*MGH, Ldl* 3, pp. 220, 228, 238) (on Petrus Pierleoni). Normally, he referred to men as *"animales"* when he regarded their state of mind as "inhuman," because their hearts had not turned "to the knowledge and confession . . . of the one and only true God." *De aedificio Dei*, chap. 17 (*MGH, Ldl* 3, p. 149). *De investig. Antichristi*, 1. 30 (*MGH, Ldl* 3, p. 340). *Tr. in Ps. 36*: 25 (*OI*, 2, pt. 2, p. 543). Cf. *Tr. in Ps. 10*: 2 (Migne *PL* 193: 789): zeal and contentiousness are characteristics of carnal men.

[84] *Tr. in Ps. 34*: 3b (*OI*, 2, pt. 1, p. 349). *Tr. in Ps. 144*: 16 (Migne *PL* 194: 967).
[85] *Tr. in Ps. 77*: 45–48 (Migne *PL* 194: 465).
[86] *Tr. in Ps. 37*: 7 (*OI*, 2, pt. 2, pp. 626–27).
[87] *Tr. in Ps. 72*: 9 (Migne *PL* 194: 342).
[88] *Tr. in Ps. 37*: 4 (*OI*, 2, pt. 2, pp. 608–12).
[89] *Tr. in Ps. 19*: 3 (Migne *PL* 193: 952).
[90] *Tr. in Ps. 9*: 15 (Migne *PL* 193: 962).

bonding, in turn, led to action. Gerhoch wrote, for example, of the "genital concupiscence by which fetuses are procreated."[91] The desire for God was equally erotic and characterized in metaphors of ardent sensuality.[92] In either case, what prompted the appetite, the "assent of the mind"?

Gerhoch found the answer in the affects. The mind, he wrote, should be shaped by the affects of the individual conforming themselves with the affects set forth in the Psalms. Like some Cistercians of his generation, Gerhoch gave exceptional weight to the affects in forming the soul. By the intellect, he wrote, one knew justice. By the affect, one held to justice. The Holy Spirit taught by inflaming the affect,[93] but, in holy things as well as in profane, ardor was heightened by delaying the consummation of desire. By delay, desire was increased. By heightened desire the intellect was enlarged, and, as the intellect widened, the affect was opened the more ardently to receive the things of heaven.[94] The affects that ignited "genital concupiscence" were also the feet by which one entered the Lord's house, where one saw the God of gods face to face.[95]

Recognizing that affects were beyond counting,[96] Gerhoch yet identified many kinds, from those of the flesh to those of the spirit. He acknowledged that, in any particular circumstance, opposing affects (for example, affects of the flesh and those of piety) might be mixed, and that emotional swerves could recur from one affect to another.[97] When he considered the ontolog-

---

[91] *Tr. in Ps. 77*: 45–48 (Migne *PL* 194: 465).

[92] Below, nn. 167–178.

[93] *Tr. in Ps. 118*: 171 (Migne *PL* 194: 834). *Tr. in Ps. 136*: 8 (Migne *PL* 194: 908–909). *Tr. in Ps.*, prologue (Migne *PL* 193: 636).

[94] *Tr. in Ps. 21*: 3 (Migne *PL* 193: 996).

[95] *Tr. in Ps. 121*: 2 (Migne *PL* 194: 847).

[96] *Tr. in Ps.*, prologue (Migne *PL* 193: 624).

[97] Gerhoch's most complete discussion of affects and their interrelationships occurs in his prologue to the *Tractates on the Psalms* (Migne *PL*, 193: 632–34). He there mentions: the *affectus pietatis, dilectionis, admirationis, congratulationis, humilitatis, moeroris, timoris, indignationis, zeli*, and *bonae praesumptionis*. Elsewhere, he mentions both bad effects and good effects.

Bad affects include the following: Affectus peccandi, *Tr. in Ps. 57*: 3 (Migne *PL* 193: 1718). Affectus carnalis, *Tr. in Ps. 36*: 38 (*OI*, 2, pt. 2, p. 580). Affectus appetendi gloriam et honorem, *Tr. in Ps. 36*: 38 (*OI*, 2, pt. 2, p. 580). Affectus carnis, *Tr. in Ps. 118*: 25. *Daleth* (Migne *PL* 194: 750). Affectus stultitiae, *Tr. in Ps. 133*: 3 (Migne *PL* 194: 891) (referring to Gerhoch's early enthusiasm for the theater and other unwholesome displays of learning, in which, he said, he was proficient beyond his fellows). Affectus ambitionis, *Tr. in Ps. 29*: 5 (Migne *PL* 193: 1254). Affectus superbiendi, *Tr. in Ps. 73*: 23 (Migne *PL* 194: 380).

Good affects include the following: Affectus charitatis, *Tr. in Ps. 18*: 11 (Migne *PL* 193: 917). *Tr. in Ps. 1*: Gloria (Migne *PL* 193: 657) (cf. affectus dilectionis, above). Affectus filialis, *Tr. in Ps. 118*: 66. *Theth* (Migne *PL* 194: 774). Affectus maternus (in Christ), *Tr. in Ps. 15*: 3; *Tr. in Ps. 68*: 30 (Migne *PL* 193: 832. Migne *PL* 194: 265). Affectus humilitatis, *Tr. in Ps. 36*: 38 (*OI*, 2, pt. 2, p. 582). Affectus devotionis, *Tr. in Ps. 35*: 7c–8a (*OI*, 2, pt. 2, p. 430) (cf. affectus pietatis, above). Affectus laudandi, *Tr. in Ps. 148*: 2 (Migne *PL* 194: 984). Affectus doloris, *Tr. in Ps. 118*: 159. *Res* (Migne *PL* 194: 826).

For additional discussions of the affects, see *Tr. in Ps. 15*: 1–3; *Tr. in Ps. 17*: 9 (Migne *PL* 193: 832, 862).

ical bonding of God and human beings, he found that, of all the affects, charity formed the mind most powerfully.[98] But the affects themselves, even that of charity, were subject to the passions. The sensual life was captive to the worldly passions of unrighteous desire, evil fear, perverse joy, and melancholy.[99] Lacking charity, these passions generated servile, vice-ridden fear of divine punishment. By contrast, if they were sanctified by charity, passions of holy desire, dread, joy, and sorrow issued in a filial, virtuous fear of the Lord.[100] Holy fear was essential to the bonding of the soul to God. Such fear, Gerhoch wrote, was the unshakable basis on which God's word was established.[101] The Christian entered the chamber of hope through the door of fear;[102] indeed, Gerhoch taught, hope was useless without fear.[103]

Gerhoch witnessed the anguish of the situation thus described, smitten with fear because of his secrets,[104] and racked with uncertainty whether he merited God's hatred or love.[105] Still, he recognized that, if not overwhelmed by worldly fear or love, terror of eternal punishment was a useful teacher and an edifying critic. He himself fled to God's mercy because he had been terrified by God's justice and humbled by the chastening blows of his harsh love. From the experience of his conversion, Gerhoch knew that, mixed with love, terror impelled man to praise and adore his Maker.[106]

Just as the soul mediated between body and spirit, affects mediated between the passions, one's inmost self, and the outward, material existence—that is, between the passive and active modes of life.[107] Certainly, affects could remain without extrinsic effects. People could misread actions as manifesting specific affects (for example, tears as manifesting contrition), when the facts were otherwise.[108] But the perfect love of God was never vain. The affect of divine goodness always had temporal effects, appropriate to each believer's place and station, even when individual persons, lacking such effects, thought that they possessed that affect and were thought by others to possess it. To be sure, the affects of divine goodness, or love, had worked differently in different believers, according to the diversity of call-

---

[98] See references in n. 97.

[99] Cf. *Tr. in Ps. 1*: Gloria (Migne *PL* 193: 657).

[100] *Tr. in Ps. 18*: 10–11 (Migne *PL* 193: 912). *Tr. in Ps. 127*: 1 (Migne *PL* 194: 863).

[101] *Tr. in Ps. 118*: 38–39 (Migne *PL* 194: 760).

[102] *Tr. in Ps. 33*: 9 (*Ol*, 2, pt. 1, p. 272).

[103] *Tr. in Ps. 54*: 1 (Migne *PL* 193: 1649).

[104] *Tr. in Ps. 18*: 14 (Migne *PL* 193: 938).

[105] *Tr. in Ps. 118*: 63. *Heth* (Migne *PL* 194: 773).

[106] *Tr. in Ps. 18*: 11; cf. *Tr. in Ps. 21*: 17 (Migne *PL* 193: 920, 1021). *Tr. in Ps. 33*: 9 (*Ol*, 2, pt. 1, p. 281). See also *Tr. in Ps. 118*: 101. *Mem* (Migne *PL* 194: 792). *Tr. in Ps. 118*: 63, 66–68. *Heth. Theth* (Migne *PL* 194: 774, 776–77).

[107] For the contrast between the affect, acting in secret, and its manifest, or extrinsic, effect, see *Tr. in Ps. 59*: 7 (Migne *PL* 193: 1757). *Tr. in Ps. 144*: 8 (Migne *PL* 194: 965).

[108] *Tr. in Ps. 113*: 136. *Fe* (Migne *PL* 194: 815).

ings in the Church, even as divine love manifested itself with different effects in the Blessed Virgin and in John the Baptist. Some were raised to prelacy in the Church. Others had neither great wealth nor high office through which to produce external effects. Yet, in all, the affect was one and the same. Each manifested, as one could, the same great affect of love; in return, each received the same crown.[109] It was as though their hearts had come together in a living circle, equidistant from the same point, which no heart could touch, because a countervailing centrifugal tendency moved all away from the center at the same time as the centripetal attraction drew them toward the center.[110]

The crucial fact was that, motivating extrinsic actions as they did, affects impelled the soul to exceed itself. The acquisitive and proud exceeded themselves by serving the affect of their own hearts, rather than that of God, "so that, out of [their] inmost affect, intent on the cravings of [their] free will, they could, not only perform sins, but even love them."[111] By the affect of ambition, they set up an idol of Diana, the huntress, in their hearts.[112] By contrast, the blessed exceeded themselves through passing over by faith into the body of Christ and yielding to the affect of God.[113] For the soul approached the delights of its spiritual marriage with Christ, not by the intellect, the senses, the body, or life itself, but by true charity.[114]

In this movement, the human affects, by free action of the will, were conformed with the heart of Christ. The members of his Body participated in his divinity, just as he participated in their humanity. Changed in being, the soul perceived truths earlier inaccessible to it, just as Mary, seeing the risen Christ, disbelieved his resurrection and mistook him for a gardener until her heart was conformed in faith according to the heart of Christ. Slow of heart to believe, disciples unknowingly discoursed with their risen Lord at Emoaeus until, their hearts burning according to the heart of Christ, they recognized him in the breaking of bread. Peter too passed from ignorance to recognition when Christ appeared on the shore of Tiberias, and, confessing his love, the Apostle showed that his heart was as Christ's.[115]

Thus, all the redeemed, moved by one and the same affect of divine love,

---

[109] *Tr. in Ps. 18*: 11 (Migne *PL* 193: 924–27, 930–31).

[110] *Tr. in Ps. 18*: 11 (Migne *PL* 193: 930). See also *Tr. in Ps. 45*: 6 (Migne *PL* 193: 1575–76), comparing God in the midst of his city with the focal point of a circle, and the related passage in *De aedificio Dei*, chap. 3 (Migne *PL* 194: 1203). Cf. *Tr. in Ps. 75*: 12 (Migne *PL* 194: 410), on Jesus in the midst of the Apostles, "vel Spiritum sanctum, quum posuit Jesus in medio discipulorum, id est in cordibus eorum, quia locus cordis medietas est animalis."

[111] *Tr. in Ps. 72*: 7 (Migne *PL* 194: 314): "obliti se transeunt extra se, implendo, non dico illa peccata solummodo ad quae videtur impellere aliqua necessitas vel trahere infirmitas humana, sed transeunt 'in affectum' non Dei sed 'cordis sui.' . . ."

[112] *Tr. in Ps. 29*: 5 (Migne *PL* 193: 1254–55).

[113] *Tr. in Ps. 68*: 11 (Migne *PL* 194: 237), "credendo in me transirent in corpus meum."

[114] *Tr. in Ps. 6*: 1 (Migne *PL* 193: 710).

[115] *Tr. in Ps. 19*: 5–7 (Migne *PL* 193: 969–72).

mixed with terror, had one heart and one soul in God, while the reprobate, enshrining their private idols, approached the altar carrying the fire of worldly desire in the thuribles of their hearts or, worse, the fire of most shameful lust.[116]

RELATIONSHIP OF THE UNDERSTANDER TO
THE OBJECT OF UNDERSTANDING

Thus far, we have examined the evidence of dependence (in the fewness of those who authentically understand and in the esthetic character of understanding) and the grounds of dependence (in the dependence of a creature on its Creator and of the redeemed on the Redeemer). We are now in a position to examine the means by which the relationship of dependence was established in a special instance—namely, in the hermeneutic relationship of understander to the object of understanding. We can also go further to investigate some consequences that that ambiguous relationship had for society as a whole. Gerhoch identified three aspects of this relationship as primary: the act of participation; the event of assimilation (through play, often characterized in erotic analogues); and the call from God, the object of understanding, to the understanding soul.

Let us draw a summary profile of participation, before we enter into the complex dynamic of play, that movement by which capacities were fulfilled and the hermeneutic reexperience of emotions in the text was authentically achieved.

Gerhoch's autobiographical passages and his extensive account of the Second Crusade and its repercussions in Germany reveal an acute historical judgment and a fine narrative ability. But discourse about participation excluded historical depth of vision. The relationship of those who had one heart and mind in God was neither spatial nor temporal. Physical closeness and distance had nothing to do with the "local movement of the body," but rather with the "spiritual movement of the mind" or heart—that is, with the affects.[117] Likewise, their relationship was not temporal. Not length of days, but strength of affect, measured their service to God.[118] Before God, events occurred simultaneously in eternity, an "everlasting today."[119] Christ himself was the seventh day that the Father sanctified, blessed, and sent into the world,[120] and events done in him partook of the "everlasting today," even when they followed in the sequence of time. Thus, while

---

[116] *Tr. in Ps. 18*: 11 (Migne *PL* 193: 930). *Tr. in Ps. 64*, chap. 32 (*MGH, Ldl* 3, p. 454). Above, nn. 45, 112.

[117] *Tr. in Ps. 67*: 2; *Tr. in Ps. 77*: 34; *Tr. in Ps. 89*: 10 (Migne *PL* 194: 165, 460, 520).

[118] *Tr. in Ps. 75*: 12 (Migne *PL* 194: 409).

[119] *Tr. in Ps. 2*: 7 (Migne *PL* 193: 664).

[120] *Tr. in Ps. 37*: 2–5 (*OI*, 2, pt. 2, p. 597). Cf. *Tr. in Ps. 35*: 9 (*OI*, 2, pt. 2, p. 438). *Expositio super canonem*, "collatio missae" (*OI*, 1, p. 11).

Christ's incarnation, death, and ascension were done once and for all, his resurrection was continual in converted sinners, "clothed in the Paschal robe of resurrection."[121] Hoping in his mercy, as had the patriarchs of the Old Testament, living people could say that they had waited upon him in the ancient Fathers, even as they now did in themselves.[122] All ages fell away during the Eucharist, when believers could return in mind to the paradise of delight and eat the fruit of the tree of life.[123]

Gerhoch called the principle of this relationship "participation." He took the term from Psalm 121:3: "Jerusalem aedificatur ut civitas, cujus participatio ejus in idipsum." The translation, "Jerusalem is builded as a city that is compact together," conceals the kind of unity that Gerhoch read into the difficult words "cujus participatio ejus in idipsum." The idipsum in which participation occurred, he wrote, was God. He sharply distinguished participation, which united, from partition, which divided. If Adam had overcome temptation, he and his offspring could have fulfilled God's blessing, "Increase and multiply and fill the earth" (Gen. 9:7), without being subject to death; for only the elect would have been born. The principle of participation would have been unneeded and unknown to the human race.

Through Adam's sin, a partition, or separation, did occur between the children of the curse, who did not wish to know God (idipsum) and who were implacably divided against one another, and the children of the blessing who strove with toil and in the sweat of their brows to eat the bread of charity. The children of the blessing felt God in common (idipsum invicem sentientes), lived peaceably in the present life, and, dying, slept peaceably in idipsum. Jerusalem was built in in idipsum only from the children of the blessing, those who spoke and knew and died in idipsum.[124]

To visualize participation, Gerhoch employed the metaphor of the circle. The edifice of the city was like a building with a round foundation. Because all points were equidistant from the center, the whole was drawn back in idipsum, to that invisible point of unity, just as the city was unified by participation in its unifying focal point.[125] Thus, Gerhoch wrote, God was the boundless mercy, the fullness of mercy, in which all the merciful participated.[126] The holiness that was inherent in God and that was God was

---

[121] Tr. in Ps. 7: 8 (Migne PL 193: 730).

[122] Tr. in Ps. 32: 22 (OI, 2, pt. 1, p. 151).

[123] Expositio super canonem, "collatio missae" (OI, 1, p. 23). A fuller consideration of Gerhoch's historical conceptions appears in my article, "The Church as Play: Gerhoch of Reichersberg's Call for Church Reform," in Festschrift Brian Tierney.

[124] Liber de aedificio Dei, chap. 1 (Migne PL 194: 1195–97). See also chap. 8, 50, 53. (MGH, Ldl 3, pp. 141, 165, 167). Tr. in Ps. 121: 3 (Migne PL 194: 847–48). Classen's judgment that Gerhoch derived his doctrine of participation from the Bible, rather than from Neoplatonic theology, appears to exclude unduly the heavy freight of Neoplatonism carried in the general corpus of Christian theology. Classen, Gerhoch von Reichersberg, p. 41.

[125] Liber de aedificio Dei, chap. 3 (Migne PL 194: 1203–1204). See above, n. 110.

[126] Tr. in Ps. 58: 18 (Migne PL 193: 1747).

conveyed as an accident to the saints, who partook of God's nature.[127] The risen Christ, preserving the integrity of human nature in divine glory, wished that his ministers be where he was and see his glory, and, seeing it, partake of and enjoy it, in the same way as bodily eyes, seeing the brightness of the sun, partake of its light, rejoicing the more fully, the more clearly they see it.[128] Yet, the glory participated to them was eclipsed by the brilliance of divine glory, even as the light of a star is eclipsed by that of the sun.[129]

Gerhoch's concept of uniform human nature also enabled him to think of nonparticipatory kinds of personal union. Common descent, for example, made it possible for him to write that, when his ancestors, Adam and Eve, sinned, he sinned in them.[130] Feeling the same thing in common (*id ipsum invicem sentiendo*) permitted compassionate bonding.[131] Adherence to the same doctrines, or commitments, established a wide range of unitive relationships. Thus, the Apostle Peter was said to preside in the reigning pope,[132] and Simon Magus lived in his followers, the simoniac clergy, or rather he daily died and left in them the stinking corpse of his sin. So, too, the spirit and power of prophets, who once preached in their own persons, returned in those who followed and imitated them.[133]

Still, bonding by common descent, feeling, or commitment did not establish the unity of heart and soul in God, as did bonding by participation. Divine and human modes of being were so utterly different that God was inaccessible to human faculties, and sacred truth, revealed to some, was incommunicable among human beings. In their normal state, human affections were like cold coals, neither burning nor enlightening. Aroused by vices, they burned without casting light. Only when kindled by grace could they burn and illuminate.[134] Likewise, it was impossible for any person to teach another to be just. Only the Holy Spirit taught justice, opening the intellect to recognize it and inflaming the heart to cleave to it.[135]

Even grace, while mediating the dialectic between divine and human being, did not extinguish it. Grace was a necessary preliminary to the bonding of hearts and souls, and that bonding itself, by participation, occurred through the mediation of Christ. Through that mediation, God the Father, being in Christ, was also in believers. In them and with them, the

---

[127] *Tr. in Ps.* 67: 16 (Migne *PL* 194: 189).
[128] *Tr. in Ps.* 15: 6 (Migne *PL* 193: 838).
[129] *Tr. in Ps.* 19: 4 (Migne *PL* 193: 962).
[130] *Tr. in Ps.* 118: 66. *Teth* (Migne *PL* 194: 777).
[131] *Tr. in Ps.* 18: 11 (Migne *PL* 193: 925).
[132] *Liber de aedificio Dei*, chap. 66 (*MGH, Ldl* 3, p. 173).
[133] *Princeps mundi* (*Liber de simoniacis*), chap. 33 (*MGH, Ldl* 3, p. 271). *Tr. in Ps.* 118: 24. *Guimel* (Migne *PL* 194: 750). *De investig. Antichristi*, 1. 74 (*MGH, Ldl* 3, p. 395).
[134] *Tr. in Ps.* 17: 9 (Migne *PL* 193: 862).
[135] *Tr. in Ps.* 118: 171. *Tau* (Migne *PL* 194: 834).

Father through Christ performed the works that their faith required to live.[136] A believer who was man because he carried the image of Adam, the earthly man, was regenerated in baptism through Christ's mediation. He became the Son of man because, putting off the old man, he now carried the image of the heavenly man, Christ.[137] "Wherever a true Christian is, there is Christ."[138]

Gerhoch's doctrine of participation can be defined more precisely. First, Gerhoch assumed that participation was isomorphic. The believer partook of Christ entirely, not in part. Christ was "whole in heaven, whole on the altar, whole in the mouth of one eating his body and drinking his blood; whole in the mouth of one believing unto righteousness; whole in the mouth of one confessing unto salvation."[139] Thus, believers participated fully in Christ's kingly and priestly anointings, for they were, with him, one Christ. So, too, when Christ sanctified himself as a sacrifice before the crucifixion, he sanctified all his followers, the members of his Body, as an "acceptable sacrifice." He consecrated them for the mystic sacrifices that the Holy Spirit consummated in the holocaust with which he inflamed their hearts.[140]

Second, Gerhoch assumed that participation was asymmorphic. There was no exchange in the mediated dialectic. The believer was changed into Christ (or God); but Christ (or God) was not changed into the believer. Thus, Christ was persecuted, abandoned, and crucified in his poor, although, as God, he was impassible.[141] To be sure, Christ, like Ulysses, appeared in different forms to different people, according to their capacities, expectations, and circumstances; but he himself was changeless, always one and the same. "I live," St. Paul had written, "yet not I, but Christ lives in me" (Gal. 2:20).[142]

Finally, Gerhoch assumed that participation was polymorphic. Christ was unity; but his Body displayed the "variety of unity."[143] Eating his Body,

---

[136] *Tr. in Ps. 34*: 22 (*OI*, 2, pt. 1, p. 386). Cf. *Tr. in Ps. 142*: 8 (Migne *PL* 194: 952): Satan works through his members.

[137] *Tr. in Ps. 8*: 5; *Tr. in Ps. 10*: 9; *Tr. in Ps. 20*: 11; *Tr. in Ps. 143*: 3 (Migne *PL* 193: 748, 808, 983, Migne *PL* 194: 956). Cf. *Tr. in Ps. 35*: 8b (*OI*, 2, pt. 2, pp. 434–35), where Gerhoch argued that, by baptismal rebirth, believers became, not men, but sons of men.

[138] *Ep. 7* (Migne *PL* 193: 497): "ubique verus Christianus, ibi Christus."

[139] Ibid.

[140] *Tr. in Ps. 26*: 1 (Migne *PL* 193: 1175). Cf. *Tr. in Ps. 8*: Gloria (Migne *PL* 193: 752), on Christ's pontifical miter and royal crown. *Tr. in Ps. 19*: 1, 3 (Migne *PL* 193: 942, 957–58). See Classen, *Gerhoch von Reichersberg*, p. 190, on Gerhoch's assertion of the priesthood of all believers, through justification by faith.

[141] *Tr. in Ps. 21*: 1 (Migne *PL* 193: 992). *Tr. in Ps. 69*: 2. *De aedificio Dei*, chap. 13 (Migne *PL* 194: 274, 1233). *De aedificio Dei*, chap. 30 (*MGH, Ldl* 3, p. 157).

[142] *Tr. in Ps. 21*: 8; *Tr. in Ps. 58*: 7 (Migne *PL* 193: 1005–1007, 1735–36). Gerhoch frequently cited Gal. 2:20. E.g., *Tr. in Ps. 22*: 5; *Tr. in Ps. 26*: 8 (Migne *PL* 193: 1062, 1200). *Tr. in Ps. 35*: 15b (*OI*, 2, pt. 1, p. 289).

[143] *Tr. in Ps. 26*: 3–4; *Tr. in Ps. 44*: 10 (Migne *PL* 193: 1187–88, 1570).

believers were "concorporated" with Christ. Drinking his blood, they were "conviscerated" and "convivified" with him in all their diversity.[144] They comprised one man, one person, who, in love, had one heart and soul,[145] even though they were scattered throughout the world.[146] They remained many diverse members, each with its own function, bound together by one mediating adhesive, "as many members become one dove."[147]

Analyzing what Gerhoch meant by unity of heart and mind in God, we came first to his principle of identity, which was defined speculatively, with reference to the order of being. That led in turn to a dialectical relationship governed by the principle of participation, which was, in fact, a branch of Gerhoch's Christology. Before authentic union could occur through participation, before the leap of spiritual understanding could be made, a third principle had to come into play, that of assimilation.

The Dynamic of Play

From the Fathers, including Augustine, Gerhoch inherited the concept of play as a rhetorical device, but, even more, as the dynamic by which participatory union was achieved through interpretation. Gerhoch's own career and temperament enabled him to express with unusual clarity the rhetoric and the dynamic of play.

Of the four varieties of play exploited by the Church Fathers—play of imitation (drawn from the theater), of conflict (drawn from the amphitheater), of endurance and skill (drawn from the circensian games), and of hazard (drawn from gambling)—that of imitation lay closest to Gerhoch's heart. For him, as for the Fathers, all these analogues of play, including notably those taken from theatrical performance, were ways of illuminating aspects of the game of love.

To be sure, Gerhoch occasionally expressed his affinity to the theater in denials. Brilliantly trained in rhetoric, he delighted in theatrical productions when he was master of the school at Augsburg, before his conversion to the common life. Later, he especially deplored the performance in churches of theatrical works, even on Scriptural themes, as a practice launched by clergy of distinguished lineage and excellent literary education who consumed the sustenance of the poor in vain luxuries. Polluted with concubinage, he wrote, they brought their women with them when they changed their churches into theaters; while they put on plays about Antichrist, they set themselves up as the abomination of desolation in the holy place.[148]

---

[144] *Tr. in Ps.* 22: 5 (Migne *PL* 193: 1062).

[145] *Tr. in Ps. 111:* 1 (Migne *PL* 194: 703). *Expositio super canonem,* "communicantes" (*OI,* 1, p. 40).

[146] *Tr. in Ps.* 4: 9 (Migne *PL* 193: 686–88).

[147] *Tr. in Ps.* 67: 14 (Migne *PL* 194: 185).

[148] *De investig. Antichristi,* 1. 5 (*MGH, Ldl* 3, p. 315).

Although he loved music, he disliked polyphony in churches; it reminded him of elaborate modulations in theatrical songs, which ought to be cast out as stinking rags.[149]

These denials, however, did nothing to conceal the degree to which theatrical play marked Gerhoch's thought and work. Indeed, when he discussed the three expository styles available to him—the exagematic, the dramatic, and the mixed—he explained why he chose the mixed style for his voluminous commentaries on the Psalms. The exagematic style of plain discourse, he said, suited factual statements. The dramatic style enabled writers of comedies, tragedies, and other genres not to speak indirectly about others but to personify them and, through the immediacy of direct discourse, to stir the emotions of their audiences. Employing the mixed style, philosophers, such as Plato and Boethius, had occasionally spoken through the disguise of personification, as had prophets and the author of the *Apocalypse*. Gerhoch followed these precedents, he wrote, because the mixed style enabled him to heighten the effect of empathetic participation; it made it possible for readers to join their affects to those of others with true devotion. Unlike the dramatic style, which merely simulated the affects of those in joy or sorrow, the mixed style enabled readers truly and devoutly to join their affects with those of others.[150]

Gerhoch considered the experience of the saved in this world a drama made up of pathos, periptery, and theophany.[151] But the encounter between reader and text was also a dramatic performance. This was true of the encounter between Scripture and readers, who identified themselves with participants in the *spectacula* of sacred history; it was also true of encounters between Gerhoch's own text, which recreated those spectacles, and the *benevoli spectatores* who read it.[152] Gerhoch acknowledged that empathy occurred, if at all, not in words but in the contemplative silence of the heart, that most inward moment of stillness and unspeakable joy when, in its sleep, the soul felt the gentle touch of its divine spouse.[153] Yet, one approached that moment through the senses. Daily immersed in the theatricality of the liturgy, Gerhoch imagined into his work the performing arts

---

[149] *De aedificio Dei*, chap. 64 (*MGH, Ldl* 3, pp. 172–73). *Tr. in Ps. 39*: 4 (Migne *PL* 193: 1438).

[150] *Tr. in Ps.*, prologue to *Pars I* (Migne *PL* 193: 631–33). *Tr. in Ps. 36* (*OI*, 2, pt. 2, p. 575). In view of Gerhoch's devotion to the memory of Pope Gregory VII, it is interesting to recall that one charge brought by the Synod of Brixen (1080) against that pope was that he was more devoted than laymen to "obscene theatrical shows." Carl Erdmann, ed., *Die Briefe Heinrichs IV* (Stuttgart: Hiersemann, 1978. *Deutsches Mittelalter: Kritische Studientexte*, 1), p. 70.

[151] See my essay, "The Church as Play: Gerhoch of Reichersberg's Call for Reform," in *Festschrift Brian Tierney*.

[152] For a review of incidents referred to as *spectacula* by Gerhoch, see the essay cited in n. 151. He addressed his readers as *benevoli spectatores* in *Tr. in Ps. 64*, chap. 73 (*MGH, Ldl* 3, p. 471).

[153] *Tr. in Ps. 4*: 7; *Tr. in Ps. 25*: 8 (Migne *PL* 193: 684, 1170).

of rhetoric, music, and theatre, even adorning some manuscripts with pictures and musical notations.[154] In his commentaries, he frequently wrote as the personification of a Scriptural figure, performing, before his *benevoli spectatores* the role of David, of Jeremiah, to whom Gerhoch felt a particular affinity, or even of Christ. These were evidently dramatic devices by which he deliberately stimulated his own empathetic participation in Scripture, as well as that of his readers. Reading became performance.

Gerhoch recognized that music, as well as personification, was a means of performance, notably with regard to the Psalms, and it too entered his dramatic repertoire. He identified psalmody with writing; to discourse on the psalms was also to sing them.[155] To discourse on the psalms, and to sing them rightly, was to take the psalmists' meanings to heart. Thus, Gerhoch strove "to form the mind according to the meanings (*sensus*) and affects (*affectus*) of the Psalms," not only by his method of discussing the matter of the Psalms, but also by his method of singing for the discipline (*exercitium*) of the mind. His object was to inflame the heart with desire for union.[156]

For Gerhoch, as for the Church Fathers, the empathetic participation elicited in the theater provided one way to speak of the soul's erotic passage from sensual experience and spiritual union. His use of the biological paradigm of assimilation, like Augustine's, profoundly complements his use of the esthetic one and, in some instances established an equivalence between the two paradigms. Gerhoch's comments on sexuality illustrate the importance of role playing, and, indeed, of role reversals in the dynamic play of love, which demanded of him the offering of chastity.

It was not possible, Gerhoch acknowledged, to crush sensuality without destroying the powers of growth and fulfillment.[157] He considered sexuality dominant in sensual existence, and a survey of his attitude toward sexuality may serve to define the complex means by which he passed from sensual experience to spiritual perception.

Gerhoch's thoughts about sexuality moved within the conventional paradox that, whereas sterility was a curse, virginity (or sexual abstinence) was a virtue.[158] True to convention, Gerhoch resolved the paradox by understanding sterility in a spiritual sense and virginity in a physical one. Con-

---

[154] *Tr. in Ps.* 37: 4 (*OI*, 2, pt. 2, pp. 608–12). Classen, *Gerhoch von Reichersberg*, pp. 115–16. On the theatrically of liturgy in Rome, see *Tr. in Ps.* 64, chap. 10 (*MGH, Ldl* 3, p. 445).

[155] See above, n. 30. See also *Tr. in Ps.* 74: 1; *Tr. in Ps.*, prologue to *Pars VIII* (Migne *PL* 194: 381, 390).

[156] *Tr. in Ps.*, prologue (Migne *PL* 193: 636).

[157] *De investig. Antichristi*, 2. 29 (Scheibelberger, ed., p. 249).

[158] A few examples suffice. On the opprobium of sterility, *Ep. 4* (Migne *PL* 193: 494). *Tr. in Ps. 34:* 27–28. (*OI*, 2, pt. 1, p. 397): sterile branches are to be cut off the vine of Christ and burned. On fecundity as a sign of the Church, *Tr. in Ps.* 2: 8; *Tr. in Ps.* 17: 47 (Migne *PL* 193: 665, 890).

sequently, nuptial metaphors and other erotic images extolling fecundity were applied to roles played in the spiritual life. In physical existence, marriage was a state of life compassionately instituted for the weak. The better way, even for the married, was to castrate oneself to works of the flesh for the sake of the kingdom of heaven.[159] Before Gerhoch hovered the "sterile virginity" of the Blessed Virgin, which became fecund by faith.[160]

To say this, of course, is to say that Gerhoch assumed a negative value that equated sexual denial in the physical order with spiritual fecundity in the invisible order. Because of that negative value, Gerhoch was able to treat spiritual marriage as an analogue of physical existence and to transfer by analogy the eroticism of the procreative act to the spiritual union of the soul with God. Quite deliberately, Gerhoch recreated in the invisible order of dependence a reversal of roles that he had abandoned in the physical one.

The distinction between voluntary physical sterility and spiritual fecundity permitted Gerhoch to distinguish between the outer man, denied physical union, and the inner man, subsumed in the ardent erotic union of heart and soul. In the area of sexual denial, Gerhoch asserted masculine dominance. He recalled that the Old Testament had excluded female animals as sacrificial offerings, permitting only males as oblations to God.[161] Women were physically inferior to men. In the Church, it was the function of men, stronger and more constant in preaching the word of God by virtue of their manliness, to write or speak according to the grace given them, or to do God's work in some other way. Weaker and more apt for service, women were not permitted to speak in the Church.[162] Even the Blessed Virgin did not write down God's words to her, but entrusted them to Apostles and Evangelists, who worthily spoke and wrote them. She was queen of the humble and chief exemplar of humility, in deferring to the Apostles and Evangelists and declining to teach men.[163] It was wrong even to mix the weaker voices of women with the stronger ones of men in chorus.[164]

---

[159] Martin Alois Fischer, "Vita Apostolica bei Gerhoch von Reichersberg" (Ph. D. diss., Innsbruck, 1971), p. 94. *De aedificio Dei*, chap. 30, 42 (Migne *PL* 194: 1271, 1298–99). *Expositio super canonem*, "Evangelium" (*OI*, 1, p. 4): the camps of the Lord are full of priests and ministers castrated for the kingdom of heaven's sake.

[160] *Liber de laude Fidei* (*OI*, 1, p. 267).

[161] *Tr. in Ps. 75*: 12 (Migne *PL* 194: 407).

[162] *De investig. Antichristi*, 2. 75 (Scheibelberger, ed., pp. 335–36).

[163] *Tr. in Ps. 64*, chap. 23 (*MGH, Ldl* 3, p. 450).

[164] On weakness: *Tr. in Ps. 21*: 1 (Migne *PL* 193: 991): ". . .humana in Christo natura, quae quasi femina a tempore mortalitatis magnam propter nos habuit fragilitatem. . ." *Tr. in Ps. 67; Expositio in Cant. Moysis*, 1 (Migne *PL* 194: 216, 1027–28). On choirs, *Expositio in Cant. Moysis*, 1 (Migne *PL* 194: 1026). Cf. *Tr. in Ps. 67*: 26 (Migne *PL* 194: 206). The Second Lateran Council (1139) forbade nuns to sing in the same choir with monks (canon 27). Karl Joseph von Hefele and Henri Leclerq, *Histoire des Conciles*, vol. 5, pt. 1 (Paris: Letouzy et Ané, 1912), p. 733. Reflecting Byzantine practice, Anna Comnena recorded that her father prescribed that there be both male and female singers in the choirs in the orphanage that he established at the church of St. Paul. *History*, 15. 7.

Remembering that the word *vir* (a male human being) was derived from *virtus* (virtue), Gerhoch was outraged by such innovations in his day as the prostitution of boys, the profanation of altars by deviant sexual practices, and theatrical performances in churches in which "men entirely degraded themselves to play the roles of women, as though they were ashamed to be men."[165] But, as we shall see, there was an evident contradiction between this criticism and Gerhoch's willingness to play feminine roles in the Church (see discussion at n. 178).

Playing roles enabled an actor to be two persons at once—himself and the character personified by him. Yet the psychological separations between male and female and between physical and spiritual coition were never complete. Every soul impregnated by God and conceiving and giving birth to his Word, Gerhoch wrote, became the spouse of God and the mother of Christ.[166] To describe the impregnating union, Gerhoch strangely combined the erotic embrace extolled in the Song of Songs (2:6) with the prophet Elisha's revival of the Shunamite woman's son. Elisha stretched himself out upon the child, mouth upon mouth, eyes upon eyes, and hands upon hands (2 Kings 4:34). Gerhoch interpreted the placing of mouth upon mouth as a life-giving kiss, the one kiss made up of two persons.[167] This union transformed the believer's countenance into conformity with God's beauty and assimilated it to the goodness of his countenance. Thus, the bodily eyes, with the other organs of physical sensation, could rest from their labors, so that the Lord's countenance could shine in Gerhoch's. The grace diffused from his lips, mouth placed upon mouth, would abound in Gerhoch's, and his hand would work in Gerhoch's. The lover's song to his beloved would be fulfilled: "Your cheeks are as beautiful as the turtledove's" (Cant. 1:9).[168]

Gerhoch imagined the affective life as female, whether it were still subject to the senses, like the Samaritan woman, bereft of five husbands and having

---

[165] *De investig. Antichristi,* 1. 5 (*MGH, Ldl* 3, p. 316). Cf. St. Cyprian, *Ep. 1:* 8 (Migne *PL* 2: 215): ". . . quisquis virum in feminam magis fregerit." On the derivation of *vir* from *virtus, Tr. in Ps. 52:* 3 (Migne *PL* 193: 1644). Another aspect of the question is indicated by Gerhoch's comment on Psalm 18: 11 (*Tr. in Ps. 18:* 11 [Migne *PL* 193: 926]): "Quis enim sapiens et gustans judicia Domini vera, non hoc sapiat in eis, quod pretiosior fuit castitas Mariae virginis, quae carnis incentiva non sentiens casto Domini amore flagravit, quam castitas Pauli apostoli, qui stimulum carnis tolerando viriliter contra eumdem pugnavit?" On what Gerhoch considered a revival of prostitution of boys in his day, *De investig. Antichristi,* 1. 74 (*MGH, Ldl* 3. p. 395). On the profanation of the episcopal chapel in Regensburg by Satanic rituals, *De investig. Antichristi,* 1. 17 (*MGH, Ldl* 3, p. 324).

[166] *Tr. in Ps. 16:* 8 (Migne *PL* 193: 851). *Expositio super canonem,* "collatio missae" (*OI,* 1, p. 24). On the metaphor of the mind as a womb, above n. 80.

[167] *De investig. Antichristi,* 2. 35 (Scheibelberger, ed., p. 267). For an analogy between the union of two persons in a kiss and the union of two natures in Christ, see *De investig. Antichristi,* 2. 2 (Scheibelberger, ed., pp. 192–93).

[168] *Tr. in Ps. 26:* 8 (Migne *PL* 193: 1200). *Tr. in Ps. 118:* 29. *Daleth.* (Migne *PL* 194: 756): "osculo tuo."

no legitimate spouse (John 4:17–18),[169] or like the spouse trembling with delight and dread: "My beloved put his hand through the orifice and my bowels quaked within me" (Cant. 5:4).[170]

The affects (feminine) were prior to the intellect (masculine), although the intellect was the loftier of the two and the one that "with uncovered face, mirroring the splendor of the Lord, is transformed from splendor into splendor, as by the Spirit of the Lord." Gerhoch captured this ambivalence when he described the soul itself as composing two kinds of speculation (*theoriae*): The first was the female level of feelings, the carnal ones being enmeshed in the obscurity of images, and the spiritual ones, stricken silent with virgin fear at the approach of the divine bridegroom and enraptured by the torrent of divine pleasure. The other was the level of intellect, the male child given birth by the sensory level, as the Blessed Virgin gave birth to Jesus. The male speculation was the stronger and the more sublime, but it received the fruits of illumination from the female, weaker than the male, to be sure, but also the more devout and the readier to serve. The sedulity of women concerning details of Christ's burial earned them the privilege of discovering his resurrection before the Apostles and of announcing it to them, although as men, stronger and more constant in preaching the Word of God, the Apostles proclaimed the resurrection to the world. Likewise, as women were not allowed to speak in the Church, so too, in the soul, what was received as a secret by the feelings ought to be kept as a secret by them and not conveyed to others; but those hidden perceptions were wellsprings from which the intellect drew waters for the advantage of others. Thus, Gerhoch concluded rather inconsistently, in the Christian, as in Christ, there was neither male nor female, but both were one in dignity and grace.[171]

In these comments, Gerhoch reflects the thinking in liturgical drama in his day for Passiontide, which prescribed that subdeacons enact the roles of the women at the foot of the cross, and of those to whom the resurrection was first revealed.[172]

Certainly, it had been conventional from classical antiquity onward to characterize the soul as female. This convention had considerable importance for Gerhoch. When he portrayed the affective faculties as female, he

[169] *Tr. in Ps.* 67: 6 (Migne *PL* 194: 172).

[170] Gerhoch applied this verse to the mind. *Expositio super canonem,* "praefatio" (*OI*, 1, p. 7).

[171] *De investig. Antichristi,* 2. 75 (Scheibelberger, ed., pp. 333–36). Cf. *Tr. in Ps.* 7: 2 (Migne *PL* 193: 725): "Una theoria dicitur, id est visio, sive contemplatio, et in hoc est virtus theoreticae vitae, ut fiat ratio humana particeps aeternae sapientiae, quae non est aliud quam ipse Dei Filius." See above, n. 20, on visual associations.

[172] O. B. Hardison, Jr., *Christian Rite and Christian Drama in the Middle Ages: Essays in the Origin and Early History of Modern Drama* (Baltimore: Johns Hopkins University Press, 1965), pp. 70–72.

was able to ascribe to them the traits that he ascribed to women: weakness, subordination, and dependence, notably in needing impregnation with form in order to bear young. Possibly, Gerhoch was able in this way to confront some of his own sexual ambivalence. He captured that ambivalence himself when he wrote that, through the union of the soul with Christ there were two beings in the flesh of one man, the bridegroom and the bride.[173] At the age of thirty-nine, Gerhoch ascribed his conversion from the secular to the religious life to terror, fearful signs, and excruciating illness visited upon him by God. He placed the decisive moment in his sixteenth and seventeenth year. Stricken then with disease and insupportable pain, he embraced the life of chastity and recovered, although the loss of his virginity remained a matter of regret.[174] Throughout his career, he endured bitter sexual temptations and anxieties, charged with guilt, a sense of pollution, and fear of punishment that even strict penance only assuaged.[175]

His painful quest for purification and forgiveness, and perhaps for erotic pleasure that would never end,[176] may well have enabled him to find some measure of his identity in ambiguous role playing. He used this device, for example, when he confessed that, by comparison with the rigor of the Apostles and apostolic men, he was a woman, unable to carry the tone in their manly chorus,[177] and when, contradicting his strictures against men playing theatrical roles of women (see previous discussion at n. 165), he portrayed himself in the roles of Thamar, Ruth, the widow whose oil Elisha multiplied, or the bride and mother of Christ.[178]

Gerhoch considered man a work of art created by God from nothing and always tending, by its natural defect, to return to that origin. It bore the image of man, Adam. Likewise, the redeemed man was a work of art, recreated by God, recalled by him from reverting to the earth and to the nothing from which he came, and in his recreated state bearing the image of the Son

[173] *Tr. in Ps. 55*: 1 (Migne *PL* 193: 1673). Gerhoch was adapting Matt. 19: 5, on the marriage of man and woman, "Erunt duo in carne una." Cf. *Tr. in Ps. 36*: 4 (*OI*, 2, pt. 2, p. 493).

[174] *Dial. de cler. sec. et reg.* (*MGH, Ldl* 3, p.. 203).

[175] E.g., *Tr. in Ps. 37*: 7 (*OI*, 2, pt. 2, pp. 626–29). *Tr. in Ps. 77*: 45–58 (Migne *PL* 194: 465). Sexual torments attacked Gerhoch even when he was at prayer (above, n. 81). He reported with admiration that, in answer to prayers for chastity, an angel had appeared to a priest dear to God and men. In the guise of a physician, the angel anointed the priest's genital area with balsam. From that moment, all carnal temptation chilled, but, in place of his corruptible seed, the priest received such increased powers in sowing the word of God as to demonstrate that he had partaken of the wisdom of Him who said, "And my fragrance was the purest balsam" (Eccl. 24:21). *De investig. Antichristi*, 1. pref. (*MGH, Ldl* 3, p. 305).

[176] *Tr. in Ps. 36*: 4 (*OI*, 2, pt. 2, p. 493): "intimi amoris aeterna voluntate substantialiter tibi coadunabitur [Christus]."

[177] *Expositio in Cant. Moysis*, 1 (Migne *PL* 194: 1026).

[178] Thamar: *Princeps Mundi* (*Liber de simoniacis*), chap. 34 (*MGH, Ldl* 3, p. 272) Ruth: *Tr. in Ps. 37*: 2–5 (*OI*, 2, pt. 2, pp. 603–604). Widow: *Tr. in Ps. 70*: 24 (Migne *PL* 194: 312). Bride of God and mother of Christ, above, n. 167.

For the description of Gerhoch as father and mother of his community, see *Annales Reicherspergenses, Chronicon Magni Presbyteri* (a. 1169) (*MGH, SS* 17, p. 491).

of man, Christ.[179] Whether he applied to the soul the metaphor of an image made like a prototype or that of metal assimilating the fire that melted it, or that of a mirror obscured by sin and misery but able once cleansed of reflecting God's beautiful countenance, open to his beauty and love (*capax tuae pulchritudinis tuaeque dilectionis*),[180] Gerhoch described the bonding relation between an active, form-giving term and a passive, form-receiving one. This was the same relation, Gerhoch believed, that existed between male and female in their procreative union.

His insistence on subordination and obedience informed these esthetic metaphors, and his use of the biological paradigm in his comments on sexuality discloses in great detail an attitude about the importance of obedient subordination in esthetic bonding that they expressed. The starting point was certainly the passive or sensual part of Gerhoch's adolescent crisis, loss of virginity, illness, and excruciating pain. Associated with these afflictions was the passion of overwhelming fear. Amidst physical and spiritual agonies, Gerhoch found a hidden active principle that elucidated his passivity, not as a means of annihilation, but as one of glorious integration. That hidden principle, or negative value, was God working in, on, and through his creatures and guiding Gerhoch toward a negative value in the moral order; namely, chastity. Finally, Gerhoch perceived his need for, and desire of, those negative values, and his capacity to embrace them. The result was an affective distance from the physical event and its concommitant fear, and an affective bonding with the negative values through the "perfect love that casteth out fear."

Oscillating, as Augustine had done, between the biological and the esthetic paradigms of assimilation, through relationships of dominance and subordination, Gerhoch was able by analogy to transfer the language of affective union from the sensual dimension to the spiritual one, and this analogic transference left him with two quite disparate roles to play as male, active and dominant by virtue of his physical identity, and as female, passive and dependent by virtue of his affective union with God.

The Call to Participation

The authentic hermeneutic experience consisted of many elements, all expressing dependence: the order of existence (including sacramental union through faith), the composition of the soul, and the erotic play by which the interpreter became one with the object of reflection. To complete the diagram of dependence, one element remains to be considered: the call that the interpreter heard from within the object, whether painting or text.

[179] On creation and recreation, see *Tr. in Ps.* 70: 20 (Migne *PL* 194: 305–307). On the images of Adam and Christ, above, n. 137.

[180] On the metaphor of molten metal, above, nn. 20, 58. On the metaphor of the mirror, *Tr. in Ps.* 26: 8 (Migne *PL* 193: 1200–1201).

Reminiscent of Augustine's teaching on the fewness of the saved, Gerhoch's doctrine that few could make the leap of understanding needed to grasp the authentic content of Scripture posited a call to play certain roles, both feminine and masculine, a call to be both submissive and dominant.

In its bonding with God, the soul was called to play a feminine role of submission. In this regard, Gerhoch emphasized the obedience and even the passivity of the interpreter's soul, needing to be moved and filled by God. The interpreter's soul, called beyond itself, received the heart and mind of Christ, whereas others, imprisoned by their own finitude, set up idols of lucre in their hearts, or filled the thuribles of their hearts with blazing lust. The call that made the leap of understanding possible was in the unspeakable joy of the soul at the touch of Christ, her bridegroom.

The soul's spiritual marriage required passivity only toward the divine spouse. Toward human beings, it required militance; because of its call to ultimate dependence on God, the soul here played masculine roles of the warrior and, especially, the prophet. Gerhoch elucidated the ensuing unity of heart and soul with the metaphor of the grapevine. Each branch, each believer, was united with Christ, the vine stock. But branches were not directly bonded with other branches; barren ones could be cut off and burned to the profit of the rest. Another aspect of this view of unity through a common focal point is indicated by Gerhoch's assertion that, when weighing the authority of a sacred text, one considered what was said, not who said it.[181]

Thus, the call to ultimate dependence in the textual interrogator's vocation, which Gerhoch himself experienced as a kind of rushing compulsion,[182] imposed manifold obligations that could run counter to obligations among believers. As dependence bred action, it impelled Gerhoch, above all, to purification through arduous self-denial, and to spiritual fecundity arising from physical and spiritual discipline. It was also a call to offices that set prophets at odds with their people: to intercede for the sins of the people; to rebuke the sinners; to fight against enemies of truth—human

---

[181] On the vine and branches, see *Princeps Mundi* (*Liber de simoniacis*), chap. 25 (*MGH, Ldl* 3, p. 263): "At vero si de vite palmes excisus fuerit, iam boni suci eius particeps esse non potest; sed nec vivit nec usum habet alium, nisi ut in ignem mittatur et ardeat." Gerhoch ascribed the authority of a text to what was said rather than to the author in *Tr. in Ps. 64*, chap. 17 (*MGH, Ldl* 3, p. 447). See also Gerhoch's distinction between an emperor, who may be heretical, and his decrees, which may defend the Church. *Tr. in Ps. 64*, chap. 18 (*MGH, Ldl* 3, p. 448). This argument is consonant with Gerhoch's view that the validity of sacraments was not impaired by the moral unworthiness of the priests who administered them (except for the priests themselves). However, it is also at least modified by statements such as the following: "... quia non est speciosa vel preciosa laus in ore peccatoris, maxime in obsequio divino quae sua sunt, non quae Jesu Christi querentis, quod est adorare auream statuam." *Tr. in Ps. 64*, chap. 5 (*MGH, Ldl* 3, p. 444). On Gerhoch's doctrine of sacramental validity, see Wolfgang Beinert, *Die Kirche, Gottes Heil in der Welt* (Münster: Aschendorff, 1973. *Beiträge zur Geschichte der Philosophie und Theologie des Mittelalters*, n. F., 13), pp. 383–85.

[182] *Tr. in Ps. 54*: 24 (Migne *PL* 193: 1673).

enemies such as Jews, heretics, pagans, and false Christians—and also against demons, spirits of the air, and unclean spirits in magic, poetry, and philosophy. The call to ultimate dependence was, consequently, a call to invite and to endure, if need be, malice, hatred, persecution, and death.

To be sure, Gerhoch's doctrine of vocation had an institutional aspect in his exaltation of clergy over laity, and in his belief that obedience through arduous self-denial was a path to salvation. The great enemies to be overcome were within. They were impurities of heart; this area of conflict required the soul to struggle boldly with itself so that it could be fit to play its role as the spouse and mother of Christ.

Scripture affirmed that God willed all persons to be saved; but, Gerhoch commented, the text implied not the indiscriminate redemption of all, but rather the redemption of individuals who feared God and did righteous works without regard to person or class.[183] Some of the redeemed were among the laity, good and religious persons, living piously in the world and awaiting the blessed hope and coming in glory of Jesus.[184] Abounding as they might in spiritual virtues, the laity still dwelt in the valleys below the clerical heights, obedient and humble of heart before the priests and religious who fought for God in sermons and writings.[185]

Gerhoch's comments on the attainment of virtue therefore chiefly applied to those set apart as spiritual warriors. The one thing needed, he argued, was to purify the soul from the fire of lust. Fasts, vigils, and prayers were essential means to that end; and the penitential cultivation of grief also assisted in achieving purity by means of virginity or chastity.[186] The Old Testament required that a new priest be purified by aspersion with water, and by having all the hairs of his body shaved. The spiritual meaning of this rite, appropriate to Christians, was that clerics could seek the perfection of cleanliness and beauty by cutting all worldly powers, goods, and cares from their souls with the sharp blade of divine love. But the roots remained. The flesh regenerated the hairs of human corruption, which needed repeatedly to be cut off with the razor of solicitude.

Exercising that solicitude was difficult enough under the constant surveillance of a religious community, and virtually impossible for those who lived in private.[187] Abuses occurred among the Hebrews when the purifica-

---

[183] *Tr. in Ps. 64*, chap. 77 (Migne *PL* 194: 56).

[184] *Tr. in Ps. 64*, chap. 152 (*MGH, Ldl* 3, p. 485).

[185] *Tr. in Ps. 64*, chap. 154, 173 (*MGH, Ldl* 3, p. 486. Migne *PL* 194: 115). On degrees of sanctification in the interplay between the *vita theorica* and the *vita contemplativa*, see Classen, *Gerhoch von Reichersberg*, p. 46. Beinert, *Die Kirche, Gottes Heil*, pp. 313, 343. Erich Meuthen, *Kirche und Heilsgeschichte bei Gerhoh von Reichersberg* (Leiden: Brill, 1959. *Studien und Texte zur Geistesgeschichte des Mittelalters*, 6), pp. 29–31.

[186] *Tr. in Ps. 64*, chap. 6–8, 116, 166 (also on false penances), 170 (*MGH, Ldl* 3, pp. 444–45. Migne *PL* 194: 76–77. *MGH, Ldl* 3, p. 495. Migne *PL* 194: 113–14.

[187] *Tr. in Ps. 64*, chap. 47–48 (*MGH, Ldl* 3, pp. 458–59).

tion of priests was neglected; and the abuses that Gerhoch saw thronging the Church in his time likewise multiplied because so few priests, castrating themselves for the sake of the kingdom, were fit and worthy to sing hymns to God, to see visions of the heavenly kingdom, and to judge unchaste old men.[188]

Purification came, Gerhoch argued, by imbibing the waters of wisdom, and with them virtues that made possible the soul's passionate concentration on eternal goods. Chief among those virtues was instant obedience expressive of dependence, which, in the common life, required abandonment of private concerns, and even one's own will, to complete the perfect work of disciples according to another's judgment and will.[189] But self-denial, including the radical discipline of the common life, preserved personal integrity; for it could never be imposed by violence. It was embraced voluntarily,[190] even as Christ was humbled by his own decision and numbered among the wicked for the glory of the Father,[191] and as a wife entered into the subordination and obedience of marriage by her free consent.[192] Yet, in quest of goodness, the individual, outward act of self-denial expressed an equally individual passionate dependence, a yearning for purity absent from human nature. Ignited by the servile fear of punishment for sin, it glowed with the filial fear at the heart of obedience.[193] It exemplified the principle that those who love in others what they do not have in themselves make those good things their own[194] and that such action is particularly true of those who are comforted by the same divine power that terrifies them.

The same call that imposed feminine passivity toward God also imposed roles of masculine aggression. Souls enlightened and transformed by this apocalyptic moment found themselves surrounded by external enemies; they had the prophetic duty of preaching for the conversion of the wicked, and the prophetic burden of being ignored or persecuted by the world. The prophetic call presented quandaries for a man who was repelled by sinfulness of bishops and popes, and who was yet bound to hierarchic obedience both by solemn vows and by the conviction that obedience was a means to holiness.

Gerhoch's doctrine of vocation to ultimate dependence obliquely

---

[188] Tr. in Ps. 64, chap. 36–39 (Migne PL 194: 30–33).
[189] Tr. in Ps. 64, chap. 107–111 (Migne PL 194: 71–74).
[190] Tr. in Ps. 64, chap. 125 (Migne PL 194: 472).
[191] Tr. in Ps. 64, chap. 89 (Migne PL 194: 62)
[192] Below, n. 234.
[193] Tr. in Ps. 64, chap. 98, 100, 110, 111 (Migne PL 194: 67–68, 73–74).
[194] Tr. in Ps. 64, chap. 96, 163 (Migne PL 194: 66, 490). Cf. the Regula canonicorum ab Amalario collecta, 1. 105 (Migne PL 105: 894–95): "Nostra nimirum sunt bona aliorum, quae etsi imitari non possumus, amamus in aliis; et amantium fiunt quaecumque amantur in nobis."

demanded conflict within institutional order; the unity of heart and soul that he preached was personal rather than constitutional. It occurred through the direct action of God in the heart of each faithful person. The goodness and wisdom of God, as well as his equity, were inaccessible to human reason, and therefore incommunicable from one person to another. In a sense, each of the faithful learned the wisdom of God not from the Church but from the hidden doctrine imparted to them by their invisible master.[195] Gerhoch therefore turned not to tradition, a creature of space and time, but to the apocalyptic moment of personal illumination.

Gerhoch devoutly revered the memory of Pope Gregory VII as a restorer of the Church, and he counted himself among the disciples of that pope in his attacks on clerical abuses, notably simony and Nicolaitism (the marriage of clergy). There is indeed something very old-fashioned in Gerhoch's fervid and tenacious attacks on these abuses, and on the Aachen Rule for canons regular, which remained current and flourishing in Gerhoch's day, even though Hildebrand had persuaded a Lateran synod to abrogate it in 1059, and Gregorian popes had on several occasions condemned it. Gerhoch's dogged loyalty to the Gregorian program is evident. Nevertheless, he gradually found himself deploring the transformation of the Roman church into a *curia*, encumbered by legalism that negated justice and immersed in forms of jurisdiction that polluted priestly hands with human blood. Rome, he grieved, had fallen captive to avarice, the worst of sins, and in the armed conflict between rival claimants to the papal throne the abomination of desolation had been set up over the tomb of Peter. Gerhoch protested against the elaboration of legal technique in the Roman see; against the corresponding increase in the dominance of legists over the activities of popes and, thus, the administration of the Church; against the regal pomp of papal legates; and against the pope's conduct of bloody warfare.[196] He at length called for a general council.[197]

Among his angriest and most persistent attacks were those against the harbingers of scholastic philosophy. Learned men, well trained in Scripture, they studied testimonies of Truth as heretics did, although they were enemies of Truth.[198] His own conflict with a pupil of Abelard, in which Gerhoch

---

[195] Cf. *Expositio super canonem*, "collatio missae" (*OI*, 1, p. 25).

[196] On legists, *De novitatibus huius temporis*, chap. 22 (*MGH, Ldl* 3, pp. 301–302). On papal legates, *De investig. Antichristi*, 1. 50 (*MGH, Ldl* 3, p. 357). On warfare, *Ep. 17* (to Alexander III) (Migne *PL* 193: 568–69). On the increasing severity of Gerhoch's attitude toward Rome, see Classen, *Gerhoch von Reichersberg*, p. 153; Meuthen, *Kirche und Heilsgeschichte*, pp. 94–97.

[197] On Gerhoch's resort to a general council, see Classen, *Gerhoch von Reichersberg*, pp. 102, 196–97, 199, 204. For his contrast between Roman church and Roman *curia*, see his letter to Cardinal Henry (Migne *PL* 193: 9–10); and *De investig. Antichristi*, 1. 67 (*MGH, Ldl* 3, p. 384).

[198] *Tr. in Ps. 118*: 3. *Aleph* (Migne *PL* 194: 734–35). On the use of Arabic numerals, see *Tr. in Ps. 71*: 15 (Migne *PL* 194: 329–30). On the conflicts between Gerhoch and representatives

was accused of heresy, sharpened his conviction that, lacking charity, these new philosophers tormented the faithful.[199] Trusting in carnal wisdom, hostile to God, they questioned belief that Christ was truly God and truly man.[200] Swollen with their empty philosophy, Gerhoch wrote, they wished to comprehend with human reason what the pious mind could only strive with faith to apprehend. Although identical with those of true believers, their sacramental signs and gestures of consecration were empty, snares for entrapping the elect, works such as had been prophesied concerning the ministers of Antichrist.[201]

Evidently, the ultimate dependence of errant popes and scholastics was not directed toward God. Thus, Gerhoch's concept of a call to ultimate dependence could subvert tradition when a leap of spiritual understanding brought prevailing norms into question. Gerhoch contrasted the "traditions and commands" of Christ with the "traditions of Pharisees, scribes and Sadducees,"[202] but the traditions of Christ (or the Apostles) needed no historical or institutional continuity. Thus, Gerhoch could regard the common life, as led by canons regular (of which he was an ardent protagonist) as a "tradition" received from the Apostles,[203] even though he believed that it had lapsed after the apostolic age and remained dormant for centuries until recent times.[204] Gerhoch's distinction between authentic spiritual tradition and questionable secular traditions enabled him to defend the conversion from paganism or Judaism to Christianity.[205] It also enabled him to denounce the traditions of Pharisees, scribes, and Sadducees, "wicked customs in the Church"[206] for as Gregory VII had pointed out, Christ did not say, "I am custom," but "I am truth."[207]

Thus, the roles that Gerhoch elected to play in the Church, expressive of a call to ultimate dependence, would have been meaningless and inauthen-

---

of the new scholastic philosophy, see Classen, *Gerhoch von Reichersberg*, pp. 33, 38–39, 51, 89, 91, 117–18, 171; Meuthen, *Kirche und Heilsgeschichte*, p. 12; and Horst Dieter Rauh, *Das Bild des Antichrist im Mittelalter: von Tyconius zum deutschen Symbolismus* (Münster: Aschendorff, 1973. *Beiträge zur Geschichte der Philosophie und Theologie des Mitelalters. Texte und Untersuchungen, neue Folge*, 9), pp. 421, 445.

[199] *Tr. in Ps. 11*: 5 (Migne PL 193: 806). *Tr. in Ps. 136*: 4 (Migne PL 194: 906–907). On Gerhoch's general isolation, see Classen, *Gerhoch von Reichersberg*, p. 321. On suspicions expressed concerning his doctrines, and formal charges of heresy brought against him, see Classen, *Gerhoch von Reichersberg*, pp. 48, 50, 52, 80, 152–53, 212, 250ff.

[200] *Tr. in Ps. 29*: 10 (Migne PL 193: 1273–74). *Tr. in Ps. 67*: 17 (Migne PL 194: 191–92). *Tr. in Ps. 35*: 7c–8a (*OI*, 2, pt. 2, p. 431), contrasting "Christian philosophy" with worldly.

[201] *Tr. in Ps. 21*: 2 (Migne PL 193: 994). *Dial. de cler. sec. et reg.* (*MGH, Ldl* 3, p. 227).

[202] *Tr. in Ps. 43*: 2 (Migne PL 193: 1534).

[203] *Dial. de cler. sec. et reg.* (*MGH, Ldl* 3, p. 233).

[204] *Tr. in Ps. 64*, chap. 161 (*MGH, Ldl* 3, p. 489).

[205] *Tr. in Ps. 146*: 9 (Migne PL 194: 977).

[206] *Tr. in Ps. 141*: 4 (Migne PL 194: 941).

[207] *Liber de aedificio Dei*, chap. 3 (Migne PL 194: 1202), quoting a statement of St. Cyprian that was current among Gregorian reformers. See Karl F. Morrison, *Tradition and Authority in the Western Church, 300–1140* (Princeton: Princeton University Press, 1969), p. 273.

ticated without conflict. To his age, he chose to personify Jeremiah, whose sufferings had been grafted on the passion of Christ, a prophet rejected by his own. Gerhoch's belief that few were called to the apocalyptic leap beyond carnal to spiritual knowledge[208] required him to teach that the few who knew the truth and lived it were pilgrims and exiles on earth. To be sure, he recognized that the diversity of gifts in the church established a subordination according to which "weak and feminine persons" prayed and "strong and virile" ones struggled manfully with written and spoken words for the Word of God. Each complemented and ministered to the other.[209] Individual contributions to the common welfare varied according to capacity, and distribution of material benefits likewise varied according to the recipient's need.[210] In the heavenly kingdom, too, each would be changed according to his own measure.[211] Not all had the purity of heart of those who would see God; there were lower degrees of blessedness appropriate to those who possessed lesser spiritual gifts.[212]

The roles of dependence that Gerhoch believed he was called to play drove him beyond this benign view. He execrated his enemies, even the most exalted, bishops who polluted with human blood the lips and hands that made the body of Christ.[213] He menaced those whom he judged to be Nicolaites and simoniacs. Despite their eminent offices in the Church, despite their assiduous performance and reception of the Eucharist, despite the glittering opulence of their churches, despite their learning and eloquence, Gerhoch raged, those who transformed the temple of God into a den of thieves did not participate in the Holy Spirit through and in Christ. They were cut off from every blessing,[214] and yet they ruled. God had chosen the weak to confound the strong,[215] but, in the historical church as in the Babylonian Captivity of the Jews, Babylon the harlot still blasphemed, drunken on the blood of saints, whom the world despised. Those who lived according to the flesh, even bishops, persecuted those who lived according to the Spirit. Babylon had been rebuilt within the walls of Jerusalem. Still captive in a foreign land, still eating the bread of their grief in the visible Church, those called to play the role of exiles dreamed of the happiness that would be theirs in the heavenly Jerusalem.[216] Their sufferings authenticated their vocation, by

---

[208] *Tr. in Ps. 64*, chap. 49, 64, 106, 120, 167 (*MGH, Ldl* 3, p. 466. Migne *PL* 194: 57–58, 71, 79–80. *MGH, Ldl* 3, p. 492).

[209] *Tr. in Ps. 58*: 18 (Migne *PL* 193: 1747).

[210] *Tr. in Ps. 67*: 16 (Migne *PL* 194: 189).

[211] *Tr. in Ps. 15*: 6 (Migne *PL* 193: 838).

[212] *Tr. in Ps. 19*: 4 (Migne *PL* 193: 962).

[213] *Tr. in Ps. 64*, chap. 62 (*MGH, Ldl* 3, p. 465). On the papal curia as guilty of blood judgment, *Tr. in Ps. 64*, chap. 2, 3 (*MGH, Ldl* 3, pp. 440–41).

[214] *Tr. in Ps. 118*: 66. *Teth* (Migne *PL* 194: 777).

[215] *Tr. in Ps. 64*, chap. 59 (*MGH, Ldl* 3, p. 463).

[216] *Tr. in Ps. 64*, chap. 1, 5, 7, 8, 39, 49, 161, 163, 172, 174 (*MGH, Ldl* 3, pp. 442–45. Migne *PL* 194: 30–31. *MGH, Ldl* 3, pp. 459–60. Migne *PL* 194: 57, 114–15). On the reconstruction

locating their ultimate dependence outside the limits of time and space, and even outside the Church, as a temporal institution.

Recapitulation

Of course, the dynamic of play within the hermeneutic experience was not exhausted by Gerhoch's portrayal of erotic form giving and form receiving within the soul. By way of summary, I shall now recapitulate the range of play indicated by Gerhoch's repertoire of metaphors and suggest some rationales of dialectical, spiritual union that it implies.

I have mentioned a number of the sensory metaphors with which Gerhoch described his assimilation by a leap of understanding: metaphors of absorption by eating and digestion,[217] and by drinking and intoxication;[218] metaphors of geometric unity achieved in a circle by centering on a common invisible point;[219] metaphors of compositional unity in song through harmony;[220] metaphors of organic unity among members of a body or between a vine, or a tree, and its branches;[221] metaphors of the union of man and woman, issuing in one kiss, and one erotic rapture.[222]

Other sensory metaphors illustrated the union of heart and soul in God. The soul was like a tool, productive only when moved by the hand of God.[223] Those who adhered to the Father of lights were one light in the Lord, as one brightness shone forth from many lamps burning in one house.[224] Similarly, there were many books, but one Scripture, written by one Spirit and so rightly considered one book;[225] many churches but one Church; and many heavens, but one Heaven.[226]

These paradoxical metaphors are all ways of illustrating by analogy how individuals, isolated in their separate identities, could become united, participating by loving obedience in a common element (*id ipsum*). As we have seen, Gerhoch's esthetic method of assimilation, elaborately complemented

---

of Babylon within Jerusalem, *Tr. in Ps. 64*, chap. 12, 25, 26, 64, 123, 124 (*MGH, Ldl* 3, pp. 446, 450–51, 466. Migne *PL* 194: 81–83). On the same subject, also described as the repaganization of the Church, see Rauh, *Das Bild des Antichrist*, pp. 440–41, 467.

[217] On the stomach of the mind, above n. 80. *Tr. in Ps. 34*: 25 (*OI*, 2, pt. 1, pp. 390–91). *Tr. in Ps. 140*: 6 (Migne *PL* 194: 957).

[218] Above, nn. 76, 79. See also *Tr. in Ps. 22*: 5; *Tr. in Ps. 35*: 9 (*OI*, 2, pt. 2, p. 440). *Tr. in Ps. 118*: 170. *Tau* (Migne *PL* 194: 834). *De aedificio Dei*, chap. 176 (*MGH, Ldl* 3, p. 200).

[219] Above, nn. 110, 124.

[220] Above, nn. 38–64. Also *Tr. in Ps. 29*: 5 (Migne *PL* 193: 1264).

[221] On the metaphor of the body, nn. 68, 140, 145–47, 230. On the metaphor of the vine and branches (also very frequent), nn. 73, 230, and *Tr. in Ps. 39*: 16 (Migne *PL* 193: 1462). On the metaphor of the tree and branches, *Tr. in Ps. 91*: 13 (Migne *PL* 194: 566).

[222] On the formation of one kiss by two persons, above n. 167. And *Tr. in Ps. 36*: 4 (*OI*, 2, pt. 2, p. 483).

[223] Below, n. 235.

[224] *Tr. in Ps. 26*: 3–4 (Migne *PL* 193: 1189).

[225] *Tr. in Ps. 26*: 2 (Migne *PL* 193: 1182).

[226] *Tr. in Ps. 150*: Gloria (Migne *PL* 194: 996–98).

by the biological paradigm, explained the psychological process by which this unity could be achieved. It also provided several rationales justifying the evident contradiction in terms that Gerhoch reached when he taught that personal identity survived—indeed, that it was redeemed—in a union that transcended personal identity. His metaphors were convincing because they implied one or another of those rationales.

The rationales for assuming that esthetic assimilation of persons sustained and subsumed personal identity are suggested by the prepositions with which Gerhoch described the relationship between God and men. Of course, the relationship had two sides, the human and the divine, and they were asymmetrical because God was not assimilated to men; men were assimilated to God and passed over into his body, but there was no reciprocal and corresponding "transumption" of God into man.[227] Men, both good and evil, were from him (*ex illo* or *ab illo*). They existed through him, with him, and in him (*per illum, cum illo, in illo*), in the general sense that all men live, move, and have their being in God (Acts 17:28). In addition, the elect moved toward God (*ad illum*) as their goal, and they were in him in the special sense that, by love, they hungered and thirsted for God as the reward of their faith, and, believing in him, they were lifted outside themselves to partake of his divinity. About the divine side of the relationship, Gerhoch could say that God was in men, that he worked with them, and that he advanced his purposes through them. The prepositions "from" (*ab* or *ex*) and "toward" (*ad*) did not apply to the divine side of the relationship, because God could be said neither to derive from nor to move toward men as the goal of his activity.[228]

The prepositions indicated five kinds of rationales for union, of which the first three and the last two were limited to the relation of the elect to God:

A rationale of origin (from: *ex*, or *ab*, and *in*: the general sense of Acts 17:28): Human beings participate in God because they derive their being from him, because he dwells in them as the life of the soul, and because sacramental union like being and life derive from his grace.

A rationale of instrumentality (through: *per*): Human beings participate in God because he acts through them. They are one with him in operation, as a tool is one with the craftsman.

---

[227] *Tr. in Ps. 17:* 37; *Tr. in Ps. 22:* 5; *Tr. in Ps. 54:* 23 (Migne *PL* 193: 883, 1051, 1669).

[228] The following texts illuminate Gerhoch's conscious use of prepositions to describe the relation of the soul to God: *Tr. in Ps. 12:* 1; *Tr. in Ps. 16:* 15; *Tr. in Ps. 39:* 16; *Tr. in Ps. 65: 7–8*; *Tr. in Ps. 65:* 30; *Tr. in Ps. 77:* 8, 12; *Tr. in Ps. 118:* 67. *Theth; Tr. in Ps. 118: 146–47. Caph* (Migne *PL* 193: 810, 857–58, 1462). Migne *PL* 194: 129–30, 214, 442–43, 448, 774, 821). Gerhoch provided a formulaic summary in his sentence, "Si enim ad vitam, quae Christus est, voluerimus pervenire, debemus ad ipsum in ipso et per ipsum currere." *De aedificio Dei,* chap. 50 (*MGH, Ldl* 3, p. 165). Cf. Gerhoch's frequent distinction between loving friends *in* God and enemies on God's account (*propter Deum*). *Tr. in Ps. 29:* 10; *Tr. in Ps. 118:* 153. *Res; Tr. in Ps. 142:* 4. (Migne *PL* 193: 1270. Migne *PL* 194: 824, 950). On Augustine's use of a similar distinction, see above, Chapter 4 at n. 75.

A rationale of intentionality (with: *cum*): Human beings participate in God because their wills conform with his redemptive plan.

A rationale of end, or direction (toward: *ad*): The elect participate in God as works, or means, participate in ends.

A rationale of transposition (*in*, with the specific sense already suggested): The elect participate in God, having been raised above the human mode of being into the divine.

Gerhoch's comments on wicked men and heretics illustrate how the first three rationales sustained personal identity. Plainly, these rationales could have served pantheistic, or extreme panentheistic, doctrines suppressing the integrity of the individual person. Although God, the source of all being and life, was everywhere present, those who were blind to his light could not see him. They were separated from him, although he was the life of their souls.[229] People detached from God were not reborn or renewed by the sacraments that they received. Their sacraments were like branches trimmed from the vine, or a hand, cut off from the body, keeping the outward form of relationship to vine or body, but emptied of the vitality that had given it life and force.[230]

To say that God worked through the wicked, and that their wills served his purposes, was not to say that their interests conformed to his. In fact, their carnal will ran directly counter to the divine will; for, in exalting the sensual thoughts and desires of their own hearts, they did not wish to be incorporated in Christ, but wished to incorporate Christ in themselves.[231] Such "animal men," priests and pontiffs who performed the sacraments and administered them to others, filled the emptiness of their spiritual vessels not with the real Christ but with another, whom they made for themselves and worshipped as an idol in the true Christ's place.[232] Consequently, the same fire of celestial wisdom that liquified the saints into its own form, melting them as gold, caused the impious to harden, like clay, in their separation from the fire.[233]

The rationales of end and transposition, applying only to the elect, likewise sustained personal integrity in the soul's assimilation to God through

---

[229] *Tr. in Ps. 77*: 7 (Migne *PL* 194: 442).

[230] *Tr. in Ps. 21*: 32 (Migne *PL* 193: 1040). *Princeps mundi* (*Liber de simoniacis*), chap. 19, 25, 29–31 (*MGH, Ldl* 3, pp. 257, 263, 267).

[231] *Tr. in Ps. 22*: 15 (Migne *PL* 193: 1051). Gerhoch added that they killed Christ in this way, and so consumed the Eucharistic elements to their own condemnation. He here adapted Augustine's statement that believers were changed into Christ, not he into them (*Conf.*, 7. 10. 16), a passage also cited in *Tr. in Ps. 17*: 37 (Migne *PL* 194: 883), and in a quotation from Hugh of St. Victor, *Tr. in Ps. 33*: 2–5 (*OI*, 2, pt. 1, p. 220). Above, Chapter 1, n. 14.

[232] *Tr. in Ps. 118*: Alleluia. *Aleph* (Migne *PL* 194: 731). On pontiffs who conveyed the Eucharistic elements to others and consumed the same elements to their own condemnation, see *Princeps mundi* (*Liber de simoniacis*), chap. 26 (*MGH, Ldl* 3, p. 264). *Tr. in Ps. 64*, chap. 172 (Migne *PL* 194: 114).

[233] *Tr. in Ps. 18*: 7 (Migne *PL* 193: 910).

loving obedience. Personal integrity was sustained, in part, because of Gerhoch's insistence that assimilation occurred according to the finite capacity of the individual soul rather than according to the infinite plenitude of God; correspondingly, it was sustained because of determinant importance that he assigned to the affects. Equally, his doctrine of the freedom of the will sustained his teaching that personal integrity was not suppressed, but that it survived and was redeemed in union of heart and soul.

The first stage of marriage, before bridegroom and bride became one body, was "a consensus of minds and an identity of wills to live together in indivisible association." Before the carnal consummation of marriage, the bride must voluntarily consent to obey the bridegroom. Thereafter, the bridegroom impregnated his wife, lest her good will remain fruitless and sterile, her love limited to the goods of her husband rather than extending to the husband himself. This worldly pattern, Gerhoch wrote, corresponded with the marriage of the soul to Christ. Voluntary consent was a necessary preliminary to their union in one body; but, in spiritual as in carnal marriage, it was also true that, surviving, the freedom of the will could lead the wife (or the soul) into harlotry and repudiation by her husband.[234]

Consequently, Gerhoch carefully defined his rationales of intentionality and instrumentality when he applied them to the elect. He employed an unmistakable metaphor of obedience. A blacksmith, he wrote, first makes the hammer, or some other tool; then he works by means of (per) the tool, and the tool works along with him. Likewise, God first created the faculty of willing as an instrument of virtue and good work, and afterward assisted the good will to work, and to cooperate with him as he wrought it and other things through it. Nor did he abandon his task before it was fully achieved. Without the artisan, the hammer can do nothing, and the free will can do nothing without God, its governor and fellow worker. In saying this, Gerhoch insisted, he did not destroy free will, but rather he enabled it to understand that it could do nothing without God, any more than branches could flourish without the vine or a hand act without the body, or any tool without being moved by the artisan's hand. Thus, Gerhoch argued, he preached both the innate freedom of the human reason, and its need to be more free from necessity, from sin, and from wretchedness, the punishment of sin, liberties that were achieved in God.[235]

The saved grasped that the integrity of personality was part of a dependent relationship between the soul and God. The metaphors of con-

---

[234] *Tr. in Ps.* 33: 2 (*OI*, 2, pt. 1, p. 179).

[235] I have conflated two similar texts concerning the freedom of the will. *Tr. in Ps. 1*: 3 (Migne *PL* 193: 647–48), and *Tr. in Ps.* 37: 22–23 (*OI*, 2, pt. 2, p. 665). See also Gerhoch's observation that the productivity of the branch (the believer) depended on the vine (Christ) and the root (God). *Tr. in Ps.* 39: 16 (Migne *PL* 193: 1462). There is also a hint of subordination in the description of Christ as the hand of the Father. *Tr. in Ps. 64*, chap. 81 (Migne *PL* 194: 58).

jugal union, hammer, branch, and hand have an essential characteristic in common with the other metaphors that I have mentioned. Certainly, all express the passivity of the soul, its need to be filled with the form, or moved by the energy of God, before its individual capacities for good could be filled. The role of obedience, or dependence, is evident. All likewise express the independence of the soul, both negatively and positively. The negative expressions of independence allude to the spiritual harlotry of an unfaithful wife; the inertness (and unproductivity) of a hammer left on the shelf; the lifelessness of a severed branch or hand; and the impairments of necessity, sin, and wretchedness. The positive expressions allude to the collaboration of separate partners in one action; the fecundation of marriage; the hammering out of visible works; the putting forth of fruit; and the manifestation in human works of God's goodness, justice, and beauty. Gerhoch wrote to the same effect when he spoke of the union of two persons in one kiss.[236]

Gerhoch's own experience of conversion heightened his sense of identity in affective union. Just as he recognized that the will could lapse from conjugal love into harlotry, so his own conversion taught him that the human will could change from wantonness to fidelity, and that obedience once withdrawn could be restored. Throughout his writings, he turned repeatedly to the parable of the prodigal son, often for a passing illustration, but occasionally for a fuller discussion.[237] When he identified himself with the prodigal son, he clearly referred the terror and guilt of his adolescent conversion to events later in his career.[238] The prodigal son had dissipated his patrimony living with harlots; however, Gerhoch wrote that he was worse than the prodigal. For he had not only wasted his substance on himself and been reduced to feeding swine. He recalled to his horror that he had also striven with might and main to set up again a tree that anathema had cut off at the roots; thus resisting the judgment of the Church, he had become an abortive and the vilest of creatures.[239] He identified the enemies and faultfinders who surrounded him with the elder brother in the parable, and the elder brother with Satan dissuading the Father (God) from showing mercy and honor to the penitent son (Gerhoch himself). Confessing his sinfulness and unworthiness, he yet begged God to affirm him as his son, purifying him inwardly with the flesh of the fatted calf (Christ) and adorning him outwardly with his best robe and ring (fame), and with sandals that would beautify his once mud-caked feet for all to see. Thus, his

---

[236] Above, n. 167.

[237] E.g., *Tr. in Ps. 70*: 19; *Tr. in Ps. 84*: 9 (Migne *PL* 194: 303, 520). *De aedificio Dei*, chap. 38 (Migne *PL* 194: 1287), a miracle of St. Remigius.

[238] Above, n. 177.

[239] *Tr. in Ps. 68*: 30 (Migne *PL* 194: 265). *De aedificio Dei*, chap. 152, 153 (*MGH, Ldl* 3, pp. 189–90).

preaching of peace would be vindicated, and others would be constrained to apply to him (with a sexual cross reference) the verse, "How beautiful are thy steps in sandals, O prince's daughter" (Cant. 7:1).[240]

Gerhoch, the psalmodist, delighted in the thought that the Father received the prodigal son with a concert of musical instruments and singers.[241] But through these parallels runs uncertainty, yearning for a manifest vindication that might never be given, and the fear that, because of his unworthiness, his prayer might be unheard in the courts of heaven.[242] Gerhoch's own uncertainty and fear are perhaps the clearest demonstration of how much more completely the demonstrative function of his method could be performed than the authenticating ones.

Thus, according to Gerhoch's doctrines about union of heart and soul in God, the essential leap of understanding took place in a dialectical relationship between separate partners, each with its own identity—the soul and God. Their separateness was mediated by participation. Participation occurred through esthetic assimilation; and assimilation required subordination of the passive partner (the soul) to the active partner (God) in loving obedience, and ultimate obedience. Esthetic assimilation kept the identities of God and soul intact and, indeed, redeemed the identity of the soul by freeing it from circumstances of necessity, sin, and wretchedness. Even so, in Christ, when humanity was subsumed into divinity, it kept its individual substance, just as water loses its fluid quality, but keeps its original substance when it freezes and stands still, like a stone.[243]

CONCLUSION

We have now diagrammed the hermeneutic circle according to Gerhoch of Reichersberg. In elaborate articulation, the doctrine of empathetic participation gave Gerhoch assurance that the hermeneutic circle would not deteriorate into the vicious one of textual ventriloquism. As the interrogator of texts unpacked the object of inquiry, he engaged in a dialectical cycle of filling the object and being filled by it in turn. Yet, this hermeneutic circle was kept from being an exercise in self-reflection. For the authentic interrogator approached his task of questioning the text with disciplined obedience, dependence, and self-emptying, going progressively beyond himself.

[240] *Tr. in Ps. 78*: 1 (Migne *PL* 194: 484–85). *Tr. in Ps. 118*: 125. *Ain.* (Migne *PL* 194: 805). For the identification of Christ as the fatted calf, and the Holy Spirit as its fat, see *Tr. in Ps. 64*, chap. 171, 172 (Migne *PL* 194: 113).

[241] *Tr. in Ps. 118*: 54. *Zain* (Migne *PL* 194: 769). For another figure that had a future in the history of conversion, see *Tr. in Ps. 67*: 2 (Migne *PL* 194: 164): ". . . quia de inimicis Dei facti sunt canes Dei bene latrantes et in custodia domus aut gregis vigilanter excubantes." See also *Tr. in Ps. 27*: 3 (Migne *PL* 193: 1228).

[242] Above, n. 174.

[243] *Tr. in Ps. 64*, chap. 90 (Migne *PL* 194: 63).

He moved by stages through the sensory qualities (the object as sign), to the intellectual or spiritual ones (the object as symbol), to the affective ones (the object as sacrament).

This progressive penetration of the text took place through the dynamic of play. The authentic interrogator assumed roles of subordination that engrossed him in the work and allowed him to be ever more deeply formed by the object of understanding. He eventually assimilated to that object through the affects, above all by love. Role playing enabled him to reexperience as his own the emotions in the object. But there was always a negative element, a hermeneutic gap, between the interrogator of the text and the unspoken content of the text.

Therefore, transformed by empathetic participation in the emotions in the work, the interrogator still retained his own identity, which he exercised in the actions that flowed from his contemplative union—that is, from his obedience to the call from within the work. Thus, the interpreter played two characters: the one, in relation to the object, submissive, affective, and form receiving, and the other, in relation to the world at large, assertive, rational, and form giving. True to the biological paradigm in his thinking, Gerhoch described these characters as male and female in an erotic relationship, the male dominating, the female yielding. In the first role, he interrogated the text; in the second, he proclaimed it. Whether in visual or in textual analysis, the hermeneutic process required these two to function as one.

Removed from its theological casing, this model of understanding recognizably survived long after Gerhoch's day. If there is much truth to the premise that Schleiermacher was the originator of the art of hermeneutics, Schleiermacher's recasting of this model demands attention. Schleiermacher's equation of understanding with interpretation, and his insistence that understanding was linguistic, that nothing that was unconstructed was understood, and that the work of art was a historical artifact (or product) in a developmental continuum have no true analogues in the pattern of understanding that we have found in works by Augustine and Gerhoch. But, then, other lines of similarity between Gerhoch's doctrines and Schleiermacher's lead back again from the hermeneutic method to the theological matrix. "Schleiermacher's Christology," as one scholar has observed, "is not based on a historicized causal relationship moving from the historical effect back to its cause, but upon the immediate existential experience of the revelation in Christ. The questions of historical criticism about the reports of the Gospels are no longer fundamental. What is central is the actual present life-relation to the present and living Christ. It is for the sake of Christ that Schleiermacher believes in the biblical reports."[244]

[244] Martin Redeker, *Schleiermacher: Life and Thought*, trans. John Wallhausser (Philadelphia: Fortress Press, 1973), p. 132.

EIGHT

Schleiermacher's Anthropology

UNLIKE GERHOCH OF REICHERSBERG, Friedrich Schleiermacher (1768–1834) was celebrated in his own day, and, despite fluctuations in appraisal, his writings have continued to exercise a wide and profound effect. Even one of his severest critics acknowledged that he "determined the nineteenth century," and that "he must certainly rank among the great names in Christian theology, being mentioned alongside Origin, Augustine, and Calvin."[1]

In this chapter, I propose to explore the residue of the hermeneutic tradition, represented by Augustine and Gerhoch, in Schleiermacher's doctrines. The discussion leads naturally to the juncture between his theology and his hermeneutics. It begins appropriately with Schleiermacher's celebrated application of the principle, "I am you," when he asserted that interpreters, if they rightly practiced the art of understanding, transformed themselves into the author of the text under review, and, indeed, that interpreters, consciously analyzing what was unconscious for the author, might reexperience the original process of composition, understanding the author better than the author understood himself.[2] Much of what follows elucidates the fact that, while Augustine and Gerhoch had distinguished the event, understanding, from its memory, interpretation, Schleiermacher equated understanding with interpretation; both, for him, were linguistic.

Clearly, the concepts set forth by the sentence, "I am you," were at work

[1] Karl Barth, *The Theology of Schleiermacher: Lectures at Göttingen, Winter Semester of 1923/24*, ed. Dietrich Ritschl, trans. Geoffrey W. Bromiley (Grand Rapids, Mich.: Eerdmans, 1982), pp. 104, 137, 259, 274. Friedrich Schleiermacher, *The Christian Faith*, trans. H. R. Mackintosh and J. S. Stewart (Philadelphia: Fortress Press, 1976), p. 5. Brian A. Gerrish, *A Prince of the Church: Schleiermacher and the Beginnings of Modern Theology* (Philadelphia: Fortress Press, 1984), p. 18. James K. Graby, "Reflections on the History of the Interpretation of Schleiermacher," *Scottish Journal of Theology*, 21 (1968), pp. 283–99. On Schleiermacher as causing a reorientation in theology, see H. J. Adriaanse, "Schleiermacher als Philosoph," *Nederlands Theologisch Tijdschrift*, 35 (1981), p. 326. On fluctuations in Schleiermacher's reputation, see Friedrich Schleiermacher, *Theologische Schriften*, ed. Kurt Nowak (Berlin: Union, 1983. Texte zur Philosophie und Religionsgeschichte), pp. 17–19.

[2] Schleiermacher, "Draft for part 2 (1826)" and "Academic Addresses (1829)," in *Hermeneutics: The Handwritten Manuscripts*, trans. James Duke and Jack Forstman (Missoula, Montana: Scholars Press, 1977. American Academy of Religion, Texts and Translations, no. 1), pp. 150, 191. Richard R. Niebuhr, *Schleiermacher on Christ and Religion: A New Introduction* (New York: Scribner's, 1964), pp. 87, 111. Martin Redeker, *Schleiermacher: Life and Thought*, trans. John Wallhausser (Philadelphia: Fortress Press, 1973), pp. 176–77, gives the genealogy of Schleiermacher's statement from Luther to Dilthey.

in the central hermeneutic proposition that interpreters could, and should, transform themselves into the author. But is this process theoretically possible? Did not Schleiermacher's insistence on a common humanity—on the proposition that every person "carries in himself a minimum of all others."[3]—demolish the integrity of the individual? Schleiermacher's early education in Moravian spirituality, his conversion as a young man to the philosphy of Spinoza, and his fascination with the teachings of Fichte produced in his thinking a conviction of cosmic wholeness. Applied to Christian doctrine, that conviction brought charges of pantheism down upon his head. It has also led recent scholars to deny that Schleiermacher's doctrine of universal love left any room for the separateness of "I" and "you," and hence for the dialogue in which each discovers oneself in the other. For individuals—whether God and man, or man and man—seemed engulfed in a common identity. Indeed, his entire doctrine of interpretation appeared to dissolve into a vicious circle of anthropology. For, he wrote, "The world expresses itself in the type of the human spirit, and this type represents itself in the world."[4]

Yet, rejecting the charge of pantheism, Schleiermacher insisted that his doctrines preserved the integrity of the individual, even while they taught a common identity. Indeed, his comments on the creation of Eve portray exactly the dialogue between "I" and "you" as distinct individuals. As long as the first man was alone with himself and nature, Schleiermacher wrote, the divinity spoke to him in various ways, but Adam neither understood nor answered. He experienced no development from the inmost part of his soul. The divinity therefore made a helpmate. In her, flesh of his flesh and bone of his bone, the first man discovered humanity and, in humanity, divinity. Living, mental (*geistvoll*) tones awakened in him; he raised his eyes to see the world. For in that moment he became able to hear and to answer the voice of divinity. To gaze upon the world and to have religion, man must first find humanity, and he achieves that only in love and through love. He embraces most ardently the person in whom the world is most clearly and purely reflected. He loves most tenderly the one in whom he believes that he finds compacted all that he himself lacks to form humanity.[5]

[3] *Hermeneutik*, 3. 6 (*Sämmtliche Werke* [hereafter *S. W.*], 1. 7, p. 147). This principle was the basis of what, in the present study, I am calling "participation," and what Richard R. Niebuhr has called "self-impartation," in "Schleiermacher on Language and Feeling," *Theology Today*, 17 (1960), p. 150.

[4] Poul Henning Jorgensen, *Die Ethik Schleiermachers* (Munich: Kaiser, 1959. Forschungen zur Geschichte und Lehre des Protestantismus, Reihe 10, Bd 14) p. 148. Siegfried Keil, "Die Christliche Sittenlehre Friedrich Schleiermachers—Versuch einer sozialethischen Aktualisierung," *Neue Zeitschrift für systematische Theologie und Religionsphilosophie*, 10 (1968), p. 320. For Schleiermacher's anthropological vicious circle, see *Schleiermachers Dialektik*, ed. I. Halpern (Berlin: Mayer and Müller, 1903), p. 126.

[5] *Reden über die Religion*, 2, p. 88 (Nowak, ed., *Theologische Schriften*, pp. 97–98).

Later, Feuerbach described the needfulness of the individual, in his separateness and finitude, as voids, or holes, in the self.[6] Schleiermacher anticipated Feuerbach's concept of this "porosity" as the negative condition of
bonding, in which the humanity of the individual was wakened to life. He
lamented illusions of self-sufficiency cherished by those who in pride over-
valued their personalities, the finite characteristics of their separate lives,
refusing in fear to acknowledge humanity's common state of dependence.[7]

Schleiermacher's defense against the charge of pantheism neither was,
nor is, convincing to many of his ablest admirers or critics. For our purposes, the central effect of this concept was the one exerted on Schleiermacher's doctrine of the hermeneutic gap. His recasting of the Biblical
account of Adam and Eve stressed mutual recognition, but the same distance
that made communication possible also was a precondition of misunderstanding or incomprehensibility.

As his thinking matured, Schleiermacher drew an increasingly sharp distinction between thought and language. By the end of his career, he
acknowledged that the distance between speaker and hearer (and thus that
between language and thought) was the fundamental precondition for hermeneutics.[8] Even when he was able to argue that the two were, in some
sense, identical,[9] he understood, as an interpreter of Scripture, the difference between letter and spirit. For, as the Apostle Paul wrote, "Our suffi-
ciency is of God, who also hath made us able ministers of the new testament; not of the letter, but of the spirit: for the letter killeth, but the spirit
giveth life" (2. Cor. 3: 5–6).[10] Even then, he recognized the special labor
necessary to understand a text written in a foreign language, as the texts of
Scripture were for him. He knew the need to master not only the standard
literary form of any given language and the elements that distinguished it
from every other one, but also the idioms, archaisms, and other peculiarities
of individual writers.[11]

The character of poetry illustrated yet another disparity between thought
and language. The effect of poetry did not depend on the logical content
that was the original basis of language, and the subject of scholarly inquiry

---

[6] Above, Chapter 2, n. 1.

[7] *Predigt über die Einigkeit im Geiste (Epheser 4: 1–3)* (*S. W.*, 2. 4, p. 704). On the relationship between Schleiermacher's theories and Feuerbach's, see Gerhard Spiegler, *The Eternal
Covenant: Schleiermacher's Experiment in Cultural Theology* (New York: Harper and Row,
1967), p. 27: "The logic of Schleiermacher's thought becomes explicit in the work of Ludwig
Feuerbach."

[8] "Academic Addresses (1829)," in *Hermeneutics: The Handwritten Manuscripts*, p. 180.
See also Duke, introduction to *Hermeneutics: The Handwritten Manuscripts*, p. 13. See below,
n. 26, concerning the *Weihnachtsfeier*.

[9] Duke, introduction to *Hermeneutics: The Handwritten Manuscripts*, p. 9. Cf. Niebuhr,
Schleiermacher on Christ and Religion, p. 81.

[10] Nowak, ed., *Theologische Schriften*, pp. 19–20.

[11] *Einleitung ins neue Testament* (*S. W.*, 1. 8, p. 1).

(*Wissenschaft*). Rather, it depended on the poet's power to force the fixed combination of elements in language into indirect, allusive patterns corresponding with the picture in his mind, and on the capacity of the reader, by a series of mimetic intellectual movements, to render present to himself the poet's frame of mind. Even the distinctive affinity of poetry to music was inadequate to explain this process. The difference between speech (Wissenschaft) and thought was analogous to that between the description of a plant in a botanical handbook and the evocative representation of a poet, conveying by *ein unbekanntes Etwas* his own thoughts immediately into the reader.[12]

The separation of language from thought was particularly marked in religion. The religious personality of each individual, Schleiermacher wrote, was "a closed entirety." Religion indeed presented itself as a great self-elaborating whole, understandable only through itself.[13] Everything that formed a continuum in human mentality lay outside the sphere of teaching. In the context of Schleiermacher's long and brilliant career as a preacher, and his persistent attention to the religious training of children, it is astonishing to discover his judgment that religious instruction was a senseless term. But he was convinced that words were only shadows of perceptions and feelings, and, without enabling others to participate in those ineffable realities, they imparted no understanding of what they said.[14] Despite his youthful impetuosity, Schleiermacher complained in his *Reden* that he was unable to arouse in others echoing tones of the supreme harmony in his religious feelings; despite words, few understood religion at all.[15]

The history of Scriptural interpretation cast the disjunction of language from thought on a far grander scale. Indeed, every holy writing of the past, Schleiermacher wrote, was a mausoleum of religion, the dead letter, a monument of the great spirit that had been there but was no longer. The person who had religion was not one who believed in a holy writing, but one who had no need of one and who, instead, could make himself, his own existence, a holy text.[16] By contrast with pagan Rome, Christian (i.e., papal) Rome had become a devotee of the dead letter, casting out religion and persecuting

---

[12] *Vorlesungen über die Aesthetik* (S. W., 7. 8, pp. 631–32, 635–39). For the view that, taken in themselves, these lectures would have deprived Schleiermacher of all right to judge esthetic matters, see Rudolf Odebrecht, *Schleiermachers System der Ästhetik: Grundlegung und Problemgeschichtliche Sendung* (Berlin: Junker and Dünnhaupt, 1932), p. 4.

[13] *Reden über die Religion*, 5, p. 268 (Nowak, ed., *Theologische Schriften*, p. 191), "ein geschlossenes Ganze." *Reden über die Religion*, 5, pp. 286–87, 293–94 (Nowak, ed., *Theologische Schriften*, pp. 200, 204).

[14] *Reden über die Religion*, 3, p. 139 (Nowak, ed., *Theologische Schriften*, p. 123). Cf. *Reden über die Religion*, 2, p. 72 (Nowak, ed., *Theologische Schriften*, p. 89).

[15] *Reden über die Religion*, 1, 3, pp. 1, 135 (Nowak, ed., *Theologische Schriften*, pp. 53, 121).

[16] *Reden über die Religion*, 2, pp. 121–22 (Nowak, ed., *Theologische Schriften*, p. 115).

those who truly glimpsed the eternal.[17] Again and again, Schleiermacher returned to his theme that conflict arose as soon as the letter was separated from Spirit; that unity in Spirit could exist in a great diversity of Scriptural interpretations; and, indeed, that the multiplication of differences, notably those of thought and expression, revealed in its beauty and majesty the work of one and the same Spirit. They were different parts of a whole, working together to one purpose and goal, which, however, was not exclusively a tranquil collective life.[18]

Augustine too had accepted multiplicity of meaning as a result of the hiddenness of Scripture. But Schleiermacher's doctrines differed from the Father's in two major regards. First, Schleiermacher's understanding of Scripture as a collection of historical documents made the barrier to understanding a matter of historical criticism, rather than one that hinged on the disparity between divine and human natures, as it had been for Augustine. It was in the nature of narrative, he wrote, that no story—including those in Scripture—could be complete.[19] More fundamentally, Schleiermacher recognized that the books of Scripture were composed under vastly different languages. The Gospels, the few pages containing reports of the life of Christ, were pieced together, partly of what his followers remembered of his oral teaching, partly of experiences had by those first nourished by his spiritual life and instructions that they formed while traveling with him.

At the end of a transition from oral to written accounts, the texts of the synoptic Gospels (but not of John) passed through other stages of revision, perhaps by editors who never knew Jesus and who were guided, not by historical accuracy, but by a wish to enhance the lyrical and dramatic character of the texts. In some instances, events could not have occurred as they were represented in the Gospels. Quite understandably, interpretations based on texts composed in this way were many and diverse, and the historical events recounted in those texts had been so overlayed with fabrications and errors that there were many places where modern interpreters could never penetrate the meaning of the disciples of God who spoke and wrote at the impulse of the Spirit.[20]

The second regard in which Schleiermacher's sense of Scripture's hiddenness differed from Augustine's was related to the Bishop's belief that Scrip-

---

[17] *Reden über die Religion*, 2, p. 64 (Nowak, ed., *Theologische Schriften*, p. 85). See Barth, *The Theology of Schleiermacher*, p. 257.

[18] E.g., *Predigt über die Einigkeit im Geiste (Epheser 4: 1–3)* (*S. W.*, 2. 4, pp. 688, 690–93, 697). *Predigt 59 am 2. Sonntage des Advents 1833* (*S. W.*, 2. 3, p. 742). Concerning the openness of dogmatic theology, see William A. Johnson, *On Religion: A Study of Theological Method in Schleiermacher and Nygren* (Leiden: Brill, 1964), p. 73.

[19] Manuscripts of 1809/10 in *Hermeneutics: The Handwritten Manuscripts*, p. 89.

[20] *Predigt 60 am 4. Sonntage des Advents 1833* (*S. W.*, 2. 3, p. 759). *Einleitung ins neue Testament* (*S. W.*, 1. 8, pp. 196, 206, 223). *The Christian Faith*, p. 601. *Life of Jesus*, ed. Jack C. Verheyden, trans. S. Maclean Gilmour (Philadelphia: Fortress Press, 1975), pp. 37 (lecture 6), 49, 55 (lecture 8). *Predigt über Phil. 2: 5–11* (*S. W.*, 2. 10, p. 493).

ture was an intermediate revelation that would be superseded by a complete revelation at the end of time. Schleiermacher's doctrine of historical progression did not anticipate a cataclysmic end of all ages, but, in another way, it did cast the shadow of incompleteness over all Scriptural interpretation. When would the time be, Schleiermacher asked, when there would be no mediation, but the Father would be all in all? It lay, he answered, outside all time. Before him stretched a progressive movement that might indeed lead to the ruin of the religion that he revered, times of destruction that were yet epochs of humanity in which, by palingenesis, Christianity might reawaken in a new and more beautiful form.[21] Under the aspect of indefinite historical movement, Schleiermacher regarded essential doctrines, including notably that of the Trinity, as incomplete and subject to continual revision.[22] The Bible was the original translation (*Dolmetschung*) of Christian feeling, and its interpretation was subject to ceaseless improvement and development. In fact, despite the power with which it was written, it did not exclude any other book from becoming a "Bible," if only it were written with the same power.[23]

It followed, therefore, that, in his search for meaning, the interpreter sought the unsaid in the text. The same hermeneutic principles applied to Scripture and to nonreligious texts and, in fact, to normal conversation. In all cases, the interpreter read between the lines in order to discover not only the sense of the words but also the thinking that lay behind particular statements.[24] In this regard, as in others, Schleiermacher found a model in Plato, who, Schleiermacher wrote, judged writing a dubious method of communication and, in his dialogues, sketched out "a few unconnected strokes," leaving the reader to reconstrue the inward connection among them that had existed in the author's mind.[25] "We now understand why in *Christmas Eve* music is rated above speech and silent devotion above both.   If there is speech, we do not have anything more than an attempt of feeling to depict itself."[26] In the community of religious feeling, Schleiermacher envisioned music without song or tone, and speech without words.[27] "You ask," he wrote, "which language is secret enough, speech, writing, action, the still mimesis of the Spirit? Every one, I answer, and you see, I have not shrunk

---

[21] *Reden über die Religion*, 5, pp. 308–309 (Nowak, ed., *Theologische Schriften*, 211–12).

[22] Niebuhr, *Schleiermacher on Christ and Religion*, p. 156.

[23] *Letter to F. H. Jacobi; Reden über die Religion*, 5, pp. 305, 376 (Nowak, ed., *Theologische Schriften*, pp. 210, 425).

[24] "Academic Addresses (1829)," in *Hermeneutics: The Handwritten Manuscripts*, p. 182. See also *Einleitung ins neue Testament (S. W.,* 1. 8, p. 7).

[25] *Schleiermacher's Introductions to the Dialogues of Plato*, trans. William Dobson (New York: Arno, 1973, reprint of 1838 ed.), general introduction, pp. 15 (on the *Phaedrus*), 17.

[26] Barth, *The Theology of Schleiermacher*, p. 210.

[27] *Reden über die Religion*, 4, p. 183 (Nowak, ed., *Theologische Schriften*, p. 146).

from the loudest. In each, the holy remains secret and concealed from the profane."[28]

Thus, Schleiermacher's maxim that the interpreter should transform himself into the author of the text preserved the individuality of the "I" and the "you," even while it posited their identity in human nature. Correspondingly, Schleiermacher's conception of the hermeneutic gap included a principle of uncertainty, such as also operated in the doctrines of Augustine and Gerhoch. But, in this respect, as in regard to the multiplicity of interpretations, they reached the same conclusion by quite different ways.

Augustine and Gerhoch posited a diversity of inspiration, including, of course, such inspiration as was vouchsafed to the understander, or interrogator, of the text. Equating understanding and interpretation, as they had not done, Schleiermacher sternly excluded supernatural inspiration from the task of interpretation.[29] To be sure, he wrote that inspiration was as important an element in hermeneutics as in any other art.[30] But his discussion of *Begeistung* and *Begeisterung* in art makes it clear that he intended the natural, organic processes and impulses of composition, just as his discussion of *Eingebung* in Scripture meant freedom in religious action, reflection, and witness.[31] Consequently, Schleiermacher's principle of uncertainty hinged on the approximate character of all understanding and on the indefinitely progressive movement of interpretation through history.[32] "And thus," Schleiermacher wrote, quoting himself against himself, "that feeling of satisfaction seems to be somewhat premature, which maintains that we might now be able to understand Plato better than he understood himself; and it may excite a smile to observe how unplatonically one who entertains such a feeling comes to the investigation of Plato, who puts so high a value upon the consciousness of ignorance."[33]

Schleiermacher went beyond recognizing the hermeneutic gap. His critical methods gave him tools for magnifying the negation of commonality that it had always been known to pose. They constituted a Verfremdungstechnik. Still, his insistence on assimilative union of an author by the interpreter required another set of methods. I shall now turn to the two

---

[28] *Reden über die Religion*, 5, p. 312 (Nowak, ed., *Theologische Schriften*, pp. 213–14).

[29] "Marginal Notes (1832/33)," "Manuscripts of 1890/10," in *Hermeneutics: The Handwritten Manuscripts*, pp. 87, 89, 216.

[30] "1819 Compendium," in *Hermeneutics: The Handwritten Manuscripts*, p. 110.

[31] *Reden über die Religion*, 2, pp. 118–19 (Nowak, ed., *Theologische Schriften*, p. 113). *Vorlesungen über die Aesthetik* (*S. W.*, 7. 8, p. 175). Barth, *The Theology of Schleiermacher*, pp. 175, 182.

[32] "1819 Compendium," "Second Address," in *Hermeneutics: The Handwritten Manuscripts*, pp. 100, 201. Niebuhr, *Schleiermacher on Christ and Religion*, p. 91. Jack Forstman, *A Romantic Triangle: Schleiermacher and Early German Romanticism* (Missoula, Montana: Scholars Press, 1977. American Academy of Religion, Studies in Religion, no. 13), pp. 100, 102.

[33] *Schleiermacher's Introductions to the Dialogues of Plato*, general introduction, p. 5.

branches of Schleiermacher's interpretive work: the isolating enterprise of criticism (*Kritik*) and the unifying one of exposition (*Auslegung*).[34]

THE TASK OF the critic was to establish the text as the author wrote it, that is, as a historical artifact. [35] To conceive of a text in this way was to consider the characteristics that defined it as the work of a particular author, in a discrete culture, at a unique moment:—in short, to accentuate its features as the product of a finite historical process that was over. The editor began with the limits within which the author worked, and against which the author may have struggled, including the capacities and rules of the language in which the text was written.[36] Among the negative values that the critic had to define were the defining limits of the text itself, as an individual work, and as the representative of a genre. The critic's task involved breaking the text apart into its components, and subjecting each of them to the same kind of analysis as the text; for "however unified a book may be, it consists of many wholes which must be separated from one another."[37] Thus, by fragmentation and analysis, the editor recovered the principles of organization by which the whole and the part were made mutually reflective. Moving from the limits of language to those of composition, the critic came, finally, to "the creative moment of the author."[38] The critic accumulated biographical information about the author. If an author had written a number of works, the critic located the particular text under consideration in the chronological series that charted the development of the author's thinking. However, the primary data about the process of thinking encapsulated in the text came from the text itself. As a work of art, the text isolated a transitional point in the flow of history and immobilized it. The "free productivity" of the author, as artist, fixed that instant in space and in time.[39] In the process, both the author's conscious convictions and unspoken thoughts and feelings were incorporated into the text, together with his methods of composition.

Thus, the critic assimilated the author's process of thinking but clarified his distance from the subject by continuing to exercise his own.[40]

In its historical character, criticism taught yet another lesson that combined estrangement with assimilation. In addition to reexperiencing the author's process of composition, the critic had to read the text, as nearly as

[34] Cf. *Einleitung ins neue Testament* (*S. W.*, 1. 8, p. 7).
[35] Cf. *Einleitung ins neue Testament* (*S. W.*, 1. 8, pp. 4, 5): the Bible is "ein geschichtliches Resultat."
[36] "Academic Addresses (1829)," in *Hermeneutics: The Handwritten Manuscripts*, p. 189.
[37] "1826/27, version of part 2," in *Hermeneutics: The Handwritten Manuscripts*, p. 169.
[38] "Academic Addresses (1829)," in *Hermeneutics: The Handwritten Manuscripts*, p. 201.
[39] *Vorlesungen über die Aesthetik* (*S. W.*, 7. 8, pp. 232–33).
[40] Barth, *The Theology of Schleiermacher*, p. 179.

possible, as did the original audience.[41] In isolating and fixing the transitional moment in a work, the author-artist never went beyond what was prepared for the intended audience. The author's free productivity was limited according to what was given in the audience.[42] Indeed, such was the effect of the impersonal norms of genre, imposed by the audience, that "an author who has written in more than one genre is to be regarded as a different author in each case, except with respect to his unique use of language."[43] Each culture provided a distinctive repertory of genres, an array of options from which the author chose one way in which to organize and express material.[44] Thus, authors of books in the New Testament wrote very differently, according to whether they were addressing a circle of Jewish or Gentile converts, or one of mixed Jewish and Gentile Christians, or, yet more precisely, Jewish readers in Palestine or in the Hellenic diaspora.[45]

Defining the original audience placed a formidable number and variety of defining limits between critic and subject, in addition to those pertaining to the circumstances of composition. Schleiermacher's reading of history convinced him that art, and not merely certain forms of art, existed only for the higher circles of society. He recalled instances, in then recent times, when attempts of political factions within the ruling order to appeal to the masses through artistic media had failed.[46] Furthermore, even though he imagined a general development of the human spirit, he believed that each national type emerged as a distinct modality within that development, that art expressed the distinguishing features of national types, and, indeed, that changes in art reflected shifts in a national existence from one period to another.[47]

Finally, his awareness that audiences changed within national groupings gave him a sense of the incompatibility of different genres and styles. To be sure, different schools in a given period and different instants in the careers of a given school could yield common elements.[48] But it was tasteless, Schleiermacher wrote, to combine in one composition elements from different periods.[49] What was truthful in one period and genre was not necessarily so in another.[50] He illustrated the disparity in judgment between two audiences by referring to a number of ancient statues, earlier called the

[41] *Einleitung ins neue Testament* (*S. W.*, 1. 8, p. 7).
[42] *Vorlesungen über die Aesthetik* (*S. W.*, 7. 8, p. 233).
[43] "Manuscripts of 1809/10," in *Hermeneutics: The Handwritten Manuscripts*, p. 85.
[44] "Academic Addresses (1829)," in *Hermeneutics: The Handwritten Manuscripts*, pp. 184–85.
[45] *Einleitung ins neue Testament* (*S. W.*, 1. 8, pp. 7, 31).
[46] *Vorlesungen über die Aesthetik* (*S. W.*, 7. 8, pp. 203–205).
[47] *Vorlesungen über die Aesthetik* (*S. W.*, 7. 8, pp. 91, 116–17, 201, 277).
[48] "Manuscripts of 1809/10," in *Hermeneutics: The Handwritten Manuscripts*, p. 85.
[49] *Vorlesungen über die Aesthetik* (*S. W.*, 7. 8, p. 267).
[50] *Vorlesungen über die Aesthetik* (*S. W.*, 7. 8, p. 614).

"Group of Lycomedes." Modern connoisseurs had assembled these separate figures into a composition representing a dramatic event. Yet exact inquiry had demonstrated that the figures in no way belonged together and, moreover, that the nature of ancient art forbade such a composition.[51] And misunderstanding was a risk in every hermeneutic exercise, one that the "art of understanding," because of its approximate and provisional character, could never entirely overcome. Any audience, including the one originally intended by the author, could labor under the vain conceit that it understood what it did not understand, but the chance of error was heightened when a work from a remote age and culture was at issue.[52]

As indicated above, the effects of Schleiermacher's criticism, as a *Verfremdungstechnik*, were particularly evident in his study of the New Testament. Earlier traditions of exegesis, represented by Augustine and Gerhoch, had sought to read the books of Scripture as works of a single author, and they had not felt a sense of historical foreignness between themselves and the revelations, events, and commands of Scripture. As an exegete, Schleiermacher too sought an immediate participation in the Spirit of the New Testament. But his critical methods had the opposite effect. He did not read the individual books as works of a single author, springing from the same origin and witnessing to a common direction and goal. Instead, he emphasized their different origins and histories, and he left Scriptural theology aside.

He entirely denied the prophetic continuity between Old and New Testaments, which had been a vital element in the argument of patristic and medieval exegetes for the authenticity of Christ's Messiahship. Even the verses of separate books in the New Testament were by no means mutually illuminating and interchangeable. Each book presented a different set of difficulties. Because the authors of numerous works were either unknown or pseudonymous, the personal credence of the writers could lend no authority to those texts. As indicated above, the synoptic Gospels had prehistories. They were the aggregate works of many hands, passing through stages of oral and literary composition before the existing texts were fixed. Not only did they tell little of the life of Christ as a whole, but it was frequently difficult to penetrate the purely literary embellishments in them to the authentic events behind the narratives.

In addition to their individual prehistories and histories, the texts had a collective historical formation and existence. Schleiermacher completed his fragmentation of Scripture by analysis of the Scriptural canon as a historical artifact. The slow and hesitant compilation of the canon was one of trial and error, exercised over a long time without benefit of any apostolic norm.

[51] *Vorlesungen über die Aesthetik* (S. W., 7. 8, p. 593).
[52] *Schleiermacher's Introductions to the Dialogues of Plato*, general introduction, p. 15. Barth, *The Theology of Schleiermacher*, p. 179.

Eventually, it included some works, such as the Apocalypse, which Schleier-macher regarded as having little value. Thus, uncertainty regarding the cri-teria of selection, inclusion, and exclusion cast a shadow over the coherence and the authority of the collective memory fixed in the canon, and the actual religious experience of the primitive Church.[53]

Plainly, Schleiermacher's fragmentation of Scripture into a miscella-neous collection of historical documents challenged the continuity between primitive Christianity and all subsequent epochs in Church history in which the canon was accepted as setting forth the only true paradigm of Christian faith and order. His critical methods stressed the historical finitude of lan-guages, of the documents in Scripture, of the creative moments in which those documents were produced and fixed, and of the audiences for which they were written. He insisted on the discontinuity of historical periods. He asserted that the authentic and normative religious instant for every person was not the reading of texts, but the individual's experience of being filled with the unmediated influence (*Einwirkung*) of God.

Schleiermacher repeatedly asserted that the same art of hermeneutics was valid for the New Testament and for all other texts. The problems, methods, and possibilities that he explored for his art in the study of the New Testa-ment, including that of immediate intimation, were, he thought, univer-sally applicable. However, the atomization that ensued through criticism of any historical text was, for Schleiermacher, counterbalanced by other methods that did enable interpreters to transcend distances of time and cul-ture, and to assimilate remote authors and audiences to themselves. Even the incommunicable moment of the individual's religious intimation (*Anschauung*) of God was a "small fragment" of a vast entirety. I now turn to the principles of exposition that, for Schleiermacher, made the transit from fragmentation to unity possible.

SCHLEIERMACHER READILY combined what he called historical and spec-ulative knowledge, but not in equal parts. The occasions on which his inter-pretations of Scripture deliberately and systematically contorted the literal sense of the text were signs of the divorce in his mind between criticism and exposition.[54] The certainty of critical method, he wrote, was of an entirely different order from the certainty of the method by which an interpreter

---

[53] *The Christian Faith*, pp. 595, 600–603. *Einleitung ins neue Testament (S. W.,* 1. 8, pp. 5, 9–10, 196, 206, 223, 470, 472). Friedrich Schleiermacher, *The Life of Jesus,* pp. xxx–xxxi, xxxvii, 49, 55. Niebuhr, *Schleiermacher on Christ and Religion,* p. 149.

[54] On historical and speculative knowledge, *Schleiermachers Dialektik,* pp. 200–204. Exam-ples of Schleiermacher's deformation of literal meaning occur in his exegesis on the creation of Eve, cited above at n. 5; in the doctrine of marriage that he extorted from Ephesians 5; and in the evasion of Christ's command to hate parents, wife, children, and kinsmen for his sake (Luke 14:26). Barth, *The Theology of Schleiermacher,* pp. 112–13. *Predigt über das Gebot Christi: um Seinetwillen zu hassen (S. W.,* 2. 4, pp. 586–607).

grasped an author's way of thinking.[55] The task of criticism was to identify parts; that of exposition, to reconstruct the whole, including the thinking that informed the author's process of composition.[56] Thus, the interpreter passed from an outward form, the actual work of art, to the picture inside the artist's mind, and, further, to the inmost beginning of shapes, or formulations, in the artist's frame of reference. Those primordial forms dwelled in the spirit of which the artist partook because he belonged to a collective life in this world.[57]

The hermeneutic schools represented by Augustine and Gerhoch employed allegory to delve beneath the surface of Scripture and to expose its hidden coherence. True to the traditions of literalism, refreshed and reasserted by Protestant reformers, Schleiermacher allowed allegory to enter his interpretive apparatus only when the text itself was allegorical. "Expressions are to be regarded as figurative," he wrote, "only when there is no other possibility."[58] But the exclusion of allegory did not exclude moralizing the letter of Scripture to suit the spirit of the interpreter's own age.

Schleiermacher's point of departure was the concept of the fragment. To be sure, he wrote, a person might find beautiful outlines and relationships enclosed in a piece of a great work of art. From the fragment, it might be possible to deduce the rules governing them. Would not the viewer, on that account, consider the fragment more a work in itself, than part of a work? Would the viewer not judge that, by comparison with the part, the whole work of art—if it was thoroughly executed in the same style—was lacking in verve, boldness, and everything that bespeaks a great spirit? Yet, an individual object displayed relationships that could not be fully understood from the object itself. The world is a work of which a person can see only one part, and, even if that fragment were complete in itself, a viewer could not form an adequate conception of the whole.[59] Schleiermacher's point in this passage is that the internal unity of a work, which may be extrapolated from a fragment, does not disclose the endless, inexhaustible unity that encompassed and related all works, and that was detected, not by critical analysis of internal, organic unity, but by religious feeling. From this perspective, every text or work of art was a fragment of a whole.

To elude the hermeneutic gap of fragmented, historical discontinuities, Schleiermacher seized upon the hermeneutic circle. Without the term, earlier writers, including Augustine and Gerhoch, had imagined a hermeneutic circle, generally formed by the premise that authors and interpreters of

[55] "Academic Addresses (1829)," in *Hermeneutics: The Handwritten Manuscripts*, p. 185.
[56] "1819 Compendium, draft for part 2 (1826)," "Academic Addresses (1829)," in *Hermeneutics: The Handwritten Manuscripts*, pp. 112, 156, 188.
[57] *Vorlesungen über die Aesthetik* (*S. W.*, 7. 8, p. 583).
[58] "Manuscripts of 1809/10," in *Hermeneutics: The Handwritten Manuscripts*, p. 87.
[59] *Reden über die Religion*, 2, p. 83 (Nowak, ed., *Theologische Schriften*, p. 95). See Odebrecht, *Schleiermachers System der Ästhetik*, p. 24.

Scriptural texts shared a common divine inspiration. Having excluded supernatural inspiration, Schleiermacher invoked the principle of a common humanity, rendered articulate through feeling. In fact, he applied his doctrine of the hermeneutic circle to several specific relationships. He started from the general principles that in its particular composition an individual work of art mirrored experience of absolute humanity and that it gave access through that experience to that absolute, and thus to the interplay of the finite humanity of the individual and the infinite humanity of the world. With these principles in mind, he applied the hermeneutic circle to the work of art itself; "each part can be understood only out of the whole to which it belongs, and *vice versa*." Schleiermacher also extended the principle that "the whole should be understood from the particulars and the particulars from the whole" to the relation of an author's works to his cultural context.[60] The principle applied, most directly of all, to the enterprise of understanding (equated with interpretation). A circle existed between the work of art and the interpreter, who had absorbed the work of art. Unlike every other work of art, the world could not be absorbed as a whole into the interpreter;[61] but, even there, interpretation was possible because of an "indwelling form of knowing" through which the individual participated in the Absolute, "infinite humanity," or "the higher World Spirit."[62]

As indicated above, Schleiermacher's critics contended that what he called a hermeneutic circle was in fact a vicious circle of anthropology. But Schleiermacher constructed defenses against that charge by his teachings on participation, movement, and vocation.

According to his expository method, the fragments that Schleiermacher established by his critical method in fact constituted a sequence of hierarchic complexity and magnitude: the author, the moment of composition, the oeuvre, the genre or school, the class or cultural context, and the general development of humanity. The hermeneutic circle located each of these elements in the context of the one that followed it, culminating in the indefinite vastness of religion and the participatory union of religious feeling.

The stress in criticism fell on the text, or work of art, as a historical document. That in exposition fell on the interpreter or spectator as, in some sense, a dweller outside of time who participated in the life of the author.

---

[60] "1819 Compendium," in *Hermeneutics: The Handwritten Manuscripts*, p. 113. Martin Redeker, *Schleiermacher: Life and Thought*, trans. John Wallhausser (Philadelphia: Fortress Press, 1973), p. 179, quoting *S. W.*, 1. 7, p. 255.

[61] *Vorlesungen über die Aesthetik* (*S. W.*, 7. 8, p. 33).

[62] Cf. Johnson, *On Religion*, pp. 31, 139. Compare Bernard of Clairvaux, *De Diligendo Deo*, 7. 22 (J. Leclercq and H. M. Rochais, eds., *Tractatus et Opuscula*, [Rome: Editiones Cistercienses, 1963, *S. Bernardi Opera*, 3], pp. 137–38): "Sed enim in hoc est mirum, quod nemo quaerere te valet, nisi qui prius invenerit. Vis igitur inveniri ut quaeraris, quaeri ut inveniaris. Potes quidem quaeri et inveniri, non tamen praeveniri. Nam etsi dicimus: 'Mane oratio mea praeveniet te,' non dubium tamen quod tepida sit omnis oratio, quam non praevenerit inspiratio. Dicendum iam unde inchoet amor noster, quoniam ubi consummetur dictum est."

But this mode of participation was possible because, in articulating a common humanity, the interpreter participated in the divine nature, which Schleiermacher defined as omnipotence and love. The almighty love that the divine nature was, Schleiermacher wrote, was not in us so long as there was anything in us that set limits to love.[63] Among those limits were space and time. The immediate participation of God was the ground of relationship between the interpreter, as subject, and the author in the text, as object.[64] But, because it annihilated historical discontinuities, it also required the interpreter to strive to transcend the finitude of individuality, to live in one and all, and to become thereby more than an individual; consequently, little was lost when the interpreter was in fusion with the universal.[65]

As he worked out his doctrine of participation, Schleiermacher was guided by the two conventional paradigms that we have traced from the beginning: the biological and the esthetic. As we have found repeatedly, these paradigms occurred in a system of thought that permitted the coincidence of opposites, or "the interconnection of antithesis."[66] Schleiermacher applied the concept of organic unity to relationship in his hierarchic sequence. An author's thinking; the moment fixed in the work; the unfolding development of an oeuvre, a genre, or cultural context; and the universal—all were conceived as having organic unity. Any organism incorporates from its beginning the specific pattern of its later development. This assumption of original, rather than acquired, nature too was built into Schleiermacher's doctrines, as, for example, when he argued that the oeuvre of Plato had an organic unity, the elements of his character and the germs of almost all his philosophic system having been present even in his earliest dialogue.[67]

Nourished by an affinity to Spinoza, the concept that individuals belonged to a developing organic whole, in which they had a common identity, enabled Schleiermacher to assume an identity between subject and object, whether between an interpreter and an author, or between a particular human being and the Absolute.[68] Analogues from sculpture illustrated his underlying assumptions that each person was "a compendium of humanity," that each personality embraced in some sense the whole human nature, and, indeed, that all human natures were fused into one with reference not to the individuating factors of being and will but to the unifying

[63] "Academic Addresses (1829)," in *Hermeneutics: The Handwritten Manuscripts*, p. 205. *Predigt über 2. Pet. 1: 3–4 (S. W.*, 2. 4, pp. 526–27).

[64] Cf. Nowak, introduction to *Theologische Schriften*, p. 24.

[65] *Reden über die Religion*, 2, p. 132 (Nowak, ed., *Theologische Schriften*, p. 120).

[66] See below at nn. 83–84. Spiegler, *The Eternal Covenant*, pp. 52, 72, 74.

[67] *Schleiermacher's Introductions to the Dialogues of Plato*, introduction to the *Phaedrus*, p. 67.

[68] Cf. Johnson, *On Religion*, p. 18.

ones of meaning and understanding.[69] Schleiermacher rejected the argument of classicists that ancient Greek sculptors had achieved the ideal type of nature against which all other representations must be judged. Surely, the Greeks had achieved exemplary perfection in the art of sculpture. It was possible, however, that the figures portrayed by ancient sculptors represented stages of genetic development rather than universal ideals. Skeletal examinations of the ancient dead did not clarify this argument. One had to recognize, however, that in European civilization sculpture was confined to peoples of the same racial type. If a sculptor decided to carve a statue of a Negro, it would be an astonishing caprice, Schleiermacher continued, but the statue itself could not be considered as outside the realm of art because it did not have the beautiful as its subject. Neither was it impossible that the career of artistic development might move toward representing its inner perfection in that very type, and the same could occur with regard to any race.[70] The closer a person came to fusion with the universal, the more fully the one participated in the other, the more completely they became one, neither party taking thought for itself, but each for the other, in such a way that they were no more human beings, but humanity.[71]

Thus, the Redeemer, the God who became flesh, planted the seed of his divine life in the souls of human beings and drew it to himself, "with heavenly, divine power."[72] Thus, through participation, Schleiermacher imagined himself as a plant, "which survives only through living assimilation and circulation."[73]

Schleiermacher employed a venerable signature of the biological model when he described the moment of understanding in erotic terms. The hermeneutic method, as he described it, consisted of intuitive, or divinatory, and comparative knowledge. "Divinatory knowledge is the feminine strength in knowing people; comparative, the masculine." The two must cleave together in one operation; "the general and the particular must interpenetrate."[74] The ecstatic moment of religious understanding was likewise a holy, conjugal embrace. "I lie on the breast of the endless world. In this moment, I am her soul, for I feel all her strengths and her endless life as my own. In this moment, she is my body, for I penetrate her muscles and her members as my own, and her inmost nerves are moved according to my sense and my reflex (*Ahndung*) as are my own."[75]

[69] *Reden über die Religion*, 2, 4, pp. 99, 234 (Nowak, ed., *Theologische Schriften*, pp. 103, 173).

[70] *Vorlesungen über die Aesthetik* (*S. W.*, 7. 8, pp. 608–11).

[71] *Reden über die Religion*, 4, p. 234 (Nowak, ed., *Theologische Schriften*, p. 173).

[72] *Predigt über Phil. 2: 5–11* (*S. W.*, 2. 10, p. 503). Cf. *Reden über die Religion*, 5, pp. 237–38 (Nowak, ed., *Theologische Schriften*, p. 175).

[73] *Aus Schleiermachers Leben in Briefen*, ed. Wilhelm Dilthey and Ludwig Jonas. Bd 1 (Berlin: Reimer, 1860), pp. 230, 336.

[74] "Draft for part 2 (1826)," in *Hermeneutics: The Handwritten Manuscripts*, p. 150.

[75] *Reden über die Religion*, 2, pp. 73–74 (Nowak, ed., *Theologische Schriften*, p. 90). Cf. Richard R. Niebuhr's reference to "a deeply feminine dimension in [Schleiermacher's] own

Almost certainly inspired by his Moravian antecedents, Schleiermacher's concept of marriage as a "fusion of two persons" in which an interpenetration of man and woman occurs informed these doctrines of hermeneutic and spiritual union.[76] It was of a piece with his interpretation of the creation of Eve, the lessons of which Schleiermacher applied to himself: "I must fuse into one being with a beloved soul, so that, in the most beautiful way, my humanity may work on humanity; so that I may know that after the resurrection of freedom the transfigured higher life may be formed in me as the old man begins the new world."[77]

The emphasis on feeling in these erotic conceptions of biological union formed a transition to the esthetic model. Schleiermacher's continual cross-references from literary to visual arts, and the stress of his expository methods on the spectator, rather than the spectacle, were effects of the esthetic model. Human sensuality was the essential organ of art, he wrote,[78] and the esthetic sense united art and religion. As the impulse to the universal, it made all knowledge art, and art, the highest knowledge.[79] Schleiermacher's attention ran to the first secret-filled moment of every sensual perception, before intimation (*Anschauung*) and feeling (*Gefühl*) divided, when sense and its object flowed, the one into the other, and became one, only to part when the perception was past. That union was indescribable and quickly over, but it was the basis of reflection and knowledge.[80] When it came in the moment of spiritual exaltation, it led to the particular way of intimation (*Anschauungsart*) that transcended humanity, and that Schleiermacher once defined as God.[81]

This esthetic perception left a feeling of utter dependence, which was both the sign and the means of the individual's unifying relationship with God.[82] But everything that could be perceived belonged to a great historical picture,

---

being." "Karl Barth's 'Schleiermacher': A Review Essay," *Union Seminary Quarterly Review*, 39 (1984), p. 132.

[76] Redeker, *Schleiermacher: Life and Thought*, pp. 64–65, 67. Barth, *The Theology of Schleiermacher*, pp. 111, 121. Cf. Thomas F. Torrance, "Hermeneutics According to F. D. E. Schleiermacher," *Scottish Journal of Theology*, 21 (1986), p. 262: "Hence it is all the more necessary that the interpreter should divine the seminal determination in the consciousness of a biblical author in order to reconstruct and reproduce it as a determination in his own consciousness and so to remodel it in his own understanding."

[77] Barth, *The Theology of Schleiermacher*, p. 123

[78] *Vorlesungen über die Aesthetik* (*S. W.*, 7. 8, p. 44).

[79] *Schleiermachers Dialektik*, p. 20. On the equivalence of the arts, see Odebrecht, *Schleiermachers System der Ästhetik*, p. 13.

[80] *Reden über die Religion*, 2, p. 73 (Nowak, ed., *Theologische Schriften*, p. 90). Johnson, *On Religion*, p. 34.

[81] *Reden über die Religion*, 2, pp. 125–26 (Nowak, ed., *Theologische Schriften*, pp. 116–17). Barth, *The Theology of Schleiermacher*, p. 258. This was not Schleiermacher's only definition of God. See Werner Schultz, "Schleiermachers Theorie des Gufühls und ihre theologische Bedeutung," *Zeitschrift für Theologie und Kirche*, 53 (1956), p. 85.

[82] Johnson, *On Religion*, p. 138. On Hegel's jibe that the prime exemplar of Schleiermacher's doctrine of utter dependence was a dog, see Robert R. Williams, "A Scholarly Note?" *The Owl of Minerva*, 14 (1982), pp. 9–10.

which represented a moment of the universal. Schleiermacher envisioned
the vast diversity of opinion and feelings as a magic circle encompassing and
playing about everything, as though it were an atmosphere filled with solvent and magnetic (or electric) powers, melting and unifying everything,
and informing all its emanations with light and truth. This, he wrote, was
the harmony of the universal; the wonderful and great unity in the world,
its eternal works of art.[83] In that dynamic unity of the endless, where all
that is finite exists undisturbed together, all opposites reciprocally penetrate
and unite.[84]

The moment of esthetic union was also the instant of exaltation and presence of mind when the concept of art arose,[85] the experience that enabled
artists, as well as heroes, lawgivers, and others to mediate between finite
human beings and endless humanity.[86] When it was over, it lost its reality
as experience and entered the sphere of memory: the religious became the
historical, as was notably the case with Judaism, which, Schleiermacher
held, had become a dead religion.[87] It did not become a dead thing, an
"incorruptible mummy," in the hands of the virtuosi, or artists, of religion,[88] who, through their feeling of utter dependence, remained able to
mediate between the endless and the finite. Nor, in Christianity, was the
historical Jesus the only mediator. For whoever grounded his religion on
the same perception embodied in Jesus is a Christian, without regard for the
school, whether he derives his religion historically from himself or from
any other. Nor did Jesus define, by the intuitions and feelings that he himself could convey, the entire scope of the religion that was to issue from his
basic intimation. For his disciples did the same, never fixing boundaries for
the Holy Spirit.[89] Such were the considerations that led Schleiermacher to
conclude: "he who does not believe does not experience, and he who does
not experience, does not understand."[90]

---

[83] Werner Schultz, "Die Idee des Spiels und die Idee der Menschheit in der Theologie
Schleiermachers," *Neue Zeitschrift für systematische Theologie*, 4 (1962), p. 351. *Reden über
die Religion*, 2, p. 92 (Nowak, ed., *Theologische Schriften*, p. 99).

[84] *Reden über die Religion*, 2, p. 64 (Nowak, ed., *Theologische Schriften*, p. 85). *Schleiermacher's Introductions to the Dialogues of Plato*, introduction to *The Sophist*, p. 252.

[85] *Vorlesungen über die Aesthetik* (*S. W.*, 7. 8, p. 86).

[86] *Reden über die Religion*, 1, pp. 10–11 (Nowak, ed., *Theologische Schriften*, pp. 57–58).
See Albert L. Blackwell, *Schleiermacher's Early Philosophy of Life: Determinism, Freedom,
and Phantasy* (Chico, Calif.: Scholars Press, 1982. Harvard Theological Studies, 33), p. 277:
"Schleiermacher felt that the chief means of widening sympathy is the most inward of all our
capacities, phantasy."

[87] *Reden über die Religion*, 5, pp. 286–87 (Nowak, ed., *Theologische Schriften*, p. 200). Cf.
Reden über die Religion, 2, pp. 99–100 (Nowak, ed., *Theologische Schriften*, pp. 103–104).

[88] *Reden über die Religion*, 4, 5, pp. 184, 203, 213, 219, 221–23, 286-87, 299, 308 (Nowak,
ed., *Theologische Schriften*, pp. 147, 157, 162, 165–67, 200, 207, 211).

[89] *Reden über die Religion*, 5, p. 304 (Nowak, ed., *Theologische Schriften*, p. 209).

[90] Schleiermacher was commenting on the statement of Augustine, as repeated by Anselm
of Canterbury, "Nor do I seek to understand in order that I may believe, but I believe in order
that I may understand." Niebuhr, *Schleiermacher on Christ and Religion*, p. 139.

Schleiermacher's doctrines of participatory bonding focused on movement. Whether in their biological or esthetic modes, they portrayed dynamic relationships. The objects of Schleiermacher's interest were the formulations of thought in the author's mind, the processes of composition encapsulated in the work, the movements of historical development in which the work figured, and the oscillations between divinatory and comparative operations in the interpreter's analysis. The metaphors of organic growth, copulation, and the oscillating current of electrical energy witness to this overriding fascination with movement. The crucial point was the fleeting moment of immediate experience when perception and feeling were one, a moment of transition that was also mediation.

Quite naturally, Schleiermacher employed the analogue of play, and especially mimetic play, to describe participatory bonding. As noted with reference to Augustine and Gerhoch, this analogue too belonged to the long tradition of thought about participatory bonding in which Schleiermacher stood.

At first glance, Schleiermacher might appear to have been hostile to the analogue of play. He took issue with Schiller's doctrine that art was "free play," the diametric opposite of serious understanding and formulation of thought, although not with the importance that Schiller gave play in the creative act.[91] Phrases such as "empty play" are frequent in his writings. On the rare occasions when he employed metaphors of play, he inclined to use them to emphasize vanity or triviality.[92] But Schleiermacher was known for his ready sense of humor, and his works exhibit a variety of experiments with play in the dramatic form of dialogues (including one of his most celebrated works, the *Weinachtsfeier*), charades, and other genres.[93] His own temperament may have made him particularly alert to Plato's "playful use of language," including irony, to the "joking spirit" with which Plato constructed the convolutions in some of his dialogues.[94] and to the dialogues themselves as "playing for time."[95]

The German language gave Schleiermacher a large repertory of words and phrases that implicitly or explicitly expressed the idea of play—*aufs*

---

[91] *Vorlesungen über die Aesthetik (S. W., 7. 8, pp. 97–101)*. Schultz, "Die Idee des Spiels und die Idee der Menschheit in der Theologie Schleiermachers," pp. 340–46, on intellectual precedents for Schleiermacher's doctrine of play. See also Odebrecht, *Schleiermachers System der Ästhetik*, pp. 107–13, 149, esp. p. 108: In play, human dignity comes to consciousness.

[92] E.g., *Reden über die Religion*, 1, 2, pp. 16, 32, 44, 54, 61 (Nowak, ed., *Theologische Schriften*, pp. 60, 69, 75, 80). *Schleiermacher's Introductions to the Dialogues of Plato*, introduction to *Phaedrus*, p. 57. For his use of the analogue of a "cat's cradle," *Predigt über Matt. 13: 22 (S. W., 4, p. 741)*.

[93] Barth, *The Theology of Schleiermacher*, p. 273.

[94] E.g., *Schleiermacher's Introductions to the Dialogues of Plato*, introduction to *Cratylus*, pp. 231, 233, 244–45.

[95] *Schleiermacher's Introductions to the Dialogues of Plato*, introduction to *Phaedrus*, p. 62.

Spiel setzen, Wortspiel, Beispiel, Wettspiel, Kampfspiel, Spielraum, eine Rolle spielen, Schauspiel, Kinderspiel, ein falsches Spiel treiben, aus dem Spiel lassen, and many others. Apart from his own temperament, the unconscious, collective associations of this repertory, the power of language to shape thought, may have influenced his thinking. Still, the importance of play in his general doctrines was far from the involuntary reflexes of temperament or linguistic conditioning. The analogue of play in music was never far from his mind and gave him a paradigm of how many became one that he frequently employed.

At the highest of all levels, Schleiermacher, inspired by his knowledge of electrical forces, described the entire world as "an eternally continuing play of opposing powers," a counterpart to "the play of special powers and personality" in the individual human being.[96] The participation of holy thoughts and feelings came only in the gentle play of rays of God's holy fire.[97] Thought arose from finite to unending through the play of human nature with ideals; art, from the free play of fantasy with ideals; and a work of art, from the inner play of pictures and thoughts.[98]

Evidently, the concept of play was associated in Schleiermacher's mind with ecstatic participation, which he considered the ground of all art, and, indeed, of life, because "all life should be art."[99] Texts and works were monuments of that play, which they also incorporated, and from within them came a call, or vocation. The esthetic basis of that call is evident in Schleiermacher's assertion that being was not thought or action, but intimation (*Anschauung*) and feeling (*Gefühl*).[100] The intensely personal feeling of absolute dependence, by which the humanity of one individual fused with, and worked upon, humanity, was the sign of this vocation.

The call from within the work was a call to the priestly office of mediation. Schleiermacher's thought turned to the example of Christ, who came so that, through community, the blessings of his presence should extend not to individual souls only but to all.[101] The Redeemer's vocation to Peter, the command to feed Christ's sheep, encased in the text of Scripture, was the common call of all Christians.[102] The earthly places to which God called individuals—their professions—were by no means distinct from this religious calling. For professions too served the entire range of God's great

---

[96] *Reden über die Religion,* 1, 2, pp. 6, 51–2 (Nowak, ed., *Theologische Schriften,* pp. 55, 79).

[97] *Reden über die Religion,* 1, p. 13 (Nowak, ed., *Theologische Schriften,* p. 59).

[98] *Reden über die Religion,* 1, p. 9 (Nowak, ed., *Theologische Schriften,* p. 57). *Vorlesungen über die Aesthetik (S. W.,* 7. 8, pp. 108, 111, 179–80). On the kinds of play represented in Schleiermacher, see the summary statement by Schultz, "Die Idee des Spiels und die Idee der Menschheit in der Theologie Schleiermachers," p. 348.

[99] *Schleiermachers Dialektik,* p. xviii. See Schultz, "Die Idee des Spiels und die Idee der Menschheit in der Theologie Schleiermachers," p. 347.

[100] *Reden über die Religion,* 2, pp. 50–51 (Nowak, ed., *Theologische Schriften,* p. 78).

[101] *Predigt am Sonntage Cantate 1823* (Joh. 21: 16) (*S. W.,* 2. 4, p. 204).

[102] *Predigt am Sonntage Cantate 1823* (Joh. 21: 16) (*S. W.,* 2. 4, p. 192).

work. Neither in the religious nor in the secular part of his vocation did a member of the Christian community bury his talent. Rather, in both parts, every person sought to nourish the souls of his brethren with comfort and truth from the fullness of the divine treasure.[103]

Christian vocation was, above all, a call to love for Christ that impelled believers in all aspects of their vocation. This was true of scholars trained in the art of understanding. "Can there be a living love for the Redeemer," Schleiermacher asked, "without assiduous occupation with the Word?"[104] But Schleiermacher did not call for passionless hermeneutics. No knowledge of past ages, of extinct languages, or of any concept that provides a fundamental and deep insight into the different parts of the divine Word can achieve a living and right knowledge of that Word, if it is acquired only to dazzle the world, or to gratify the human spirit by pursuing research into the divine Word as one would on some other human concern. So loveless an enterprise of scholarship could never answer the call to feed the Lord's sheep, for the scholar's endeavor was of concern to himself alone.[105] Only when everything in one's soul was subordinated to love of Christ, and ruled and penetrated by that love, did one achieve a truly divine wisdom (*Weisheit*), knowledge (*Wissenschaft*), and art (*Kunst*).[106]

Always presupposing an equation of understanding with interpretation, Schleiermacher's search for the creative process within the text was, therefore, a means of entering into the play of forces in the world, as it directed the minds of author and interpreter. The fusion of personalities that occurred might well have an intellectual component—such as historical knowledge, facility in alien languages, and mastery of critical methods—but its closure, through love, was affective.

Schleiermacher's doctrine of participatory bonding followed convictions, represented by Augustine and Gerhoch, in these ways, and also in its portrayal of bonding as mimetic and conflictual. When the called entered into the sanctuary of true knowledge, they received a heavenly lyre and a magic mirror in order to accompany their silent vision (*Bild*) with divine sounds, and to gaze upon it, forever, always the same in countless forms.[107] As priestly mediators, those who gazed on the image in the magic mirror, mirroring themselves in the eternal world, could become in turn mirrors of the eternal world, as did Spinoza.[108] In their writings, they could exhibit mirrored likenesses of themselves, as did Plato.[109]

Schleiermacher carefully distinguished creative reproduction from

[103] *Predigt am Sonntage Cantate 1823* (Joh. 21: 16) (*S. W.*, 2. 4, pp. 197, 205).
[104] *Predigt am Sonntage Cantate 1823* (Joh. 21: 16) (*S. W.*, 2. 4, pp. 196–97).
[105] *Predigt am Sonntage Cantate 1823* (Joh. 21: 16) (*S. W.*, 2. 4, pp. 197–99).
[106] *Predigt am Sonntage Cantate 1823* (Joh. 21: 16) (*S. W.*, 2. 4, p. 200).
[107] *Reden über die Religion*, 3, p. 171 (Nowak, ed., *Theologische Schriften*, p. 140).
[108] *Reden über die Religion*, 2, p. 55 (Nowak, ed., *Theologische Schriften*, p. 80).
[109] *Schleiermacher's Introductions to the Dialogues of Plato*, introduction to the *Symposium*, p. 289.

mechanical copying. The copyist, he wrote, was entirely excluded from art. But a reproduction, as in painting, was a product of the same artistic moment as the original, though on a subordinate level.[110] Likewise, a sculptor, who conceived the idea of a work, might act mimetically in forming the picture in his mind. The clay model that he made was only a reproduction of the inner picture, a transition between the original in his mind and the mechanical copy of the model, which latter was the work, not of the sculptor, but of the artisan who executed it in stone.[111]

The object of hermeneutic inquiry, therefore, was to reproduce the living processes of thought in the mind of the author so completely that the interpreter could imitate the author's thinking and style, writing "on a given subject in the same way as another would have treated it." The perfect reproduction captured the identity between the antitheses of subjective and objective in the original work.[112] Indeed, Schleiermacher's fundamental insistence that the interpreter assimilated the thinking of the author and the expectations of the originally intended audience demanded the practice of hermeneutics as a mimetic art.[113]

Having identified nature with human nature, Schleiermacher taught that nature art and, indeed, that art, rather than imitating nature as classical estheticians held, prescribed rules to nature and was the canon of nature.[114] This principle reached beyond the literary, visual, and performing arts, for, as always, Schleiermacher used esthetic principles to illuminate moral responsibility. Art's prescription of laws to nature elucidated the transformation of human nature into divine by the imitation of Christ. The original likeness of human nature to God had been darkened and obliterated by sin, which separated human beings from God. Christ's voluntary self-emptying and subservience was the model for all who, having among themselves the mind that Christ had, restored that likeness and entered into communion with God.[115] The immediate experience of Christ, perceived and felt by his imitators, produced moments in the history of religion as art; and religion's works of art were exhibited as though the entire world were a gallery of religious scenes. Likewise, all history was an endless gallery of the noblest works of art, eternally multiplied through a thousand shining mirrors, every individual work being a reflection of the Spirit of the universal.[116]

---

[110] *Vorlesungen über die Aesthetik* (*S. W.*, 7. 8, p. 87).

[111] *Vorlesungen über die Aesthetik* (*S. W.*, 7. 8, p. 57).

[112] "Draft for part 2 (1826)," in *Hermeneutics: The Handwritten Manuscripts*, p. 154.

[113] Cf. also "Academic Addresses (1829)," in *Hermeneutics: The Handwritten Manuscripts*, p. 186.

[114] *Vorlesungen über die Aesthetik* (*S. W.*, 7. 8, p. 149). Karl F. Morrison, *The Mimetic Tradition of Reform in the West* (Princeton: Princeton University Press, 1982), p. 324.

[115] *Predigt über die an uns Alle gerichtete Aufforderung, dem Leiden Christi ähnlich zu sein (1. Pet. 2: 20–22)* (*S. W.*, 2. 4, p. 238). *Predigt über Phil. 2: 5–11* (*S. W.*, 2. 10, pp. 493, 497, 510–11).

[116] *Reden über die Religion*, 3, pp. 140–41, 172–73 (Nowak, ed., *Theologische Schriften*, pp. 124, 141–42).

Finally, Schleiermacher remained true to convention by teaching that the play leading to participatory union involved conflict. He insisted that controversy was opposed to the nature of true religion, lamented divisions in Christianity, and denounced the polemical attitude of sectarian Christianity toward everything outside itself and toward departures from historical ideals within itself, hostility exemplified, he judged, in the oppressiveness of the Roman Church.[117] Yet, even when he did not enter "the contests (*Kampfspiele*) of philosophical and theological athletes," he observed and learned from both sides, not only when he was a young man, but also throughout his career.[118] He included polemics and apologetics in the course of study that he prescribed for theological education. In his own irenic way, he provoked and engaged in controversies throughout his life, and the periodic revisions of his major writings resulted from conflicts over doctrine and ecclesiastical polity. It is evident by now that Schleiermacher's views of the world, of the human soul, and, specifically, of the interpretive method all portrayed general harmony made up of the opposition of parts. The contrary powers interpenetrated and became one, even as in dialectic, the two arguments converged in closure.[119]

SCHLEIERMACHER'S THEOLOGY placed the task of interpretation in a yet wider context. For, as in the doctrines of Augustine and Gerhoch, so also in Schleiermacher's, conflict was the necessary authentication of participatory union. His doctrines concerning the imitation of Christ in self-denial and self-emptying took up the ancient themes of conflict against the soul and struggle against the world, "that area in which sensual and natural powers rule alone, where pleasure and aversion are at work, or force and power." The world withstood the kingdom of God, "where all is acceptable for the power of love, where this true and eternal divinity reigns, and all becomes and arises through it. . . ." Nor were Christians permitted to take up the world's weapons—including human knowledge and art—to fight for the kingdom of God, for, in so doing, they would dim the light and increase the darkness.[120] The call from within the text was thus a call to conflict and suffering, a call to bear Christ's cross as did the martyrs in the first centuries of Christianity.[121]

---

[117] See *Reden über die Religion*, 5, pp. 245, 285, 291, 292 (Nowak, ed., *Theologische Schriften*, pp. 179, 202–205). For the metaphor of a picture gallery as used by Hegel and Ortega, see Chapter 11 n. 10. See also Chapter 1 n. 76.

[118] *Aus Schleiermachers Leben in Briefen*, Bd 1, p. 82, a letter that Schleiermacher wrote at the age of 21 to his father.

[119] See Friedrich Kaulbach, "Schleiermachers Idee der Dialektik," *Neue Zeitschrift für systematische Theologie und Religionsphilosophie*, 10 (1968), esp. pp. 228–33 and p. 247, on the "identity of the process."

[120] *Predigt am Sonntage Cantate 1823 (Joh. 21:16) (S. W., 2. 4, p. 201). Predigt über 2. Pet. 1: 3–4 (S. W., 2. 4, p. 529).*

[121] *Predigt über die an uns Alle gerichtete Aufforderung, dem Leiden Christi ähnlich zu sein*

"Here is the land of conflict and strife," Schleiermacher wrote, "and since there can be no conflict and strife without suffering, what more beautiful goal can we set for ourselves than always to suffer for the sake of doing good?"[122]

Schleiermacher's theology so diminished the concepts of sin and evil,[123] that the antitheses of good and evil, as the ultimate poles of struggle, no longer held. In his theology, the interpreter's labor and participatory union took place in the conflict against finitude and, supremely, against death. The great war was against blind instinct, thoughtless habit, dead obedience, everything inert and passive—all symptoms of stifled humanity and freedom. This struggle of life against death, the first and last enemy, was the task of the moment and of the centuries, the great, unceasing work of redemption performed by everlasting love.[124]

Summary

Some students of Schleiermacher have argued that he excluded the dialectic of the "I–you" relationship by positing a fundamental unity of being: all were one. His theories of criticism point to the same conclusion, but by the opposite route. For they indicate that the "I–you" dialogue was impossible because of discontinuities in human existence—that is, in the basic dimensions of history, time, and space.

On the whole, Schleiermacher's heirs have divided his legacy. They have regarded it as presenting a choice, rather than a whole inheritance. For they have generally parted into two camps: on the one hand, those who follow the principles of his critical theories, analytically fragmenting and deconstructing works of art as historical documents or artifacts, and, on the other, those who embrace his expository doctrines, in which identity and individuality combine. The first places stress on the object, that is, on the spectacle; the second, on the interpreter, or spectator. The first, the critical method, is historical; the second, the expository, is antihistorical. No one could question that many of Schleiermacher's antihistorical conclusions were timebound and, precisely, infused with the enthusiasms of the Romantic movement. But the antiquated savor of his conclusions does not taint the doctrines that, arising from age-old tradition, transcended the limits of his

---

(1. Pet. 2: 20–22). Predigt über das Gebot Christi: um Seinetwillen zu hassen (Luk. 19:26) (S. W., 2. 4, pp. 233–34, 586).

[122] Predigt über die an uns Alle gerichtete Aufforderung, dem Leiden Christi ähnlich zu sein, (1. Pet. 2: 20–22) (S. W., 2. 4, p. 243).

[123] See Redeker, Schleiermacher: Life and Thought, pp. 165–66.

[124] Reden über die Religion, 2, pp. 103, 111 (Nowak, ed., Theologische Schriften, pp. 105, 109). Predigt am Todtenfeste 1821 (1. Joh. 3:14) (S. W., 2. 4, p. 334). Schleiermacher's contortions of Christ's calls to hatred are to be understood from this point of view, which defined any limits to love as signs of human imperfection. See above, at nn. 81–86, and Predigt über das Gebot Christi: um Seinetwillen zu hassen (Luk. 14:26) (S. W., 2. 4, pp. 590, 592, 595).

age. It does not discredit his assumption of a universal humanity, the proposition (in the tradition within which he worked) that there were objective techniques of apprehending that common humanity, or the method of analysis and synthesis that Schleiermacher formed out of traditional elements for empathetic participation in the humanity of others.

Those who deny Schleiermacher's antihistorical, synthetic propositions were anticipated by the ancient Skeptics in their debate with Plato. Given the predicaments of communication, they assert the impossibility of apprehending one's own mentality, much less that of another, especially at the distance of centuries. For those who press this case to its logical extreme, only the decomposition of texts as artifacts is possible; the author, his creative processes, and the expectations of the intended audience are inaccessible and may not enter into critical judgment. To them, Schleiermacher's insistence that the interpreter reexperience the thinking of author and original audience seem a flight of subjectivity, or "an unjustifiable psychologizing of the interpretive task."[125] For them, it is folly to think of the interpreter as mediator between separate human lives, and of understanding as an act of mediation between subjective and objective aspects in a work of art.

It is more difficult to deny these mediating functions if the entire range of understanding, including the affects, is kept in view, if, for example, the virtue of compassion is sought in human relations, not least through historical inquiry. The exclusion of affective bonding is not possible in any case if critical inquiry is considered, as it was by Schleiermacher, an act of love. Criticism fragments; love unites. But is there a call to love in critical analysis? The assertion that criticism should be completed by love was for Schleiermacher an escape from the vicious circle of anthropology to the hermeneutic circle of authentic knowledge. It has proved to be a great stumblingblock in Schleiermacher's legacy.

[125] Cf. Gerrish, *Prince of the Church*, p. 23. Werner Schultz, "Schleiermachers Theorie des Gefühls und ihre theologische Bedeutung," *Zeitschrift für Theologie und Kirche*, 53 (1956), p. 92.

CONCLUSION

THE DOCTRINES OF Augustine, Gerhoch, and Schleiermacher concerning interpretation elucidate two points: first, the complex frame of reference that was thought to verify the sentence, "I am you," and, second, the continuity of that frame of reference in a Western hermeneutic tradition. The verifying structure can be briefly summarized. Beginning with a distinction between flesh and spirit, it was deduced, ultimately, from Plato, and, in various guises, it posited an ironic tension between archetype and image, on the participation of the image in the archetype, and on the actual presence of the archetype in the image of likeness. Further, the verifying structure consisted of two tiers: the first, of logical, or empirical, analysis; the second, of affective assimilation. The profound mystical elements characteristic of the "Platonic" hermeneutic tradition occurred on the second tier. Understanding was understood as a mediating act between separate modes of existence, as well as between separate lives; the understander mediated being itself, insofar as knowledge was identical with being.

To speak of continuity in the tradition is to evoke a mixed picture of differences and similarities. Schleiermacher's departures from the theological propositions of Augustine and Gerhoch were massive. He defined God as a human way of seeing. His Christology is a branch of anthropology. His world had neither primordial forms (within or outside God's mind) from which all existing things derived, nor any fixed goal toward which all life moved. He replaced the doctrine of the end of the world with one of indefinite transition. His historical doctrines produced effects like those that I have already noted in Feuerbach's psychology and in twentieth-century literature. Of these, one was the reduction of the conflict between good and evil from a moral antithesis to an empirical relativism. Another was the exclusion of divine inspiration from the interpreter's (or artist's) act of creative mediation, and its replacement by organic processes, and freedom, of composition. A third was the "historical flattening" of interpretive, or narrative, levels. The range of four levels of Scriptural interpretation, employed by Augustine and Gerhoch, reduced itself to two in Schleiermacher's hands. He excluded allegory; and his appraisal of historical distance between the books of the Old Testament and those of the New persuaded him that they were by no means mutually reflective in any analogical, or anagogical, sense. A fourth difference was his insistence on recovering the original intent and understanding of the author. Augustine considered them irrelevant, or beyond the reach of the Scriptural interpreter. But Augustine and Schleiermacher agreed that the interpreter could recover from the text depths of meaning of which the author was unaware. These departures enabled Schleiermacher to equate understanding (as a linguistic endeavor) with interpretation, as Augustine and Gerhoch could not do. Other differences—including some bearing on the composition of the soul and, thus, on the psychology of perception—could be mentioned. But these suffice to indicate the magnitude of change in the tradition produced, in part, by a shift toward empirical and historical norms.

Massive differences in hermeneutic method need to be weighed against abiding similarities. Perhaps the most fundamental of them was the assumption of the universal uniformity in human nature on which the intersection of identity and individuality depended. The concept of understanding as mediation required this assumption of a common ground of being and a common humanity. A cluster of similarities specifically concerned the task of understanding understanding: the insistence that the text (or work of art) be understood as a whole, in the light of the internal correlation of parts and whole; that the text (or work of art) was a fragment of what the work manifested, the rest being made up of negative values in the work; and that, in addition to the distinction between word and meaning, there was a further one between meaning and the preverbal word, or thought. The three authors also shared the assumptions that, in the hermeneutic circle, the interpreter interrogated the text through an act of self-emptying, or dependence, opening himself to be filled with the positive and negative contents of the text; and that the closure of the hermeneutic circle occurred through a participatory bonding of the interpreter with the author, or spirit, in the text, a bonding that was esthetic and affective. A distinguishing mark of all three writers was the conviction that that bonding was erotic, analogous to the coupling of male and female, and that the mediation that made it possible occurred in the dynamic of play.

This complex of ideas enabled Augustine, Gerhoch, and Schleiermacher to conceive of understanding as a tool that enabled language to function in a sacramental way, as well as in significatory and symbolic ones. Bonding occurred through understanding the sacramental capacity of language, and many of the similarities in the teachings of the three writers concerned the nature and limits of the unitive play through which that capacity was realized. I have noted that the mediating play, and its effects, were regarded as mimetic, in response to a call to the interpreter from within the text (or work of art). When bonding by empathetic participation was specifically at issue, our three authors consistently thought of the capacity of the interpreter, as spectator, rather than of the nature of the text, or spectacle; for, as the metaphors of filling indicated, the shape of what the interpreter imbibed was given by the contours of his own mind, the receiving vessel, rather than by the material received or by its origin.[1]

---

[1] Cf. Niebuhr, "Schleiermacher on Language and Feeling,'" p. 156: "Technically, [the indi-

The predominance of the esthetic paradigm of assimilation through dominance and subordination over the biological one is notable in the three writers. In this regard, it duplicates the predominance of the esthetic paradigm that we found in works of Joyce, Pirandello, and Mann, and provides an index to the continuity with which currents within the Western intellectual tradition have magnified spiritual values, especially when attained with great suffering, over material ones. Yet, here again we have seen that the theologians, preoccupied with the salvation of the entire world, elucidated their thought with the universal, biological paradigm as well as with the more restrictive esthetic one, whereas the twentieth-century men of letters, portraying artists whose salvation entailed withdrawal from the masses, employed the biological paradigm only to set it aside.

Because bonding was esthetic, the three authors also concurred in thinking that the assimilative event of understanding was esthetic, just as they imagined that participation was dialectical. It followed that an essential component of bonding was conflict, both as the dialectical way to union and as the outer contours of finitude to be struggled against in love. Conflict defined bonding as its authentication, the most dramatic evidence in the world of events that "every determination is a negation" (*omnis determinatio est negatio*).

Finally, as the three authors explored sacramental bonding through language, they affirmed that the actual event of understanding was the fleeting experience of unity at the moment of perception. What followed was not the manifestation but what could be said about the manifestation, divided from the event as a historical account is from experience, or as the memory of love is from love.

The common tradition linking these understandings of the event and the experience of understanding, as they were set down by Augustine, Gerhoch, and Schleiermacher, is emphasized by the fact that they were all interpreters of Scripture, the last two consciously in the Augustinian line.[2] Thus, they deliberately reflected, albeit in quite different ways, the norms of doctrine and exegesis framed in the early Church. Their hermeneutic methods, however, raised a further issue. All three authors habitually illuminated their methods, as well as their doctrines, by cross-references to arts in different media. Schleiermacher's doctrines led to the conclusion that art was inconceivable without religion and, indeed, that it was, in a sense, identical with religion.[3]

---

vidual author] must be considered as just one of innumerable vessels through which the language expresses and maintains itself."

[2] See Niebuhr, "Karl Barth's 'Schleiermacher': A Review Essay," p. 134: "Schleiermacher also understand himself to be thoroughly in the Augustinian-Reformed tradition. . . ."

[3] See Mariana Simon, "Sentiment religieux et sentiment esthétique dans la philosophie religieuse de Schleiermacher," *Archives de Philosophie*, 32 (1969), pp. 69, 74, 77, 84. Odebrecht, *Schleiermachers System der Ästhetik*, pp, 184, 190, 198.

The issue to which I now turn is whether the three writers reflected a common cultural assumption when they applied the same hermeneutic principle of mediation to the literary and the visual arts. This subject leads, further, to the question of whether the assumption of a common esthetic bonding, unlimited by artistic genre or medium, has remained current in Western culture.

One guiding principle is evident, namely, that art was not considered autonomous. The consistent emphasis on art, including the art of understanding, as mediation posited that the work of art must be understandable, not only to its maker, but also to its intended audience. Thus, Schleiermacher contended, religious paintings through the ages repeated the same subjects but exhibited fundamental changes in portrayal and style. The continuity of subject and variety in representation, he wrote, could be explained not with reference to the piety, character, or skill of the artist, but, instead, with regard to the expectations and demands of the collective world in which the artist lived and for which he painted. The individual understanding of the artist was part of the "species consciousness" of all human beings, particularly of those in artist's time and culture. Artists of any era would have painted for no one, if they had not painted in the styles and genres given them by their environment. Thus, in painting, as in rhetoric, the emotional stimulus of art, the cycle of expectation and discovery that permitted empathetic participation, had absolutely no basis in art.[4] There could be no question of art for art's sake, or of an autonomous art or work.

For Schleiermacher, the same principle applied to all human endeavors. All possible branches of knowledge (*alle mögliche Wissenschaften*), he wrote, belonged to the same system, organically united by principles of coordination and subordination. The idea of the whole was mediated through the parts. The act of mediation was performed by the art of understanding, articulated in speech. Being common, speech absorbed the speakers into its impersonal unity, forming and conforming their thoughts according to the rules and possibilities of language. But being articulated by particular men and women, it also established the individual and singular in what was said.[5] Together with his principles of criticism and exposition, this conception of the unity of knowledge passed into Wilhelm Dilthey's theory of *Geisteswissenschaften*. Dilthey, who was Schleiermacher's biographer and in a sense his disciple, conceived of the world of knowledge, not as segmented, autonomous realms of specialist inquiry, but as an interlocking

---

[4] *Vorlesungen über die Aesthetik* (*S. W.*, 7. 8, pp. 186–89, 213–15). See Niebuhr, "Schleiermacher on Language and Feeling," p. 153. See Odebrecht, *Schleiermachers System der Ästhetik*, p. 32: "Der ästhetische Wert liegt nicht in der objektiven Darstellung, sondern in der schöpferischen Dynamik, die von der Darstellung rückwärts zum Zentum der Schöpferkraft führt, beim Produzierenden sowohl wie beim Nacherlebenden." Also, p. 152: "Nicht das Werk, das Wirken ist der Wert."

[5] *Vorlesungen über die Aesthetik* (*S. W.*, 7. 8, pp. 43, 51).

system of discourse that centered on the mediative event of understanding articulated in speech, an event that was both collective and individual. From Dilthey, this preoccupation with hermeneutics as a key to collective institutions passed into sociology and other disciplines, including the history of art. Yet many of Dilthey's successors have discarded his view that understanding did not solve, but rather deepened, the riddle of life, not least in social conflict as the necessary authentication of empathetic union.

PART IV
UNDERSTANDING UNDERSTANDING:
THE INVISIBILITY OF ART

Now I want you to see the pictures
  in the painted arcades
  all stretched out in long array.
It will be a little wearying
  for you
  to survey everything
With your neck bent back
  and your face atilt.
[But] whoever sees these [pictures]
  recognizing what is true
  in the empty figures
  feeds [his] faithful mind
With an image that for him
  is not empty.

Paulinus of Nola,
Carmen 27, 511–15.
CSEL 30, p. 285.

NINE

The Hermeneutic Gap in Painting

A living leaf poised on the berry bough
heavy with a handful of harvest moons,
this silent warbler sees only the mite,
that form of motion alive in the golden light
transfusing this cluster and all it attracts
to become the fruit of perfection.

You who have paused to participate in the pattern
consider that in the moment of your attention
you too were clustered here
and ask who delighted in watching you.

Richard Kay, "On Watching a Bird and Fruit
Painted in Colors on Silk by Wu Ping,"
Saltatim (Lawrence, Kansas: Ergo, 1967), p. 1

WE HAVE NOW considered the understanding in the enterprise of understanding words. From words, or participation in another through the sense of hearing, we turn to pictures, participation through sight—the sense that, with hearing, lies at the base of all thought about esthetic understanding. Here, as in earlier discussions, we shall find that, even when the esthetic paradigm of assimilation predominated, it was complemented, through a common link of eroticism, with the biological paradigm. The analogy of composing with engendering was never entirely out of mind. As before, we shall find that the union of "I" and "you" was thought to come about through play—indeed, through play that was recognized both as a means to understand and as the fleeting event and experience of understanding itself.

In one of his most poignant episodes, Virgil portrayed Aeneas's arrival, as a weary exile, in Carthage. While he waited for his fateful audience with Dido, the queen, he saw on the walls of the temple of Juno murals depicting the war that had destroyed his city and cast him and his companions into their calamitous voyage. He recognized the representations of his fellow Trojans, of their Greek enemies, and of himself in events long past. Wracked with sobs and bathed in tears, "he fed his soul on the empty painting" (*Aeneid* I: 446–93). The fullness of Aeneas's heart and the emptiness of the murals stand in contrast; they are brought together by Aeneas's performance, or reliving, of earlier experience that he projected into the murals. Much the same performance was captured by the Christian poet, Paulinus of Nola (353–431), when he portrayed a viewer of religious paintings, feeding his faithful mind on an image empty perhaps to unbelievers but by no means empty for him when he recognized the truth in the hollow figures (see the epigraph to Part Four). Interpretation of art occurs in the emptiness of painting, just as it does in the silence of words. The gap in which this performance took place is the subject of the following chapters; but it is wise to remember that all interpretation, in whatever void, to some degree falsifies its object.

But wait. Our discussions of Augustine, Gerhoch, and Schleiermacher have yielded references to words as empty vessels; the term "empty words" is common. The emptiness of words was grasped as silence; the silence of art as emptiness. Are these not analogues but synonyms for the same thing?

The visual arts, like the literary ones, were powerful means of bonding. A tradition that persisted, though it was often denied, held that poetry and painting were cognate arts. Poetry, it maintained, was painting that spoke and painting, silent poetry.[1] Plato observed at the very outset of Western philosophy that words were as silent as paintings.[2] References also crossed. To become one through understanding with the subjects of words or of paintings, a person had to shut the eyes and "wake to another way of seeing, which everyone has but few use."[3] As we shall see, the Iconoclastic Dispute was one chapter in a debate that continues even now between some theorists who equate words and pictures and others who assign them to different orders of perception.

In fact, each medium had its own kind of emptiness, its own kind of silence. What they had in common was that they made the absent present through voids; but it was a conventional and false analogy, a confusion of categories, that equated those voids. To pass, even in written texts, from words to the voice in the words and then to the power of the voice (1 Cor. 14:11) was an exploration entirely different from that in the hollowness of painting, because the hermeneutic gaps in the two enterprises belonged to different orders. My contention is this: Grasping the content of the verbal

---

[1] Cf. Giovanni Battista Armenini, *On the True Precepts of the Art of Painting*, I. 3, trans. Edward J. Olszewski (New York: Burt Franklin, 1977), p. 93. The linguistic character of art has been repeatedly asserted in many areas of art history. See, for example, Richard Brilliant, *Visual Narratives: Storytelling in Etruscan and Roman Art* (Ithaca, N.Y.: Cornell University Press, 1984); Mario Praz, *Mnemosyne: The Parallel between Literature and The Visual Arts* (Princeton: Princeton University Press, 1974); Norman Bryson, *Word and Image: French Painting of the Ancien Régime* (Cambridge: Cambridge University Press, 1983). On "visual language," see, for example, Nathan Knobler, *The Visual Dialogue: An Introduction to The Appreciation of Art* (New York: Holt, Rinehart and Winston, 1966?).

[2] Above, introduction to Part Three.

[3] Plotinus, *Enneads*, 1. 6 (Loeb ed., vol. 1, pp. 256–58). For a graphic description of the soul being saturated by the object of vision, and thus participating it, see *Enneads*, 58. 10–11. (Loeb ed., vol. 5, pp. 270–74).

statement brought a hermeneutic of understanding into play. Grasping the content of the visual representation brought into play a hermeneutic of calculated misunderstanding. The issue was a hermeneutic double game.

Because the concept of painting's "deficiencies" is crucial in my discussion, preliminary definition may be helpful. Painting was thought to have "deficiencies" in the comparison of art with nature (or life). It was also thought to have "deficiencies" by comparison with other arts (such as sculpture and poetry), which approximated nature more closely than the medium of painting allowed. Whereas nature could speak and poetry discourse, painting was silent, and whereas nature and poetry could harbor and express mixed emotions and the simultaneity of events, painting was limited to the representation of single-mindedness and isolated gestures at moments that were extracted from an action and frozen in a "snapshot" effect. Where nature (and sculpture) were three-dimensional, painting was flat and, in that sense, as well as in its silence, empty. Where nature provided light, painting required light to be seen, although through its colors it simulated the effects of light. Where nature moved, painting was inert (or immobile). These characteristics of media formed inescapable parts of any method of understanding applied to painting. As we shall see, the deficiencies of the media—the empty spaces in which interpretation played its falsifying games—were capable of being used in different ways, as they were, for example, by iconoclasts, who moved from the lifelessness of paintings to the charge of idolatry, and by iconodules, who moved from the hermeneutic gap of painting's "deficiencies" to a hermeneutic circle that led in and through paintings to the realities that they both concealed (in their "deficiencies") and revealed (in their positive values).

Thus far, discussion of verbal arts has repeatedly turned to three levels of understanding, which can, generally, be described as consideration (a sensory perception), meditation (abstract rational discourse), and contemplation (affective union). Bonding occurred when understanding reached the contemplative state. Writers, such as Augustine, Gerhoch, and Schleiermacher, who portrayed bonding through words found that the hermeneutic gap was caused by a logical fallacy—the violation of the law of contradiction. For an interpreter can make sense of "I am you" only if "I" can be both "I" and "not-I" simultaneously.

In philosophy and theology, this logical fallacy became a proposition of truth. But the ancient and continuing warfare between philosophy and poetry hinged on the fact that the arts of imagination required calculated deception. Thus, in painting as in poetry, two deliberate fallacies of perception were added to this logical one. *Pathetic fallacy* denotes the attribution of life, will, or temperament to lifeless things or forces (as in the "savagery" of a raging torrent).[4] *Affective fallacy* refers to the transference of the read-

---

[4] John Ruskin, who invented the term, argued that "pathetic fallacy" was distinctive of

er's (or viewer's) emotions to the object of contemplation. In either case, the object of contemplation becomes a mirror of the contemplator's mind. The pathetic fallacy was at work in Paul Klee's (1879–1940) concept of "living pictures," and Wassily Kandinsky's (1866–1944) regard for "every work of art" as "the mother of our emotions."[5] With paintings of great visual realism before his mind's eye, Hegel also observed the affective fallacy at work: "This awakening of all feelings in us, the dragging of the heart through the whole content of life, the realization of all these inner movements by means of an external object whose effect rests only on deception— all this is what . . . is seen to be the peculiar, preeminent power of art."[6]

Philosophers and theologians denied that the imaginative arts (especially poetry and painting) could be used as means toward authentic knowledge, precisely because their effects depended on the conscious deployment of these fallacies—that is, of misunderstanding. For this reason, they denounced poets and painters alike as liars.

Thus, while the central role of fallacy may have excluded from painting the philosophical distinction between demonstrative knowledge and authentic understanding, it did not draw a line between visual and verbal arts. Yet, such a line did exist for the very reasons that so long led to the classification of painting among the servile, or manual, arts, and philosophy, among the liberal, or intellectual, ones. The medium of painting was capable of practice, but it could not frame theories. Even its capacity to represent theories was indirect, by way of figures and analogies, rather than direct, in speculative analysis. When, in the eighteenth century, a science of esthetics eventually came into being, it arose not among artists or in the media of art but among philosophers and in words. Thus, despite its own restless, self-critical nature, painting lacked the pairing of practical and theoretical endeavors that could dictate abstract, guiding principles to itself, to individuals for the conduct of their lives, or to society. It remained without discourse, a servant, as the hand serves the mind or an artist, a patron.

This distinction between verbal arts, which depended on understanding, and visual arts, which depended on the calculated use of fallacies (or misunderstanding), has consequences for any discussion of hermeneutics, including one of the hermeneutics of empathy. For the verbal and visual

---

modern Europe but not of the ancient or medieval culture. The student, Ruskin wrote in a way that appears to discount all allegory before modern times, "will find the modern painter endeavoring to express something which he, as a living creature, imagines in the lifeless object, while the classical and medieval painters were content with expressing the unimaginary and actual qualities of the object itself." *Modern Painters*, vol., 3, p. 4, chap. 13 ("Of Classical Landscape").

[5] Paul Klee, *On Modern Art*, trans. Paul Findlay (London: Faber and Faber, 1974), p. 33. Wassily Kandinsky, *Concerning the Spiritual in Art*, trans. M.T.H. Sadler (New York: Dover, 1977), p. 1.

[6] *Vorlesungen über die Aesthetik*, Bd 1 (X, 62) 5th ed. of *Jubilaeumsausgabe* (Stuttgart: Fromann, 1971), p. 78.

arts vary, in the cognitive strategies by which they can fit clues together into their respective hermeneutic circles.[7] A hermeneutic gap in narrative or in discourse has duration; there is a space between its opening and its disposition, a space in which clues accumulate with the telling. A hermeneutic gap in visual perception has no duration; clues must be simultaneous. This difference exists because language advances, whereas visual arts arrest. Language works by spells; it moves discursively to persuade, inform, direct, or enchant. The visual arts work by marvels; they arrest to amaze, imply, inspire, or entrance. Further, behind these considerable differences stands a yet more fundamental one; whereas speech is dynamic, the visual arts divide the dynamic function of doing (by the viewer) from the static one of being (by the work of art). Finally, the distinction between necessity and contingency comes into play. Language is universal in the community and necessary to its identity and self-knowledge, "the universally communicated unity of the many selves."[8] It enables each person to assert his individuality and yet to fuse his thinking and feeling with the thinking and feeling of others. The twofold effect allows the person, as individual, to perceive himself objectively as others perceive him. By contrast, art is contingent, occasionally accidental; and works of art express an isolated, or alien, self-consciousness. For this reason, art, as a speculative (or theoretical) enterprise, is dependent upon the cognitive strategies of language to record, explain, and interpret what words cannot express.[9] A double her-

[7] The "language of art," as a term used by Gombrich, Collingwood, and others to indicate the interpretive, signifying power of art is different, at least in degree, from Joshua Reynolds's definition of "the language of art" as "the power of drawing, modelling, and using colors." E. H. Gombrich, *Art and Illusion: A Study in the Psychology of Pictorial Representation* (Princeton: Princeton University Press, 1969), p. 291. R. G. Collingwood, *The Principles of Art* (New York: Oxford University Press, 1958), section 12: "Art as Language," pp. 273–85; p. 298: ". . . art and language are the same thing. . . ." Joshua Reynolds, *Discourse 2*, in *Discourses in Art*, ed. Stephen O. Mitchell (Indianapolis: Bobbs-Merrill, 1965), p. 14. See also *Discourse 4*, pp. 46–47, "the powers exerted in the mechanical part of the art have been called the language of painters." Reynolds also recognized the discrepancy between the content of art that was "so difficult to express in words," and the "mysterious and incomprehensible language" of commentators on art. *Discourses 7, 8*, in *Discourses on Art*, pp. 94, 134. Correspondingly, Reynolds argued that "no art can be engrafted with success on another art," although they had the same origin and were governed by corresponding "rules and principles," because they worked in different media, and addressed different senses. *Discourses 7, 13*, in *Discourses on Art*, pp. 109, 203.

[8] G.W.F Hegel, *The Phenomenology of Mind*, trans. J. B. Baillie (New York: Harper and Row, 1967), p. 717.

[9] An example of the difference between visual and verbal images is the disparity between Oscar Wilde's novel, *The Picture of Dorian Gray*, and Ivan Albright's painting of the same name (in the Art Institute of Chicago), an imaginative recreation of the portrait described by Wilde. See Chapter 12, after n. 22. Compare Armenini's comment on words as a preservative of art. *On the True Precepts of the Art of Painting*, I. 2, p. 94: "By means of the written word, which spreads throughout the world, not only are the arts rendered easier and less wearisome, but they are also preserved more firmly and alive in the memory of posterity, which cannot happen if entrusted only to the works and tongues of the practitioners." Armenini had in mind ancient works of art that were known only through texts. Cf. Wright Morris on the subordi-

meneutic, one part applying to verbal images and another to visual, the first leading to decipherment and interpretation and the second to unconstrued emotion, is at issue.

Thus, I cannot follow the argument that all understanding, including that of visual images, is linguistic and, by extension, a branch of literary criticism. (See also Chapter 10, after n. 49.)

Although visual arts may aspire to the condition of language, which allows narrative and discourse, and although the verbal and visual arts are mutually reflective enterprises, they make up distinct hermeneutic codes. In 1982, the German artist Joseph Beuys (1921–86) conducted a seminar in Kassel, West Germany. At the end, he rode over the blackboards on a bicycle, blurring and connecting with tiretracks and flecks spun off from the wheels the chalk notations that he had made day by day. Three years later, the blackboards and the bicycle were assembled and exhibited in New York. The reviewer who lamented the absence of an English translation of Beuys's German notations, and yet perceived the visual beauty of the lines left by bicycle wheels, sensed the discrepancy between verbal and visual codes in the same work.[10] The translation that he called for from German into English was analogous to the transformation of verbal and visual images into one another.

The contrast between the development of calligraphy as a pictorial art in Oriental and Islamic traditions and the lack of a corresponding development in the West indicates an aversion or a technical impediment to such a merger of visual and verbal codes in Western culture. Scholars have analyzed Western paintings as "pictographs" and "hieroglyphs" and have fruitfully employed "the language of art" as an analytical tool. They speak of "reading" pictures. These ways of thinking undeniably assist in semiotic, psychological, and sociological inquiries. The fact remains that Western art lacks the linguistic characteristics of pictographic or hieroglyphic texts, including the elements that make them generally intelligible—for example, common standards of grammar and syntax, the interplay between spoken

---

nation of photographs to verbal commentaries in "Photographs, Images and Words," James Alinder, ed., *Untitled 25. Discovery and Recognition* (Carmel, Calif.: The Friends of Photography, 1981), p. 31: "Images of interest are scrutinized like poems. Predictably, the verbal scrutiny will prove to be what gives the photograph its image. The 'readings' will be subtle, as filled with insight, as bizarre as the talents of the writer. . . .it is better that the photograph have no commentary at all than that it appear to be necessary to the picture. The ambiguity that is natural to the photograph lends itself to conflicting interpretations, but if the viewer's first impression is not his own, he may never come to have one that is. In the photograph this is a real loss for an imaginary gain." For references to divisions between conceptual and perceptual artists in New York and Los Angeles ("the literate, conceptual rationale" and "the perceptual, tactile level"), see Lawrence Weschler, *Seeing is Forgetting the Name of the Thing One Sees: A Life of Contemporary Artist Robert Irwin* (Berkeley: University of California, 1982), pp. 47, 61, 78.

[10] *New York Times*, 17 January 1986.

and written language, a large and flexible vocabulary, discourse, and linguistic permanence. A true pictographic text can be pronounced, and the etymology of its words is part of its content. But neither is true of features in Western art that, by analogy, are called "pictographic."[11]

"If you can explain a painting," Renoir is said to have remarked, "it isn't a work of art."[12] In the following chapters, I shall first establish that the distinction between bonding through verbal understanding and bonding through visual misunderstanding reinforced and distorted by verbal associations was part of the heritage of late antiquity. Later, I shall attempt to elucidate the career of the distinctive hermeneutic gap in the visual arts, centering on the pathetic and affective fallacies, and its corresponding hermeneutic circle, in the post-Renaissance era. The discussion of the late Roman and Byzantine stages of that career will be drawn from texts about art. The discussion of later stages will rest on the evidence of art itself.

Although my primary subject will be contemplative bonding, toward which the visual and verbal arts may converge, the materials to be reviewed will also re-introduce into the discussion the levels of consideration (looking at pictures) and meditation (thinking or discoursing about pictures).

THE CENTRAL PARADOX of our subject was that, like words, visual art made the absent present through its inarticulateness, its voids. By way of introduction, I wish to illustrate the importance of distinguishing visual from verbal codes, and the continuing power of the pathetic and affective fallacies in unlocking the visual code, by reference to one instance—the Christmas crèche. Both in distant and in recent times, the crèche elucidates the point that what reveals a living reality within the object is something other than the object itself. It is a dynamic read with love or hatred into the object, a dynamic that literary tradition may have planted in the viewer's mind. Discernment of the invisible content in the emptiness of the object occurs not when the object is made, or even when it is seen, so much as when it is felt. Thus, just as Christian exegetes sensed no need to recover the intent of any author of a Scriptural text, so too artists were regarded as irrelevant to understanding or feeling the contents of their works. For, although they represented the highest mysteries of religion, artists might

---

[11] See the statement by Jean Dubuffet in *Jean Dubuffet: Forty Years of His Art* (Chicago: University of Chicago Press, 1984), p. 11: "Les paroles n'ont souvent pour effet que de brouiller les communications. Le langage des peintures va mieux sans paroles." Cf. Reynolds, *Discourse 13*, in *Discourses on Art*, p. 205: "It is, I know, a delicate and hazardous thing . . . to carry the principles of one art to another." See also V. A. Kolve, *Chaucer and the Imagery of Narrative: The First Five Canterbury Tales* (Stanford: Stanford University Press, 1984), p. 1: ' As Ralph Cohen has reminded us, words are finally nothing like pigments; extension in time is not the same as extension in space; verbal and visual organization are not interchangeable. The 'sister arts' of poetry and painting are not, and cannot ever be, the same."

[12] Alfred H. Barr, Jr., *What is Modern Painting?* rev. ed. (New York: Museum of Modern Art, 1956), p. 46.

themselves be ignorant mechanics, mired in impurities of life as inert and deadly as the materials with which they worked. Accordingly, Plato insisted that artists were ignorant of the deep, invisible realities that they represented. Thus, what people embrace or loathe in a crèche is not the crèche that their eyes see, or yet the artist in the work, but an interplay of frictions that stirs their hearts. The love or hatred by which "symbolic speech' is taken to heart is blind.[13] The bonding effect is in the spectator, not in the spectacle, in pathetic and affective fallacies, rather than in visual perceptions, or verbal connotations.

I begin at the Supreme Court of the United States. My point of departure is the Court's judgment in the case of *Lynch* v. *Donnelly*, otherwise known as "the nativity scene case," which was decided on 5 March 1984. The object of the suit had been to prevent the city of Pawtucket, Rhode Island, from including a crèche as part of a Christmas display on public property. By a majority of five to four, the Court rejected the suit. Speaking for the majority, Chief Justice Burger determined that the crèche did not violate the constitutional prohibition against an established religion any more than did the painting in the Supreme Court chamber itself of Moses receiving the Ten Commandments, or the exhibit of more than 200 paintings on Christian subjects in the National Gallery. A "crèche, like a painting, is passive," he said. As a national holiday, established by long usage and by law, Christmas was distinct from religious observances. So the crèche, too, was secularized in the context of the Christmas season, and in its physical setting of a display that also included a large assortment of other nonreligious objects, not least a talking wishing well. The crèche served "legitimate secular purposes," Justice O'Connor concurred, "as a typical museum setting, though not neutralizing the religious content of a religious painting, negates any message or endorsement of that content."

The four dissenters found that, by including the crèche, the display did indeed indicate solidarity of government with "the Christian message of the crèche, and dismissal of other faiths as unworthy of similar attention and support." Speaking for the dissenters, Justice Brennan stated that, while the mayor of Pawtucket had offered to include a menorah in future displays, it was his stated purpose "to keep Christ in Christmas." The exhibit of a "life-sized display depicting the biblical description of the birth of Christ" in a conspicuous place behind a white picket fence did not serve a secular purpose. The crèche, Justice Brennan continued, originated in a devotional exercise of St. Francis of Assisi, and it could only be "understood as a mys-

---

[13] The crèche at Scarsdale, New York, was reportedly described as "symbolic speech" by Marvin E. Frankel, an attorney for Scarsdale, arguing before the Supreme Court. *New York Times*, 21 February 1985. Because the eight voting members of the Court tied, they were unable to resolve the Scarsdale case, automatically affirming the ruling by a lower court that allowed the exhibition of the crèche. *New York Times*, 28 March 1985.

tical recreation of an event that lies at the heart of Christian faith." "The religious works on display at the National Gallery . . . ," he said, "present no risk of establishing religion. Their message is dominantly secular. In contrast, the message of the crèche begins and ends with reverence for a particular image of the divine." Contradicting the majority's argument from custom, Justice Brennan indicated that, until the middle of the nineteenth century, Puritans and other Christian sects in the United States had long opposed the celebration of Christmas itself—not to speak of religious images—as sacrilege.

Justice Blackmun and Stevens concurred with Justice Brennan. They added that the majority decision of the Court was offensive to Christians, because it denied "the sacred message that is at the core of the crèche, and relegated a "sacred symbol" to the role of a commercial ornament.[14]

The striking thing about these opinions is how little attention the Justices paid to the crèche as an object. The issue was not what artists intended, nor yet what people saw when they looked at the object with their eyes, but what people saw inside the object when they looked at it with their hearts and minds.

In fact, the same thing was true of the crèche erected by St. Francis of Assisi and referred to by Justice Brennan. The surviving accounts indicate that Francis only set up in the open air a manger filled with hay, to which he led two live animals, an ox and a donkey. No images or human actors made up a scene. At the manger, some of Francis's brethren sang; in joy, a host of people clustered round, lighting the night with their torches as though it were day; Mass was celebrated, and Francis, serving as deacon, chanted the Gospel. The miracle of the crèche was seen only by two men. During the Mass, John of Greccio, a friend and follower of Francis, Francis's agent in producing the drama, saw something where there was nothing—a child was lying in the manger. John saw Francis go to it and, taking it in his arms, waken it, even as he wished to waken Christ in the hearts of a negligent people.[15]

There are two points to be made. The first is that Francis's crèche was composed largely of blanks to be filled in by imagination as the enactment of a liturgical drama, the Eucharist, proceeded. The chanted words of the Gospel explained the mute tableau. Francis may have known precedents derived from the grotto of the nativity of Bethlehem, where at Christmas the Crib was reverently adored as early as the fourth century, and from the Church of Santa Maria Maggiore, in Rome, where during the Christmas Mass a consecrated Host was placed on the altar that contained wooden frag-

---

[14] *Supreme Court Reporter*, 104, no. 11 (1 April 1984. *Lynch* v. *Donnelly*), pp. 1355–87.

[15] Thomas of Celano, *First Life of St. Francis*, I. 30. 84–87. Bonaventura, *Life of St. Francis*, 10. 7. See the imitative miracle recounted in the *Little Flowers*, chap. 42.

ments revered as parts of the manger. But these precedents, too, employed no visual portrayals of the nativity.

This corresponds with Francis's own opposition to images as *objets de luxe*. According to legend, Francis received his call to holiness from a painted crucifix that moved its lips and, "calling him by name, said 'Francis, go, repair my house, which, as you see, is falling utterly into ruin.' "[16] But Francis's own devotion to absolute poverty excluded the arts. He allowed only rough, poor, unadorned churches to be built; and, during the early decades of the Franciscan Order, his brethren excluded almost all pictorial decoration. The decoration (about 1300) of the Upper Church in Assisi with an elaborate program of frescoes showing scenes of Francis's life marked a permanent schism between rigorists in the Order, who wished to maintain the rule of poverty as laid down by Francis, and laxists, who wished to mitigate that rule, inter alia by introducing costly ornaments, such as painting, carved work, books, and decorated vestments.[17]

The second point is that the miracle at Greccio was a surprise. It occurred when John saw an infant in the emptiness of the crib. Evidently, the major visionary in this event was Francis himself, and his seeing, which was not physical seeing, was one astonishment among many in which, by the ardent love and compassion with which he contemplated Christ, he was thought to have been "wholly changed into Jesus," bearing the marks of the crucifixion.[18] Contrary to rules of logic and natural order, Francis became what he beheld in the crib and in the speaking crucifix; but what he saw in those works of art was more than, and in fact negated, the work of art itself.

In his own way, Keats captured this experience of surprise that both fulfills and negates art when he contemplated the "pipes and timbrels" and "wild ecstasy" on a Grecian urn.

> Heard melodies are sweet, but those unheard
>   Are sweeter; therefore, ye soft pipes, play on;
> Not to the sensual ear, but, more
>   endeared,
>   Pipe to the spirit ditties of no tone.

From the discussion thus far, it would appear that the effect of a painting does not necessarily depend on its content, which is also to say, its style. The placement of Francis's manger in the open air, also suggests that the physical context, adverted to by the Supreme Court in *Lynch* v. *Donnelly*, may also be neutral. In the eighth century, a Frankish writer was amazed that Byzantines put icons, which they revered as holy, in places of gross

[16] Thomas of Celano, *Second Life of St. Francis*, 6. 10.

[17] Alastair Smart, *The Assisi Problem and the Art of Giotto* (Oxford: Clarendon, 1971), pp. 1–7, and, on the fresco showing the crèche at Greccio, pp. 185–87.

[18] *Little Flowers*, on the stigmata, chap. 3.

impurity, such as streets and public squares.[19] John Ruskin (1819–1900) was a major apostle of esthetics and art history in Victorian England, and yet, even in the awe-inspiring context of St. Peter's in Rome, art did not soften a robust Anglican aversion to what Ruskin called "a mixture of paganism and papacy" acquired in childhood. His taste ran to Gothic. "The characters [in St. Peter's] I was not prepared for," he wrote, "were the clumsy dullness of the façade, and the entirely vile taste and vapid design of the interior. We walked round it, saw the mosaic copies of pictures we did not care for, the pompous tombs of people whose names we did not know, got out into the fresh air again with an infinite sense of relief, and never again went near the place, except to hear music, or see processions and paraphernalia."[20]

Like Martin Luther in 1510, Ruskin found little pleasing in Rome. Despite context, Ruskin was not able to establish a link between the magnificent art of papal Rome and his own life. He was unable to perform the kind of speculative play by which art and life surprisingly fused at Greccio, when Francis took Jesus to his heart and moved toward the moment when, seeing without sight, the two became one.

> Love looks not with the eyes, but with the mind.
> And therefore is wing'd Cupid painted blind.[21]

Even in the few remarks made thus far, we have uncovered witnesses to the terrible power gained by art through pathetic and affective fallacies, as a means of understanding—that is, understanding that by inward performance goes beyond interpretation to participation. Whether in *Lynch* v. *Donnelly*, or in the crèche at Greccio, or in Ruskin's aversion to the supreme achievements of the Roman Renaissance, the testimonies are clear that art has the power to reform and purify, or to harm and corrupt. Even those who approve art recognize that it destroys in order to create, and that this destruction comes about by the negative side of composition: omission. Through the performance of a game that pathetic and affective fallacies engender—changing the object of contemplation into a mirror of the contemplator's mind—what is omitted can signify more than what is included. As our instances have suggested, the power of a word or a picture to change life for good or ill often is released by something that is not in the picture at all, and that may never have been imagined by the artist. Such is the case with all great symbols. By speculative play, the viewer eliminates barriers between himself and the thing symbolized—reduces the odds, one might say—and finally becomes one with it, eliminating even the act of elimination. With that union, as texts considered in earlier chapters have indicated,

---

[19] *Libri Carolini*, 4. 26 (*MGH, Conc. 2, Suppl.*, p. 225).

[20] John Ruskin, *Praeterita: The Autobiography of John Ruskin* (Oxford: Oxford University Press, 1978), vol. 2, chap. 2. sect. 33, 34, pp. 246, 248.

[21] Shakespeare, *A Midsummer Night's Dream*, I. i. 234.

the viewer is transformed into another person. This promise of transformation through art was the unspoken issue in *Lynch* v. *Donnelly* as it has been in iconoclastic movements that have punctuated Western history.

There is an amazement at the convergence of art and life where, by the pathetic or by the affective fallacy, objects become symbols, all the more terrible because it is seen by not being seen and present by its absence. This wonder disclosed to love's blind yearning can, perhaps, stir more primal emotion if it appears in a violated, than in a perfect, work, and in one from a distant world. Such wonder flashed out at Rainer Maria Rilke when he turned aside to see it in an archaic torso of Apollo, another fragment of vanished lives. As Rilke's eye passed over the wounded stone, he felt that the gaze of the statue's lost head penetrated the whole. The light of its absent, but ruthless, eye, Rilke wrote, irradiated the torso, like a lamp, with fecund, predatory strength. Uncannily, there was in the headless fragment no place that did not see the viewer; and from the voiceless stone Rilke thought he heard an unspoken, lordly call: "You must change your life."[22] But these silent words only seemed to come from the emptiness of the torso.

[22] Rainer Maria Rilke, "Archäischer Torso Apollos," in *Der neuere Gedichte, anderer Teil* (Leipzig: Immsel, 1908), p. 1. See also Velasquez's use of the multiple ambiguity between contemplating a work of art and contemplating the reality that it represented in his painting, *Christ after the Flagellation, Contemplated by the Christian Soul* (soon after 1631) (now in the National Gallery of Art, Washington, D. C.), ambiguity playing here between the relationship portrayed in the picture and the relationship between the viewer and the picture.

TEN

Participatory Bonding through Painting: The Iconoclastic Dispute (ca. 726–843)

JOHN RUSKIN, who invented the term, believed that the pathetic fallacy was a characteristic of modern artistic expression, but not of ancient or medieval painters.[1] However, the task of the present chapter is to indicate the importance of the performance engendered by the pathetic and affective fallacies in a great controversy of late ancient, or early medieval, culture— namely, the Iconoclastic Dispute. That conflict arose in the eighth century, in Byzantium, and, inciting great political and military strife, eventually drew into the debate scholars and princes even in distant regions of the West. I hope, in the process, to locate the distinction between verbal and visual hermeneutics at a crucial moment in the career of the classical tradi- tion and, further, to elucidate some modes of visual bonding that were asserted and challenged during the long struggle.

The power of visual arts to make absent things present depended on a particular way of understanding, which, for reasons already stated (Chapter 9), I consider calculated, stylized misunderstanding. One characteristic of that way of understanding was the assumption that signs could actually mediate to an interpreter the thing signified, and not merely communicate knowledge about it. The distinction between communion and communica- tion is crucial. By communion, the knower became one with the thing known; understanding as interpretation shaded into understanding as par- ticipation, or compassion. In the classical tradition, a second basic assump- tion concerning the ways in which painting made absent things present was that the mediation of the sign was possible because painting deceived the eye and, thereby, beguiled the mind into its empathetic performance. In as much as the effect of art depended upon deception, Christian writers could by no means easily conclude that the same hermeneutic process applied to the understanding of verbal signs and the calculated misunderstanding of visual signs.

In the early Church, the question arose slowly and late whether the pic- torial arts too could be used in love's game of hide-and-seek to unfold the

[1] *Modern Painters*, vol. 3, pt. 4, chap. 13, "Of Classical Landscape."

secrets and the application of Scripture.[2] The question arose for Christians, as it had done for Jews, because it was thought that God had written with his own hand on tablets of stone a commandment against making and venerating images, just as he also forbade adultery, murder, theft, and other social offenses. Because of this prohibition, the devotional use of images by Christians began late in Church history, probably in the third century, certainly before the late fourth. There are many visual souvenirs of the ironies generated by the debate between iconodules and iconoclasts as it progressed through the ages. Two of the most direct are a pair of fragments from an altarpiece by Josse Lieferinxe (painted in 1497). The one depicts St. Sebastian affronting the pagans by destroying their idols; the other, St. Irene ministering to the wounded Sebastian beneath an image of the Blessed Virgin.[3] The irony is not only in the replacement of pagan by Christian images, depicted in these paintings, but also in the existence of the altarpiece itself as a devotional object.

Amply developed arguments for and against the devotional use of images were set forth during the ferocious and protracted Iconoclastic Dispute in the Byzantine Empire during the eighth and ninth centuries. Inventive as they were, the adversaries in that dispute inherited and reworked much earlier positions.

While I do not wish to discount the conflict as a political (and military) war, my concern is with the ideas that it called forth. One key element of the dispute was the degree to which tradition—in this case, the tradition of using images devotionally—could legitimately supplement Scripture, such as the prohibition in the Second Commandment against graven images. Was the traditional use of images a tool by which people grasped the life hidden in the words of Scripture?

There was evidence that viewers absorbed physiologically what they saw. Had not a pregnant woman who saw a Negro deliver a black child? Scripture itself recorded that Jacob had produced striped, speckled, and spotted cattle by exposing his flocks to colored rods when they conceived.[4]

EVEN WHILE THEY celebrated the grisly deaths of martyrs for resisting idolatry, venerators of images invented legends to demonstrate that those closest to Christ in his earthly work had commemorated holy lives in art. The tradition of the Gospel was one with that of painting. The Virgin herself, they said, had embroidered a tapestry of Christ and the Apostles, and

---

[2] Above, Chapter 4 at n. 13.

[3] Philadelphia Museum of Art, nos. 765, 767. See also Antonio Vivarini's (fl. 1440–1476/84) painting of St. Apollonia destroying an idol, (Kress Collection, National Gallery of Art, Washington, D.C.).

[4] On the pregnant woman, Theodore the Studite, *ep.* 2. 36. On Jacob's flocks (Gen. 30:37–41).

the evangelist and physician, Luke, had painted icons of the Virgin and Christ. Indeed, they argued, holy images had been made not by hands but by direct action of divine powers. Latter-day painters were described as working under heavenly inspiration.[5] Ironically, revered icons depicted deaths inflicted on martyrs for refusing reverence to idols.

But this argument was understated. For iconodules also believed that pictures were more than illustrations; they were illuminations. They not only portrayed what the words were about; they also penetrated the veil of the words to the hidden meaning. They were "the eyes of what is said."[6]

The function of pictures was to instruct the mind by arousing the emotions. Early Christians had censured pagans for having frescoes painted on the walls of their houses to inflame carnal passions; for having painted tablets of lascivious subjects in their bedchambers—for example, a scene of Aphrodite locked in the arms of her lover—so that, grappling in their own voluptuous embraces, they could look up and reinflame their ardor; for thronging public places with vividly erotic pictures so that their eyes had already vicarously shared in the debaucheries portrayed before their bodies joined.[7]

Christian defenders of religious pictures chose kindlier illustrations; but they agreed that the function of pictures was to begin a friction in the mind exciting affects of desire and love.[8] Gentler loves might be aroused by images of the Virgin. Love might also be expressed in grief, as it was by Gregory of Nyssa, who could never look at a picture of Abraham's intended sacrifice of Isaac without weeping.[9] "Shall we not weep," asked one patriarch of Constantinople, "when we see an image of our crucified Lord?"[10] Love might be expressed in exultation stirred up by scenes of the struggles and agonies of saints, prophets, and martyrs, a joy fulfilled in emulation— that is, in fear and anger against the enemies of the faith, including those

[5] See Edward James Martin, A History of the Iconoclastic Controversy, (London: SPCK, 1930), p. 103. On Pope Paschal I's assertion that, because no one could call Jesus "Lord" without being moved by the Holy Spirit, no one could paint Jesus as Lord without being moved by the same power. G. Mercati, Note di Letteratura biblica e cristiana antica (Rome: Vatican, 1901. Studi e testi 5), p. 229. Martin, Iconoclastic Controversy, pp. 191–92.

[6] Theodore the Studite, "Second Refutation of the Iconoclasts," chap. 19 (Catharine P. Roth, trans., St. Theodore the Studite on the Holy Icons [Crestwood, N.Y.: St. Vladimir's, 1981], p. 55).

[7] Gregory of Nyssa, Life of Moses, 2. 71 (Jean Daniélou, ed., Grégoire de Nysse: Vie de Moïse [Paris: Cerf, 1955. Sources chrétiennes, vol. 1bis], p. 51). Clement of Alexandria, Exhortation to the Greeks, chap. 4 (Loeb ed., pp. 136–38).

[8] John Damascene, Adv. Const. Cabalinum, chap. 2 (Migne PG 95: 313, 325).

[9] Ernst Kitzinger, "The Cult of Images in the Age before Iconoclasm," Dumbarton Oaks Papers, 8 (1954), p. 137 refers to Oratio de deitate filii et spiritus sancti (Migne PG 46: 572). Gerhart B. Ladner, "The Concept of the Image in the Greek Fathers and the Byzantine Iconoclastic Controversy," Dumbarton Oaks Papers, 7 (1953), p. 4.

[10] Tarasius at Nicaea II, Actio 4 (Mansi 13: 12).

false brethren who rejected the sacred icons.[11] Finally, love might be expressed in fear and trembling aroused by a picture of Christ coming in majesty at the Last Judgment, attended by angels, with rivers of fire pouring forth from his throne and devouring sinners.[12]

Another argument followed over the proposition that religious paintings were, in fact, a kind of Scripture: that there was no essential discrepancy between verbal and visual communications of God's Word. Writers and painters produced the same narrative of Scripture. Indeed, art thrust history in the face of viewers; they could see Abraham's knife against Isaac's flesh.[13]

One of the earliest and most persistent arguments for the devotional use of images was that they instructed the unlearned, that they were "silent writing," or "the books of the illiterate."[14] In fact, painting for popular consumption was also a method of persuasion, deployed by the ruling orders. Even in the fifth century, Paulinus of Nola commented that he had used religious paintings (with explanatory verbal captions) to divert illiterate pagans from drunken revels at the shrine of St. Felix.[15] Likewise, early in the Iconoclastic Dispute, Pope Gregory II rebuked the Emperor Leo III for having deprived his people of a wholesome diversion through pictures, and thereby consigned them to such frivolities as gossip and the playing of harp, cymbals, and flutes.[16]

Like other arguments, still to be mentioned, this one derived from pagan defenses of idolatry against Christian attacks: namely, pagans said, prudent rulers had invented idols to exert control over the vast, ignorant, and unruly majority. The rulers knew that the images had neither sensation nor divinity, but they hoped that their awe-inspiring presence would by terror restrain the mob from crime and impiety. It was easy for Christians to refute this argument, when it came from the mouths of pagans, by asking why, if idols did prevent crime, laws continued to be necessary, or why, if idols failed to prevent crime, the deception of idolatry was permitted to continue.[17] However, when later generations of Christian writers defended sacred images as instructional aids, they used a similarly condescending argument. The testimonies of Church Fathers and great prelates and the architectural remains of the imperial court demonstrate that, through all

[11] Nicaea II. *Actio* 1 (Mansi 12: 1013). *Actio* 4 (Mansi 13: 19, 31, 127, 131 and freq.). John Damascene, *Adv. Const. Cabalinum*, chap. 7 (Migne *PG* 95: 323).

[12] John Damascene, *Adv. Const. Cabalinum*, chap. 8 (Migne *PG* 95: 324).

[13] Nicaea II, *Actio* 4 (Mansi 13: 9–11).

[14] Kitzinger, "The Cult of Images," p. 136.

[15] *Carm.* 27, 11. 580–95 (*CSEL* 30, p. 288).

[16] Mansi 12: 977.

[17] Arnobius, *Adversus Paganos*, 6. 24–26 (*CSEL* 4, pp. 235–37). On the effects of awe-inspiring imperial statues, see Kitzinger, "The Cult of Images," p. 91, referring to Gregory Nazianzenus.

that was sumptuous and exquisite, the learned and the powerful too refreshed their most intimate spirituality from the wellspring of art.

The crucial fact was that defenders of sacred images were not content to regard them as illustrations, as visual aids to reading. Rather, they insisted that pictures were not merely about the people depicted, as words in a text are about a subject, but that, in some senses, they were equivalent to, or identical with, the subjects. The image, they taught, was greater than the word;[18] it offered certitude beyond the power of words. For the icon tablets and the materials painted on them were in some way "alive."[19] Priests mingled Eucharistic elements with pigments scraped from icons, thus administering the living sacrifice to the faithful.[20] In a less complete identification, the imperial cult taught that the honors, or affronts, rendered to an image were deemed to be rendered directly to the subject.[21]

Defenders of sacred images soon found themselves repeating arguments that, generations earlier, defenders of idolatry had used against Christians: By likeness, the presence of the subject was manifested in the image, and the prototype was in the copy—Christ was venerated in, but not with, his image. The images were surrogates for their subjects—God was worshipped through his image. An effluence, or power, of the subject inhabited the image by virtue of consecration. Without reference to consecration, this last argument took a distinctive form when it was argued that God imprinted an image of himself in saints, and that an image of that image was imprinted in icons of the saints.[22] This doctrine derived in part from the Neoplatonic concept of God as the beauty from which derived the beauty in all beautiful things, and it suggested "by implication, at least, [that] the work of the artist [was] an extension of the divine act of creation."[23]

[18] Nicaea II, *Actio* 4 (Mansi 13: 19, 102).

[19] Nicaea II, *Actio* 4 (Mansi 13: 15).

[20] On the mingling of pigments with Eucharistic elements, see the letter of Michael II to Louis the Pious (824) (*MGH, Conc.* 2, pt. 2, p. 479).

[21] Martin, *Iconoclastic Controversy*, pp. 64, 209.

[22] Arnobius, *Adversus Nationes*, 6. 8 (*CSEL* 4, p. 220). For the descent of these ideas from Dionysius the Areopagite, see the general discussion in Martin, *Iconoclastic Controversy*, p. 139. On the argument that the prototype was in the copy, see Theodore the Studite, *First Refutation*, chap. 2, 5, 9, 11, 12, 20. On the argument that images were surrogates for their subjects, see Theodore the Studite, *Second Refutation*, chap. 16, 17, 24, 25, 26, 28. The power of consecration to confer a sacral character on icons is the most elusive of the three in Christian writings. An account of how John the Faster, bishop of Constantinople (d. 595) declined a request that he bless an icon may indicate that the blessing of icons was a recognized practice in his day. Much later, Pope Hadrian I recorded that it was usual in the Roman Church for icons to be anointed with chrism. The counterargument of the *Libri Carolini* that icons could neither sanctify nor be sanctified addresses the contention of the Council of Nicaea (787) that icons were like the consecrated elements of the Eucharist. For Pope Hadrian's statement and the counterargument, see *MGH, Conc.* 2, *Suppl.*, p. 34, chap. 39, and *Libri Carolini*, 4. 16 (*MGH, Conc.* 2, *Suppl.*, pp. 87–88). On the intricate history of the creation, alterations, and eventual oblivion of the *Libri Carolini*, see Ann Freeman, "Carolingian Orthodoxy and the Fate of the *Libri Carolini*," *Viator*, 16 (1985), pp. 65–108.

[23] Kitzinger, "The Cult of Images," p. 141.

It became hard to distinguish between arguments defending the veneration of images and those defending the veneration of the saints' actual physical remains, their relics. Identical kinds of miracles were attributed to icons
and relics.

Scriptural commentators never lost sight of the fact that, in words, they
did not read God, but rather read about him.[24] The interrogative, stochastic
elements of play derived from that uncertainty. By contrast, defenders of
religious images gradually came to teach that their emotions were stirred
not only by the memories and associations aroused by pictures but by the
very presence of the subjects in the pictures. This equivalence or identity
evaded interrogation. Dealers with words remained conscious of ever
moving toward God through an elimination of carnal and spiritual barriers.
But, in the emotional bonding with what they found in pictures, venerators
of icons could feel that they had eliminated not only those barriers but even
the act of elimination itself. Not stochastically, but fully, they imagined
themselves into the picture, participating in the Passion of Christ, in the
struggles and agonies of the saints, and in their holiness.

THOSE OPPOSED TO the veneration of images held firmly to the argument
that the Word of God had banished pictorial imagination from the Church.
Religious images, they contended, were a pagan, or demonic, invention.
God forbade it in the Old Testament; Christ destroyed idolatry; and the
martyrs struggled to the death against it. But, with his malice and guile,
Satan had reintroduced the images into the Church.

In effect, the opponents of the veneration of religious images repeated St.
Jerome's (ca. 340–420) blanket condemnation of heretics. Whatever silver
and gold of word and understanding they had by nature, Jerome had
written, heretics turned into idols that they made out of their own heart.[25]
Their objections depended, however, not merely on the willful distortion of
Scripture by heretics to conform with their own understanding, but equally

---

[24] Cf. Clifford Geertz, *Local Knowledge: Further Essays in Interpretive Anthropology* (New
York: Basic Books, 1983), p. 110: "But the point is that he who chants Quranic verses—
Gabriel, Muhammad, the Quran-reciters, or the ordinary Muslim, thirteen centuries further
along the chain—chants not words about God, but of Him, and indeed, as those words are His
essence, chants God himself."

[25] *Comm. in Oseam Proph.*, 1. 4. 12 (*Corp. Christ., ser. lat.* 74, p. 43): "Cumque ita cor
loco suo motum fuerit, ligna et lapides deos putat et adorat opera manuum su-
arum.   Principium enim fornicationis, idolorum inventio. Numquam haeretici suo errore
satiantur, non cessant a fornicationis turpitudine, et cotidie non custodiendo legem et scripturas sanctas, Dominum derelinquunt, insaniunt et inebriantur; et perdito mentis iudicio,
adorant idola quae de suo corde finxerunt, fornicationisque spiritu possidentur." Also *Comm.
in Oseam Proph.* (*Corp. Christ., ser. lat.* 74, p. 106): "Haereticorum terra fecunda est, qui a
Deo acumen sensus et ingenii percipientes, ut bona naturae Dei cultum verterent, fecerunt ex
his idola." See, further, 1. 2. 3; 1. 2. 9; 2. 10. 2 (*Corp. Christ., ser. lat.* 74, pp. 19, 22. 107).

on the failure of the iconodules to recognize the deficiencies of painting and, correspondingly, the lack of equivalence between paintings and texts.

When they argued that the image was greater than the word, iconodules embraced one position in an ancient debate over which bodily sense was superior, sight or hearing. Their position defended the superiority of sight, on the ground that sight resulted in immediate perception, without the intervention of mental processes, including reference to memory. The impact of vision on the emotions was therefore direct.[26] Their opponents upheld the superiority of hearing, reinforced by the testimony of the Apostle Paul that "faith cometh by hearing" (Rom. 10:17). Their position was precisely that hearing engaged the critical and synthetic processes of understanding. Though words might deceive, the unspoken truth within the soul could winnow true from false in spoken words. By contrast, defenders of hearing argued, vision, in its externality and materialism, permitted the mind to be entranced by mere appearance, and seduced by concupiscence of the eyes.

The argument that hearing gave access to the life-giving spirit within words led those opposed to the veneration of images to the first "deficiency" of painting—namely, that it was empty, or lifeless. In its rhythmic pattern of line and color, a painting could give the illusion of life. But, by contrast with the reality that it portrayed, that illusion was static, not transitory. Unlike sculpture, painting could not be viewed in the round. Indeed, a thing of the surface, without depth, the illusory likeness itself was subject to deterioration by retouching or cutting, discoloration, darkening by grime and soot, and, of course, deliberate destruction.[27]

Thus, for opponents of veneration, images were not texts, any more than seeing and hearing were identical. Hearing and seeing were one only for God in his perfect simplicity,[28] and images were void of the Spirit that enlivened the letter of Scripture.[29] They objected that paintings deceitfully used material objects to represent spiritual realities. Iconodules answered that there was no difference between a parchment hide that Scripture was written on, and a wooden tablet that carried a picture. Both were material

---

[26] This proposition was the essence of the frequently repeated argument that paintings were the books of the illiterate. For a much later statement, see Giovanni Battista Armenini, *On the True Precepts of the Art of Painting*, I. 3, trans. Edward J. Olszewski (New York: Burt Franklin, 1977), p. 102: ". . . poetry requires study, time and knowledge to be understood, whereas painting stands always revealed to persons of every quality and type. Writings do not help him who lacks memory or judgment; but painting is always apprehensible and is understood by all but the completely blind." On the inadequacy of this argument to elucidate the work of the senses in post-Renaissance painting, see Chapter 11.

[27] On the recognition, even by iconodules, that icons were material objects subject to deliberate destruction, see Martin, *Iconoclastic Controversy*, pp. 112, 141.

[28] Augustine, *Tr. in Ev. Johan.*, 99. 3–4 (*Corp. Christ., ser. lat.* 36, pp. 583–85).

[29] *Libri Carolini*, 1. 19 (*MGH, Conc. 2, Suppl.*, pp. 29–30).

surfaces, they said, marked with colors made of matter.[30] Far different from the life-giving text, images were inert, dead matter given form by a dead art discovered by heathen.[31] To be sure, they might appear to reproduce the games of conflict, imitation, and skill by which believers approached God through his Word. But the iconodules employed the analogues of mimetic play inappropriately, not, as the Fathers had done, to emphasize the life that they drew from the Spirit or the text of Scripture. An opponent of the veneration of images wrote more perceptively than he knew when he argued that it was foolish to use images in the Church on the model of iconodulism in imperial ceremonies. Why not take models also, he asked, from theatrical shows or mimes, or from the cruelties that occurred in gladiatorial games?[32]

Pictures portrayed instants in conflict. But, unlike the actions themselves, they were mute as well as inert and discontinuous. Silence was a second disability of painting. Far from being "speaking images," narratives in which viewers "read" the struggles, passions, and triumphs of the saints, pictures were as little self-explanatory as mimes. At mimes, as Augustine had written, a public crier "had to explain . . . what the dancer wished to convey during the performance . . . for if anyone unacquainted with such trifles goes to the theater and no one else explains to him what these motions signify, he watches the performance in vain."[33] Similarly, in the eighth century, a viewer needed captions to decide whether the icon was to be venerated because the subject was a saint, or destroyed because the subject was a pagan divinity.[34]

In the emptiness of their two-dimensionality and silence, paintings lacked the power of discourse to command, criticize, and, above all, question. Thus, in their "snapshot effect," they could not portray the long testing of virtue against vice in the spiritual formation of the saints. After choosing to depict a sensational instant, artists filled their panels with impious acts, the atrocities of wars, cruelties of wicked men, and monstrious outrages of wild beasts.[35] Although they might represent individual scenes, they did not have the power to replicate the counterpoint of prefiguration and fulfillment in the continuing warfare that composed sacred history.[36] Finally, in their visual precision, images lacked the numinous vagueness of words. Consequently, artists represented subjects differently. There were iconographic confusions in the portrayals of Peter and Paul. A troubling anachronistic

---

[30] John Damascene, *Adv. Constant. Cabalinum*, chap. 3, 7 (Migne *PL* 95: 316, 323). See also the letter of Pope Gregory III, Nicaea II, Actio 4 (Mansi 13: 95).

[31] Council of Hieria (754), *Horus* (Mansi 13: 273, 275, 277). On painting as an "evil art," col. 324.

[32] *Libri Carolini*, III. 15 (*MGH, Conc. 2. Suppl.*, pp. 133–34).

[33] Augustine, *De Doctrina Christiana*, 2. 25. 38 (*Corp. Christ., ser. lat.* 32, p. 60).

[34] *Libri Carolini*, 4. 16. 21 (*MGH, Conc. 2, Suppl.*, pp. 205, 213).

[35] *Libri Carolini*, III. 22 (*MGH, Conc. 2, Suppl.*, p. 149).

[36] *Libri Carolini*, 1. 16, 17, 30 (*MGH, Conc. 2, Suppl.*, pp. 39, 42, 60).

combination of historical events in paintings demonstrated that the spiritual identities of saints could not be portrayed in the material fixity of art as they could be in the discursive freedom given by words in allegorical exegesis.[37] An artist was forced to choose one iconographic option to the exclusion of all others. He could not represent Moses both as a youth and as a man of forty. When texts of Scripture conflicted, he could represent only one of them; he could not, for example, represent Moses' encounter with the Lord in the fire both on Mt. Sinai and on Mt. Horeb, both in the whole mountain ablaze with fire and in the burning bush (Deut. 4:11, Exod. 3:104), although all narrative versions were grist for the verbal allegorists' mill.

Likewise, pictures played the game of imitation. But, in this regard, too, they manifested a "disability" of painting—its powerlessness to represent invisible subjects. Again, the iconoclasts draw on a long tradition. Clement of Alexandria reproached pagans and idolaters with having "turned heaven into a stage. The Divine has become a drama, and what is sacred you have acted in comedies under the masks of demons, travestying true religion by your superstition."[38] Also writing against the pagans, Lactantius (ca. 260–ca. 340) added: "For whatever is simulation must necessarily be false; nor can anything receive the name of a true object which gives truth the lie by deception and imitation. But if all imitation is emphatically not a serious matter, but, as it were, a game and jest, then there is no religion in images, but a mime of religion."[39]

Beginning in the fourth century, opponents of the veneration of images turned these same arguments against the Christian venerators of images. The imitative play of images, they said, intruded the practices of pagans into the Church,[40] changing the glory of the incorruptible God into corruptible images. Mosaic and fresco decorations were executed with full regard to dramatic effects of position and lighting. Some priests placed the Eucharistic bread in the hands of images of Christ, allowing communicants the sense of taking his Body from Christ directly.[41] In the eighth century, iconoclasts drew on this legacy to argue that art used deceptive likenesses of pictures to entice human spirits from the service of God to the adoration of material creation.[42]

Finally, their opponents acknowledged, the venerators of images played

---

[37] See also Augustine, *De Consensu Evang.*, 1. 10. 16 (Migne PL 34: 1049).

[38] Clement of Alexandria, *Exhortation to the Greeks*, chap.4 (Loeb ed., p. 134).

[39] Lactantius, *Divine Institutes*, 2. 19 (Migne PL 6: 344–45).

[40] Kitzinger, "The Cult of Images," p. 93, quoting Epiphanius of Cyprus.

[41] Michael II to Louis the Pious (824) (*MGH, Conc.* 2., p. 479).

[42] E.g., *Libri Carolini*, 1. 7; 2. 26–27 (*MGH, Conc.* 2, *Suppl.*, pp. 24–25, 85, 89). Cf. Augustine, *De fide et symbolo*, 7. 14 (Migne PL 40: 188). According to Augustine, it was blasphemous (*nefas*) to put up an image of God the Father, circumscribed by material form, in a Christian church.

the game of skill. In this regard, the skill was not that of the spiritual race, manifesting the power of God, but that of art's self-concealment. The credit of texts depended upon the credit of its author, and this was notably true of the authors of, and commentators upon, Scripture. But the makers of icons might be uneducated artisans, men of polluted hands, motivated by a sinful love of gain.[43] (One is reminded of the celebrated papal audience at which a member of the Curia disparaged Michelangelo by saying that artists were "ignorant of everything except their art.") In the early days of the Church, a Christian apologist had argued that the effect of pagan idols depended entirely upon the artist's skill in concealing the various processes of manufacture. But, he said, if you could go inside the smooth, majestic exterior of an idol, you would see the plates that made up that exterior, and the dovetails, clamps, and brace-irons that held them up, not to mention the lead strips that filled in the chinks.[44]

Correspondingly, opponents of venerating images in the Church knew that surprises opened through the emotional impact of pictures were all contrived. Painting was two-dimensional. Because it was an object of one surface, a painting, far more than a statue, depended for its effect on its angle, distance, and point of vision. Even as mechanisms of illusion, paintings, as they actually are, are not as they appear to be from the intended perspective. The spectator perceives the illusion of an illusion. The effects of pictures, iconodules as well as iconoclasts knew, depended upon the industry, experience, and skill with which the artist rendered himself and his art transparent. These came about through the deliberate placement of pictures in architectural settings that gave the theatrical impact of concealment and revelation, and through techniques manipulating lifeless objects to produce calculated optical illusions of vivacity, like those produced, for example, by mosaicists with tricks of proportion, plotting colors, and setting tesserae at angles to catch light in a prescribed way.[45] Thus, unlike the unfettered power of the word, which went forth to the ends of the earth, the power of a painting or mosaic was limited to one small place, and not to understanding but to calculated misunderstanding.

Iconoclasts recognized the iconodules' play as manipulation in a literal sense, not only in the manufacture, but also in the veneration, of icons. Although her husband, the emperor Theophilus (829–42) imposed strict iconoclastic policies on the Empire, the empress Theodora secretly venerated icons. Once, surprised by a court jester in the act of kissing the images, she made the excuse that she was playing with dolls. At a relatively mod-

---

[43] Council of Hieria (754), Horus (Mansi 13: 248–49).

[44] Arnobius, Adversus Nationes, 6. 16 (CSEL 4, p. 228). Cf. Clement of Alexandria, Exhortation to the Greeks, chap. 4 (Loeb ed., pp. 132–33).

[45] Cf. Libri Carolini, 1. 2, 9–10; 2. 13. 27, 31; 3. 15 (MGH, Conc. 2, Suppl., pp. 13, 26, 73, 84, 102, 133).

erate stage in the iconoclastic movement, sacred images were actually allowed as mementos and decorations, provided they were hung too high to be reached by venerators.[46]

Evidently, those opposed to the veneration of images said, the venerators deceived themselves, as pagan idolaters had done, "by voluntary blindness," worshipping the works of their own hands.[47] Because of art's terrible power to deceive, all the elements of play—conflict, imitation, and skill—blocked off the problematic but hope-filled openness of Scriptural exegesis. Interrogation was evaded. Like the spectacles of the heathen, the illusions of Christian images depended on the spectator, and on his willingness to be surprised by pictures. Opponents of images, might have repeated the words of an early apologist against the heathen: "Take away the spectator, and you will have shown [their] emptiness."[48] Far from being an extension of God's creative, life-giving act, the work of the artist began in dead matter and ended in the assured fading and decay of material things. Unlike the text of Scriptures, opponents of images argued, images prevented an escape from the vicious circle of mortal needs to regeneration, refreshment, and security through union with the very source of life.

Moses turned aside to see a great vision. God appeared to Moses in the burning bush, Augustine wrote, using a corporeal form exactly so that it would signify something and then pass away.[49]

THE BURDEN OF the arguments against the veneration of sacred images was that the parallel between visual perception and verbal interpretation—summed up in the premise, "poetry is like painting"—was false. Their weight did not fall on paintings as decorative patterns on flat surfaces, as allegories, or emblems, as devices to instruct, delight, and arouse, or even as mnemonic representations. It fell precisely on the viewing of paintings as an act of recapitulation, or performance, and, iconoclasts argued, it resulted from willfully misunderstanding the "deficiencies" that gave rise to pathetic and affective fallacies. Though they glittered in reflected light, icons were creatures of dark matter, illuminated, rather than illuminating. The "deficiencies" of painting delivered lifelessness where words delivered spirit, surface instead of depth, appearance (or even the illusion of an appearance) instead of reality, muteness instead of discourse, fixity instead of diversity, and localized instead of universal presence. Icons were dark, silent, empty, and inert (or immobile). It was a grave error to espouse the textuality of paintings; for the interpretation through verbal discourse

[46] Martin, *Iconoclastic Controversy*, pp. 173, 210.

[47] Arnobius, *Adversus Nationes*, 6. 14 (*CSEL* 4, p. 226).

[48] Pseudo-Cyprian, *De spectaculis*, chap. 8 (*CSEL* 3, pt. 3, p. 11). *Libri Carolini*, 1. 17 (*MGH, Conc.* 2, *Suppl.*, p. 41).

[49] Augustine, *De Trinitate*, 2. 6. 11 (*Corp. Christ., ser. lat*, 50, p. 96).

operated through a hermeneutic quite different from the hermeneutic of seeing. The latter did not respect the hermeneutic gaps of Scripture that intruded uncertainty upon the exegete, as, interrogating the text in a cycle of self-emptying and assimilation of the other, he received a multiplicity of answers. Instead, the hermeneutic gaps of painting were produced, not by negative values in Scripture, but by those of the medium of painting itself. The hermeneutic cycle in painting was idolatrous, exactly because it required the pathetic and affective fallacies as self-worship, rather than the self-emptying and assimilation of the other.

By contrast, the arguments of iconodules, while admitting the force of constructive misunderstanding, still asserted the textuality of paintings, and likewise affirmed that Scriptural exegesis and sacred art were variants of the same hermeneutic enterprise. The negative values—including the "deficiencies"—of painting were the openings through which a viewer entered the work of art and penetrated and performed the content that the iconodules argued was hidden there and that the iconoclasts denied. The cross-references to the visual arts noted in our discussions of Augustine, Gerhoch of Reichersberg, and Schleiermacher have already indicated the assumption of parallel hermeneutics in the verbal and in the visual arts. Indeed, Gerhoch's description of spiritual bonding with Christ by contemplating a painted crucifix (discussed in Chapter 7 at n. 19) recapitulated, in broad outline, the major propositions set forth by iconodules in the eighth century.

To say this much is to say that the foes and the advocates of veneration differed in their concepts of bonding through hermeneutic play. The enemies of veneration restricted bonding through play to verbal discourse, for, in their view, the dialectic in understanding pictures was only an apparent one, between the mind and what it read for itself into lifeless matter. For their part, advocates of veneration imagined the same dialectic at work in contemplation, whether of Scripture's hidden truth, or of the life implanted, by likeness, in a painted image, and entered into through the door of its darkness, silence, emptiness, and inertia.

Of course, the consequences were not merely doctrinal or esthetic. Characteristically, factions wished to remold the life of the world according to the art of their thoughts. The violence of metaphors taken from amphitheater, theater, and circus was retranslated from metaphor to action. Conflicting games of love became social revolutions, and not only in the civil wars of Byzantium. The same arguments that I have mentioned were repeated, virtually unchanged in the Reformation.[50] Also repeated was the firmness unto death. We are told, for example, of a woman in sixteenth-

---

[50] Charles Garside, Jr. *Zwingli and the Arts* (New Haven: Yale University Press, 1966), pp. 91 (St. Bonaventura), 111–15, 172–73.

century Holland who refused to venerate a wooden crucifix as her Lord and God. "This is a wooden god," she said. "Throw him into the fire and warm yourselves with him." As she was led out to be strangled, she again refused the crucifix. "This is not my lord and my God; my Lord God is in me and I in him." The executioner began his work. She lowered her eyes and fell asleep.[51]

The Iconoclastic Dispute, therefore, was one episode in a continuing tension between what have been described as the rigors of "word-centered Christianity" and the "iconic character of authentic Christianity."[52]

Some other general propositions about bonding through the pathetic fallacy in the visual arts can be drawn from the specific evidence of the Iconoclastic Dispute.

First, bonding through the calculated misunderstanding of visual perception is not universally acknowledged. Even those nurtured in the same cultural tradition may differ over whether such bonding is possible. The icon painter, Lazarus, and those who commanded that his hands be pressed between red-hot irons were of one culture, but different minds.[53] Thus, understanding was an event that occurred in three contexts: those of the associations attaching to the painting and its subject, of the tradition in which the viewer stood, and of the personal convictions and goals of the viewer.

Second, there were many reasons to deny bonding through the visual arts. Certainly, religious prohibition against graven images was normative for the iconoclasts, and it was reinforced by the conviction that sacred images derived from an alien, pagan tradition. However, iconoclasts also refused to enact the pathetic fallacy because they held to the logical distinction between spirit (life) and matter (death), to the fundamental "deficiencies" of painting (as contrasted with life or with speech), and to their unwillingness to concede that visual deception in painting could lead to intellectual or spiritual truth. The analogies that iconodules drew between spiritual and material things, they held, were false; and the iconodules ratified their false analogies only by applying to the icons the names of the saints or sacred events that they depicted. The use of the same name for a saint and for an icon representing him did not indicate, much less prove, identity.[54] The validity of using analogy to transform verbal into visual data (or *vice versa*) long continued to provoke controversy.

Third, Iconodules contended that the "lie" of art led to truth by a her-

[51] George Hunston Williams, *The Radical Reformation* (Philadelphia: Westminister, 1962), pp. 345–46, on the execution of Wendelmoet Claesdochter (1527).

[52] David Tracy, *The Analogical Imagination: Christian Theology and the Culture of Pluralism* (New York: Crossroad, 1981), pp. 207, 214. See also p. 205.

[53] Martin, *Iconoclastic Controversy*, p. 208.

[54] Cf. Martin, *Iconoclastic Controversy*, pp. 173, 186.

meneutic of calculated misunderstanding. Generally, iconodules paid little attention to the artist and, consequently, to two kinds of bonding mentioned earlier: the bonding of artist to work and of artist to subject. The exceptions to this rule were icons miraculously made "without hands," and other images attributed to divine or apostolic origin. Their attention concentrated, rather, on the bonding between archetype and image, and on that between knower and known.

Thus, they only exceptionally took into account methods of association that hinged on origin. Most commonly, their methods of association were likeness (the archetype is in the image by likeness), contiguity (the viewer absorbs the subject of the icon by physical contact, which included both acts of veneration and digesting flakes of paint from it), and contrast (the venerator is bonded to the subject of the icon through the image as instrument or catalyst). Theology permitted some iconodules to press association by likeness to the level of natural association. They portrayed the world as a continuous hierarchy of images descending from Christ as the immediate image of God through stages (including humankind) to the material icon or statue.[55]

Even in this chain of nature, participatory bonding occurred in likeness, by contiguity, and through contrast. Reinforced by philosophical and theological texts, the iconodules' method of association persisted for centuries.

Fourth, the participation of the knower in the known occurred through affective bonding. To be sure, the Iconoclastic Dispute concerned a specific kind of art—sacred images. But the veneration, or adoration of images as an act of worship was, as we shall see, not limited to religious cult. Although iconodules and iconoclasts alike considered (or looked at) and meditated upon icons, only iconodules employed them as stimuli of contemplation. The word *worship*, with its connotations of honor, service, devotion, and desire, generally illuminates the state of contemplative absorption. For students of esthetics, it also poses the question of how far a painting can be "emancipated from its ritualistic context" without losing sight of the very functions that it was made to perform.[56]

Fifth, evidently, not all knowers participated equally in the objects of their knowledge. Even Jacob's flocks, conceiving before the colored rods, brought forth young striped, speckled, or spotted (Gen. 30:39 [see n. 4]). Thus, the performance that led to participatory bonding (when it occurred) was isomorphic, asymorphic, and polymorphic, according to the capacity of the knower, not according to the nature of the known. Moments in the career of this proposition have already appeared in our discussions of Augustine, Gerhoch, and Schleiermacher.

[55] E.g., John Damascene, *Orat. III* (Migne *PG*: 1337, 1340–41).

[56] Cf. E. H. Gombrich, *Art and Illusion: A Study in the Psychology of Pictorial Representation* (Princeton: Princeton University Press, 1969), p. 191.

An important distinction has emerged from the discussion thus far—namely, that between paintings as the objects of interpretation and paintings as the objects of feeling. But it is remarkable that, even as this distinction emerged and developed, there was no corresponding reflection on the techniques by which paintings produced their esthetic effects. The positive values of style, however, important they were to the patrons of sacred art, were hardly mentioned in the Iconoclastic Dispute. It is as though the actual paintings (and mosaics) were incidental to the uses to which they were put and, in some sense, transparent.

This position drew much strength from the heritage of Plato, who contended that, despite their skill, poets and artists had no understanding of the subjects that they depicted, and who consistently taught the meagerness of art and its images, except as they became transparent manifestations of true beauty. To say this much is also to say that the contemplation of icons went beyond sensory impressions, and beyond esthetic judgment. Love was essential to the kind of contemplation, or worship, at issue in the Dispute. Thus, the esthetic participation of iconodules, and the repugnance that their enemies felt toward sacred images, arose, not from sensation, but from passion, not from the sensory feelings directly stimulated by the painting as an object, but from the erotic states of mind that it indirectly provoked. This paradoxical invisibility of art, and the distinction between art's address to the senses and to the affects, was not limited to distant antiquity. It pertained to the deficiencies of painting—silence, darkness, emptiness and inertia (or immobility)—and to their effects as components in works of art. In the next chapter, I consider a later period in its history.

ELEVEN

Art as Iconoclasm:
The Contemplative Tradition in
Western Art

Therefore it is believed that those patches or spots which appeared on walls that were formerly all white gave rise to the grotesques. When one gazes at these spots, diverse fantasies and strange fanciful forms seem to take shape. Not that they are really there; they are, instead, spontaneously created in our minds, which, transforming these whimsicalities, seem to take delight in these forms.

Giovanni Battista Armenini, *On the True Precepts of the Art of Painting*, III. 12, ed. and trans. Edward J. Olszewski (New York: Burt Franklin, 1977), p. 262.

SILENCE, EMPTINESS, darkness, and immobility are aspects of the holy. They also characterize the medium of painting. They were considered "deficiencies" of painting as long as art was regarded as a rival or correlate of nature, as it was throughout the Renaissance.

Eventually, from the mid-nineteenth century onward, the correlations between art and nature snapped. Once art was considered to be autonomous (that is, independent of nature), what had been considered the "deficiencies" of painting could be made its very subjects. To achieve this was to disarm the hermeneutic of calculated misunderstanding that we have described. For the misunderstanding that led to bonding presupposed the work of pathetic and affective fallacies in stylized responses; and they, in turn, depended on painting's "deficiencies." After the correspondence between nature and art was broken, the medium could present itself as it was, and not as a tool for deceiving the eye and beguiling the heart into misguided performance with sham representations. To dispense with the function of art as visual representation entailed laying aside its erotic powers, although the direct appeal to the feelings (as sensation) was retained and accentuated. The play of conflict, skill, and chance between viewer and painting could hardly continue as before when the central element, the game of imitation, was withdrawn. Thus, the place that art had in the contemplative tradition from antiquity until the nineteenth century weakened, notably in styles that departed from visual realism. Such is the overarching theme of the following chapters.

THE TEXTURE OF the subject is rich, and it entails a qualitative change from the previous discussion. The central point of dispute in the Iconoclastic Dispute was spiritual bonding. By contrast, the history of Renaissance and post-Renaissance art displays a secular range of bonding. Celebrated writings by Leon Battista Alberti (1404–72) and Giovanni Battista Armenini (ca. 1533–1609) provide soundings of this change. As they discuss how painters can "capture the minds" of viewers, they stress exactly the physical, technical, and even mechanical characteristics of paintings of which adversaries in the Iconoclastic Dispute generally took little notice. Persuaded that the effect of art depended on its power to make works like nature's, Alberti and Armenini emphasized the skill and learning of the artist, style, and the physical placement and condition of pictures. Although the supernatural effects of venerating religious images still provoked comment,[1] the primary interests of Alberti and Armenini lay with such secular kinds of bonding as those between the artist and nature (his subject), between the artist and his work, and between the viewer and the painting.

Still, performances engendered by the pathetic and affective fallacies, so vital to the erotic effect of art, continued to be the catalyst of esthetic bonding. As we shall see, the fallacies rested on ancient fictions which required the artist to deceive the eye, presenting "to plain sight what does not actually exist."[2] These fictions, as earlier, demanded reciprocating action and reaction, by artists and by viewers, in turning "the forms of things unknown"

> . . . into shapes and giv[ing] to airy nothing
> A local habitation and a name.[3]

Apart from fictions, one reality was identified by Alberti and Armenini as essential to esthetic bonding in their day: iconoclasm. All the prescriptions that Alberti and Armenini entered concerning style and display posit the failure not only of medieval artists but also of the majority of their own contemporaries to deceive the eye and captivate the heart. Of course, they cast their most burning scorn on medieval compositions for the "barbarism" of their harsh, trivial, and segmentary character. Action followed theory in the destruction of medieval compositions by enthusiasts of the new style, including Giorgio Vasari (1511–71), who took time away from

[1] Giovanni Battista Armenini, *On the True Precepts of the Art of Painting*, III. 2, trans. Edward J. Olszewski (New York: Burt Franklin, 1977), p. 218.

[2] Daniel V. Thompson, Jr., *Cennino d'Andrea Cennini: The Craftsman's Handbook*, chap. 1 (New York: Dover Press, 1960), p. 1.

[3] Shakespeare, *A Midsummer Night's Dream*, V. i. 7.

composing panegyrics on Renaissance artists in order to dismantle medieval altarpieces. A late, but by no means the least, victim of humanist iconoclasm was Duccio di Buoninsegna's *Maestà*, installed with great splendor on the high altar in the cathedral of Siena in 1311, deposed to a lower place in 1506, and sawn apart in 1711.

Just as styles that arose in the Renaissance defined themselves by contrast with earlier styles, and continued to suppress them until the middle of the nineteenth century, nonrepresentational styles later defined their own objectives and characters by iconoclastic rejection of their predecessors, even when the general momentum of their work appeared, in the late twentieth century, to demand the elimination of fine art itself.

My points are that, throughout the history of Western art, esthetic bonding was sought, that style was considered either a device of or an impediment to bonding, and that the active enterprise of bonding included both production and suppression. While iconodule and iconoclast confronted each other as enemies in eighth and ninth century Byzantium, they were united in the same person during and after the Renaissance. The performance of erotic games of art concentrated less in the viewing than in the making of an object.

The paradox of art as iconoclasm leads beyond the sphere of action to the sphere of contemplation encompassing it. Our subject, affective participation, is contemplative. To be sure, the hermeneutic of verbal or of visual images can be applied to discursive mental activity: to consideration, or description, and to meditation, or analysis. But contemplation is a nondiscursive state in which the mind recollects its faculties, not to exercise, but to forget them. Discrimination and love are essential. By discrimination, the mind chooses the object of contemplation, forsaking all others; by love, it cleaves to that object. The sleep of contemplation is a purposeless, calm, dreamlike absorption in the beloved.

HOW ARE WE to distinguish the two approaches—through verbal and visual images—to the same iconoclastic, contemplative end? Problems encountered in earlier discussions (especially Chapter 9) continued, like all eternal questions, to be urgent and inexhaustible. I have attempted to indicate a hermeneutic flaw in arguments that consider art a subordinate, illustrative branch of literary culture and, consequently, embrace the proposition that "language is the universal medium in which understanding itself is realized.[4] To do so is to discount the presence in visual art of a system of

---

[4] Hans-Georg Gadamer, *Truth and Method* (New York: Crossroad, 1985), p. 350. Compare the kind of imaginative meditation that could hold spectators "for hours at a stretch, if contemporary [i.e., eighteenth-century] testimony is believed, in front of the painting." See Michael Fried, *Absorption and Theatricality: Painting and Beholder in the Age of Diderot* (Berkeley: University of California Press, 1980), pp. 122–23, 131.

erotic methods, concepts, and exigencies of deliberate, stylized misunder-standing that connect and complement each other without corresponding to the seemless web of understanding verbal language, and thus (mistakenly, I argue) to identify the erotic game of art with "the sacred seriousness of language [and] its beautiful well-measured game."[5]

In the present chapter, I propose to consider the tradition of esthetic bonding from a viewpoint that does not envelop visual art as a branch of literary criticism. Instead of employing paintings to illustrate philosophical or religious propositions, I shall continue the discussion of nonverbal ele-ments in art, including its iconoclastic ones, that enabled viewers to enter into affective union in and through paintings.

From the beginning, however, it must be evident that paintings did not ensnare the unprepared or, perhaps, the unwilling. The games of visual and verbal hermeneutics could exclude, or reflect, one another; the Iconoclastic Dispute illustrated the perennial fact that even they were not independent of the cultural context in which they happened to be played. In 1838, Thomas Babington Macaulay (1800–59) traveled to Italy, having just returned with the profits of four years' service in India in his pockets. His sweeping knowledge of classical and modern literature, together with his own literary abilities, had already made him a celebrated figure, but breadth neither of cultural sympathy nor of esthetic sensibility enlightened his comments on the artistic treasures gathered before him. He "wandered through" the Capitoline Picture Gallery in Rome without taking special note of any painting. He was "distracted by the multitude and magnificence of the objects" in the Vatican Museum, but what struck him was the splendor, immensity, and profligate variegation of the swarming exhibits that "made the whole seem a fairy region." Macaulay, perhaps, "looked at pictures as a man of letters, rather than as a connoisseur." But he did look at, without meditating upon or contemplating, them. Intense cultural prej-udices, which expressed themselves in other ways, may have contributed to his esthetic blindness. They certainly lay behind his preemptory dismissal of "all the mystic daubs of the Germans," and his comment that Raphael's *Vision of Ezechiel*, in the Pitti Palace, "was so fine that it almost reconciled me to seeing God the Father on canvas."[6]

Cultural traits that repelled Macaulay from esthetics and from German history enabled his elder contemporary, Hegel to distinguish several modes of "sympathy and communion" with art. Ancient statues, he wrote, were "corpses in stone," abandoned by the spirit that once animated them, just as ancient hymns were words emptied of belief. In antiquity, they had par-

---

[5] Friedrich Schleiermacher, "On Translation," trans. André Lefevere, in A. Leslie Willson, ed., *German Romantic Criticism* (New York: Continuum, 1982), p. 22.

[6] G. Otto Trevelyan, *The Life and Letters of Lord Macaulay*, vol. 2 (New York: Harper, 1875), pp. 26, 32, 354–55.

ticipated in a living world, objects and means of cult by which worshippers penetrated their internal reality. Hegel and his contemporaries viewed them externally in the context of elements of the dead world in which they once existed. Historical study did not enable scholars to participate in a life that was over, but only to represent it and to assimilate, as conscious memory, the external manifestations of the spirit that had informed the ancient worlds. They could know and enjoy, but not worship, the images.[7]

Yet, Hegel continued, historical scholarship remained ignorant of "the true and real nature of a work of art" so long as it rested content with technical and external aspects. Scholarship at a more theoretical level also had its cost; for "the beauty of art does in fact appear in a form which is expressly contrasted with abstract thought and which the latter is forced to destroy in exerting the activity which is its nature. . . . Reality as such, the life of nature and of mind, is disfigured and killed by comprehension." Hegel was convinced that art was a thing of the past for his age. His own time, he said, was given over to ideas, enjoyment, and criticism, rather than to the genuine truth and life of art as event. The owl of Minerva—the reflective powers of philosophy—took wing as dusk was falling on the creative life of an epoch.[8]

Even so, an exalted mode of esthetic sympathy and communion was possible to the philosopher who realized that all works of art manifested a universal spirit, and that all cultural epochs were self-portraits of that spirit as it confronted, recognized, and thus negated itself in order to advance to a new historical embodiment. "This way of becoming," Hegel wrote, "presents a slow procession and succession of spiritual forms, a gallery of pictures, each of which is endowed with the entire wealth of Spirit. . . ."[9]

The contrasting examples of Macaulay and Hegel suggest the elaborate correspondences between the two games of art and language, and between them and the wider cultural matrix that had to exist before the eroticism of the pathetic and affective fallacies could take hold. Hegel's comments also

---

[7] *The Phenomenology of Mind*, trans. J. B. Baillie (New York: Harper and Row, 1967), pp. 753–54. See also *Vorlesungen über die Aesthetik*, Bd 1, (X, 15–16, 45–47, 350–52) 5th ed. of *Jubilaeumsausgabe*. (Stuttgart: Fromann, 1971), pp. 31–32, 61–63, 366–68.

[8] *Vorlesungen über die Aesthetik*, Bd 1. (X, 17–18), pp. 33–34. Hegel's reference to Minerva's owl occurs in the preface to his *Grundlinien der Philosophie des Rechts*, characteristically with a metaphor drawn ſ om painting. Eva Moldenhauer and Karl Markus Michel, ed., *Werke in zwanzig Bänden*, Bd 7 (Frankfurt a. M.: Suhrkamp, 1970), p. 28: "Wenn die Philosophie ihr Grau in Grau malt, dann ist eine Gestalt des Lebens alt geworden, und mit Grau in Grau lässt sich nicht verjüngern, sonder nur erkennen; die Eule der Minerva beginnt erst mit der einbrechenden Dämmerung ihren Flug."

[9] *Phenomenology of Mind*, p. 807. Cf. José Ortega y Gasset, "The Dehumanization of Art," in *The Dehumanization of Art and Other Writings on Art and Culture* (Garden City, New York: Doubleday, 1956), p. 45, writing of art as a farce, "much as in a system of mirrors which indefinitely reflect one another no shape is ultimate, all are eventually ridiculed and revealed as pure images." The absence of erotic content for Ortega is evident. See also Schleiermacher, above, Chapter 8, n. 117, and Chapter 1, n. 76.

indicate the variety of fallacies that could be invested in the same object, for example, by worshippers, art historians, and philosophers. Macaulay's comments resonate with religious and cultural iconoclasm. Far more radically, Hegel's portrayal of history as a sequence in which what is becomes the negation of itself—the repeated "Golgotha of the Absolute Spirit"— portrayed iconoclasm as necessary in the inexorable renewal of life. The subject calls, if not "for an erotics of hermeneutics," then for a hermeneutic of eroticism.[10]

THE RENAISSANCE LEGACY:
INTERPLAY OF SENSATIONS AND PASSIONS

I turn to four paintings that represent the event of contemplation (Plates I– IV). All of them were made during the seventeenth century, following in the wake of "tenebrism" as represented by Caravaggio (1569–1609): Jusepe de Ribera, *The Sense of Touch*, ca. 1612–15 (Norton Simon Foundation, Pasadena)[11]; Rembrandt, *Aristotle with a Bust of Homer*, 1653 (Metropolitan Museum, New York); Luca Giordano, *Carneades with a Bust of Paniscus*, ca. 1658–60 (Coll. Stanley Moss)[12]; and Adriaen van der Werff, *Children Playing before a Sculptural Group with Hercules*, 1687 (Alte Pinakothek, Munich).[13]

Although three of the works, those by Rembrandt, Giordano, and van der Werff, were painted within a period of forty years (1653–87), the four pictures, taken together bracket a span of about eighty years. During that time, Ribera established himself as a dominant figure in the Neapolitan school and found an ambitious and able successor in his pupil, Giordano. Rembrandt's austere style fell out of fashion, as he himself declined into poverty and ignominy, to be succeeded by the svelt and ornamental style of van der Werff, who, from early manhood on, was acclaimed as the greatest of Dutch masters, and whose career was resplendent with wealth and glory. Van der Werff's painting is by far the smallest of the four, and this disparity in size accentuates the massive esthetic shift indicated by the contrast between the simplicity of the three much larger works and van der Werff's small,

[10] Cf. Naomi Schor, "Fiction as Interpetation: Interpretation as Fiction," in Susan R. Suleiman and Inge Crosman, eds., *The Reader in the Text: Essays on Audience and Interpretation* (Princeton: Princeton University Press, 1980), p. 182.

[11] Published in Craig Felton and William B. Jordan, *Jusepe de Ribera, lo Spangnoletto, 1591–1652* (Fort Worth: Kimbell Art Museum, 1982), cat. no. 1 (color plate, and black-and-white print, with a reference to a cognate painting in the Prado).

[12] Published in Clovis Whitfield and Jan Martineau, eds., *Painting in Naples (1606–1705) from Caravaggio to Giordano* (Washington, D.C.: National Gallery, 1982), pp. 169–70. I am obliged to Professor Jay Gates for this reference.

[13] Pictured in *Alte Pinakothek München: Erläuterungen zu den ausgestellten Gemälden* (Munich: Bayerische Staatsgemäldesammlungen, 1983), pp. 562–63.

PLATE I. Jusepe de Ribera, *The Sense of Touch*.
Courtesy The Norton Simon Foundation.

densely populated canvas with its agitation, heavy symbolism, and discon-
nected, multiple areas of action.

Evidently, the paintings set up two asymmetrical relationships in which
understanding is implied: the first, between the contemplator and the contemplated, and the second, between the painting and the viewer. In the first,
the subject is the contemplated, a sculptural fragment. In the second, the
subject is the contemplator of the first relationship—for example, Aristotle,
rather than the bust of Homer. I turn now to the asymmetry in the paintings.

Contemplative union is evident. In the design of the paintings, the "I" of
the contemplator becomes one with the "you" of the contemplated head.
Each, fragmentary in its own way, participates in a union that includes them
both; each is expanded thereby to play a role in an unseen, but integral,
pattern.

PLATE II. Rembrandt (Rembrandt Harmensz van Rijn), *Aristotle with a Bust of Homer*. The Metropolitan Museum of Art, New York. Purchased with special funds and gifts of friends of the Museum, 1961. (61.198)

Despite their differences, the four paintings portray a common method of contemplation. That method is subject of the three earlier paintings. It appears at the left of van der Werff's work, in the figure of a young man holding a female bust, a caesura or pause, in the encircling violence. The method, entirely familiar in mystical disciplines, is an exercise in concentration that begins with a physical object, and then passes from the bodily sensations or rhythms (such as breathing), to inward visualization, and, finally, beyond meditation to abandonment of intellect. This practice was frequently represented in paintings of saintly rapture, of the Magdalene, for example, Jerome, and Francis of Assisi. The contemplative figures in the four paintings under discussion have closed their eyes, or—in the case of Rembrandt's *Aristotle*—look with an abstracted gaze, not at but beyond or through the objects of contemplation, a gaze paralleled by the god-intoxicated stare of Poussin's poet (in *The Inspiration of the Epic Poet*, Louvre). They study those objects through their hands, and, more exactly, through the prehensible faculty of their hands. Finally, in all four instances, the

PLATE III. Luca Giordano, *Carneades with a
Bust of Paniscus*. Stanley Moss and Company, Inc.

object of concentration is a sculptural fragment, a head, specifically a portrait bust in the paintings by Rembrandt and Giordano; and the sculpture
and the contemplator face one another.

Plate V underscores the inwardness of this pose by contrast. Contemporary with the four paintings of contemplative subjects, the portrait of
Antoine Coysevox represents quite a different mental attitude. The animated, outward gaze of the sitter away from the carving emphasizes, by
contrast, the withdrawn, inward contemplation in the other portraits reproduced here, despite the prehensile gesture of the studying hand that they
all share. Unlike the other subjects, Coysevox is plainly not imagining himself into the emptiness of the sculptured head.

Comparison with gestures in yet other paintings will underscore the dis-
tinctiveness of this common gesture. The possible contrasts are many: for
example, Titian's portrait of Jacopo Strada in his opulence, leering toward

PLATE IV. Adriaen van der Werff, *Children Playing
before a Sculptural Group with Hercules*.
Munich, Alte Pinakothek.

an unseen companion as he grasps a female figure, one commodity among
many in his treasure room (Kunsthistorisches Museum, Vienna); Lorenzo
Lotto's portrait of Andrea Odoni, swathed in a fur-lined robe, as he stands
in a clutter of sculptural fragments, a book, and coins and, with a gaze of
calm self-satisfaction, extends an Egyptian statuette toward the viewer
(Hampton Court); Giovanni Cariani's *Portrait of an Antique Collector*, evidently interrupted with calliper in hand as he measured a male torso, and
looking directly, with some boredom, at the intrusive viewer (formerly
Bowood, Lansdown Collection).

These celebrated pictures will readily come to mind. I supplement them

PLATE V. Circle of Pierre Mignard (French, 1612–95),
Portrait of the Sculptor Antoine Coysevox.
The Portland Art Museum, Portland, Oregon, gift of
Mr. and Mrs. Edwin Binney 3d.

with illustrations of several less familiar works. Werner van den Valckert
(ca. 1580–1630) portrays a man, presumably an artist, looking toward the
viewer as he points at a lay figure; as in the three paintings already mentioned, discourse between the subject and the viewer is suggested (J. B.
Speed Art Museum). Michael Sweert's *The Artist's Studio* (1652) represents a discourse underway, in the midst of a mindless accumulation of
sculptural fragments, as the artist's assistant carries still more, jumbled in
his apron, to the pile (Detroit Institute of Arts). While the young man at
the center of the painting is inspecting the putto in his right hand, his inspection is clearly part of the general bustle, and his grasp of the figure lacks the
caressing, tracing movement represented in the four pictures with which I

began. Finally, Gillis Tilborch the Younger (1625–78) portrays a number of entirely uncontemplated sculptures in *A Picture Gallery with the Artist and his Patrons*, including the female bust held aloft by one of the visitors, which the artist regards with a suspicious glance and the other figures ignore (Helen Foresman Spencer Museum, University of Kansas).

Thus, in a common, stylized fashion, the rapture of expression in our four paintings portrays the erotic nature of contemplation; the tranquillity of the outward poses implies intense, inward ardor. Far from voiding the passions, contemplation concentrated them in love. For the four artists, the rapt subjects of these pictures were related to their other works, which conveyed affective intensity in a variety of ways, not least by presenting the nude, or evocatively undraped body, as the object of contemplation. All four were celebrated for their paintings of themes from classical mythology and from Scripture, in which they employed the device of the disclosed body to capture and direct the erotic instincts of the viewer, in scenes of tranquillity or conflict, of triumph or agony. The habit of addressing the passions through art, and of spiritualizing physical desires entrapped by "the concupiscence of the eyes," belonged to the social context in which these paintings were made, though no uniform consensus prevailed. The continuing dispute over the nudes in Michelangelo's *Last Judgment* for the Sistine Chapel provides an index. Although some nudes were modified by draperies under Pope Paul IV, Pope Clement VII intended to destroy the fresco, and El Greco offered to repaint the *Last Judgment* in a more decorous fashion, yet the defenders of Michelangelo's work insisted that there was nothing in it that was not spiritual.[14]

Thus, both because of the nature of contemplation itself, and because of prevalent theories of art that accepted the sensual as a manifestation of and a gateway to the spiritual, these paintings, even in their reflective calm, imply an erotic content. Such is particularly obvious in the painting by van der Werff, where the contemplative young man turns his affects aside from the merely physical presence of the woman beside him to the spiritual presence in the sculptured head. In a powerful symbolic fashion, it is the central element in Rembrandt's painting. For the glittering chain worn by Aristotle that bisects the composition is love, "Homer's golden chain, which reacheth down from Heaven to earth, by which every creature is annexed, and depends on his Creator."[15] The symbolic message is that "Homer's golden chain" of love was shared, both by poetry and by philosophy in their accesses to universal order.

[14] Anthony Blunt, *Artistic Theory in Italy, 1450–1600* (London: Oxford University Press, 1973), pp. 118–19. Kenneth Clark, *The Nude: A Study in Ideal Form* (Princeton: Princeton University Press, 1971), pp. 26–27.

[15] Robert Burton, *The Anatomy of Melancholy*, ed. Floyd Dell and Paul Jordan-Smith (New York: Tudor, 1955), p. 623.

The works to which I have alluded for contrast underscore another common feature of the asymmetry in the four "contemplative" paintings, apart from the mood of withdrawal—namely, the importance of the fact that the fragmentary object of contemplation is the head. Although portraits represented specific men or women, and not ideal or generic types, there is, for our purposes, no distinction between the portraits of Homer and the young Pan, in the works by Rembrandt and Giordano, and the anonymous heads in those by Ribera and van der Werff. The head was the seat of reason, which ruled all the senses and combined and unified the disparate impressions of the senses into a whole that could be the object of thought. It was also the locus of four senses, only the sense of touch being generally dispersed through the body. The prehensile gestures in the paintings by Ribera, Giordano, and van der Werff draw attention precisely to the four senses in the head.

It is notable, however, that all four painters represent this exploration as a face-to-face asymmetry between a living person and a lifeless sculptural fragment; but the person was as unseeing and unseen as the work of art. No contemplator is studying the senses' interrelation through the mind in an actual human body, either his own or another's. For these paintings allude to the physiology of understanding only as part of esthetic apprehension.

By making the head the object of sightless contemplation, the four painters pointed toward the faculties and the art of contemplation itself. By constructing an asymmetry between the sculptural fragment and the contemplator, the artists posed a universal hermeneutic situation as a problem in art. Turning aside from outward vision, the contemplators presented the data of feeling to the inward vision of the mind's eye. Given the nature of concentration, this turning inward can only be regarded as a flight from distraction, and thus a censure of the vagrant sense of sight. Such is the universal situation.

As far as its application in art is concerned, the conviction dominating the asymmetry in our four paintings is clear. It is that beauty is not a physical quality of an object—its form or color, for example—but that it is *in* the physical qualities. We perceive that hidden, or enclosed, beauty through the attraction or repellence of our feelings, provoked through the senses. A salient feature of the paintings under discussion is that they portray the penetration of physical qualities, not only as pictorial statements about what the intense act of contemplation looked like, but as an exercise in reciprocal exchanges between the sense of sight and touch, which is also to say between the arts of painting and sculpture, exchanges in which the non-theoretical sense of touch is made to serve the theoretical sense of vision or, more precisely, as we shall see, the theoretical, inward vision of the mind.

The question that they pose is: How are tactile (or kinesthetic) data trans-

formed into visual images? The answer involves the forgetfulness of contemplation, and the movements of visual and motor imitation, the recapitulation by the eye of what it sees, the caressing, tracing movement of the
hand over what it feels. The paintings locate these two acts, forgetfulness
and imitation, at a particular moment in the process of thinking, whether
in philosophy or in art—that is, at the moment of previsualization.

The theme of forgetfulness is abundantly clear in the paintings themselves, in the closed books concealed by draperies behind the bust of Homer,
the neglected canvas, the withdrawal from encircling commotion. I shall
suggest later that the combination of contemplative forgetfulness with imitation, at the moment of previsualization, has, in fact, been a primary
impulse in the history of Western art. For the present, however, I wish to
round out my discussion of confrontation of painting and sculpture in our
four contemplative works.

The distinction between painting and sculpture is explicit in the paintings
by Ribera, which depicts a stretched and figured canvas in the foreground,
and by van der Werff, which couples the arts of drawing and carving in one
composition. It is implicit in all four works, because the asymmetry
between contemplator and contemplated in them derives from the imitation
of sculpture by paintings. As cognate arts of visual imitation, painting and
sculpture shared some values and objectives, as well as the disabilities of
silence, emptiness, darkness, and inertia. Neither, for example, was able to
represent process. However, the fundamental distinction between painting,
the art of drawing with colors, and sculpture, an art of carving from, or
pouring, bulk engendered rivalry. Painting had the greater plasticity. It
could portray a vast array of subjects, in limitless combination and variety.
It could depict any imaginable setting for those subjects, and command the
entire spectrum of visual effects from the most minute detail to the greatest
vagueness and ambiguity of visual perception. Further, it allowed alterations, even in the major elements of compositions. However, the flatness of
its surface limited the effect of a painting to a single focal point, and to quite
restricted angles and ranges of vision.

By contrast, sculpture did not merely represent such physical properties
as mass, weight, relief, and the balance of stresses; they were inherent in
its materials. Being three-dimensional, a statue could be, and was intended
to be, viewed from many focal points and angles and ranges of vision, and
it also possessed tactile values that contributed to its simulation of life. Its
power to simulate life was enhanced by the fact that it presented different
silhouettes, as living creatures did, according to the spectator's point of
view.

Descartes (1596–1650), a contemporary of Ribera, Rembrandt and Giordano, wrote about the extraordinarily vivid effects that were produced by
automata in grottoes and fountains in the French royal gardens. Hydraulic

pressure made some play on instruments or utter words. Visitors, he wrote, stepped on tiles of the pavement that set the mechanism in action. "If they approach a Diana bathing, they will cause her to hide in the reeds; and if they pass further to pursue her, they will cause a Neptune to advance and menace them with his trident. Or if they go in another direction, they will make a marine monster come out and spew water into their faces, or other such things, according to the whims of the engineers who made them."[16] Descartes's argument was that the human body was a statue, a machine, inhabited by a reasonable soul.

Sculpture, too, had the deficiencies of its media. It was incapable of the complex designs, the combinations of subjects, and the range of visual effects that the plasticity of painting made possible. Because the sculptor's materials were both heavy and fragile, his works demanded compactness. Once the carving of a statue had been well advanced, few alterations in the major conception were possible. The greatest deficiency of sculpture when compared with painting was its lack of color. It was far from unknown for paints or stains of different colors to be used to achieve polychrome sculpture. But, for the contemplative, reinforced by the assumption that colorlessness was a norm in classical Greece, this last, most crucial, deficiency was an advantage.

A century after our four paintings had been completed, Sir Joshua Reynolds (1723–92) commented on the absence of color from statuary. True to tradition, Reynolds believed that, in their works, ancient sculpture left enduring models of the imitation of nature, and yet had refrained from giving their statues the colors that nature gave their subjects. Firm in his own ignorance of ancient polychroming, Reynolds continued: "If the business of sculpture was to administer pleasure to ignorance, or a mere entertainment to the sense, the Venus de Medicis might certainly receive much improvement by color; but the character of sculpture makes it her duty to afford delight of a different and, perhaps, of a higher kind; the delight resulting from the contemplation of perfect beauty; and this which is in truth an intellectual pleasure, is in many respects incompatible with what is merely addressed to the sense."[17]

The colorlessness of sculptural fragments in our paintings thus returns us to the asymmetry of contemplation in the paintings, and, indeed, to the contemplation of the beauty that was in the physical qualities of works of art, not among them. The deficiencies of painting and sculpture also point to the reason why our painters placed contemplative absorption at the

[16] René Descartes, *Treatise of Man*, trans. Thomas Steele Hall (Cambridge, Mass.: Harvard University Press, 1972), p. 22.

[17] *Discourse* 10, in *Discourses on Art*, ed. Stephen O. Mitchell (Indianapolis: Bobbs-Merrill, 1965), p. 146.

moment of previsualization, and the means by which one penetrated those qualities to partake of the beauty that they both concealed and manifested.

The deficiencies of painting, amplified by imperfections of the sense of sight, required that bodily sight be discounted in the contemplative union. Sculpture, with its tactile character, made possible immediate perception of the object of contemplation through the sense of touch. Through touch, the contemplator could experience all three dimensions of the statue; he could feel himself into the statue. By contrast, painting required the viewer to regard its works at a distance. The viewer absorbed the picture through the mediation of visual images that were subject not only to organic dysfunctions (uncorrected by exercises, lenses, or surgery), but also by perfectly normal binocular disparity and rivalry. Painters were altogether aware of these organic anomalies in the act of seeing, of visual displacement of color that occurs in viewing compositions, and of the blurred and highly selective images that the eye transmits to the brain. Motor images formed by the hand moving over a solid object were direct; visual images formed by the eye in its darting, roving movement across a world of surfaces were indirect.

The contemplative poses in the four paintings—with eyes shut or cast in an unseeing gaze, and hands tracing the contours of the sculptures—specifically evade the effects of eye-hand coordination. The reason is that eye-hand coordination is action, rather than contemplation. Thus, when it occurs, as in the manual labor of painting or sculpture, eye-hand coordination in fact excludes the contemplative state. The familiar antithesis between active and contemplative states can easily be illustrated by comparing our four contemplative works with others that portray artists at work, not in the flamboyant exhibitionism of some self-portraits, but in quiet, intense, and even reverent concentration.

The four contemplative paintings under discussion do imply some means at the juncture of paintings and sculpture that enabled tactile, or kinesthetic, images to be transformed into visual ones. As I indicated, that transformation occurred at the moment of previsualization, which is to say before the picture took shape in the mind or on the easel. Our paintings express an esthetic understanding born of habit, and, especially, habits that established reciprocity between motor and visual images. Born of repeated imitation, comparison, and correction, those habits ingrained ways of relating new experiences to received norms, of callibrating transformations and displacements in norms, and of bringing about the convergence of subject and object. The habits were rooted in spatial relationships—such as proportion (or magnitude), contiguity, and shape—and in organic coordination. The formation and reformation of these habits occurred for painters and sculptures, not only in touching and in seeing, and in the formal discipline of copying works of other artists, but also in sketching. Sketching was the border point between previsual and visual, between motor and visual images. By "sketching," I refer not to careful drawings intended to be preliminary to finished works (much as a sculptor's *modello* in clay would be), but to swift, almost involuntary, and desultory outlines made, much as one gestures with the hand tracing outlines in the air. In such sketches, images are performed, rather than executed.[18]

The four paintings extend what should be included in this common ground of performance. It was natural that Ribera, Rembrandt, Giordano, and van der Werff combined paintings and sculpture in these portrayals of contemplation, in works drawn in strong contrasts between light and shade. For all were expert practitioners of engraving, a hybrid of carving and drawing, that served contemplation with colorlessness and suggestiveness, which it took from both.

I have now come to the point at which the two asymmetries—the one in the picture, and the other, between the picture and the viewer—overlap. "I fear," Reynolds wrote, "we [painters] have but very scanty means of exciting those powers over the imagination which make so very considerable and refined a part of poetry.   It is true, sketches, or drawings as painters generally make for their works, give this pleasure of imagination to a high degree. From a slight, undetermined drawing, where the ideas of the composition and character are, as I may say, only just touched upon, the imagination supplies more than the painter himself, probably, could produce; and we accordingly often find that the finished work disappoints the expectation that was raised from the sketch; and this power of the imagination is one of the causes of the great pleasure we have in viewing a collection of drawings by great painters. These general ideas, which are expressed in sketches, correspond very well to the art often used in poetry," which Reynolds went on to identify as "indistinct expressions," freely set forth by the allusiveness of words, but, on the whole, excluded from painting by the need to render "a determined form," or distinct image, to the viewer's eye.[19]

The preceding discussion should make evident that my contention is twofold. I contend that Reynolds was right when he identified the source of poetry's evocative power in the license it gave readers to move into the gaps of the text and expand it there, each according to his own way or mood. I also contend that Reynolds was mistaken in the contrast that he drew between the gaps opened by the allusiveness of verbal images in poetry and his denial that the media of painting opened corresponding gaps in the very midst of painting's "distinct images." It now remains to indicate reasons for thinking that empathetic participation in painting was possible exactly

[18] See E. H. Gombrich, *Art and Illusion: A Study in the Psychology of Pictorial Representation* (Princeton: Princeton University Press, 1969), p. 189, on Leonardo's use of sketches in this way.

[19] *Discourse 8*, in *Discourses on Art*, p. 138.

because the imagination could play in the open spaces between elements that composed the "determined forms" of painting.

In the process, I hope to indicate also that, as in earlier centuries, while esthetic apprehension of poetry depended upon a hermeneutic of under- standing, that of painting depended upon a hermeneutic of calculated mis- understanding informed by eroticism through pathetic and affective falla- cies.

The discussion of the asymmetry between painting and viewer will go beyond our four contemplative paintings, but we must begin with them. The most evident traces of calculated misunderstanding, in respect of this second asymmetry, are the fictions of visual realism and the completeness (or perfection) of the work of art, which later ran counter to doctrines about the deficiencies of art.

The four paintings imply and parody a number of fictions, including that of the artist's inspiration, but none more evidently than the fiction that art imitates nature. The pathetic and affective fallacies of the "living" work of art depended on the proposition that, by self-concealment, the painter's art deceived the eye of the viewer. Yet, it was evident to writers and to painters that painting captured the hearts of viewers not by imitating but by departing from nature, by eliminating details so as to focus the attention of the beholder, by correcting the defects and disproportions of nature (espe- cially in portraiture), and by rendering visible (through allegory and sym- bolism) what could not be seen, including states of mind. It would be a grave mistake, wrote a patron of Poussin, to paint things as the eye sees them.[20]

Our four paintings parody the illusion of natural imitation. The accept- ance of illusion as illusory is apparent in their theatricality. In different ways, this is equally true of the exaggerated proscenium effect in van der Werff's crowded painting, in the unnatural dramatic splendor of Rem- brandt's *Aristotle*, and in the austere elimination of detail in the three ear- lier works. It is apparent in the uniformity with which light appears to stream from beyond the upper left corner of each picture, and from the varieties of brushwork in different areas of every canvas. It is evident, above all, in the imitation not of nature but of art.

In this last regard, the four paintings play upon a multiple irony. Our first asymmetry, between contemplator and contemplated in the picture, focuses on a work of art, which is itself an imitation. What is imitated may have been a living person, as in the case of portrait busts. It may have been another work of art, as it would have been if, as seems likely from the heft, a light cast rather than a heavy carving in stone is represented. The actual subjects of Rembrandt's bust of Homer and of Giordano's Paniscus were undoubtedly casts or engravings. Portfolios with engravings of classical

[20] Gombrich, *Art and Illusion*, p. 313.

works of art were part of the painter's stock-in-trade. The painting by Sweerts, showing a disorderly agglomeration of sculptural fragments, is reminiscent of long-standing practice. A century before Sweerts, Armenini, commenting on the difficulty of travelling great distances to study original works of sculpture, remarked on the easy availability of wax or gesso copies, occasionally in miniature. The copies were inexpensive and, because of their lightness, easy to handle and move. "I have seen studios and chambers [throughout Italy] . . . full of such well-formed copies," he wrote. "Looking at these, it seemed to me that they were the very works found in Rome."[21] The point, however, is that such collections of engravings and casts were also common among connoisseurs, and that familiarity with sculpture through replicas in media other than the original ones conditioned esthetic judgments of patrons and artists alike.

The esteem for ancient statuary exemplified in these paintings drew its sanction from the belief that, in antiquity, sculptors "being indefatigable in the school of nature, have left models of that perfect form behind them which an artist would prefer as supremely beautiful," the bases of all that had raised and kept modern art out of barbarism.[22] But, as already noted, the presumed absence of colors from ancient statues appeared a notable departure from the imitation of nature. In the controversy between ancients and moderns in the seventeenth century, other deficiencies of ancient sculpture were alleged, including lifeless insipidity and the incongruity of serene facial expressions in representations of violent action.

Even those who revered ancient sculpture, therefore, found that its success involved, and required, not imitation only, but also departures from nature. Emulating nature included rivalry as well as simulation. Thus, the imitation of art by art was an epicycle of illusion, riding on the great illusory circle of the doctrine that art imitated nature. By portraying the imitation of art by art, the four paintings under review define layer after layer of illusion, the copy in the painting of the sculptural image of the original, with every probability of another stage—the copy (engraving or cast) of the sculpture—intervening between painting and statue. Each layer of illusion lacks features essential to its prototype, keeping only superficial resemblance. The representations of human figures in these paintings, less elaborately, repeat the irony that art imitates nature on the surface, but negates the essence, of things.

Painting, an enterprise of one surface, also exposed the second great fiction, the perfection of the work of art—another characteristic that literary and visual arts had in common. "In the greatest classics . . . the triumph of form is always unsteady, always partly flawed, partly accidental. And yet

---

[21] *On the True Precepts,* I. 8, p. 132.
[22] Reynolds, *Discourses,* 3, 6, in *Discourses on Art,* pp. 30, 85.

with a secret lost even to the author, the work works."[23] My concern is not with flaws in individual paintings, but with the general sentence of failure that the idea of perfection imposed upon the enterprise of painting. The goal of perfection and the sentence of failure provoked incessant rivalry in art, and the rapid change and proliferation of styles. The "incessant change" in painting as in poetry "is only possible because the appreciator accepts the illusion as illusory,"[24] and, it should be added, defective. Art was never able to cast off its finitude, never able to transcend its limits, because each advance carried those limits with it.

Among the most tenacious limits on the perfectibility of art were the exigencies of the medium, paint. Immensely flexible as they are, these limits, or "deficiencies," cannot be transcended without abandoning the enterprise of painting. Such is one "reason why the perfection of illusion was also the hour of disillusionment."[25] But it is also the case that, in the asymmetry between painting and beholder, the deficiencies of silence, emptiness, darkness, and inertia provided openings for empathetic participation in and through painting.

In the era of our four contemplative works, the perfection of a painting was thought to consist in invention (the choice of subject), composition (the manner of treating subjects), and disposition of masses (the deployment of color, or of light and shade). Even the most skillfully achieved effects were lost if the painting was badly displayed. Bad lighting or hanging pictures too high, too low, or at too great a distance from viewers, Armenini wrote, frequently distorted the perspective in the works and obscured even the most expert paintings.[26] Thus, as regards empathetic participation, the painting's correspondence to its environment should be considered, together with the painterly techniques of invention, composition, and disposition of masses.

Correlations clearly exist between silence and invention, emptiness and composition, darkness and the arrangement of masses, and inertia and the display of the painting. I shall now attempt to suggest how these correlations appear in the four works with which I began, and how, as general characteristics of painting, they invited empathetic participation.

Like God, theorists wrote, the artist made something where there had been nothing. But, just as theologians taught that without God's unseen but universal presence, the world would return to the void from which it came, so too paintings betrayed the fact that they owed their form not to

[23] David Tracy, *The Analogical Imagination: Christian Theology and the Culture of Pluralism* (New York: Crossroad, 1981), p. 200.

[24] Christopher Caudwell, *Illusion and Reality: A Study of the Sources of Poetry* (New York: International Publishers, 1966), p. 43.

[25] Gombrich, *Art and Illusion*, p. 278.

[26] *On the True Precepts*, II. 11; III, 5, pp. 204, 232.

their visible materials but to the will of the artist, which was invisible but everywhere present in them. Yet, their deficiencies were their strengths.

The silence of paintings was a form of concealment that gave them the power to suggest many things. Reynolds expressed a general position when he wrote that artists should choose subjects that viewers could readily identify, especially from ordinary experiences of life or from their knowledge of classical literature and Scripture. Thus, he said, through common knowledge, they would engage common sympathy.[27] Still, even though representational painting required distinct images, invention—the choice of a subject—had a suggestive power. Titles were frequently inadequate or misleading clues to subjects, when they did not actually conceal them. The artist could name his work as an afterthought, with nonchalance or irony.[28] A painting could be named and renamed by others after it left the artist's hands. The title of van der Werff's work, *Children Playing before a Sculptural Group with Hercules*, is certainly inadequate to the subject chosen by the artist. Even when titles correspond completely, or approximately, with subjects, the concealing muteness of the painting may disclose general connotations far beyond the particular image.

For example, by their asymmetry between the lifeless works of a past culture and living viewers, our four paintings present the tragic pathos of the transience of life and art. This theme is most evident in van der Werff's painting, with its elaborate and precious parallels of hunter and victim (Hercules and the aged woman; cat and bird; tempests of nature, or life, and the stormy force of nature and unsuspecting people about to be engulfed by it); but the theme of mortality is also starkly set forth in the other paintings. In them, it appears with an anonymity of time and place that enables a viewer to apply it to his or her own circumstances.

The evocative concealment of silence was used by painters in many ways. Following the precedent of the ancient painter, Parrhasios, some artists veiled their canvases with *trompe l'oeil* draperies (e.g., Titian, *Portrait of Filippo Archinato*, Philadelphia Museum of Art). Anamorphic and allegorical paintings provided other means by which silence, concealing the subject, could be made expressive. Poussin, Brueghel, and many others explored the further possibility of immersing the subject as a small and almost imperceptible figure in vast landscapes or bustling panoramas. All these devices, like the ones employed in our four paintings, counterbalanced silence and invention so as to attract and fix the attention of the viewer.

The correlation of emptiness and composition (the way of treating sub-

---

[27] *Discourse 4* in *Discourses on Art*, p. 40. Illuminating parallels with the following argument appear in Amos Ih Tiao Chang, *The Tao of Architecture* (Princeton: Princeton University Press, 1956), esp. pp. 9, 12, 21, 71 ("creative forgetfulness"). See above Chapter 2.

[28] Cf. Reynolds's account of how Giovanni da Bologna named a sculptural group. *Discourse 10*, in *Discourses on Art*, p. 152.

jects) contributed to the same effect. Composition governed the number and deployment of figures. Emptiness was an attribute of the grand style, which, aiming at the rapture of the sublime, demanded the reduction of figures, detail, and ornament that could distract attention from the subject. Emptiness characterizes composition of the paintings by Rembrandt, Ribera, and Giordano. In each, figures are reduced to two, fused by the attitude of contemplation into one. At first glance, the thickly figured painting by van der Werff might appear to be an exception. But, even there, the diverse and segmented actions, including the contemplative figure, is bracketed between two voids—to the left, the profound shadow out of which a Silenus bust regards the transience of youth and light and, to the right, the lowering sky. The voids are joined by an empty vault. Even the confined and threatened area of human endeavor is pierced by a shadow, an intrusion of the void. The theatricality of all four paintings, therefore, requires emptiness for its effect, emptiness of composition accentuating the emptiness of physical vision in the subjects.

As already indicated, emptiness—the absence of figures—was a characteristic demanded of the grand style, but it was also sanctioned by the doctrine that paintings required incompleteness to achieve their effect. Incompleteness might be included by the reduction of figures, or by techniques of style, such as the roughness of Rembrandt, the "crudely daubed strokes and blobs" of Titian's late style, or the "odd scratches and marks . . . this chaos, this uncouth and shapeless appearance" of Gainsborough's work that "at a certain distance assume[d] form" and great beauty.[29]

Titian, in one of his most profound works, depicted the power of emptiness, joined with composition, to engage empathetic participation. True to age-old convention, in *The Vanity of All Earthy Things*, he portrayed *Vanitas* as a beautiful woman turning her mirror to the spectator (Alte Pinakothek, Munich). The mirror displays the transient wealth of this world, but not the face of the spectator. In this way, Titian employed a cardinal deficiency of painting, its emptiness, to enable every viewer, being shocked by the absence of his reflection, to imagine that it should be there.

When correlated with the deployment of masses through the use of color, the third deficiency of painting, darkness, also reinforced the capacity for contemplation. Titian's *Vanity* is a remarkable example of how this deficiency, too, could be made an enticement to contemplation; for, despite the bright expanses of her sleeve and flesh tones, the beholder's eye is captured by the dark mirror, unrelieved, except to the viewer at closest range, by the shadowy goods it displays. In our four pictures, the arrangement of masses

[29] Gombrich, *Art and Illusion*, pp. 195, 196, 200. Reynolds, *Discourse 4*, in *Discourses in Art*, p. 220.

through the deployment of color (or light and shade) establishes powerful irregular rhythms.

Simplicity of composition in the three earlier paintings limits those rhythms to the blank backgrounds and to the curves of arm and drapery that draw the sculpture and the contemplator into a single pattern. Screening the arm of his artist in its dark sleeve, Ribera assimilated the lightness of his hands to that of the sculptured head; and, showing both faces in profile, he established a further parallel between the shadow on the lower part of the carving and the dark beard of the artist. Giordano deployed masses to a similar effect. Depicting both heads in three-quarter profile, he arranged Carneades's cloak in such a way as to echo the outline of Paniscus's head and shoulders. Further, he used the contrast between the lightness of Carneades's left arm and the darkness of his cloak to cut horizontally across the vertical axis of the picture.

The irregular rhythms established by the masses of light and shade in Rembrandt's painting are very elaborate. The eye is attracted by Aristotle's flamboyant sleeves, linked by "Homer's golden chain" of love. But the sleeves are divided by the black column of Aristotle's inner vestment, continuing, embellished, and completed by the beard and hat that encircle his face. Glittering against that black column, the chain of love establishes a diagonal from upper left to lower right, dividing the picture into two segments, the upper one, dominated by Aristotle's head, and the lower, dominated by Homer's bust. The shimmering pleats of the sleeves divide each of those segments, the upper one vertically, the lower one horizontally.

Enough has been said about van der Werff's composition to indicate that in it, as in Titian's *Vanity* and in these three other works, although the bright masses attract the eye, the dark ones detain it.

Our four paintings, now reinforced by Titian's *Vanity*, point to a general fascination of darkness. The common allegiance of Ribera, Rembrandt, Giordano, and van der Werff to the *tenebrosi* belonged to a persistent current in Renaissance and post-Renaissance painting. Varnish was applied to deepen colors, and, as it discolored, to darken them. The technique of *sfumato*, developed by Leonardo and Giorgione, was continuously developed, not only by Caravaggio and the other tenebrosi, but by later artists who made "picture[s] so dark that [they] cannot be seen without a peculiar light and then with difficulty." One such artist, Reynolds recalled, was a flower painter who affected to work in "the true Italian taste," painting "as black and dirty as he could," leaving "all clearness and brilliancy of coloring" to those who pandered to the common taste.[30] The fascinating illusion of mass

---

[30] *Discourses 4, 8*, in *Discourses on Art*, pp. 53, 136. Howard Hibbard, *Caravaggio* (New York: Harper and Row, 1983), p. 150. On Constable's revulsion from this attitude, see Gombrich, *Art and Illusion*, p. 53. The entire previous discussion underscores the effort, described by Fried in regard to eighteenth-century French painting to negate the presence of the beholder, and thereby to capture his attention. I hope to emphasize here that the paradoxical

through darkness also induced painters to draw attention to their principal subjects by shifting light away from them, or even by casting them off center and in heavy shade, as Veronese did in his *Martyrdom of St. Sebastian* (Church of San Sebastiano, Venice), and as van der Werff did when he placed the Silenus brooding over the fated transience of life from the edge of darkness.

The disabilities of silence, emptiness, and darkness thus provided means of concentration, openings by which the viewers' attention could be engaged and hermeneutic gaps in which their imagination could play. By contrast, the disability of inertia, or immobility, in its correlation with display, was a means of distraction. This effect came about partly through the nature of the painting as a physical object that could be seen only in a physical environment. The correspondence of object to environment necessarily modified the experience of seeing.

In this regard, our four paintings give us little evidence, except for the facts that Rembrandt painted his *Aristotle* for the collection of Prince Antonio Ruffo, and that *Carneades* originally belonged to a set of ten paintings of philosophers, all by Giordano. The salient fact is that, in these cases, paintings were intended to be seen as parts of collections—that is, as individual elements among many in galleries, including sculpture, curiosities, and other treasures. They could also be regarded as components of architectural or decorative schemes in churches, palaces, common dwellings, and other structures.

As physical objects, paintings deteriorated. In the mid-sixteenth century, Armenini lamented the enormous loss of paintings in fresco and on canvas, including many of the most excellent contemporary works, which loss he had witnessed over the space of twenty years, and which daily increased.[31] Apart from deliberate destruction or mutilation, moisture was the great enemy of frescoes, but it also took its toll in the sagging and rotting of canvas. Airborn particles of smut and grime, notably from candles used to illuminate paintings, covered their surfaces and became incorporated in the paint and varnish. Discoloration and darkening also occurred with the yellowing of pigments and varnish. Restoration of deteriorated paintings frequently resulted in mutilation, partly because of the scouring with which they were cleaned and partly because of the repainting to which they were subjected.

Leonardo's *Last Supper* was only one masterpiece that experienced natural

---

use of negation to attract and fix the attention was part of the whole strategy of understanding art, rooted in the medium of paint, and centering on the hermeneutic gap. Fried alluded to the enticing effect of using darkness and arrangement of figures to construct the hermeneutic gap (though not by that name) when he wrote that the beholder's attention was attracted by "retarding the viewer's grasp of what is taking place and thereby heightening the dramatic impact of the composition." Fried, *Absorption and Theatricality*, p. 157. See also pp. 31, 43 (on the seventeenth-century antecedents), 67, 75, 103, 108.

[31] *On the True Precepts*, I. 1, pp. 83–84.

decay, abuse, and inept restoration. Goethe recorded how, in his day, it continued (through copies) to be "an object of wonder," even though the work that Leonardo left had "almost ceased to exist."[32] Goethe's contemporary, Reynolds, lamented the state of "old pictures, deservedly celebrated for their coloring [that were] often so changed by dirt and varnish" that they had to be studied for what they once were, rather than for what they had become.[33]

Conditions of display also impeded contemplative exercises. Protective coverings or draperies concealed some paintings.[34] Illumination was a severe handicap that can still be experienced in many churches and galleries. Armenini's regret, in the sixteenth century, that excellent pictures lost their effect through bad lighting is echoed in comments in nineteenth-century guidebooks such as "best light before noon," "good light only at midday," and "not visible except on very bright days." Occasionally, candle sconces were affixed to picture frames, although the burning candles obstructed a full view of the paintings, and begrimed and endangered the canvases themselves. The paradox is that artists painted great masterpieces on commission specifically for places where, they knew, the works would be rendered invisible, for example, by backlighting, distance, or architectural obstructions.

The overarching impediment to contemplation, however, was the diminution of the individual painting by its total environment. Whether as altarpieces, as pawns in the game of collection, or as elements in architectural ornamentation, paintings were displayed generally with other objects of luxury, "not in any logical order, but as decoration—a magnificent and unusual decoration indeed," as a guidebook to the Gallery of the Pitti Palace observes, "which was intended to convey an impression of wealth and splendor, with its beautiful pictures in rich frames set close together so that the walls are brilliantly impressive, animated as they are by vivid colors and gleaming gold."[35]

Yet distraction was not the whole story. Such galleries, being places of power, were also places of awe. Their prodigal ostentation expressed

[32] "Observations on Leonardo da Vinci's Celebrated Picture of the Last Supper," in John Gage, *Goethe on Art* (Berkeley: University of California Press, 1980), p. 166.

[33] Reynolds, *Discourse 2*, in *Discourses on Art*, p. 18. Cf. the forthright statement by the late twentieth-century painter, Robert Irwin: "After going through the Louvre twenty times and the National Museum and the Prado and whatever—I can't remember the names of the ones in Amsterdam and Florence—well, after a while it got to the point where I'd enter a room and just twirl around and go to the next one and twirl and then the next one. . . . I mean, it got to the point where if I ever saw another fucking brown painting. . . . I was so fucking tired of brown paintings, I mean they all looked exactly the same!" Lawrence Weschler, *Seeing is Forgetting the Name of the Thing One Sees: A Life of Contemporary Artist Robert Irwin* (Berkeley: University of California, 1982), p. 35.

[34] Veiled pictures are frequently depicted in seventeenth-century paintings. See the reference to veiled pictures by Titian, Correggio, and Giulio Romano in Armenini, *On the True Precepts*, III. 10, p. 256.

[35] Anna Maria Francini Ciaranfi, *The Pitti Palace and Gallery in Florence* (Florence: Arnaud, n.d.), p. 13.

worldly might that few could wield. As the idealization of art advanced, the opulence of these galleries also was thought to declare another sublimity, more hidden but no less fascinating and dreadful. For collections of art came to be regarded as places of spiritual exaltation, where the soul was purified by "heavenly unction . . . as when the fullness of divine quintescence flows over it."[36]

Paintings that depict galleries, real and imaginary, illustrate both the awe-inspiring magnificence achieved in this way, and the extreme difficulty that viewers experienced in seeing individual paintings that were hung in such profusion and proximity. Paintings moved into the context of a gallery from another setting achieved quite different pictorial functions, for example, when a painting taken from an altar ceased to be a visual component of ritual and became instead a little gleam in a dazzling and shining blaze of self-glorifying reverence. But precisely in this difficulty of concentration—the partial invisibility of the painting—there lay an important factor in the contemplative tradition of Western art.

Plates VI and VII illustrate two ways in which the method of exhibition modifies and may obscure the sense of a painting. In Plate VI, Rubens's *The Apocalyptic Woman* appears as a liturgical object, installed above the distant high altar in Freising cathedral, for which it was commissioned. Because of the size and quality of the engraving, Rubens's picture is identifiable under a magnifying glass. Plate VII shows the same painting (with a curved top in the center of the cluster of pictures at the right) as an historical document. The painting by Maass shows it in the secular context of the Alte Pinakothek (Munich), where it is still to be seen, though hung in a different arrangement, similarly encompassed and modified by other paintings on sacred and profane themes.

Architectural settings and galleries were themselves works of art. In them, as in paintings and statues, the part was controlled or overpowered by the whole, its environment. They were works, moreover, that embodied the very deficiencies of painting and sculpture. To be sure, as in those two "representational" arts, the media imposed specific characteristics on those deficiencies. Silence appeared in the bewilderment or vastness of structure; emptiness appeared both in the slowness with which each object slowly disclosed itself (if at all) to the approaching viewer, complicated by individual visual impairments, and in the paradox by which multiplicity of detail negates itself into the void of an indistinct impression. Darkness existed in the fact that components of the environment "killed" each other, as well as in the conditions of display.

The relation between whole and parts in an architectural setting or gallery belonged to an order of magnitude entirely different from the relation

---

[36] Peter Böttger, *Die Alte Pinakothek in München: Architektur, Ausstattung und museales Programm* (Munich: Prestel, 1972), p. 124, on the Hofgartengalerie in Munich (1787).

PLATE VI. Franz Josef Mörl and/after Cosmas Damian Asam,
"Das Innere des Freisinger Domes nach der Umgestaltung
durch die Brüder Asam, 1724," in Josef Heckenstaller,
*Dissertatio Historica de Antiquitate et aliis quibusdam
Memorabilibus Cathedralis Ecclesiae Frisingensis*
(Munich, 1824). Archiv des Erzbistums München und Freising.

between whole and parts in a painting. The whole of which an individual
painting was part in part was made up by aggregation; the whole within a
painting, by composition.

The great difference, however, pertained to the fourth deficiency—that
of inertia, or immobility. Viewers perceived the immobility of paintings in
one way, by moving into and out of the focal point in front of the works.
They perceived that of statues in a second way, by circling statues in the
round or by passing reliefs. In both cases, the viewers moved outside of the

PLATE VII. J. Maass, *View of the Rubens Gallery in the Alte Pinakothek,*
Munich (1895).
Munich, Staatsgemäldesammlungen.

work of art. But, in architectural settings and galleries, viewers moved
inside and through the work of art, and—as gallery paintings indicate—
they became kinetic components of those aggregated works, participating in
the whole.

Evidently, the previsual sequence of observation, copying and digesting,
portrayed in our four paintings, could and did occur under these circumstances. Under them, the enterprise of contemplation, with its twofold
reflex of forgetting and imitating, therefore became subject to constraints
not present in the contemplation of isolated objects. It was evident that the
appearance of paintings changed as they were moved from one position to
another both because of the lighting, and because of associations with
neighboring works detected by the viewer's restless eye. Styles blurred in
the complex visual patterns, and so did colors. Reynolds knew that colors
made individual pictures stand out from all the others in a gallery and enabled them to capture and detain the vagrant glance of the viewer as he
passed. But he also knew that, however glorious a painting by a Flemish
artist might be, it seemed "cold and gray" when put beside a Titian.[37]

[37] *Discourses 4, 8,* in *Discourses on Art,* pp. 44, 134.

Moving within and through a building, or gallery, as a work of art, the viewer's eye became selective; the contemplative effects might be delayed. From boyhood on, nurtured by his father's interests and collection, Goethe lived among artists and developed his own painterly abilities by sketching from life and from engravings, by visiting collections, and by forming his own collection of graphics and casts, which eventually amounted to more than 26,000 pieces. In his autobiography, he identified two events as crucial to his esthetic education: his visit to the Painting Gallery in Dresden (February/March 1768), and to the gallery of sculptural casts at Mannheim (October 1769). The walls of the Dresden Gallery were thickly hung with pictures. Goethe commented that the Mannheim collection made up "an irresistible mass," "a forest of statues through which one was forced to wind."[38] Despite his rapture with the Dresden collection, he mentioned no painting that specifically captivated him. Predisposed to what he judged the natural realism of Flemish painters, exemplified by Jan Weenix's (1640–1719) power to "give life to lifeless creatures" in pictures of the hunt,[39] he deliberately avoided the antiquities and "the Italian masters" in Dresden, an extraordinary collection of works painted between the fifteenth and the eighteenth centuries.[40] In the thick sculptural forest at Mannheim (complete with rotating pedestals and variable light effects), he did admire four specific works, but the effects were delayed. Despite its impact on his later sense of art, the visit to Mannheim left few immediately observable marks. Indeed, Goethe recalled deliberately forgetting the burdensome images of the casts, returning to them much later by a long circuitous route.[41]

With similar selectivity and delayed effects in mind, Reynolds wrote about the abstraction of memory. All the devices employed by the artist to draw spectator's attention to his painting (and away from others), Reynolds wrote, should be so unobtrusive "that no remains of any of these subordinate parts occur to the memory when the picture is not present."[42]

Thus, the "deficiencies" of silence, emptiness, darkness and inertia in the environment of paintings, as well as in the paintings themselves, engaged the empathetic participation of viewers, but they produced their effects upon the viewer as a kinesthetic element within the work of art, not as an observer outside it. Such viewing was selective. It had delayed, abstract effects. These characteristics of viewing played together with other aspects of the act of viewing—for example, the combination of styles, the transference of colors, and other visual and intellectual displacements. Whereas contemplation of a work of art from outside, face to face, was static, contem-

---

[38] *Dichtung und Wahrheit*, III. 11.
[39] Ibid., III. 14.
[40] Ibid., II. 8.
[41] Ibid., III. 11.
[42] *Discourse 4*, in *Discourses on Art*, p. 42.

plation of a work of art in and through correspondence with its environment encompassed novelty, variety, and contrast.

In both, however, the fragmentary character of the work of art was essential. Its deficiencies enticed the viewer to enter into it, to expand its fragmented state, to complete the fragment, remake it into a form, by empathetic, erotic participation in its hidden content, design. We have seen that, in painting, the deficiencies of silence, emptiness, and darkness enabled concentration, while that of immobility bred distraction. But we have also seen that immobility in painting subsumed the deficiencies of the works of art, the environments, in and through which paintings were viewed. The conclusion is evident that through immobility, the most complex deficiency of all, Western painting achieved its impulse for iconoclastic change through the passionate mimetic rivalry of art and that imitative rivalry was characterized by the twin reflex of forgetfulness and copying.

Some such perception was at the heart of Hegel's portrayal of history as a gallery of self-portraits, each representing a stage at which the Absolute Spirit recognized and negated itself. Only a slight shift of mood transforms this powerful metaphor of common meaning in all periods of history into the meaningless void intended by Ortega when he described the historical career of painting as a structure of mirrors, each indefinitely reflecting the others, every image nothing more than a passing shadow.[43]

The discussion thus far has exposed some of the complexities in esthetic bonding as it occurred through the contemplative experience of painting. I believe that enough has been said to underscore the distinction between the rational hermeneutic of auditory images, or words, and the affective (or erotic) hermeneutic of visual ones, in paintings. The contrast between participation through understanding and participation through calculated misunderstanding—both modes of esthetic bonding—is summed up in Reynold's statement that "art is better learnt from the works themselves than from the precepts which are formed upon those works."[44] The discussion has dealt entirely with materials between the Renaissance and the eighteenth century. To what degree, if at all, was the kind of bonding game hitherto described possible after the advent of nonrepresentational painting, or to "minds fuddled with slides and photographs"?[45] This question poses the subject of the next chapter.

[43] Above, n. 8.

[44] *Discourse 6*, in *Discourses on Art*, p. 81.

[45] John Pope-Hennessy, "Self-Portrait of an Art Historian as a Young Man," *New York Times*, 8 December 1985.

TWELVE

The Ascendancy of Sensations over Passions: Departures from Visual Realism

The first man who began to speak, whoever he was, must have intended it. For surely it is talking that has put "Art" into painting. Nothing is positive about art except that it is a word. Right from there to here all art became literary. We are not yet living in a world where everything is self-evident. It is very interesting to notice that a lot of people who want to take the talking out of painting, for instance, do nothing else but talk about it. That is no contradiction, however. The art in it is the forever mute part you can talk about forever.

Willem de Kooning (1951), in
Herschel B. Chipp ed., *Theories of Modern Art:
A Source Book by Artists and Critics* (Berkeley:
University of California Press, 1970), p. 556.

THE CONTEMPLATIVE TRADITION in Western art was an erotic tradition. Violent and exalted, eroticism took many forms, but it was always present in that moment when the contemplator took to his heart the object of his desire. When this kind of absorption occurred in the asymmetry of viewer and painting, it generally hinged on invention, that is, on the subject portrayed. When it occurred in the asymmetry of artist and painting, it hinged on the manifold experience of previsualization, that is, on the instant of choosing the subject. The pathetic and affective fallacies played a role in both asymmetries.

Plainly, the game of contemplative eroticism has continued to be possible in those varieties of Western art that engage the passions, and thus the pathetic and affective fallacies, through the subject. This is true, for example, of many kinds of religious art, of some symbolist and surrealist paintings, of Picasso in a number of his works, and, most consistently, of branches of art in which Renaissance traditions of pornography continue.

In the diverse spectrum of Western painting since the middle of the nineteenth century, however, many components have systematically eliminated visual equivalence between nature and art. Consequently, the erotic game of correspondence—of pathetic and affective fallacies—that viewers could play between the subject in a painting and their physical and mental desires became limited. The tendency toward subjectless paintings broke away from the play between the sensory (or physiological) impressions and the passions that had been basic from antiquity onward. Subjectless paintings retained a sensory effect and aimed at direct appeal to the feelings, without any clear results for the intentionality of the passions. Thus, the rules governing the complex mimetic interplay of sensation and affect—an interplay that, over the centuries, the calculated, stylized misunderstandings served by visual realism had made habitual, and even trivial—no longer held. However, eroticism and mimetic play did continue in the rivalry of the artist with his predecessors in the question for novelty, contrast, and skill.

There was a further consequence. As the scope for performance of the pathetic and affective fallacies became more limited, it also became more private. The possibilities that a subjectless painting could have a common public meaning diminished. Decipherment, interpretation, and affective bonding belonged to the private encounter between viewer and painting. Thus, whatever public meaning existed came to be, and to be understood, not through visual images, but through words—that is, not through direct experiences of art, but through discourse about art.

In the present chapter, I shall primarily consider not the areas of art where invention has kept the game of erotic bonding in its repertoire, but those where the rules of invention, together with erotic play, have become attenuated. The importance of bonding to the evolution of artistic forms and the shift from art as a common visual experience to "talk" that "put[s] 'Art' into painting," will thereby stand out all the more clearly.

"IMITATION," Armenini wrote, "is nothing more than a diligent and judicious contemplation of the works of others so that through this scrutiny one may become like other excellent artists."[1] But we have seen that, through its combination of forgetfulness and imagination, mimesis was also a means by which painters became unlike other artists. The question is whether, since the mid-nineteenth century, contemplation and the hermeneutic gap that it closes have been limited to style: whether, in other words, contemplation is no longer sought in the asymmetry of painting and viewer.

At first glance, this assumption would appear to be ill founded. What is the evidence *contra* and *pro*? The evidence *contra* consists of style itself, and of philosophical, or religious, commitments.

There is a great caution against critical judgments of disruption. For what appears at the event to be an abrupt denial of inherited norms may turn out to have fulfilled them, once enough time has passed for its antecedents to

---

[1] Giovanni Battista Armenini, *On the True Precepts of the Art of Painting*, I. 8, trans. Edward J. Olszewski (New York: Burt Franklin, 1977), p. 130.

be traced. A striking reversal of judgment has occurred in the history of painting. In time, the French Impressionists have come to be seen not as radicals but as conservatives, and it has become possible to argue that Degas and Monet completed a process that began with Giotto, and that Cézanne labored "to re-establish a lost tradition."[2] The same process of tracing roots has revealed the extraordinarily slow and partial nature of other "revolutions," whether the cultural one of the Renaissance, many of whose salient features have now been tracked to the twelfth century, or the scientific one of the early twentieth century, which is recognized to have begun as a slow groundswell in the seventeenth century, with remote anticipations in the fourteenth.[3]

Just as, in music, Schönberg traced the genealogy of his twelve-tone method of composition to Beethoven and, beyond, to the classicism of the seventeenth and eighteenth centuries, advocates of the abstract style in the visual arts have traced their intellectual descent through impressionism to mannerist painters, such as Michelangelo and El Greco, and further back to the "symbolism" of Giotto and his contemporaries.

Renaissance painting betrays a variety of styles, at least one in fact for each great painter—styles, moreover, that employ many of the very devices by which the Renaissance legacy is said to have been liquidated in the twentieth century: the attack upon the pictorial surface, the cult of surrealism, the acceptance of chance in execution, and composition by massing planes of color rather than by lines. By its very use of geometry and mathematical structure, Renaissance painting also implied the opposite alternatives, taken up in its Baroque sequel. "The principles of impressionism," Wölfflin argued, were already at work in the art of Velasquez and Rembrandt.[4] Elements of style that came to fulfillment in the nineteenth and twentieth centuries were also contained in the "inexplicitness" of faces in paintings by Giorgione, followed by the "dematerialization" of the subject in portraits by his student, Titian, and, more completely, by El Greco into planes and masses of color evocative of conceptual associations rather than physical ones.[5] Finally, in the mixed styles of Renaissance paintings, two-dimensionality coexisted and even flourished alongside the three-dimensionality of vanishing-point perspective. They appeared conterminously, as in anamorphic paintings (e.g., Holbein's *Ambassadors* contained anamorphic segments), or when, as frequently happened in manuscript illuminations,

[2] Eric Newton, *European Painting and Sculpture* (Baltimore: Penguin, 1964), pp. 232, 234.

[3] See, especially the discussion of the concept of scientific revolution in Stephen Toulmin, *Human Understanding. The Collective Use and Evolution of Concepts* (Princeton: Princeton University Press, 1977), pp. 98ff., 322–23 and passim.

[4] Heinrich Wölfflin, *Principles of Art History: The Problem of the Development of Style in Later Art*, trans. M. D. Hottinger (New York: Dover, n.d.), pp. 21–22.

[5] John Pope-Hennessy, *The Portrait in the Renaissance* (New York: Bollingen Foundation, 1966), pp. 132, 138, 153–54.

human figures were portrayed in the round, against a two-dimensional background. Two-dimensionality normally characterized the first stage in the preliminary sketches by which paintings were made, mechanical and architectural diagrams, and wood-cuts not to mention the remnants of folk art that survive. In itself, therefore, the return of two-dimensionality to modern painting does not reflect a way of seeing foreign to the Renaissance, and, indeed, the juxtaposition of two- and three-dimensionality on the same canvas (for example, by Picasso and Max Ernst) had Renaissance precedents. Far from unidirectional movement of style leading toward the end of the Renaissance legacy, therefore, the history of painting offers a number of styles that existed simultaneously, and pictorial devices that have been employed by extremely diverse, eclectic styles, in the Renaissance and in the nineteenth and twentieth centuries.

Beneath the multiplicity of styles, there runs a richly varied, but continuous stream of thought. For this reason, Morpurgo-Tagliabuë has been able to survey the various schools of contemporary esthetics, and to conclude that, although they look like islands cut off from one another, they are in fact an archipelago, united by basic critical assumptions that are invisible on the surface.[6] In the same way, it has been possible to find a cognitive strategy persisting beneath stylistic changes from Caspar David Friedrich (1774–1840) to Jackson Pollock (1912–56) and Mark Rothko (1903–70).[7] To mention the names of Friedrich, Pollock, and Rothko is also to allude to the contemplative tradition, in its varied forms.

Among the Expressionists and Abstractionists, there was a direct contact with the Neoplatonic spirituality of the late Middle Ages and the Renaissance through literary texts and religious associations. They followed in the intellectual commitments of Dürer and Michelangelo. Neoplatonism took countless forms. Some of them worked strangely in the mind of Van Gogh, whose religious motivation led him to an early, brief, and unfortunate experience as a lay preacher, and never left his intuitive life. Others inspired Kandinsky and collaborators on *der Blaue Reiter*. In yet another theosophical school of thought, they illuminated Mondrian's thinking about the nature and purpose of art. He too equated visual naturalism with materialism, which denied man's spiritual nature. Mind found the realities of the world, Mondrian thought, by turning inward. There, the artist saw, not naturalistic shapes, but living rhythms. Mondrian wished to convey what he saw by creating an arrangement of lines and colors (or "noncolors," such as gray) bound together by exact proportions, and, therefore, by a labile equilibrium. The spiritual reality that the artist saw, and that he meant his

[6] G. Morpurgo-Tagliabuë, *L'Esthétique contemporaine. Une enquête* (Milan: Marzorati, 1960), p. xv. Professor Paolo Cherchi kindly drew my attention to this study.

[7] Robert Rosenblum, *Modern Painting and the Northern Romantic Tradition* (New York: Harper and Row, 1975).

painting to impart by setting up reverberations in the viewer's mind, Mondrian argued, was exactly that rhythm, fluctuating with no final resolution.[8]

Rothko too worked in the tradition that we have described. "The people who weep before my pictures," he wrote, "are having the same religious experience I had when I painted them." The establishment of the Rothko Chapel, "where a group of his paintings might function in a quasi-religious way," demonstrated that this empathetic, indeed sacramental, closure was more than a fiction in the artist's mind,[9] but it was not the same kind of closure as had been sought, for example, in Goethe's age.

WHAT, THEN, IS the evidence that warrants doubting that the contemplative tradition in Western art survived the artistic revolutions of the nineteenth century, except in the critical, self-transforming imitation of art by art? It is worth repeating the consequence, that the hermeneutic gap in painting would consist primarily, if not entirely, in "the riddle of style."[10]

One kind of evidence is the rarity of paintings that portray the event of contemplation. In earlier centuries, ecstasies were abundantly portrayed. One exception to the dearth of such representations in recent times is Gauguin's *Nirvana: Portrait of Meyer de Haan* (ca. 1889, now in the Wadsworth Atheneum, Hartford). Gauguin painted this portrait under eclectic religious impulses that he had absorbed from his friendships with Van Gogh and Jacob Meyer de Haan (1852–1895), who was widely read in the quasi-mystical philosophy that inspired the synthetist group.

Even this particular testimony to the survival of the contemplative tradition indicates a profound change from the works previously discussed. By contrast with the four contemplative works we have considered, the artist in Gauguin's portrait is depicted in a state of inward isolation. He does not hold or regard any object outside himself (e.g., a sculptural fragment). His hand rests on his own heart. The figures behind him are fictions of his self-absorption, and they flee. For the state of mind portrayed is not contemplation, in the sense hitherto applied, as an ecstatic union of knower and

[8] The importance of Neoplatonism in the thought of these Expressionists, and of Plasticists, suggests that caution should be used in arguing that the "Platonic-Christian" idealism, together with its tools of allegory and analogy, has grown bankrupt and void in modern painting. Cf. Karsten Harries, *The Meaning of Modern Art. A Philosophical Interpretation* (Evanston: Northwestern University Press, 1968), pp. 14–15, 156, and passim.

[9] Rosenblum, *Modern Painting and the Northern Romantic Tradition*, p. 215. Compare the remark of Callistratus, *Descriptions* 2, in the third and fourth century after Christ, that the sculptor Scopas had imparted to a statue the divine frenzy within him, and that, to the viewer, art translated imitation into reality. (Loeb ed., Philostratus, *Imagines*, pp. 381–82). See above Chapter 1, n. 75.

[10] E. H. Gombrich, *Art and Illusion: A Study in the Psychology of Pictorial Representation* (Princeton: Princeton University Press, 1969), p. 6, applied the phrase "riddle of style" to the fact that, although the visible world is one, the artistic styles of representing it have profligately varied through the centuries.

known, characterized by discernment and love. Instead, Gauguin has portrayed a state of mind cultivated not in the Christian but in the Buddhist tradition: In Cézanne's words, "the great Buddhist invention, Nirvana, solace without passions, without anecdotes—colors!" Like contemplation, Nirvana was a state of self-forgetting beyond intellect; unlike contemplation, it was void of being and of nonbeing, void even of divine relationship, wisdom, and intent.

The single instance of Gauguin's exoticism points to a comprehensive discontent with the content of meaning in Western art. The vital fact in this change was insistence on the autonomy of art. This blow ended the hypothetical rivalry between nature and art. It invalidated all theories that the power of art to draw the heart through life's whole range of meaning hinged on deception. Furthermore, it removed the grounds for affective bonding by the viewer in and through the painting by calculated misunderstanding.

The revulsion against academic theories that impelled painters as diverse as Courbet and Cézanne and their followers was also a rejection of the concepts of ideal beauty and of the sublime, inherent in doctrines that art imitated nature. Reynolds had considered the ability to detect ideal beauty in a painting the proper task of esthetic judgment. However, that power was not merely innate. It required "a cultivated and prepared artificial state of mind," working through the natural impulses of sensuality and love of the sublime.[11]

Repudiating the sublime entailed barring acquired artificiality of mind together with the representational functions of art through which the mind, educated to the task, could apprehend ideal beauty. Of the components in Reynold's definition, only sensuality was left. Perception of a painting ceased to be a process of detection, of penetrating the deceptions of art to apprehend the realities of nature. It became, instead, a sensory event, or impression, passing and swiftly over. Art, quite intentionally, repudiated the prerequisites for a collective repertoire of pathetic and affective fallacies. Contemplation was replaced by enjoyment. Like all sensory impressions, it was private, "my" experience, which others could duplicate, but not share. The artist became a recorder of sensory impressions, rather than what Leonardo had called "an interpreter between nature and art," who, through philosophical study and scientific observation, had transformed his mind "into the very mind of nature."[12]

The artist's work thus became inward and, to some degree, incommunicable. The reduction of esthetic perception to sensuality, which followed from excluding the sublime and exalting the immediate appeal to the feel-

[11] Joshua Reynolds, *Discourses 8, 13, 15,* in *Discourses on Art,* ed. Stephen O. Mitchell (Indianapolis: Bobbs-Merrill, 1965), pp. 128, 192, 237.
[12] Kenneth D. Keele, *Leonardo da Vinci's Elements of the Science of Man* (New York: Academic Press, 1983), p. 131.

ings, also had consequences for paintings as works of art. The distinctions of style, including notably the grand style, which was calculated above all to convey the sense of the sublime, fell by the wayside. Invention, the choice of subjects—a major prerequisite for the shared, commonly stylized, pathetic and affective fallacies of a community—became a matter of indifference. Gradually, the emphasis on sensory impression, together with awareness that those impressions were expressed and imparted by the manipulation of line and color, led to the radical simplification and in time, for some artists, to the elimination of the subject. The same considerations freed artists from the academic canon of unified composition. The sensory effect of a painting was thought to come not from the number and disposition of figures but from the interplay of color and line. The canvas thus broke up into areas of color. Composition became a thing of fragments. Regarding artists in earlier centuries, Cézanne wrote: "They are capable of contemplating detail. All the rest of the picture will always follow you, will always be present. It is as though you could hear the whole melody of it in your head, no matter which detail you happen to be studying. You cannot tear anything out of the whole. . . . They did not paint patchwork as we do." Bafflement, rather than understanding, became a stated objective.

Before the artistic revolutions of the nineteenth century, what began in sensuality was thought capable of moving through stages of meditation on art's deception to contemplation of the natural truths that deception made it possible to disclose. Innovations, represented by the names "Courbet" and "Cézanne," cast this proposition aside as fictional, and an impairment of art's true objects and powers. The artful search for meaning in and through paintings was a vain hermeneutic, if direct sensory effect was the meaning that a painting had, or if paintings, as self-contained and self-explanatory monads, were the meanings that they had.

Art was not correlated with nature, but with history.[13] The persistent systematic displacements from meaning to sensation applied to the affective hermeneutic of art were possible only because the innovators of the nineteenth century knew the history of art with unprecedented completeness. Quite different circumstances attended the rational heremeneutic of words.

Although they derided great museums as "necropolises of art," innovators still discovered in those relatively new foundations dossiers, as it were, of previous experiments. New, inexpensive devices of pictorial reproduction enlarged the geographical sample of materials available to artists in their rivalry with their predecessors. By the same channels, non-European elements—especially the collections of Asianists and anthropologists—opened to artists ways of manipulating line and color that stood in powerful and instructive contrast with European precedent. An interplay between

[13] Gombrich, *Art and Illusion*, pp. 393–94.

painting and photography also disclosed visual effects unknown to earlier generations and provided yet another body of evidence with which earlier artistic achievements were compared.

But all these materials passed through literary filters—that is, through volumes of scholarly analysis, journals, correspondence, and debate. Schleiermacher, Hegel and others had already drawn a line between art and the scientific (or historical) study of art. The achievement of nineteenth-century innovators in painting was to establish this distinction within the enterprise of painting itself. Their comparative, historical study in the Gallery of the Louvre and in other collections inspired Impressionists to abandon the single-image painting, with its monocular focus, which made full sense only when seen from one vantage point, well-defined by the artist. Their comparative historical studies and syntheses also prompted their experiments with light, which were equally experiments with multiple images in one frame, and the precedents that they built upon precedents opened the way to even more sweeping multiplicity among Cubists and Abstractionists in their fascination with making rhythm visible, and among photographers, like Edward Steichen (1879–1973), influenced by them.

Comparative knowledge of art history in the nineteenth century has given modern and contemporary art the character of a widening series of reactions. A painting by Rothko presupposes the experiments in abstraction from the Impressionists on, and, by extension, it defines itself as an innovation only with reference to the entire course of representational art in the West. It has meaning not so much in itself as in a manifold context of understanding and feeling that has matured for centuries.

Thus, even though critical comparison had the effect of distinguishing between present art and past, it also had the effect of making historical—that is, verbal—discourse part of the composition. A picture became a document, or statement. It could be "read" as a pictograph or hieroglyph. In fact, a picture, like a poem, became "what happens when it is read,"[14] a sensory experience weighed "on the scales of words."[15]

Contemplation of the sublime in nature through art was thought to take the viewer out of himself; it was said to overpower and possess the entire mind, confound the judgment, and eclipse all that was merely reasonable or pleasant, even as it also imparted greatness of soul. However, replacing the correlation between nature and art with that between history and art excluded this experience of timelessness. The object was anything but the "sleep" of contemplation. The calculated misunderstanding of visual images that shaped pathetic and affective fallacies and made art a gateway

[14] Christopher Caudwell, *Illusion and Reality: A Study of the Sources of Poetry* (New York: International, 1966), p. 40.

[15] Hans-Georg Gadamer, *Truth and Method* (New York: Crossroad, 1985), p. 359. See the basic definitions elaborated in Chapter 9.

to nature had permitted affective participation between the viewer (including the artist as viewer) and the subject that escaped the finitude of time. Thus, Schleiermacher wrote that viewers could reexperience the creative process by which a work had been composed. By contrast, the correlation between history and art, accentuating verbal discourse, also accentuated understanding (not calculated misunderstanding) as interpretation (not as affective participation). The event of seeing became bound to the moment in which the sensation occurred, and subordinate to the verbal understanding available to the viewer in his finite situation. It was not necessary for understanding to accompany seeing. The viewer was not thought to penetrate in and through the picture, or to participate in the timelessness of its primordial, hidden contents.

Instead, the picture was thought to become contemporary with the viewer through his experience. The "play of art,"[16] was an event of contemporaneity, not of timelessness. It occurred in the physical encounter by which the viewer "participated in the action" of the painting. "All in all, the creative act is not performed by the artist alone; the spectator brings the work in contact with the external world by deciphering and interpreting its inner qualifications and thus adds his contribution to the creative act."[17] As a result, the spectator does not participate in a hidden beauty or reexperience the original process of composition. What he sees is what he sees; he expands the "creative act" by his seeing; and, as viewers increase in number, the "creative act" ramifies, not by silencing the judgment in awe, but by multiplying direct experiences and perhaps (but not necessarily) decipherments and interpretations.

Supplanting the correlation between nature and art with another between history and art had one further consequence for hermeneutics. The autonomy of art, in its historical situation, limited the questions of art to those arising from painterly techniques and media. Painting was freed of the "illusion" or "deception" of representation and, thereby, from the necessity of meaning. The "deficiencies" of painting could be considered such only when compared with the capacities of nature. They constituted a hermeneutic gap only when they were thought to form an enigma of representation. Once the autonomy of art was realized, the "deficiencies" that had earlier been judged enigmatic were able to become, among others, the subjects of painting. The riddle of style replaced the enigma of meaning.

Some artists, to be sure, invented ways to overcome, or to appear to overcome, the exigencies of painting, moving from collage to relief to the three-dimensionality of sculpture, composing the vibrations of op art and kinetic art, adding sound and other effects to those of painting in multimedia com-

---

[16] Gadamer, *Truth and Method,* pp. 108–18.
[17] Marcel Duchamp (1957), quoted by Helen Franc, *An Invitation to See* (New York: Museum of Modern Art, 1973), p. 10.

positions, happenings, and environments. The Impressionists' discoveries in the representation of shimmering light and the Nonobjectivists' in that of rhythms were early responses to this impulse.

But others embraced the exigencies of the medium. The silence of painting evolved into the elimination of narrative and of identifiable subjects; its emptiness, into the "empty" paintings of Rothko and Barnett Newman; its darkness, into dissolution of masses, for example, by Pollock, Noland, and Castellani, and by Reinhardt in his all-black paintings. The process of elimination by which these former "deficiencies" became the subjects of painting led some to attempt the elimination of elimination itself, in which the absence of painting became the subject.

Transforming what had been deficiencies of painting into its subjects entailed denying the fragmentary character of the work of art. Lacking "deficiencies" by comparison with nature, it was possible for the silence, emptiness, and darkness to be complete in themselves, rather than voids enticing viewers to enter into the work of art and expand it by empathetic participation.

The character of a fragment had been essential to the effect of paintings as objects of contemplation, the basis on which viewers moved, by empathetic participation, from fragment to form. To deny the fragmentary character of a painting and to reconstruct its hermeneutic gap around the riddle of style had implications for the fourth "disability" of painting—its inertia (or immobility), including its correspondence with its environment. Acceleration and proliferation in stylistic innovation were two. But they expressed and strengthened a prior and greater implication, which has been called the desacralization of art.

Detachment from nature, the sublime, and ideal beauty, together with the exposure of forgeries, copies, and misattributions rendered the painting and its effects creatures of transient circumstances, perishable in their significance, as well as in their physical existence, rather than effluences of preternatural and enduring inspiration. The environment of viewing paintings correspondingly changed. Instead of galleries designed for permanent exhibition, museums redesigned galleries as exhibit spaces that, in their anonymous decor, could accommodate either permanent or changing exhibits. The display of paintings, as in the Palatine Gallery at the Pitti Palace, "not in any logical order, but as decoration to the rooms" ceased. Instead, as was appropriate for documents or specimens, logical arrangements were imposed, corresponding with the historical origins of the paintings and dispersing and illuminating the works so that they could be "read," without the obscurity, mutual cancelation, and visual displacements inevitable in earlier modes of display. Galleries became laboratories, rather than places of awe, laboratories for the ever self-extinguishing and self-renewing "play of art." They were not designed to impart the "feeling of solemnity" that struck Goethe when he visited the Painting Gallery in Dresden, a feeling, Goethe continued, "which so much the more resembles the sensation with which one treads a church, because the ornaments of so many a temple, the objects of so much adoration, as now re-erected here, serve the sacred purposes of art."[18]

It is now possible to identify some differences between Goethe's perception of the sacred in Dresden and the "quasi-religious" empathy experienced by visitors to the Rothko Chapel. The naturalism that Goethe cherished in Dutch paintings, the ideal beauty that, he believed, they mysteriously imparted and concealed as fragmentary revelations, and the power of older religious paintings to be rededicated to "the sacred purposes of art" had no place in Rothko's work or in emotional responses to it.

Instead, the "quasi-religious" experiences of Rothko and the viewers of his paintings demanded a direct sensory perception, including the proportion of scale between painting and viewer; conscious decipherment and interpretation; and the acceptance of silence, emptiness, darkness and inertia—not inertia of the work of art, but of the continual moment of self-negation by viewers as they entered into and expanded "the creative act," the hermeneutic situation. There is no room for the concept of the painting or of the viewer as fragmentary.

It is also possible to understand why, in its exaltation of silence, emptiness, darkness, and inertia, Western art departed from the contemplative tradition, rather than entering into it the more fully, as did Chinese art, for example, in which expression was achieved "through *absence* of brush and ink."[19] For the divorce of art from nature prevented those elements from leading in and through the riddle of style to the enigmas of life.

I CONTEND THAT esthetic bonding through imitation underlay major, even iconoclastic, changes in style in recent generations; that the correlation of nature and art was replaced by one of present and past art; and that rational understanding as interpretation became prior to, or even supplanted, calculated misunderstanding as affective participation.

Two examples will illustrate these contentions: Gustave Courbet's (1819–77) *The Stonebreakers* (1849) and Picasso's *Guernica* (1937). The first was an exercise in extreme naturalism; the second, in abstraction.

Courbet painted *The Stonebreakers*, inspired by the hopes and failure of the Revolution of 1848. The impact of the work derived exactly from the realism with which Courbet portrayed his subjects. Courbet himself alleged that he saw nothing but a historical representation in the picture. But other viewers at once recognized a symbolic, or allegorical, message in it: namely,

[18] *Dichtung und Wahrheit*, II. 8.
[19] Gombrich, *Art and Illusion*, p. 208.

that toil had reduced laborers to faceless, degraded anonymous objects, but objects of vast, if latent, power. Some viewers found the picture a ludicrous caricature. Others were repelled by it. Immediately, a friend of Courbet acclaimed the picture as the first monument to the laboring class. It was perhaps an exaggeration when he added that the workers of Courbet's village, Ornans, wished to hang the work as an altarpiece in their church, but it is a fact that the painting became a symbolic focus for socialist and communist thought about art, and, until destroyed by an air raid on Dresden in 1945, an icon revered as the object of pilgrimage.

The scandal that *The Stonebreakers* raised—reinforced by Courbet's *Funeral at Ornans*, exhibited with it in 1850—was due precisely to Courbet's use of traditional methods to achieve an untraditional naturalism. After his arrival in Paris (1840), Courbet had painstakingly studied the great Renaissance paintings in the Louvre, analyzing and copying sections of them day after day to master their techniques of composition. He appropriated methods of the Neoclassicists. Yet, to viewers who read it allegorically, and took the message to heart, *The Stonebreakers* conveyed a vivid degradation foreign to Velasquez, to Titian, even to Caravaggio, and to the other artists whose works he sketched in the Louvre. This achievement made Courbet's naturalism (depending on the critic's viewpoint) a deformation or a reformation of earlier varieties of realism and also gave it its profound allegorical resonance in socialist ideologies.

Through his painting, Courbet effected an iconoclasm as complete as he did, toward the end of his career, by destroying the Vendôme column during the heyday of the Paris Commune. The iconoclastic effects of his painting derived from the esthetic bonding with earlier paintings that he achieved through carefully developed habits of previsual and visual apprehension. The pathetic and affective fallacies that they evoked sprang not primarily from the positive values of *The Stonebreakers*, but from the ideological— that is, verbal—modes of interpretation in which viewers read it.

One twentieth-century painting ranks with Courbet's *Stonebreakers* as an instantly recognized symbol of collective values—Picasso's *Guernica*, a work acclaimed as prophetic and deeply allegorical. It is paradoxical that Courbet's contemporaries condemned or praised him for having cut loose from tradition by his naturalism, while some, at least, of Picasso's have judged him to be a revolutionary precisely through his adherence to, and recasting of, tradition.

Picasso began sketches for his painting almost immediately after the destruction of the city of Guernica by Picasso's enemies, the Fascists, during an air raid (26 April 1937), an incident in the Spanish Civil War. He completed the work in less than two months, as a protest, both partisan and universal, against the atrocity.

Picasso lacked the affection for philosophy, the intense personal spirituality, and the revulsion against "materialism" in art that placed other abstractionists in the Neoplatonic tradition. But, through the closest companions that he had as a young man in Barcelona, and later in Paris, he deeply sensed the conflict between matter and spirit that impelled them into Abstractionism. For that reason, the works of El Greco and Gothic sculpture had a lasting attraction for him. He sought the same verities in them as he did in ancient sculpture, in geometric forms, in the illumination of medieval manuscripts, in Mannerist paintings of seventeenth century, and in the shapes of shells, and animals, and microscopic creatures.

He was seeking to discover the underlying structure of all things by which, like Kandinsky and Mondrian with their philosophical convictions, he meant principles of movement, or rhythmic construction. *Guernica*, one of his best documented paintings, is also one of the clearest combinations of mimetic impulses and abstract representation. For there, he employed symbols, themes, and gestures drawn from ancient, medieval, and Renaissance art with a style from which colors (except shades of grey) were excluded, together with naturalistic perspective. His allusions to some specific compositions of earlier centuries are explicit. *Guernica* is a work, furthermore, true to the Cubist style, in which proportion existed only among the elements of the composition, and bore no relation to visual reality, and the forms were entirely unmodeled and allusive.[20] The old and the new are epitomized in a symbol that presides over the entire composition, an eye with a lightbulb as its pupil. In his first sketches, Picasso put a sun where the eye now is. His later changes combine that symbol for light (or rational understanding) and justice with the eye, another symbol of rational knowledge. For our purposes, it is also pertinent that, in the mimetic tradition, the enlightened eye was symbolically interchangeable with the mirror. Picasso had employed the light and the mirror as symbols of truth in an earlier series of Minotaur etchings; he here repeated that usage. The artist himself emphasized that *Guernica* was unique among his works in its symbolic, or allegorical, message, but there are in fact many other examples of his reuse of symbols in ways that are allegorical, though less saturated with allegorical meaning than *Guernica*.

Viewers read different messages in *Guernica*, as they had in *The Stonebreakers*. To some, it was incomprehensible. To others, it was a notably pathological specimen of a revolting style, a symptom of social disintegration. But, to those attuned to Picasso's style or ideology, *Guernica* became a powerful symbol. It was capable of becoming such even to viewers who brought to the painting literary associations and ideologies foreign to those of Picasso himself. One of these, a Greek poet, associating the picture with the fall of Constantinople, in 1453, asked a pertinent question.

[20] See Anthony Blunt, *Picasso's 'Guernica'* (New York: Oxford University Press, 1969).

Picasso, did you know
or did you not?
You leant on Byzantium as you created *Guernica*.

Byzantium
in its last glory
as the last Konstandinos,
King Paleológos,
like victory-death
charged amid your horses.

   Equally like him
your horses feel
the fall of that City,
this is why they are so dead
in their incomparable vigor.

When I see the painting
I envisage you,
an undoubted
Byzantine.[21]

Both *The Stonebreakers* and *Guernica* belong to a genre of painting delib-erately intended to produce moral action by arousing esthetic judgment—the genre of political, or social, art.

Their intent and their effects were ideological. The iconoclasm of style, naturalist and Cubist, was achieved by esthetic bonding that the artists formed by imitating, and assimilating, the styles of past artists. But these sympathies of admiration and rivalry did not engage the viewer. The esthetic qualities of the works, produced not only by style, but by the use of somber colors and by the immense sizes of both paintings, were subor-dinate to ideological sympathies. Their esthetic effects impelled viewers to moral action only after they were read, deciphered, and interpreted through the filter of words. The calculated misunderstanding by which, in previous generations, one passed in and through the deficiencies of painting to empa-thetic participation, transcending the finitude of history, is absent.

In stylistic iconoclasm, *The Stonebreakers*, *Guernica*, and the prolifera-tion of schools that they represent, reveal an ancient legacy. Do they belong to the contemplative tradition in Western art? Courbet and Picasso could at least respond as Wittgenstein did when told that his work was "not philos-ophy." "My arguments," he is supposed to have answered, "may not be

---

[21] Kóstas Kindínis, "Guernica," *Poems: Reinvestigations and Descent from the Cross*, trans. Kimon Friar (Minneapolis: Nostos, 1980), p. 34.

'philosophical' in any previous definition of the word, but they are the 'legitimate heirs' to what was previously known as 'philosophy.' ''[22]

THE ANTECEDENTS of artistic representation of movement (e.g., Marcel Duchamps's *Nude Descending a Staircase,* 1912, now in the Philadelphia Museum of Art) were present in literature about the relation between art and nature long before they were realized in paintings and longer still before they were realized in photography. Similarly, the hermeneutic effects of disrupting the correlation and rivalry between nature and art were explored in nineteenth-century writings, decades before they became evident in painting. At that moment of transition, when authors could move both in the intellectual world that was passing and in the one that was coming to be, they clearly perceived that the autonomy of art weakened affective participation in and through paintings, and that the calculated esthetic misunderstanding basic to participation was being subordinated to understanding as verbal interpretation.

Oscar Wilde's (1856–1900) *The Picture of Dorian Gray* (1891) is the narrower and more superficial of the two works that I shall discuss. It is a kind of morality play. It expresses the same devotion to art for its own sake (not for the sake of beauty as a moral good) that had given Wilde a certain distinction while he was still an undergraduate at Oxford, and the same morbid fascination that, two years after *Dorian Gray*'s publication, made his *Salome* an international scandal. A very handsome young man, Dorian Gray, has his portrait painted. He became corrupt, but the physical signs of chronic debauchery and the ravages of age appeared on the portrait, instead of on his body. In a last outburst of depravity, he attacked the portrait, which he acknowledged as his soul; he instantly died and the marks of evil deformed his body, leaving the portrait once more the image of the outer beauty that had been his.

Many lines of meaning run through this story, including inevitably the relation between creator and image. The painter revealed himself, the secret of his own soul, on the canvas. The artist-creator, in this case, did not produce his own image, though he invested the image with the expressive likeness of his artistry and love. The artist's devotion to Dorian Gray infused the portrait with a living ideal that made it possible for Dorian's wish to be granted, and for the portrait to become "the most magical of mirrors." The portrait was more than a mirror reflecting the surface. Wilde's primary concern was the divorce between surface and symbol, contrary to the nature of art, which is actually both. The split between the romantic passion and the

---

[22] Toulmin, *Human Understanding,* pp. 241–42; cf. pp. 146–47. Correspondingly, Heidegger also insisted that philosophy had always been a Greek enterprise, and that it remained so in his hands. Cf. Martin Heidegger, *Was ist das—die Philosophie?* (Pfullingen: Neske, 1956).

Greek perfection, between soul and body, had led, in Wilde's terms, to "a realism that is vulgar, an ideality that is void." Dorian Gray's soul was transposed from his body and located in the portrait; surface and symbol, body and soul, reality and spirit were sundered. Wilde's point was, further, that art and life (or nature) had been split apart, and this was the lesson of his morality play.

It is dangerous, Wilde says, to read the symbol. Art mirrors the spectator and not life. It depends upon the pathetic and affective fallacies. But the burden of his story is that to acknowledge this rule, to expect no hidden unity beneath the surface, to live in narcissistic self-admiration invites destruction. It is also that the modern world leaves no alternative to spiritual desolation.

The ultimate vacuity of being, beauty, and truth, and the emptiness of the forms of life that occurred because ideal and existence were irreconcilably split drove Dorian on until he murdered the artist who had painted "the most magical of mirrors," and fatally attacked the portrait, his own soul.

With meticulous care, Wilde examined three kinds of esthetic bonding, three areas in which the pathetic and affective fallacies occurred: those between the subject of the portrait and the portrait (pp. 11, 30, 105, 117),[23] the artist and the work of art (pp. 12, 62, 127), and the reviewer and the work of art (p. 39). Wilde developed a fourth, that between the artist and the subject, as the core of an affective triangle between the artist in love with the subject, the subject in love with himself in the portrait, and the portrait itself. In passing, Wilde alluded to a natural sympathy of "chemical atoms" between the portrait and the subject—a "horrible sympathy" by which atom called to atom "in secret love of strange affinity" (pp. 105, 117), an archaic survival of the alchemical sympathies in which John Donne believed he had found scientific analogies for affective bonding (see Chapter 3, after n. 9). But this allusion to sympathetic magic, or alchemy, was incidental.

Wilde's principal contention was that esthetic bondings occurred through the sensations, not through natural affinity. Art was not, he thought, a convergence of universal beauty with material form. A painting was no more than its material form and color. Art was "simply a method of procuring extraordinary sensations" (p. 236). A painting concealed, rather than embodying, the artist and his creative passion (p. 127). The effect of art, and thus the degree of esthetic participation that could be achieved, lay in the measure to which the spectator found himself mirrored in the work of art—that is, the degree to which art became for the spectator "a form of autobiography" (cf. pp. viii, 12).

[23] References are to the Modern Library edition (New York: Random House, 1926).

The destruction of Dorian's "autobiography," his portrait, was his own death. Sympathy (bearing the connotations of empathy) was, for Wilde, reduced to subjective isolation in the pathetic and affective fallacies. What appeared to be sympathetic affinity was in fact the projection of the spectator rebounding back to him from the object of his glance, as from a mirror, and stimulating his senses.

Clearly, Wilde anticipated the doctrine that the viewer did not reexperience the original creative process of the artist, but rather expanded it in a new, historical, and therefore transient situation.

Significantly, he cast his narrative against a background of play. Play is everywhere, in the form of drama, music, puppetry, hunting, and players at a game passing counters; there is the play of love and, above all, the play of representational art. By invoking play so frequently and in such diverse forms, Wilde did more than indicate the luxurious social context of his story. He accentuated the double nature of human beings and the importance of pathetic and affective fallacies in their lives. For, as he wrote, they were spectators of the play in which they were also actors, narcissistically enthralled, and perhaps destroyed, by "the mere wonder" mirrored in the spectacle that was themselves (pp. 111–12).

Wilde concerned himself primarily with the divorce between life and representational art. He believed that this was only part of a much wider disintegration, that of a culture that drew its symbolic meanings in words. He pointed to this broad bewilderment of philological culture at the very crux of his story. Dorian's corruption began with the insinuation of Lord Henry's words, words that, unlike music, created another world, instead of another chaos, in him. His corruption was sealed by words, by the reading of a book about the decay of beauty. "Dorian Gray had been poisoned by a book" (p. 162).

More than twenty years before Wilde published *The Picture of Dorian Gray*, another Englishman had described the disintegration of philological culture in mimetic terms. That man was C. L. Dodgson (Lewis Carroll, 1832–98). His work was *Through the Looking-Glass* (1872). Dodgson was admirably qualified to consider the area of transformation in which visual and verbal images turned into one another. He would have liked to be an artist: he was in fact an accomplished photographer. He was by profession an Anglican deacon, a mathematician, and a philosopher. He was among the earliest students of the branch of philosophy that came to be known as symbolic logic, in which mathematical symbols are used instead of words. As a mathematician, he lived in a world where Euclidean geometry no longer held the field. Other, equally plausible, geometries had been invented according to which parallel lines could meet and straight lines described circles, or which established any number of finite dimensions, thus allowing two or more objects to occupy the same space at the same time. As a cleric, he became embroiled in the furious dispute that disrupted the Church of England and led to the secessions of Manning and Newman to Rome, a dispute that raised, not only ecclesiastical obedience, but also the metaphysical questions of space, time, movement, and corporality that were embedded in the doctrine of transubstantiation, and the new problems that Darwin's concept of evolution presented to the theological doctrines of creation, fall, redemption, and Second Coming.

Dodgson could see that the coherence of the world expressed in visual and in verbal mirages had vanished. The canons of proportion and mass, of space and time, of beauty, and, thus, of meaning had not been invalidated. A worse fate had overtaken them. They had become ambiguous. Opposites had become identical. Other conterminous canons had emerged beside the former canons; much of the incoherence in Dodgson's stories occurs through his very skillful juxtaposition of the old canons with the new.

Like Wilde, Dodgson portrayed the spectator's perception as normative. Unlike Wilde, he represented the understanding, not sensation, as dominant. The crux of his narrative was the perplexity that spectators interpret the same visual or verbal images in quite different, and even in contradictory, ways, and that an individual mind can be baffled by the sensory images that it receives. What is nonsense to some is sense to others. Some can, and others cannot, believe impossible things. Unicorns think that children are fabulous (i.e., mythic) creatures.

Subject and object may exist in different dimensions. No matter how fast runners may go, they may never pass the trees and other things around them (as they perceive them).

Overarching these general propositions is Dodgson's theory that visual images, the things that one sees or thinks one sees, are known by verbal images—that is, by the names attached to the visual images. Verbal understanding intrudes itself into visual perception. The Fawn and Alice walked together as friends until, having left the wood of forgetfulness, they recalled their own, and each other's names, and the mutual fear encased in those names. The name of a song is not what the song really is, and portmanteau words (words of multiple connotations) intervene between things and the understanding of those things.

Dodgson cut through the miscomprehension caused by imposing verbal images on visual images when he wrote that the best way to explain a thing was to do it (*Adventures in Wonderland*, chap. 12). But the invincible quandary was that the world of direct sensory experience was known through the looking glass of words. The looking-glass world was incoherent, judged by the standards of actual existence. To be sure, it had its own coherence—the coherence of universal madness, perhaps that of a game (meaningless outside itself) in which everyone plays according to the rules. Like Wilde, Dodgson skillfully underscored his ideas with metaphors of play, whether drawn from chess, or knightly duels, croquet, cards, or riddles that had no answers.

Indeed, one submits to be played by the game. All meaning consists in the regulated movement of play, and at the moment of play. When one refuses to submit to being played by the game and unmasks the artificiality of order, the game, with all its coherence and correspondence, ends, and only its meaningless instruments (e.g., a scattered pack of cards) are left (*Adventures in Wonderland*, chap. 12).

Which is insane—the world of direct perception, or the world in which the name becomes the thing? Dodgson put the question differently. He asked which was the reality and which, the dream. Tweedledum and Twee-dledee reduced Alice to tears by insisting that she was not real, but only a figment of the Red King's dream, and, on awaking, Alice herself asked who dreamed it all. "He was part of my dream, of course—but then I was part of his dream, too!" (chap. 12). As one reads Dodgson's concluding verses on children,

> Dreaming as the days go by,
> Dreaming as the summers die:
>
> Ever drifting down the stream—
> Lingering in the golden gleam—
> Life, what is it but a dream?

one senses a disquieting reality in the apparent incoherence of the Red Queen's query: "What do you suppose is the use of a child without any meaning? Even a joke should have some meaning—and a child's more important than a joke, I hope" (chap. 9).

Dodgson employed an ancient theme in literature, which was gaining new force, when he implied that dreams might be a way to knowledge outside that accessible to rational discourse; he was a link between the ample literature of oracular dreams and miraculous visions and the modern psychological and psychiatric study of dreams. He was greatly interested in psychic research, and his writings, and his own life, have yielded fascinating materials both to Freudians and to Jungians.

Dodgson and Wilde portrayed the quandary of relating visual and verbal images in different ways. Still, they both sensed the discrepancy between esthetic perception and verbal expression. More plainly than Wilde, Dodgson characterized words as the means by which we impose form, and therefore meaning and intelligibility, on the visual world. But language, he affirmed, was not a mirror of reality; it created its own quite arbitrary and ambiguous game of fictions that existed inside the world of being, perhaps without touching it at any point. Verbal and visual images commanded dif-

ferent repertories of pathetic and affective fallacy. Dodgson left the possibility that the world of names might be a barrier to true knowledge from
which we could escape only through the power of dreams—that is, in the
realm of previzualization when one sees without the sense of sight, and is
not played by the game of language.

CONCLUSION

As LITERATURE AND THEOLOGY were pervaded by historical standards of judgment from the eighteenth century onward, the possibilities of esthetic bonding were seen to narrow. This constriction occurred because human existence itself, and with it human knowledge, came to be seen as creatures of finite historical situations that could not recur. Human actions and feelings, confined to nonrecurring situations, could not teach by example; they were inimitable; they could not be reexperienced or performed by spectators.

The same narrowing occurred in the history of painting, but in a distinctive fashion. Whereas literature and theology were verbal enterprises, painting engaged both visual and verbal perceptions. Painting labored under the exigencies of two media, those of the painter and of the author. Thus, the game of bonding through understanding combined the hermeneutic of visual, with that of verbal, images. The "deficiencies" of painting were fundamental to the formation of the hermeneutic gap and, therefore, to the whole endeavor of understanding in art. It diminishes the complexity of the hermeneutic play in art to portray that enterprise as fundamentally linguistic. For to "read" a painting as a hieroglyph or pictograph is to discount a range of apprehension, unknown in verbal discourse, that could not be deciphered or interpreted, but that could only be done or experienced. It is also to blur the distinctions between pathetic and affective fallacies accessible through words and those accessible through visual images. As Jackson Pollock commented on his painting, *The She-Wolf*, "Any attempt on my part to say something about it, to attempt explanation of the inexplicable, could only destroy it."[1]

This twofold game of apprehension in art has existed throughout the period that we have considered, but with significant changes. As long as art was regarded as a second, imitative nature, a sympathy was thought to run between art and the "inexplicable" order, or ideal beauty in nature and outside of time. After art came to be regarded as autonomous, the "inexplicable" included sensory perceptions of the artist and the sensory responses of viewers, both of which were limited to particular historical situations. The game set in motion by the hermeneutic gap in painting no longer circled around the perennial enigmas of nature or life, but around the time-bound riddle of style. Visual apprehension was informed by verbal understanding.

[1] Quoted in Franc, *An Invitation to See*, p. 83.

Yet, the "inexplicable" in style retained some measure of its iconoclastic legacy from the "inexplicable" in the rapport between nature and art. The mimetic absorption of earlier ways of visual expression through the interplay of forgetting and copying lay at the heart of the rapid proliferation of styles in the nineteenth and twentieth centuries. Art converged with iconoclasm, and amorous with malevolent sympathies.

Much has been said in the preceding chapters about the iconoclasm of innovators. But, in the evolution of values in painting, as in biological evolution, the mimetic struggle for survival was by no means one-sided. My account would be incomplete if I did not, at least briefly, indicate the iconoclasm of those hostile to particular innovative styles. I shall not speak of the destruction of paintings by the Nazi regime, or of other iconoclastic campaigns that, like the Nazis', belonged to immense networks of convictions and goals that had nothing to do with art. Instead, I shall rest content with an episode in the life of one man, an incident when the pathetic and affective fallacies issued, not in bonding, but in revulsion.

In 1954, the House of Commons commissioned Graham Sutherland to paint a portrait of Winston Churchill. With every mark of esteem, the House presented the portrait to Churchill on the occasion of his eightieth birthday. Despite its glittering pomp, the occasion was tense. When he saw the picture a few days before the ceremonial presentation, Churchill had been horrified by what he considered the simian features on the canvas. He spoke of publicly condemning and rejecting the gift. In the event, Churchill concealed his violent reaction and accepted the picture; but, because his loathing continued to fester, his wife secretly ordered it destroyed in 1955 or 1956. The portrait was a very celebrated work in the oeuvre of a major twentieth-century painter, and it was highly regarded by many critics. Having been commissioned by the House of Commons as a signal honor to Churchill, it was a public monument of considerable interest. Between 1956 and her death (1977), Lady Churchill naturally received many requests to see or exhibit the picture. Only in 1965 did she tell the members of her family that it had been destroyed, and in 1978, after her death, her executors announced its fate to the public at large.[2]

Churchill's anger notably represents the failure of a viewer to pass from relationship to identity with a picture. An artist himself, Churchill was offended not by the technical qualities of the painting, but by the discrepancy that Sutherland's style introduced between the values that Churchill saw in the visible picture and those in the invisible image that he cherished of himself. The style violently frustrated the pathetic and affective fallacies that he expected to experience in the portrait. It was not possible for him to

[2] This is the account given by the Churchills' daughter, Mary Soames, in *Clementine Churchill* (Boston: Houghton Mifflin, 1979), p. 445–46, 501–503. I am indebted to Mr. Christopher Blunt for this reference.

pass from visible to invisible because, as a sign and symbol, and perhaps even as sacrament, the painting mocked a need for empathy that the painter did not feel.

The reasons behind Churchill's violent response, bearing as they do on the role of style in empathetic participation, elucidate a much wider phenomenon. They cast some light on the conflict between older points of view, represented by Churchill, and newer ones, represented by Sutherland. From the latter, the contemplative tradition has become attenuated in Western art, as in other enterprises of formal thought, including literature and theology, because the play of human existence has come to be regarded as historical rather than metaphysical. Thus, the assumption of a universal hermeneutic of art, depending on calculated, stylized misunderstanding rooted in pathetic and affective fallacies, has been dispelled.

However, one metaphor links its present, attenuated forms, with its earlier, the metaphor of the game. It was natural that a game should consistently be recognized as the point at which visual apprehension intersected with verbal understanding. Common human experience demonstrates that visual and verbal perceptions are transformed into one another by the imitative, comparative, and critical performances or enactments of play, notably of play for stakes.

A game has always been at issue, a collective enterprise with and against others. But change has modified even this enduring metaphor. In the sixteenth century, Armenini scorned a writer who had classed painting among servile and trivial diversions of life. Affirming art's power, by benign deception, to teach virtue, inspire piety, and confer everlasting fame, he declared that the offensive writer did "not know any of the cards [in the game of art], although it has more than any game."[3] By contrast, Francis Bacon (in 1963) judged art to be a pastime played by man to divert himself from the futility of existence, played competitively, with increasing virtuosity, "so that he can make life a bit more exciting."[4] Bacon's irony, empty of love's renewing vigor and freshness, was anticipated in the game metaphors of Wilde and Dodgson; the sardonic emphasis on virtuosity for its own sake shared by all three men would not be softened by applying Reynold's assertion that, because the distinction of an artist depended on hard work, "not upon a trick, he is free from the painful suspicions of a juggler, who lives in perpetual fear least nis trick should be discovered."[5]

If a wider view is taken, and the subject of painting is considered the dynamics of the human mind, neither deception nor diversion is adequate to define the objects of the game. Then, one confronts common human

[3] *On the True Precepts*, I. 3, p. 102.

[4] Herschel B. Chipp, ed., *Theories of Modern Art: A Source Book by Artists and Critics* (Berkeley: University of California Press, 1970), p. 621.

[5] *Discourse 2*, in *Discourses on Art*, p. 25.

needs that abide throughout time, erotic needs; and the predicament at the core of thought and feeling is posed, not by the limitations of medium or imagination, but by perennial desires, violent and unsatisfied by the surrounding world. What is fragmentary in the "I" yearns for unity with the "you." Such desires ignite contemplation; through the responsory of needful call and giving answer, never silenced and always urgent, they have driven Western art forward in its restless course, and the evolution of moral good.

We shall never really know what motives, other than esthetic repulsion, led Lady Churchill to destroy the Sutherland portrait, or what combination of offended propriety and agitated memories inflamed those motives. Yet, the parallel with Dorian Gray recalls the equivalence, expressed also in sympathetic magic, between image and subject. Thus, it also illustrates the cost for players in the hermeneutic double game of word and vision, for societies as well as individual persons, whose bonding to images of past luck makes every new throw a loss.

EPILOGUE ON DISCARDED ALTARPIECES

ALMOST AT THE very beginning of this book, we considered John Donne's verses on the delight that painters take "not in made work, but whiles they make" (Chapter 3, n. 79). All that we have said locates the bonding of the "I" and the "you" in art in the creative act, but we have also seen that the creative act may occur, not once only, but many times. It may occur, as Donne wrote, when a painting is first made. Or it may occur repeatedly, as often as viewers imaginatively reexperience the creative instant when artist and painting both were one and began their separate existences. In neither case could the painting be a memory of a past act, the memorial of a bonding that had taken place and was over, for in both the instant and the experience of bonding were in progress.

Some measure of the change described in the preceding chapters exists in a comparison of disputes over altarpieces. I have refrained from discussing religious painting since the Iconoclastic Dispute. The reason is that, on balance, a discussion of such art would necessarily survey a category of work that is exceptional, due partly to the general conservatism of style in religious art, and partly to the liturgical functions for which many religious paintings were made as visual components. If it is not denatured by being placed in a secular environment (such as a museum), religious art is one with its "ritualistic context."[1]

However, a brief comparison of controversies over altarpieces may serve to underscore the narrowing by nonfigurative styles of the scope for a hermeneutic grounded in pathetic and affective fallacies and return us to religious art, the point of our departure.

In 1986, an altarpiece by Willem de Kooning (1904-   ) was removed from St. Peter's Lutheran Church, in New York. The painting, a large triptych, consisted of irregular, sinuously interlacing bands of blue, yellow, and red on a white ground. True to the artist's practice of action painting, it lacked title as well as subject, nor, as his wife commented, did he "stick in a cross or any of the symbols." Although it was intended to have a kind of religious "consciousness" about it, its religious character was objectively recognizable only by its position in a place of worship.

The triptych's admirers found that it deepened their "experience of worship," because it embodied St. Peter's commitment to late twentieth-century architecture, art, and music in its liturgies. The work's detractors

---

[1] E. H. Gombrich, *Art and Illusion: A Study in the Psychology of Pictorial Representation* (Princeton: Princeton University Press, 1969), p. 191.

asserted that it impeded concentration, looking "like graffiti," and posing, for those who sought meaning, "a personal Rorschach test." In either case, the scope for pathetic or affective fallacy included only esthetic sentiments; the avoidance of subject and figure excluded the viewer from entering into, and reliving, a commonly recognizable scene, or participating in the lived reality of persons depicted. Neither the positive values nor the "deficiencies" of painting pretended to manifest secrets, or any tragic, or ironic, inner meaning. They only disclosed themselves; they were their own meaning. It was evident to both sides that the triptych's "highly abstract style [was] an intensely and even private form of expression," and that, being private, it might be unable to enhance collective devotion.

A learned observer drew a parallel between the dispute over de Kooning's triptych and that over the nudes in Michelangelo's *Last Judgment*, the great fresco behind the altar in the Sistine Chapel. The parallel has only limited validity. To be sure, in each case, detractors contended that the painting undermined the ritual functions of the room where it stood. An analogy could run between the charge that, being lascivious, Michelangelo's picture was inappropriate to the Sistine Chapel and that, being distracting in its meaninglessness, de Kooning's was inappropriate to St. Peter's in New York.

Still, the nature of the objections differed. Objections to Michelangelo's nudes concerned not subjectlessness but his treatment of the subject, which was considered to violate norms of dignity, propriety, and decorum. Objections to de Kooning's abstraction turned on the emptiness that was the subject of the triptych, an emptiness that appeared unintelligibly to counterfeit graffiti.[2]

A similar contrast appears by comparing the dispute over de Kooning's triptych with rejections of other altarpieces. El Greco volunteered to repaint the *Last Judgment* in a more decorous style, but his own *Martyrdom of St. Maurice* (1580–82) was rejected because it violated decorum in another way—namely, by subordinating the subject, the martyrdom, to the decorative possibilities of style, thereby "remov[ing] the desire to pray before" the representations of saints (El Escorial).[3] Other points of comparison are offered by Caravaggio's *Inspiration of St. Matthew* (1602), commissioned and rejected for the altar of the Contarelli Chapel (destroyed, formerly in the Kaiser Friedrich Museum, Berlin), and his *Death of the Virgin* (ca. 1605–1606), commissioned for and rejected by Santa Maria della Scala (now in the Louvre). These paintings were, like the others mentioned, denounced for their lack of decorum, the first, for portraying St. Matthew as an illiterate and graceless peasant with a protruding foot, the second for displaying

---

[2] *New York Times*, 25 February 1986.
[3] Jonathan Brown, "El Greco and Toledo," in Jonathan Brown et al., *El Greco of Toledo* (Boston: Little Brown, 1982), p. 98.

the legs and feet of the Virgin's corpse bare, and possibly also for Caravaggio's use of a prostitute, his mistress, as the model for "the overly explicit womanliness of Mary," in this painting, as in the also rejected *Madonna with St. Anne* (1605–1606, now in the Borghese Gallery, Rome).[4]

The contrast between the criticisms of altarpieces by Michelangelo, El Greco, and Caravaggio, and those of de Kooning's underscores the conclusions in the preceding chapters. For, while, in the sixteenth and seventeenth centuries, the ultimate address of painting was indirectly to the passions by way of the senses, that, in subjectless abstraction of the twentieth century, is directly to the senses. Passions are common in human nature; the pathetic and affective fallacies that they engender may be collective, if not common. Sensations are private; and, as the dispute over de Kooning's triptych indicates, a collective experience deriving from immediate sensation, if possible at all, must be filtered through the images of words—that is, through a hermeneutic of interpretation, rather than through one of passion.

[4] Howard Hibbard, *Caravaggio* (New York: Harper and Row, 1983), pp. 143–44, 191, 197, 202.

THE CALL FROM WITHIN
THE WORDS

ONLY A FEW of the contents of the words, "I am you," have been unpacked in this essay; many, perhaps very many and splendid ones, remain to be discovered. At any rate, I have considered some of the ideas contained in those three monosyllables—the simplest of words—and I have sketched, after a fashion, ways in which those ideas formed great enterprises in literature, theology, and art. Because the sentence is a riddle or a bafflement to many, I have tried to explain how it could be understood. The major part of my task, in fact, has been to disclose the twofold movement of understanding that made the sentence intelligible, a movement that began with the definition of an area of perplexity (the hermeneutic gap) and led to a closure that engaged the heart as much as, or more than, the mind (the hermeneutic circle).

I began with the sentence, as a concrete, but minute, artifact of culture. As is the case with fragments, the sentence led to a greater whole—namely, to patterns of understanding by which interpreters made the sense of the sentence. Those patterns were dominated by two paradigms used for organizing ideas about assimilation, two paradigms that grew out of the primordial distinction between body and spirit, and that focused on the fundamental acts of human creativity: procreation and composition. I have called them the biological and the esthetic paradigms. Both were essays in strife as well as in unity; for both portrayed consummation of union through dominance, whether the dominance of male over female, or of artist over matter. But even those patterns proved to be fragments of a yet wider world, and I turned from them to the ways of understanding the enterprise of understanding itself, based on what Hegel called the two theoretical senses: hearing and sight. The understanding heart, by its sympathy and compassion, has been the major actor in my story. But evidently in the movement toward unity through dominance, empathetic participation of the "I" in the "you" could be inspired by malevolent, as well as by amorous, sympathy. Desire, envy, rivalry, and hatred could blend with, or replace, the gentle urgencies of love. Rare as they are, references to the cannibalism of God set a measure that ferocity could reach. Understanding could be equated with passion as well as with decipherment and interpretation. Thus, conflict had its part to play in closing the circle between "I" and the "you."

Closure always began with a gap, or need: all wisdom begins in wonder. The need expressed in the sentence "I am you," are the primal ones of human existence. For that reason, the responses that they provoked were erotic, in all the forms in which love reveals and disguises itself. And, in those responses, another level of need came to bear; for the materials that were used had their own limitations. Media that addressed hearing and sight, the two senses that, above all, make human communication possible, were most inadequate to close the gap. Words were silent; painted images, empty. Arising in common human need the erotic responses of literature, theology, and painting consisted both in the formal (or positive) characteristics of the works and in the "deficiencies" of art. Both were included in the task of art to conceal itself; both belonged to the interpreter's task of reading between the lines; both explained the paradox that, while there is more to a painting than you can see in it, there is also less to a painting than you do see in it. Thus, the bonding of "I" and "you" moved in and through works of art, by stages of sensory perception, decipherment, interpretation, and, finally, affective contemplation, a journey that was not open to all.

Ways of thinking that denied or negated the passions suppressed the needs of the passions. This was notably true of historical interpretation and analysis, as it ceased to be regarded as a study of universals, and indeed a branch of theology or of philosophy teaching by examples, and became, instead, a study of finite and passing situations. As a study of situations, historical analysis requires and conveys detachment of the observer from the spectacle of life. In each endeavor considered in this essay—literature, theology, and art—the ascendancy of historical analysis has attenuated the range of meanings that the sentence, "I am you," could have. There, rational understanding, as decipherment and interpretation, has survived; but empathetic understanding, as participation, has declined. Such naturally would be the consequence of defining the basic question, the hermeneutic gap, of an enterprise so as to exclude basic human needs. The distinction between knowing and loving is akin to that between history and art.

Formal disciplines that require detachment also require a degree of deafness to the call within the words, "I am you." Other disciplines that assume the universality of passion allow the call to be heard.

The sentences "I am I" and "you are you" are grammatically correct, but logically they lead nowhere because of their circularity. The sentence, "I am you" is both grammatically and logically correct. However, it raises difficulties if one imagines that personality—what constitutes an "I" and distinguishes it from every possible "you"—is unique and therefore incommunicable. If one assumes that personal identity is incommunicable (that a person can be either "I" or "you" but not both "I" and "you"), the "I" and the "you" stand as separate entities forever distant from one another. Thus conceived, the detached symmetrical egoism of "I am I" and "you are you" is unbridgeable.

Absorption was a modeling process that combined acts of internalization and bonding projection without falling into the vicious circle of Narcissism. If there had been no psychological advance beyond "I am I" and "you are you," the ironic distance between hearts could not have been closed. To be sure, the "I" could have sought a basic likeness with the "you." This is projection. But without self-critical internalization, true bonding would have been out of the question. Without it, the "I" might have found, in anger or in sadness, that the "you" was only a mystified projection of itself.[1] If they coincided in time, the "I" and the "you" could have engaged in partnership, in reciprocal actions, or in dialogue. If they lived in different ages, or if they exemplified unrequited love, the "I" could have been a metaphor of the "you."[2] But parallel lives do not intersect; and the distance that characterizes the irony of metaphors cannot be resolved into a real identity between the metaphor and the object to which it refers. The ideas that I have discussed aimed at more than mystification, dialogue, or metaphor.

Assuming a common, inward existence prior to the mutual, outward one, the fragmentary "I" sought something of itself in the "you"; it also sought something of the "you" in itself. Love is a game of chance performed by trial and error. In such games as in any modeling process, thought and experience are constantly tested against each other. A critical act of absorption performed this testing function in the cyclical interplay of internalization and projection. Absorption was thought to take a specific form, imitative mediation. It operated through a reproductive system of signs, symbols, and sacraments, separately or in combination. Such tools of critical modeling were social; they were outward. Signs, symbols, and sacraments were tools that made possible the mimetic movement of the "I" toward closure with the "you." But the effects of modeling varied according to the personal choice and character of the individual "I." In other words, absorption varied according to the kind and intensity of bonding that any given "I" could achieve through imitation. The common identity of individual and species, of painting and genre, had a parallel in this movement by trial and error

[1] Cf. Plato, *Phaedrus*, 255: "the lover is his mirror in whom he is beholding himself, but he is not aware of this." Feuerbach and his contemporary, Bruno Bauer, regarded the Christian doctrine of God as a projection of the human mind. On Feuerbach, see above, Chapter 5 at nn. 105, 108. See Bauer's *Die Posaune des jüngsten Gerichts über Hegel den Atheisten und Antichristen: Ein Ultimatum* (Leipzig, 1841, reprinted Aalen: Scientia, 1969), p. 148.

[2] The metaphor "is" the thing designated in a hypothetical way; but, of course, it "is not" really the thing itself. As metaphor, the "I" would be a hypothetical "you." On the importance of this hypothetical use of metaphor, especially the relation between *mythos* and *mimesis*, see Paul Ricoeur, *The Rule of Metaphor: Multi-disciplinary Studies of the Creation of Meaning in Language*, trans. Robert Czerny et al. (Toronto: University of Toronto Press, 1977), pp. 244–46.

toward closure. For however personal and one-sided it might be, the internalization, absorption, and bonding projection by which each fragmentary "I" was expanded by becoming "you" as well as "I" diversified and widened the collective life that signs, symbols, and sacraments conveyed. Personal and social processes of transformation recapitulated and reverberated within one another. Individual modifications occurred, as Darwin wrote, for the benefit of the species; they were the means of social reform and renewal, which is also to say, of moral evolution.

In its very origins erotic, the structure of thought that permitted one to be, not either "I" or "you," but both "I" and "you" also allowed the "I" to be both male and female in the process of modeling, or reproduction, by which the "I" was expanded by being transformed into the "you." Qualities equated with femininity amounted to psychological internalization of the "you." The "I" was male in giving form, female in its capacity to receive and nurture form, and in its compassion. Through the centuries, male dominance and female submission was an ever-repeated aspect of this erotic metaphor. Discussions of processes within the individual mind, and of bonding among persons, easily employed the analogue of procreation to elucidate strategies of reproductive mediation between "I" and "you." By extension, this sexual analogue with the coordinated interplay of internalization and projection eventually gave rise to theories of the genetic renewal, or cognitive evolution, of society.

The intricate poetic strategy of modeling summed up in the sentence "I am you" was cast and recast into many versions. In all of them, doctrines coalesced around enigmatic assumptions about transition from visible to invisible modes of existence, about rendering present what was absent. Those assumptions made sense in discussions of art and love, but, to return to our point, they were hard to apply in kinds of discourse that were not atuned to the passions, or that assumed mutual, but not common, existence. Not all categories of ideas can be analyzed by the same methods. Poetic truth can be at odds with the literal truths of philosophy or history. Long ago, Wilhelm Dilthey dreamed that methods of social sciences might be used to unravel the riddle of life, by advancing the enigmatic search for "you" in "I" and for "I" in "you." But it remains to be seen whether the methods of the social sciences can or should serve that task, great and necessary as it may be. Commonly their methods assume a plurality of structures arranged in polar opposition. There is social order, providing the possibilities and limits of what is thinkable. There are the discrete mental frames of reference guiding individual persons. There is the internal order of each literary work. The distances among these different structures can be mediated. They can be mediated by conflict, or by deliberate or unconscious resemblance. Mediation establishes relationship, but detachment remains.

At their points of greatest resemblance, the structures are homologous, but separate, entities. Together the "I" and the "you" constitute a collective "we." The methods of the social sciences generally exclude the possibility that separate entities (or structures) may be identical.

Older methods have been used to explore various kinds of internalization, assimilation, and projection. However, even philosophers and historical writers over the centuries who were convinced that the sentence "I am you" expressed both poetic and literal truth left many issues open. Outside the formulas of religious or political denominations, they did not exhaust the consequences for moral action that followed from the ironic coupling of "I" and "you." By contrast, implications in metaphysics and epistemology were fully developed inside and outside the limits of dogma. The Greek strand in Western culture asserted: "I am you," The Jewish strand commanded: "Love your neighbor as yourself." But who was the "you," the neighbor?

Here, as so often, the blending of Hellenism and Hebraism was incomplete. The reasons were practical, as well as intellectual. The institutions that conveyed ideas had claims of their own, claims of allegiance to family, cult, class, party, nation, or state. Authors and their audiences acted and reacted upon one another within these visible, finite associations. They shared many motives for assigning a common identity to "I" and "you" within them. The lessons of metaphysics and epistemology could readily be put into practice, when tailored to suit finite social contexts. But the motives for going beyond such associations were not always compelling either for an author or for his audience. Indeed, humanity's social and political nature forcefully bent the ideas summed up in the sentence "I am you" to its own, practical uses. When he threatens to burn the risen Christ as a heretic, the Grand Inquisitor in Dostoevsky's novel, *The Brothers Karamazov*, personifies the common discrepancy between institutional apparatus and informing vision. In this case, the discrepancy lay between the transcendent need for freedom preached by Christ and the apparatus of miracle, doctrine, and coercive authority with which the Church "corrected" Christ's work to suit the pragmatic needs of this world, replacing the ideal of freedom with that of obedience.

Thus, discussion of the moral consequences implied by the proposition, "I am you," has been pursued chiefly in the contexts of social and political order, always led by dominance, its pillar of fire. Only partial surveys have been achieved, generally without regard for the "deficiencies"—the silence and emptiness—of verbal and visual arts. Dogma, or ideology, has no patience with its own finitude. Western culture is characterized by its individualism. Still, it has also nurtured contrary doctrines. Egoism and collectivism are two poles in Western thought, each with its own promises, each, when put into practice, with its own costs. Theories examined in this essay stand at different points along the spectrum between the poles of egoism and collectivism, combining their promises and perhaps, in practice, compounding their costs. However, a complex web of interdependence undeniably enables life to exist and expand.

With every year, the fragility of that web becomes more evident. It would seem wise, therefore, to examine earlier visions of interdependence, framed in beauty, moved by love, and joined by compassion, and to profit from their experience in the world, however flawed they may have been in theory or in practice. New and urgent motives have arisen for each "I" to hear the call of every "you" outside the confines of social and political commitments, to feel the likeness that both relates and assimilates separate entities to one another, and to believe that through mediating likeness even discordant, polar opposites surrender in love each to each, parts of a single, illuminating, and fecund harmony, surprising and terrible in its power.

INDEX

Library of Congress Cataloging-in-Publication Data

Morrison, Karl Frederick.
I am you.

Includes bibliographical references and index.
1. Empathy in literature. 2. Empathy in art.
3. Empathy—Religious aspects—Christianity—History
of doctrines. I. Title.
PN56.E62M67   1988   909'.09821   87-36042
ISBN 0-691-05510-6 (alk. paper)